A Desktop Guide for Nonprofit Directors, Officers, and Advisors

Avoiding Trouble While Doing Good

A Desktop Guide for Nonprofit Directors, Officers, and Advisors

Avoiding Trouble While Doing Good

Jack B. Siegel

John Wiley & Sons, Inc.

This book is printed on acid-free paper. ♾

Published by John Wiley & Sons, Inc., Hoboken, New Jersey.

Published simultaneously in Canada.

For general information on our other products and services, or technical support, please contact our Customer Care Department within the United States at 800-762-2974, outside the United States at 317-572-3993 or fax 317-572-4002.

Wiley also publishes its books in a variety of electronic formats. Some content that appears in print may not be available in electronic books.

For more information about Wiley products, visit our Web site at http://*www.wiley.com.*

Library of Congress Cataloging-in-Publication Data:

Siegel, Jack B.

A desktop guide for nonprofit directors, officers, and advisors : avoiding trouble while doing good / Jack B. Siegel.

p. cm.

Includes bibliographical references and index.

ISBN-13: 978-0-471-76812-8 (cloth/cd-rom : alk. paper)

ISBN-10: 0-471-76812-X (cloth/cd-rom : alk. paper)

1. Nonprofit organizations—Management. I. Title.

HD62.6.S557 2006

658.4'22—dc22

2005031930

Printed in the United States of America

10 9 8 7 6 5 4 3 2 1

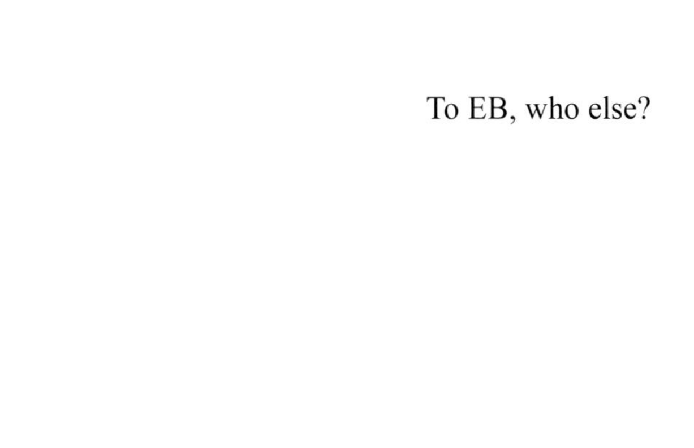

To EB, who else?

CONTENTS

Because of the rapidly changing nature of information in this field, this product may be updated with annual supplements or with future editions. Please call 1-877-762-2974 or email us at *subscriber@wiley.com* to receive any current update at no additional charge. We will send on approval any future supplements or new editions when they become available. If you purchased this product directly from John Wiley & Sons, Inc., we have already recorded your subscription for this update service.

ABOUT THE AUTHOR

Jack B. Siegel is an attorney and CPA, holding an LLM in Taxation from New York University and a Masters of Management from Northwestern University. Mr. Siegel received his law degree from the University of Wisconsin, where he was a member of the Wisconsin Law Review. Mr. Siegel practiced law for ten years with Foley & Lardner, and he was a partner on the firm's tax team. In addition to other tax and corporate work, Mr. Siegel advised nonprofits on such diverse matters as UBIT, private foundation status, physician joint ventures, investment matters, low-income housing tax credits, tax-exemption, and corporate structures. Subsequently, as assistant general counsel with a major nonprofit low-income housing tax credit syndicator, Mr. Siegel helped structure tax credit transactions.

Mr. Siegel currently heads Auto Didactix LLC and Charity Governance Consulting LLC, a division of Auto Didactix LLC. Charity Governance provides consulting services to charitable organizations, focusing on board training, governance manuals, and special projects involving legal, accounting, and financial matters. Auto Didactix LLC develops and distributes professional training software for lawyers, accountants, and financial professionals. This *Guide* grew out of Mr. Siegel's multimedia, interactive program *Avoiding Trouble While Doing Good: A Guide for the Non-Profit Director and Officer.*

He has also authored *Taxation of Bankruptcy*, published by the American Institute of Certified Public Accountants, *Tax Deferred, Like Kind Exchanges of Real Property*, a multimedia, interactive program, and *TaxProf*, a computer-based tutorial for the first federal income tax course, which is now in its seventh edition.

Mr. Siegel served as a member of President Clinton's transition team in 1992, with the Treasury Tax Policy Cluster. He has served as an instructor in the Public Finance Ministry of Taiwan Academy of International Taxation, presenting a course on the U.S. taxation of financial assets. He has also taught as an adjunct professor of law for IIT-Chicago Kent's School of Law LLM Tax Program.

He has spoken extensively on tax, governance, and legal matters, having presented courses on the taxation of S corporations, real estate, partnerships, tax-exempt financing, ethics and professional responsibility, and other tax-related matters. He has most recently made presentations on nonprofit governance for ALI-ABA, ARNOVA, CAPLAW, Massachusetts Continuing Professional Legal Education, and nonprofit seminars.

Mr. Siegel is a member of the American Bar Association (Tax and Business Law Sections), the American Institute of Certified Public Accountants, ARNOVA, and the Association of Consultants to Nonprofits. He maintains the Charity Governance blog at http://charitygovernance.blogs.com. Mr. Siegel can be contacted at guide@charitygovernance.com.

COVERAGE, CONVENTIONS, AND ACKNOWLEDGMENTS

Coverage: The first responsibility of nonprofit boards and officers is to ensure that scarce resources are used in the most effective and efficient way possible to accomplish the nonprofit's mission. Those charged with oversight and management are understandably focused on the nonprofit's core mission. Too often, they view legal, accounting, and tax issues as burdensome distractions. This can be both costly to the mission and embarrassing to those in charge. *A Desktop Guide for Nonprofit Directors, Officers, and Advisors* offers answers and relief to decision makers and their advisors. It addresses nonprofit governance, bringing a practical and fresh look to the boardroom. Coverage includes:

- Assessing the decision to serve.
- Identifying the players.
- Understanding legal duties and responsibilities.
- Reading and analyzing financial statements.
- Learning how to obtain and maintain federal tax-exempt status.
- Considering the deduction for charitable contributions, planned giving, and related reporting and substantiation requirements.
- Addressing state registration and reporting requirements, including Internet solicitation.
- Identifying other benefits of nonprofit status (e.g. property tax exemptions, favorable postal rates, and securities law exemptions).
- Exploring fundraising, pledges, restricted gifts, endowments, and federal grants.
- Identifying and protecting against event and operational liabilities.
- Analyzing director and officer indemnification, directors' and officers' insurance, and operational insurance coverages.
- Evaluating an organization using a variety of methodologies.

These are broad categories. The *Guide* addresses many specific topics and issues including Sarbanes-Oxley reforms, internal controls and fraud prevention, lobbying and political activity, the GAO audit standards, payments in lieu of taxes, the IRS intermediate sanctions, donor advisory boards, planned giving, IRS Form 990, employment practices, record retention policies, CAN-SPAM, and many other topics that are driving decisions in the independent sector today. The goal is to provide those on the frontlines with a desktop reference, answering commonly asked questions.

Those using the *Guide* will find the table of contents and index helpful entry points. Few readers will read the entire *Guide* from front to back. That is fine. All would benefit, however, by reading the first five chapters. Those chapters contain the core content, which apply to all nonprofits. Chapters 6 and 7 pertain to tax matters. Those chapters are must reading for those who serve organizations that do not have a tax advisor—although the need for a tax advisor will be clear after completing those chapters! The first half of Chapter 13 contains a 250-question survey that is designed as a summary of all the information presented in the *Guide*. All readers are encouraged to use this survey to perform a legal and financial audit on their organizations. Much of the remaining material in the *Guide* will also be useful to most organizations. For example, Chapter 11 covers common operational risks, including those arising from employment, volunteers, and fundraising events. Directors and officers should be interested in the discussion of directors' and officers' insurance in Chapter 12, including sample policy language. All of this material addresses governance in a larger sense, but the first five chapters focus specifically on boards, officers, and what they should be doing to discharge their duties.

Conventions: Pronouns are used in the masculine gender for clarity and simplicity unless the context requires otherwise. All charitable organizations and people named in examples throughout this *Guide* are fictitious unless the context indicates otherwise. While the *Guide's* intended audience includes advisors to nonprofits, the *Guide's* text assumes the reader is a director, executive director, or officer.

Acknowledgments: I thank my editor, Susan McDermott, for her enthusiastic support for the project. I am also grateful to Dexter Gasque, senior production editor, for his patience with my inexperience in the production process. Finally, I thank my wife, Evelyn Brody, professor at Chicago-Kent College of Law, who read the manuscript making extremely helpful comments and suggestions.

DISCLAIMER

This book does not constitute legal, tax, accounting, or other professional advice, nor does this book create an attorney-client, accountant-client, or other relationship between the author and publisher, on the one hand, and the reader, on the other. The services of a qualified lawyer, accountant, or other professional should always be sought when professional advice is required. The publisher and the author make no representations or warranties with respect to the accuracy or completeness of the contents of this work and specifically disclaim all warranties, including without limitation warranties of fitness for a particular purpose. No warranty may be created or extended by sales or promotional materials. The advice and strategies contained herein may not be suitable for every situation. Neither the publisher nor the author shall be liable for damages arising therefrom. The fact that an organization or Web site is referred to in this work as a citation and/or a potential source of further information does not mean that the author or the publisher endorses the information the organization or Web site may provide or recommendations it may make. Further, readers should be aware that Web sites listed in this work may have changed or disappeared between when this work was written and when it is read.

This book is aimed at a nationwide audience, and consequently, when addressing issues governed by state law, it makes generalizations when highlighting specific issues. The resolution of those issues will be highly dependent on the law of the relevant jurisdiction and the specific facts. Where this book does make reference to specific case and statutory authorities, the intent is to illustrate the issues addressed by the law and how different jurisdictions have approached issues.

This book is not a comprehensive treatise. Even when reference is made to the laws of a specific state, that reference is often an isolated one which does not necessarily take into account other provisions of that state's laws. While considerable effort was devoted to researching the content of this book, the research techniques used in writing this book differ significantly from those that would be employed if the author were representing a particular nonprofit or other client. Moreover, when professionals advise clients, thcy do so with a specific set of facts in mind. It is expected that those involved with a particular nonprofit will undertake additional work and seek additional advice when resolving specific issues and problems facing them and their organizations.

With the exception of references to the Internal Revenue Code, all statutory references are to statutes appearing on Web sites (generally state and federal government sites). While this would be unacceptable for actual client legal research, it is perfectly acceptable for purposes of this book. Case and statutory citation is designed to highlight different approaches to issues. Once receiving direction from this book, anyone undertaking advisory legal work still must thoroughly review applicable statutes and case law, as well as treatise-like secondary legal works.

On a more positive note, the purpose of this book is to provide a starting point for directors and officers of nonprofits and their advisors. When used in that spirit, the reader will discover that the book is an excellent resource for identifying and framing issues.

FOREWORD

They're not gonna catch us. We're on a Mission from God

ELWOOD BLUES[1]

Thus, to do a great right, you may do a little wrong, and you may take any means which ends to be attained will justify, the amount of the right, or the amount of the wrong, or indeed the distinction between the two, being left entirely to the philosopher concerned.

CHARLES DICKENS[2]

Don't say I didn't warn you

When your train gets lost

BOB DYLAN[3]

As you review this *Guide*, you will learn how directors can be held accountable by courts, state attorneys general, the IRS, and even their fellow board members, to name just a few of those who will be watching the decision process. But you will also learn that in the vast majority of cases, directors and officers really have very little to worry about, even if they participate in a decision that in hindsight is a bad or even dumb one.

So why worry about legal, financial, and regulatory issues if you are unlikely to find yourself financially accountable? Why not just go to the meetings and rubberstamp the executive director's proposals? The answer to these questions is quite simple: The issues discussed in this *Guide* will help you and your fellow directors and officers make better decisions.

Recent anecdotal evidence does suggest an increase in the number of actions being brought against nonprofit directors and officers. Even though directors and officers may not be held monetarily liable, they may still have to incur significant legal fees when disputing a claim. And even if they are indemnified or have their legal fees covered by a directors' and officers' insurance policy, nobody wants the bad publicity or additional time commitment that often accompanies one of these

---

1. THE BLUES BROTHERS (MCA 1980).
2. OLIVER TWIST, Chapter 12 (1838)
3. *It Takes a Lot to Laugh, It Takes a Train to Cry, on* HIGHWAY 61 REVISITED (Columbia 1965).

entanglements. The directors of the New York Stock Exchange,[4] the Art Institute of Chicago,[5] the United Way of the National Capital Area,[6] American University,[7] and a host of other marquee organizations have all come under the spotlight in recent years because of board decisions and practices. As just one example of how scandal can adversely impact a director, the *Wall Street Journal* reported that one of the former directors of the New York Stock Exchange stepped down from the General Electric board amid turmoil over his role in the NYSE-compensation imbroglio involving former NYSE chairman, Richard Grasso.[8]

The directors and officers of both for-profit and nonprofit organizations encounter similar governance issues and concerns, but make no mistake: nonprofit directors and officers face a unique environment. At the most fundamental level, nonprofits do not have shareholders. While many directors and CEOs of large publicly held corporations may at times envy that fact, nonprofit directors know all too well that the absence of shareholders also means the inability to raise equity capital.

The differences between nonprofits and for-profits go well beyond shareholders. You may know how to read financial statements for business entities, but do you understand the special rules that apply to nonprofit financial statements? You may be able to prepare your own tax return using TurboTax, but do you understand the federal tax rules applicable to nonprofits, very few of which have anything to do with collecting revenue? While cash is cash in the business world, in the nonprofit world a charity may not be able to spend cash if it is part of a restricted fund. Do you really understand how such restrictions can limit an executive director and the board of directors? Have you thought about the risks and compliance issues that a nonprofit assumes when sponsoring a street fair, fun run, raffle, or other fundraiser? And don't forget that nifty Internet site that your nonprofit developed to increase contributions and get the message out. Does it pose issues that should be of concern to you as a director or officer?

By taking the time to consider the answers to these and other questions, you will improve the organization's decision-making process. Even though your personal assets may not, as a practical matter, be subject to exposure, you and the organization will avoid compliance issues raised by regulators when they discover practices that violate rules and regulations. Of equal or arguably greater

---

4. B. White, *Grasso, Spitzer Take It Personal,* WASH. POST, May 26, 2004; and *The People's Lawyer Strikes Again*, ECONOMIST, May 26, 2004.
5. Complaint filed by the Securities Exchange Commission against Conrad P. Seghers and James R. Dickey in the United States District Court for the Northern District of Texas (Dallas Division), June 16, 2004; SEC Litigation Release No. 18749, June 17, 2004; and N. Weinberg & B. Condon, *The Sleaziest Show on Earth*, FORBES MAG., May 24, 2004.
6. PRICEWATERHOUSECOOPERS, UNITED WAY OF THE NATIONAL CAPITAL AREA FORENSIC ACCOUNTING INVESTIGATION (Aug. 7, 2003); and J. Salmon and P. Whoriskey, *Audit Excoriates United Way Leadership*, WASH. POST, June 25, 2004.
7. See the discussion in Chapter 6.
8. J. Lublin & K. Kranhold, *Financier to Quit GE Board Over Role at NYSE*, WALL. ST. J. Feb. 8, 2005.

importance, your decisions as a board member are likely to result in better utilization of the nonprofit's scarce resources.

This *Guide* could have easily included a reference to the Sarbanes-Oxley Act of 2002[9] in its title, given the *Guide's* focus on better governance. Even though many in Congress and the nonprofit community have been willing to draw from the various corporate reforms mandated by Sarbanes-Oxley, those reforms were designed with large, publicly traded companies in mind. Anyone who takes the time to read the regulations promulgated by the SEC will quickly see the complexity and cost that comes with compliance, making many of the reforms inappropriate for many small and medium-sized nonprofits. Already people are talking about a backlash, with corporate executives and business groups calling for regulatory retrenchment[10] and some companies electing to go private in an effort to escape costly regulatory burdens.[11] While this *Guide* will consider audit and compensation committees and a number of other Sarbanes-Oxley reforms, its perspective goes well beyond those sometimes limited and often costly reforms.

Sarbanes-Oxley has largely become a boondoggle for accountants and consultants and, more importantly, a checklist that some boards and executives can now hide behind in lieu of addressing difficult cultural and ethical issues that go to the core of how business is conducted in the United States. If you doubt this, simply take a look at American International Group, one of the "bluest" of the blue chip companies. On March 15, 2004, Maurice Greenberg, its Chairman and CEO, and Howard I. Smith, its Vice-Chairman and CFO, both signed Exhibit 31 to AIG's annual Form 10-K filing, thereby making the financial certifications required by Section 302 of Sarbanes-Oxley.[12] A little over a year later, the front page of the *Wall Street Journal* carried the following headline: *AIG Admits 'Improper' Accounting: Broad Range of Problems Could Cut $1.77 Billion Of Insurer's Net Worth, A Widening Criminal Probe.*[13] The article reports that the improper accounting that the company admitted to had occurred over the last decade, presumably including the period covered by the two certifications made. Mr. Greenberg was forced to resign amidst investigations by multiple governmental agencies.[14] AIG's stock price dropped 29% during the turmoil.[15] In short,

---

9. Pub. L. 107-204, 116 Stat. 745 (2002).
10. K. Eichenwald, *Reform Effort At Businesses Feels Pressure*, N.Y. TIMES, Jan. 14, 2005.
11. C. Deutsch, *The Higher Price of Staying Public*, N.Y. TIMES (Jan. 23, 2005); and M. Ligos, *When Going Public May Not Be Worth It*, N.Y. TIMES, June 3, 2004.
12. Securities and Exchange Act of 1934—Rules 13a-14 and 15d-14. The SEC amended Form 10-K and Form 10-Q to incorporate the certifications.
13. I. McDonald, T. Francis, and D. Solomon, WALL ST. J., Mar. 31, 2005. See also Press Release, American International Group, AIG Delays Form 10-K Filing to Complete Review (Mar. 30, 2005).
14. C. Johnson and B. White, *AIG in Damage Control: Cooperation Counts in Investigations*, WASH. POST, Apr. 1, 2005. This and other articles make reference to investigations by New York Attorney General Eliot Spitzer, the United States Justice Department, and the Securities and Exchange Commission. Mr. Spitzer announced that his office would not pursue criminal charges against Mr. Greenberg. See D. Starkman, *Greenberg Avoids Criminal Charges: Former AIG Chief Could Face Civil Lawsuit Over Stock Sales*, WASH. POST, Nov. 26, 2005.
15. P. McKay, I. McDonald, and J. Lahart, *AIG Investors Are Learning A Hard Lesson: Accounting Woes' Unknown Depth Takes a Toll on Insurer's Shares, Has Value-Oriented Pros Divided*, WALL ST. J., Apr. 4, 2005.

what quickly become routine sign-offs are not nearly as effective as Congress and various regulators would prefer us to believe. Those truly concerned with improving governance in their organizations—be they for-profits or nonprofits—should eschew the sophistry offered by the Sarbanes-Oxley talisman and opt for a broader examination of how their organizations are governed. Good governance cannot be mandated; there must be buy-in from those charged with governing. That belief underlies this *Guide* and the prescriptions it offers.

CHAPTER 1

SETTING THE STAGE: SOME PRELIMINARIES

Send lawyers, guns, and money, Dad, get me out of this.

WARREN ZEVON[1]

You may be passionate about addressing literacy problems in your community, or perhaps the senior partner in your advertising agency or law firm has told you that you will be serving on the board of directors of a business association that sponsors an annual street festival. Then again, a friend who is chairman of an inner-city hospital might have tapped you for service on the hospital's board—or your generous contributions to the local opera company may have been noticed, causing the company's development director to ask you to serve as a board member.

There are many routes to service as a director or officer of a nonprofit. Whatever your route to service, you need guidance. This is true even if you are an attorney or accountant because like it or not, the other board members will assume you are an expert in nonprofit law, regulation, and taxation. That will be true even if you limit your practice to divorce or admiralty law, or to auditing Fortune 500 companies.

This *Guide* is designed to help you fulfill your responsibilities by providing you some needed information. It covers a wide range of topics, including (1) how nonprofits are legally organized, (2) the roles, responsibilities, and duties of directors and officers, (3) the basic tax rules affecting nonprofits and donors to charities, (4) the laws regulating fundraising, (5) organizational risks, and

1. *Lawyers, Guns and Money*, on EXCITABLE BOY (Asylum 1976).

(6) steps that you can take to protect yourself from liability as a volunteer director or officer. To spur discussion within your own organization, the *Guide* concludes with an organizational self-evaluation that summarizes the many issues it covers.

The challenges facing those who run nonprofits are daunting. The primary mission of nonprofits is to educate students, treat the sick, feed the hungry, provide legal services to the disadvantaged, display art and perform music to enlighten, and serve the community in any number of other ways. Yet, nonprofit directors, officers, and employees must seek contributions and grants, comply with complicated tax laws, report to a variety of governmental agencies, protect assets, maintain records, manage multiple risks, and stand accountable to various constituencies.

The only way those running nonprofits can succeed in achieving their primary missions is to act in concert with each other in developing systems and controls to successfully complete all secondary tasks. This means that the board and the executive director must be partners, exhibiting mutual respect for each other. In many instances, the organization is the brainchild of the executive director who saw a need, nurtured an idea to meet that need, found the funding to build an organization to implement the vision, and selected the directors. In other words, the executive director is often a very strong-willed person. The natural tendency will be for the board to defer to the executive director.

That deference can be a fatal mistake, although few realize this until it is too late. As visionaries, executive directors tend to be mission focused, viewing much of what we will consider in this *Guide* as burdensome detail, red tape, and administration that interferes with the mission. One has only to reflect on the many scandals that have plagued the nonprofit sector during the last decade to realize that the headlines are rooted in failure to pay attention to secondary aspects of running an organization: risk management, control, red tape, and administration. There were no conflict-of-interest or gift-acceptance policies in place. Financial controls were inadequate. The organization operated without budgets or acceptable financial reports. There were no procedures to ensure compliance with restrictions in gifts. Investment policies and procedures were either nonexistent or poorly conceived. In almost every instance, one question, often unstated, lurks: Where was the board of directors?

The law clearly assigns duties to directors. Based on the belief that only so much can be asked of what are often volunteers, the law has regrettably gone too far in relieving directors of liability for breach of those duties. This does not mean that volunteers must live up to the law's low expectations by shirking their legal duties. As should be evident, board members should be actively engaged in the organization's governance, asking tough questions, and demanding that controls be put in place and adhered to. That does not mean that the directors and the executive director need be locked into a never-ending battle. Quite the contrary: By ensuring that adequate controls and reporting are in place, the board is actually freeing the executive director to focus on mission.

Are Nonprofit Directors Really Afraid of Liability? The Trustees of the Tampa Museum of Art Paint a Different Picture

* * *

Want to improve nonprofit governance? Lots of people do, and they prove it by making all sorts of proposals, but holding directors responsible is on absolutely nobody's agenda. Directors can ignore the financial statements. They can miss all of the meetings. They can approve transactions evidencing blatant conflicts of interest while ignoring statutorily mandated validation procedures. They can refuse to even acknowledge internal controls. While not universally true, a likely regulatory response will be removal rather than accountability through monetary liability, and even removal is relatively rare.

Why the resistance to mandating that directors act responsibly? "Everybody knows that if there is any possibility that a director will be held liable, nobody will serve as a volunteer director." That is the gospel. Nobody is willing to question something that is so obvious. But is it so obvious?

Consider the trustees of the Tampa Museum of Art. When the museum wanted to expand, it sought funding from the city of Tampa to the tune of $29.8 million.[2] The museum had raised $31 million as part of a capital campaign and hoped to raise another $20 million.[3] Tampa Mayor Pam Iorio was not satisfied, however, with the adequacy of the funding package. She literally asked the museum's trustees to guarantee their decision process as a condition to financial participation by the city. Specifically, the mayor asked the trustees to *personally* cover operating losses through 2015 with a $9 million guarantee.[4]

Given the old saw about directors refusing to serve if they are held to *any* level of accountability, the entire board of trustees would have been expected to resign on the spot, but that did not happen. You might assume, therefore, that the trustees engaged in a lengthy debate that went on for days, if not months. That did not happen. Did they spend hours in their lawyers' offices discussing asset protection trusts? Apparently not. Rather surprisingly, they quickly agreed to the guarantees.

There will be some who argue that the museum's directors were just a bunch of rich people who would have donated that sort of money to the museum over the next ten years. The recent fundraising experience of New York City's Museum of Modern Art (MoMA) suggests that there is some truth in that perception.[5] At the same time, it is one thing to give money to build a building. It is quite different to agree to underwrite a decision if it turns out to be a bad one in hindsight. If the operating deficits materialize, does the museum then dig a $9 million hole in the museum's lobby and name it after the trustees? People like to fund successes. They do not like to fund disasters, but that is exactly what the museum's trustees agreed to do should losses materialize.

Would a smaller pool of volunteer directors necessarily be a bad thing? Not if it forced a consolidation of charities providing duplicative and inefficient services. Board sizes presumably would also shrink, eliminating 50-person boards that prove to be inefficient and unwieldy.

* * *

---

2. M. Manning, *Museum Trustees Take It Personally*, Tampa Bay Bus. J., Feb. 27, 2005.
3. *Id.*
4. *Id.*
5. H. Eakin, *A Very Modern Art, Indeed*, N.Y. Times, Nov. 7, 2004.

So we come to our first major case. Surprisingly, the origins of this story are not in some state attorney general's efforts to identify and correct board misdeeds but in the New York Office of Parks, Recreation, and Historic Preservation (OPRHP). Back in 1969, the Saratoga Performing Arts Center (SPAC), a Section 501(c)(3) organization that sponsored an annual performance series at an amphitheatre located in Saratoga, New York,[6] entered into a 50-year rent-free lease (with a 50-year renewal option) with OPRHP.[7] The New York City Ballet was one of the two principal resident companies participating in the series. On February 12, 2004, SPAC's board of directors decided to terminate the ballet's summer residency following the 2005 season. OPRHP recognized that the board's decision was contrary to the entire rationale underlying the lease; consequently, it wanted some explanations. As regulator and funder, OPRHP sent in a team of auditors to assess the decision process. What the auditors found was a very poorly run nonprofit with major control and governance failures at virtually every level of the organization.[8] Specifically, the team found that:

- Corporate minutes were incomplete, lacked detail, and did not record vote tallies.[9]
- Executive compensation was too high as measured against a comprehensive benchmark study of 55 similar organizations.

---

6. New York State Office of Parks, Recreation, and Historic Preservation, with the support of the Bonadio Group, Preliminary Audit Report—Saratoga Performing Arts Center, Inc. (Nov. 22, 2004). SPAC issued a formal response to the Preliminary Audit. *See* Letter from Stephen M. Serlin, Chairman of the Board of Directors of Saratoga Performing Arts Center to Paul Laudato, Chief Counsel, New York State Office of Parks, Recreation, and Historic Preservation (Dec. 20, 2004). OPRHP issued a final audit report in 2005. See New York State Office of Parks, Recreation, and Historic Preservation, Final Audit, Saratoga Performing Arts Center (Mar. 16, 2005). In its formal response to the Preliminary Audit, SPAC's board of directors stated:

> The Board sees no advantage in engaging in a protracted audit process or debate to question or confirm a set of findings with which the Board essentially agrees.

The board did take some issue with the Preliminary Audit's conclusions regarding the reasons behind the termination of the New York City Ballet, as well as with the conclusion that the president's compensation was excessive. In the case of the termination, the board contended that whatever methodology is used, it believed that the New York City Ballet required significant underwriting. The board's response also addressed a number of other issues in the Preliminary Audit, seeming to express some disagreement over more minor points. The Final Audit took issue with both the board's assessments regarding the financial analysis and the president's salary.

7. Saratoga Performing Arts Center, Inc. and National Museum of Dance, Combined Financial Statements for the Years Ending December 31, 2004 and 2003, Note 4.
8. OPRHP, Preliminary Report, *supra* note 6. *See also* R. Pogrebin, *Saratoga Center Cited for Mismanagement*, N. Y. Times, Nov. 23, 2004.
9. The wording in the OPRHP, Preliminary Report *supra* note 6, was ambigious. The comment did seem to be general in nature, but placed specific emphasis on the minutes for the meeting where the decision regarding the ballet was made.

- Reimbursement policies were sloppy, with some of the records apparently incomplete.[10]
- The president's wife, functioning as the development officer, was the second highest paid employee despite documented evidence of inadequate fundraising plans, efforts, and results.[11]
- SPAC fell short on building its endowment, relying too heavily on ticket sales. The auditors found no evidence of a planned giving program.
- SPAC had no investment or spending policy with respect to its endowment, limited as it was.
- There was no evidence of a long-term business plan despite the president's pledge to create one after his responsibilities had been significantly reduced, leaving him additional time for developing a plan.[12]
- There may have been internal control deficiencies with respect to how large cash payments to some performers were made.
- The decision to terminate the New York City Ballet was based on incomplete financial data, which, had the analysis been complete, might have actually shown that the New York City Ballet carried its weight or at least have come much closer than SPAC had suggested—it is hard to say because the audit report is unclear on the various revenue sources that the auditors apparently viewed as closing a perceived gap in funding.[13]
- Board members did not receive advance notice that the decision involving the New York City Ballet was on the agenda. Not even half of the board members attended the meeting at which the decision was made to drop the ballet.

---

10. OPRHP, PRELIMINARY REPORT, *supra* note 6, at 3 (Executive Summary—Findings and Recommendations 3 and 7).
11. OPRHP, PRELIMINARY REPORT, *supra* note 6 (Executive Summary—Findings and Recommendations 1 and 3), and (Findings and Recommendations 3 and 5).
12. OPRHP, PRELIMINARY REPORT, *supra* note 6, at 11 (Executive Summary—Findings and Recommendation 8).
13. OPRHP, PRELIMINARY REPORT, *supra* note 6, at 3 (Executive Summary—Findings and Recommendation 2), provides:

> SPAC's decision to eliminate the residency of the New York City Ballet after the 2005 season was based on financial information which was inaccurately and incompletely presented. The $900,000 "accounting gap" between ticket sale revenues and production costs did not portray the complete financial condition of the ballet program as it did not include directed gifts in support of the ballet program (as identified in SPAC's own financial records) nor were nearly identical balance sheet gaps by the Philadelphia Orchestra, the other principle summer tenant, disclosed to the public. Moreover, the audit found that the NYCB's commitment to its Saratoga residency included a $700,000 subsidy of its own (made up from NYCB's own development efforts) and that the average attendance at a ballet performance at SPAC was higher than per-performance attendance at the NYCB's Lincoln Center home (excluding "The Nutcracker").

For additional background information, see R. Pogrebin, *City Ballet's Summers in Saratoga Springs Are Dancing on the Edge*, N.Y. TIMES, Aug. 16, 2004.

- SPAC's decision to drop the ballet was a fundamental change in mission, yet the board and officers never sought the input of a number of SPAC's constituencies, including its landlord (New York State).
- Some fundraising events and balls lost money—although this is often characteristic of these sorts of events.
- Board members provided significant services to SPAC on a fee basis, raising conflict-of-interest questions.[14]
- There was no evidence of job descriptions for SPAC employees.

Something clearly was wrong with SPAC. The report focused on the board's lack of independence and involvement.

Other boards that do not want to make the same mistakes should take the time to read the OPRHP preliminary report, asking whether their organization would receive a clean bill of health if subjected to such close scrutiny. Those boards that are feeling sheepish or even embarrassed when faced with that question might want to start with the checklist in Chapter 13, but they would be better served by first reviewing the entire *Guide*. By no means does this *Guide* provide all of the answers, particularly because personalities run organizations and interact with each other while doing so, generating competition, goodwill, conflict, humor, envy, admiration, bitterness, and a whole host of other emotions. This *Guide* does, however, address virtually every fault raised in that truly amazing report.

1.1 THE NEED FOR ACTION

Many of the covered topics are ones that people, particularly some executive directors of nonprofit organizations, do not like to discuss. As a businessperson, lawyer, accountant, or other professional, you are probably accustomed to asking tough questions in your day-to-day professional life. If you are like many professionals, you probably view your participation as a volunteer director or officer as an opportunity to "kick back" and do some good. Don't!! William Bowen, the president of the Andrew W. Mellon Foundation, makes a strong case in his 1994 book, *Inside the Boardroom: Governance by Directors and Trustees*, that the most important input from a volunteer director is his tough-mindedness.[15]

---

14. OPRHP, PRELIMINARY REPORT, *supra* note 6 at 13 (Executive Summary—Findings and Recommendations 6 and 12).

15. William G. BOWEN, INSIDE THE BOARDROOM, GOVERNANCE BY DIRECTORS AND TRUSTEES 131–33 (John Wiley & Sons,1994). Mr. Bowen actually poses a paradox, noting that many individuals agree with his basic proposition that business executives often check their analytical apparatus and toughness at the boardroom door. At the same time, Mr. Bowen is quick to second the observation of one commentator, who said "[business] CEOs tend to be the best board members; they are more likely than others to understand how complex organizations function."

United Way of America and William Aramony, the Granddaddy of Scandals

* * *

Probably the most publicized example of nonprofit mismanagement in recent years involved United Way of America (UWA) and its executive director, William Aramony. UWA is the national umbrella organization that supports nearly 1,400 independent local United Ways across the country.[16] According to its Web site, UWA provides these member organizations with advertising, training, corporate relations, research, networks, and government relations. The member organizations support UWA by providing voluntary funding equal to less than 1 percent of the funds the members raise.[17] In 1992, stories of excessive compensation paid to Mr. Aramony began to appear in the popular press, resulting in an uproar.[18] People were surprised to learn that the president of a nonprofit organization received a salary of $390,000 per year, plus $73,000 in additional compensation. The stories in the press reported trips on the Concorde, local travel in chauffeured limousines, and stays while visiting New York City in a $430,000 condominium purchased by a UWA subsidiary.[19]

In 1994, Mr. Aramony was indicted, charged with diverting hundreds of thousands of dollars in funds for his personal use. The jury convicted Mr. Aramony on 25 counts, and he was sent to prison. The Fourth Circuit Court of Appeals subsequently affirmed most of the convictions, although it vacated two of them.[20]

In an editorial, *The Washington Post* asked the pertinent question: "Where was [the United Way of America's] board while its staff was flying the Concorde to Europe? The board has traditionally been composed largely of leading figures from the corporate world—people who brought prestige to it, but put little time into it."[21]

* * *

There are many reasons that directors check their good judgment at the boardroom door. Here are three possible explanations: First, too many directors take what might be called the "books-on-tape" approach to board membership, showing up once a month to hear the executive director tell a nice story about all of the good things the organization is doing. These meetings tend to be very relaxing with lots of carbohydrates consumed in the form of morning buns, scones, and doughnuts. If the directors are really lucky, they will receive a plate of

16. United Way of America *available at* http://national.unitedway.org/aboutuw/mission.cfm (last viewed Mar. 18, 2005).
17. The "less than 1 percent" claim was originally made on a Web page that is no longer available. The United Way of America's 2003 IRS Form 990 shows approximately $22 million in membership dues. This is less than 1 percent of the $3.59 billion that United Way indicates was raised by member organizations through the annual campaign, gifts, corporate sponsorships, and government grants in 2003-04.
18. C. Shepard, *United Way Head Resigns Over Spending Habits*, WASH. POST, Feb. 28, 1992; and *Aramony Convicted of Using Charity Money to Support Playboy Lifestyle,* WASH. POST, Apr. 4, 1995.
19. C. Shepard, *Perks, Privileges and Power in a Nonprofit World*, WASH. POST, Feb. 16, 1992.
20. United States v. Aramony, 88 F3d 1369 (4th Cir. 1996); and United Way of America, Vacco v. Aramony, N.Y.L.J., Aug. 7, 1998 (Sup. Ct. N.Y. County July 13, 1998).
21. S.J. Vitell and D. L. Davis, *United Way's Breach of Trust*, WASH. POST, Apr. 7, 1992.

scrambled eggs and bacon[22] or a catered lunch of oversized sandwiches and fancy chips, but eating is not what governance is about, nor is passively watching a slick PowerPoint presentation.

Second, too many board members equate governance and fundraising, assuming that they have discharged their duties if they raise enough money. While the lifeblood of many organizations is money, fundraising is not governance. Those who are good at fundraising would do everybody a favor by not demanding positions on boards unless they are willing to read financial statements, think about personnel issues, allocate resources, review budgets, and take on the other difficult decisions that come with governing an organization.

Third and finally, some executive directors can be power hungry, carefully guarding their prerogatives and fiefdoms. The board may want information that is not forthcoming from the executive director. With only limited time to devote to the organization, few board members are willing to rock the boat, particularly if the executive director uses food and PowerPoint as part of the pacification process.

Does this mean that the board should be at war with the executive director? Absolutely not, but there should be some institutional tension. The board does not exist to rubber-stamp every proposal that the executive director makes. No executive director is infallible. The truly good ones recognize this, causing them to seek input and advice from their boards. One nonprofit recently was reported to be in dire financial straits.[23] Its former chairman functioned as the de facto executive director. Not surprisingly, one board member reported that "[he] screamed and hollered, and there were certain things he wanted done, and he was a powerful guy."[24] According to a newspaper account, "[he] drove out the treasurer, fired the development director and wound up the only person allowed to write the league's checks."[25] This organization was the victim of a kickback scandal, resulting in the indictment of the former chairman and the attorney he had handpicked as counsel to the organization.[26] The attorney subsequently pled guilty, and the former chairman pled guilty to a charge involving a similar scheme, but a different organization.[27] The other board members had a problem that was readily apparent based on the quotes given to the newspaper. They should have either governed or resigned, but it is fairly apparent that at least

---

22. One board had a chairman who was a leading heart surgeon. The board meeting was held at a local club. Eggs were available on the menu, but everyone ordered fruit after the surgeon gave the cue when he ordered oatmeal.
23. C. Spivak and D. Bice, *Debts Threaten Athletic League: Facing Bankruptcy, PAL May Have to Sell Building*, MILWAUKEE J.-SENTINEL, Feb. 9, 2005.
24. J. McBride, *With George at Helm, Athletic League's Financial Health Deteriorated*, MILWAUKEE J.-SENTINEL, Dec. 2, 2003.
25. *Id.*
26. G. Zielinski, *Sostarich Pleads Guilty in George Scandal: He Admits to Kicking Back Legal Fees to Ex-Senator*, MILWAUKEE J.-SENTINEL, Jan. 30, 2004.
27. G. Zielinski, *George Pleads Guilty to Fraud: Four Other Counts Dismissed; Ex-Senator to Cooperate*, MILWAUKEE J.-SENTINEL, Jan. 22, 2004.

some of the other members were too passive, apparently failing to provide the tension that was clearly required under the circumstances.

The explanations for lackluster board performance should not be taken as excuses or justifications. Put plainly, if you are a member of a board, it is your duty to either actively involve yourself in the governance of the organization or submit your resignation. Not only are you opening yourself up to embarrassment and potential liability if you do not take your position seriously, but more importantly, you are wasting resources that others have entrusted you to protect, and you are diminishing the value of the independent sector in the eyes of the public.

THE MUSEUM OF MODERN ART: A FUNDRAISING JUGGERNAUT. BUT WOULD LESS HAVE BEEN MORE?

* * *

In anticipation of the reopening of the Museum of Modern Art in November 2004, The *New York Times* ran a lengthy article entitled "MoMA's Funding: A Very Modern Art, Indeed,"[28] focusing on how MoMA financed the $858 million construction of its new facilities. A significant portion of the financing for this project came from a large board of trustees with members who made seven- and eight-figure pledges. Total contributions from the trustees exceeded $500 million, averaging more than $7 million per trustee. Every museum hopes that its permanent collections and curatorial staffs make it the envy of other museums throughout the world, but there is little doubt that most executive directors who read this article were even more envious of MoMA's fundraising capacity. Like a California wildfire, the news leapt from the museum world to other nonprofits, also making MoMA the envy of social service agencies, universities, hospitals, and countless other equally worthy nonprofits.

In fact, on the same day that the article appeared, Independent Sector, a nonprofit trade association, began its annual conference in Chicago. During a discussion of the ideal board size, one gentleman from the audience (a very corporate-looking lawyer: no weekend-casual dress for this prosperous fellow), took the mike, extolling MoMA's fundraising capacity. He essentially argued that no nonprofit should limit its board size if it can find directors who can raise the sort of money described in the *Times* article. Word had spread. Audible gasps were heard from many of the 125-plus attendees when the tanned lawyer repeated the numbers. The undercurrent from many in the audience was, "Hear, hear. This gentleman is absolutely right. The staff of the Senate Finance Committee[29] has no business telling us to limit our board size to 15 members. One size does not fit all."

Unfortunately, the dark-suited messenger failed to report the article's subtext. The *Times* article included the following facts: There is now a "powerful new emphasis on net worth." To raise the money that it did, MoMA added a number of celebrity business executives to its board who are not recognized as traditional collectors and may not fully understand MoMA's historical context or mission. There has also been an apparent shift in power with

28. H. Eakin, *A Very Modern Art, Indeed*, N.Y. Times, Nov. 7, 2004, *supra* note 5.
29. Staff of the S. Fin. Comm., DISCUSSION DRAFT ON PROPOSED REFORMS FOR EXEMPT ORGANIZATIONS (2004).

the movement in the direction of professional managers and away from curators. There was also discussion of cost overruns. One person was quoted in the article as having said, "[The new building] ran away with the budget." The logical question: Is fundraising capacity skewing MoMA's mission?

No one will know the answer to that question for several years, but there certainly was a lot of speculation over the size of the gift shops and restaurants. Many were questioning MoMA's jaw-dropping $20 admission price before the reopening. While MoMA was successful in tapping the pocketbooks of its trustees, it also incurred over $235 million in additional debt to finance the project, bringing its total outstanding debt to over $398 million.[30] That debt and the staff needed to run a larger facility have to be funded somehow. Will this mean more blockbuster shows of big-named artists at the expense of smaller, more intimate shows highlighting the works of newer and lesser known artists? The *Times* article suggest the answer is "No." In fact, the article suggests that there may be fewer blockbusters if desired attendance levels can be reached without resort them. But will there be room for many lesser-known contemporary artists, or will MOMA's collection be frozen in the Twentieth Century? Striking the proper balances is what defining, fostering, and protecting mission are about.

Let's return to our corporate lawyer and many of those at the session on governance. Governance and fundraising are not the same things. As a couple of people in the audience pointed out, large boards are unwieldy, and their members lose a sense of responsibility. Those observations are fact, not opinion. Large boards also tend to shift power to the executive director, which can actually weaken the institution by eliminating an important check on the executive director. In other words, a large board may be good for fundraising but not for governing. There are plenty of ways to reward big donors, including granting naming rights and appointing major benefactors to donor-advisory committees. Those in the room who argued against smaller boards were confusing fundraising with governance.

* * *

1.2 PART OF THE BIGGER SCHEME

You may view yourself as "just a minor player on the scene." Nothing could be further from the truth. Assuming your organization is a tax-exempt entity, it is just one of over 1.54 million tax-exempt organizations that were on the Master File of Tax-Exempt Organizations of the Internal Revenue Service (IRS) at the end of Fiscal Year 2004.[31] There are undoubtedly additional organizations that are nonprofits but these have not obtained tax-exempt status for one reason or another. The nonprofit sector's share of national 1998 income was 6.1 percent, or just over $440 billion. The total number of paid employees in this sector of the economy that year was 10.9 million.[32] The point: You might be a volunteer, but nonprofits play a vital role in our society. Your efforts are important.

30. H. Eakin, *supra* note 5.

31. *See* Internal Revenue Service, *Table 22—Tax-Exempt Organizations and Other Entities Listed on the Exempt Organization Business Master File, by Type of Organization and Internal Revenue Code Section, Fiscal Years 2001–2004*, reprinted in PUBLICATION 55B, IRS DATA BOOK (FY 2004).

32. URBAN INSTITUTE, THE NEW NONPROFIT ALMANAC & DESK REFERENCE (2002).

1.3 ASSUMPTION

The title to this *Guide* includes a reference to executive directors and advisors but the *Guide*'s real focus is on "volunteer" or pro bono service, with special focuses on the role of directors and the partnership between the board and the executive director. The *Guide*'s typical reader will be a director—sometimes referred to as a trustee. If the organization does not have a professional staff, the typical user may also be serving as an officer who carries out the board's directives. As a consequence of this focus on "volunteer" service, the *Guide* will not always draw the sharp distinction that the law draws between directors and officers. Having just described the intended audience, let's be clear: This *Guide* will prove to be invaluable to lawyers, accountants, and advisors to nonprofits. Even those who are already knowledgeable about certain topics covered in the *Guide* will undoubtedly have gaps in their knowledge that other parts of the *Guide* can fill.

1.4 GENERALITY OF COVERAGE

Although the discussion of the federal income tax aspects of nonprofits will be applicable to nonprofits throughout the United States, the discussion regarding director and officer duties, corporate governance, operational risks, fundraising, and other matters governed by state law should be viewed as a general discussion with the understanding that the specific rules will vary from state to state.

Nevertheless, the discussion will alert you to the basic issues that will arise in whatever legal jurisdictions your organization is organized and operates. In many cases, there are far more similarities than differences among state laws. When appropriate, differences in state law will be noted, but when it comes to particular issues affecting your organization, you will still need to consult with qualified legal counsel.

1.5 USING QUALIFIED PROFESSIONALS

This *Guide* will provide you with practical insights into the issues facing volunteer directors and officers, but it is not meant as a substitute for the advice of a qualified attorney, accountant, or other professional. Many of the rules that are discussed have exceptions, complex definitions, subparts, and subtle nuances. If each rule were discussed in detail, this *Guide* would quickly become a treatise. The objective is to alert you to issues that you need to know about to better manage your nonprofit's operations and assets while keeping everyone out of trouble.

Unfortunately, many nonprofits try to cut corners when it comes to legal, accounting, and other professional services. Often this is a case of being "penny-wise and pound-foolish." The argument goes something like this: "We are a social services agency. Every dollar we spend on lawyers and accountants is a dollar less that we can spend on the needs of those we serve." The problem with this argument is that others have entrusted the board and officers with making sure that the money from contributions and grants is not wasted or stolen. Like it or not, that means the organization must tolerate some level of expenditures on lawyers, accountants, and administrative overhead. There will still be those who disagree. The simple retort: "Fire those in charge of disbursing the money—just leave the money in a bag and tell needy people to help themselves." In the long run, truly qualified advisors save organizations money and protect assets.

1.6 BEFORE STARTING A NEW ORGANIZATION

Throughout this *Guide*, the examples assume that the organization in question is an established one with staff, financial resources, and a clearly articulated mission. However, there will undoubtedly be people who review this *Guide* as they contemplate starting a new organization. The organization in question will mostly likely be charitable in nature. With that in mind, let's now briefly address the considerations in starting a charity.

(a) START BY LOOKING FOR AN EXISTING CHARITY. Organizing and operating any organization takes time, effort, and money. Simply building the organizational architecture does not provide any benefit to the needy or the sick. These organizational efforts do not improve the school system or bring art to a new or wider audience. So before starting a charity, be sure that there is a need. If you google a phrase such as "medical research," "contemporary dance," or "food bank for the homeless," you will discover that there are existing organizations already providing the services in question. While everyone likes to be the big kahuna, you may actually be far more effective by teaming up with an existing organization. The downside: You may have to establish credibility by performing menial tasks assigned to new volunteers before you can make policy. Those tasks may entail stuffing envelopes, updating mailing lists, packing cartons of food, or pounding nails and sawing two-by-fours. Do not forget, however, that those tasks await you as the organizer of a new organization unless you have a long list of volunteers.

By working with an existing charity, your time and money are much more likely to impact mission. A good case can be made that we have too many charities with many providing duplicative services. Each one of these charities develops a fundraising program, assembles a board and staff, implements a system of internal controls, and pays outside advisors. For the most part, all of these expenditures represent overhead that is necessary but that siphons dollars away from the mission. Consider taking advantage of the economies of scale offered by an existing charity.

There is a clear lesson here for people who want to start a charity: Think long and hard before building a new wheel.

A New Trend toward Consolidation

* * *

Over the last several years, there have been a number of widely reported stories of fraud perpetrated against charities with "marquee" names. One fraud that comes to mind involved the American Cancer Society's Ohio Division and the embezzlement of nearly $6.9 million dollars through wire transfers to a Swiss bank account.[33] Fortunately for the society, the fraud was quickly discovered and the bulk of the money was recovered. During the spring of 2004, an executive with the St. Clair Goodwill in Port Huron, Michigan pled guilty to two counts of embezzlement, admitting to stealing $750,000 from the charity over a 20-year period.[34]

Here is a hypothesis about these frauds. When people think about the Goodwill Industries or the American Cancer Society, a large, national organization comes immediately to mind. However, many reported frauds involve local chapters of nationally known organizations. The appeal of local chapters is understandable because the chapter structure permits the national organization to add an influential banker, attorney, accountant, union leader, and other prominent members of the local community to its fundraising efforts through the allure of board membership. Those local faces are good for fundraising. Face-to-face appeals are undoubtedly more effective than phone calls from telemarketers located in the charity's office in Washington, D.C. or India.

There is a cost to the resulting decentralized structure, however. While the national organization may be a large one, the local chapters are relatively small, particularly if the branches go deeper than the state level. Each of these organizations must implement a system of internal controls. That should mean checks and balances in the accounting system. Structurally, such a system requires at least two "finance or accounting" types so that someone is always watching the person who has custody or expenditure authority over the organization's assets. Three people would be preferable so that the recordkeeping function is kept separate from the custody and expenditure functions.[35] As the St. Clair Goodwill incident at least suggests, however, these chapters simply may not be large enough in terms of financial resources to be able to support a large administrative staff. None of the newspaper accounts indicate whether the St. Clair chapter had more than one accountant, but one has to be suspicious about whether there were "deep" financial controls. From a practical standpoint, small organizations simply do not generate the volume of financial transactions that are often necessary to make a solid system of financial controls economically viable.

Large organizations that utilize local chapters need to take at least one of two basic courses of action to ensure the adequacy of internal controls. The first course is the obvious one: Consider consolidating local chapters into state or regional chapters. If the national organization believes this will hurt fundraising, it should appoint the lawyer, accountant, and community leader to an advisory board to keep them involved.

A second course of action is to adopt a "lockbox" approach with the local chapters left in place but the national organization adopting and enforcing a system of internal controls covering local operations. This system could include a staff of internal auditors who periodically

---

33. M. Gallagher and V. Radcliffe, *Internal Controls in Nonprofit Organizations: The Case of the American Cancer Society, Ohio Division*, 12 NONPROFIT MGMT. & LEADERSHIP 313 (Spring 2002).

34. A. Mullins, *Ex-Goodwill Executive Admits Stealing $750,000*, TIMES HERALD.COM, Apr. 30, 2004; and A. Mullins, *Ex-Goodwill Worker Stole 'Substantially'* TIMES HERALD.COM, Dec. 18, 2003.

35. We consider all three functions in Chapter 5.

review local accounting controls, a standardized system of internal controls, a uniform chart of accounts, prepackaged accounting and reporting systems, and centralized investment of funds. With the lockbox in place, money is collected at the local level but remitted into segregated accounts maintained by the parent organization.

Obviously, much thought and planning must go into determining the particular features for a given organization. Overall, the lockbox approach is designed to leave the local fundraising structure in place while imposing a cost-effective control system from above. The national organization will have to develop a system to ensure that locally raised money is returned to the local community. In achieving that result, the umbrella organization should resist the temptation to impose a "handling" fee that exceeds the actual cost of the control system.

As just one example, the United Way of Chicago and the United Way of Suburban Chicago recognized the potential cost savings that could be achieved through a consolidation of their operations, resulting in a decision to merge. The following is an excerpt from a press release[36] issued by United Way of Metro Chicago:

> On January 1, 2004, United Way entities throughout the Chicago area become United Way of Metropolitan Chicago. This restructuring, a full-scale effort to impact more lives in the community, has succeeded in lowering costs and increasing operational efficiency, so more donor dollars are available to fund community health and human service programs. The consolidation centralizes all support staff functions, but does not change the fundamental activities of United Way in each community it serves—that is raising funds and distributing them locally.
>
> "The consolidation will eliminate duplication and dramatically increase efficiencies and effectiveness so we can direct more donor dollars to improving peoples' lives," said R. Eden Martin, Board Chairman of United Way of Metropolitan Chicago. He said the consolidation has already put in place changes that will yield an annual savings of nearly $3.0 million in administrative costs, which means an 18% reduction in expenses. As a result, more donor dollars can go to United Way-funded programs. "We're extremely pleased with these immediate results of our efforts, and expect to see more positive results as time goes on," he said.

* * *

(b) CONSIDER PARTNERING OPPORTUNITIES. There may be a reason that there is not a contemporary dance company or a school of medieval art in your community. There may be no need or demand for the services in question. To quickly assess whether the need exists, try identifying a successful entity that is in close geographic proximity to your community. Give the executive director a call, and see whether he has ever considered extending the organization's service area. This organization may already have a detailed study that outlines why expansion to your community is not warranted or feasible. These insights could save you wasted time and resources. That contact could also expose "partnering" opportunities. For example, suppose you are located in rural Connecticut, 75 miles outside New York City. You are interested in classical music but are tired of making the trek into New York City. You and friends consider starting a symphony

36. Press Release, United Way Metro Chicago, "Chicago Area United Way System Completes Its Transformation" (Dec. 19, 2003).

orchestra. That is going to require a lot of money. Instead of almost certain failure, why not contact an institution located in New York City to see whether it has ever considered an "outreach" program? You can offer organizational skills, a new source of funds, and a possible venue for a two-or-three concert summer series. The series probably will not include performances by the New York Philharmonic, but you might be able to find students from Juilliard or other schools who are looking for a venue. That's an opening that you may be able to build into a more substantial series.

(c) IDENTIFY FUNDERS. All too often, people interested in starting a charity begin the process by asking the attorney to "draw up the papers." That is the wrong place to start. After identifying an unfilled need, begin by determining how much financial support there is for your idea. If you and several like-minded friends have only a few thousand dollars to contribute, you will not get very far. Unless you can obtain legal and accounting services pro bono, you are probably looking at a minimum cost of $2,500 to $5,000 in professional fees to shepherd a new organization through the formation and tax-exemption process.

That cost will be much higher if you do not have a business plan—yes, a business plan—for the charity. Even though the charity may be a nonprofit, if it is to succeed, it must be run like a business. At a minimum, you should have the following information before contacting a professional to help with the organizational process:

- A clearly defined mission and the specific activities that will fulfill that mission.
- A detailed assessment of need in the contemplated service area (e.g., identify the number of children with the life-threatening disease or who cannot read at grade level).
- A detailed assessment of how the community is likely to react to the organization and its activities, particularly if the activities will be controversial (e.g., a halfway house for sex offenders or drug addicts).
- A list of individuals and organizations already providing similar services in the contemplated service area with as much detail about these existing service providers as is available (e.g., clinics that treat AIDS patients and the number of persons served).
- A list of directors and officers as well as their qualifications.
- A five-year budget with a very detailed one-year budget.
- A list of any required government approvals or licenses with necessary contacts and approval and license applications.
- A list of potential and committed funders and sponsors. If grants are contemplated, you should have a full understanding of what information must be provided to each potential funder and of the application and funding processes.

- If the organization will require ongoing funding, a detailed plan describing fundraising plans and assessing associated costs.
- An assessment of what resources the organization will need to fulfill its mission (e.g., music teachers, special needs facilities for handicapped clients). If physical facilities are required, identify the cost, lease terms, and availability. If specialized personnel are required, identify their availability and cost.
- An assessment of insurance costs and needs.

You can certainly pay a consultant to assist you in assembling this information, particularly when it comes to fundraising and obtaining grants. Much of the legwork can and should be undertaken, however, by the organizers.

(d) RETAIN A QUALIFIED ATTORNEY. You should contact a qualified attorney once the business plan is in place and the organization and its activities appear to be viable. At that point, you and the attorney can begin the organizational process, which should include the following steps:

- Form a nonprofit corporation (or other appropriate entity) by filing articles of incorporation with the appropriate state agency (most likely the secretary of state). Do not let the attorney handle this process alone. Be sure to review all documents, focusing on governance and the organization's needs.
- Name or elect an initial board of directors.
- Hold an organizational meeting with the initial board of directors appointing officers and adopting organizational bylaws
- Obtain a taxpayer or employer identification number.
- Prepare and file an application for tax-exempt status with the IRS. The attorney will help you with this process, but if you have taken the preliminary steps already suggested, you should be able to prepare many of the required schedules yourself.
- If required, file an initial registration with the charity regulator in the states in which the organization is organized, soliciting funds, or doing business.
- If required, obtain workers' compensation coverage.
- File all necessary applications, registrations, exemptions from or permits required by sales and use tax, employment tax, and property tax laws.
- File and obtain any special licenses (e.g., for a day care center or charter school).
- If contracting with paid fundraisers, make sure that the fundraisers and related contracts comply with applicable state and federal laws.

- Schedule and provide notices for regular board meetings and, if a membership organization, necessary membership meetings.
- Begin working with a qualified accountant to set up an accounting system, including a system of financial and internal controls.

To reiterate, do not call an attorney until you have completed the initial steps just described. Every attorney who works with tax-exempt organizations has horror stories to tell about the client who called before the business plan was in place. Good attorneys will tell this client that either the attorney can do the legwork or the client can, but if the attorney does the legwork, the client will receive an exorbitant legal bill. All too often, the inexperienced client pushes forward, asking the attorney to write descriptive material that the client could just as easily have written. Despite the warnings and carefully crafted engagement letter, this client is almost always shocked when the bill arrives.

(e) ADVICE TO THE WEALTHY. Every advisor who specializes in charitable organizations has had a wealthy person ask about setting up a foundation. The inquiry often occurs in conjunction with the sale of a closely-held business, an IPO, or thoughts about the person's legacy. Many people like the sound of their surname followed by the phrase "Family Foundation." Granted, this discussion will not discourage most people who have the glimmer of a family foundation in their eyes from forming a foundation, particularly when the person is worth hundreds of millions of dollars and has very specific charitable missions firmly in mind. However, the wealthy need to recognize that family foundations are very expensive from an administrative standpoint. These foundations are subject to complex and unforgiving federal tax rules that forbid self-dealing, political activity, certain business holdings, and certain expenditures. The foundation will require regular legal advice to avoid the pitfalls posed by these and other rules.

With that in mind, wealthy individuals and families should at least consider alternatives to the family foundation, particularly when the contemplated gift or bequest will not exceed $10 million. The following alternatives should be considered:

- Making restricted gifts to a public charity or charities that carry out programs that are of interest to the donor.
- Making a gift to or creating a fund administered by a community foundation.
- Setting up a donor-advised fund with a commercial entity such as Fidelity Investments or the Vanguard Group.
- Establishing a supporting organization.[37]

---

37. Forming a supporting organization may become more difficult because the Senate Finance Committee has considered proposed legislation that would prevent charitable organizations that look like family foundations from availing themselves of "supporting organization" status as a means to avoid private foundation status. At the May 20, 2005 meeting of the Exempt Organizations Subcommittee of the American Bar Association

Each of these alternatives provides the tax advantages associated with charitable giving, creates a legacy, provides younger family members with the opportunity to participate in the family's philanthropic endeavors, and, in many cases, offers more flexibility than a family foundation. We will consider several of these alternatives in more detail in the section of Chapter 7 that pertains to private foundations and in Chapter 10.

1.7 CONCLUDING THE PRELIMINARIES

William Bowen's sentiments are worth keeping in mind. Volunteering as a nonprofit director or officer permits you to devote your energies to a cause you believe in while providing what should be a pleasant diversion from your day-to-day professional activities. While you might be tempted to check your professional judgment at the nonprofit boardroom door, don't.

Your contribution to a nonprofit organization will be greatly enhanced by relying on your hard-hitting business judgment. This *Guide* will provide you an overview of the legal, accounting, and regulatory issues that confront nonprofits, permitting you to better focus that judgment.

Tax Section, one government official indicated that the IRS had centralized the processing of applications for those organizations trying to take advantage of what are now apparently suspect categories of supporting organizations. This official indicated that processing of these applications had all but ground to a halt as the IRS considered how to deal with the "supporting organization" issue in the wake of congressional concerns.

CHAPTER 2

BEFORE SIGNING ON

Here I am at the end of the road and at the top of the heap.

POPE JOHN XXIII, ON SUCCEEDING PIUS XII[1]

Being asked to serve on a board is often a boost for the old ego. Before you agree to sign on as a volunteer director or officer, you should address a few details. Most will be nothing but common sense, but having a checklist certainly will not hurt.

Here are two basic pieces of advice. First, avoid the one-man show: The executive director who desires agreement and demands adulation. Second, make sure you are interested in and committed to the organization's mission. If you are not, worry not. The organization can find someone else who is.

Before committing, be sure to ask yourself why you are agreeing to serve. There would be far more vacancies on boards if only those with the "purest of hearts" served. Many people join boards to network, but anyone joining for this reason should ask, "Will I have the time to make a meaningful contribution to the organization?" Those who answer "no" might actually be better off declining membership. Putting in "face-time" is one thing, but people eventually notice those who make a significant contribution and those who do nothing. Nobody wants to be noticed for shirking their responsibilities or skipping meetings and events.

2.1 "GIVE, GET, OR GET OFF"

While many organizations want your time and judgment, there is no question that what some organizations want is either your money or your ability to raise money.

1. TIME, Nov. 24, 1958.

In an article discussing a dispute between the Chicago Museum of Contemporary Art and the estate of a former chairman, a development officer is quoted as having said:

> We seek four basic commitments....They [trustees] should go to board meetings, serve on at least one committee, attend exhibition openings and performances, and most important, contribute to the MCA's financial support....A trustee either gives money, helps us get it, or gets off the board.[2]

This very candid comment regrettably reflects reality despite sounding crass[3] and confusing governance with fundraising. Directors who like the perks and visibility associated with certain organizations should be sure that they are willing to pay the "admission" price, both in terms of money and time devoted to oversight.

2.2 ASK QUESTIONS

Before agreeing to serve, you should ask questions about what the organization does and what will be expected of you. At a minimum, you should want to know how often and when meetings are held, whether you will be expected to serve on any board committees, what events you must attend, and whether fundraising is required.

If you are a professional, you should tactfully ask whether the organization expects you to provide your expertise to the organization free of charge. This is an important issue if you are an attorney, an accountant, or a public relations professional. Even if you do not have the requisite expertise in nonprofit law, accounting, or taxation, the organization may be expecting you to corral someone with that expertise. If these are the expectations, establish the rules of the game upfront. Otherwise, you could create an embarrassing situation for everyone when you send your first bill for professional services. In addition, be sure to consider the potential for conflicts of interest before taking on such an engagement.

---

2. A. Artner, *$5 Million MCA Pledge Foundered In Power Feud, Ex-Chairman, Wife Reportedly at Odds With Museum Chief*, CHIC. TRIB., Jan. 11, 1998.

3. For a more recent restatement of the "Give, Get, or Get Off" adage, see J. Graves, *Between a Board and a Hard Place; Volunteer Directors of Arts Groups, Not Paid Staff, Face the Ultimate Responsibility*, TACOMA (Wash) NEWS TRIB., Mar. 13, 2005. Graves writes,

> TAM's board, like many, uses a sliding scale, said vice president Judith Nilan. Each donor is expected to raise or give a certain amount. The museum calculates these in advance, and can afford to admit only a certain number of members at lower levels so the board can meet its annual group donation of $100,000.
>
> "Most boards have a give-or-get policy, and if they don't, they should," Donnelly said. "What are you there for, your good looks? I'm serious. You bring your skills and talents to a board, but the organization needs resources."

2.3 REVIEW MATERIALS

Before agreeing to serve, take time to review written information about the organization. You should review the organization's:

- Annual report.
- Fundraising brochures.
- Financial statements.
- Membership information.
- Articles of incorporation and bylaws.
- IRS Form 1023, Application for Federal Exempt Status (which is a publicly available document).
- Most recent IRS Form 990 (considered in Chapter 6).
- Web site, if it has one.

2.4 MEET WITH THE EXECUTIVE DIRECTOR AND OTHER OFFICERS

If at all possible, schedule a brief meeting with the organization's executive director to learn more about the organization and what will be expected of you. If you know any of the other directors, be sure to ask them for a candid assessment of what being a director of this particular organization is all about. Be sure to ask about pending litigation. There is no point jumping onto the *Titanic*. Directors' and officers' liability insurance coverage and indemnification are definitely two protections that you will want to ask about before agreeing to serve.

2.5 REVIEW OTHER RESOURCES

There are any number of steps that you might take to find additional information about an organization that has asked you to serve as a volunteer director or officer, including the following:

- Contact the state attorney general (or other agency with a regulatory role) to request copies of information that is available to the public.
- Contact the Better Business Bureau in your city, or check to see whether the organization has been reviewed by the BBB Wise Giving Alliance.
- Check the IRS Web site at http://www.irs.treas.gov/basic/bus_info/eo/eosearch.html to learn about the organization's tax-exempt status.
- Check the GuideStar Web site at www.guidestar.org. As of June 1, 2005, GuideStar maintained data on over 1.5 million exempt organizations, including charities, membership organizations, civic leagues, political groups, and others.
- Run a search on the Web.
- Run a Lexis/Nexis or Factiva search if you subscribe or otherwise have access to either of these services.

- If the organization has issued tax-exempt bonds or other securities (e.g., partnership interests in low-income housing tax credit projects), review the offering statement.
- Attend a meeting of the members, if there are members.

2.6 STEP ASIDE IF THE INFORMATION IS NOT FORTHCOMING

There will be instances when the organization's executive director does not answer your questions fully or locate the requested documents (even following repeated requests). It goes without saying that this is an important piece of information in and of itself. You should avoid any organization if its leaders do not want you to know what the rules of the game are or what the organization really does.

An unwillingness to provide information may not necessarily mean that something is askew. However, it may indicate that the organization is a one-man show. As you will see time and again, that is a show you may want to miss.

Obtaining and reviewing all of this information is not just a question of self-protection. You will also be in a better position to perform your duties as a volunteer director or officer if you have reviewed the indicated material and talked with the people in charge. In most cases, you will find that everything is in order, speeding your review.

2.7 YOUR ROLE

You have certain functions and responsibilities as a nonprofit director or officer. The best way to understand these duties and responsibilities is to first ask those who are asking you to volunteer what they expect you to do. You should then review the information referred to earlier in this chapter. If you know that you will not be able to fulfill your duties and responsibilities, you should admit that upfront, and refrain from volunteering. In the long run, everyone will be better off if you do not serve. If you do decide to serve, you are responsible for overseeing the assets and activities of the organization. As the next chapter makes clear, there will be people watching how you discharge your duties.

CHAPTER 3

ORGANIZATIONAL BASICS

Be the first to move for adjournment; this will make you popular; it is what everyone is waiting for.

HARRY CHAPMAN[1]

But delegation requires greater accountability and tigher control.

PETER F. DRUCKER[2]

---

1. JAMES B. SIMPSON, SIMPSON'S CONTEMPORARY QUOTATIONS REVISED EDITION (HarperCollins 1997), attributing the quote to Harry Chapman in the Greater Kansas City Medical Bulletin (1963).
2. *Management Lessons of Irangate*, WALL ST. J., Mar. 24, 1987.

We now consider organizational issues associated with charitable and other nonprofit organizations. This means first drawing a distinction between nonprofit and tax-exempt entities and then defining the term *nonprofit organization* and your role as a director or officer. We then consider the role of members. We also examine the role played by state attorneys general. They (or some agency with similar powers and authority) are charged with regulating nonprofit organizations at the state level. Having defined the players, we then consider conduct of meetings, maintenance of minutes, major events in the life of a nonprofit, and various other issues.

3.1 NONPROFIT VERSUS TAX-EXEMPT STATUS

People frequently use the terms *nonprofit* and *tax-exempt organization* interchangeably. In many cases, the organization that they are referring to can be described by both terms. However, the two terms do have different meanings, and consequently, do not necessarily include the same organizations.

A *tax-exempt organization* generally is organized as a nonprofit entity. However, not all nonprofit entities will qualify for tax-exempt status. An organization must meet the requirements of Section 501(c) of the Internal Revenue Code to be recognized as a tax-exempt organization for federal tax purposes. In most cases, the organization must file IRS Form 1023 or 1024 as a first step in the recognition process.[3]

A nonprofit entity, on the other hand, is organized and operated under the laws of a particular state, usually pursuant to state statutes governing nonprofit corporations. It is not required to file for tax-exempt status but often does. Furthermore, not all nonprofit organizations are charitable organizations, as we will see in Chapter 6.

3.2 THE CORPORATE FORM IS THE PREVALENT ONE

Nonprofits can be organized as unincorporated associations, corporations, charitable trusts, or limited liability companies. Many nonprofit organizations start out as unincorporated organizations. Two good examples are the local garden club and a grade-school boosters' club. This may be sufficient for conducting business for a garden or boosters' club because there is probably not a lot of revenue involved or exposure to liability.

3. Churches and their integrated auxiliaries are not required to file for Section 501(c)(3) tax-exempt status. There is a procedure for granting group exemptions when a central organization has one or more subordinate organizations under its general supervision or control. This exemption is often used where there is a national organization with local chapters. If the central organization has an exemption, the subordinate organizations need not apply for exemption, but the central organization must provide the IRS with information regarding each subordinate organization either when the original application for group exemption is filed or if the subordinate organization is subsequently added to the group, as part of an annual filing that the central organization submits to the IRS at least 90 days before the close of the central organization's accounting period. *See* IRS Publication 557, Tax-Exempt Status for Organization (Rev. Mar. 2005), for additional details.

As an organization's activities become more involved, it will likely choose the corporate form because it provides a well-grooved organizational form. This is probably due to the fact that all but two states have a comprehensive nonprofit corporation statute; Delaware[4] and Kansas[5] provide for nonprofit corporations to be formed under their general corporation statutes. Furthermore, most people are much more familiar with the corporate organizational form than the other forms. Most important, people like the corporate form because it provides limited liability. As you will see, however, that does not mean that directors and officers will necessarily escape liability if they breach their duties. Assuming no breach of duties, limited liability in this context means that someone suing the corporation can look only to the nonprofit's assets to satisfy the claims. Some states separately provide statutory protection to members of unincoporated associations.

The charitable trust is also a viable organizational form, often recommended by estate planners who are charged with creating a vehicle to implement the client's charitable desires. If the trust format is utilized, it most likely will be for organizations that do not actively conduct a charitable activity. Instead, the organization's primary activities are likely to be fundraising, investing its endowment, and distributing funds to individuals (e.g., a scholarship fund) or to other charitable organizations (grantees).

The limited liability company is a relatively new form of entity, so there are probably more questions than answers under state law regarding the qualification and use of these entities as nonprofits.[6] It is possible to obtain tax-exempt status for certain limited liability companies. Affiliated nonprofit organizations are using limited liability companies as part of their corporate structures.

The feature that most distinguishes nonprofit corporations from business corporations is the absence of shareholders. Like their for-profit counterparts, nonprofit corporations have directors and officers. Under most nonprofit corporate laws, a nonprofit corporation can be organized as either a member or "nonmember" organization. In some cases, members are functionally equivalent to shareholders. However, the better term is *stakeholder,* and there may well be other stakeholders who are not members. Moreover, not all "members" are members in the legal sense: those with the right to elect directors. For example, an art museum may have membership categories that provide members of the public with certain privileges for different levels of contributions, but the board is self-perpetuating. The art museum may also have nonmember stakeholders, which could include students of a fine arts school run by the museum.

Membership is a fluid concept, tailored to the particular needs of the organization. For example, many hospital-affiliated groups utilize membership as a means

---

4. Del. Code, Title 8, Chapter 1. For example, see Section 215, which addresses member voting rights in non-stock corporations.
5. Kan. Stat. § 17-6001. The Web site of the Kansas secretary of state refers to the same statutory provision for both for-profit and nonprofit corporations.
6. The IRS exemption process clearly contemplates limited liability companies qualifying as charitable organizations. *See* IRS FORM 1023 (Rev. 10-2004), Part II, Question 2.

to establish parent–subsidiary relationships. That is the "impersonal" world of controlled nonprofit corporate groups.

3.3 THE PLAYERS

We turn our focus to the different players in the nonprofit corporate environment. In terms of governance, the two most important groups are the directors (designated trustees by some organizations) and officers. In smaller, more volunteer-centric organizations, there is likely to be overlap between the two groups, with the directors also filling the various officer positions. This is perfectly appropriate when there is no paid staff. When nonprofits have staffs, many of the officer positions are filled by paid employees rather than board members. Even then, there may be some overlap. For example, the organization's secretary may be a volunteer board member when there is not a general counsel who might otherwise fill that position. The organization may also draw a distinction between the president (a board member functioning as chair of the board) and the executive director (a paid staff member functioning as the chief executive or the chief operating officer). Nonprofit corporation statutes provide for great flexibility, permitting each organization to tailor the relationship between the board and the officers to fit the organization's particular needs and culture.

(a) THE BOARD OF DIRECTORS. The board of directors is responsible for managing the nonprofit's affairs. This does *not* mean carrying out day-to-day activities such as raising funds, paying salaries, performing activities that further the organization's exempt functions (e.g., teaching if the organization is devoted to education), or maintaining an accounting system. *Managing the affairs of the corporation* means providing oversight, setting long-term policy, objectives, and direction, and allocating resources. The directors should *not* be interacting with the organization's staff on a day-to-day basis except to the extent required by formal board requirements (e.g., the audit committee meeting with the treasurer in preparation for a board meeting).

(i) Oversight versus Operations. The board should serve as a check on the officers and staff. This means monitoring corporate spending, compliance with applicable laws, and progress toward meeting budgets and missions.[7] To illustrate

7. *See* Office of Community Services of the Administration for Children and Family Services of the U.S. Department of Health and Human Services, Information Memorandum No. 82 (2005), which provides an excellent description of the relationship between a board and the executive director, stating in Q & A 7:

> Boards establish policy, Executive Directors execute policy.
>
> Boards set agency mission, Executive Directors accomplish agency mission.
>
> Boards set performance targets, Executive Directors guide work to achieve targets.
>
> Boards and Executive Directors evaluate agency performance, Both are accountable.
>
> Boards supervise directly only one employee—the Executive Director.

Each of these sentences is the heading of a larger discussion that is very much worth reviewing.

the distinction between the board and staff, consider an organization that has a complaint for sexual harassment filed against it. If the organization is relatively large and this is an isolated incident, the board certainly wants to be kept informed about the lawsuit, but the board should leave the details to the appropriate officers and staff members, particularly if the organization has in-house legal counsel. If, however, the suit involves allegations against the nonprofit's executive director or there are a number of complaints, the board needs to become more proactive, possibly appointing a special committee to investigate and make recommendations to improve the work environment.[8] Even then, the staff should be charged with implementing the recommendations.

If board members find themselves running operations in their capacity as board members, organizational changes may be in order at either the board or the staff level. Sometimes the board members become too involved, interfering with the staff. If this is the case, the board should ask itself why this is happening. The board might rightfully conclude that the staff is not up to the task, in which case staff-level changes are in order. However, the board should be circumspect before concluding that the problem is the staff. Almost everyone who advises nonprofits has seen instances when a board's second-guessing and interference impedes the staff. This is often a problem in homeowner associations. Frequent management turnover is often a sure sign that the board is meddling.

(ii) Chair of the Board. State statutes do not thoroughly address all aspects of board operations. For example, the Revised Model Nonprofit Corporation Act[9] (Revised Model Act) is silent on the question of whether there must be a chair of the board. Nevertheless, boards frequently designate a chair. There is a running debate as to whether the chair should be an independent director or the organization's executive director/president.[10] From a governance standpoint, there

---

8. Appointing a special litigation committee may be particularly warranted when a number of the directors have conflicts with respect to the litigation.

9. The Revised Model Nonprofit Corporation Act (RMNCA) was adopted by the American Bar Association's Business Law Section Subcommittee on the Model Nonprofit Corporation Law in 1987.

10. *See* NATIONAL ASSOCIATION OF CORPORATE DIRECTORS, REPORT OF THE NACD BLUE RIBBON COMMISSION ON BOARD LEADERSHIP (2004), in which the executive summary acknowledges this debate, stating:

> Some leading corporate governance experts have advanced cogent arguments for separation of the chair and CEO roles. Others have argued convincingly for the effectiveness of the combined form. The range of views on this Commission mirrors this controversy.

The Blue Ribbon Panel argues that the question is not so much one of separation of functions but more a question of making sure that where there is not a separation between the CEO and the chair of the board, that "there be a designated leadership role for an independent director to serve as a focal point for the work of all the independent directors." The New York Stock Exchange takes a similar approach in its listing standards, with such standards being subject to SEC approval. *See* NYSE, LISTED COMPANY MANUAL § 3.30A, providing as follows:

> To empower non-management directors to serve as a more effective check on management, the non-management directors of each listed company must meet at regularly scheduled executive sessions without management.

The accompanying commentary requires a nonmanagement director to preside at each meeting.

should be institutional tension between the board and the organization's officers. Consequently, an independent chair is preferred, with that independence permitting the board to be an active participant in the governance process rather than serving as a rubberstamp for the officers' decisions. The word *tension* is used in a structural sense, which will become clearer as you review this Guide. In practice, the chair of the board and the executive director should have a close working relationship akin to a partnership.

(iii) Board Membership. The members of the initial board of directors are usually named in the corporation's articles of incorporation. Subsequent changes in the board's composition are usually made in accordance with the corporation's bylaws. The board can be self-perpetuating, or it can be chosen by the organization's members, or even a combination. While generally not required, staggered or rolling terms should be considered so that the entire board is not up for election at the same time, thus preserving institutional memory. State laws may explicitly allow for staggered terms[11] or indirectly allow for such terms by permitting the organization's bylaws to define director terms and classes.

State nonprofit corporation acts generally impose few, if any, qualifications for directors. The Revised Model Act requires that directors be individuals but otherwise leaves qualification requirements to the articles of incorporation or bylaws.[12] Notwithstanding the absence of general qualification requirements, many organizations face what might be described as secondary qualification requirements. If the organization will seek government funding, its organizers need to be cognizant of qualification requirements imposed by the government agency providing the funding. For example, nonprofits seeking funding under the federal government's Community Services Block Grant program must administer those grants through what is termed a tripartite board.[13] This generally

---

Both the Blue Ribbon Commission and the NYSE Listing rules focus on publicly-held companies. Their viewpoints may reflect the "cult of the CEO" that is so prevalent in UNITED STATES business today. Both groups recognize the importance of an independent board but, due to realities, are either unwilling or unable to completely pry the controlling hands of the CEO from the board's throat. Neither group is an impartial observer. The NYSE is competing with other exchanges for listings so there is only so far it can go in mandating governance reforms. The Blue Ribbon Commission has more than a few current and former CEOs as commission members, so there may have been a built-in predisposition toward the CEO perspective. Given that potential bias, it is difficult to see why an independent board chair is not preferable to special meetings of independent directors, particularly because both the NYSE and the Blue Ribbon Commission view independence as a key part of the governance process.

---

11. For an example, see Alaska Stat., Title 10, Chapter 10.20, § 10.20.096, which provides:

    Election and terms of directors. At the first annual election of directors and at each annual meeting thereafter the members shall elect directors to hold office for the terms provided in the bylaws. Each director holds office for the term for which elected and until a successor is elected and qualified. The terms of office of directors may be staggered.

    RMNCA § 8.06 also provides for staggered terms, which need not be uniform.

12. RMNCA § 8.02.
13. 42 U.S.C. 9910.

means that at least one-third of the organization's board be democratically selected representatives of low-income individuals and families who reside in the neighborhoods being served and one-third must be elected officials holding office at their time of selection.

Other nonprofits that receive state or local government funding may be required to designate slots on the board for labor, government, and community group representatives, with the requirements depending on the type of mission being funded. Organizations that claim supporting organization status under federal tax law[14] may be required to demonstrate that their boards are responsive to the supported organizations.[15] This may mean that a majority of the directors must be appointed by the supported organization.[16] Whatever the source of these types of secondary qualification requirements, organizations and their legal advisors should keep them in mind when drafting governing documents and when holding elections.

The board should scrupulously adhere to schedules and procedures for director elections to avoid any questions as to whether directors are duly elected. While these requirements can seem needlessly rigid, noncompliance can be problematic. In one instance, the bylaws called for elections to be held on the second Tuesday of the month. For some reason, the local chapter held the election on the third Tuesday of the month. The state umbrella organization declared the election of a slate of controversial directors invalid because the election occurred during a meeting held on the third Tuesday of the month.[17] There have been reports of disagreements and disputes between this particular state organization and the person behind the local election, demonstrating that disputes over technicalities are often subterfuges for larger policy differences.

Not surprising, some boards lose track of time and forget to hold scheduled elections. Fortunately, many state statutes provide that directors duly elected continue to be qualified as directors until their replacements are elected, thereby eliminating many potential problems.[18] Boards should not rely, however, on these types of backstops.

Most state statutes require a minimum number of directors, often three,[19] but this is by no means universal. Unless there is a very good reason, boards should be composed of an odd number of directors to avoid building the possibility for a deadlock into the legal structure—although there could be circumstances in which potential for deadlock is a means to protect minority interests.

---

14. I.R.C. § 509(a)(3).
15. Treas. Reg. § 1.509(a)-4(f) and (g).
16. Treas. Reg. § 1.509(a)-4(g)(1)(i).
17. K. Semple, *Discord in New York Branch of Disabled Veterans Group*, N.Y. TIMES, May 10, 2005.
18. For example, Section 108.10(e) of the Illinois General Not For Profit Corporation Act of 1986 provides that "[e]ach director shall hold office for the term for which he is elected and until his successor shall have been elected and qualified."
19. Charities organized as trusts can have one trustee under the laws of most states.

There are pros and cons to large and small boards. Large boards provide a deep pool of talent and workforce. However, small boards may be less bureaucratic, often getting to the heart of the matter much quicker. Many museums and performing arts groups have large boards because a significant portion of their revenue comes from charitable contributions raised through the efforts of board members.[20] While this is a long-standing practice, these groups should consider donor-advisory boards as an alternative to reward and recognize their large donors (and keep the board a manageable size). As an alternative, groups that must have large boards should consider vesting significant but clearly defined power in an executive committee, subject to full-board oversight.

Although state nonprofit statutes do not generally define donor-advisory boards, these statutes do not preclude them. This mechanism can be an excellent method for tapping the fundraising abilities or special insights or expertise of people who are too busy to serve effectively as board members. Nonprofits can use these informal constructs to formally recognize people who have something to offer the organization without overloading the board with too many members. Keep in mind that most experts on organizational behavior believe any board with more than 15 members is inefficient and unwieldy.[21] This may be why the staff of the Senate Finance Committee recommended limiting boards to a maximum of 15 directors in *Charity Oversight and Reform: Keeping Bad Things from Happening to Good Charities* prepared for a hearing held on June 22, 2004. As a

---

20. For example, GuideStar lists over 50 names under the caption Board of Directors for the Museum of Modern Art. Some of these appear to be officers and more limited trustees. The Lyric Opera of Chicago also has a very lengthy list of directors, requiring two columns filled with dozens of names.

21. The National Center for Charitable Statistics did an analysis of charities in the 1998–2000 period using data obtained from GuideStar. It found that the mean number of directors was slightly less than 11, with only 37 percent of the organizations reporting 11 or more directors. A number of business associations have addressed board size. For example, the BUSINESS ROUNDTABLE, PRINCIPLES OF CORPORATE GOVERNANCE (May 2002), shows a preference for smaller boards, stating:

> Boards of directors of large, publicly owned corporations vary in size from industry to industry and from corporation to corporation. In determining board size, directors should consider the nature, size, and complexity of the corporation as well as its stage of development. The experience of many Roundtable members suggests that smaller boards are often more cohesive and work more effectively than larger boards.

The Council of Institutional Investors recommends no more that 15 directors in a publication entitled Corporate Governance Policies (Apr. 2005), stating:

> Absent compelling, unusual circumstances, a board should have no fewer than 5 and no more than 15 members (not too small to maintain the needed expertise and independence, and not too large to be efficiently functional).

As the well-known expression goes, "as goes General Motors, so goes the UNITED STATES economy." That may not be as true following the invasion by foreign carmakers during the last two decades, but GM is still a multibillion-dollar company, and its Corporate Governance Guidelines, provide:

> The Board in recent years has averaged 13 members. The Board believes that a board ranging in size from 10 to 14 is appropriate.

The cited sources focus on the appropriate board size for public companies, but these prescriptions all seem to focus on group dynamics and efficiencies. There is every reason to assume that the same group dynamics are at work regardless of whether the entity is a nonprofit or business organization. See ABA COORDINATING COMMITTEE ON NONPROFIT GOVERNANCE, GUIDE TO CURRENT AND EMERGING STANDARDS OF NONPROFIT

final thought, any nonprofit which is still using the anachronistic term "women's board" should seriously consider designating what is in fact often an advisory board as "friends of" or other more appropriate term.

BOARD COMMITTEES

A board, particularly a large one, should consider using committees as a means to make the board meetings more productive. At a minimum, a board should have an audit committee that is responsible for selecting and consulting with the corporation's outside auditors and addressing related matters involving the organization's financial statements and internal controls.[22] The board should also consider establishing a compensation committee if the organization has paid staff. If the organization has an endowment, the board will also want to establish an investment committee to formulate policies and review investment results. This is particularly important in this age of hedge funds, derivatives, and synthetic securities.[23] All boards should also have a nominating committee that identifies candidates for membership if for no other reason than that new members mean relief for existing members who, for whatever reason, decide that they would like to pursue other activities.

The number and formality surrounding board committees depends largely on the size of the organization and its board. Although state statutes often contain very formal definitions and limitations when it comes to committees, small groups often ignore these formalities (without assuming too much risk). Typically, an issue comes up at a meeting and the board appoints two or three interested directors to investigate the matter and report their findings at the next board meeting. There will and should be more concern about complying with statutory requirements when larger organizations are involved, particularly if a

---

CORPORATE GOVERNANCE: GOVERNING AND BEST PRACTICES IN WAKE OF SARBANES-OXLEY (Mar. 10, 2005 draft), in which the authors observed:

> For many Section 501(c)(3) nonprofits, large boards may have resulted from a desire to increase donations and fundraising, since contributing or raising money for the organization is often an explicit or implicit expectation of nonprofit board members. For national 501(c)(6) trade and other associations that have a federated structure (i.e., with relationship with local affiliates or chapters), large boards may result from the desire to have representation from each affiliate or chapter.
>
> In the wake of current recommendations for smaller, more effective, "working" boards, some nonprofits may need to review their assumptions about the appropriateness of having large or prospective donors/fundraisers serve on their boards. If monetary contribution or fundraising is a primary reason for certain board spots, are there other structures, such as an advisory board or fund-raising committee, that could fulfill this purpose without the increased time and potential liability demands of board service? Are all board members willing and able to make the necessary commitment to serve as active overseers of corporate operations, including through active committee involvement?

Too often, when people elevate fundraising capacity as the key factor in board size while minimizing the importance of governance, the subtext is that money entitles those with it to control the organization. Unfortunately, being entitled does not always translate into actual exerise of control or oversight.

---

22. California law mandates an audit committee for charitable organizations that receive $2 million or more in annual gross revenues per year. *See* Ca. Gov. Code § 12586(e)(2).
23. *See* Susan M. Mangiero, RISK MANAGEMENT FOR PENSIONS, ENDOWMENTS, AND FOUNDATIONS (John Wiley & Sons, 2004).

statute mandates the committee or it is a standing committee. In these instances, the board should consider a committee charter.

Probably the most critical issue facing any board and its committees is delegated authority. Are committees supposed to make recommendations to the board, or do the committees have delegated authority to act without any further approval by the board? The Revised Model Act[24] and many state nonprofit corporation statutes permit the delegation of authority to committees. This means that when a board creates a committee, it should focus on what power it is delegating, if any. Because of the full board's ongoing oversight responsibility, delegation of authority to a committee does not by itself relieve the board from its general duties.[25]

In some states, committees can include nonboard members.[26] Doing so can serve the complementary purposes of spreading the organization's work to other volunteers and developing future board members. If nonboard members are permitted to serve on committees, the board should be particularly careful in chartering the committee so that the board's powers are not exercised by nonboard members, who may not be subject to the same duties as the board members. This possibility could explain why some states require a majority of the members of a committee to be board members or prohibit nonboard members from serving on a committee.

The committees that boards should at least consider include those discussed in the following sections.

The Executive Committee

Large boards sometimes appoint an executive committee to meet on a more regular basis than the entire board. The board may delegate certain powers to this committee. For example, the executive committee may be put in charge of formulating the agenda for board meetings, making more routine decisions, and bridging the gap between the full board and the organization's officers and staff. Certainly, this structure is permissible under many state nonprofit statutes. In fact, the New York statutes permit very broad delegation of powers to an executive committee.[27] However, any board that finds itself creating an executive committee should first ask itself whether there is truly a need for one or whether the better antidote for the problems posed by a large board would be just shrinking the size of the full board.

If the board opts for an executive committee, all board members should assume that they are in all likelihood equally responsible for the decisions of the

---

24. RMNCA §§ 8.01(c) and 8.25(d).
25. RMNCA §§ 8.25(f) and 8.30.
26. For example, Section 108.40 of the Illinois General Not For Profit Corporation Act of 1986 permits nonboard members to serve on board committees.
27. N.Y. Consol. L. Chapter 35, Article 7, § 712.

board, as the next section will make clear.[28] As a practical matter, this means that the charter for the executive committee should require the committee to keep the full board completely informed of the committee's activities and all fundamental decisions be made by the full board (statutes typically list those fundamental corporate acts that cannot be delegated to a committee) such as amending the bylaws. This may require that the executive committee's charter expressly define either the decisions that are reserved for the full board or decisions that are being delegated to the executive committee.

There are undoubtedly executive committees that are self-perpetuating committees, appointing their own members. There often is no legal prohibition against this, but anyone who serves on the larger board should ask why there is a need for the larger board, or more importantly, why he is serving as a director. All too often self-perpetuating committees are where the real power in any organization resides. Such a committee may be symptomatic of a one-man show and the problems attendant to it but with a hydra-headed person.

The Audit Committee

Every board should give serious consideration to an audit committee. This committee is charged with selecting the organization's independent auditor, reviewing the auditor's opinion and management letter, focusing appropriate attention on internal and financial controls, and resolving disputes between management and the independent auditors over financial statement presentation. We take up the issue of Sarbanes-Oxley–style[29] reforms in Chapter 5. There we look closely at the question of independence when it comes to audit committee membership. As you will see, there is a move toward mandating audit committees for larger charities, as is now the case under California law.[30]

Other states may follow California's lead.[31] The California statute contains very specific limitations as to who qualifies for audit committee membership,

---

28. Alaska is among the few states that expressly provides for an executive committee in its statute. What is interesting about its formulation is the explicit statement that the executive committee does not alter the duties of nonexecutive committee directors. Alaska Stat., Title 10, Chapter 10.20, § 10.20.111 provides:

> If the articles of incorporation or the bylaws so provide, the board of directors, by resolution adopted by a majority of the number of directors fixed by the bylaws, or, in the absence of a bylaw fixing the number of directors, the number stated in the articles of incorporation may designate two or more directors to constitute an executive committee, which, to the extent provided in the resolution or in the articles of incorporation or the bylaws of the corporation, may exercise the authority of the board of directors in the management of the corporation. The designation of the executive committee and the delegation of authority to it do not relieve the board of directors or any member of the board from responsibility imposed by law.

Section 712 of Article 7 of Chapter 35 of the New York Consolidated Statutes contains similar language regarding the status of the directors who are not members of the committee. It is difficult to reconcile the right to broadly delegate authority with no reduction in the level of responsibility assigned to the board members as a whole.

29. Sarbanes-Oxley Act of 2002, Pub. L. 107-204, 116 Stat. 745 (2002).
30. Cal. Gov. Code § 12586(e)(1).
31. Massachusetts, New York, and Texas had audit-related legislation pending as of June 1, 2005.

with an eye toward eliminating potential conflicts and maintaining independence.[32] If statutorily mandated audit committees become the norm, nonprofits—particularly those nonprofits operating in multiple jurisdictions—will have to closely monitor membership requirements.

The Finance Committee

There is absolutely no question that the full board of directors should devote a portion of each regular meeting to a discussion of the organization's finances. This discussion should focus on the organization's financial statements and adherence to the current budget, but that discussion is not sufficient. The board should want a smaller group focusing on the organization's financial condition and requirements in greater detail. This means assessing the organization's long-term financial needs, devising alternative forms of financing, budgeting, and planning for capital expenditures. These functions are best assigned to a finance committee. Obviously, this committee's membership should include the board members with the appropriate financial knowledge and experience, but committee membership may be an excellent opportunity to educate several board members who are less sophisticated when it comes to finances. This committee should work closely with the appropriate officers and employees in performing its assigned tasks.

The Compensation Committee

Both state charity regulators and the IRS have become quite active in assessing whether officer compensation arrangements are reasonable. The IRS is now in charge of administering a very formal regime (intermediate sanctions) for determining whether compensation paid to directors, officers, and others having substantial influence over the organization is appropriate. To meet the burdens imposed by this regime, charities are advised to use comparables and compensation consultants. Moreover, boards should be documenting the decision process. A standing compensation committee is clearly becoming an essential governance tool, if only to protect the full board's precious meeting time from rambling and lengthy debates. The compensation committee should be primarily responsible for developing compensation packages for the executive director and other key executives, reviewing overall levels of compensation throughout the organization, and reviewing pension and other benefit plans.

The compensation committee should operate under a charter, which at a minimum authorizes the committee to retain outside compensation consultants, restricts committee membership to independent directors, establishes ground rules governing the relationship between the executive director and the committee, and assigns primary responsibility for compliance with the intermediate sanctions to the committee, although the intermediate sanctions may still require full board involvement.

---

32. Cal. Gov. Code § 12586(e)(2).

While a charter may seem like a needless formality, a controversy that came to a head during the fall of 2005 at American University aptly illustrates why committee charters are important.[33] The controversy centered on a 1997 contract with the university's president and his rights to certain fringe benefits and reimbursements. Newspaper accounts indicated that there was a lack of clarity over the roles played by the chair of the university's board of trustees, the compensation committee, and the full board in negotiating and approving the contract. This led some to argue that the contract was invalid when a larger controversy erupted.

OTHER COMMITTEES

As already noted, when appropriate, the board should have an investment committee. We consider the function of that committee in more detail in Chapter 4. In Chapter 10, we consider gift-acceptance policies. If the organization has a large endowment or planned giving program, the board should consider a standing committee to administer the organization's gift-acceptance policy. Depending on the circumstances, the board may want to consider conflicts, litigation, and other committees.

(iv) A Director Is a Director. As a general rule, state nonprofit corporation statutes do not sanction or permit different classes of directors, with some classes having more power or different duties than others.[34] A director is a director. This often leads to some concern on the part of those who serve on boards because of their mission expertise rather than their legal or financial expertise, which they themselves often perceive to be nonexistent.

---

33. For the details, see the discussion of American University in Chapter 6

34. The Delaware Chancery Court may have initiated a trend toward holding directors with special expertise to a higher standard of care. When it decided *In re Emerging Communications Shareholders Litig.*, Civil Action No. 16415 (Del. Ch. Ct. June 4, 2004), the court absolved a number of directors from liability, but held one director liable, stating:

> Muoio is culpable because he voted to approve the transaction even though he knew, or at the very least had strong reasons to believe, that the $10.25 per share merger price was unfair. Muoio was in a unique position to know that. He was a principal and general partner of an investment advising firm, with significant experience in finance and the telecommunications sector. From 1995 to 1996, Muoio had been a securities analyst for, and a vice president of, Lazard Freres & Co. in the telecommunications and media sector. From 1985 to 1995, he was a securities analyst for Gabelli & Co., Inc., in the communications sector, and from 1993 to 1995, he was a portfolio manager for Gabelli Global Communications Fund, Inc.
>
> Hence, Muoio possessed a specialized financial expertise, and an ability to understand ECM's intrinsic value, that was unique to the ECM board members (other than, perhaps, Prosser). Informed by his specialized expertise and knowledge, Muoio conceded that the $10.25 price was "at the low end of any kind of fair value you would put," and expressed to Goodwin his view that the Special Committee might be able to get up to $20 per share from Prosser. In these circumstances, it was incumbent upon Muoio, as a fiduciary, to advocate that the board reject the $10.25 price that the Special Committee was recommending. As a fiduciary knowledgeable of ECM's intrinsic value, Muoio should also have gone on record as voting against the proposed transaction at the $10.25 per share merger price. Muoio did neither. Instead he joined the other directors in voting, without objection, to approve the transaction.

To illustrate this point, consider Joe Gray, a renowned child psychologist. As a board member of a social services agency that provides counseling to troubled teenagers, Joe is legally just as responsible for financial decisions made by the board as is the local CPA who also serves on it. As a practical matter, if Joe is an intelligent person who pays attention and asks thoughtful questions at board meetings, he can reasonably rely on the advice and recommendations of the board member who is a CPA or a banker.

Here is a bit of advice for the "Joes" of the world: Do not be afraid of financial issues or hide behind what you claim to be a lack of expertise. Those who may oppose you on a mission-related issue will often do so without openly debating the merits but will instead disguise their opposition using financial issues as the subterfuge. If you are unwilling to analyze the numbers because you are numbers phobic, you may end up losing a policy debate that you could have easily won.

Recall the case in Chapter 1 involving the Saratoga Performing Arts Center. The state audit was triggered when the board decided to drop the New York City Ballet for financial reasons. As it turned out, the board's decision to eliminate the New York City Ballet was arguably "flawed and was presented based on inaccurate and incomplete information.[35] If you were the arts advocate on this board who supported keeping the ballet, you needed to understand financial issues to be able to assert your position. In that particular case, this might have meant finding your own financial experts to build the case supporting your position, but you had to at least understand that there was a financial issue that was open to debate.

(v) Board Decisions. State statutes and corporate bylaws set forth the necessary number of votes required for board action, but the statutory provision is typically a default rule that can be altered by the organization's governing documents. Not surprisingly, majority rule normally is controlling—but be careful to distinguish between a majority of the directors in office, a majority of the authorized number of directors, and a majority of the directors present at a meeting with a quorum.

The court then went on to somewhat undercut its "special expertise" rationale by posing an alternative basis for liability and then concluding that Muoio had not carried his burden with respect to either alternative. However, the strong language in the preceding quote clearly suggests that this particular judge is willing to factor director expertise into the liability determination.

There will be those who are quick to point out that this decision arose in the context of a takeover transaction in a business context. The problem with that argument is that directors of Delaware nonprofit corporations are subject to the same standards of care because they are governed by the same statutory regime. Many other state nonprofit corporation acts contain language similar to that found in Section 102(b)(7) of the Delaware General Corporation Law. You should note that this discussion has been placed in a footnote because it is simply too soon to even identify a clear trend. Nevertheless, *Emerging Communications* is now in the judicial domain. Under the right circumstances, a judge can cite it as authority for penalizinga director with expertise.

---

35. *See supra* footnotes 7 through 14 of Chapter 1 and the accompanying text.

Under the Revised Model Act, there must be a quorum present for a vote. The Revised Model Act bases the percentage required for a quorum on the number of directors in office immediately before the meeting begins,[36] but the articles of incorporation certainly could focus on the authorized number of directors (assuming state law so permits, which is likely).[37] Under the Revised Model Act, a quorum cannot be fewer than the greater of (1) one-third of the directors in office or (2) two directors.[38]

Typically, the board determines whether there is a quorum when the meeting starts. This is appropriate, but care should be taken that there is a quorum present each time the board votes. Given the focus on the time when a vote is taken, a slate of directors who oppose an action that they believe is likely to be passed can prevent the board from taking action if they leave immediately before the vote and their absence breaks the quorum.[39] Anyone wanting to employ this technique should first make sure that the applicable state law follows the Revised Model Act and that the internal bylaws do not provide another rule. Moreover, directors breaking the quorum should also consider whether leaving before a crucial vote could be construed as a breach of their duties to the organization. For example, suppose the vote is over the approval of a refinancing that is necessary to avoid a default by the organization. The departing directors might disagree with approving the loan, but do they have a duty to offer a better alternative or at least permit the directors wanting to approve the loan the opportunity to vote, given the fact that there has been a full and open discussion?[40]

When it comes to extraordinary matters, such as a vote to dissolve the corporation or merge with another organization, a two-thirds or more vote may be required by statute, the articles of incorporation, or the bylaws. It also may be necessary, depending on the terms of the articles of incorporation, bylaws and state statutes, to obtain the consent of the members or the state attorney general before taking certain actions.[41] Among the actions that may require higher percentages of director votes or require outside approval from a regulator or a court are decisions to dissolve, liquidate, or merge the nonprofit; to move the organization's

---

36. RMNCA § 8.24(a).
37. *See* RMCA § 8.24(a), Official Comment.
38. RMNCA § 8.24(a).
39. RMNCA § 8.24(b).
40. *See* RMNCA § 8.24(b), Official Comment
41. For example, see the Nonprofit Corporation Law of the Missouri Revised Statutes § 355.676. See New York Attorney General, A Guide to Mergers and Consolidations of Not-For-Profit Corporations under Article 9 of the New York Not-For-Profit Corporation Law (2004), which provides a very helpful overview of the procedures that must be followed and the approvals that must be obtained for a merger or consolidation involving New York nonprofits. It is available on the Web at www.oag.state.ny.us/charities/forms/merger.pdf.

assets out of state or change the state of incorporation; or to sell substantially all of the organization's assets.[42]

Many state statutes permit written consent resolutions, allowing the board to take action without a formal meeting. In many states, actions taken by written consent must be unanimous. Under some state statutes, directors can conduct meetings by telephone or video conference.[43] However, this is not yet universal. There is no question that board meetings over the Internet and by videoconference will become increasingly commonplace as state legislatures modify their laws.

It is critical that the board count only duly-elected directors when determining whether there is a quorum. Directors sometimes send a substitute when they cannot attend a meeting. This is often true of senior lawyers in large law firms, who should know better. Unless state statutes or the bylaws specifically provide otherwise (which is not often the case),[44] the substitute is not a director, and consequently, cannot be counted toward the quorum determination nor vote. Moreover, under the Revised Model Act, a director cannot vote by proxy (in contrast to the ability of a member of the nonprofit to grant a proxy).[45]

(vi) Trustees Functioning as Directors. Some organizations, particularly educational institutions and museums, have a board of trustees rather than a board of directors. Is there a difference? That may depend in large part on organizational form. Under state law, charities can be organized as trusts as well as corporations. By way of example, Stanford University is organized as a trust under California law,[46] while Harvard University is organized as a corporation.[47] In all likelihood, both boards of trustees bring the same level of care to discharging their duties.

---

42. See, for example, Section 65.534(7) of the Oregon Revised Statutes, requiring notification by a public benefit corporation of the Oregon Attorney General in the event of a planned sale lease, exchange or other disposition of all or substantially all of the nonprofit's property unless the transaction is in the usual and regular course of the nonprofit's activities, or a waiver is obtained from the Oregon Attorney General.

43. As an example, Florida grants relatively broad authority for meetings by teleconference or voice over Internet protocols. *See* Florida Statutes, Title XXXVI, § 617.0820(4), providing:

> Unless the articles of incorporation or the bylaws provide otherwise, the board of directors may permit any or all directors to participate in a regular or special meeting by, or conduct the meeting through the use of, any means of communication by which all directors participating may simultaneously hear each other during the meeting. A director participating in a meeting by this means is deemed to be present in person at the meeting.

44. Under Texas law, a director may send to the meeting a proxy who has the powers of a director. *See* Article 1396-2.13 of the Texas Nonprofit Corporation Act.

45. RMNCA § 7.24.

46. See Stanford Facts 2005, University Governance, indicating that the university is a trust with corporate powers under the laws of the state of California. This document is *available at* http://www.stanford.edu/home/stanford/facts/board.html.

47. See Harvard Guide, The Early History of Harvard University, stating that "On June 9, 1650, the Great and General Court of Massachusetts approved Harvard President Henry Dunster's charter of incorporation." This document is available at www.hno.harvard.edu/guide/intro.

Under traditional distinctions between corporate and trust law, trustees of a trust are ostensibly held to a higher standard of conduct in discharging their duties than are directors of a corporation. This is clearly true in the case of trusts used as estate planning devices, as well as employee plan trusts that are subject to the Employee Retirement Income Security Act (ERISA). A debate is raging currently among regulators and scholars as to whether trustees of a charitable trust are or should be held to the same standards as trustees or directors of a nonprofit corporation. In a perfect world, organizational form would not be determinative. Individuals performing equivalent functions should be held to the same standard regardless of title. Whether this is the view that a particular court will adopt is open to question, however.

For those organizing a nonprofit corporation, here is some good advice: Refer to your directors as *directors* rather than as *trustees*.[48] The word *trustee* has longstanding connotations and may result in a higher standard of care being imposed on the individuals serving as trustees. So, even though being referred to as a trustee may carry more stature than being designated a director, being referred to as a director may, in a very practical sense, reduce exposure to liability.

(vii) Resignation and Removal. There will be times when a director wants to resign before the expiration of his term or the board members (or the nonprofit's members if so empowered) decide they would like to remove a director. Not surprisingly, resignation is fairly straightforward. State statutes and bylaws permit directors to resign before the expiration of their terms. In most cases, resignation is not controversial, but there can be an issue when policy is disputed. Almost everybody has been involved in an argument in which one of the parties in the heat of the moment screams, "I've had enough; I quit." What happens when during the course of a lengthy, seven-hour meeting a director yells "I quit" when walking out the door at 2 A.M.? Typically, if that director was the obstacle to the desired action, the remaining directors will call for an immediate vote on the controversial issue. The next morning, when emotions have cooled, the director who walked out will make a phone call to find out what happened only to learn that the board approved the controversial matter after this director left. "What do you mean, you accepted my resignation? I didn't resign!" If much is at stake, there is likely to be a lawsuit over whether that director resigned, whether there was still a quorum, or whether the board had adequately accepted the resignation. The bylaws should clearly outline the procedures for resignation, preferably requiring a formal written document signed and dated by the resigning director.

---

48. It is unusual to find a provision in a state nonprofit corporation statute that affirmatively permits the directors to be designated by a title other than director, but see Section 224 of Title 12 of the Louisiana Revised Statutes, which provides as follows:

> The directors may be given any title deemed appropriate, but shall be subject to all the provisions relating to directors.

In the absence of a procedure calling for a written resignation, the board should be very circumspect about relying on a resignation uttered in the heat of the moment. Although at least one court has held that a resignation may be oral in the absence of formal procedures,[49] another court has ruled that such utterances do not constitute an effective resignation, stating:

> For the board members to interpret the resignation messages as creating "instant vacancies" points to the presence of impermissible arbitrary and capricious conduct as a mater of law...particularly in light of the animosity and dissension that had prevailed among the parties immediately prior to the dispatch of the resignation and withdrawal messages. The expression "act in haste and repent in leisure" recognizes the very human phenomenon of impulsive utterances that ought not be elevated to the level of considered and meaningful conduct.[50]

Those with a penchant for the dramatic should avoid well-planned "hasty" utterances; there is no guarantee that another court will be as understanding of human nature.

The Revised Model Act provides the board the ability to remove a director without cause, requiring a two-thirds vote unless the articles or bylaws provide otherwise.[51] Obviously, involuntary removal can pose a socially awkward situation, making an informal request for resignation the preferable route if removal is predicated on repeated failures to attend meetings or similar circumstances. Short terms for board membership might be a better way to rid the board of nonperforming directors.

The majority should first closely examine the nonprofit's articles or bylaws before it seeks to remove a director or faction of directors on the basis of disagreements over policies. If emotions or money are involved, the majority had better follow notice and required procedures before removing a director because it can expect a lawsuit contesting the validity of the action. Even when the majority has the necessary votes, it should factor in how various constituencies will react and how the action will look in the press.

The board should carefully examine the nonprofit's articles of incorporation and bylaws before removing a director who is elected by the members or is designated by an outside body such as a governmental agency. State statutes typically provide that, in the absence of a provision in the articles or bylaws to the contrary, only the group that has the power to elect that director has the authority to remove that director.[52] This same approach is generally applicable when filling the resulting vacancy.[53]

---

49. Eurich & Matthews v. Korean Foundation, 176 N.E.2d 692 (Ill. App. 1961).
50. Matter of Kane v. Board of Trustees of Great Neck Library, 629 N.Y.S.2d 637 (N.Y. Sup. Ct. 1995).
51. RMNCA § 8.08(h).
52. In the case of members, see RMNCA § 8.08(e). In the case of designated directors, see RMNCA § 8.09.
53. RMNCA § 8.11.

So far, we have focused on internally motivated resignations and removals. Most state statutes provide procedures for judicially approved removal of directors,[54] granting not only the corporation[55] but also the state attorney general the right to commence removal proceedings. While attorneys general have been reluctant to sue directors for monetary damages, there is less reluctance on their part to threaten judicial removal procedures to obtain resignations when boards are not adequately performing their oversight function. Typically, state statutes permit judicial proceedings to be initiated when there are allegations involving fraudulent or dishonest conduct, or gross abuse of authority or discretion. However, some statutes also permit such proceedings when removal is in the best interest of the corporation,[56] providing the other directors (and the attorney general, if empowered to act on behalf of the corporation) with leverage when there has been gross neglect or incompetence rather than dishonest behavior.

(viii) Board Vacancies. When filling board vacancies other than through regularly scheduled elections, the board should follow the procedures outlined in the articles of incorporation or bylaws. This is particularly important in determining the remaining term of the person filling the vacancy. It is common for the bylaws to provide that the replacement director holds office during the uncompleted portion of the term—thereby not disrupting a staggered-term structure. However, there can be instances when the bylaws provide for a permanent replacement to be selected at the next regularly scheduled election.

There can be confusion when there are multiple resignations, leaving less than a quorum of directors in office. Typically, state statutes permit the remaining board members to select replacement directors on the basis of a majority vote if the resignations make obtaining a quorum impossible.[57]

(b) THE OFFICERS. The different state statutes vary as to the required officers and their designations. Most organizations will have a president, vice president, treasurer, and secretary, although a vice president often is not legally required. Note, that it is the functions—not the titles—that are mandated.

The officers are selected in accordance with the terms of the articles of incorporation and bylaws. Normally, the board selects the officers, but in some nonprofits power resides with the members. State statutes and the bylaws usually set terms, but in most cases an individual can be reappointed to a position.

The bylaws, particularly bylaws based on forms used by large law firms, often contain detailed descriptions of officer duties and responsibilities. Before agreeing to serve as an officer, the individual should carefully read the description of the duties set out in the bylaws to determine what the position actually entails.

---

54. RMNCA § 8.10.
55. When there are members, some state statutes grant the members the right to initiate judicial removal proceedings, requiring a certain percentage of voting members to approve such action.
56. Wis. Stat., Chapter 181, § 181.0810(1)(b).
57. RMNCA § 8.11(a)(3).

For example, consider a description of the treasurer that requires the treasurer to establish a system of accounts, maintain the books and records of the corporation, invest funds, write checks and authorize wire transfers, and work with outside auditors. This may be an appropriate description if the treasurer is a paid employee who functions as the organization's chief financial officer. If, however, the treasurer is a volunteer board member who simply makes a report at each meeting, but who relies on an outside accounting firm to create and maintain the books and records, this volunteer should request that the bylaws be modified to reflect this fact. Otherwise, someone could point to the broad language in the bylaws if there were ever an issue, arguing that this person had not adequately discharged his duties as stated in the bylaws.

(i) The President. The role of the president varies from organization to organization. In an organization that simply raises and disburses money or engages in limited activities through surrogates, the president is often a board member who is charged with setting meeting agendas and running board meetings.

In organizations that are more operational in nature, the president may be called the executive director, responsible for the organization's operations. As already noted, the board in these situations may have a separate chair who acts as an intermediary between the board and the executive director. The executive director may also hold a director position, but the organization will best be served by an independent chair who is not an employee.

(ii) The Vice President. The vice president usually runs the board meetings and the organization in the absence of the president. In many organizations whose officers are volunteers, the position of vice president is often viewed as the future-president-in-training position. As is the case with many business organizations, however, a large nonprofit may have a number of paid vice presidents. The vice president tag then serves as a means to designate who is in charge of the organization's information technology, fundraising, human resources, curatorial, and other functional activities. This moniker may establish the line between those employees whose compensation is reviewed by the board and those whose compensation is set by the designated officers within the limits of a board-approved budget.

(iii) The Treasurer. The treasurer is responsible for the financial affairs of the corporation, and, as a consequence, reports to the board about financial matters. As with the president, the treasurer's role will vary. If the nonprofit is a small, board-run organization, the treasurer is likely to be a board member responsible for managing bank accounts and investments, working with the outside accountants on tax and financial statement preparation, and reporting on financial matters to the board. In an organization with large, ongoing operations, the treasurer may be the compensated chief financial officer responsible for a wide array of financial matters and supervising a number of employees.

In a hospital system or a large educational institution, there may be a treasurer and a controller who both report to the chief financial officer. In this case, the treasurer typically is responsible for financial planning, banking relationships, cash management, insurance and risk management, and capital budgeting. The controller, on the other hand, typically is responsible for maintaining the accounting systems and internal controls, preparing financial statements, preparing operating budgets, and reporting to the government. Obviously, several of these functions overlap, and responsibility for a particular function may vary between organizations.

(iv) The Secretary. The secretary is responsible for maintaining the corporate records, including the minutes of board meetings. In fact, many state statutes mandate that minutes be kept, although these statutes rarely set forth a required level of detail. In an organization with substantial operations, the role of secretary is often performed by the organization's general counsel.

(c) MEMBERS. State nonprofit statutes provide for member and nonmember organizations. It is typical for the articles of incorporation to state whether the organization is a membership or nonmembership organization[58] and to establish membership classes, if appropriate. The bylaws will then define the details of membership.

(i) Advocacy versus Affinity. You are probably a member of several nonprofit organizations including art museums, historical societies, zoological societies, theater companies, and public radio and television stations (a "friend"). If you have ever read the fundraising categories for an arts group, you know that the different classes of membership usually equate with different levels of contribution, but this is not how the word *member* is used in the law. These types of memberships are referred to as *affinity* memberships and carry no legal rights other than a contractual right to the promised benefits.

Only those who have the right to vote for the board are members in the legal sense. Membership is almost universal in mutual-benefit nonprofit corporations (such as social clubs and labor organizations) and is often a feature of advocacy groups but is not so common in charities. Advocacy can be broken down into two broad categories: (1) *issue advocacy* and (2) *commercial and economic advocacy.* The first category of organizations includes environmental, abortion-rights, and gun-advocacy groups, among others. These groups may have nonvoting members but are typically characterized by a voting membership. The organizations in this group focus on the issues of the day. The second category includes labor unions, trade associations, and community groups such as the Jaycees or the Rotary. Members of these groups share a common economic interest such as

---

58. *See, e.g.*, Wis. Stat., Chapter 181, § 181.0202(1)(f).

protecting workers, accrediting members, promoting legislation favorable to the members, or acting as the "business" community at large.

(ii) Membership Requirements and Rights. State nonprofit corporation statutes provide a great deal of flexibility when it comes to defining membership requirements and rights. As a practical matter, the organizers of any membership organization can pretty much create whatever legal framework they want in structuring the internal governance requirements of their organizations, at least from the standpoint of corporate law.

The organizers should give very careful consideration to the role of members when considering corporate governance. Will the board be self-perpetuating, or will the members elect the directors? Will the members elect the officers, or will the directors appoint them? This careful consideration is particularly warranted in states where membership confers standing to sue or to withhold consent to certain actions.[59] In the absence of a state statute granting members standing to sue, some courts have been willing to grant standing under what they consider to be the right set of circumstances.[60] Assessing whether this should be a concern in a particular jurisdiction is another example of why seeking the advice of qualified legal counsel is important.

When the organization may take positions on issues, the rules should be very clear in setting forth the requirements that must be satisfied before the organization takes a formal position on an issue. Is a vote of the members required? If so, does majority vote control? If there is significant dissent from the majority position, must that dissent be formally reflected? How much advance notice must be given before a vote is taken? Will the organization pay the costs incurred by different factions in trying to influence the membership? If there is a newsletter, do competing factions have equal access to it? All of these questions clearly must be answered in the case of issue-of-the-day groups, but they apply equally to many groups of a more commercial nature. For example, a trade association primarily engaged in accrediting its members should have procedures in place to address changes in accreditation standards. Given the possible antitrust ramifications of its accreditation activities, this sort of organization must be particularly circumspect in assessing motivations when changing these standards.

Some membership organizations provide for the expulsion of members. For example, an association of museums may adopt an ethical standard for its member organizations. If one of these organizations fails to comply with that standard,

---

59. *See, e.g.*, Wis. Stat., Chapter 181, § 181.0741, providing as follows:

> A derivative proceeding may be brought in the right of a corporation or foreign corporation to procure a judgment in its favor by one or more members having 5 percent or more of the voting power or by 50 members, whichever is less, if each of these members meets all of the following conditions:...

60. *See* Weaver v. Wood, 680 N.E. 2d 918 (Mass. 1997); Carl J. Herzog Foundation v. University of Bridgeport, 699 A.2d 995 (Conn. 1997); and Jensen v. Duluth Area YMCA, File No. C3-02-603462 (Minn. Ct. App., Nov. 16, 2004).

there should be rules in place for determining whether grounds for expulsion have been met, as well as rules that address due process considerations. For example, is the member subject to expulsion entitled to a hearing? Can the member apply for reinstatement?

(iii) Member Decision Making. State nonprofit corporation statutes generally devote considerable space to addressing decision making by members, granting the organizers considerable leeway in formulating the process. Anyone advising a membership organization should assume that some deviation from stated procedures has taken place, meaning that it is necessary to review the articles of incorporation and bylaws to fully ascertain member decision-making rights. Both the drafters of state statutes and organizers have recognized that obtaining member participation can be difficult because the number of members can be high (e.g., hundreds of thousands or even millions) and the membership can be geographically dispersed. Consequently, state statutes tend to be more permissive when it comes to proxies, absentee ballots, and minimum quorum requirements. Under the Revised Model Act, there is a quorum of members if 10 percent of the votes entitled to be cast on a matter is represented at a meeting of members (unless the articles of incorporation or bylaws provide otherwise).[61] In Pennsylvania, the quorum determination is based on the members present at the outset of the meeting rather than at the time of the vote,[62] demonstrating again why individual state law must be reviewed.

The Revised Model Act provides that members can act by written consent but that the action need be approved by 80 percent of the voting power.[63] The Revised Model Act also permits members to vote by proxy[64] and voting agreements.[65]

MEMBERSHIP LESSONS FROM THE SIERRA CLUB

* * *

Does immigration to the United States damage the environment? That question became a central issue in the 2004 campaign for several positions on the Sierra Club's board of directors. Although the outsiders who waged the battle for seats on the Sierra Club's board disputed many of the claims made about their positions and motives, the ensuing dispute captured newspaper headlines and clearly galvanized those opposing the outside

---

61. RMNCA § 7.22(a).

62. See Penn. Consol. Stat., Title 15, § 5756(a)(2), which provides:

> The members present at a duly organized meeting can continue to do business until adjournment, notwithstanding the withdrawal of enough members to leave less than a quorum.

63. RMNCA § 7.04(a).

64. *Id.*

65. RMNCA §7.30.

forces. According to an article in the April 22, 2004, edition of the *New York Times*,[66] the establishment slate candidates finished "at least 95,000 votes" ahead of what had been characterized as the dissident slate. So why might advocates for restrictions on immigration want to attach themselves to the Sierra Club?

The answer to this question is probably rooted in creative marketing. The Sierra Club is a high-profile organization with large mailing lists, money, a solid reputation, and very open membership requirements. It is this last point that poses the interesting governance issue. "Give us your name, address, and a check[67] for $25 and you can be a voting member." This is a logical strategy for attracting members and money, but it can open an organization up to a philosophical hijacking.

Imagine the cost of starting a new organization, building national recognition and the muscle to implement your views on public policy, and developing a large list of faithful contributors. That could take years. For $100,000, however, a small group can effectively "buy" 4,000 votes in an existing organization. For $1 million, an organization can buy 40,000 votes. In short, when properly orchestrated, a smaller group can undertake a hostile takeover of a larger one, particularly if the larger organization has a passive membership.[68]

Many lawyers and organizers give little thought to membership requirements when drafting the articles of incorporation and bylaws for new nonprofits. The focus in the organizational stage is likely to be on how to attract members with low membership fees and exciting premiums. Given the recent Sierra Club experience, it may be time for lawyers and organizers to spend more time focusing on member governance issues.

The Sierra Club election puts into focus the membership construct, starkly posing the question of what rights members should have. The answer to this question is not the same for all nonprofits. An organization such as the Sierra Club is an advocacy organization whose members should have lots of input into the positions it takes because the organization purports to represent the membership's viewpoint. Like an advocacy group, an art museum also has members but it also has other constituencies and serves purposes other than just producing an "art" experience for its current members. This suggests that an art museum's membership should not necessarily have as much input into the museum's operations as the members of an advocacy group. This could explain why museum and public television members have little, if any, input into organizational governance. As consumers, they pay money and

---

66. F. Barringer, *Establishment Candidates Defeat Challengers in Sierra Club Voting*, N.Y. TIMES, Apr. 22, 2004.

67. According to its IRS Form 990, the Sierra Club is a Section 501(c)(4) organization. Consequently, membership dues are not tax-deductible. However, it is possible to make a tax-deductible contribution to the Sierra Club Foundation, a Section 501(c)(3) organization, that is associated with the Sierra Club. The reference to the $25 in dues is generic and is not meant to suggest that the Sierra Club's membership dues are $25.

68. The Sierra Club dispute resulted in litigation, with a California court issuing at least two opinions in the matter. *See* Club Members for an Honest Election v. Sierra Club, Statement of Decision and Order Granding Defendant's Motion for Summary Judgment, Case No. 429277 (S.F. Sup. Ct. February 23, 2005); and Club Members for an Honest Election v. Sierra Club, Order Granting Defendants' Special Motion to Strike in Part, Case No. 429277 (S.F. Sup. Ct. February 23, 2005). The discussion in the text accompanying this footnote is meant as general comment rather than one specific to the *Sierra Club* case. Yet, the court, in its first opinion, quotes one director as having stated:

> ...And, uh, once we get three more directors elected, the Sierra Club will not, no longer be pro-hunting and pro-trapping and we can use the resouces of the $95-million-a-year budget to address some of these issues. And the heartening thing about it is that, in the last election, of the 750,000 members of the Sierra Club, only 8 percent of them voted. So, you know, a few hundred, or a few thousand people from the animal rights movement joining the Sierra Club—and making it a point to vote—will change the entire agenda of that organization.

At least one of the parties recognized the potential influence that a relatively small number of people could exert on the organization.

generally get a slightly better consumer experience than the general public. Although referred to as members, in many organizations, these individuals are not members as that term is used in state statutes.

With that distinction in mind, let us consider several approaches to structuring membership input. If an organization wants to avoid a philosophical hijacking as a result of its membership structure, it could require membership for a certain period of time (possibly a year) before a member can vote. This might strike some as undemocratic, but nothing requires that an organization be democratic. If you do not like it, start your own organization (or so the Supreme Court implied in 2000 when it issued a major decision involving the Boy Scouts of America).[69]

A second approach is to permit members to vote but to have a split board with some board members elected by the members and others by the board. This provides the members the opportunity to make their views known to those running the organization but permits a group of insiders and professionals to control the organization. This approach is not so democratic, but it avoids chaos, allows members to comment, and keeps the organization moving forward. If the professionals become too detached from the "unwashed" members, the "great unwashed" can cut off funding.

A third approach is to permit members to vote for all directors but to require that a candidate should have been a member of the organization for a set period of time (e.g., five years). This ensures that candidates for directors have had a long-standing interest in the organization, making it far less likely that they are seeking to hijack the organization. After all, how can one of us hijack us? Of course, this is not foolproof. Think of the 1960s radicals who had a neocon conversion during the Reagan 1980s. This solution also poses a problem when the big-name celebrity or public figure takes what the organization views as a positive interest in the group. Mr. Hot Young Celebrity wants to be on the board and will donate $10 million after being elected. This possibility suggests that any provision defining qualifications for board membership might include a board override (possibly requiring a two-thirds vote of the board).[70]

A fourth approach providing for staggered director terms was in place in the Sierra Club's organizational structure. In theory, this would have meant that it would take more than one election cycle to gain control of the board. But the existing circumstances posed a problem for those trying to maintain control. A few incumbents were already sympathetic to the insurgents' cause, and so control was at stake in the 2004 election.

A fifth approach, suggested by an article in the *Chronicle of Philanthropy*,[71] moves us out of the legal realm. According to this article, one reason that the Sierra Club was vulnerable to a philosophical hijacking was its large but passive membership.[72] Earlier in its history, the membership was closely knit and included much socializing among the members. In recent decades, this aspect of the organization has largely been lost. Many members dutifully remit their annual membership fees, and that is it. So the lesson is to keep the membership engaged. Of course, this will cost time and money to accomplish. This approach also may warrant keeping the membership small and limiting it to the truly committed. Of course, doing so runs counter to the natural inclination to become bigger so that those running the organization have more resources under their control. Boards that want a smaller, more focused membership must also keep an eye on the organization's professional staff, a group that may believe their salary levels depend on a larger membership.

---

69. Boy Scouts of America v. Dale, 530 U.S. 640 (2000).

70. Do not forget the admonition in the first chapter: The primary focus of each director should be on oversight rather than fundraising, at least as a legal matter.

71. S Greene, *Hostile Takeover or Rescue?: Sierra Club's Board Candidates Fight to Shape the Group's Future*, CHRON. OF PHILAN., Apr. 15, 2004.

72. *Id.* One person quoted in *Chronicle* article suggested that of the 700,000 Sierra Club members, "just 30,000 are actively involved."

To summarize, a single approach to membership will not fit all organizations. While organizations and their lawyers should focus carefully on legal solutions to the membership issue, organizations and their directors and officers should not overlook the fifth approach. Determining how to keep the membership engaged, particularly in an advocacy organization, is the central issue. Finally, museums, theater groups, and other entertainment nonprofits might reap benefits if they provide a voice to their members. Contributions from the public members could increase significantly if the public members had some input into the organization's direction rather than feeling that they are just prepaying their admissions and getting desirable entry times at blockbuster shows.

The Sierra Club saga obviously holds important lessons for both nonprofit boards and their advisors. While not an apparent issue in the battle for control of the Sierra Club, foundations and others making grants to membership organizations need to take the potential for instability caused by members into account when writing grants and contracts. A grantor makes a multiyear grant with certain expectations as to how the money will be utilized. Unless those restrictions are tightly drafted, the grantor could find itself committed to fund grant payments to an organization that has been philosophically hijacked.

* * *

(iv) Constitutional and Due Process Overlay. Whenever more than one person is involved in an organization, conflict, disputes, and disagreements are a distinct possibility. Over the years, various conflicts have occurred within membership organizations. These can arise over membership requirements, positions on issues, rights when leaving the organization, and expulsion. By and large, the courts have taken the position that people and organizations have a constitutional right to freedom of association,[73] as well as freedom not to associate. Although not universally so, the courts have stayed away from imposing their views on membership organizations.[74] When the courts have been asked to intervene, they have viewed themselves as enforcing a contract between the members. In other words, the courts have served as referees or arbiters of disputes but have shied away from forcing external notions as to appropriate policy on membership organizations.[75] Where there are clear rules, the courts have essentially told unhappy minorities, "Start your own organization if you don't like this one."

This is not to say that courts will not require some level of fair play. For example, in one case in which a museum was to have its accreditation suspended by a trade association of museums, the court stated that the museum in question was

---

73. NAACP v. Alabama ex rel. Patterson, 357 U.S. 449 (1958).

74. *See* E. Brody, *Entrance, Voice, and Exit: The Constitutional Bounds of the Right of Association*, 35 U.C. Davis L. Rev. 821, 856-865 (2002).

75. *See, e.g.*, Hispanic College Fund v. NCAA (In. Ct. App. 2005), in which the court went even further, stating:

> Absent fraud, other illegality, or abuse of civil or property rights having their origin elsewhere, Indiana courts will not interfere with the internal affairs of voluntary membership associations. See footnote Ind. High Sch. Athletic Ass'n, Inc. v. Reyes, 694 N.E.2d 249, 256 (Ind. 1997). This means our courts will neither enforce an association's internal rules nor second-guess an association's interpretation or application of its rules.

See also the Sierra Club cases cited in *supra* note 68.

entitled to notice and a hearing as a matter of "fair play."[76] As one commentator has pointed out,

> [C]ourts more closely scrutinize exclusion or expulsion from commercial and professional associations, such as membership in a medical association necessary for hospital privileges. The public policy recognizes the interests of third parties—for example, consumers and patients—as well as the interest of the would-be member to practice his or her trade. The courts' authority in this area, however, is not rooted in the Fourteenth Amendment's Due Process Clause, but rather in their inherent equity powers.[77]

In addition to minor interventions, the courts in several notable instances have engaged in what some perceive to be major intrusions of a constitutional nature. For example, is there a constitutional right to leadership in a particular organization? In most cases, no, as one litigant found out in 2000 when the Supreme Court held that the Boys Scouts of America may exclude a gay person from its leadership ranks because the litigant's status as a gay male conflicted with the Boy Scouts' view of gays.[78] In an earlier unanimous decision, however, the Supreme Court upheld a Minnesota antidiscrimination statute as applied to a local chapter of the Jaycees, an organization that barred women as voting members.[79] It is difficult to imagine such a decision, given Justice Brennan's initial framing of the issue:

> There can be no clearer example of an intrusion into the internal structure or affairs of an association than a regulation that forces the group to accept members it does not desire. Such a regulation may impair the ability of the original members to express only those views that brought them together. Freedom of association therefore plainly presupposes a freedom not to associate.[80]

So how should the two cases be reconciled? Volumes have been written in an effort to do just that. Suffice it to say that the *Jaycees* case involved an organization that broadly represents the community and business leaders, an organization that providers local businesspeople networking opportunities while taking on projects to serve the greater community. On the hand, the Boys Scouts of America is arguably more value laden and far less associated with business networking. If an organization wants to set membership requirements that exclude protected classes of people or groups that some view as warranting protection,

---

76. Vanderbilt Museum v. American Association of Museums, 449 N.Y.S. 2d 399 (Sup. Ct. Suffolk Cty.1982).
77. E. Brody, *supra* note 74, at 833
78. Boy Scouts of America v. Dale, 530 U.S. 640 (2000). It is noteworthy that 43 nonprofit groups filed amici curiae briefs in support of the Boys Scouts of America. Some of these groups likely were in tune with Mr. Dale from a gay rights' perspective but were concerned about limiting potential intrusion on their own rights to define membership requirements. *See also* Hurley v. Irish-Am. Gay, Lesbian & Bisexual Group, 515 U.S. 557 (1995), denying a gay activist group the right to march in a St. Patrick's Day parade despite the fact that the parade took place on public streets.
79. Roberts v. United States Jaycees, 468 U.S. 609 (1984). *See also* New York Club Ass'n v. City of New York, 487 U.S. 1 (1988); and Bd. of Dirs. of Rotary, Int'l v. Rotary Club of Duarte, 481 U.S. 557 (1987).
80. *Id.*

it should review these and a number of other cases before setting membership requirements. This is particularly true if the organization focuses on commercial issues or constitutes a public accommodation. Most important, the members should undertake some soul searching before excluding classes of people.

Another area in which courts have been willing to intervene on constitutional grounds involves mandatory membership organizations that engage in permitted political speech that is unrelated to the organization's primary activity. For example, certain states require lawyers to be members of state bar associations and workers may be required to be union members. On occasion, bar associations take positions on controversial public issues (e.g., the death penalty) that go beyond their primary regulatory function. Likewise, labor unions are permitted to engage in political activity, but their primary purpose is to represent workers in labor relation matters. In these instances, the courts have not prevented the organization from taking a position despite disagreement by some who are represented by the organization, but have required that the portion of mandatory dues that financed the expressive activity be refunded to those members who so request a refund.[81]

Other issues come up with respect to membership organizations that raise complex constitutional issues. For example, states and the federal government ban corporations from contributing to political campaigns. There are, however, limits on such bans with respect to certain membership organizations. Finally, the state is loathed to regulate churches. What is important to remember is that as a general proposition, membership organizations generally must comply with their established rules but are largely free to establish those rules.

(v) Corporate Affiliated Groups. Lawyers advising nonprofits have found the membership construct to be very useful for structuring affiliated groups of nonprofits formed in states that do not permit a nonprofit corporation to issue stock. In these structures, the *parent,* or controlling entity, is the sole member of the *subsidiary entity.* This member is given the power to appoint directors to the board of the subsidiary entity.

Charitable organizations are not permitted to make distributions of assets or income to private, noncharitable interests[82] This is the rule for charitable organizations, but under certain circumstances, a tax-exempt entity can make liquidating distributions to its members.[83] Those statutes providing for distribution tend

81. United States v. United Foods, 533 U.S. 405 (2001)—ads for food products; Bd. of Regents of Univ. of Wis. Sys. v. Southworth, 529 U.S. 217 (2000)—student fees; Keller v. State Bar of Cal., 496 U.S. 1 (1990)—state bar association; and Abood v. Detroit Bd. of Educ., 431 U.S. 209 (1977)—labor union.

82. For an example, see Section 1005 of Chapter 35 of the New York Consolidated Laws, which does provide for distribution to members upon dissolution but carefully carves charitable assets out of that regime through a distinction between Type B (broadly speaking, charitable) and other organizations.

83. For an example, see Section 1005 of Chapter 35 of the New York Consolidated Laws, which does provide for distribution to members upon dissolution but carefully carves charitable assets out of that regime through a distinction between Type B (broadly speaking, charitable) and other organizations.

to focus on distributions as part of a plan of dissolution. If the parties contemplate the subsidiary paying "dividends" to the parent/member, they should check state law before proceeding.[84] Some states prohibit "distribution" payments to members under certain circumstances. This applies equally well to two charitable entities aligned in a parent-subsidiary configuration through the membership construct.[85] It may be possible to use a single-member limited liability company as an alternative to a corporate subsidiary, but this alternative is relatively untested.

Federal income tax law prevents Section 501(c)(3) organizations from engaging in certain activities. On occasion, these activities are conducted through another entity that is affiliated with the Section 501(c)(3) organization through a membership structure.

(d) THE REGULATORS—STATE ATTORNEYS GENERAL. A state's attorney general is generally the person who represents and protects the interests of the public with respect to charitable organizations. The California Attorney General does a nice of job summarizing the role of this office under California law.

> The California Attorney General acts as the legal overseer of California charities. The Attorney General has the duty of protecting the interests of all public beneficiaries of charities within his jurisdiction. The Attorney General may conduct investigations and bring legal actions to protect the assets of California charities and insure the assets are used for their intended charitable purposes. Most California charities must register and file annual financial reports with the Attorney General's Registry of Charitable Trusts.[86]

---

84. Section 181.1302(3) of Chapter 181 of the Wisconsin Statutes permits interim distributions if certain conditions are satisfied, including that the distributee be exempt under Section 501 of the Internal Revenue Code. This provision is notable because many states do not permit interim distributions even to other charitable organizations.

85. See Fla. Stats., Title XXXVI, Chapter 617, § 617.0505(1), which provides as follows:

> A dividend may not be paid, and any part of the income or profit of a corporation may not be distributed, to its members, directors, or officers. A corporation may pay compensation in a reasonable amount to its members, directors, or officers for services rendered, may confer benefits upon its members in conformity with its purposes, and, upon dissolution or final liquidation, may make distributions to its members as permitted by this act. If expressly permitted by its articles of incorporation, a corporation may make distributions upon partial liquidation to its members, as permitted by this section. Any such payment, benefit, or distribution does not constitute a dividend or a distribution of income or profit for purposes of this section.

The Florida legislature passed legislation changing the statute to permit distributions to a parent entity following an opinion by Florida's attorney general confirming that the statute did not permit interim distributions, but Florida Governor John Ellis Bush vetoed the legislation because he viewed the changes as being too broad. *See* Governor John Ellis Bush, Veto Message (May 20, 2004), available at http://www.vote_smart.org/veto_letters/pdf_bush_fl_sb2056.pdf; Fla. Sen. B. 2056 (enrolled Apr. 26, 2004); and Fla. Atty Gen., Op. No. 99-23, (1999).

86. California Attorney General, Attorney General's Guide for Charities at 1 (1988), available at http://caag.state.ca.us/charities/publications/gfc.pdf.

In some states, this role is performed by district attorneys or special boards or commissions. For present purposes, the state charity regulator is referred to as the *attorney general.*

Protecting the public interest generally means ensuring that a charity's assets are devoted to charitable purposes, making sure that there is no prohibited self-dealing, bringing civil actions to stop acts outside of the organization's authority (referred to as *ultra vires* acts), seeking to remedy the wrongdoing by errant directors and officers, seeking accountings, and approving (or participating in court-supervised proceedings for) certain transactions such as mergers and dissolutions.[87] Under some statutes, the attorney general has the power to ask the courts to replace directors (or even boards) who fail to properly discharge their duties but may lack the power to subsequently intervene, assuming that the board is functioning in accordance with its articles of incorporation, bylaws, and state law.[88]

Many state statutes expressly limit the attorney general's authority over religious organizations.[89] Any grant or exercise of such authority would raise obvious questions under the "establishment" clause of the United States Constitution.[90] This reluctance to regulate religious activities also finds its way into exemptions from charitable solicitation laws[91] and property tax levies, as well as the procedural restrictions on the IRS in raising tax-exemption and related

---

87. See *In re* Barnes Foundation, Opinion of the Court of Common Pleas of Montgomery County, Pennsylvania (Jan. 29, 2004), for a discussion of the role of the attorney general.

88. *See* State of Minnesota v. Medica Health Plans, File No. MC 01-004100 (Aug. 17, 2005), in which the Minnesota Attorney General brought suit against the board of a nonprofit health care insurer alleging breaches of their duties. The attorney general had been instrumental in appointing this board several years earlier to replace the organization's then existing board in light of a highly-publicized scandal. The new board operated under an agreement with the attorney general. After several years, an audit demonstrated that the new board had performed admirably, but the attorney general argued that the new board had hijacked the company. The court apparently viewed the case as a power struggle rather than a case involving breaches of duties. Given the absence of wrongdoing, the court dismissed the case, noting that although appointed through the efforts of the attorney general, the board was free to act independently of the attorney general going forward.

89. For example, see Cal. Corp. Code § 9230(a). The 2001 SUPPLEMENT TO THE CALIFORNIA ATTORNEY GENERAL'S GUIDE FOR CHARITIES provides:

> The Attorney General has limited oversight functions for corporate changes made by religious corporations, other than dissolution. (Corporations Code §§ 9230(a) and (c). Despite confusing provisions in California statutes regarding consent to religious corporation mergers (Corporations Code § 9640), the Attorney General's statutory power over religious corporations is essentially limited to enforcement of the criminal laws and to disposition of assets on dissolution....

This supplement is available at http://caag.state.ca.us/charities/publications/supplement2001.pdf.

90. U.S. CONST., amend I, providing "Congress shall make no law respecting an establishment of religion, or prohibiting the free exercise thereof..."

91. This deference to religious organizations may be undergoing change. In 2005, the Massachusetts legislature considered legislation that would require religious organizations to register with the state if they are involved in charitable solicitation. *See* Mass. Sen. Bill 1074 (2005).

issues when the charity involved is a religious organization and the conduct is questionable.[92]

Many state statutes give the attorney general the authority to require nonprofits to report certain information to the attorney general. An attorney general will learn about potential problems by (1) reviewing required annual filings, (2) reviewing certain transactions that must be brought to the attention of the attorney general (e.g., mergers and dissolutions), (3) reading newspaper articles, and (4) responding to tips from concerned insiders, as well from such whistle-blowers as disgruntled employees and disappointed charitable beneficiaries.

Historically, the focus of the attorney general has been on fundraising fraud. In more recent years, however, the focus of state attorneys general has shifted to mismanagement, according to a 1996 report by the Nonprofit Coordinating Committee of New York.[93] This report was based in part on interviews with a number of state attorneys general. In summarizing these interviews, the report states:

> The state officials who spoke with us have been shifting attention and resources to these more pervasive problems [mismanagement, waste, and inefficiency]. In the past five years, they have come to think that the underlying problem [with respect to the pervasive problems] is governance....They believe that when there are problems with misappropriation of funds, or excessive compensation, or mismanagement, or waste, there are almost always also problems with whether the board is providing adequate oversight.[94]

This suggests that the state attorneys general who were interviewed see their function as a check on boards of directors. Although the Nonprofit Coordinating Committee report is now almost a decade old, at recent nonprofit organization conferences, several enforcement officials echoed the report's conclusion regarding enforcement trends.

(e) STANDING. The traditional role of the state attorney general is to protect the interests of each charity's charitable class or beneficiaries, defined as those people or institutions who are the intended beneficiaries of the organization's activities. For example, the students at a university are a key component of the school's beneficiaries or charitable class. In the case of a hospital, patients or potential patients are its beneficiaries or charitable class.

Traditionally, a charity's charitable class or beneficiaries lack the right (standing) to bring lawsuits against a charity that they believe is not fulfilling its mission

---

92. *See, e.g.*, IRS Tech. Adv. Mem. 2004-35-020 (2004) for an example, but do not be misled. The IRS will address clear-cut violations of the law by religious organizations. *See* Bob Jones University v. United States., 461 U.S. 574 (1983); and Bob Jones University v. Simon, 416 U.S. 725 (1974). In Foundation of Human Understanding, 88 T.C. 1341(1987), the court noted "We can only approach this question with care for all of us are burdened with baggage of our own unique beliefs and perspectives."

93. Peter Swords and Harriett Bograd, The Nonprofit Coordinating Committee of New York, Accountability in the Nonprofit Sector: What Problems are Addressed by State Regulators (1996), available at http://www.bway.net/~hbograd/ag_prob.html.

94. *Id.*

or duties to the class.[95] Normally, only the state attorney general has this power, but this has not stopped members of charitable classes from trying to bring actions against charities. In one notable case, the court held that the beneficiaries of a nonprofit corporation were entitled to bring an action against the organization's directors for breaching their duties to the nonprofit.[96] In that case, the patients of a nonprofit hospital were permitted to sue for injunctive relief but not monetary damages. As noted, the bulk of the authority is against such suits,[97] but courts have allowed beneficiaries to bring suit in more than just a few isolated cases.[98] When standing is granted, the party seeking to bring the suit usually is able to establish that it has a special interest with respect to the charity, there is fraud or misconduct on the part of the directors, the attorney general is unavailable or ineffective, or the acts complained of are extraordinary.[99] Courts are much less likely to grant standing when the dispute is over policy, direction, or judgment calls (i.e., the board acted within the scope of its authority and consistent with the charity's stated mission, but someone simply disagrees with the action taken).

Louisiana College

* * *

On December 6, 2004, the Commission on Colleges of the Southern Association of Colleges and Schools (SAC) placed Louisiana College, a private Christian college located in Pinesville, Louisiana, on a 12-month probation, stating:

> Probation is the Commission's most serious sanction, short of loss of membership, and can be imposed on an institution for failure to correct deficiencies of significant non-compliance with the Core Requirements or the Comprehensive Standards of the Principles of Accreditation of the Commission, failure to make timely and significant progress toward correcting the deficiencies, or failure to comply with Commission policies and procedures. The imposition of Probation is an indication of the gravity of non-compliance with the Principles. Probation may be imposed upon initial institutional review, depending on the judgment of the Commission of the seriousness of the non-compliance or in the case of repeated violations recognized by

95. In the *Barnes Foundation* litigation that concluded in 2005, the Barnes Foundation was the sole party to the judicial proceeding, although the students were permitted to submit an amicus curiae brief.
96. *See* Stern v. Lucy Webb Hayes Nat'l Training School for Deaconesses Sibley Hospital, 367 F. Supp. 536 (D.D.C. 1973).
97. *See* Milton Hershey School and Hershey Trust Company v. Milton Hershey School of Alumni Association, 867 A.2d 674 (Pa. Commw. 2005); Alco Gravure v. Knapp Foundation, 479 N.E. 2d 752 (N.Y. 1985); and Jones v. Grant, 344 So. 2d 1210 (Ala. 1977), involving faculty members, students and staff who brought an action for an accounting against a college, board members, and certain officers.
98. *See* Smithers v. St. Luke's-Roosevelt Center, 281 A.D. 2d 127 (N.Y. 2001).
99. *See* Robert Schalkenbach Foundation v. Lincoln Foundation, 91 P.3d 1019 (Arz. Ct. App. 2004); and M. Blasko, *Standing to Sue in the Charitable Sector*, 28 U.S.F.L. Rev. 37 (1993).

the Commission over a period of time. The maximum consecutive time that an institution may be on Probation is two years.[100]

Naturally, the college's students, faculty, and alumni were concerned about the college's future, resulting in the filing of a lawsuit on or about January 11, 2005, challenging the selection of the college's new president. This suit revealed a deep divide between the two factions.

One group, which apparently dominated Louisiana College's board of trustees, reportedly wanted to move the college in the direction of fundamentalist Baptist religious teachings. The other faction wanted to stop such movement. According to one account, the faction opposing movement toward fundamentalism was concerned that some of the trustees were micromanaging the college and stifling academic freedom.[101] The Southern Association's probation decision appears to have been rooted in this conflict—although SAC refused to take sides or reveal the specific factual basis for its decision.[102]

According to *Inside-Higher Ed*, Rory Lee, the college's former president, retired in March 2004, at which time a search committee was appointed to find a new president.[103] In September 2004, the committee selected Malcolm Yarnell as the new president. However, he withdrew his name two months later over governance issues that arose during his contract negotiations. At that time, the trustees expanded the selection committee from 9 to 17 members. Apparently the expansion shifted the committee's composition sufficiently to result in its nomination of Joe Aguillard as a candidate for the presidency. Mr. Aguillard was apparently acceptable to the faction favoring a move toward fundamentalism, but he was not acceptable to the faculty, which voted 52–12 against his appointment[104] and issued a vote of no confidence in the board of trustees.[105]

The plaintiffs in the lawsuit argued that the bylaws did not permit the college's trustees to reconstitute the search committee. The trustees took the position that once Mr. Yarnell withdrew his name, a new search process had begun, permitting the appointment of a new search committee. Those filing the lawsuit argued that because Mr. Yarnell had not signed a contract, the original search had not been completed, meaning that the search committee could not be reconstituted under the terms of the college's bylaws.[106] The trustee-defendants argued that the alumni and former college officials lacked standing to bring the suit.

According to a January 12, 2005, article from the *Associated Baptist Press*, Mr. Johnson, the chair of the college's board of trustees, sought advice on the procedural question. The article states:

> Johnson said he sought an opinion from the parliamentarian of the Louisiana Baptist Convention, which appoints trustees. "In his opinion, and according to Robert's Rules (of Order), this (special) committee is valid, was duly formed, and is appropriately

---

100. Commission on Colleges Southern Association of Colleges and Schools, Questions Regarding the Status of Louisiana College, Pineville, Louisiana (Dec. 17, 2004).

101. D. Lederman, *A Fight over Fundamentalism*, Inside Higher Educ., Jan. 10, 2005.

102. Southern Association of Colleges and Schools, Special Committee Report Louisiana College (Sept. 1–3, 2004). This report notes that "final action on the report rests with the Commission on Colleges."

103. *See Fight over Fundamentalism, supra* note 101.

104. E. Peters, *New LC Chief Meets with Faculty, Students*, Town Talk, Jan 19, 2005. One article describes this as a "straw vote." *See* B. Nolan, *Louisiana College Names New President Over Protests Split 17-13, Trustees Select Conservative*, Times-Picayune, Jan. 19, 2005

105. *See* Faculty of Louisiana College, Resolution (Dec. 8, 2004).

106. C. L. Thompson, *"Ready to Lead" – Louisiana College Elects New President*, Baptist Message Online, Jan. 20, 2005; *Louisiana College Names New President, supra* note 104; and G. Warner, *Louisiana College Trustees Nominate President, but Lawsuit May Block Vote*, Biblical Reporter, Jan. 7, 2005.

charged with bringing Dr. Aguillard's name before the board—with or without recommendation," Johnson said.[107]

If Mr. Johnson had a question about interpreting his organization's bylaws, why did he not ask his organization's general counsel instead of some lawyer affiliated with another organization?

This suit aptly demonstrates the importance of the procedures and the terms in organizational bylaws. There is little doubt that the college's bylaws made for some very tedious reading. The language did not change once the lawsuit was filed, but it suddenly took on great importance as the fulcrum over which a major policy dispute was waged. Like SAC, the court did not address the merits of the dispute over the basic direction of the college, but its decision interpreting the bylaws determined who controlled the college's direction. The court ruled in favor of the college's trustees, dismissing the lawsuit with prejudice.

* * *

3.4 ORGANIZATIONAL DOCUMENTS

Organizational documents are the legal documents defining an organization's legal structure, the relationships between those who are charged with governing and running the organization, and the procedures for managing and governing the organization and those relationships. In a corporate setting, these documents are the articles of incorporation and the bylaws. In a trust setting, the primary organizational document is a trust instrument entered into between the settlor and the trustee(s). In the case of larger trusts or trusts engaged in operations, the trustees may also adopt bylaws.

(a) USING FORMS. Twenty years ago, there would have been a reference to Appendix A and Appendix B at this point in the narrative, with the two appendices composed of sample articles of incorporation and bylaws. Today, including those samples would be a waste of paper given the availability of hundreds, if not thousands, of samples on the Web. Just google *nonprofit articles of incorporation* and *nonprofit bylaws,* or variations thereof. This will be a very useful exercise if you have never reviewed these types of documents. However, if you are charged with forming a nonprofit corporation, do not rely on what you find. Each document you find will have been tailored to a unique situation, although many of the provisions in different documents will be similar, if not identical, to each other. For drafting purposes, however, you and your counsel should review a legal form book tailored to the particular jurisdiction, one that has alternative clauses addressing the same issue.

---

107. *Trustees Nominate President*, *supra* note 106.

Many state nonprofit corporation statutes contemplate more than one type of nonprofit. For example, there are "all-purpose" nonprofits,[108] but depending on the state of incorporation, there can also be specific nonprofit codes governing religious corporations,[109] mutual benefit corporations,[110] condominium associations,[111] and chambers of commerce and trade associations,[112] among others. Although each of these types of organizations may be classified under the nonprofit rubric, each may be subject to different state tax regimes, as well as different levels of oversight by the state's attorney general or charity regulator. It is critical that the correct legal "vessel" be chosen. Importantly, an organization may choose to incorporate in a state with a favorable legal regime even if it operates in another state (where it will register to "do business" as a foreign corporation).

As you review a form, you should begin to see the need to tailor it to the particular organization's unique circumstances. If you are a lawyer looking for a good form book, call your state bar association because many bar associations publish form books tailored to the state's nonprofit corporation laws. Unless you are an experienced nonprofit lawyer, when it comes to drafting, you should make sure the organizers retain a qualified lawyer.

(b) CORE DOCUMENTS. As noted, the two core organizational documents for nonprofit corporations are the articles of incorporation and the bylaws. The articles of incorporation can be viewed as the face of the organization because they are subject to public filing requirements. The bylaws are generally not subject to public filing requirements.

Most nonprofit corporation statutes provide a great deal of latitude as to whether general governance provisions are placed in the bylaws or the articles of incorporation. By tradition, unless the statute mandates inclusion in the articles of incorporation, the bylaws set out the operational details. Again, the specific circumstances should dictate. For example, the organizers might decide that changes to the bylaws should generally require majority approval, but there may

---

108. In California, the secretary of state defines a "nonprofit public benefit corporation" as follows:

> [A] corporation organized primarily for charitable purposes and which plans to obtain state tax exempt status under Section 23701d of the Revenue and Taxation Code and/or federal tax exempt status under Section 501(c)(3) of the Internal Revenue Code or organized to act as a civic league or a social welfare organization and which plans to obtain state tax exempt status under Section 23701f of the Revenue and Taxation Code and/or federal tax exempt status under Section 501(c)(4) of the Internal Revenue Code.

109. For example, see the Illinois Religious Corporation Act.

110. In California, the secretary of state defines a "nonprofit mutual benefit corporation" as

> A corporation for other than religious, charitable, civic league or social welfare purposes and planning to obtain tax exempt status under provisions other than Sections 23701d, 23701f, 501(c)(4) or not planning to be tax exempt at all.

111. For example, see the Illinois Condominium Property Act.

112. California law makes specific allowance for chambers of commerce and boards of trade, consumer cooperative associations, and nonprofit medical, hospital, and legal services corporations.

be one issue that the organizers believe should require an 80 percent vote before a change is made to it or that requires member approval and board approval. If the articles already impose that higher threshold, that issue might be better addressed through the articles of incorporation.

(i) Articles of Incorporation. The organizers of a nonprofit corporation must file articles of incorporation with the appropriate state authority, typically the state's secretary of state. Once these have been filed, the organization exists as a distinct legal entity. If it is already nearing the end of the year, the incorporators may want to delay incorporation until after December 31 if that is an option, thereby avoiding various tax return and other filings that are often required even though the corporation is still a shell—that is, it has no assets, employees, or operations. Alternatively, the entity might select a fiscal year.

In some states, the filing office reviews the articles of incorporation before accepting them in an effort to identify any errors or missing information. In other states, the filing office accepts whatever is filed. Although filing offices that conduct reviews can be annoyingly petty, a thorough review ensures that no foot faults that could turn into future problems occur. The key is to understand the regulatory process and anticipate delays. There is nothing more frustrating than needing a nonprofit corporation to be in legal existence on a specified date only to miss that date by a day or two. This is a lawyer's issue, but it is an important one when incorporation is tied to a bond issuance, merger, or property closing. Some states provide for informal prescreening. Several states permit the incorporators to specify a delayed effective date for the nonprofit's existence, permitting convenient and more certain early filings.[113]

The articles of incorporation contain statutorily mandated information such as the corporation's name, the names of its initial directors, its purpose, whether it is a membership corporation, the name and address of its principal office and registered agent, and a dissolution clause.[114] The required information varies

---

113. *See* RMNCA § 2.03(a).

114. *See, e.g.*, RMNCA § 2.02, which provides as follows:

> (a) The articles of incorporation must set forth:
>
> (1) a corporate name for the corporation that satisfies the requirements of section 4.01;
>
> (2) one of the following statements:
>
> (i) This corporation is a public benefit corporation.
>
> (ii) This corporation is a mutual benefit corporation.
>
> (iii) This corporation is a religious corporation.
>
> (3) the street address of the corporation's initial registered office and the name of its initial registered agent at that office;
>
> (4) the name and address of each incorporator;
>
> (5) whether or not the corporation will have members; and
>
> (6) provisions not inconsistent with law regarding the distribution of assets on dissolution.

from state to state, which is one of the reasons that just getting a form from the Internet is problematic.

Both the state's charity regulator and the IRS[115] are concerned that charitable assets remain committed to charitable purposes once so earmarked. As a consequence, either the articles of incorporation or state law must address what happens to assets held by a charitable corporation upon its dissolution. If state law does not statutorily impose limitations, the articles of incorporation must contain a provision adequately limiting what happens to the assets upon the nonprofit's dissolution before the IRS will approve an application for Section 501(c)(3) tax-exempt status.[116] All of this sounds easy, but at the May 2005 meeting of the American Bar Association's Tax Section, one representative from the IRS indicated that somewhere around 30 percent of the corporations applying for exempt status must modify their articles of incorporation following IRS review because the applicant failed to satisfy the "organizational" test.

If the would-be Section 501(c)(3) organization will be a private foundation, the tax rules require that it be subject to limitations on investment activity, self-dealing, and other matters that fall under the private foundation excise tax regime.[117] Under the tax rules, state law must impose these limitations on the private foundation by statute, or the organization's governing documents must contain limiting language.[118] Consequently, the articles of incorporation for many private foundations contain rather lengthy provisions designed to comply with this requirement.

---

115. The IRS focuses on the dissolution provisions because Treas. Reg. § 1.501(c)(3)-1(b)(4) provides as follows:

> An organization is not organized exclusively for one or more exempt purposes unless its assets are dedicated to an exempt purpose. An organization's assets will be considered dedicated to an exempt purpose, for example, if, upon dissolution, such assets would, by reason of a provision in the organization's articles or by operation of law, be distributed for one or more exempt purposes, or to the Federal government, or to a State or local government, for a public purpose, or would be distributed by a court to another organization to be used in such manner as in the judgment of the court will best accomplish the general purposes for which the dissolved organization was organized. However, an organization does not meet the organizational test if its articles or the law of the State in which it was created provide that its assets would, upon dissolution, be distributed to its members or shareholders.

116. *See* Rev. Proc. 82-2, 1982-1 C.B. 367. The instructions to IRS Form 1023 contain a list of states having statutes that adequately address dissolution in their enabling statutes, but keep in mind that there may be reasons to add specific language to the articles of incorporation even though the applicable state statute provides mandatory "default" language. Moreover, there are considerations other than tax ones when drafting a dissolution clause that will be included in the nonprofit's articles of incorporation. The IRS has, however, offered the following language as an acceptable example for tax purposes:

> Upon the dissolution of (this organization), assets shall be distributed for one or more exempt purposes within the meaning of section 501(c)(3) of the Internal Revenue Code, or corresponding section of any future Federal tax code, or shall be distributed to the Federal government, or to a state or local government, for a public purpose.

117. I.R.C. § 508. We consider the tax aspects of private foundation status in detail as part of Chapter 6.

118. *See* Rev. Rul. 75-38, 1975-1 C.B. 161, and IRS Form 1023, Appendix B, for additional details, particularly information as to which states have incorporated mandatory provisions into their statutes.

(ii) Bylaws. Either the initial directors or the corporation's members adopt bylaws for the governance of the corporation. The bylaws are longer and more detailed than the articles of incorporation, specifying procedure for electing officers and directors, removing directors, dates for annual meetings, officer duties, director and officer indemnification rights, director and officer removal procedures, and a number of other matters pertaining to governance. At the same time, the bylaws are usually easier to amend than the articles. The board should examine the bylaws periodically, and adopt revisions as necessary to facilitate smooth operations.

(c) STATUTORY DEFAULT PROVISIONS. Many nonprofit corporation statutes contain what are best described as *default provisions,* specifying the rule when a particular issue is not addressed in an organization's governing documents. Typically, each of these default provisions is prefaced with the phrase "Unless the articles of incorporation or bylaws provide otherwise." For example, Section 8.24 of the Revised Model Act provides:

> Except as otherwise provided in this Act, the articles or bylaws, a quorum of a board of directors consists of a majority of the directors in office immediately before a meeting begins. In no event may the articles or bylaws authorize a quorum of fewer than the greater of one-third of the number of directors in office or two directors.

The Revised Model Act also permits director consent resolutions, "[u]nless the articles or bylaws provide otherwise." These two examples are hardly unique. Provisions pertaining to committees,[119] notices of meetings,[120] required officers,[121] board vacancies,[122] and countless other issues rely on similar default rules. In fact, the Revised Model Act contains literally dozens of default provisions.

When read in the abstract, the default provisions in the Revised Model Act and most state statutes make good sense: Majority controls; committees can be created; vacancies shall be filled; and so forth and so on. So why not keep the bylaws simple and just rely on the statute to fill in the gaps? The answer is that people run nonprofits. Majority rule is fine unless there is a natural or institutionally mandated division on the board. In that case, the organizers may want to protect the views of the minority directors by requiring at least a two-thirds affirmative vote before certain actions can be taken, or the organizers may want to limit who can serve on compensation or audit committees by imposing an "independence" requirement. These types of issues make customization advisable and necessary.

---

119. RMNCA § 8.25(a).
120. RMNCA § 8.22(a).
121. RMNCA § 8.40(a).
122. RMNCA § 8.11(a).

(d) AMENDMENTS. Both the articles of incorporation and the bylaws are subject to amendment. This is perfectly appropriate and necessary if the governing documents are to continue to facilitate governance as circumstances change. Two cautionary notes should be made about amendments. First, the amendment provision needs to be more elaborate when different actions require different levels of approval. For example, imagine an organization whose various constituencies have built a provision into the bylaws that requires at least 80 percent of the directors to approve a sale of a particular asset. If the provision in the bylaws regarding amendments requires a majority vote for amendments, it may be possible for a majority of the directors to amend the bylaws to reduce the more than 80 percent requirement to a majority requirement, thereby undoing the originally negotiated agreement. Of course, those opposing the sale are likely to seek court relief, arguing that the bylaws should be construed to require at least an 80 percent vote to amend that provision, but there is no guarantee a court will grant such relief. Good practice dictates making the appropriate references to different levels of approval in the provisions of the bylaws and articles of incorporation that address amendments. This can be particularly important in membership organizations that may allocate decision authority between the members and the directors. Amendment provisions should be drafted to prevent end runs around these allocations of authority.

Second, when amendments are made to the articles of incorporation or the bylaws, the documents should be restated and new copies should be provided to the appropriate individuals with instructions to destroy old copies. Typically, organizations do not restate documents following each amendment. At some point several years down the road, there will be a disagreement over whether a particular document contains the most current terms. If the parties can get past the disagreement, they decide to restate the documents. It is better to restate the documents on an ongoing basis. There no longer is any excuse in this age of word processing. Furthermore, all documents should be clearly dated, and the drafter should be identified.

(e) DIRECTOR REVIEW. Each director should take the time to read the organizational documents. Even a cursory review provides an overview of the nonprofit's internal rules governing corporate decisions and operations. Despite this recommendation, few directors will actually take the time to review them. Whether or not a director actually reads these documents, each director should obtain a copy of the organization's organic documents before agreeing to serve as a director. At some point during a director's tenure, some controversial issue is bound to arise. Having the articles and bylaws readily available provides the director an edge when deciding how to assert his point of view, permitting him to jockey for position without prematurely playing his hand through a request for legal documents.

(f) MORE THAN BOILERPLATE. People often refer to the articles of incorporation and the bylaws as just boilerplate. A cursory reading of these documents could easily lead someone to that conclusion, but forming a nonprofit corporation is hardly a boilerplate affair. Different groups of organizers often share different views regarding the board's role, the need for members, the supervisory role of affiliated organizations, and electoral procedures. Even the seemingly simple task of drafting a purposes or dissolution clause in the articles of incorporation can be a time-consuming one.

Terra Museum of Art and the Purposes Clause

* * *

The Terra Museum of American Art was founded in 1980 by Daniel J. Terra, who died in 1996. According to legal documents, the museum had a $450 million net value, which was comprised in part of a $100 million collection that included works by Mary Cassatt, Winslow Homer, Georgia O'Keefe, and John Singer Sargent.[123] Terra established the museum because he could not find an existing museum that was willing to take his collection of some 600 works of art and keep it intact. The museum first opened in Evanston, Illinois, but was subsequently moved to a building located on Chicago's Michigan Avenue. The museum opened a satellite facility in Giverny, France.

In 1999, the museum was drawing 135,000 visitors per annum, a relatively small number given its location in the third largest city in the United States. Not surprising, it was losing about $1 million per year. This precipitated Judith Terra, Daniel's widow and the museum's president, to propose that the museum be moved to Washington, D.C.[124]

Two directors brought suit to stop the move, asserting that Judith Terra's desire to move the museum was motivated by her desire to obtain a prominent place in the social circles of Washington."[125] In other words, they were arguing that she was breaching various duties she owed to the museum as a director and officer.

Judith Terra and several directors then filed an appeal from the lower court's decision in August 2001, alleging "payoffs, coercion and every type of Chicago-style malfeasance."[126] They argued that the museum needed to move because of financial circumstances.

What made this dispute particularly interesting was the presence of the Illinois attorney general, who joined the dispute by siding with the plaintiff's efforts to stop the museum from moving its collection outside of Illinois. The attorney general arguably overstepped his role in overseeing the charitable sector by taking sides in what was in essence a disagreement over the museum's direction, but this demonstrates how state officials often take action based on provincial motivations rather than legal rights and duties. The attorney general was acting under the Illinois Charitable Trust Act, arguing that he was exercising powers under that act to protect charitable assets.[127] A number of attorneys general have taken this position

123. Buntrock v. Judith Terra, 810 N.E. 2d 991(Ill. App. 2004).

124. J. Yates and R. Becker, *Terra Fight Turns to Battle over Widow's Motives: Action by Illinois Attorney General Adds Fuel to Efforts to Keep Art Collector's Michigan Avenue Museum from Shutting*, CHI. TRIB., Oct. 8, 2000.

125. Complaint at ¶ 32, Buntrock *supra* note 123.

126. E. Slater, *Chicago's Litigious Art of Possession: Museum Directors are Suing Judith Terra for Trying to Move her Late Husband's Collection to Washington, D.C.*, L.A. TIMES, Aug. 4, 2001.

127. *See* Illinios Charitable Trust Act § 15.5

under similar statutes,[128] making it particularly important that purposes clauses be drafted broadly enough to prevent the attorney general from injecting himself into the board's rightful domain over policy judgments.

The Circuit Court of Cook County approved a settlement in July 2001 that kept the Terra collection in Chicago for 50 years, although the museum could partner with another museum in the Chicago area.[129] Under the settlement, all members of the Terra Museum's board were required to resign and replacements were appointed. An Illinois Appellate Court upheld the settlement in May 2004.[130] A significant portion of the collection was lent to the Art Institute of Chicago.[131]

Notice that the fight was essentially over the museum's purposes and whether the purposes clauses permitted it to move its assets out the state of Illinois. This is a case in which the entire dispute could have been avoided had the museum's organic documents more clearly addressed these issues. In an implicit warning to those charged with drafting purposes clause, the Illinois Appeals Court noted: "The Foundation's articles of incorporation constitute the starting point for ascertaining these purposes."[132]

* * *

3.5 MEETINGS

Typically, board meetings occur regularly (monthly, quarterly, or semiannually). Meetings should be conducted in accordance with the rules set out in the articles of incorporation and bylaws or others the board agrees upon. Many people mistakenly assume that meetings must be conducted in accordance with *Robert's Rules of Order*,[133] but the board can adopt whatever rules it wants to govern the conduct of meetings so long as the rules are consistent with the articles and bylaws. The board might agree on some simple rules that keep the

---

128. *See* Banner Health System v. Lawrence E. Long, 663 N.W.2d 242 (2003); State ex rel. Butterworth v. Intracoastal Health Sys., Inc., No. CL 01-0068 AB (Fla. Cir. Ct. Feb. 27, 2001); In re Manhattan Eye, Ear & Throat Hospital, 715 N.Y.S.2d 575 (N.Y. Sup. Ct. 1999); NEW HAMPSHIRE ATTORNEY GENERAL, REPORT ON OPTIMA HEALTH (Mar. 10, 1998); and Queen of Angels v. Younger, 136 Cal. Rptr. 36, 40-41 (1977). Professor Evelyn Brody, a widely-respected and leading authority on nonprofit law, disagrees with the tenor of these cases, concluding:

> The role of the attorney general and courts is to guard against charity fiduciaries' wrongdoing, and not to interfere in decisionmaking carried out in good faith. To this end, an attorney general is vested with the authority to seek to correct breaches of fiduciary duty that have not otherwise been remedied by the board. However, the attorney general is not a "super" member of the board.

E. Brody, *Whose Public? Parochialism and Paternalism in State Charity Law Enforcement*, 79 IND. L. JOUR. 937 (2004). While Professor Brody does an excellent job of explaining how charitable trust acts and state corporate law defining director duties can be harmonized, no one should rely on her conclusions when drafting a purposes clause. As noted in the accompanying text, the clause should be broad enough to provide the board with flexibility to change an organization's direction, but narrow enough to prevent the state's attorney general room from acting as a "super" member of the board.

129. J. Yates, *Judge to OK Museum Accord; Appeal Likely Challenge Is Seen from Terra Widow*, CHI. TRIB., July 25, 2001.
130. *See* Buntrock, *supra* note 123.
131. J. Yates and C. Storch, *Terra Giving Up, Closing Doors in '04; Treasures to Go to Art Institute*, CHI. TRIB., June 21, 2003.
132. *See* Buntrock, *supra* note 123.
133. HENRY M. ROBERTS III, WILLIAM J. EVANS, DANIEL H. HONEMANN, & THOMAS J. BALCH, ROBERT'S RULES OF ORDER: NEWLY REVISED 10TH EDITION (HarperCollins 2000).

meeting moving forward while avoiding intricate procedures. In fact, unless board members want to wade through more than 600 pages of highly technical rules, they should avoid *Robert's Rules*.[134] These rules go well beyond making and seconding motions and calling the question. Although *Robert's Rules* does specifiy alternative rules for small boards and committees,[135] those alternatives are not set forth in one location, making it difficult to find the alternatives rules without reviewing the entire set of rules. Moreover, many organizations that blindly adopt *Robert's Rules*, do so without specifying whether the modified rules will apply.

If your organization adopts *Robert's Rules*, be prepared to deal with different types of subsidiary and privileged motions, committees of the whole and their two alternative forms, assignment of the floor, and divisions of questions. *Robert's Rules* or a variant thereof may be perfectly appropriate for a legislative body or council, but the members of a 12-person board of directors would be much better engaged devoting the time they would otherwise spend learning and navigating these rules to a more thorough review of the organization's financial statements. A board should avoid casually adopting *Robert's Rules* if the board will then default to much simpler informal procedures. If there is ever a controversial matter, some members of the board who are unfamiliar with the intricacies of *Robert's Rules* may have to contend with one board member who has taken the time to learn the rules and is then in a position to exploit that knowledge by demanding that informality give way to the formality mandated by the rules.

(a) A RECOMMENDED MEETING FORMAT. An agenda should be circulated in advance of the meeting. Other material, such as financial statements, draft minutes, and committee reports, might also be usefully distributed in advance. In addition to providing an outline for the meeting, a formal agenda also serves another important purpose. Under state statutes and governing documents, members and directors must receive advanced notice regarding certain decisions. The agenda provides the secretary with the opportunity to provide any required-advanced notice; or at least the opportunity to prevent the board from inadvertently acting on a matter that requires formal notice.

There is no right or wrong procedure for conducting a board meeting. Every board develops its own meeting style, and, for the most part, that is just fine. Whatever the format, it should be one that permits an expeditious but thorough discussion of the issues before the board. If your board has not arrived at a satisfactory format yet, you might want to consider the following format:

- *Call to order.* The secretary should determine whether there is a quorum.
- *Approval of the minutes.* Ideally, the secretary will have distributed in advance the minutes of the previous meeting so that board members have

134. Additional information pertaining to *Robert's Rule's* is available at http://www.robertsrules.com.

135. HENRY M. ROBERTS III, *supra* note 133, at 9.

adequate time to review the minutes. Board members should be given the opportunity to suggest any corrections, and the minutes should then be approved by formal vote.

- *Reports from the president or CEO.* The president, CEO, or executive director should make a brief report regarding relevant matters that have transpired since the last meeting, leaving out agenda items that are scheduled to be addressed later in the meeting.
- *Report from the treasurer.* The treasurer or other officer responsible for the financial statements should make a financial report. Ideally, board members will have been provided with the monthly (or other periodic) financial statements and budget variances before the meeting, but if that is not possible, full statements should be distributed at the meeting to each board member present. The treasurer should report on major expenditures since the last meeting as well as material budget variances.
- *Reports from standing committees.* If standing committees make regular reports, the agenda should include these reports as agenda items. Otherwise, a committee chair should ask to be added to the agenda when the committee has something to report. The board chair may want to routinely ask each committee chair about the status of matters before the committee so that matters do not fall by the wayside.
- *Scheduled new business.* The board should then discuss new business items that have been placed on the agenda by advanced request.
- *Other business.* Any new business that has not been scheduled as an agenda item should then be addressed.
- *Adjournment.* The board chair should adjourn the meeting, noting the time, date, and place for the next board meeting.

The next question that often comes up is whether proposed board actions must be couched in the form of a formal motion and whether motions must be seconded. Unless there are agreed-upon procedures, the board is not required to make decisions based on formal motions, nor must motions be seconded before the decision is submitted for a vote. A formal motion does signal that a decision is before the board, alerting the secretary that a decision is being made that should be reflected in the minutes for the meeting. A good secretary will interject if the person framing the motion has not clearly stated or defined the question being considered, inevitably leading to sounder decisions.

Although requiring a second is a nice formal touch, there generally is no legal requirement that motions be seconded. However, when someone has added new business to the agenda or raised new business at the meeting, the board might want to ask that the person raising the new business put the requested action in the form of a motion and require this motion to be seconded before the board discusses the matter. If the new business is out of sync with the board's general sentiment, requiring a second is an excellent way to avoid wasting a lot of time on a matter that only one person believes should lead to a decision. Requiring that motions of this nature be seconded forces board members to informally vet ideas before meetings (assuming that open-meeting laws do not preclude informal discussions). In many cases, seconding screens out proposals that lack the necessary support. If the proposal's advocate feels particularly strong about the proposal, an initial rejection may lead that person to reformulate the proposal. Everybody will appreciate that valuable meeting time was not wasted in a rambling bull session.

(b) MEETING MINUTES. The organization's secretary should prepare minutes for each board meeting, which should be approved at the next board meeting. If the organization's secretary is not a lawyer or is unfamiliar with legal phrasing and issues, draft minutes should be reviewed by the organization's counsel (before the minutes are circulated) to make sure that the minutes are written with a view toward potential litigation. This could be important if, for example, personnel matters or transactions involving potential conflicts of interest were discussed at the board meeting.

At a minimum, the minutes should identify the directors who attended the meeting, specify whether there was a quorum, and summarize the topics discussed so that at a later date the board does not have to reinvent the wheel. The minutes should also reflect the decisions that were made.

People, particularly lawyers, disagree over the exact level of detail that is advisable. There are those who want to keep the description brief for fear that the minutes will be used as evidence in any subsequent litigation, but others argue for lengthy descriptions in an effort to establish that business judgment was exercised. In view of recent case law, the more detailed approach is the more prudent one. In one landmark decision, the Delaware Supreme Court[136] held the directors accountable because they had not exercised sufficient care when approving a merger offer. While the specific facts are not relevant, the following references in the court's opinion illustrate why detailed minutes are important:

- "Again, the facts of record do not support the defendants' argument. There is no evidence: (a) that the Merger Agreement was effectively amended to give the Board freedom to put Trans Union up for auction sale to the highest bidder; or (b) that a public auction was in fact permitted to occur. The minutes of the Board meeting make no reference to any of this. Indeed, the record compels the conclusion that the directors had no rational basis for expecting that a market test was attainable, given the terms of the Agreement as executed during the evening of September."
- "As has been noted, nothing in the Board's Minutes supports these claims. No reference to either of the so called 'conditions' or of Trans Union's reserved right to test the market appears in any notes of the Board meeting

136. Smith v. Van Gorkom, 488 A.2d 858 (Del. Supr.1985).

or in the Board Resolution accepting the Pritzker offer or in the Minutes of the meeting itself."

- "There is no evidence of record that the October 8 meeting had any other purpose; and we also note that the Minutes of the October 8 Board meeting, including any notice of the meeting, are not part of the voluminous records of this case."

In short, the Delaware Supreme Court said to the board, "You may remember discussing these things, but the formal record does not support your recollections." Other courts have since focused on the minutes.[137] Even though these cases have arisen in a commercial context, the Delaware statute applies equally to Delaware nonprofit corporations.[138] As a consequence of this developing trend in the law, the portion of the minutes that records major decisions should include a description of the alternatives considered, as well as the factors that led to a particular choice between alternatives.[139] When decisions involve a review of contracts, reports, studies, financial information, or expert input, the minutes should catalog what documents the board reviewed.

Each director should review the minutes for each meeting, particularly when a director disagreed with an action taken by the board. Under some state statutes, a director who is present at a meeting is deemed to have consented to any action taken by the board at that meeting unless the disagreement is reflected in the meeting minutes or the director files a written statement with the secretary indicating his disagreement.[140] Properly documenting this disagreement can protect the director from liability arising out of the decision in question.

---

137. *See, e.g.*, *In re* Walt Disney Company Derivative Litig., 825 A.2d 275 (Del. Ch. Ct. 2003), in which the court stated:

> The minutes of the meeting were fifteen pages long, but only a page and a half covered Ovitz's possible employment. A portion of that page and a half was spent discussing the $250,000 fee paid to Russell for obtaining Ovitz. According to the minutes, the Old Board did not ask any questions about the details of Ovitz's salary, stock options, or possible termination. The Old Board also did not consider the consequences of a termination, or the various payout scenarios that existed. Nevertheless, at that same meeting, the Old Board decided to appoint Ovitz president of Disney. Final negotiation of the employment agreement was left to Eisner, Ovitz's close friend for over twenty-five years.

Perhaps the board discussed the matter in detail, but the absence of a written record worked to the board's disadvantage. On the other hand, the Delaware Chancery Court ruled in favor of the board when the minutes contained sufficient detail to indicate the board had exercised due care. See *In re* Caremark International Inc. Derivative Litig., 698 A.2d 959 (Del. 1996).

138. *See also* His Way, Inc. v. Malcomn McMillin, Case No. 2004-CA-00133-COA (Miss. App. Ct. 2005), in which a Mississippi court concluded:

> In the instant case, the chancellor was justified in finding the corporate records and minutes of His Way, consisting of over 100 pages, "constitutes the best evidence of who were members...."

The dispute in this case involved control of a nonprofit organization with approximately $2 million in assets. The central issues in dispute were whether there were members and if so, who those members were. Much of the discussion focused on minutes, but the facts provide another example of why adherance to corporate formalities and membership requirements is critical.

139. K. Graham, The Scope and Content of Corporate Minutes (O'Melveny & Meyers 2004).

140. Illinois General Not For Profit Corporation Act of 1986 § 108.65(b).

(c) EXECUTIVE SESSIONS. Some nonprofits may be subject to open-meeting laws or have provisions in their bylaws that permit members to attend board meetings (e.g., homeowners' associations). Typically, the board has the authority to meet in an executive or closed session when sensitive matters are discussed, such as litigation strategy or employment decisions. The board should be very careful about what it discusses during these sessions. People on boards often exhibit a strong penchant for secrecy, particularly when the issues are unpleasant or controversial. The board should resist the temptation to cover topics in executive session that are not specifically designated as being within the scope of executive sessions. Some statutes require the board to limit executive sessions to *discussions* of permitted issues, with a requirement that actual decisions be made in a regular session.[141]

(d) THE INTERNET AND MEETINGS. Some states have modified their state statutes to permit board meetings by teleconference so long as all members can hear and participate concurrently.[142] The logical next step in the progression is a meeting held through an Internet chat utility, with a participant typing comments that appear on the other participants' screens. Far fewer states have formally addressed this sort of arrangement. California permits participation "through use of electronic transmission by and to the corporation," distinguishing electronic transmission from telephone and video conferences.[143] Presumably, *electronic transmission* includes an Internet chat utility, but only if the members can communicate concurrently and

---

141. *See, e.g.*, Illinois Condominium Act, § 18(a)(9), which provides as follows:

> that meetings of the board of managers shall be open to any unit owner, except for the portion of any meeting held (i) to discuss litigation when an action against or on behalf of the particular association has been filed and is pending in a court or administrative tribunal, or when the board of managers finds that such an action is probable or imminent, (ii) to consider information regarding appointment, employment or dismissal of an employee, or (iii) to discuss violations of rules and regulations of the association or a unit owner's unpaid share of common expenses; *that any vote on these matters shall be taken at a meeting or portion thereof open to any unit owner....* [empahsis added].

142. N.Y. Consol. L., Chapter 35, § 708.

143. *See* Cal. Corp. Code § 5211(a)(6), which provides:

> Members of the board may participate in a meeting through use of conference telephone, electronic video screen communication or electronic transmission by and to the corporation (Sections 20 and 21). Participation in a meeting through use of conference telephone or electronic video screen communication pursuant to this subdivision constitutes presence in person at that meeting as long as all members participating in the meeting are able to hear one another. Participation in a meeting through use of electronic transmission by and to the corporation, other than conference telephone and electronic video screen communication, pursuant to this subdivision constitutes presence in person at that meeting if both of the following apply:
>
> (A) Each member participating in the meeting can communicate with all of the other members concurrently.
>
> (B) Each member is provided the means of participating in all matters before the board, including, without limitation, the capacity to propose, or to interpose an objection to, a specific action to be taken by the corporation.

each member has the opportunity to propose or object to a specific action to be taken by the corporation.[144]

At times a board may want to act between meetings. For example, the board may need to provide input into negotiations to settle a lawsuit or consummate a contract. Often board members provide their input through e-mails. It is easy for a board to generate dozens of e-mails in an afternoon when a deadline looms, but in the absence of specific statutory authority or case law, this type of communication should not be viewed as a board meeting even in the case of a statute like that of California, which contemplates "electronic transmission." Even though e-mail is fast, it is not concurrent. This does not necessarily preclude the board from taking action. Many state statutes do permit boards to act by unanimous written consent. In the absence of specific statutory or case law to the contrary, e-mails could be construed as a writing. In focusing on the "written" requirement for consent actions, however, remember that the decision under many state statutes must be unanimous. This means that if one board member disagrees, the board legally cannot bind the organization even though a majority of the directors approve an action through e-mail communication.

Given the convenience of e-mail, some boards will inevitably take "emergency" actions through e-mail votes regardless of whether this is permissible from a legal standpoint. Your board should not do this, but expediency could carry the day. If this happens, particularly if there is no unanimous consent, the board should validate the action at the next board meeting. Even if legally permissible, any vote by e-mail should be appropriately reflected in the board meeting minutes file. Remember that if the decision is a controversial one, someone could challenge the validity of an action taken by e-mail if the statute does not clearly contemplate vote by e-mail. This could prove problematic if a corporation or its officers have warranted the authority of the corporation to act or the other party has detrimentally relied on the authority of the corporation to act. In other words, unless the board is absolutely certain that that no one will challenge its action, it should schedule a telephonic or in-person meeting of the board rather than rely on e-mail.

Boards and their counsel should regularly survey applicable law with respect to these issues because the states have been updating their laws to facilitate actions by e-mail and other means. For example, in 2002, Minnesota amended its nonprofit corporation statute to permit directors to take action authenticated by electronic communication, which presumably includes e-mail.[145] Under certain circumstances, such action need not even be by unanimous consent. Wisconsin

---

144. *Id.*

145. *See* Minn. Stats., Chapter 317A § 317A.239, which provides as follows:

> 1. Method. An action required or permitted to be taken at a board meeting may be taken by written action signed, or consented to by authenticated electronic communication, by all of the directors. If the articles so provide, an action, other than an action requiring member approval, may be taken by written action signed, or consented to by authenticated electronic communication, by the

has a similar but clearly not identical provision in its statutes, providing that a writing includes electronic means[146] and that signature includes an electronic signature.[147] However, to the extent that an action can be taken without unanimous consent, Wisconsin requires that it must be signed by at least two-thirds of the directors in office,[148] demonstrating why it is critical to review the applicable state statutes.

As a final thought, those running organizations should not become too enamored with all the new technologies. Although people are free to drift off or doodle on a scratch pad when attending a meeting in person, communicating over the Web or a telephone line provides far greater opportunity for inattention. Almost everyone has been on a conference call when they have hit the mute button to conduct other unrelated business with an associate. There is still something to be said for in-person communication.[149]

3.6 MAJOR EVENTS

The two major transactions in the life cycle of a nonprofit are its birth and its death. It should come as no surprise that these are the two times that state law imposes a variety of requirements on the nonprofit and those charged with its formation or dissolution.

---

number of directors that would be required to take the same action at a meeting of the board at which all directors were present.

2. Effective time. The written action is effective when signed, or consented to by authenticated electronic communication, by the required number of directors, unless a different effective time is provided in the written action.

3. Notice liability. When written action is permitted to be taken by less than all directors, all directors must be notified immediately of its text and effective date. Failure to provide the notice does not invalidate the written action. A director who does not sign or consent to the written action is not liable for the action.

Section 317A.011 defines the *electronic communication* as "any form of communication, not directly involving the physical transmission of paper, that creates a record that may be retained, retrieved, and reviewed by a recipient of the communication, and that may be directly reproduced in paper form by the recipient through an automated process."

---

146. Wis. Stat., Chapter 181, § 181.0821(1r).
147. Wis. Stat., Chapter 181, § 181.0821(1m)(a).
148. Wis. Stat., Chapter 181, § 181.0821(1r).
149. In Chapter 5, we consider a financial crisis that hit the Milwaukee Public Museum in 2005. As a consequence of that crisis, the new chair of the board "decreed that board members could attend meetings only in person, not by phone." *See* A. Lank and D. Umhoefer, *Hands-Off Board Hurt Museum: Members' Lax Attendance, Cruise-Control Attitude Contributed to Financial Crash*, MILWAUKEE J.-SENTINEL, June 25, 2005. Earlier in the article, the *Journal-Sentinel* reports that the board approved a $26 million budget in 2003, the largest in its history, with only 8 of its 25 members in the room. Seven other members assented by phone, according to the article.

(a) FORMATION. We considered many of the issues that must be addressed as part of the incorporation process when we considered the articles of incorporation earlier in this chapter. Two additional points are worth making. First, the organizers should be careful when entering into contracts on behalf of a nonexistent entity because the organizers could be held personally liable in the event that the formation process fails.[150] When acting in a representative capacity, the organizers should make sure that anyone they are dealing with knows that they are acting on behalf of a nonexistent entity. If at all possible, any contract should specifically state that the other party's recourse lies exclusively with the nonprofit once it is formed. Immediately following formal incorporation, the organizers should have the new entity's initial directors adopt a consent resolution formally assuming any liabilities that the incorporators incurred as part of the incorporation process.

Second, incorporation or formation focuses on the legal existence of the entity. At this time, the organizers should also focus on obtaining tax-exempt status under both federal and state law (see Chapter 6), registering with the appropriate state charity officials in both the state of incorporation and any state in which the organization will engage in solicitation or in "business" (see Chapter 9), perfecting any property tax exemptions (see Chapter 8), and addressing insurance needs (see Chapter 12).

(b) DISSOLUTION. Both state regulators and the IRS focus heavily on the dissolution of nonprofit organizations, particularly charities. As previously noted, both sets of regulators are committed to making sure that charitable assets remain committed to the charitable sector, albeit in a different form or titled to a different charity. State regulators therefore focus on several major events in the life cycle of a nonprofit, including an outright dissolution as well as mergers and sales of substantially all of the assets that the organization holds. Typically, state statutes contain very detailed limitations on these transactions, requiring that members, the attorney general, and others be notified. New York requires court approval for some of these transactions, as do some other states.

A board should seek legal counsel whenever it contemplates any transaction that in substance is a liquidation of a nonprofit. This is particularly important because this is one area in which some states expressly hold directors personally

150. Section 2.04 of the RMNCA addresses preincorporation liability, providing as follows:

> All persons purporting to act as or on behalf of a corporation knowing there was no incorporation under this Act, are jointly and severally liable for all liabilities created while so acting.

This language appears in many nonprofit corporation acts.

accountable if they authorize an inappropriate distribution or transfer of the nonprofit's assets.[151]

Most state statutes provide for voluntary dissolutions. The procedure depends on whether the corporation is a membership or nonmembership organization. In either case, the board generally is required to adopt a plan of dissolution. If there are no members, the decision often can be made by a majority of the directors.[152] If there are members, they must approve the decision: under one formulation, by two-thirds of the votes cast or a majority of the voting power, whichever is less.[153]

Dissolution appears to be a relatively simple process, but at least two factors can add a great deal of complexity to the process. First, if the organization has restricted assets, it must make sure that their disposition and subsequent use adhere to the terms of the restrictions. For example, if an educational institution holds a $2 million scholarship fund, it must make sure that the subsequent use of those assets following a merger with another institution continues to comply with the restrictions. If the assets were acquired by bequest, court approval may be necessary, particularly if the proposed transferees will not be able to use the assets in accordance with the restrictions. In some states, the attorney general may require notification and the opportunity to review the proposed transfer or disposition. As should be apparent, state laws differ, making retention of knowledgeable legal counsel essential. It may be advisable to obtain agreements with transferees that they will honor the restrictions. In some cases, the organization may want to approach the attorney general with a prepackaged plan that the

---

151. For example, Section 108.65(b) of the Illinois General Not For Profit Corporation Act of 1986 makes directors liable for distributions not authorized by Section 109.10 (operating distributions), as well as distributions as part of a dissolution unless the distribution is authorized under Article 12, which governs dissolutions. Section 108.65(c) does limit this liability where the director has relied on financial statements in good faith, providing as follows:

> A director shall not be liable for a distribution of assets to any person in excess of the amount authorized by Section 109.10 or Article 12 of this Act if he or she relied and acted in good faith upon a balance sheet and profit and loss statement of the corporation represented to him or her to be correct by the president or the officer of such corporation having charge of its books of account, or certified by an independent public or certified public accountant or firm of such accountants to fairly reflect the financial condition of such corporation, nor shall he or she be so liable if in good faith in determining the amount available for any such distribution he or she considered the assets to be of their book value.

For additional examples, see N.Y. Consol. L, Chapter 35, §§ 719 and 1005; Mo. Rev. Stats, Chapter 355, § 355.426; Ind. Stat., Title 17, Art. 17, Chapter 13, § 4; and Wis. Stat., Chapter 181, § 181.0833, but less clearly than the other statutes cited here. A number of states do not address the question of director liability for unlawful distributions. These states apparently prefer to handle the liability issue through their basic statutory provisions regarding director liability. For example, while there could be a provision expressly imposing liability on directors of Kentucky nonprofit corporations for unlawful distributions, it is not readily apparent despite a provision in the statutes providing that directors can limit their liability through the articles of incorporation. *See* Ky. Rev. Stat. §§ 273.248, 273.300, 273,303, and 273.307 of Chapter 273 of Title XXIII.

152. *See* RMNCA § 14.01.

153. RMNCA § 14.02(a).

attorney can approve, but read on before requesting prepackaged approval from an attorney general.[154]

State attorneys general are supposed to be involved in the dissolution (or merger or sale) process to add oversight, making sure that the assets (or the value they represent) remain committed to the charitable sector. This involvement is often statutorily mandated even when there are no restricted assets. In recent years, a number of state attorneys general have used their approval power to further political ambitions, making demands on the nonprofits that go well beyond protecting assets. This is where the second complexity can arise. No one should

---

154. Consider Section 15.5 of the Illinois Charitable Trust Act, which provides as follows:

Sec. 15.5. Termination and transfer of certain trusts.

(a) If a trustee who is subject to this Act determines that the continued administration of a trust has become impractical because of the trust's small size or because of changed circumstances that adversely affect the charitable purpose or purposes of the trust, then after notifying each named charitable organization, if any, for the benefit of which the trust was created and after obtaining the consent of the Attorney General, the trustee may amend the terms of the governing instrument of the trust to the extent necessary to terminate the trust and to transfer the trust assets as provided in subsection (c) or (d). The Attorney General shall consent to the termination of the trust and the transfer of the trust assets only after having determined that the termination and transfer are necessary or appropriate, in the case of termination because of the trust's small size, to implement the charitable purpose or purposes of the trust or, in the case of termination because of changed circumstances, to fulfill the general intent of the donor of the trust as expressed in the governing instrument of the trust.

(b) For purposes of subsection (a), the term "small size" shall mean a trust for which the annual expenses of administration, including the trustee's fees, the investment management and accounting fees and excise taxes would, if charged entirely against income, exceed 25% of the income of the trust, and the term "changed circumstances" shall mean a condition in which the charitable purpose or purposes of the trust shall, in the judgment of the trustee, have become illegal, unnecessary, incapable of fulfillment, or inconsistent with the charitable needs of the community.

(c) Subject to subsection (d) with respect to a trust terminated because of the trust's small size, the trustee shall transfer the trust assets of the terminated trust to a community foundation or similar publicly-supported organization described in Section 170 (b)(1)(A)(vi) of the Internal Revenue Code of 1986, to be administered, in the case of termination because of the trust's small size, in implementation of the charitable purpose or purposes of the trust or, in the case of termination because of changed circumstances, in accordance with the general intent of the donor of the trust as expressed in the governing instrument of the trust.

(d) If a trust terminated because of the trust's small size was created for the benefit of a named charitable organization which has established an endowment fund and if the principal of the endowment fund is under its irrevocable terms no more expendable by the organization than is the principal of the trust under the terms of the governing instrument of the trust, the charitable organization may direct the trustee to transfer the trust assets of the trust to the endowment fund, to be administered in implementation of the charitable purpose or purposes of the trust.

(e) A trustee need not obtain the approval of any court in order to terminate a trust and to transfer the trust assets as provided in this Section.

(f) The provisions of this Section are an alternative to and not in abrogation of any other course of action provided by law. A trustee shall not incur any civil or criminal liability by reason of acting in accordance with this Section.

Keep in mind that Illinois' Charitable Trust Act defines *trustee* broadly, meaning that simply holding property for charitable purposes can subject an entity or an individual to the statute. Notice clauses (e) and (f), which set up the possibility of alternative approaches.

be surprised if the personal objectives of an attorney general are interjected, particularly if the charity seeking approval is a hospital, museum, or other highly visible entity that provides tangible benefits to the community. In these cases, the charity and its board might want to consider court approval if that is an alternative. Before approaching either the courts or the attorney general (or other regulator), the charity and its board should first anticipate regulatory complexities and develop a comprehensive strategy.

This chapter has focused on nonprofit corporations, but those charities operating in trust form also need to be concerned when contemplating the equivalent of a corporate dissolution. Many states have statutes that subject charitable trusts to comparable approval procedures for major transactions such as a dissolution or sale of substantially all of the trust's assets. Again, this is an area in which trustees can be subject to personal liability for failing to comply.

Finally, nonprofit corporations should take care in complying with annual state filing requirements such as those requiring an annual report to be filed with the state's secretary of state. Many state statutes provide for involuntary dissolutions when nonprofit corporations fail to comply with these requirements.

The Dispute Is Never Actually Over Legal Doctrine: Shorter College and the Greater Baptist Convention

* * *

In May 2005, the Georgia Supreme Court held that the attempt by the trustees to dissolve Shorter College, a small Baptist college in Rome, Georgia was invalid.[155] The legal question was a very technical one, but the underlying policy dispute had great significance to the parties involved.

The Shorter College trustees wanted to sever ties with the Greater Baptist Convention because they believed that the convention was asserting too much influence over the college. The dispute apparently had its genesis in a warning from the Southern Association of Colleges and Schools, the body that accredits Shorter.[156] Not surprisingly, the policy dispute focused on the influence of religious doctrine on Shorter's curriculum.[157] The existing trustees of the college wanted to sever ties to the Baptist Convention, which was a particularly dicey proposition because the convention held the power to appoint the trustees.

Initially, the existing trustees tried to alter the selection process for trustees, but that proved to be unsuccessful when the Baptist Convention countered the effort.[158] Recognizing the difficulties of severing ties under the circumstances, the "old" board of trustees decided to dissolve Shorter, but the dissolution was what might best be described as a wooden one.

---

155. Shorter College v. Baptist Convention of Georgia (Ga. Sup. Ct. 2005).

156. T. Bartlett, *Georgia Supreme Court Overrules Baptist College's Bid to Cut Ties with State Convention*, CHRON. HIGHER EDUC., May 24, 2005.

157. M. Dadigan, *After the Ruling, Shorter's Future Is Murky: What Now? College, Trustees, Students Wonder*, ROME NEWS-TRIB., May 29, 2005.

158. *Ga. Supreme Court Disallows College's Break From Convention*, BAPTIST PRESS, May 23, 2005.

The trustees simply reincorporated the school using a new legal entity as the repository for the assets, employees, and all other attributes of the existing institution. However, the organic documents provided a different procedure for appointing trustees that left out the Greater Baptist Convention.

Despite the obvious transparent nature of the old board's ploy, the trial court held that the dissolution was valid. An appellate court subsequently reversed[159] the trial court, and the Georgia Supreme Court upheld the appellate court's decision. The supreme court applied a "substance-over-form" analysis, concluding that although the legal vessel had changed the college was still the same college. It required that there had to be a "winding up of the business and affairs" of the entity before dissolution could occur. This supposition is dubious in the context of charitable organizations, as the dissenting opinion pointed out. The law generally requires that the assets be transferred to another charitable institution, which does not necessarily require that the business and affairs related to those assets cease.

The lessons for those organizing nonprofits, particularly ones controlled by other entities, are very important. First and foremost, the organizers must think about an exit strategy from the outset. Every one who participates in the formation of a new entity wants to believe that it will be successful, existing and growing into perpetuity. Unfortunately, that does not always happen, meaning that those forming the entity should give serious thought to what happens to and who controls the entity's assets if liquidation or sale becomes a necessity. In this case, Shorter College voluntarily submitted to the control of the Greater Baptist Convention in 1959, presumably to obtain additional funding. At that time, those agreeing to the affiliation probably should have given greater consideration to how that affiliation could be undone.

Second, when an affiliation exists between two institutions, the parties should consider what happens when the controlled entity begins to develop its own identity. As a legal matter, the Greater Baptist Convention clearly controlled Shorter College, but if it exercised that control, what was going to happen to the staff who ran the college?[160] If they were to resign, the convention would face some very practical problems. The legal arrangement between any controlled group of entities should have some safety-valve provisions built into it so that as the controlled entity develops its own identity, the controlling entity cannot simply reject that identity out of hand. In many instances, the parent entity provides the funding as part of the formation process, and consequently, will not want to provide for a governance structure that lessens its grip. In those instances, the people behind the scenes will reject out of hand any safety valve in the governing documents. This is fine to a certain extent, but every one should at least consider the issues. While the controlling entity can exercise control over a legal entity, that control will not necessarily constrain those running the entity from rebelling or resigning.

Finally, if the Greater Baptist Convention did gain actual control over Shorter College's board of trustees by appointing trustees who were more in line with the convention's thinking, those trustees needed to remember that their legal duties ran to the college, and not to the Baptist Convention. As a general matter, this holds true for any director appointed to the board of a subsidiary entity by the parent entity. In this particular case, if newly appointed trustees take actions that result in the loss of accreditation, the Georgia Attorney General might have a basis for bringing suit against them for breach of their duties. While existing students would run into questions of standing, it is not inconceivable that aggrieved students might not be granted standing to sue the trustees.

---

159. Baptist Convention v. Shorter College, 266 Ga. App. 312, 596 S.E. 2d 761 (2004).

160. This reality may be why the "old" board got as far as it did without being replaced. Admittedly, this is speculation, but the Greater Baptist Convention may have been reluctant to be too heavy handed because it faced the question of who was going to run Shorter College if the administration resigned in protest.

In this case, it was not the Georgia Attorney General who entered the fray to force his view of policy matters on Shorter College. Like the cases in which state attorneys general have entered the fray after receiving notice of a dissolution, however, this one cloaks much larger differences over policy as a dispute over technical corporate legal doctrine.

* * *

(c) OPERATIONS. The remainder of this *Guide* focuses on operational issues. Some of these issues involve state nonprofit corporate law. When appropriate, we consider the relevant corporate statutes. As you will see, most of the discussion focuses on a wide range of other laws. Those laws can pose various problems for nonprofit directors and officers. When grappling with operational issues, the board and the officers must keep in mind the institutional framework outlined in this chapter. Failure to do so can only compound any problems facing the nonprofit. With that in mind, let's next consider the duties imposed on boards and the interplay between those duties and operations.

CHAPTER 4

LEGAL DUTIES AND OBLIGATIONS

Duty largely consists of pretending that the trivial is critical.

JOHN FOWLES[1]

This ain't no party, This ain't no disco
This ain't no foolin' around...

TALKING HEADS[2]

1. THE MAGUS (Modern Library Ed. 1998)
2. *Life During Wartime,* on STOP MAKING SENSE (Sire 1984).

Do you think that the AIG, Marsh & McLennan, MCI, Enron, WorldCom, Tyco, and Health South debacles have little meaning for the nonprofit world? You could not be more wrong if you do. Government officials, prosecutors, and business leaders are rethinking corporate governance in view of these and other recent scandals. Those who regulate nonprofits are taking advantage of the resulting publicity to spark a discussion of governance reforms in the nonprofit community. The next time a scandal hits a nonprofit, there will be far less tolerance for sloppy governance on the part of the board. The rules of the game are changing.

This chapter addresses the issues posed by recent corporate governance lapses. It focuses on the duties of care and loyalty as well as the implications that self-dealing and conflicts of interest pose. The legal doctrine and terminology used to define director duties and obligations is often vague, relying on terms such as *prudent person, business judgment,* and *reasonable*. These terms are intentionally vague, providing regulators, courts, and juries the sort of flexibility necessary to allow the "eyes on the scene" to punish behavior motivated by bad intentions and protect behavior motivated by good ones. Unfortunately, this vagueness makes articulating hard and fast rules defining the line between acceptable and unacceptable conduct difficult.

The examination of director and officer duties begins with a case study to immerse you in the basic issues. We then briefly consider relevant terminology and four other case studies. We next examine in detail two important topics — investment decisions and conflicts of interest. Following the discussion of conflicts, we consider a common situation that poses potential conflicts: the decisions by a volunteer director to become a paid employee. We will then conclude this chapter with two lists of suggested actions, one for directors and the other for officers. By then, you will appreciate the suggested "do's" and "don'ts."

4.1 A WELL-KNOWN CASE

Let's begin by considering an example based on a well-known case to gain a better understanding of director duties and obligations. Smithville Hospital is a nonprofit hospital serving Green County located in State C. The hospital is run by a very strong-willed administrator, Mary Nightingale. Fred Jones is one of the hospital's 20 board members.

The board's investment committee is responsible for managing the hospital's $10 million endowment. That committee is headed by Manny Mony, the hospital's chief financial officer and a board member. Fred Jones also serves on that committee. The investment committee meets once a year for about 30 minutes, with the committee members approving Mony's report. Often the written report is not made available to the board until several months after the meeting. Most board members never read the report because Mony tells the committee and the board that everything is just fine.

The board generally sees no need to question Mony about the returns on the hospital endowment because he graduated first in his class at the Green School of Business, a highly regarded Ivy League business school. As it turns out, all is not as Mony has portrayed it. One of the directors, Susan Banker, is the president of Five Spot Bank. She is also Mary Nightingale's niece. Half of the hospital's endowment is held in non-interest-bearing checking accounts maintained at the Five Spot Bank. Last week, the FDIC took over Five Spot Bank after it ran into financial difficulties. The hospital will likely lose all but $100,000 of the $5 million deposit. The attorney general of State C learns about the likely loss after the *Tenville Tattler* runs a front-page exposé. The attorney general brings suit against all of the directors for breach of their duty.

As a practical matter, Fred Jones is unlikely to be held liable for the hospital's losses, as surprising as that may be in light of his conduct. Regulators are generally hesitant to pursue directors of nonprofit organizations, often expressing concern that pursuing volunteer directors will deter other members of the public from serving on nonprofit boards and concern that widely publicized scandals could adversely affect the willingness of donors to continue contributing. However, Jones and the other directors may have crossed the line in this case. These facts are based on (but embellish) the facts in *Stern v. Lucy Webb Hayes National Training School for Deaconesses Sibley Hospital,*[3] probably the most celebrated case involving the liability of nonprofit directors,[4] with the court determining that the defendant directors had breached their fiduciary duties of care and loyalty. The court focused on the fact that the directors had failed to monitor the activities of those charged with investing the organization's funds. There was a complete absence of oversight. The defendant directors treated decisions regarding the opening of new accounts and the review of the annual audit report as mere formalities. The outside directors serving on the investment committee deferred to the judgment of the person charged with making investments without asking any questions.

Making matters worse, a significant portion of the organization's capital had been invested in bank and checking accounts that bore little or no interest. Certain members of the board had financial interests in the bank, posing questions of self-dealing. The court ruled against the directors. Although there was no loss of principal, the organization was subjected to lost opportunities for income. The take-away point from *Lucy Webb Hayes* is that doing nothing can be a basis for a finding against the directors, particularly when there is self-dealing. The board and its investment committee could have avoided trouble had they treated

3. 381 F. Supp. 1003 (D.D.C. 1974).
4. The directors were designated as trustees in the case.

investment decisions as more than a mere formality to be ratified without any discussion or questioning.

Equally troubling, if not more so, were the conflicts of interest. Under many state nonprofit laws, transactions exhibiting conflicts of interest are not necessarily prohibited; state law often permits the board to avoid liability by adopting guidelines that require, among other things, that the parties directly involved in the transaction recuse themselves from the decision-making process and fully disclose the relationships.[5] What is notable about the *Lucy Webb Hayes* decision is the refusal of the court to assess monetary damages (although some costs were awarded to the plaintiffs). In fact, the court refused the requested injunctive relief of removing the offending directors. Instead, it simply required all directors to read the court's opinion.

4.2 DIRECTOR DUTIES AND RESPONSIBILITIES

A director of a nonprofit corporation has two basic duties: the duty of care and the duty of loyalty. As a general rule, a director will be deemed to have discharged these duties if his actions are informed, reasonable and he acts in the best interests of the nonprofit. On the other hand, if the director repeatedly misses meetings, makes decisions without the necessary information, or uses his insider status to the nonprofit's disadvantage, the director has likely breached his duties to the nonprofit. Not surprisingly, the demarcation between good and bad behavior can, at times, be difficult to ascertain or generalize.

An oft-quoted article by former SEC Commissioner Harvey J. Goldschmid best summarizes the distinction between the duty of care and the duty of loyalty:

> Allegations of neglect, mismanagement, and improper (but disinterested) decision-making are dealt with under the duty of care and the business judgment rule. Fraud, self-dealing, misappropriation of corporate opportunities, improper diversions of corporate assets, and similar matters involving conflicts between a director's or officer's interest and the corporation's welfare are considered under duty of loyalty statutes and case law.[6]

In formulating a director's duties, Section 8.30(a) of the Revised Model Nonprofit Act[7] provides as follows:

> A director shall discharge his or her duties as a director, including his or her duties as a member of a committee:
>
> (1) in good faith;

---

5. At least 49 states have addressed the question of conflicts of interest in the nonprofit context. *See* MARION FREMONT-SMITH, GOVERNANCE NONPROFIT ORGANIZATIONS: FEDERAL AND STATE LAW REGULATION at 219 and Appendix, Table 3 (Belknap Press 2004).
6. H. Goldschmid, *The Fiduciary Duties of Nonprofit Directors and Officers: Paradoxes, Problems, and Proposed Reforms,* 23 J. Corp. L. 631 (1988).
7. The Revised Model Nonprofit Corporation Act (RMNCA), first referred to in Chapter 3, was adopted by the American Bar Association's Business Law Section Subcommittee on the Model Nonprofit Corporation Law in 1987.

(2) with the care an ordinarily prudent person in a like position would exercise under similar circumstances; and

(3) in a manner the director reasonably believes to be in the best interests of the corporation.

What is surprising about this formulation is that it makes no reference to the duty of care or the duty of loyalty. While other sections of most nonprofit corporation statutes address the duty of loyalty, often with rules pertaining to director conflicts of interest, very few statutes refer expressly to a "duty of care" or "duty of loyalty." The statutes may use the words "prudence," "reasonable," or "good faith" when describing how directors are to act, with the duties of care and loyalty embodied in these words. Although nonprofit corporations are statutory creatures, the duties of care and loyalty have largely been shaped by judge-made common law. Let there be no doubt, however; these duties are clearly present and applicable.

Under most state statutes,[8] a nonprofit director must discharge his duties in good faith and in a manner which the director believes to be in the organization's best interests. In many states, the director is held to a "reasonable person" standard, which means the director must exercise the care an ordinarily prudent person would exercise under similar circumstances. For illustrative language, consider New York law, which requires a director to discharge his duties "in good faith and with that degree of diligence, care and skill which ordinarily prudent men would exercise under similar circumstances in like positions."[9] This standard generally applies to directors regardless of whether they are compensated or not.[10]

Later in this chapter, we consider liability shields available to directors. These are provisions in state statutes that limit the monetary liability of directors, sometimes available only to uncompensated directors, but not always. Typically a liability shield is only available if the director's conduct did not rise to the level of gross negligence or willful misbehavior. People sometimes merge the duties and the liability shield—concluding, for example, that a director has a duty not to be grossly negligent. That is simply the wrong way to analyze the relationship between director duties and liability shields. A director's duties are independent of any shield from liability. The comments to the Revised Model Act make this clear, explaining:

Two distinguishing factors of nonprofit corporations are that their directors may be serving without compensation and are attempting to promote the public good. Courts may take these factors into consideration in determining whether

8. As of 2004, 43 states had adopted a duty of care in some statutory form. FREMONT-SMITH, *supra* note 5, at 207 and Appendix, Table 3.

9. N.Y. Consol. L., Chapter 35, § 717.

10. But for a contrary holding, see George Pepperdine Foundation v. Pepperdine, 271 P.2d 600 (Cal. Ct. App. 1954), cited in FREMONT-SMITH, *supra* note 5, at 204, holding that it would be a gross injustice to hold a volunteer director to as high of a standard as a paid director. For contrary authority, see Matter of Neuschwander, 747 P.2d 104 (Kan. 1987); and Lynch v. John M. Redfield Foundation, 9 Cal. App. 3d 293 (Ct. App. 1970).

directors are liable with respect to performance of their duties. This does not mean that directors can ignore their responsibilities because they are volunteers or have no economic interest in the corporation or its operations.[11]

(a) THE DUTY OF CARE. The *duty of care* focuses on the decision-making process. A director has the duty or obligation to be informed, ask questions, participate in deliberations, and exercise judgment.[12] This does not mean that the director must ask every possible question, engage in endless deliberations, and consult with countless outside experts and consultants. The duty of care is tempered by a "reasonableness" standard. Moreover, many state statues specifically provide that a director is entitled to place reasonable reliance on information provided by employees of the nonprofit, as well as on opinions from experts such as lawyers and accountants.

The required effort will vary with the significance of the decision. Consequently, much more time, consideration, and deliberation is required of a board considering whether to double the organization's physical plant than of a board deciding whether to approve the settlement of a minor dispute involving $5,000. Although state statutes imposing fiduciary duties may not specifically address the question of illegality, implicit is a duty to refrain from illegal activity or approving actions by the nonprofit that are known to be illegal.[13] Consequently, directors who knowingly vote to ignore sales tax "because we are a small charitable organization that is unlikely to be caught" have breached their duty of care.

There is no question that boards and individual directors can delegate authority to other individuals and entities without violating the duty of care. In fact, a board might actually be in breach of its duty of care if it eschewed delegation. The law demands oversight from nonprofit boards rather than performance of day-to-day management activities. A board must rely on the organization's officers and employees to carry out the functions of the organization.

The law draws a distinction between *delegation* and *abdication* of responsibilities and duties. Abdication of duties is simply not permissible. *Abdication* can take one of two forms: The board or a director can affirmatively cede authority to someone else. For example, a board might tell the CEO, "You handle everything, don't even report back to us." This is an extreme example, but it illustrates an affirmative abdication of oversight responsibilities. The second form of abdication arises through neglect. Consider the director who has that position because he made a significant financial contribution to the organization but who has no interest in reviewing financial statements or governance. He does nothing, in effect abdicating his share of the process to the other directors.

---

11. RMNCA § 8.30, Official Comment.
12. American Law Institute, Principles of the Law of Nonprofit Organizations, Prelim. Draft No. 3, § 30 (2005).
13. *Id.*, §§ 2.01(b) and 4.01 (1992).

(b) THE DUTY OF LOYALTY. Under most state statutes,[14] a director has a duty to act in the best interests of the nonprofit corporation, requiring the director to use the organization's funds and property to advance the nonprofit's mission rather than the director's private interests. A potential conflict of interest between the *duty of loyalty* and a board member's private financial interests can arise when the board member engages in financial transactions with the nonprofit organization.

Almost everybody is familiar with the duty of loyalty to the extent that it focuses on conflicts of interest when the director sells services or products and the nonprofit is a consumer of those services or products. More ambiguous conflicts arise from *duality of interests*. Unfortunately, there are no easy ways to address these conflicts, but because they do exist in the real world, let's consider two common examples. The first involves the director who serves on a nonprofit board not as a true volunteer but because he holds another position, referred to as an ex-officio board member. This could be the mayor who, by reason of his office, is automatically a director, the county employee who serves as the county's representative on the board, or the labor union representative who occupies the designated spot on the board for organized labor. This director has a clear conflict from the outset: Does he owe duty of loyalty to the nonprofit or to his other office? If he receives confidential information as a director of the nonprofit, must he maintain the confidence? There is not a good answer to this question. Probably the best way to deal with conflicting loyalties is for the nonprofit and the other organization to formulate the procedures for dealing with this type of conflict at the outset.[15] Without an agreement in place, the other members of the nonprofit's board and its officers are likely to "work around" the ex-officio member, keeping him off key committees such as an executive or finance committee. That will defeat the purpose behind the ex-officio position.

The second conflict is a very real one, but one with which most nonprofits will likely decide to live. This one involves the director who is well connected in the community and, consequently, sits on a number of nonprofit boards. Often each organization looks to this director for his fundraising abilities. However, if he is

---

14. As of 2004, 48 states had codified the duty of loyalty in some statutory form. See FREMONT-SMITH, *supra* note 5, at 218 and Appendix, Table 3.
15. See Illinois Clean Energy Community Foundation v. Filan, Director of the Budget, 392 F.3d 934 (7th Cir. 2004), where the state of Illinois sought to force the ex-officio directors of an Illinois nonprofit corporation to turn over $125 million of the nonprofit's assets to the state. Although the case focused on whether this would constitute an unconstitutional taking, it also addressed alternative arguments that are rooted in dual loyalties. Writing for the court, Judge Posner concluded:

> All the state is left to argue is that the appointment of five-sixths of the foundation's trustees by state officials made the foundation a state agency. Not so. By whomever appointed, the trustees of a charitable foundation have a fiduciary duty to conserve the foundation's assets. 760 ILCS 55/15(a)(2); see also Schweickart v. Powers, 613 N.E.2d 403, 410 (Ill. App. 1993); *In re* Wabash Valley Power Ass'n, Inc., 72 F.3d 1305, 1319 (7th Cir. 1995); Blue Cross & Blue Shield Mutual of Ohio v. Blue Cross & Blue Shield Ass'n, 110 F.3d 318, 324 and n. 1 (6th Cir. 1997); Boston Children's Heart Foundation, Inc. v. Nadal-Ginard, 73 F.3d 429, 433-34 (1st Cir. 1996); Louisiana World Exposition v. Federal Ins. Co., 864 F.2d 1147, 1151-52 (5th Cir. 1989). That no doubt is why the trustees authorized this suit—biting the hand that appointed them, as it were.

raising funds for one nonprofit's capital campaign, will those efforts diminish his effectiveness when called upon to raise funds for another nonprofit's capital campaign six months later? In other words, how often can he go to the proverbial well and be able to fill the bucket to its capacity? As noted, most nonprofits will live with this conflict. Organizations may want to be more selective, however, when the person they are seeking for their board already sits on the board of another entity engaged in similar activities.[16] To illustrate, the Green Art Museum may not want Olivia Horvath on its board if she is already on the board of the Red Art Museum because Horvath's contacts are likely to say, "You just hit me up for the arts. I also give to the medical community, so enough for the arts for now." Obviously, there are exceptions; for example, Horvath may be prepared to write a check for $50 million to each museum. It bears repeating, however, that governance and oversight should be the primary reasons for board membership.

(c) THE DUTY OF OBEDIENCE. The duties of loyalty and care are the two primary duties that are imposed on directors. A third, more controversial one is the *duty of obedience,*[17] which requires a director to act in furtherance of the organization's mission. This duty has its roots in trust law and focuses on carrying out the purposes imposed by those who funded the trust (referred to as the *settlors).* For at least two reasons, this duty is troublesome when transferred to a corporate setting. First, there are far more stakeholders when the charity is engaged in significant ongoing operations, so to the extent that the duty of obedience is a duty to the stakeholders, the meaning of that duty becomes far more difficult, if not impossible, to ascertain as the categories of stakeholders increase. Second, the mission must often change if the organization is to be remain relevant. For these reasons, many experts have argued that the duty of obedience is not a separate duty but is subsumed in the duties of care and loyalty.[18] Yet, some state attorneys general recognize it as a specific duty.[19]

4.3 STANDARDS FOR JUDGING BEHAVIOR

Relatively few court decisions involving the breach by nonprofit directors of their duties of care and loyalty have been reported, let alone cases in which

16. Clearly, other facts explain why a nonprofit would not want a person on its board when that person already serves as a director of a competitor organization. Consider the potential for conflicts if the same person served on the boards of two nonprofit hospitals competing in the same market area.
17. Daniel L. Kurtz, Board Liability: A Guide for Nonprofit Directors at 84-85 (Moyer Bell Ltd. 1989)
18. See Fremont-Smith, *supra* note 5, at 225–26.
19. See, for example, New York Attorney General, The Regulatory Role of the Attorney General's Charities Bureau (2003), which states:

> The common law duty of obedience includes the obligation of directors and officers to act within the organization's purposes and ensure that the corporation's mission is pursued. There is no explicit reference to the duty of obedience in the N-PCL. However, the duty may be inferred by the limitations imposed upon corporate activities as set forth in the purposes clause of the certificate of incorporation (N-PCL §§ 201, 202 & 402(a)(2)) and the directors' and officers' obligations as the corporate managers of the not-for profit organization (N-PCL § 701 & 713). EPTL § 11-2.3(b)(3)(B) explicitly refers to the needs of a trust's beneficiaries.

directors of nonprofits have been found liable for these breaches. This should not, however, lead a director to ignore these duties in shaping his conduct. Many cases are settled at the administrative or the trial court level, meaning that they are not widely reported in the law books. No one should draw the conclusion that state attorneys general are ignoring bad behavior on the part of nonprofit directors. When a state attorney general does act, the results often include negative publicity in local newspapers, attorney fees, cash settlements to cover damages, removal of entire boards or individual directors,[20] and, most important, a decline in contributions and grants to the nonprofit. At the annual 2004 National Association of Attorneys General–National Association of State Charities Officials (NAAG-NASCO) public conference, a panel that included a number of state regulators was unanimous in pointing out the increased scrutiny that their offices are bringing to board governance, with a newly found willingness to step in when there are breaches of duty. Included in the materials distributed to those attending was a rather lengthy list of actions taken against a wide variety of charities and their officers and directors during the prior year.

(a) BUSINESS JUDGMENT OR ORDINARY PRUDENCE. Directors obviously want to know where the line is between actions that protect them from liability and those that can result in liability. Many state statutes incorporate and courts apply the "business judgment" rule, reflecting a historical tendency to defer to directors' judgment (avoiding a finding of liability). On the other hand, the business judgment rule is not available in the absence of the exercise of judgment. The *business judgment rule* is often referred to as a standard of conduct guiding directors in discharging their duties ("exercise reasonable business judgment"), but it is best thought of as a defense or evidentiary rule that shifts the burden of proof to those questioning a decision made by a board. Despite the absence of a profit motive in the nonprofit sector, the rule still carries the business judgment imprimatur in the nonprofit world.[21]

---

20. At a 2005 nonprofit law conference, the head charity official for one large state indicated that director removal is the usual remedy when volunteer directors engage in objectionable behavior. This was not a surprising comment.

21. In her discussion of the relationship between the common law business judgment rule and the duty of care, Ms. Fremont-Smith notes that the Revised Model Act does not preclude the application of the business judgment rule in the nonprofit context. See FREMONT-SMITH, *supra* note 5, at 209–10. She indicates that under the existing doctrines, if the decision under consideration involves a business judgment (i.e., a decision), the courts in jurisdictions that have adopted the business judgment rule are instructed to apply a "highly deferential" standard of review that simply requires the director to show a rational basis for the decision. Otherwise, the courts are instructed to apply a "reasonable basis" standard that is a less deferential standard for reviewing decisions by directors. Whether a particular court will adhere to these distinctions is clearly open to question. Some courts might conclude that the highly deferential rational basis standard can never apply in the nonprofit context because nonprofits are not businesses. Other courts might refuse to apply a common law gloss when there is a statute setting a standard for review, arguably preempting any common law standard. These distinctions are largely irrelevant for purposes of guiding behavior on a prospective basis. Directors should strive to make decisions by exercising their good judgment after a thorough assessment of the facts, pros and cons, and alternatives. Any director who follows that advice should have little to worry about.

Whether the rule is viewed as a standard of conduct or imposition of an evidentiary burden, the essence of the rule focuses on whether the process by which a decision was reached was flawed rather on whether the decision, in hindsight, was the right one. To illustrate the distinction, assume that a board decides to hire a new executive director. If the board defines the characteristics it seeks in the successful candidate, retains an executive search firm, conducts several interviews, undertakes background checks, and then makes its selection following a lengthy discussion, the law will defer to this decision even if the person hired turns out to be a thief or is ineffective. On the other hand, if the board hires a friend of the board's chair without asking any questions or reviewing this person's qualifications, the law is much less likely to defer to the decision because the process by which the decision was reached was not a reasoned and disinterested one. Many courts still extend great deference to the decisions of boards.

Given the confusion surrounding the business judgment rule, it is better to refer to the duty of care most often imposed on directors as a *prudent, reasonable,* or *ordinary person* standard. With that in mind, the line between good and bad conduct is tied to the quality of the process rather than the quality of the outcomes. The business judgment rule serves as an admonition to both judges and potential plaintiffs to avoid second-guessing board decisions if the process by which the decisions were reached was sound. This leaves plenty of room for decisions that turn out to be bad ones.

The director who wants to fulfill his duties should take the following steps: (1) attend board meetings, (2) thoroughly review proposals, (3) seek expert guidance when the matter dictates, and (4) ask questions. In other words, the director should be making *informed* decisions. This is what the standard set out in Section 8.30(a) of the Revised Model Act requires. New York,[22] California,[23] and Ohio[24] are just a few states that have adopted this standard as part of their nonprofit corporation statutes.

Not surprisingly, the business judgment, prudent person, or reasonable person formulations of the duty of care do not protect those guilty of criminal activity, acts taken in bad faith, and acts that reflect reckless, wanton, or willful misconduct.[25] Behavior predicated on those acts is referred to as *malfeasance.*

It is at this point that the distinctions between duty and liability become blurred—and understandably. A director whose conduct is malfeasant should expect to be held accountable. Even though many state nonprofit corporation statutes contain specific provisions limiting the monetary liability of directors, these limitations on liability make exceptions for liability predicated on wanton

22. N. Y. Consol. L., Chapter 35, § 717.
23. Cal. Corp. Code § 5230.
24. Rev. Ohio Code, Chapter 1702.30, § 1702.30.
25. Illinois General Not For Profit Corporation Act of 1986 § 108.70.

and willful breaches of duty.[26] Even if the director is not required to make monetary recompense, directors and boards who are accused of malfeasance may well be subject to adverse publicity as well as investigation by the state's attorney general or other government bodies. For example, recall the scandal involving United Way of America and William Aramony discussed in Chapter 1.

(b) OTHER STATUTORY DUTIES THAT CAN LEAD TO LIABILITY. So far we have focused on duties imposed on directors under state statutes governing nonprofits and possible standards for assessing whether there have been breaches of those general duties. At the end of this chapter, we examine specific statutory shields that nonprofit directors can invoke against imposition of liability. Both state law and the Internal Revenue Code impose on directors specific duties and obligations that are not eligible for general limitations on monetary liability. For example, under the workers' compensation statutes in some states, directors can be held liable if the nonprofit fails to comply with requirements that such coverage be in place. Directors also have been held liable for a nonprofit's unpaid wages. Obviously, these exposures vary from state to state. As a general rule, many state legislatures are particularly concerned about protecting workers and their rights. Consequently, directors must be particularly cautious when dealing with labor-related matters as a matter of self-preservation.

Chapter 6 considers federal income tax issues in detail. As you will see, the tax law imposes a number of excise taxes on what are termed *foundation managers*[27] and *organization managers*,[28] with both of these categories including members of the board. These taxes can be an issue if the board approves acts of self-dealing or other prohibited transactions (in the case of a private foundation) or if a charity's board approves a financial transaction with an insider that provides the insider benefits that exceed the value received by the charity for the services or property provided by the insider. The Internal Revenue Code contains its own set of limitations on these types of liability (usually tied to the level of knowledge or participation in the prohibited act), but liability under the Internal Revenue Code is unaffected by state statutes otherwise limiting director liability.

The Internal Revenue Code also imposes liability on *responsible persons* in the event that an employer does not remit trust fund taxes that it is required to collect.[29] Trust fund taxes include income tax wage withholdings and the employee's share of FICA and Medicare taxes. State law may impose comparable liability with respect to amounts required to be withheld from wages for state purposes. As a practical matter, officers need to be far more concerned about exposure to "responsible person" liability than directors because of the focus on

26. As of 2004, January 1, 2003, 31 states had adopted provisions that shielded directors from liability in the absence of malfeasance of the sort described in the text. *See* FREMONT-SMITH, *supra* note 5, at 226 and Appendix, Table 3. Of these states, 16 require the director to be a volunteer.

27. I.R.C. § 4946(b)(1).

28. I.R.C. § 4958(f)(2).

29. I.R.C. § 6672.

responsibility for actual collection and remittance, but under the right set of circumstances a board member could find himself characterized as a responsible person because of the focus on function rather than title.

(c) LIABILITY ARISING FROM JOINT VENTURES AND SUBSIDIARIES. Over the last few decades, many nonprofit organizations have been increasingly willing to enter into affiliations with for-profit entities or even form their own for-profit subsidiaries. It is not at all unusual in these cases for members of the nonprofit's board or its officers to serve as directors or in another formal advisory capacity to these ventures and entities. When accepting such a role, directors and officers should recognize that different standards of conduct can apply to their activities with respect to the commercial venture. Moreover, to the extent that shields offer protection to nonprofit directors and officers from liability, those shields are unlikely to provide protection to the extent that a liability arises from actions taken by the directors/officers in their capacity as directors or officers of a for-profit venture, albeit affiliated with the nonprofit.

For example, a federal district court denied a motion to dismiss a civil lawsuit alleging violations of antitrust law prohibiting tying arrangements when the bylaws of a for-profit subsidiary of a trade association conditioned access to services on membership in a trade association.[30] The suit named the directors of the for-profit subsidiary; it is not clear from the court's opinion that these directors served because they were directors or otherwise affiliated with the trade association. In fact, listings on various Web sites did not show board overlap. However, according to the court, the defendants acknowledged that the jurisdiction's liability shield did not apply to for-profit directors serving as directors of a wholly owned subsidiary of a nonprofit. The court then rejected a request to extend the shield as a matter of public policy. Given the broad statement in this opinion, others serving in a representative capacity for a nonprofit should assume that any liability shield will not be applicable to the extent that liability arises from their activities with the for-profit entity. With that in mind, these individuals should review appropriate directors' and officers' liability insurance policies to make sure they are adequately protected.

4.4 THE STANDARDS AS APPLIED TO COMMON DECISIONS

You must consider concrete examples to truly understand the line between good and bad conduct. With that in mind, let's consider four examples, each addressing a common decision faced by nonprofit boards.

(a) EXERCISING DUE CARE—COMPENSATION. Many nonprofit boards must set compensation, particularly for the executive director and other senior officers.

30. Jay Reifert v. South Central Wisconsin MLS Corporation, Memorandum Order (W.D. Wis. 2005).

The directors often are not knowledgeable about compensation levels in the nonprofit's industry. One charge leveled at boards composed of wealthy donors is that they tend to overcompensate the executive director and other key officials because the directors base the decision on their own standard of living. Setting compensation goes well beyond just pulling a number out of thin air or blindly accepting what the executive director recommends.

Consider Albert Gonzalez, the chancellor of BigTime U, a four-year college with an enrollment of 1,000 students. He has submitted a proposal to the school's 19-member board of trustees regarding his 20X6 compensation package. In 20X5, enrollment continued its five-year decline, causing the school to dip into its reserves to fund current operations. Nevertheless, Gonzalez's proposal calls for a 20 percent pay increase (to $700,000) plus perks valued at $300,000. Chancellors at comparable institutions are paid $200,000 per year, with fringe benefits valued at $50,000.

The trustees are local businesspeople and alumni. Most know the chancellor socially. As in past years, they approve his proposal after just 25 minutes of discussion. They do not consider comparables or the impact the increase will have on the school's financial condition. The attorney general has learned of the situation at Big Time U through media coverage of student protests over tuition increases and has contacted the trustees, threatening a suit to recover $750,000 from them in damages unless they vote to reduce Gonzalez's salary to $200,000 (and his fringe benefits to $50,000).

The attorney general's threat should not come as a surprise. Although the specific facts are different, this example is inspired by Adelphi University and its president.[31] The New York State Board of Regents removed and replaced 18 of the 19 trustees for "blindly, recklessly and heedlessly" setting the president's compensation.[32]

In addition, New York's attorney general[33] brought suit against certain trustees to recover losses from the mismanagement of university assets, among other things. All legal disputes were settled, with former trustees paying Adelphi $1.23 million and assuming more than $400,000 in legal fees.[34] The former president also made payments to the university as did an insurance company that had indemnified the former trustees, with its payments totaling $1.45 million.[35] Neither the former trustees nor the president admitted to any wrongdoing.[36]

31. Vacco v. Diamandopoulis, 715 N.Y.S.2d 269 (N.Y. App. Div. 1998).
32. Committee to Save Adelphi v. Diamandopoulos, Before the Board of Regents of the University of the State of New York (Feb. 5, 1997); and R. Hernandez, *Regents Turn Adelphi Case Over to Vacco*, N.Y. TIMES, Mar. 12, 1997.
33. *See* Vacco, *supra* note 31.
34. D. Halbfinger, *Lawsuits over Ouster of Adelphi Chief Are Settled*, N.Y. TIMES, Nov. 18, 1998.
35. *Id.*
36. *Id.*

The lesson: Be very careful if the organization's chief executive officer runs the organization as a fiefdom. A board can avoid trouble by:

- Creating an independent compensation committee to review officer compensation.
- Retaining outside compensation consultants to advise on and structure compensation packages. The executive director should not be the one recommending or retaining the consultants that ultimately make the recommendation to the board.
- Reviewing surveys of compensation paid by comparable institutions.
- Requiring that the executive not be present at compensation committee meetings or during board discussions of the executive's compensation.

If an executive director objects to these controls, each director should give serious consideration to resigning. If an individual director is outvoted by other directors who blindly approve the executive's pay package, the dissenting director should at least request that his dissent be recorded in the meeting minutes.

Setting compensation is a recurring issue for nonprofits. As the directors of the New York Stock Exchange (a nonprofit corporation organized under New York law) learned in late 2003, compensation is an issue that can generate significant heat for an organization if the public and regulators perceive that the board did not do an adequate job in setting the level of compensation.[37] Even more recently, the trustees of American University received criticism for how the president's compensation was set, as well as with the level of compensation.[38] There was even disagreement over whether the full board, the compensation committee, or the chairman of the board was responsible for the controversial contract, leading some to argue that the contract was invalid. The president paid the ultimate price for the flawed process, with the board dismissing him.

The IRS has a number of tools that it can use to challenge compensatory arrangements that it views as excessive. From the organization's standpoint, the IRS can raise the private benefit and inurement doctrines to question whether the organization should continue to qualify for tax-exempt status. From the recipient's standpoint, the IRS can raise the relatively new intermediate sanctions to force the individual to pay back the excess compensation or face confiscatory taxes.[39] Penalties under the intermediate sanctions can also be imposed on what are termed "organization managers," which include directors and officers who

37. Then SEC Chairman William Donaldson, after testifying before Congress (U.S. House Financial Services Committee), told reporters, "What we're talking about now is the [NYSE] governance procedures, which has to do not only with Mr. Grasso as the chief executive officer, but the board of directors of the stock exchange and the procedures they have in place." *See Grasso's Pay Costs Him His Job*, FORBES.COM, Sept. 17, 2003.

38. For details, see the discussion of American University in Chapter 6.

39. I.R.C. §§ 4958(a) and (b).

"knowingly participate" in the transaction (unless such participation is not willful and is due to reasonable cause).

While the regulations that have been issued to implement the intermediate sanctions are quite elaborate, at their core, these regulations are driving at the same issue posed by the private benefit and inurement doctrines: an inquiry as to whether transactions between the organization and the people providing goods and services to the organization are priced at market rates and are in the best interests of the organization. The intermediate sanctions and the prohibitions against private benefit and inurement place a burden on the charity and the recipient to prove fair market value. As a practical matter, the organization and the recipient will carry this burden if both adhere to the procedures for determining compensation outlined above. In practice, there is a dovetailing of state corporate and federal tax law. We take a closer look at these tax rules in Chapter 6.

(b) EXERCISING DUE DILIGENCE—INVESTMENTS. Directors must demand facts and probe the information they are given before they make any important decision, particularly when it pertains to investments of the organization's assets. This is a lesson that should be borne in mind by Community Givers, a local charity that supports a number of community educational, health, and civic betterment organizations, when it is approached by John Starr. Mr. Starr tells the president of Community Givers that if it invests $1 million with his company, Golden Eggs Investors, for 6 months, Golden Eggs will pay Community Givers the $1 million at the end of the six-month period, plus at least another $1 million. The president is skeptical, but Mr. Starr presents a list of "marquee" organizations that are very satisfied early participants.

The president of Community Givers then makes a few phone calls and confirms the investment results. Only then does the president propose to the board that Community Givers make the investment. The board, composed of local business and community leaders, generally follows the president's advice. At the board meeting, the board devotes about 20 minutes to the proposal, unanimously approving it. Two months after Community Givers makes the investment, Golden Eggs files for bankruptcy, the SEC indicts Mr. Starr for securities fraud, and the state attorney general brings suit against the directors.

These facts raise the same issues that were addressed by the Foundation for New Era Philanthropy pyramid-scheme scandal of the mid-1990s. Very reputable charities and individuals agreed to invest their funds with New Era on the premise that an anonymous matching donor would double the investment and return the resulting proceeds to the charity. This was an obvious Ponzi scheme. Nevertheless, more than 150 charities and individual donors agreed to participate, losing tens of millions.[40] Participants included a major university, a well-known investment banker,

---

40. Trying to arrive at a final number is difficult because there were at least two proceedings, one of which resulted in a settlement. See S. Pressman, *On Financial Frauds and Their Causes*, AM. J. ECON. & SOCIOLOGY (1998).

and a highly visible philanthropist.[41] Many of the participating charities claimed to have undertaken due diligence, but newspaper accounts suggest that the due diligence claims did not match what actually happened. Albert Meyer, an accounting professor at Spring Arbor College, fought against his college's participation, retaining his common sense. The president of Spring Arbor, apparently concerned about missing an opportunity, is quoted as having said, "I have indicated to [New Era's] Mr. Bennett that Albert's actions should in no way be interpreted as coming from Spring Arbor College." [42]

The *Philadelphia Inquirer* interviewed several investors, with one explaining, in the face of the investment's obvious absurdity, "I think the reason why we and all the other organizations got sucked into this was that we all really believed this organization was set up by Sir John Templeton to give away $1 billion.... We could not figure out where else the money was coming from." [43] And so the story goes.

The Community Givers board should be nervous about a lawsuit by the state attorney general. Assuming that state law requires directors to act in good faith with the care an ordinarily prudent investor in a similar position would exercise under similar circumstances and in a manner the director reasonably believes to be in the best interests of the corporation, the directors have breached their duties. Although the directors may have acted in good faith, a prudent person does not take on a "double-your-money-in-six-months" investment scheme with just 20 minutes (or even a half an hour) of deliberation.

As previously noted, there is a potential problem for the attorney general. Many state nonprofit corporation statutes relieve directors of monetary liability for breaches of duties unless the breach represents intentionally reckless or wanton behavior. The attorney general may have an easy time finding a lack of common sense but a much more difficult time showing that the action was intentionally reckless. Escaping monetary liability does not mean, however, that the directors escape embarrassment or removal.

Even some very-well established nonprofit boards did not seem to learn the lesson from the New Era episode. Both the *Chicago Tribune*[44] and the *Wall Street Journal*[45] have reported that the Art Institute of Chicago lost millions of dollars in a hedge fund investment scheme that had all of the classic warning signs: (1) an inexperienced promoter, (2) a proprietary investment plan, and

41. S. Stecklow, *Trustees Filing Identifies 46 Creditors That Made Money Before New Era's Fall*, WALL ST. J., June 19, 1995; and S. Stecklow, *Incredible Offer: A Big Charity Faces Tough New Questions about Its Financing*, WALL ST. J., May 15, 1995.

42. S. Stecklow, *Incredible Offer*, *supra* note 41.

43. P. Dobrin, *New Era Played on Dire Need for Cash, and Nonprofits Swallowed Their Doubts*, PHILA. INQ., May 21, 1995.

44. B. Rose, *Art Institute Names New Adviser on Investments*, CHI. TRIB., Mar. 12, 2002; T. Corfman and B. Rose, *Art Institute Investment Strategy Raises Questions*, CHI. TRIB., Dec. 16, 2001; and B. Rose, *Museum Defends Investing Strategy: Art Institute Orders Full Audit in Wake of Losses*, CHI. TRIB., Dec. 12, 2001.

45. J. Dugan, T. Burton, and C. Mollenkamp, *Chicago Art Museum Learns Lesson about Hedge Funds—Despite Pledges of Security, a $20 Million Loss*, WALL ST. J., Feb. 4, 2002.

(3) claims of high returns with little risk. The finance committee and the board of trustees approved the investment.[46] The board of trustees was comprised of some of Chicago's most powerful people, including a number of wealthy individuals and high-profile executives and board chairs.[47]

Unlike the New Era situation, the Art Institute example does not appear to have involved a Ponzi scheme. Instead the promoters seemed to have had a poor investment strategy, one which may not have been the one originally described to the trustees.[48] Apparently, the SEC was more concerned with what the promoters told the investors as the value of the fund declined than with the specific investments, but that is not entirely clear.[49] Nevertheless, it is surprising that the trustees of a large institution were willing to make such an investment. The Illinois attorney general did not commence an action against the trustees, but the Art Institute has since reformed its investment policies.[50]

We take a more detailed look at investment decisions and management toward the end of this chapter. Although there is no reason that investment decisions should require any more or less care than any other decisions, these decisions have always received close scrutiny by both boards and the law, probably because they involve the one core function of the traditional trustee: stewardship of assets.

(c) AVOIDING CONFLICTS OF INTEREST—SELLING ASSETS. Conflicts of interest can have serious ramifications for both a nonprofit and its directors and officers. State nonprofit legislation frequently places a heavier burden on directors and officers who have dealings with their organizations. When a real estate broker, investment banker, lawyer, accountant, marketing executive, physician, or other professional or businessperson serves as a nonprofit director, that person (and fellow directors) must be cautious if that person sells goods or services used by the nonprofit. Those who serve on museum and university boards must also be cognizant of other less obvious conflicts. While the temptation is understandable, board members should refrain from seeking preferential treatment for their children in a university's admissions process or using inside information about upcoming museum exhibits to acquire artworks.

Conflicts have been particularly troublesome in hospital conversions, as the directors of Holy Grail Hospital, a nonprofit hospital organized in 1918, will now discover. Holy Grail received an offer from Big Corporate Medicine, a publicly traded corporation with a market capitalization of $50 billion, to purchase

46. *Id.* The article uses the term "blessed" to describe the decision.

47. *Id.*

48. T. Corfman and B. Rose, *Art Institute Investment Strategy, supra* note 44.

49. The SEC filed a civil suit against the promoters that detailed the underlying facts but not very clearly. *See* Plaintiff's Original Complaint, Securities and Exchange Commission v. Conrad P. Seghers and J. Dickey, Civil Action No. 3:04 CV 1320-K (N.D. Tex.), filed June 16, 2004. It appears that the promoters did intend to invest the money, but that investments did not work out.

50. *See* B. Rose, *Art Institute Names New Adviser, supra* note 44.

all of Holy Grail's assets for $250 million. Holy Grail serves an inner-city community, and 60 percent of its caseload is charitable.

Holy Grail's board has ten directors. Four of them are community leaders, one is the hospital's chief operating officer, and the remaining five are doctors on the hospital's staff. Big Corporate Medicine has offered the CEO and each doctor a lucrative position with it. The board is considering whether to approve the sale of the hospital's assets to Big Corporate Medicine. As part of their deliberations, the directors must decide whether to change Holy Grail's corporate purpose from providing health services to the inner-city community to making grants to community health organizations.

The four outside directors realize that the five doctors and the chief operating officer have conflicts of interest given the employment offers from Big Corporate Medicine. While each believes the sale makes sense, the four outside directors tell the six insiders that they will not vote for a sale unless Holy Grail obtains a fairness opinion from a nationally recognized investment banker.

Can the four outside directors protect themselves from a suit by the state attorney general by obtaining a fairness opinion? This is a difficult question, which warrants a very careful review of the applicable state law. Most advisers would certainly be more comfortable with a vote in favor of the sale if the board obtained a fairness opinion. However, the number of directors who receive benefits from the buyer after the transaction may taint the transaction despite a favorable fairness opinion.

During the last two decades, there have been a number of proposed sales and joint ventures involving nonprofit hospitals, including the Sisters of Charity of St. Augustine Health System of Canton, Ohio, the Eastern Mercy Health System of Fort Lauderdale, Florida,[51] and the Massillon Community Hospital of Massillon, Ohio.[52] There have been other transactions that have come under regulatory scrutiny.[53]

In the case of the Sisters of Charity of St. Augustine (CSA), the community trustees voted to oppose a joint venture with a for-profit entity involving Timken Mercy Medical Center of Canton, Ohio after apparently expressing some reservations about the transaction.[54] The local trustees were then dismissed by CSA.[55] There is no indication that the Ohio Attorney General ever intervened to stop the transaction, apparently not finding the need to protect the charitable

51. J. Greene, *Power Struggles with System Leads to Hospital Board's Ouster*, MOD. HEATHCARE at 8, Aug. 12, 1996. *See generally* E. Hale, *Selling or Selling Out? How Community Hospitals are Changing Hands*, GANNETT NEWS SERV., Oct. 13, 1996.

52. Press Release, Office of then Ohio Attorney General Betty D. Montgomery, "Massillon Community Hospital Backs Off from Proposed Sale to Columbia/HCA: Nonprofit Hospital will Accept Bids from Other Potential Buyers" (Apr. 17, 1997).

53. R. Kutter, *Patients or Shareholders?*, ST. PETERSBURG TIMES, Nov. 14, 1996.

54. B. Japsen & S. Lutz, *Catholic System Drops Local Board Members*, MOD. HEALTHCARE, May 29, 1995.

55. Editorial, *Ceding Local Control is the Price of be Paid for System Advantages*, MOD. HEALTHCARE, June 5, 1995.

beneficiaries. The arrangement was approved by the Vatican pursuant to canon law procedures.[56]

In the Fort Lauderdale case, the board of directors was dismissed. A group of directors then filed suit against the hospital system.[57] What is particularly interesting about this case is that it did not involve a conversion to for-profit status, but rather a merger of the hospital in question with a larger nonprofit hospital system.

In the case of Massillon Community Hospital, the board members decided to re-bid the sale in view of an imminent lawsuit by Ohio's attorney general. The attorney general's press release describes a conflict of interest involving the hospital's chairman taking a position with the new for-profit hospital. Of more interest, the attorney general acknowledged that her job was not to tell the community who should operate its nonprofit hospitals, but rather to make sure that the charitable beneficiaries are protected.

As a result of alleged abuses throughout the county, more than half of the states have adopted statutes regulating nonprofit hospital conversions.[58] Boards must grapple not only with issues of fairness, particularly when apparent conflicts of interest exist, but also with the question of how to utilize the sale proceeds. Setting aside state law requirements for a moment, the following steps constitute best practices for dealing with conflicts:

- The organization should have a written conflict-of-interest policy that is distributed to each director, officer, and employee at least once a year. Each person should be required to sign the policy and the organization should keep records of how it has enforced the policy.
- The bylaws or other governing document should place an affirmative duty on each director, officer, and employee of the organization to disclose any conflicts of interest on a timely basis.
- A director with a conflict should recuse himself from the considerations.
- A director with a conflict should not be present when the board considers the matter except to answer any questions.

We consider conflicts of interest in more detail later in this chapter.

(d) RESISTING FOUNDER'S SYNDROME—DIVERSIFICATION. Not every board will face what experts refer to as "founder's syndrome," but many will. *Founder's syndrome* occurs when the board and officers defer to a nonprofit's founder,

---

56. B. Japsen, *Vatican Allows Columbia, CSA to Complete Deal*, MOD. HEALTHCARE, Nov. 6, 1995.

57. B. LaMendola, *Holy Cross Ex-Trustees Suing Nuns Over Ouster*, SUN-SENTINEL, Sept. 20, 1996); Editorial, *Both Sides In Holy Cross Dispute Must Back, Work Out Problems*, SUN-SENTINEL, Aug. 10, 1996; B. LaMendola, *Sisters Say Hospital Didn't Show Enough Mercy; Ousted Board to Sue Nuns to Control Profitable Center*, SUN-SENTINEL, Aug. 7, 1996; and B. LaMendola and E. Forman, *Nuns Oust Board, Take Control in Hospital Dispute*, SUN-SENTINEL, July 30, 1996.

58. M. Fremont-Smith and J. Lever, *State Regulation of Health Care Conversions and Conversion Foundations*, B.N.A. HEALTH L. REP., May 11, 2000.

often the organization's principal benefactor or the person whose ideas, energy, and personality launched the organization. Founder's syndrome should come as no surprise: The founder probably selected the board. If the founder's continued financial support is necessary for the nonprofit's continued survival, associates will naturally ask, "Who are we to question the person putting up the money?" This logic is to be expected, but directors must remember that under state law, their duties run to the organization, not the founder.

With this in mind, let's consider Big Foundation, an organization with a $75 million endowment, composed of $40 million in index funds and $35 million in PrivateLabel Corporation stock.[59] Jules and Flannery Levy, the founders of the PrivateLabel business, hold the remainder of its stock. Big Foundation makes grants to further literacy skills. Its board is composed of the following five members: Mr. and Mrs. Levy, their attorney, Steve Brody, Sarah Walchek, the head of the school board, and Sean Flynn, an industrialist, who has committed his charitable life to literacy causes.

As of late, PrivateLabel has run into financial difficulty due to competition from cheap foreign labor. Walchek and Flynn have spoken with an outside consultant, who is not sure whether PrivateLabel will be able to rectify the situation. Consequently, Walchek and Flynn have proposed a sale of the Foundation's PrivateLabel stock. Mr. and Mrs. Levy oppose such a sale because it would weaken their control of PrivateLabel Corporation. Assume that a prudent director would vote for a sale of the PrivateLabel stock under the circumstances.

This hypothetical illustrates several problems that foundation directors face when both they (or related parties) and the foundation hold the same investment assets. In their capacity as directors, these individuals owe a duty to the foundation. The first question these directors should have asked was whether the entity's investment assets were properly diversified. A good case can be made that holding a significant portion of Big Foundation's assets in one company is imprudent.

The obvious problem is that Mr. and Mrs. Levy also have an interest in controlling PrivateLabel, so they instinctively will oppose a sale. Although they are likely to vote in accordance with their personal interests (that is human nature), they should recognize that as directors, they must focus on the foundation's best interests when they make decisions. Because they funded the foundation, a regulator may be more predisposed to cut them some slack, but the Levys should not count on that.[60] Their attorney, Steve Brody, faces a similar but probably more difficult decision. He has managed to create a conflict for himself. As Mr. and

59. This example is designed to make a point about corporate law and director duties. In all likelihood, this situation would not occur because of tax law restrictions on excess business holdings by private foundations. *See* I.R.C. § 4943. However, the example nicely illustrates how the interests of founders can conflict with the interests of a charitable organization.

60. In 2004, the Illinois Attorney General filed suit against Gary Bielfeldt and members of his family, alleging mismanagement of the investment assets held by the Bielfeldt Foundation, among other allegations. Mr. Bielfeldt had funded the foundation.

Mrs. Levy's attorney, his allegiance should always be to them. However, he is also a director, subject to objective standards that require loyalty to Big Foundation.

Steve Brody is obviously in a difficult position: Turning down a client's request to serve as a director of an entity affiliated with the client is always difficult. This illustrates why some law firms prohibit their lawyers from serving as directors of client organizations or parties related to client organizations. Many lawyers agree to serve in these situations and do a fine job. If you are a lawyer or other adviser and are asked to serve on the board of a charity organized by your client, be sure to keep your eyes open and anticipate problems that could arise. It may actually be much easier to disappoint the client at the organizational stage by declining the request than having conflicting loyalties later.

Unless they have some very compelling reasons, the two outside directors should vote to sell at least some portion of the PrivateLabel stock. As already noted, Big Foundation's holdings pose serious diversification issues. Legally, Steve Brody and the two outside directors are in the same position, but as a practical matter, the two outside directors will have a much easier time discharging their duty by voting for diversification. Although these facts are not the same as those that confronted two foundations that held significant amounts of Reader's Digest stock in 1996, those foundations and their directors faced similar issues.[61]

Between 1996 and 1997, Reader's Digest stock lost more than half of its value (from $51 to $24.37 per share).[62] According to a February 1998 article in the *New York Post,* the New York Attorney General began a preliminary investigation into conflicts of interest arising out of the situation.[63] This investigation eventually resulted in a restructuring of the ownership by the two large foundations.[64] According to New York Attorney General Eliot Spitzer, "The charitable entities that will receive the money will now be in a position to control their charitable ends in their own way without being dependent in any way on any control by Readers' Digest."[65] The *New York Times* nicely summed up the conflict, stating:

> The endowment gifts, heavily invested in Reader's Digest stock, were administered for the recipient by seven organizations under restrictions that impeded the selling of Digest stock. The shares plummeted in the 1990's as the stock market took off, but the arrangement buttressed Reader's Digest at a turbulent time. The recipient groups, however, could only watch as they missed better investment opportunities.[66]

---

61. For federal income tax purposes, these foundations were classified as "supporting organizations" rather than "private foundations."
62. J. Barshay, *Macalester's Stock Lagging, As Reader's Digest Shares Go, So Goes College Endowment Fund,* STAR. TRIB., May 22, 1997.
63. J. Elsen, *Vacco Probes Why Mag's Woes are Hard to Digest,* N.Y. POST, Feb. 4, 1998. See also J. Barshay, *Macalester's Stock Lagging, supra* note 62 and V. Stehle, *Falling Price of Reader's Digest Stock is Big Blow to Wallace Funds,* CHRON. OF PHILAN., Feb. 26, 1998.
64. R. Blumenthal, *13 Institutions Obtain Control of Vast Bequest,* N.Y. TIMES, May 4, 2001.
65. *Id.*
66. *Id.*

As you should see, founder's syndrome can be a problem. Similar problems can exist when an organization is headed by a strong executive director. The initial reaction of outside directors is to show great deference to the executive director. However, a director's function is to cast a critical eye.

4.5 DIRECTOR RIGHTS

As a director, you have certain duties under state nonprofit corporation statutes, but you also have certain rights. The specifics vary from state to state, but directors generally have the following rights:

- To receive advanced notice of board meetings.
- To review financial statements.
- To receive meeting minutes.

Unfortunately, state statutes can be vague when it comes to granting rights to access information. In fact, the Revised Model Act grants information access rights to members[67] but curiously does not address director rights to access. The Maine statutes are quite explicit in granting directors access to books and records.[68] Other state statutes are not so specific. For example, a lawsuit is currently pending in the Tennessee and Mississippi courts related to one director who was asked to sign a confidentiality agreement before she could review foundation records.[69] She refused to sign the agreement, and the other director allegedly barred her from making copies. Let's hope that the court will address

---

67. *See* RMNCA §§ 16.02 and 16.03.

68. In 2002 Maine added Section 715 to the Maine Nonprofit Corporations Act (Chapter 13-B), providing as follows:

> Books; Records of Accounts. Each corporation shall keep correct and complete books and records of accounts and shall keep minutes of the proceedings of its members, board of directors and committees having any of the authority of the board of directors and shall keep at its registered office or principal office in this State a record of the names and addresses of its members entitled to vote. All books and records of a corporation may be inspected by any officer, director or voting member or the officer's, director's or voting member's agent or attorney, for any proper purpose at any reasonable time, as long as the officer, director or voting member or the officer's, director's or voting member's agent or attorney gives the corporation written notice at least 5 business days before the date on which the officer, director or voting member or the officer's, director's or voting member's agent or attorney wishes to inspect and copy any books or records. The only proper purpose for which a voting member may inspect and copy books or records under this section is the purpose of enabling the member to fulfill duties and responsibilities conferred upon members by the articles of incorporation or the bylaws of the corporation or by law. The corporation may require the officer, director or member or the officer's, director's or member's agent or attorney to pay the reasonable cost of the copies made and may impose reasonable restrictions on the use or distribution of the records by such a person.

69. Affidavit of Tommye Maddox Working, State of Tennessee and Tommy Madox Working, as Trustee v. Robin Costa (7th Cir. Ct. Davidson Cty. Tenn.) at ¶ 5; and J. Hamburg, *$100M Charity Caught in Tug of War*, THE TENNESSEAN, Oct. 5, 2003. The article quotes the director who was seeking information as having said, "I faxed, e-mailed and mailed letters out. I was asking for information that any board member should receive about a company that they're on the board of."

issues pertaining director rights as it tackles the even tougher issues posed by this dispute.

The fact that state law often is silent or grants limited rights to directors does not preclude the articles of incorporation or bylaws from clarifying or enlarging the list of director rights. As a matter of best practice, the organizers of a nonprofit should consider explicitly providing directors access to financial statements, committee reports, meeting minutes, director and member contact information (subject to a requirement that it be used only for official business), CPA audit and management letters, organizational documents, and other relevant information.

As a director, you should have reasonable access to the executive director and other officers. If you are not able to exercise these rights or are denied access to information, you should reassess your decision to serve. Moreover, in some cases resignation may not be sufficient—the circumstances could require demanding that the board take action, informing the attorney general, or even going to court.

4.6 A FURTHER LOOK AT INVESTMENT DECISIONS

Whether an organization holds reserves for contingencies or a large endowment to finance future activities, its directors and officers will face investment decisions. Legal rules and standards govern how a nonprofit's board handles these decisions. For the most part, these rules and standards focus on process rather than specific investment assets.

(a) WHAT THE PROCESS IS NOT. One point needs to be emphasized from the outset: Investing a nonprofit's financial assets is not a game, hobby, sport, or a chance to experiment with a new and trendy investment vehicle. Many individuals like to "play" the market or invest in real estate. That is fine, but board meetings should not become de facto investment club meetings. Even when the board decides to retain the investment function in-house, that function should be delegated to the appropriate board committee or officers. Under no circumstances should the board be engaged in discussions of whether Home Depot or General Motors is under- or overvalued or whether a new IPO is a good investment.

Along these same lines, directors should be very wary when they hear a fellow director say, "My broker doubled my money last year," or "My brother knows someone who has an unbeaten track record." Investment decisions should be systematic and considered, not anecdotal. The road to poor investment performance is littered with stories of someone else's stellar performance. In fact, several of the more notable investment scandals that have hit nonprofits in recent years occurred because "someone knew somebody who knows a lot about this stuff."

One of the most dangerous pairings is a board largely composed of financial neophytes and a couple of "savvy" directors who talk a good game. The neophytes are often intimidated when the talk before the meeting turns to how well a couple of the board members are doing in the market. Add BMW ownership, and the neophytes often turn over the investment function to the "people in the know." Much of this talk is just that, being no more credible than much of the banter in grade school locker rooms. People love to talk about their "doublers" but rarely mention their losses.

(b) RESERVES OR ENDOWMENT? Before authorizing any investment activity, a nonprofit's board must understand why the organization holds the funds that the board now must decide how to invest. If the organization is holding a reserve for potential repairs to its physical plant, emergency program needs, or as a cushion to cover higher than expected expenses, the investment decision should be simple and straightforward. The focus should be on liquidity and safety rather than investment return. Certainly, the board could invest in long-term Triple-A rated corporate bonds and receive a higher return, but liquidating a bond portfolio on short notice can result in capital losses if interest rates have risen in the interim and result in high transaction costs. When the tsunamis hit South Asia and India in December 2004, the relief organizations needed immediate access to large amounts of cash to purchase medicine, food, and supplies. Investing funds set aside for such an emergency in illiquid real estate would have been a mistake.

Funds that are held for short-term purposes should be held in an appropriate combination of money market funds, insured certificates of deposit, and short-term United States Treasury instruments. If the investment balance is large enough (in excess of $50,000 or $100,000), the organization might want to ladder the maturities of these investment instruments to obtain a slightly higher return. *Laddering* simply means staggering the terms, with the maturation of perhaps 30 percent of the investments within 30 days, 40 percent in six months, and 30 percent in one year. How a particular investment ladder is structured depends on how likely it is that all funds will be needed immediately for an emergency. For example, a condominium association building a reserve for snowplowing could safely invest the reserve funds in a certificate of deposit with a six-month maturity if the investment is made in April. However, when the certificate of deposit matures in November, the money should be transferred to a money market or checking account.

Some nonprofits have the good fortune to have an endowment. As used in this portion of the *Guide*, *endowment* refers to a pool of money set aside for investment with the intention of using the return from the investment(s) to fund part of the organization's ongoing operations, mission, special programs, or capital expenditures. An endowment is intended to provide predictable revenue, permitting the organization to make longer term operating commitments without having to worry about funding the commitment each year from program revenue and current contributions and grants. A good example is an endowed chair at a state university. The university may decide that the economics department should have one professor who devotes teaching and research to game theory, but it might be reluctant to hire a qualified candidate because of long-term trends in state funding. To solve the problem, the university's development officer might ask a willing alumnus to endow a chair through a $2 million gift.

The university's trustees must make an investment decision. The $2 million investment needs to generate sufficient return to fund the game theory professorship on an ongoing basis. This means investing to minimize the risk of loss but generating enough income or gain so the position can be funded even in the face of rising price levels. A real estate investment is not an appropriate investment for funds set aside for disaster aid by a relief organization, but investing in real estate could be appropriate in the case of an endowed position at a university, particularly if there are dozens of such positions.

To summarize, the difference between a cash reserve and an endowment comes down to time horizons. In many cases, the institution hopes that it will not have to expend its cash reserve but holds it because the principal balance either is scheduled for expenditure or could be needed on a minute's notice. In these instances, the organization must have a short time horizon and a low tolerance for risk, making the investment process relatively simple. When the institution holds assets as part of an endowment, the investment process becomes much more complex and long-term in its focus.

(c) INVESTING ENDOWMENT—THE STANDARD. In theory, the standard that applies to director decisions with respect to endowments should be no different than the standard that applies to other decisions by the directors: This generally means that directors are required to exercise reasonable care and diligence in making investment decisions. Because the investment activities of fiduciaries have long been subject to scrutiny in other legal contexts—pension administration under Employee Retirement Income Security Act (ERISA) and estate administration come immediately to mind—the formulation of the standard that applies in the nonprofit context could become entangled with other legal formulations of what constitutes due care. For example, under ERISA, a fiduciary must discharge its duties "with care, skill, prudence, and diligence under the circumstances then prevailing that a prudent man acting in like capacity and familiar with such matters would use in the conduct of an enterprise of a like character and like aims."[70] The Uniform Management of Institutional Funds Act (UMIFA), adopted by 47 states and the District of Columbia,[71] formulates the standard as follows:

> In the administration of the powers to appropriate appreciation, to make and retain investments, and to delegate investment management of institutional funds, members of a governing board shall exercise ordinary business care and prudence under the facts and circumstances prevailing at the time of the action or decision. In so doing they shall consider long and short term needs of the institution in carrying out its educational, religious, charitable, or other eleemosynary purposes, its

70. 29 U.S.C. 1104(a)(1)(B).

71. The full act is available at http://www.nccusl.org/Update/uniformact_factsheetcs/uniformacts-fs-umifa.asp.

> present and anticipated financial requirements, expected total return on its investments, price level trends, and general economic conditions.[72]

No doubt experienced lawyers could find differences in the standards of conduct proscribed under nonprofit corporation statutes, ERISA, and UMIFA. To the extent that differences exist, they are probably rooted in whether the conduct is evaluated subjectively or objectively. In other words, under some general duty of care formulations, the director must act in good faith or exercise "business judgment."[73] However, the prudent person standard is more objective in its formulation—the director may have acted in good faith and there may be logic to the decision, but 90 of 100 persons in the same situation would not have made the particular decision, making the decision problematic.

As a practical[74] matter, there probably is no meaningful distinction between the standards when it comes to making day-to-day decisions, particularly if the directors rely on investment advisers and standard investment practices. Directors of nonprofits should focus on applicable nonprofit corporation statutes defining their duties as well as the applicable versions of UMIFA, meaning that directors may be subject to two standards that have considerable overlap.[75] Even though the provisions of ERISA may not be directly applicable, if there is a challenge to director conduct, there is little doubt that the case law that has developed under ERISA will at least be cited.

Dancing with the One Who Brung Ya

* * *

On December 8, 2004, Illinois Attorney General Lisa Madigan filed suit against Gary Bielfeldt and members of his family to recover alleged losses incurred by the Bielfeldt Foundation.[76] Madigan sought to recover $30 million in alleged investment losses and somewhere around $9 million in brokerage and management fees allegedly received by Gary

72. UMIFA § 6.
73. J. Lockhart, *Fiduciary Duty to Diversify Investments of Benefit Plan as Required by Section 404(a)(1)(C) of ERISA*, 155 A.L.R. 349 (1999, updated Feb. 2004).
74. Any differences may be diminished as the currently proposed changes to UMIFA are adopted by the states.
75. The committee working on the revision of UMIFA was leaning at a late December 2004 meeting toward aligning the standard under UMIFA with the general standard under nonprofit corporation statutes. Even if the final version of UMIFA does align the two standards, it will take several years for the change to work its way through individual state legislatures.
76. Verified Complaint for an Accounting, Surcharge of Trustees, Reimbursement of Commissions and Management Fees, Reimbursement of Substantial Trading Losses, Removal of Trustees, and Other Equitable Relief, Illinois v. Bielfeldt Foundation, filed December 8, 2004.

Bielfeldt, a related entity, and members of his family.[77] The attorney general has since dropped the related entity as a defendant in the litigation.[78]

According to newspaper accounts, four of the five family members who were directors resigned in July 2004 as part of an effort to cooperate with the attorney general's requests regarding the foundation's governance.[79] The one remaining family member who stayed on as a director (Carlotta Bielfeldt) stepped down as president. The directors who resigned were replaced by independent members of the community.[80]

A significant portion of the losses were alleged to have been attributable to investments in commodities futures, which the attorney general has described as risky investments.[81] According to a *Copley News Service* analysis, the foundation had paid members of the Bielfeldt family $21 million for investment advice and other services over a 19-year period in which the foundation had paid out over $26 million in grants.[82]

By all accounts, the family is legitimate and hard working and has made significant contributions to a number of well-known local charities, including the University of Illinois Foundation, the Glen Oak Zoo, the Peoria Symphony, and the Lakeview Museum.[83] Even Melissa Merz, spokesperson for the attorney general, stated:

> The Bielfeldts have made very important contributions to their community. The intention of this action is not to discourage philanthropy or the establishment of foundations.[84]

The attorney general's complaint focuses on the fiduciary aspects of the case, with a heavy emphasis on Section 15 of the Illinois Charitable Trust Act.[85]

What is troubling about the attorney general's position is that Section 15, by its own terms, does not seem to create any duties but looks to other sources of law. By not referencing those other provisions specifically, the attorney general appears to be attempting to pull a standard of conduct out of thin air. Some standard clearly governs director conduct, but the attorney general should have pointed to the specific standard so that the conduct can be measured against it. This is not to say that the alleged misconduct did not violate the law.

From a legal standpoint, the subject that must be addressed is the relationship between the Charitable Trust Act and the Illinois Not For Profit Corporation Act and the duties imposed on directors under the Not For Profit Act. In other words, using the words *fiduciary* and *trustee* carries certain connotations that are litigation favorable to any attorney general. But are those connotations really the proper ones if the standards set out in the Illinois Not For Profit Corporation Act are controlling? This question should not be taken to suggest that the Bielfeldt directors do not have questions to answer about their conduct. Both the alleged losses and fees are large by almost anybody's standards.

Are the unpaid directors not allowed to look to Section 108.65 of the Illinois Not For Profit Corporation Act, which provides directors a great deal of discretion (because only wanton and willful misconduct is vulnerable)? The directors arguably had conflicts of interest, but

---

77. *Id.* at ¶ 2. *See also* D. Meinert, *Illinois AG Seeks to Repay Foundation Assets*, Copley News Serv., Dec. 9, 2004.

78. M. Ramsey, *Bielfeldt Brokerage Off the Hook in Charity Lawsuit*, Copley News Serv., Apr. 21, 2005.

79. D. Meinert, *New Members Named to Bielfeldt Foundation: Change Comes after AG's Office Confirmed it Was Reviewing Board's Financial Dealings*, Copley News Serv., Oct. 15, 2004.

80. *Id.*

81. Verified Complaint for an Accounting, Surcharge of Trustees, *supra* note 76, at ¶¶ 2 and 17; and D. Meinert *supra* note 77.

82. D. Meinert, *Foundation Loses Millions under Bielfeldts; Peoria Family Charges $21 Million to Manage Its Own Charitable Foundation*, Peoria J. Star, Sept. 2, 2003.

83. *Id.*

84. D. Meinert, *Illinois AG Seeks to Repay Foundation*, Copley News Ser., Dec. 9, 2004.

85. *See* Section 15, *supra* note 154 to Chapter 3; and Verified Complaint, *supra* note 76, at ¶¶ 31–48.

under the Illinois Not For Profit Corporation Act, the resulting transactions are assessed based on the facts at the time they were entered into, not in hindsight.[86]

Although many people reflexively view commodities investments as highly speculative and inappropriate for charitable foundations, this may be a case of "you dance with the one who brung ya." Gary Bielfeldt apparently made his fortune trading bonds and engaging in the commodities business,[87] so it should not be surprising that his family would not view commodity futures as inappropriate investment assets for "its" foundation. This raises an interesting question when it comes to evaluating director conduct. As already noted, the Illinois Not For Profit Corporation Act relieves volunteer directors from monetary liability so long as their behavior is not willful or wanton.[88] Is that standard applied to the "every person" director (an objective standard), or is the standard applied by taking into the account the life experience of the directors under the microscope (a subjective standard)? While the typical director might be regarded as malfeasant by approving a commodities investment strategy for the typical foundation, given the experience and past successes of the parties involved in the Bielfeldt case, the decision might not have been reckless from their viewpoint.

Moreover, under the modern prudent investor rule, investments are not viewed in isolation but in relation to the rest of the portfolio.[89] The foundation might have invested in derivative instruments to hedge the performance of other investments. Again, this is not to say that the Bielfeldts do not have to explain what appear to be significant losses, but they may actually have been diligent in their decision process, and the process by which decisions were made should be the focus, not whether the decisions were good or bad in hindsight.

The Bielfeldt Foundation is a private foundation subject to excise taxes on jeopardizing investments.[90] Commodity futures are closely scrutinized for purposes of this tax.[91] The attorney general may look to the Internal Revenue Code to support her basic position that the investments were inappropriate, but she may run into one problem. According to one newspaper account, the Bielfeldt Foundation obtained a private letter ruling from the Internal Revenue Service in 1992 blessing an investment strategy that was to include commodities futures (up to 10 percent of the portfolio).[92] As the article notes, the more recent commodity futures activity appears to exceed that 10 percent limit, but it is possible that the foundation obtained a second ruling or a legal opinion or has some other basis for arguing that the activity does not violate the jeopardizing investment limitations in the Internal Revenue Code.

---

86. Illinois General Not For Profit Corporation Act of 1986, § 108.60(a), provides as follows:

> Director conflict of interest. (a) If a transaction is fair to a corporation at the time it is authorized, approved, or ratified, the fact that a director of the corporation is directly or indirectly a party to the transaction is not grounds for invalidating the transaction.

Undoubtedly the Illinois Attorney General will have to deal with the relationship between the Illinois Charitable Trust Act and the Illinois Not For Profit Corporation Act of 1986 as the case proceeds to trial and through a likely appellate process. That should be an interesting process to watch, providing a better understanding of director duties under Illinois law.

87. T. Kellner and R. Lenzner, *One Hand Giveth ...*, FORBES.COM, Oct. 27, 2003; and G. Dougherty, *Peoria's Bielfeldts to Fight State Suit*, CHI TRIB., Dec. 10, 2004.
88. Illinois General Not For Profit Corporation Act of 1986, § 108.70(a).
89. Uniform Prudent Investor Act (1994), § 2(b), which has been adopted in 43 states and the District of Columbia. While its terms apply to trustees and trusts, the act's basic principles are generally consistent with the law applicable to those charged with managing investments in a third-party capacity.
90. I.R.C. § 4944. We consider the tax aspects of private foundations in Chapter 6.
91. *See* Treas. Reg. § 53.4944-1(a)(2), referring to commodity futures as investments that will be "closely scrutinized."
92. D. Meinert, *supra* note 82. According to this article, the ruling that was attached to the foundation's 1992 tax return blessed investments of up to 10 percent of the portfolio in commodity futures. Although the author has not seen that ruling, research turned up only one 1992 private letter that even remotely mentioned the issues that were apparently addressed in the ruling referred to in the article, IRS Priv. Ltr. Rul. 92-37-035 (1992).

What should now be apparent is that investment decisions clearly pose "duty of care" issues, as well as issues under various state statutes and the Internal Revenue Code. You should now understand why having a well-thought-out and documented investment process is prudent. What makes the investment decision process particularly perilous is the fact that people, including regulators, question the process only when things go wrong. Inevitability, that means that those who made the decisions are faced with the burden of hindsight.

* * *

(d) TRANSLATING LEGAL STANDARDS INTO ACTUAL CONDUCT. So what do *prudence* and *ordinary care* mean in terms of investment decisions? First and foremost, they mean developing a set of standards that guide investment decisions. This process first requires assessing the desired level of risk that the board believes is appropriate under the circumstances. The novice might assume that no amount of risk should be tolerated. This could lead to an investment strategy that limits investments to short-term United States Treasury securities. Such a strategy clearly would be inappropriate for most endowments and could lead to charges of imprudence because it does not strike an appropriate balance between risk and the institution's needs.

(i) Risk-Reward Analysis: Asset Allocation Models. To ascertain the proper mix of investments, the board should use an asset allocation model that considers the risk and expected returns from various assets so that the resulting investment portfolio optimizes investment return in view of the board's tolerance for risk in the portfolio.[93] Developing an appropriate allocation model is an exercise in mathematics, requiring an analysis of rates of return, covariances, standard deviations, and other statistical measures. For this reason, most nonprofit boards will want to rely on a professional investment manager who can translate the board's objectives into a mathematically sound investment strategy and in terms that the average board member can understand.

In practical terms for many endowments, this means having a diversified portfolio consisting of an appropriate mix of equity securities, debt, real estate, and miscellaneous investments that could include commodities, options, oil and gas participations, and interests in venture capital and hedge funds. Diversifying within an asset class minimizes the risk from a particular asset in that class. For example, a board would be imprudent to hold 100 percent of its assets in Wal-Mart stock. That should not be interpreted as a slight against Wal-Mart; it simply acknowledges the fact that any company can suffer an unexpected setback. This is the reason that both individual and institutional investors diversify their stock portfolios. In fact, diversification is one of the underlying motivations for investments in mutual funds and market index funds. However, just investing in United

---

93. Susan M. Mangiero, Risk Management for Pensions, Endowments, and Foundations at 59–61 (John Wiley & Sons 2004).

States equities is arguably[94] not sufficient due to what is termed *systematic risk*,[95] which is a characteristic of all markets. *Systematic risk* describes the general tendency of prices in a particular market to be positively correlated. In colloquial terms, a rising tide raises all boats (and the reverse). A particular company may report unexpectedly good earnings, but if the general market is depressed, the effect of that good news on the company's stock price is likely to be dampened. To eliminate systematic risk, it is necessary to spread equity investments across different equity markets (e.g., United States and foreign), as well as across different classes of assets. While the United States stock market may be depressed, the international market for gold or the United States commercial real estate market may be generating positive investment returns.

(ii) Diversification. To understand how diversification works, let's consider an example that Laurence Siegel used to illustrate diversification in a paper published by the Ford Foundation entitled *Investment Management for Endowed Funds*.[96] Ibbotson Associates, the well known financial research firm, provided the historical data. Mr. Siegel assumed a portfolio comprised equally of an investment in the S&P 500 stock index and intermediate-term bonds. Over the period from 1926 to 2000, the S&P 500 stock index returned an 11 percent annual return, but in any given year, the 11 percent return was subject to a 20.2 percent standard deviation (a measure of the annual variations in the 11 percent average return). Intermediate-term bonds produced a lower 5.3 percent compound annual return, but that annual return was subject to less fluctuation (a 5.8 percent standard deviation). Now assume that a nonprofit faced with a deciding how to invest its $10 million endowment wants to be able to spend 8 percent per year from its endowment fund without invading the $10 million principal balance. If it invests 100 percent of its assets in bonds, the money will be relatively safe, but it will not meet its investment or spending objectives. If it invests 100 percent of its money in stocks, on average, it will more than exceed its objectives, but its portfolio's return will be subject to wider fluctuations in a given year. This will be a problem if the nonprofit wants to insulate its operations from temporary but unpredictable shortfalls in investment income. In short, investing 100 percent of the nonprofit's assets in either of the two investment opportunities is problematic.

If the organization decided to invest equally in stocks and bonds, it would expect to earn somewhere around an 8 percent annual return. Its expected return would be subject to greater risk than a portfolio composed of all debt, but it would be subject to less risk than a portfolio composed entirely of stocks. Looking

94. *Arguably* is a necessary qualifier because some investment professionals believe that United States investors can diversity internationally by investing in certain United States multinationals.

95. Susan M. Mangiero *supra* note 93, at 67.

96. This illustration is based on an example and data taken from the Ford Foundation publication. *See* L. Siegel, *Investment Management for Endowed Institutions* (Apr. 2001), available at www.fordfound.org/publications/recent_articles/docs/investman.pdf.

to the historic returns discussed in Mr. Siegel's paper for the period 1926 through 1996,[97] the risk to the 8 percent return in a given year would be between the 5.8 percent and 20.2 percent measures of risk. In fact, we would expect the measure of risk to be 13.7 percent (the mean). However, for the period between 1926 and1996, the fifty-fifty portfolio produced an 8 percent compounded return but with a measure of only 11.2 percent risk. Two different things happened when the organization moved to the fifty-fifty portfolio. First, the portfolio's return and measure of risk changed. This aspect of change is due to simple averaging and has nothing to do with the effects of diversification. Second, the effects of diversification came into play. In this case, the effects of diversification are the ability to receive an 8 percent expected return with slightly less risk (2.5 percentage point—13.7 percent expected measure of risk minus the 11.2 percent actual measure of risk) than expected.

The 8 percent return/11.2 percent risk is said to be on the efficient frontier, a term associated with Harry Markowitz and William Sharpe, two economists who received the Nobel Prize for their work in developing modern portfolio theory. The reason why an investor can obtain a given return while assuming lower risk than might be expected is due to the fact that the returns on different asset classes exhibit different degrees of covariance. In less mathematical terms, rates of return on stocks and bonds don't move in lockstep fashion. In a year when the bond market is down, the stock market might be up. An investment advisor's primary mission is to help the organization assemble a basket of investment assets that maximizes expected return in view of specified risk tolerances by taking advantage of covariances between the returns on the different assets.

What these numbers indicate is that if the organization wants to be able to spend at a rate of 8 percent, it must forgo some of the safety associated with a portfolio entirely of bonds. By diversifying, the organization should be able to meet its 8 percent objective, and a diversified portfolio allows it to obtain significant risk-reduction benefits (in other words, more certainty that it will meet its objectives each year) by taking advantage of the fact that annual fluctuations in asset returns often cancel out each other. We have focused on a relatively simple portfolio, but no matter how complex the portfolio and underlying investment strategy, this analysis illustrates the basic principles.

We undertook the preceding analysis because diversification is an important element in determining whether a board has discharged its duty of care. The law is quite clear: The appropriateness of a particular investment is not assessed in isolation but in terms of the portfolio and the risk inherent in the portfolio.[98] As an illustration, while many people consider a leveraged investment in commodity futures to be very risky, such an investment in the context of an overall investment strategy and portfolio may be perfectly appropriate.

---

97. It is unclear why Mr. Siegel made a slight change in his measurement period in mid-analysis. It throws the comparisons off slightly, but the basic point is nevertheless clear.

98. UPIA, *supra* note 89.

(iii) Pulling the Pieces Together into a Process. Much has been written about managing an endowment. People almost inevitably offer a number of steps that the management process should encompass. Whether a specific program entails three, five, or seven steps is irrelevant, all will touch on several basic themes. However the steps are defined, the substance of the process should include the following:

- *Assessing how much the organization is seeking in income from the endowment for the organization's current program activities.* This analysis asks the board to balance the inherent conflict between the needs of current stakeholders and those of future generations. The board can pay out 15 percent of its endowment each year, but that almost inevitably means that the principal balance will be dissipated. Even if the board cuts the number back to 8 percent, it still must determine whether it wants to maintain purchasing power. Moreover, an institution's donors might limit the spending rate through restrictions they impose on gifts.
- *Analyzing the organization's tolerance for risk.* There is risk when anyone makes an investment. Some of this risk is attributable to economic uncertainty. Some of it is due to principal-agent issues: Can the investor trust the agent to do what the agent says it will do with the money? Some of the risk is attributable to markets and the nature of the asset. The organization must assess its tolerance for all of these risks. For example, a very conservative organization might want to deal only with long-established institutional trust companies because of perceived low principal-agent risk. That is a legitimate position, but it has implications. For example, selection of a corporate trustee could foreclose investments in hedge funds and could mean higher fees.
- *Establishing investment objectives.* The organization must set its investment objectives, taking into account its spending goal and its tolerance for risk. As part of this process, the organization should decide whether it will use broad indices or stock selection and whether it will invest in illiquid or riskier assets such as derivatives, real estate, hedge funds, commodities, venture capital, and foreign currencies. The organization or its advisers must then construct an asset allocation model to balance its objectives, needs, and risk tolerances.
- *Making investment decisions.* The organization or its advisers must then execute the investment plan by buying and selling investment assets. As part of this process, the organization should periodically rebalance its portfolio so that it remains aligned with its objectives.
- *Reviewing the results.* Most important, the organization must review the results. Even if it has delegated the investment process to a third-party adviser who delegates investment authority to individual managers and

reviews their performance, the organization must still review the overall results.

(iv) Delegation versus Abdication. As should now be clear, once investment management and advice move beyond somebody's brother-in-law's hot tip, the investment process can become complex, requiring expert advice. This is the reason that many boards retain professional investment managers and advisers. At one time, there was a question whether a fiduciary could delegate investment authority to a third party. By and large, that is no longer an issue. Section 5 of UMIFA provides for broad delegation of investment authority but recognizes that the terms of a particular gift or state law applying to particular institutions (e.g., a public university) may impose specific limitations. The law regarding trusts now permits delegation of investment management functions in most jurisdictions.

Under some circumstances, delegation may be the only prudent course of action if the organization lacks the personnel with the requisite skills to manage its investments. Assessing risk tolerances and setting a spending rate may appear to be a task that the organization must do by itself, but experts who have been through the process with other institutions can provide the nonprofit a framework for making these seemingly personal decisions; think of the consultant as a financial psychologist. Experts may also be brought into the review process. After all, does a board know whether the 9 percent return it received last year is an acceptable return vis-à-vis the performance of other investments?

Delegation, however, does not mean abdicating authority to others. The organization must be involved in the entire process, asking questions, managing risk, reviewing performance, and defining objectives. On balance, the nonprofit's board should not undertake this role for the organization. It should delegate the investment process to an investment committee or the appropriate officers. As is the case when authority is delegated to committees and employees, the board should demand periodic reports and exercise oversight.

(v) Investment Managers and Advisers. Many boards quickly discover that their decision process focuses on selecting advisers, communicating the board's risk tolerances and return objectives, and evaluating the adviser's performance rather than selecting specific investments. In fact, in ascertaining whether the directors have discharged their duties when they have delegated investment authority to an outsider, the courts have generally looked at the delegation and review process rather than investment results.[99] As is true with virtually all board decisions, the courts are unwilling to find breaches of duty if the board takes a proactive approach, asks questions, follows up when there are issues, and reviews and applies objective and conflict-free procedures when selecting investment professionals.

---

99. Liss v. Smith, 991 F. Supp. 278, 294 (S.D.N.Y. 1998).

The board that decides to rely on professional investment managers has a number of options. The simplest approach is to select a large corporate trust company or an established money management firm to manage the endowment for a fee. This firm will build a portfolio composed of equities, debt securities, and other assets that adheres to the nonprofit's investment policies and risk tolerances. This manager will provide regular written reports to and meet with the board or the organization's investment committee. This one-stop approach makes the most sense for nonprofits with small endowments because their investment choices are often limited to marketable securities.

Organizations with large endowments clearly have more options available. A large university or foundation might retain an adviser to help it devise an investment strategy that specifies that assets will be invested in a number of asset categories. This adviser can then recommend investment management firms that will be responsible for managing the portion of the portfolio that is allocated to particular asset classes. In other words, one firm might manage the United States equities, another international equities, a third investments in corporate debt, and a fourth investments in real estate. The management function can be sliced into even smaller slices with one firm managing investments in United States energy stocks and another responsible for investments in stocks of United States consumer goods. The thinking is that buying specialized investment expertise will improve overall return. However, this complexity can add significant cost, both in terms of monitoring costs by the organization and higher fees for presumed expertise.

Even if the nonprofit decides to work with just one or two managers, if it allocates a portion of its endowment to investments in hedge funds, venture capital, commodities, and other more specialized investments, it should seriously consider turning over those specialized components of its investment portfolio to specialist firms.

No matter what approach the organization takes, it must assess qualifications. Here are a few tips:

- Contact similar organizations to ascertain how they have approached investment management issues.
- Contact the Commonfund[100] and The Investment Fund for Foundations,[101] both nonprofits that specialize in advising nonprofits on investment management issues.
- Review directories and services that track investment managers. Standard & Poor's offers a number of directories as well as a Web-based database.[102]

---

100. The Ford Foundation provided a $2.8 million grant in 1969 (or thereabouts) to facilitate the formation of the Commonfund. The Commonfund's Web site is located at http://www.commonfund.org/Commonfund/About+Us/About_Commonfund.

101. The Web site is www.tiff.org.

102. See SUSAN M. MANGIERO, *supra* note 93, at 24.

- Review publications and services that track investment manager hirings and firings. *Pensions & Investments* is one notable publication, with both paper and online products.[103]
- Consider sending a formal *request for proposals* to a list of candidates or publishing it in a magazine such as *Pensions & Investments*.
- Narrow the list of candidates to a manageable number and then interview the firms.
- Review the information obtained from the interview process, focusing on personnel qualifications, investment philosophies, track records over extended time horizons, performance reports, relationship management procedures, representative clients, fee structure, internal controls over the process, firm stability and personnel turnover, and other relevant considerations.
- If the manager is hiring other managers to direct certain portions of the portfolio, examine the fee arrangements between the manager and those it delegates work to. Nonprofits should avoid organizations that make recommendations and receive referral fees from those being recommended or selected.
- Negotiate the terms of the arrangement with the finalists, including fees—but be realistic.
- Make a selection, keeping in mind that changing managers is expensive, so the selection should be a carefully considered one.

These recommendations assume that the nonprofit is looking for one investment manager to manage its portfolio. As noted, there are other models, but each requires similar steps. If a nonprofit is working with an adviser who simply recommends managers, the nonprofit should focus on any referral fees paid to the advisor.

(vi) Risk Management. The board must utilize risk management techniques to protect the organization's endowment from a wide variety of risks, particularly as it delegates parts of the process to third parties. Some best practices include:

- *Performing background checks on all persons and entities that receive delegated authority.*
- *Reviewing insurance and bonds.* Investment organizations should have fidelity insurance, as well as errors and omissions coverage. The nonprofit should ask about this coverage and even request to review the policies.
- *Using written contracts when authority is delegated.* The rules should be clear so that if there are mistakes or errors, the nonprofit is in a position to

103. *Id.*, at 27. The Web site for *Pensions & Investments* is http://www.pionline.com.

take legal action. For example, if an investment manger ignores investment restrictions, the nonprofit should be in a position to recover any resulting loss. When the nonprofit is asked to agree to a written contract (particularly one that is a standardized form), the person signing it on behalf of the nonprofit should focus on any arbitration or other clauses that could limit the nonprofit's rights should there be a dispute. Arbitration clauses are quite common in brokerage contracts and are viewed by brokerage firms as providing them an advantage.

- *Requiring personal guarantees.* If the organization is dealing with a large trust company or an established money manager, it is unlikely that the principals will personally guarantee contract terms. However, when dealing with a small or new organization, consider asking the principals to stand behind the contract by personally guaranteeing key terms of the contract.
- *Focusing on who has title and custody of the assets.* If investment authority is delegated, the organization should consider placing asset custody with a third-party corporate custodian. Under no circumstances should the assets be titled in anybody's name other than the nonprofit's unless the assets are held in a clearly designated trust account that protects them from claims by third-party creditors and clearly and effectively restricts their use.
- *Requiring independent verification of asset balances.* If a third party holds the assets, the organization should have procedures in place to audit and verify asset balances.
- *Curbing speculation with derivatives.* Derivatives are a risk management tool when used by someone who understands them. When viewed as investments rather than hedging devices, derivatives can expose an investment portfolio to unacceptable risks. If investment authority is delegated, the organization must undertake due diligence to make sure that the investment manager has procedures to protect against unauthorized speculation with derivatives.
- *Reviewing fee arrangements down the chain of delegated authority.*

As noted, books have been written on the investment process. If your board is just beginning to focus on investment issues, it might want to obtain *Prudent Investment Practices: A Handbook for Investment Fiduciaries* prepared by the Foundation for Fiduciary Studies, with technical assistance from the American Institute of Certified Public Accountants. This book outlines a 5-step investment process and then provides 27 steps for implementing that process. Also of interest is *Risk Management for Pensions, Endowments, and Foundations* by Susan M. Mangiero (John Wiley & Sons, 2005). She provides a more comprehensive examination of the risk management issues associated with the investment process, including a discussion of the finance theory underlying modern investment management.

(e) CORPORATE TRUSTEES AND CHARITABLE BENEFICIARIES. Charities are often the beneficiaries of trusts, with a corporate trustee managing investments and administering the trust. Although the charity's directors may believe that the investment process is outside of their control, they should nevertheless make sure that the charity is adequately monitoring the corporate trustee. There have been a number of cases in recent years in which corporate trustees have increased fees—thereby reducing the amount payable to the charitable beneficiary—even though the trust agreement did not permit unilateral increases. This practice may not be widespread, but a number of publicized cases have involved large financial institutions.[104] This problem has been attributed to two decades of consolidation in the financial services industry with corporate trustees being subject to acquisition by money center financial institutions that are removed from the local communities and their charitable institutions. When charitable trusts have brought legal action, they have often been successful.[105] For example, Security Pacific National Bank was the trustee of 2,500 trusts that fixed its fee by contract. Notwithstanding that the fee could be changed only by order of the probate court, Security Pacific increased its fee nine times during a 15 year period without obtaining court approval. The trust beneficiaries included more than 450 charitable organizations.[106] A class action lawsuit was brought on behalf of the beneficiaries contesting the fee increases. The plaintiffs successfully recovered $111.5 million in damages.[107]

Fees are not the only issue, however, that should be of concern. At least two corporate trustees were accused of improperly converting common trust fund accounts to proprietary mutual fund accounts, triggering capital gain taxes.[108] In both instances, the trustees settled the dispute, making multimillion payments. Since those conversions, the tax law has been modified, permitting tax-free

---

104. B. Wolverton, *Loss of Trust: Donors, Foundations Say Banks Mishandle Charitable Accounts*, CHRON. OF PHILAN., Apr. 14, 2005; and P. Horn, *Legal Fight Could Hurt Trust's Giving: Wachovia Wants a Bigger Fee, Plus $5 Million for Work from the Past*, PHIL. INQ., Jan. 25, 2004.

105. *See* B. Wolverton, *supra* note 104. The *Chronicle* article listed multimillion dollar settlements or court orders involving Wells Fargo & Company, Northern Trust Bank of California, and Bank of America. In fairness to the named institutions, the disputes often arose out of the actions of a predecessor organization that the named institution had acquired—offering a lesson to all companies engaged in acquisitions regarding due diligence. Two trusts established by John D. Rockefeller, Jr. ended up in litigation with Bankers Trust Company of New York over fees. *See* In the Matter of the Petition for Judicial Settlement of the Intermediate Account of Proceedings by Bankers Trust Company of New York, as Trustee under the Indentures of Trust established by John D. Rockefeller, Jr., dated October 16, 1922, for the Benefit of the New York City Baptist Mission Society, 784 N.Y.S.2d 923 (N.Y. Sur. Ct. 2004).

106. B. Wolverton, *supra* note 104.

107. Nickel v. Bank of America National Trust, 290 F.3d 1134 (9th Cir. 2004); and 991 F. Supp. 1175 (1997).

108. B. Wolverton, *supra* note 104, referring to litigation involving First Union and Bank One. For additional details, see R. Arnold, G. Jordan, & P. Napolitano, *Advanced Litigation Risk Management for the Corporate Fiduciary*, TRUSTS & ESTATES, May 2001.

transfers from common trust funds to mutual fund accounts.[109] While this amendment of the tax code certainly eliminates the tax cost of conversion, it does not eliminate the opportunity for financial institutions that are acting as trustees to make the switch to increase their fee income,[110] again making it imperative for charities that are trust beneficiaries to monitor trustee activities.[111] Disputes also can arise when the trust holds assets that create potential conflicts of interest.[112]

The *Chronicle of Philanthropy* reports that careful monitoring can pay for itself, pointing to Shriners Hospital for Children, an organization that has 22 hospitals around the country.[113] According to the *Chronicle,* the hospitals are beneficiaries under charitable trusts having a combined value of $450 million. During a two-year period, Shriners collected several million dollars as a result of its monitoring activities, uncovering overcharges, failures to distribute income, and inappropriate charges for taxes. This requires some effort, with Shriners assembling a team of employees to monitor trust activity, including one employee whose job is to review trust documents on a full-time basis.

Those setting up trusts can eliminate potential problems by paying careful attention to trustee fees and other administrative and discretionary matters at the outset of the relationship. Drafting the terms of the trust is technically outside the purview of the charitable beneficiary, but often it knows about the donor's intentions regarding the charity. In those instances, the charity should at least consider advising the donor regarding some administrative issues. The following are among the terms that whoever is responsible for negotiating the trust

109. The Small Business Jobs Protection Act of 1996 includes Section 1805(h), Nonrecognition Treatment for Certain Transfers by Common Trust Funds to Regulated Investment Companies, which amended the tax treatment of conversions into mutual funds under Section 584 of the Internal Revenue Code of 1986.

110. See Howard A. Amer, Assistant Director of the Division of Supervision and Regulation, Board of Governors of the Federal Reserve System, Ltr. No. SR 97-3 (Feb. 26, 1997), stating:

> The change to the tax laws that now permits a tax-free conversion has enabled banking organizations to eliminate some of the duplicative administrative and operational costs associated with offering common trust funds to fiduciary customers and mutual fund investment products to other customers. *Some banking organizations may also recognize that conversion provides an opportunity to generate additional income by charging fees for providing trustee services to customers and additional fees for rendering investment advisory services to the mutual fund in which their fiduciary customers have invested. Income can also be generated from shared fee arrangements with unaffiliated mutual fund providers.* [emphasis added]

111. R. Arnold, G. Jordan, & P. Napolitano, *supra* note 108.

112. B. Wolverton, *supra* note 104, discussing a lawsuit by Pittsburg's McCune Foundation against Cleveland's National City Bank. According to the *Chronicle* article, family members were concerned that some of the foundation's assets were invested in the bank's own stock. The lawsuit was dismissed, but the foundation continued to complain about the matter, resulting in some accommodation by National City.

113. B. Wolverton, *Close Monitoring of Charitable Trust Adds Up to Big Sums for One Group*, CHRON. OF PHILAN., Apr. 14, 2005.

agreement should consider whenever a corporate trustee will administer a charitable trust:[114]

- The fee arrangement should be carefully defined.
- Procedures for adjusting the fee arrangement should be addressed. If the parties will rely on statutorily determined fees, they should address what happens when the statute is modified.
- The settlor, cotrustees, or the charitable beneficiary should have the right to replace the corporate trustee in the event of a merger or other consolidation that results in a larger institution or one that is not headquartered in the community acquiring the corporate trustee.
- The trust agreement should provide for a detailed accounting at least annually. The accounting should show how fees and income distributions are calculated.
- The trust agreement should address investment decisions by the corporate trustee involving proprietary investment products (such as a family of mutual funds sponsored by the trustee or an affiliate) as well as assets that could pose conflicts of interest (investments in the trustee's own stock or in companies in which a person affiliated with the trustee has a beneficial interest.)
- If there will be cotrustees, the trust agreement should address the procedures for replacing them.

In view of the recent class action litigation, many corporate fiduciaries have begun to insert language into their fee agreements limiting the rights of the beneficiaries to bring legal action against the corporate trustee. There is clearly a question of whether these waivers will be upheld to the extent that the behavior in dispute involves breaches of fiduciary duties.[115] Rather than forcing the charitable beneficiary to resort to future litigation, the best course of action is to address these provisions at the outset, demanding that they be eliminated. To do this, the donor must take the time to read the fine print.

---

114. This checklist focuses on the issues raised by the discussion in the text. The typical trust agreement involving a corporate trustee requires that a number of other issues be addressed.

115. RESTATEMENT (THIRD DRAFT) OF TRUSTS § 78, Comment, provides as follows:

> Even express authorization...would not completely dispense with the trustee's underlying fiduciary obligations to act in the interest of the beneficiaries and to exercise prudence in administering the trust. Accordingly, no matter how broad the provisions of a trust may be in conferring power to engage in self-dealing or other transactions involving a conflict of fiduciary and personal interests, a trustee violates the duty of loyalty to the beneficiaries by acting in bad faith or unfairly.

There is little reason to assume that this sentiment will change in the final version. Although courts need not necessarily follow the American Law Institute's restatements of the law, courts often look to these restatements when adjudicating legal disputes.

4.7 ANOTHER LOOK AT CONFLICTS OF INTEREST

When nonprofits run into trouble, the cause is often rooted in conflicts of interest that have not been adequately addressed. Regulators at both the state and federal levels recognize this fact. Not surprising, virtually every state[116] addresses conflicts of interest, often imposing additional burdens on the parties as they discharge their duties.[117] Pursuant to legislative mandate, the IRS recently adopted a set of rules that apply to transactions between charities and insiders, including directors, employees, and substantial donors. These rules are designed to ensure that dealings with insiders are priced at arm's length and further the organization's charitable purposes. Against this backdrop, let's take a closer look at the duty of loyalty and conflicts of interest.

(a) NEED FOR A CONFLICT-OF-INTEREST POLICY. Every nonprofit should adhere to the procedures outlined in applicable state statutes for handling conflicts of interest. These rules take two basic forms, those that prohibit certain transactions under any circumstances[118] and those that validate certain transactions if specified procedures are followed. Those procedures are generalized, applicable to all organizations subject to the statute. Given that fact, the nonprofit should adopt a written conflict-of-interest policy that contains not only the provisions outlined in the applicable state statute but also specific rules reflecting the organization's unique characteristics and circumstances as well as requirements imposed by other regulatory bodies.

A conflict-of-interest policy serves two basic purposes. First, it establishes rules, providing the organization with a clear basis for disciplining anyone who violates the prescribed rules. Second, and arguably more important, a conflict-of-interest policy serves as an educational tool, sensitizing and reminding those in the organization of the importance of avoiding conflicts. Remember, however, that all conflict-of-interest policies have limitations. As laudable as they may be, they will not stop a wrongdoer. The organization should build monitoring into its system of internal controls to detect violations of the policy. Consider the engineering professor at George Washington University who was accused of using companies that he owned to improperly divert federal grant money for personal purposes.[119] The university had a conflict-of-interest policy in place, but the policy apparently did not stop behavior that violated the policy. To the

---

116. According to FREMONT-SMITH, *supra* note 5, at 218, as of January 1, 2003, 39 states had adopted a conflict-of-interest provision in their state nonprofit corporation statutes. Another 12 jurisdictions had a conflict-of-interest provision in their general business corporation statutes. According to FREMONT-SMITH, *supra*, these business corporation statutes are relevant in the nonprofit context because there is no nonprofit corporation statute.

117. *See, e.g.*, N.Y. Consol. L., Chapter 35, § 715.

118. Twenty-eight states and the RMNCA specifically prohibit loans from a nonprofit to a director. See FREMONT-SMITH, *supra* note 5, at 226.

119. P. Fogg, *Grand-Theft Auto: An Automotive Expert Is Accused of Stealing Federal Grant Money to Bankroll His Lifestyle*, CHRON. HIGHER EDUC., Feb. 4, 2005.

university's credit, the questionable transactions were detected through routine audit procedures. Nevertheless, the university subsequently agreed to pay $1.8 million to the federal government to resolve the matter.[120] The professor pled guilty to embezzlement.[121] To be effective, a conflict-of-interest policy must work in conjunction with financial and internal controls, something that we consider in Chapter 5.

Let's now consider five case studies illustrating the issues surrounding conflicts.

(i) The Community Organization—Case 1. Conflicts come in all shapes and sizes. If an organization's executive director and existing board are properly focused, they will look for a variety of professionals and businesspeople to serve on the board. This provides the organization ready access to specialized knowledge and experience. However, all too often, when the nonprofit needs more than a quick judgment or assessment, the board member who possesses the specialized knowledge is in the business of selling services, posing a conflict. Consider Non-Violent Suburban Kids, a nonprofit corporation seeking to eliminate violence in public high schools in the greater Albertsville area. Non-Violent has established contacts in each of the 75 suburban high schools. Guidance counselors at participating schools receive special training in identifying students who could engage in violent behavior on school campuses. Identified students are referred to Non-Violent's treatment facility on both an institutionalized and outpatient basis, depending on each student's particular needs.

Toren Ruffin, an investment banker, and Josey Herron, a local real estate developer, serve on Non-Violent's board. Because of increased demand for Non-Violent's services, the board is considering expanding its existing facility. This involves building a new 500,000 square foot facility and issuing tax-exempt bonds to finance it. Herron has submitted a proposal for the construction of the facility, and Ruffin has suggested that Non-Violent use his firm to underwrite the financing.

The conflicts here are very clear for both Herron and Ruffin. In all likelihood, they need to recuse themselves from the decision process if state law sets procedures for validating transactions embedded with conflicts. More generally, an organization considering a project that will require professional services may even want to consider selecting directors who are not associated with potential contractors, but in many cases, executive directors might believe this is an easy way to obtain discounted services.[122] Before agreeing to serve, professionals

---

120. P. Fogg, *George Washington U. to Pay $1.8 Million to Avoid Prosection in Embezzlement Case*, CHRON. OF HIGHER EDUC., Apr. 21, 2005.

121. Press Release, Department of Justice, "Former GWU Professor Pleads Guilty to Embezzling More Than $900,000 from Federally Funded Program" (Apr. 13, 2005).

122. At a recent meeting of nonprofit consultants, one executive director indicated her only reason for having an attorney and accountant on "her" board of directors was to obtain pro bono legal and accounting services, disdainfully dismissing any oversight role that these professionals might provide. She clearly is very practical and also clearly running a one-woman show. One can only wonder what governance problems are bubbling just below the surface in that organization.

should ascertain whether their good judgment is being sought or just free services. They should also anticipate foreseeable conflicts that could pose problems.

(ii) The Art Museum—Case 2. Museums face particularly difficult challenges in addressing conflicts of interest because the people who serve on museum boards often have a strong interest in collecting the types of objects the museum collects. Although this can result in knowledgeable and active directors, it also poses potential conflicts between directors and the museum's mission, as David Walken, an avid collector of the artwork of Spanish painter Joaquin Sorolla, should have recognized when he was deciding whether to accept a position as a trustee of the Museum of Significant Spanish Arts. Sorolla is relatively unknown in the United States. Assume:

- The museum decides to sell two works by Sorolla from its permanent collection. Walken buys the works at an auction run by an independent auction house.
- Walken votes at a trustees' meeting to have the museum hold a major Sorolla retrospective.
- Walken loans a Sorolla painting from his private collection to the museum to display in its Sorolla retrospective.
- Walken decides to buy Sorolla's *Infants Eating on the Beach in Malaga.* The museum is interested in expanding its collection of Sorolla's work.

Each of the proposed actions poses a conflict for Walken, and they would be best dealt with through full disclosure. In each instance, Walken should disclose to the other trustees his interest in collecting Sorolla before the board takes action. In all likelihood, he will at least need to recuse himself from participating in the decision and, depending on the particulars of state law, may be required to demonstrate that the transaction is fair and in the best interests of the museum.

Walken should not participate in the museum's decision to sell the two Sorolla paintings even if the sales are through an independent auction house. His decision may not be objective because this action places two coveted Sorollas on the market and within his grasp. It might actually make sense for the museum to expand its Sorolla holdings rather than sell them—but can Walken be truly objective?

Have you ever noticed that when a museum holds a retrospective, the commercial art galleries in the city often exhibit art by the same artist? The reason is quite simple: Museum retrospectives create interest in an artist and add to the artist's reputation. Of course, this often translates into increased market value. If Walken is permitted to vote on whether the museum should hold a Sorolla retrospective, people may ask whether he voted to further the museum's mission or to increase the value of his Sorolla collection. Walken should refrain from voting.

The loan of the Sorolla painting poses a similar problem. Does this loan further the museum's mission, or is Walken just looking for free advertising in anticipation of a future sale of the painting? Will someone say, "That must really be an important piece of art since it was part of the retrospective"? And what if the museum finds itself competing with Walken for the same work of art? He clearly has a conflict here, and he cannot ignore his duty of loyalty to the museum.

A strict reading of the law may permit some of these actions because the private benefit is not tangible. Even the law does not always recognize these sorts of inchoate conflicts, but that is a short-run perspective. If museum trustees vote to further their own interests, the museum could find its reputation tarnished. This could result in other institutions refusing to loan the museum works of art for exhibitions and potential donors deciding to donate money and objects to more "ethical" museums. Eventually, the public may catch on and stop frequenting the museum. In an effort to protect their reputations, many museums have adopted ethical codes promulgated by professional associations. While potential trustees may find these codes restrictive, these same trustees undoubtedly gain many intangible benefits from serving as trustees of prominent institutions. Before agreeing to serve, potential trustees must balance compliance with ethical limitations against the intangible benefits that might accrue to trustees.

(iii) The Hospital—Case 3. Both state charity regulators and the IRS have devoted considerable time to conflicts between nonprofit hospitals and physicians who serve on hospital boards. These conflicts arise when the physician is either an employee of the hospital or proposing a joint venture with it. In a traditional business setting, the equityholders in the business have a natural incentive to maximize their own return. Nonprofit hospitals have no equityholders. This is apparent in the case of Dr. Fran Marr, a leading oncologist on the staff of Good Treatment Hospital, a regional nonprofit hospital located in Wellsville. She is also a member of Good Treatment's board.

Dr. Marr has devised a new test that is 300 percent more effective in screening for breast cancer than existing tests. Being quite entrepreneurial, she has formed a for-profit venture to administer and interpret the test results. She has asked Good Treatment to invest $1 million in her for-profit venture. Good Treatment has traditionally shied away from such investments, but there is pressure for it to invest in this venture because the hospital's CEO suspects that Dr. Marr will refer patients who test positive to Good Treatment for care. With 600 new beds to fill, the hospital needs all of the referrals it can get.

State law may well contain conflict-of-interest procedures as part of the nonprofit corporation statutes. These procedures could require Dr. Marr to recuse herself from the decision-making process. Even if the state statutes do not contain specific procedures for dealing with conflicts of interest, Dr. Marr has a common law duty of loyalty as a director that could be enough to require her recusal.

Setting aside state law considerations, Good Treatment's bylaws may contain additional procedures for handling conflicts. If Dr. Marr and Good Treatment

Hospital fail to comply with either state law or the hospital's bylaws, another director may have the right to bring a derivative suit on behalf of the corporation, or the state attorney general may consider taking action.

As you will see shortly and in Chapter 6 in the discussion of federal tax aspects of tax-exempt entities, such an arrangement between Dr. Marr and the hospital raises issues under the private inurement and intermediate sanction provisions.[123] The IRS could step in or even challenge Good Treatment's tax-exempt status. The nonprofit novice is often surprised to learn that the IRS even addresses corporate governance issues, but the IRS views governance issues as critical in ascertaining whether an organization is entitled to tax-exempt status. In fact, the IRS has gone so far as to issue a model conflict-of-interest policy that every organization should at least consider in assembling its own policy.

Finally, when dealing with organizations that provide health care services, the parties need to be concerned with Medicare and Medicaid fraud issues. Before agreeing to an investment or joint venture, the board should ask whether the arrangement with an insider poses problems under Medicare or Medicaid, particularly because violation of these laws can result in criminal prosecution.

(iv) The Foundation "Slush" Fund—Case 4. The Grace Foundation was founded ten years ago when Janis Cavett, a wealthy Wall Street bond trader, decided to established the foundation with a $100 million gift. Its assets have since grown to $400 million. Cavett, who died five years ago, did not specify a particular charitable focus for the foundation's philanthropic activities, but she favored gifts to organizations funding conservation activities and environmental research. Because Janis had no family, her former assistant, Mavis Watson, and ten independent directors now control the foundation

The directors receive no compensation for their services even though they are expected to devote about 100 hours per year to the foundation and its affairs. Watson believes that the directors are entitled to some reward for their time, so she has segregated $1 million of foundation annual income, permitting each director to specify a charity or charities to receive a $100,000 gift.

Governance experts have debated whether this arrangement poses unacceptable conflicts for the directors or whether the directors have any specific duties when making their selection. To the uninitiated, this may seem like a peculiar arrangement, but it is not. One study of foundations funded in conjunction with hospital and health care provider conversions (from nonprofit to for-profit entities) found that roughly one in eight of these organizations permitted its directors to make discretionary grants, with the median grant being $50,000.[124] According to this study, "[n]early all of the foundations (9 of 10) that give this authority to board members have conflict of interest policies that limit the involvement of

123. See the discussion of the intermediate sanctions (I.R.C. § 4958) in Chapter 6.

124. Grant Makers in Health, The Business of Giving: Governance and Asset Management in Foundations Formed in Health Care Conversions (Feb. 2005), *available at* http://www.gih.org.

board members in decisions about grants when the board member has a material interest in the potential recipient."

To a large extent, the legal issues associated with such discretionary funds depend on the specific circumstances. To illustrate, let's consider the following variations on the basic facts:

- *Donation to the Green Contemporary Art Museum.* Assume that Jorma Taylor, one of the ten Grace Foundation directors, requests the foundation to make a \$100,000 donation to the Green Contemporary Art Museum and that the museum honors the donation by naming a hall after Taylor. This transaction raises some troubling questions. First, the donation is outside the foundation's traditional area of interest. Consequently, are the foundation's assets being used to further Taylor's interests at the expense of the foundation's mission? Second, Taylor, not the foundation, is being publicly recognized. As will be discussed in a subsequent chapter, the IRS does not appear to view naming rights as being significant enough to jeopardize a donor's charitable contribution deduction. Could the IRS view this, however, as compensation to Taylor (arguably the flip side of the deduction question), resulting in taxable income to him and possible adverse tax consequences to the foundation? Setting aside the tax issue, might the state's attorney general argue that this is a diversion of charitable assets? Certainly, there is logic to that argument, particularly if the transaction is viewed as an indirect payment to Taylor, but that logic is at least debatable because the \$100,000 ultimately benefits a charity. Suppose that instead of naming a hall after Taylor, the museum simply invites him to a dinner to honor donors?
- *Satisfaction of a Legally Binding Pledge.* Assume the same facts as in the prior situation but that Taylor had made a legally binding pledge to the Green Contemporary Art Museum. Further assume that nothing is named in Taylor's honor. This is probably the most problematic case because Taylor already has a binding obligation that the foundation's assets are satisfying. Instead of charitable recipients having \$200,000 in assets following this transaction, they have only \$100,000 in assets. The state attorney general could certainly argue that Taylor breached his duty of loyalty, particularly because the \$100,000 benefited an art museum rather than a conservation or environmental cause. Moreover, the satisfaction of Taylor's pledge could constitute an act of self-dealing under the private foundation excise tax regime,[125] a regime we will consider in Chapter 6.

---

125. Treas. Reg. § 53.4941(d)-2(f) provides as follows:

> In addition, if a private foundation makes a grant or other payment which satisfies the legal obligation of a disqualified person, such grant or payment shall ordinarily constitute an act of self-dealing to which this subparagraph applies.

- *Other Board Members Must Approve the Recommendation.* Assume the same facts as in the prior example except that the other board members must review, evaluate, and approve Taylor's recommendation and that Taylor does not participate in this decision. From a conflict-of-interest standpoint, this is probably the best possible approach. Rather than each director acting alone, the decision is clearly one of the board acting on behalf of the foundation. However, even if the recommending director leaves the room during the board's deliberations, does the "back-scratching" element in the arrangement pose a problem? After all, how likely will that director vote for the next director's recommendation if the returning director learns that his recommendation has been rejected?

There is no doubt that such arrangements will continue. In part, this explains why everyone would like to be a foundation director or, better yet, a foundation president. As one former foundation president observed, "I was never as good looking, or a better dancer than when I had yoodles of money to give away." The slush fund may just be another perk that comes with having money to give away, but those who are lucky enough to find themselves with that perk should consider structuring the arrangement to avoid adverse tax and corporate law consequences as well as the appearance of impropriety.

(v) Social Entrepreneurship—Case 5. Many nonprofit conferences have focused heavily on *social entrepreneurship* in recent years. Social entrepreneurship represents a move away from traditional philanthropy—raising money and then giving it away. This new school of philanthropy focuses on joining philanthropy and for-profit ventures in creative ways to further charitable mission. For example, a social services agency might decide to open a restaurant that employs only homeless individuals. Or a conservation group might open a resort that highlights and furthers its conservation efforts. Often, these activities are conducted as joint ventures with for-profit entities. In those cases, the nonprofit must be particularly careful in structuring the arrangement so that the venture furthers the nonprofit's mission rather than simply providing private benefits to those who own the for-profit entity.

To illustrate the potential issues, consider Teen Literacy, a highly-regarded Section 501(c)(3) organization that operates five after-school literacy centers throughout the urban Philadelphia area. Not only does Teen Literacy work to improve reading skills of at-risk teenagers, but it also provides assistance to students with their math and writing homework. Martha Lyons, Teen Literacy's executive director, has been a pioneer in using teenagers to provide assistance to other teenager, with the result that Teen Literacy has won numerous awards for its highly successful program. In fact, Teen Literacy has received a Department of Health and Human Services (HHS) grant for $500,000 during each of the last five years. The grant money has been used to purchase computers, supplies, and insurance, as well as to rent space for Teen Literacy centers. Abby Duncan is a marketing executive that has served on the Teen Literacy board since the inception of the organization ten years ago. She and Lyons have become good friends and strong allies in the fight for teen literacy.

About two years ago, Duncan had an epiphany: Why not offer fee-based college preparatory services on the weekends, when the centers are otherwise unused? She approached Lyons with a business plan that called for Teen Literacy to contribute $50,000 to a newly-formed for-profit corporation. The plan also called for Duncan and Lyons individually to each contribute $50,000 to this new venture. Teen Literacy, Duncan, and Lyons were to each receive a one-third interest in Teen College Prep, Inc. (TCP). Under the plan, TCP would sub-lease space in the existing centers for $10,000 per year. Pursuant to terms of the leases, TCP agreed to provide its services by employing teachers from the local schools. TCP also agreed to provide these services at a 50 percent discount from the rate charged by for-profit providers in suburban locales.

After much discussion, the Teen Literacy board approved the venture. As part of the approval process, the board held a special two-hour meeting. Although both Duncan and Lyons were present for the first hour of the meeting to explain the business plan and answer questions, they were not present during the second hour, when the remaining ten members of the board discussed and then unanimously approved the proposal.

Last month, Teen Literacy received a letter from HHS's inspector general indicating that an audit had uncovered the following problems: (1) government-funded computers were used by TCP without payment, (2) at least $200,000 of government-funded Teen Literacy staff time was devoted to TCP activities, and (3) Teen Literacy had not been reimbursed by TCP for a portion of insurance premiums funded with government grant money despite the fact that TCP had been added as a named-insured on Teen Literacy's insurance policies. The auditor also noted that there was not sufficient adult supervision during weekday afternoon hours at Teen Literacy centers. Upon further investigation, the auditor determined that this apparently was due to a number of high school teachers switching from volunteer status with Teen Literacy to employee status with TCP.

When the board received a copy of the inspector general's report, it began its own investigation. Martha Lyons resisted, but finally made financial statements for TCP available to the board. Much to the board's surprise, the notes to the statements indicated that Lyons had entered into a management contract with TCP. She and Abby Duncan have each received $50,000 a year under these contracts, reducing TCP's net income to $2,000 per annum. The Teen Literacy employee who had notified the inspector general about potential abuses (who Lyons had dismissed) has since gone to the newspapers.

As these facts amply illustrate, when a board decides to venture into social entrepreneurship, the conflicts analysis should extend far beyond making sure that the nonprofit receives fair value in return for its capital contribution. Even when insiders are not involved, the board must make sure that the for-profit activities are consistent with and further the nonprofit's mission.

As a condition of funding any for-profit venture, the board should make sure that the agreements mandate timely financial reports to representatives of the nonprofit who have no financial interest in the venture and who are not subject to supervision by people having such an interest. The board also needs to think beyond the initial start-up phase, making sure that it has knowledge of and input into management agreements, leases, and contracts related to the for-profit venture. It also needs to monitor the impact of the for-profit venture's activities on the nonprofit's mission. As this case illustrates, the needs of the for-profit venture can directly conflict with the nonprofit's core mission: In addition to financial resources, TCP also drained valuable volunteer personnel from Teen Literacy's programs and placed Teen Literacy's federal grant in jeopardy.

Ideally, the managers of, suppliers to, and other investors in the for-profit venture should not be insiders. The absence of insider conflicts means that everybody on the nonprofit's team is reviewing the arrangement with complete objectivity. Unfortunately from a governance standpoint, insiders are often involved in for-profit enterprises. This may be necessary to keep people who are involved with the nonprofit from leaving the nonprofit to pursue for-profit activities. It may also be necessary because people employed by the nonprofit possess special skills. That certainly can be the case when the for-profit venture involves exploiting intellectual property or scientific or medical knowledge. In these instances, the nonprofit's board must be prepared to closely monitor the for-profit's activities and the relationship between the two entities on an ongoing basis. In other words, the board's oversight responsibility extends well beyond the initial decision to pursue the venture.

Many nonprofits are actively pursuing joint ventures with for-profit entities. Although this particular case is fictional, it was inspired by several known cases that have generated litigation or unfavorable publicity for the organizations in question. Consequently, the lessons from this case are extremely important to organizations that engage in ventures involving social entrepreneurship.

(b) LOANS TO DIRECTORS AND OFFICERS. According to a 2004 study conducted by the *Chronicle of Philanthropy*, 19 states and the District of Columbia either prohibit or restrict loans from charitable organizations to their directors and officers.[126] For example, the New York Not-For Profit Corporation Act specifically prohibits loans by a nonprofit to an officer or director, with an exception for certain chartered educational institutions.[127] The *Chronicle* reported that "New York State officials had ordered the officers and directors of three dozen

126. H. Lipman and G. Williams, *Assets on Loan: Nonprofit Groups Lend Millions to Officials, Chronicle Study Finds*, CHRON. OF PHILAN., Feb. 5, 2004.

127. N. Y. Consol. L., Chapter 35, § 716.

charities to repay a total of $1.3 million in loans."[128] In California, a charity must obtain approval from the state's attorney general or a court before it can lend to an officer or director of the charity, with a special rule for certain primary residence loans.[129]

Even when no specific prohibition against such loans exists, the directors still must consider their duty of loyalty and any requirements that must be followed to validate an otherwise tainted transaction. When not prohibited, these loans are probably most justifiable when they are used to assist a new executive with the purchase of a primary residence, although even that is somewhat suspect. If a commercial mortgage lender will not make a mortgage loan to an executive because the executive's income is insufficient, for example, why should the nonprofit have any less concern about repayment? Nevertheless, the private sector has a practice of assisting executives with housing, so these loans may be justifiable on competitive grounds.

Loans to officers and directors also can create an impediment for a board, making it reluctant to fire an executive if the executive might resist repaying the loan after dismissal. More basically, an executive should not be able to hide behind unauthorized expenditures of charitable assets for personal purposes by claiming that the amounts are loans. In a number of instances, below-market loans have been used to transfer charitable assets to officers and directors in blatant contravention of state and tax rules prohibiting private benefit. Any director asked to approve such a loan should vote against it and seriously consider resigning as a director.

4.8 MOVING FROM A VOLUNTEER DIRECTOR TO A PAID EMPLOYEE

On occasion, an organization decides to hire a volunteer director as a full-time employee. At that time, the director and the organization must make the transition while steering clear of potential conflicts inherent in the process. The obvious solution is for the director/employee to resign as a director before the board even considers the matter.

Let's assume, however, that the director does not resign until he is retained as an employee, or, more likely, he continues as a director following employment. Not surprising, the particulars of state law govern the transition. As already noted, directors have a duty of loyalty that focuses on conflicts of interest, requiring the director to place the nonprofit's interests above his own when potential conflicts exist.

If a particular state has a statute that outlines the procedures to be followed when a director has a conflict of interest, the board and the interested directors

---

128. G. Williams, *New York Charity Officials Repay $1.3 Million in Loans*, CHRON. OF PHILAN. Jan, 5, 2005.

129. Cal. Corp. Code § 5236; and CALIFORNIA ATTORNEY GENERAL, ATTORNEY GENERAL'S GUIDE FOR CHARITIES at 46 (1988), available at http://caag.state.ca.us/charities/publications/gfc.pdf

should follow those procedures closely. For an example, consider Section 715 of the New York Not-For-Profit Corporation Law.

> Section 715. Interested directors and officers.
>
> (a) No contract or other transaction between a corporation and one or more of its directors or officers, or between a corporation and any other corporation, firm, association or other entity in which one or more of its directors or officers are directors or officers, or have a substantial financial interest, shall be either void or voidable for this reason alone or by reason alone that such director or directors or officer or officers are present at the meeting of the board, or of a committee thereof, which authorizes such contract or transaction, or that his or their votes are counted for such purpose:
>
> (1) If the material facts as to such director's or officer's interest in such contract or transaction and as to any such common directorship, officership or financial interest are disclosed in good faith or known to the board or committee, and the board or committee authorizes such contract or transaction by a vote sufficient for such purpose without counting the vote or votes of such interested director or officer; or
>
> (2) If the material facts as to such director's or officer's interest in such contract or transaction and as to any such common directorship, officership or financial interest are disclosed in good faith or known to the members entitled to vote thereon, if any, and such contract or transaction is authorized by vote of such members.
>
> (b) If such good faith disclosure of the material facts as to the director's or officer's interest in the contract or transaction and as to any such common directorship, officership or financial interest, is made to the directors or members, or known to the board or committee or members authorizing such contract or transaction, as provided in paragraph (a), the contract or transaction may not be avoided by the corporation for the reasons set forth in paragraph (a). If there was no such disclosure or knowledge, or if the vote of such interested director or officer was necessary for the authorization of such contract or transaction at a meeting of the board or committee at which it was authorized, the corporation may avoid the contract or transaction unless the party or parties thereto shall establish affirmatively that the contract or transaction was fair and reasonable as to the corporation at the time it was authorized by the board, a committee or the members.
>
> (c) Common or interested directors may be counted in determining the presence of a quorum at a meeting of the board or of a committee which authorizes such contract or transaction.
>
> (d) The certificate of incorporation may contain additional restrictions on contracts or transactions between a corporation and its directors or officers or other persons and may provide that contracts or transactions in violation of such restrictions shall be void or voidable.
>
> (e) Unless otherwise provided in the certificate of incorporation or the by-laws, the board shall have authority to fix the compensation of directors for services in any capacity.
>
> (f) The fixing of salaries of officers, if not done in or pursuant to the by-laws, shall require the affirmative vote of a majority of the entire board unless a higher proportion is set by the certificate of incorporation or by-laws.

Under this statute, the director/employee would not have a problem so long as the terms of the arrangement were fully disclosed in good faith to the other board members, the director/employee's vote was not the deciding one, and any other terms in the nonprofit's certificate of incorporation or bylaws regarding interested directors were satisfied. If the decision process does not comply with applicable requirements, the burden of demonstrating that the contract is fair and reasonable shifts to the director/employee. The terms of the contract should be disclosed to the other directors in written form and the decision should be recorded in the minutes.

Now assume that state law does not provide the safe harbor that New York law does. In all likelihood, the burden of demonstrating that the contract is fair rests with the director/employee. Obviously, there will be some uncertainty, which can be significantly reduced if the following steps are taken:

- Full disclosure of the contract terms is made in writing to the other directors.
- The vote is recorded in the minutes.
- The director/employee does not take part in the vote.
- The presence of the director/employee is not required for a quorum.
- The director/employee is not in the room when the matter is discussed (except to respond to questions) or when the vote is taken.
- The parties obtain data regarding compensation paid by other organizations in comparable situations.
- If the compensation arrangement is the result of a recommendation from an outside consulting firm, the director/employee should not be involved in the process of selecting that firm.
- Both the nonprofit and the director/employee have independent counsel.
- The director/employee does not sit on any boards affiliated with the other directors.

Must all of these requirements be satisfied to avoid trouble? Probably not, but that depends on the facts and circumstances. For example, if the compensation of the director/employee is $25,000 per year, separate legal counsel probably is not necessary. But keeping with the general philosophy evidenced throughout this *Guide,* these procedures will both keep people out of legal trouble and produce sound decisions on the part of the board.

To emphasize the point, consider the problems facing Richard Grasso and the New York Stock Exchange. One of the New York Attorney General's major objections to the arrangement is that Mr. Grasso sat on the board of a corporation whose chairman of the board headed the NYSE compensation committee, [130]

130. Press Release, "New York Attorney General, Former NYSE Chief Sued Over Excessive Pay Package" (May 24, 2004); and Summons at ¶¶ 25-31, People of the State of New York v. Grasso, Langone, and NYSE (N.Y. Sup. Ct. May 23, 2004).

although that board member has vigorously denied any wrongdoing.[131] Only time will tell whether that becomes a problem for Mr. Grasso, but people certainly have focused on the potential for corporate "back-scratching." Just to be clear, even when state law does provide a safe harbor like the one in the New York statute, the nonprofit should view the best practices steps.

The selection of outside compensation consultants is an important component in any compensation process. When the executive director selects the compensation consultants and those consultants make a presentation to the board about the executive director's compensation package, there will be questions as to whether there was good faith disclosure. Is the consultant providing an objective assessment or one that makes the case for compensating the person who retained the consultant? In the wake of the Sarbanes-Oxley Act of 2002,[132] NYSE rules now require that executive compensation for NYSE-listed companies be determined by an independent committee that controls the retention of compensation consultants involved in the process.[133] Nonprofit boards should consider the NYSE rule as a best practice.

4.9 RELIEF FOR DIRECTORS AND OFFICERS

In the mid-1980s director and officer insurance coverage premiums skyrocketed. Many organizations were unable to afford the rates, and some insurance companies refused even to write coverage.[134] Both the states and Congress recognized that this posed a problem for volunteer directors and officers as well as other volunteers. This resulted in a number of legislative changes.

(a) STATE RELIEF. Thirty-seven state[135] legislatures have enacted special provisions that relieve nonprofit directors from liability for their decisions.[136] You have already had a preview of these statutes in the section of this chapter describing director duties and the standards for judging the exercise of those duties. Many liability shields protect nonprofit directors from monetary liability if their behavior is not criminal, grossly negligent, or wantonly reckless. These shields are available for breaches of the duty of care but not the duty of loyalty.[137] They often explicitly require that the director have acted in good faith. Some courts have woven the duty of loyalty and good faith together, holding that actions taken in bad faith constitute a breach of the duty of loyalty. In some cases, only uncompensated directors can avail themselves of this protection.[138]

---

131. C. Johnson, *Spitzer Suit Includes Ex-NYSE Compensation Chairman*, WASH. POST, Nov. 3, 2004.
132. Pub. L. 107-204, 116 Stat. 745 (2002).
133. NYSE, LISTED COMPANY MANUAL, Rule 303A.05, Compensation Committee (Nov. 3, 2004).
134. H. REP. NO. 105-101, Part 1 (1997).
135. *See* FREMONT-SMITH, *supra* note 5, at 227–28.
136. *See, e.g.*, N.Y. Consol. L., Chapter 35, § 720-a. This provision is limited to uncompensated directors of Section 501(c)(3) organizations. It was enacted into law in 1986.
137. *See* RMNCA Alternative § 8.30. *See also* Del. Code, Title 8, Chapter 1, § 102(7), *infra* note 157.
138. Illinois General Not For Profit Corporation Act of 1986, Chapter 805, § 108.70(a).

As a practical matter, these shields provide volunteer directors of nonprofit organizations with extraordinary protection against monetary liability for decisions that they make in their capacity as directors— too much protection, one can easily argue. The shields make it unlikely, as a practical matter, that a director who undertook only a cursory review of financial statements or a consultant's report will be held monetarily accountable for a bad decision. Nevertheless, a director who wants to be involved with a nonprofit organization should recognize that these shields do not protect him against removal as a director, injunctive relief, or prohibition from serving on other nonprofit boards. Nor will a shield against monetary liability protect a director against public humiliation or embarrassment. Moreover, when the director holds his position because he is a paid employee of another organization (e.g., a public employee or elected official who is appointed to a board), a shield against monetary liability will not protect the director from possible loss of his primary position through termination or public recall. Quite apart from a determination of actual liability for damages, it can cost a great deal of money to successfully invoke a shield against monetary liability.

Again, for clarity's sake, it is important to separate duty from liability. What is often difficult to reconcile is a finding that a director breached his duty but is shielded from monetary liability for that breach. This is admittedly an unsatisfactory result if the objective is to punish or deter less than exemplary behavior, yet the legislatures of many states have made the decision that it is better to have people volunteer without risk of monetary exposure for doing a mediocre job than to have nobody doing a superlative job. This is arguably the wrong balance to strike, but many state regimes clearly strike it.

Many states have separately enacted statutes permitting nonprofit organizations to indemnify officers and directors against certain liabilities and to reimburse them for legal and other litigation expenses.[139] Anyone relying on indemnification authorized under statute must review the specific statute because the costs that can be indemnified vary widely among the states. Some states limit indemnification to attorney's fees and court costs while other states include settlement payments. Several states permit a director to be indemnified for the cost of a judgment against the director.

In practice, directors and officers often find the right to indemnification to be hollow protection. First and most important, indemnification provides no protection when the organization has insufficient assets. Second, state statutes rarely mandate indemnification but permit nonprofits to provide it. These statutes can limit director or officer indemnification once the person's conduct rises to a certain level. For example, several states require the director to successfully defend his conduct before attorney's fees can be reimbursed. This can effectively eliminate the right to indemnification. Third, some indemnification provisions provide

---

139. Illinois General Not For Profit Corporation Act of 1986, Chapter 805, § 108.75.

indemnification to directors and officers but permit the board to decide after the fact whether indemnification will be awarded. At that time, the director or officer seeking indemnification may be the scapegoat or a pariah. Fourth—and finally—some states require any indemnification to be approved by a court or a regulator. Being entitled to indemnification is never undesirable, but directors and officers should not count on it for true protection. We consider indemnification in greater detail as part of Chapter 12. The better form of protection is a directors' and officers' insurance policy, something we also consider in Chapter 12.

(b) FEDERAL RELIEF UNDER THE VOLUNTEER PROTECTION ACT. In 1997, Congress enacted the Volunteer Protection Act[140] to provide protection to volunteers including unpaid directors and officers of nonprofits. Congress found that:

> Volunteer service has become a high risk venture. Our "sue happy" legal culture has ensnared those selfless individuals who help worthy organizations and institutions through volunteer service. The proliferation of these types of lawsuits is proof that no good deed goes unpunished.
>
> The litigation craze is hurting the spirit of volunteerism that is an integral part of U.S. society. From school chaperones to Girl Scout and Boy Scout troop leaders to Big Brothers and Big Sisters, volunteers perform valuable services. Rather than thanking these volunteers, our current legal system allows them to be dragged into court and subjected to needless and unfair lawsuits. In most instances, the volunteer is ultimately found not liable, but the potential for unwarranted lawsuits creates an atmosphere in which too many people are pointing fingers and too few remain willing to offer a helping hand. The need for relief from these debilitating lawsuits has increased over the last two decades. Until the mid-1980s, the number of lawsuits filed against volunteers could have been counted on one hand although the law permitted such suits. Volunteers had little reason to worry about personal liability.

The Volunteer Protection Act provides that a volunteer of a nonprofit organization or government entity is generally relieved of liability for harm caused if:

- The volunteer was acting within the scope of assigned responsibilities.[141]
- The volunteer was properly licensed, certified, or authorized by the state in which the harm occurred if such authorization is required.[142]
- The harm was not caused by willful or criminal misconduct, gross negligence, reckless misconduct, or a conscious, flagrant indifference to the rights or safety of the individual harmed by the volunteer.[143]
- The harm was not caused by the volunteer operating a motor vehicle, vessel, aircraft, or other vehicle for which the state requires the owner or operator to possess an operator's license or maintain insurance.[144]

---

140. Pub. L. 105-19, as codified at 42 U.S.C. Chapter 139.
141. 42 U.S.C. 14503(a)(1).
142. 42 U.S.C. 14503(a)(2).
143. 42 U.S.C. 14503(a)(3).
144. 42 U.S.C. 14503(a)(4).

The Volunteer Protection Act defines *nonprofit* as including Section 501(c)(3) organizations and any nonprofit organized and conducted for public benefit and operated primarily for civic, educational, religious, welfare, or health purposes.[145] The act's history indicates that this definition includes trade and professional associations.[146] Under the act, a volunteer can receive reasonable reimbursement or allowance for expenses actually incurred without losing the status as a volunteer.[147] The act also contemplates honorariums to the extent the awards do not exceed $500 per year.[148]

The scope of the Volunteer Protection Act is not entirely clear. Litigation will inevitably be necessary to determine its outer limits. Most important for this chapter, the law explicitly states that it does not affect any civil action brought by the nonprofit itself or by a government entity against any volunteer of such organization or entity.[149] It also does not affect the liability of any nonprofit organization or government entity with respect to harm caused by a volunteer, making general liability and other insurance coverages a necessity.[150] Finally, the act permits states to opt out of it to the extent that the lawsuit involves citizens of that same state.[151] New Hampshire appears to be the only state to have opted out to date.[152]

The Volunteer Protection Act preempts state law to the extent that it provides more protection to volunteers than provided under a particular state's law,[153] but this is a bit misleading to the extent that the focus is on limiting liability. The act provides that state laws can condition the limitation of liability upon the adoption of risk management procedures, volunteer training, and provision of a source for economic recovery such as insurance without treating these items as state limitations on the act.[154] Consequently, to fully understand the scope of the Volunteer Protection Act as it relates to a nonprofit operating in a particular state, it is necessary to review the laws of the particular state.

Although the Volunteer Protection Act is probably of some assistance to volunteers who cause physical injury to third parties (e.g., the ski-patrol volunteer who further harms an injured skier while providing medical assistance), any protection that it provides to directors who neglect their duties to the nonprofit is largely illusory. After all, the act does not bar the organization itself or a state attorney general from bringing an action against the director.[155]

---

145. 42 U.S.C. 14505(4).
146. H. Rep. No. 105-101 (1997).
147. 42 U.S.C. 14505(6)(A).
148. 42 U.S.C. 14505(6).
149. 42 U.S.C. 14503(b).
150. 42 U.S.C. 14503(c).
151. 42 U.S.C. 14502(b).
152. 1998 NH ALS 129. See S. Gravely and E. Whaley, *A Patchwork of Protection: Sources of Volunteer Immunity for Medical & Public Health Volunteers*, Health Law. Wkly, Apr. 8, 2005.
153. 42 U.S.C. 14502(a).
154. 42 U.S.C. 14503(d).
155. 42 U.S.C. 14503(b).

Nevertheless, there may be instances in which the act provides protection to volunteers acting in their capacity as nonprofit directors. One court has held that the executive director of a nonprofit youth center could not recover unpaid wages under the Fair Labor Standards from the volunteer directors because the Volunteer Protection Act served as a shield to liability.[156] The case specifically holds that the act applies to claims rooted in contract, not just tort law. Moreover, the court also held that the act applies to liability under federal and individual state law. Although none of those directors likely argued with the result, it is questionable whether the court even needed to raise the Volunteer Protection Act. It is hornbook corporate law that the directors of a corporation are not liable for its obligations (unless there is a statute that specifically imposes liability on the directors).

4.10 GOOD FAITH: A STORM ON THE HORIZON FOR NONPROFIT DIRECTORS

In most speeches and articles discussing the liability of nonprofit directors, the speaker or the author points to liability shields under many nonprofit corporate statutes, concluding that there is little risk that liability will ever be imposed because of evidentiary burdens highly favorable to directors. By and large, that is a reasonable conclusion, particularly given the seeming reluctance of state attorneys general to seek monetary recompense from directors. Nevertheless, directors should not be lulled into a false sense of security. State regulators are well aware that although not stealing money, many volunteer directors regularly miss board meetings, fail to give financial statements even a cursory review, and do not regularly review reports prepared for directors. These regulators do not like it, particularly when this sort of inattention leads to losses through embezzlement and overreaching by employees and other insiders who are more attentive to their own needs than those of the nonprofit.

Unfortunately for errant directors, the broad protection ostensibly provided by existing liability shields may be eroding. Over the last several years in extreme circumstances, the Delaware courts, regarded as the judicial bell cows of the corporate governance world, have been willing to hold directors who failed to review financial statements or basic documents and reports when making decisions liable for breach of their duties of care. The Delaware statute conditions availability of its liability shield on good faith conduct.[157] The "good faith" requirement has permitted the Delaware courts to deny protection from the

---

156. Armendarez v. Glendale Youth Center, Inc., 256 F.Supp.2d 1136 (D.C. AZ 2003).

157. Del. Stat,. Title 8, Chapter 1, § 102(b)(7), provides as follows:

> A provision eliminating or limiting the personal liability of a director to the corporation or its stockholders for monetary damages for breach of fiduciary duty as a director, provided that such provision shall not eliminate or limit the liability of a director: (i) For any breach of the director's duty of loyalty to the corporation or its stockholders; (ii) *for acts or omissions not in good faith or which involve intentional misconduct or a knowing violation of law*; (iii) under § 174 of this title; or (iv) for

shield despite the absence of criminal or reckless conduct.[158] The recent cases may have arisen in a business context, but the statutory language at issue is equally applicable to Delaware nonprofit corporations. Moreover, several states have based their liability shields on similar language.[159] Even when a liability shield does not expressly refer to "good faith" conduct,[160] a court certainly could read such a requirement into the statute.

> any transaction from which the director derived an improper personal benefit. No such provision shall eliminate or limit the liability of a director for any act or omission occurring prior to the date when such provision becomes effective. All references in this paragraph to a director shall also be deemed to refer (x) to a member of the governing body of a corporation which is not authorized to issue capital stock, and (y) to such other person or persons, if any, who, pursuant to a provision of the certificate of incorporation in accordance with §141(a) of this title, exercise or perform any of the powers or duties otherwise conferred or imposed upon the board of directors by this title. [emphasis added]
>
> The shield is dependent upon the incorporators (or an amendment to existing articles) including a provision containing the shield in the nonprofit's articles of incorporation.

---

158. *In re* Emerging Communications Shareholders Litig. (June 4, 2004); *In re* The Walt Disney Company Derivative Litig., 825 A.2d 275 (Del. Ch. 2003); *In re* Caremark Int'l, 698 A.2d 959, 967 (Del. Ch. 1996); and Smith v. Van Gorkom, 488 A.2d 858, 872-73 (Del. 1985). The Delaware Chancery Court subsequently ruled that the Disney directors had not violated their duties, although the court did note that some of the behavior exhibited by certain directors was less than exemplary. See *In re* The Walt Disney Company Derivative Litig., Opinion and Order dated (Aug. 9, 2005). While there has been some debate as to whether this decision represents a return to more conservative views regarding director duties, those who would dismiss the line of cases finding liability would be well advised to focus on Judge Chandler's preface to his opinion, where he writes:

    > Recognizing the protean nature of ideal corporate governance practices, particularly over an era that has included the Enron and WorldCom debacles, and the resulting legislative focus on corporate governance, it is perhaps worth pointing out that the actions (and the failures to act) of the Disney board that gave rise to this lawsuit took place ten years ago, and that applying 21st century notions of best practices in analyzing whether these decisions were actionable would be misplaced.

    For similar cases outside of Delaware, see *In re* Abbott Laboratories Derivative Shareholders Litig., 325 F.3d 795 (7th Cir. 2003); and Pereira v. Cogan, 294 B.R. 449, 462 (S.D.N.Y 2003).
159. *See, e.g.,* Tex. Stat., Chapter 22, § 22.221(b), providing as follows:

    > A director is not liable to the corporation, a member, or another person for an action taken or not taken as a director if the director acted in compliance with this section. A person seeking to establish liability of a director must prove that the director did not act:
    >
    > (1) in good faith;
    >
    > (2) with ordinary care; and
    >
    > (3) in a manner the director reasonably believed to be in the best interest of the corporation.

    Florida State Chapter 617, Section 617.0830 provides that a director shall perform assigned duties in good faith, among other things, and then shields a director who complies with the statutory requirements. Section 65.357 of Chapter 85 of the Oregon Revised Statutes contains similar (but not identical) language, as does Section 6C of Chapter 180 of the General Laws of Massachusetts. Section 15A:6-14 of Title 15A of the New Jersey Permanent Statutes adopts an approach similar to that adopted by Section 102(b)(7) of the Delaware Statutes.
160. For example, Section 108.70 of the Illinois Not For Profit Corporation Act of 1986, provides as follows:

    > Limited Liability of directors, officers and persons who serve without compensation.
    >
    > (a) No director or officer serving without compensation, other than reimbursement for actual expenses, of a corporation organized under this Act or any predecessor Act and exempt, or qualified for exemption, from taxation pursuant to Section 501(c) of the Internal Revenue Code of 1986, as amended, shall be liable, and no cause of action may be brought, for damages resulting from the exercise of judgment or discretion in connection with the duties or responsibilities of such director or officer unless the act or omission involved willful or wanton conduct.

While no one can predict the future, it is a good bet that sometime in the next five years, an attorney general facing a set of facts that is particularly disturbing will decide to use the Delaware case law to make an example of a group of nonprofit directors whose inattention has resulted in a significant and highly public loss.[161] Instead of simply asking for resignations, this attorney general may seek monetary recovery from these volunteer directors, arguing that the state's liability shield is inapplicable because the directors did not act in good faith.

The recurring response by the nonprofit community to any effort to increase director responsibility through threat of monetary liability has been to argue that this would reduce the number of volunteers. That is also essentially why liability shields for directors of business corporations were enacted. The Delaware courts are still willing to accept business judgment that turns out to be wrong, but these courts are starting to refuse protection to directors who are passive or inactive: directors who fail to exercise business judgment. Does this mean that the standard has changed? According to E. Norman Veasey, the former Chief Justice of the Delaware Supreme Court, not really.[162] He approvingly quotes[163] a speech by Vice Chancellor Strine of the Delaware Court of Chancery:

> I won't pretend that directors don't have reason to be concerned . . . but the legal reality today is identical to the legal reality a year ago: Independent directors who apply themselves to their duties in good faith have a trivial risk of legal liability. Let me repeat that: If you do your job as a director with integrity and attentiveness, your risk of damages liability is minuscule.

In others, beware, but do not be afraid.

4.11 AVOIDING TROUBLE AS A DIRECTOR

The following are some basic steps you can take as a director as part of an overall effort to discharge your duties to the nonprofit:

- Attend board meetings.
- Follow the procedures outlined in the articles of incorporation and bylaws.
- Review meeting minutes and committee reports.

---

161. *See* Walt Disney Company Derivative Litig. (2005), *supra* note 158. As noted, Judge Chandler refused to find liability in this case, but clearly indicated that the facts in *Disney* arose before the recent corporate governance movement, at least suggesting that equivalent behavior might not escape monetary punishment next time.

162. E. N. Veasey, *A Perspective on Liability Risks to Directors in Light of Current Events*, INSIGHTS, Feb. 2005. Chief Justice Veasey, in acknowledging the recent cases, notes that they do pose issues for directors, but he believes that these cases must be evaluated in the context of their specific facts. He specifically states,

> The concept of good faith has been in our jurisprudence and statutory law for a long time. It works as part of the articulation of the business judgment rule that applies to the directors' decisionmaking process and it is part of the directors' statutory oversight responsibility. This was true well before *Caremark* and *Disney*.

163. *Id.*

- Promptly disclose any conflict(s) of interest between you and the organization.
- Ask that experts be retained when the board is required to make a decision that requires information and judgment that is outside the board's experience and expertise.
- Review the financial statements.
- Review the IRS Form 990 (tax return).
- Insist on annual budgets, internal accounting systems, and frequent financial reports.
- Review the audit reports and management letters prepared by the independent auditors.
- Foster an atmosphere that encourages employees to come forward with problems.
- Insist on compliance with all applicable laws, even though this may cost the organization funds that otherwise could go to program-related activities.
- Be leery of the one-man show.

4.12 AVOIDING TROUBLE AS AN OFFICER

The following are some basic steps you can take as an officer as part of an overall effort to discharge your duties to the nonprofit:

- Do not exceed your authority.
- Make sure the description of your duties in the bylaws or your employment contract is consistent with what you actually are expected to do on a day-to-day basis.
- Keep the board of directors informed.
- Respect the board of directors.
- If problems arise, inform the directors. We (as a society) have had considerable experience with cover-ups; they generally do not work and lead to more trouble.
- Adhere to mandated procedures and policies.
- When you do not have the expertise, retain an expert.
- Promptly disclose any conflicts of interest between you and the nonprofit.

4.13 THE LITMUS TEST FOR GOOD CONDUCT

What amazes many lawyers who advise nonprofit organizations is what happens to the judgment of businesspeople once they become volunteer directors and officers. Their hard-hitting judgment flies right out the window, and they do things that they would never do in their own business or professional lives. For example, most businesspeople complain about taxes, but their businesses comply with sales and use tax requirements. Once they are on a nonprofit board, these same people often try to play fast and loose with the tax authorities to generate some additional cash for the organization, forgetting that in some states the directors and officers can be held liable for the organization's unpaid taxes. Much more time could be spent discussing the duties of a nonprofit director or officer. But when push comes to shove, the best and most economical advice is for people to keep their common sense when they walk into the nonprofit boardroom and stay engaged.

CHAPTER 5

FINANCIAL STATEMENTS, INTERNAL CONTROLS, AND SARBANES-OXLEY

A truth that's told with bad intent
Beats all the lies you can invent

WILLIAM BLAKE[1]

1. *Auguries of Innocence,* in ENGLISH POETRY II: FROM COLLINS TO FITZGERALD (Harvard Classics 1909–14).

The executive director of a graduate-level nonprofit management program recently indicated that his program did not emphasize financial statements or accounting systems. This director reaffirmed the common impression that consumer sovereignty runs all too rampant in higher education. While obviously taking the course of least resistance, this director is not doing his students a favor by giving them what they want rather than what they need. The director indicated that the students would prefer another course in fundraising. That is fine, but here are just a few questions for the students and the boards they will eventually serve:

- How will you be able to make a case that you need additional funding if you cannot show donors and grant makers why your organization's current resources are insufficient?
- Once you have raised the money, how will you make sure that an unscrupulous employee does not use your ignorance of internal controls to steal money from the organization?
- How will you monitor whether costs are being contained without budgets and analysis of budget variances?
- How will you respond to a donor who refuses to continue contributing to your organization because a similar organization has lower overhead costs?
- How will you respond to regulators who are asking for increasingly more financial information?
- How will you develop planned giving programs if you do not understand basic finance and tax concepts?
- How will you develop performance measurements that show how your organization is converting its resources into accomplishments?

- How will you know whether your organization is heading toward a financial crisis?
- How will you know what resources you can use for unrestricted purposes?

Asking for more resources is inappropriate when a nonprofit cannot responsibly manage what it already has. Nobody can manage anything without the ability to read financial statements or rely on financial controls to assure that the output from the accounting system is complete and accurate.

This *Guide* does not constitute a course in financial accounting. In fact, it assumes that you can already read basic financial statements. Your instincts will serve you well even if you are not familiar with financial statements; they are easier than the number-phobic make them out to be. This chapter will sensitize you to some of the differences between financial accounting for business entities and nonprofits. There are important differences, and you need to understand how they affect the interpretation of nonprofit financial statements.

We also examine internal controls and fraud prevention. As used here, internal controls include all policies and procedures used to protect assets, ensure reliable information and reports, promote efficient operations, and urge adherence to company policies. Although MBA programs generally include at least one course on financial accounting, many of these programs do not even touch on the design of accounting systems. This is too bad, because a well-designed accounting system is an important weapon in any organization's arsenal against insider and third-party fraud. Unfortunately, the newspapers are filled with cases in which employees have stolen large sums of money from nonprofits with marquee names. This is a recurring problem that you, as a director or officer, must be willing to focus on even if someone else actually designs the system of financial controls. This is one of the reasons that independent auditors submit a management letter to the board each year with their audit report.

Theft at Chicago Public Television Station: Internal Controls Matter

* * *

An employee of Chicago Public Television station WTTW (Channel 11) stole more than $550,000 from the station over a period of three and one-half years.[2] The employee was sentenced to a prison term of four and one-half years.[3]

According to newspaper accounts, the employee was the station's accounts payable manager.[4] She submitted checks for management approval, convincing management that

---

2. S. Esposito, *Ex-Channel 11 Employee Admits Theft from Station*, Chicago Sun-Times, July 28, 2004.
3. *Id.*
4. Associated Press, *Ex-PBS Employee Gets Prison for Theft*, Aug. 20, 2004.

the amounts were owed.[5] The checks were generated by computer, apparently permitting the employee to somehow substitute her name for the vendor's name. The employee then deposited the checks to her account. After the theft was discovered, WTTW retained PricewaterhouseCoopers to conduct a forensic audit to determine the extent of the thefts and presumably to make recommendations on how to close holes in the accounting system.

Many Chicago-area contributors were probably distressed to learn of this problem because the station runs rather lengthy on-air fundraising campaigns several times a year. Given the apparent need for funding, those contributors were probably surprised to learn that such a large theft went unnoticed for so long. Although the facts are still not entirely clear, it appears that the theft was discovered after the employee made a mistake while perpetrating the scheme: The employee apparently substituted her name on a check for a payment that was actually owed.[6] The theft was discovered after she retired.[7] One can only wonder how long the scheme would have continued undetected had the employee not made a mistake or retired.

An executive from the station who was asked about the matter described the station's staff as "closely knit" and the theft as a "betrayal."[8] She indicated that this experience had been emotionally difficult for everyone at the station. The employee had been employed by the station for 30 years.[9] These comments are not at all surprising in the case of employee thefts. Thefts are often perpetrated by long-time, trusted employees. That is one of the reasons the thefts go undetected for so long.

* * *

5.1 WHERE ACCOUNTING RULES COME FROM

The accounting rules applicable to nonprofit organizations are promulgated by the Financial Accounting Standards Board (FASB), the same organization that sets the accounting standards applicable to business entities. The primary enforcement mechanism is the audit function. A certified public accountant can render an unqualified or "clean" opinion with respect to audited financial statements only if the statements were prepared in accordance with generally accepted accounting principles (GAAP).

With the exception of individual state statutes and requirements under federal grant programs,[10] no general requirement mandates audited financial statements for all charitable organizations. Yet, demands from lenders, grant makers, and donors often force a nonprofit with significant revenues, assets, or activities to make audited financial statements available. If the nonprofit receives federal money, it also may be required to undergo audits. This is also true if a nonprofit

5. S. Esposito, *supra* note 2.
6. *Id.*
7. *Id.*
8. *Id.* Confirmed by a telephone conversation with a WTTW station executive.
9. R. Feder, *Channel 11 Fugitive Surrenders to Police*, CHICAGO SUN-TIMES, Jan. 23, 2004.
10. As you will see in Chapter 9, many states regulate charitable solicitation. More than a few states require audits when contributions or assets exceed certain dollar thresholds. There is a trend toward expanding mandatory audit requirements.

wants to participate in certain fundraising campaigns, such as the Combined Federal Campaign sponsored by the federal government to coordinate the workplace charitable solicitation of federal employees,[11] or wants to receive the seal of approval from some private concerns that evaluate charities.

Consider yourself fortunate. Thirty years ago, you would have had far greater difficulty reading nonprofit financial statements because they were prepared using the arcane principles of fund accounting. Fortunately, the accounting profession rejected fund accounting, and nonprofit financial statements now look very similar to those prepared for business entities. The one obvious difference is that the statement of financial position for a nonprofit entity does not show an equity balance because there are no equityholders. Instead, this statement presents a balance for net assets.

5.2 THE THREE NONPROFIT FINANCIAL STATEMENTS

Nonprofit organizations prepare three financial statements: (1) the statement of financial position (the balance sheet), (2) the statement of activities (the income statement), and (3) the statement of cash flows.[12] As is true of the financial statements for business entities, nonprofit financial statements also include footnotes that explain accounting practices and disclose important supplemental information. The footnotes should not be ignored when reading financial statements. In fact, the footnotes often contain the most important disclosures, including discussion of lawsuits and other contingent liabilities.

To help you learn how to read the financial statements for nonprofits, we examine the financial statements for a hypothetical nonprofit, Community Help. This particular nonprofit provides relief services by taking in money from a variety of sources and disbursing it to people in need of assistance. These disbursements do not have a predictable flow, requiring this organization to maintain a fairly high degree of liquidity.

(a) STATEMENT OF FINANCIAL POSITION. The *statement of financial position* is equivalent to a business organization's balance sheet; it provides relevant information about the nonprofit's assets, liabilities, and net assets at a particular moment in time. The statement of financial position focuses on net assets rather than shareholder equity, as explained earlier. Quite simply, more assets are better than fewer assets, and fewer liabilities are better than more liabilities.

All financial statements are rooted in *historical dollar values.* Although the cash balance reflects the value of cash as of the date of the statements and

---

11. 15 C.F.R. 950.203(a). Part 950 of Title 15 to the Code of Federal Regulations sets out the rules that govern all aspects of the Combined Federal Campaign. *See also* Exec. Order No. 12404, 3 C.F.R. (1983); and Exec. Order No. 12353, 3 C.F.R. (1982).

12. Financial Statements of Not-for-Profit Organizations, Statement of Fin. Accounting Standards No. 117, ¶ 6 (Fin. Accounting Standards Bd. 1982).

marketable securities are valued at their readily ascertainable value,[13] the balances for inventories[14] and buildings may bear little relation to their current value. Moreover, the balance sheet for a going concern does not adequately reflect the value of work-force-in-place, donor mailing lists, and other intangible assets. In reviewing financial statements, you will want to focus on the due dates for the liabilities. The footnotes accompanying the financial statements can be particularly helpful on that account.

Nonprofit financial statements add a third dimension to the analysis, making them different from more conventional business financial statements. You must focus not only on the relationship between assets and liabilities (reading down the statement) but also on the restrictions on those assets (reading across the statement).

The statement of financial position categorizes assets into the following three categories: (1) unrestricted, (2) temporarily restricted, and (3) permanently restricted. This focus on restrictions is not some irrelevant accounting convention but reflects the legal restrictions on the entity's assets. *Unrestricted net assets* represent net assets that are neither permanently restricted nor temporarily restricted by donor-imposed stipulations. As this definition suggests, the board can use unrestricted assets as it likes.

Temporarily restricted assets are those assets attributable to:

- Contributions and other inflows of assets whose use by the organization is limited by donor-imposed stipulations that either expire by passage of time or can be fulfilled and removed by actions of the organization pursuant to those stipulations.
- Other asset enhancements and diminishments subject to the same kinds of stipulations.
- Reclassifications to (or from) other classes of net assets as a consequence of donor-imposed stipulations, their expiration by passage of time, or their fulfillment and removal by actions of the organization pursuant to those stipulations.[15]

Probably the best example of a temporarily restricted asset is a pledge that will be satisfied over multiple periods.[16] Another example is a $100,000 fund whose income must be reinvested until the fund's value equals $200,000, at which time the $200,000 will be used to fund a special performance.

---

13. ACCOUNTING FOR CERTAIN INVESTMENTS HELD BY NOT-FOR-PROFIT ORGANIZATIONS, Statement of Fin. Accounting Standards No. 124, ¶ 7 (Fin. Accounting Standards Bd. 1995). Investments in affiliated entities are accounted for differently. See REPORTING OF RELATED ENTITIES BY NOT-FOR-PROFIT ORGANIZATIONS, Statement of Position 94-3 (Am. Inst. of Certified Pub. Accountants 1987).
14. Inventories are supposed to be valued at lower of cost or market, but determining the market value of tangible personal property can be difficult and subjective, particularly if the property is not a readily marketable commodity.
15. ACCOUNTING FOR CONTRIBUTIONS RECEIVED AND CONTRIBUTIONS MADE, Statement of Fin. Accounting Standards No. 116, Appendix D, (Fin. Accounting Standards Bd. 1993).
16. *Id.*

Permanently restricted assets are those assets attributable to:

- Contributions and other inflows of assets whose use by the organization is limited by donor-imposed stipulations that neither expire by passage of time nor can be fulfilled or otherwise removed by actions of the organization.
- Other asset enhancements and diminishments subject to the same kinds of stipulations.
- Reclassifications from (or to) other classes of net assets as a consequence of donor-imposed stipulations.[17]

If a donor contributed $1 million to a charity and provided that the principal was to be invested and held in perpetuity but the income was to be made available annually to the charity, the $1 million would be classified as permanently restricted. By contrast, if by resolution, the board of directors of the charity decided to treat a pool of unrestricted assets as an endowment, agreeing that only income from the pool could be spent, this board-designated endowment would nevertheless be classified as unrestricted because the board can always alter its decision.

These examples are relatively straightforward, but the distinction between unrestricted, temporarily restricted, and permanently restricted assets can become quite complex. For example, when restricted assets are used to finance capital expenditures, the organization might report the release of the restrictions as the newly-acquired asset is depreciated or when it is placed in service.[18]

Looking at Exhibit 5.1 for the statement of financial position for Community Help, you should notice that Community Help has $75 million dollars in cash and equivalents. Has the board or a donor committed those assets to long-term plans? Even if they are uncommitted, would Community Help's board want to liquidate those assets to fund current operations? These are questions that should be of concern to the board, particularly if the quality of the receivables has deteriorated or future events could result in a sharp decline in contributions.

Community Help is flush with net assets, a significant portion of which is unrestricted. However, that does not mean that it is financially healthy. Although the organization has more than $57 million in cash, Community Help also has $109 million in accounts payable and another $41 million in long-term debt that will come due within the next year.

17. *Id.*
18. AICPA, Audit and Accounting Guide for Not-for-Profit Organizations, § 9.08 (2001).

STATEMENT OF FINANCIAL POSITION
AS OF DECEMBER 31, 20X5 (IN THOUSANDS)

	Unrestricted	Temporarily	Permanent	20X5	20X4
Current Assets					
Cash and Cash Equivalents	$ 57,275	$ 17,642	$ 927	$ 75,844	$ 71,509
Investment (Note 10)	$ 119,053	$ 6,892	$ 7,801	$ 133,746	$ 109,084
Receivables (Net of $24,471 B/D Allow.)					
Trade	$ 93,864	$ 7,176	$ 0	$ 101,040	$ 110,093
Contributions, Current (Note 4)	$ 25,039	$ 61,081	$ 17	$ 86,137	$ 69,824
Other	$ 0	$ 0	$ 3,169	$ 3,169	$ 2,491
Inventories (Net Of $6,631 for Obsolescen	$ 60,073	$ 307	$ 0	$ 60,380	$ 47,572
Other Assets	$ 6,698	$ 137	$ 563	$ 7,398	$ 7,016
TOTAL CURRENT ASSETS	$ 362,002	$ 93,235	$ 12,477	$ 467,714	$ 417,589
Investments (Note 8)	$ 338,874	$ 12,323	$126,295	$ 477,492	$ 416,159
Contributions Receivable (Note 4)	$ 1,426	$ 8,862	$ 958	$ 11,246	$ 8,300
Prepaid Pension (Note 12)	$ 14,977	$ 0	$ 0	$ 14,977	$ 16,989
Land, Building, & Equip, Net (Note 5)	$ 318,491	$ 0	$ 0	$ 318,491	$ 304,619
Other Assets	$ 19,330	$ 208	$ 1,071	$ 20,609	$ 7,111
TOTAL ASSETS	$1,055,100	$114,628	$140,801	$1,310,529	$1,170,767
Current Liabilities					
Accounts Payable and Accrued Expenses	$ 109,538	$ 1,506	$ 0	$ 111,044	$ 89,161
Current Portion of Long-Term Debt	$ 41,390	$ 0	$ 0	$ 41,390	$ 21,847
Postretirement Benefits (Note 13)	$ 6,034	$ 0	$ 0	$ 6,034	$ 5,458
Other Liabilities	$ 8,378	$ 641	$ 1,987	$ 11,006	$ 8,780
TOTAL CURRENT LIABILITIES	$ 165,340	$ 2,147	$ 1,987	$ 169,474	$ 125,246

EXHIBIT 5.1 STATEMENT OF FINANCIAL POSITION FOR COMMUNITY HELP

Statement of Financial Position
As of December 31, 20X5 (In Thousands)

	Unrestricted	Temporarily	Permanent	20X5	20X4
Long-Term Debt (Note 6 and 7)	$ 90,053	$ 0	$ 0	$ 90,053	$ 98,185
Postretirement Benefits (Note 13)	$ 45,048	$ 0	$ 0	$ 45,048	$ 43,112
Other Liabilities	$ 33,647	$ 276	$ 15	$ 33,938	$ 29,005
TOTAL LIABILITIES	$ 334,088	$ 2,423	$ 2,002	$ 338,513	$ 295,548
NET ASSETS (Notes 3, 8, 9, and 11)	$ 721,012	$112,205	$138,799	$ 972,016	$ 875,219

Commitments and Contingencies (Notes 6, 7, 12, 13, & 14)

SUBJECT TO ROUNDING ERRORS

Exhibit 5.1 Statement of Financial Position for Community Help *(Continued)*

If you were a director or officer of Community Help, you should focus on the quality of its $94 million in unrestricted trade receivables and $25 million in unrestricted pledges. Community Help also has another $60 million in inventories, but those inventories will not generate cash if Community Help uses them to support free services.

$57 Million in Cash

Community Help has $57 million in cash—not a small sum. If the organization has a fairly predictable stream of contributions, its directors should not be too worried about meeting the payables and current portion of the long-term debt, particularly with $119 million in unrestricted current investments. Nevertheless, the board should focus on the apparent gap between cash and current liabilities. This gap could be a problem if Community Help is forced to liquidate long-term investments that are otherwise earmarked for new programs as opposed to covering the gap with receivables that represent unrestricted charitable pledges.

In short, as a director or officer, you should consider the current portion of the organization's liabilities and how the organization will repay them. Will the organization look to current balance sheet assets or revenue from future contributions and activities?

Current Debt

Community Help has $150 million in *current debt,* which is debt that will come due within the next year. The board should ask management how it plans to fund this debt. To ask this question is not to suggest that Community Help is in financial peril. In fact, it appears to have a variety of resources that it can use to fund the repayment of the current debt, including significant investment assets, operations that generate significant amounts of cash, and receivables.

Community Help's board should ask management which of these resources it intends to tap to fund the current debt. This choice could affect Community Help's long-term plans and missions.

Future Cash from Operations

Management could be looking to cash generated from future operations to fund the shortfall described (current liabilities minus cash). Unfortunately, the directors will not be able to assess the amount of cash that future operations will generate by looking at the statement of financial condition. In fact, no financial statement provides information about future operations. As already noted, but worth repeating, financial statements report *historical* events. However, to the extent that Community Help's directors believe that the past is a predictor of the future, they should examine the statement of activities and the statement of cash flows to assess whether future operations will generate cash to fund the shortfall between balance sheet cash and current liabilities. More important, the board should require that the officers clearly present and substantiate Community Help's business plan. This will mean providing the board with budgets.

Quality of Receivables

The calculation of the shortfall in current assets is very conservative: Current assets have been limited to cash. A more realistic formulation includes receivables. To assess the quality of receivables, Community Help's board should review Note 2 to the financial statements, which provides as follows:

2. Contributions Receivable

At December 31, 20X5, the Organization anticipates collection of outstanding contributions receivable as follows:

(In thousands)	
Amount receivable within 1 year	$86,136
Amount receivable in 1 to 5 years	11,635
Total contributions receivable before reserve for uncollectible amounts	97,771
Less reserve for uncollectible amounts	(390)
Total contributions receivable, net	97,381
Less current portion	(86,136)
Contributions receivable, net, noncurrent	$ 11,245

Amounts presented above due after December 31, 20X6, have been discounted to present value using published U.S. Treasury Bill rates. At December 31, 20X5, the Organization had commitments from donors for conditional contributions approximating $.85 million. These pledges will be accrued in future periods as the conditions are met.

The information in this note is somewhat inconsistent with the actual financial statements. The definition of "contributions" is unclear, which should cause Community Help's board to ask for clarification.

As suggested, Community Help's management could look to the current portion of the receivables to fund the cash shortfall. Note 2 does not dissect all aspects of the accounts receivable balance. The board should ask management to discuss the quality of the $94 million in trade receivables. Specifically, the board should ask to see an aging schedule (an analysis of accounts receivable classified by how long they are past due); older receivables are less likely to be collected.

Investment Assets

It may well be that Community Help's management and board recognized long ago the current relationship between its cash position and current debt. They may have chosen to invest a portion of incoming cash in short-term investments to boost the return on assets. This would be sound financial management.

To gain a better understanding of Community Help's investments, its board should review Note 8 to the financial statements, which provides in pertinent part as follows:

At December 31, 20X5, the aggregate carrying amount of investments was as follows:	
(In thousands)	
U.S. government securities	$102,274
Corporate bonds and notes	79,425
Foreign obligations	6,279
Common stocks	272,444
Mortgage and asset-backed securities	102,593
Other	48,222
Total investments at fair value	611,237
Less current portion	(133,745)
Investments, long term	$477,492

If necessary, Community Help could meet the "cash minus current debt" shortfall from maturing investments.

Again, if you are not familiar or comfortable with financial statements, step back and think about the analysis, which is based on a simple question: Will Community Help be able to satisfy its existing liabilities if it must rely on its current assets? To answer that question, we examined its assets to determine what would be available to meet liabilities. The results of this analysis may be disturbing or troublesome, but the analysis is straightforward.

(b) STATEMENT OF ACTIVITIES. The *statement of activities* is akin to an income statement; it is designed to show the effects of the organization's transactions and events that change the amount and nature of the organization's net assets. While the statement of financial position is a snapshot at a given moment, the statement of activities provides a detailed analysis of income, expenses, gains, and losses over a given period of time. Notwithstanding the different temporal focus, the analysis continues to focus on the distinction between items that are unrestricted, temporarily restricted, and permanently restricted.

Income is shown as increasing net assets, and expenses are shown as decreasing net assets. Rather than calling the resulting amount *net income,* the statement refers to the result as a *change in net assets.*[19] Special rules apply for in-kind

19. Accountants distinguish between the following three basic types of transactions for purposes of revenue recognition: (1) exchange transactions, (2) contributions, and (3) intermediary transactions. These distinctions can become highly technical, but for our purposes, an *exchange transaction* is one in which the organization receives something of value in consideration for giving something of roughly equal value. A *contribution* is a payment to an organization that is not contingent upon the recipient organization providing reciprocal value. For example, an organization that hires an employee and receives the employee's services in exchange for the payment of salary has engaged in an exchange transaction. The classic example of a contribution to a charity is a cash donation. Subject to the rules relating to pledges, contributions of cash and property are

contributions to museum collections, which permit a museum to exclude the contributions from revenue if certain conditions are met.[20]

In addition to the statement of activities, an organization is required to provide expense information about its different functional activities.[21] This information can be provided either in a separate statement or in footnotes. Exhibit 5.2 depicts the statement of activities for Community Help.

(i) Activities and Liquidity. Again, our focus is on addressing the shortfall between the $57 million cash balance and the $150 million in current liabilities. Community Help has several sources that can be used to cover this shortfall. Charitable contributions obviously represent one source. Last year Community Help took in $290 million in contributions, but can it count on that level of contributions this year? Even if it can, are those contributions already committed to programs and services? These are questions that every board should ask.

$93 Million Shortfall

As we examine the statement of activities, our focus is still on the shortfall between Community Help's cash balance and its current liabilities. Those reading the financial statements will inevitably look to the statement of activities to assess whether the organization is generating sufficient funds to pay the current liabilities as those liabilities become due because this statement presents revenues and expenses for the just-completed period. If Community Help has been in existence for some time, this statement will provide some insight into what is now likely to happen, but remember that the statement of activities, like all financial statements, is *historical* in nature. Past performance is often an unreliable predicator of future results.

---

included in revenue in the period received. Contributed property is valued at fair market value. Exchange transactions also impact the income statement, but the timing of revenue recognition differs with the recognition of contributions.

An *intermediary transaction* involves an organization that receives funds but has no discretion over how they are spent: The organization is acting as the disbursement agent. To illustrate, assume the United Means runs a workplace giving campaign that permits the donor to designate a specific charity as the beneficiary of a contribution. United Means books the transaction as an offsetting asset and liability, with nothing flowing through its income statement. *See* Transfers of Assets to a Not-for-Profit Organization or Charitable Trust That Raises or Holds Contributions for Others, Statement of Fin. Accounting Standards No. 136 (Fin. Accounting Standards Bd. 1999). As a further illustration, assume a social services agency receives a grant from the federal government, but it is required to disburse equal amounts of that money to participants in the agency's programs. Once again, the transaction has no impact on the income statement. *Id.*, Appendix, Example 3.

---

20. Accounting for Contributions Received and Contributions Made, *supra* note16, at 13, 26, and 27. To qualify for this treatment, the contributed assets must be (1) held for public exhibition, education, or research in furtherance of public service rather than financial gain, (2) protected, kept unencumbered, cared for, and preserved, and (3) subject to an organizational policy that requires the proceeds from sales of collection items to be used to acquire other items for collections. Alternatively, the organization can capitalize its collections, in which case the contribution must be reflected in the income statement.
21. Financial Statements of Not-for-Profit Organizations, *supra* note 12, at 26.

Statement of Activities
For the Year Ended December 31, 20X5 (In Thousands)

	Unrestricted	Temporarily	Restricted	20X5	20X4
Operating Revenues and Gains					
Contributions from Units	$ 33,252	$ 74,567	$ 0	$ 107,819	$103,075
Contributions for Use in Next Year	$ 0	$ 35,854	$ 0	$ 35,854	$ 30,915
Legacies and Bequests	$ 37,467	$ 2,998	$ 4,974	$ 45,439	$ 26,284
Services and Materials	$ 6,929	$ 7,771	$ 0	$ 14,700	$ 17,443
Grants	$ 6,077	$ 38,191	$ 0	$ 44,268	$ 39,323
Other	$ 61,747	$ 16,456	$ 1,298	$ 79,501	$ 68,988
Products and Services					
Relief	$ 572,347	$ 0	$ 0	$ 572,347	$544,541
Program Materials	$ 51,863	$ 798	$ 0	$ 52,661	$ 51,162
Contracts	$ 19,144	$ 0	$ 0	$ 19,144	$ 14,181
Investment Income (Note 10)	$ 43,910	$ 667	$ 605	$ 45,182	$ 42,561
Other Revenues	$ 22,932	$ 334	$ 0	$ 23,266	$ 31,328
Net Assets Released from Restrictions	$ 173,431	–$174,684	$ 1,253	$ 0	$ 0
TOTAL OPERATING INCOME	$1,029,099	$ 2,952	$ 8,130	$1,040,181	$969,801
Operating Expenses:					
Program Services	$ 895,457	$ 0	$ 0	$ 895,457	$860,873
Supporting Services					
Membership and Fundraising	$ 36,712	$ 0	$ 0	$ 36,712	$ 33,735
Management Services	$ 50,065	$ 0	$ 0	$ 50,065	$ 44,618
Total Supporting Services	$ 86,777	$ 0	$ 0	$ 86,777	$ 78,353
TOTAL EXPENSES	$ 982,234	$ 0	$ 0	$ 982,234	$939,226
CHANGES IN NET ASSETS FROM OPS	$ 46,865	$ 2,952	$ 8,130	$ 57,947	$ 30,575

Exhibit 5.2 Statement of Activities for Community Help

STATEMENT OF ACTIVITIES
FOR THE YEAR ENDED DECEMBER 31, 20X5 (IN THOUSANDS)

	Unrestricted	Temporarily	Restricted	20X5	20X4
Nonoperating Expenses					
Investment Income in Excess of Amount Designated for Current Ops (Note 10)	$ 37,372	$ 300	$ 1,181	$ 38,853	$ 30,505
CHANGE IN NET ASSETS	$ 84,237	$ 3,252	$ 9,311	$ 96,800	$ 61,080
Net Assets, Beginning of the Year	$ 636,776	$108,955	$129,487	$ 875,218	$814,142
Net Assets, End of Year	$ 721,013	$112,207	$138,798	$ 972,018	$875,222
SUBJECT TO ROUNDING ERRORS					

EXHIBIT 5.2 STATEMENT OF ACTIVITIES FOR COMMUNITY HELP *(CONTINUED)*

Moreover, the statement of activities is an effort to measure economic income using a number of accounting conventions and principles. It is not a measure of cash flow. Therefore, the $96 million increase in assets (net income number) does not necessarily represent a corresponding $96 million increase in cash and other liquid assets.

$108 Million in Contributions

Charitable contributions represent one source that most organizations use to cover a shortfall. The $108 million in contributions (excluding refugee relief) for the just completed year suggests that this is a good place for Community Help to find additional revenue. This may be exactly how management plans to deal with the $93 million shortfall. However, if you were a board member, you would ask a number of questions to determine whether the $108 million level will be repeated and, if so, whether those contributions can be used to cover the shortfall between the cash balance and current liabilities.

In planning to meet current liabilities, the board needs to know whether the $108 million in charitable contributions comes from a one-time fundraising drive or ongoing fundraising activities. The directors should ask management for a five- or ten-year history of fundraising activities. Even if Community Help can count on the same level of contributions, those contributions will not necessarily be available to meet the cash shortfall because they could already be committed to existing or planned programs. The board should review the footnotes for additional details.

Service Fees in Excess of Expenses

Community Help cannot look to the net income from services as a source of additional cash because its total revenue from relief services ($527 million) falls far short of its total costs for rendering those services ($895 million). Is this bad management? Probably not. Community Help is providing its services on a subsidized basis, looking to contributions to meet the shortfall. This shortfall is probably consistent with the organization's charitable mission. This fact illustrates the reason it is not always appropriate to apply for-profit measurements to the nonprofit world. A better measurement in this case might be the number of people served, the cost of service per person, or the percentage of people served to the total who need assistance. Although the directors of any nonprofit should ask hard-hitting questions concerning funding and liquidity, they also should ask the executive officers whether the organization is meeting its charitable objectives.

Past Performance Is No Guarantee of Future Performance

As noted, an organization's financial statements are historical in nature; that is, they report *past performance.* This fact cannot be stressed enough. Although people use financial statements to attempt to predict future performance by examining and extrapolating trends, no one can predict the future. As a board member, you should avoid the often incorrect belief that last year's contributions or fees from services will repeat or grow at a certain rate. For example, the revenues for the major relief organizations showed a sharp increase for 2004 and 2005 because of contributions targeted for South Asian tsunamis and Hurricane Katrina relief. In budgeting for 2006, the boards of these organizations would be making a mistake if they assumed that 2006 revenues would continue at 2004 and 2005 levels (assuming no major natural disasters).[22] For a more common example, consider the organization that conducts a massive capital campaign in Year 2. The board would be deluding itself if it budgeted for a comparable level of contributions in Year 3. In fact, the board should probably assume that Year 3 contributions will drop below Year 1 contribution levels (assumed to be at long-term historic averages) because some of those who contributed to the capital campaign in Year 2 might well reduce their regular contributions in Year 3 (cannibalization of the donor base).

The best way to monitor an organization's financial position and performance is on an ongoing basis. Do not focus only on the annual statements. You should ask questions at monthly board meetings and request monthly statements, budget updates, and variances from budget.

(ii) Liquidity Is Again the Problem. The problem with the statements of financial position and activities is that both provide only a partial picture of the organization's cash position. Under nonprofit accounting rules, pledges must be accounted for as current period revenue, increasing both net assets and revenues. However, a pledge is not readily spendable, and the expense for depreciation does not represent a current expenditure of cash. The statements of financial position and activities are therefore somewhat misleading to the untrained eye. This point can be extended to all other transactions that result in increases in revenues or assets but that are not cash based.

Although the statements of financial position and activities provide an economic measure of organizational finances, these statements do not clearly indicate where cash is coming from and where it is going, which is problematic because all organizations ultimately must survive on cash flow.

(c) STATEMENT OF CASH FLOWS. Nonprofits are required to include a statement of cash flows as part of their financial statements.[23] This statement shows the sources and uses of cash. It answers many of the questions left unanswered by the statements of financial position and activities.

---

22. Later in 2005, there were major natural disasters in Pakistan and Central America. A number of relief organizations acknowledged that contributions for these relief efforts were coming in at a slower rate than they would have liked. *See* B. Condon, *Red Cross, Red Ink*, FORBES.COM, Oct. 26, 2005; N. Wallace and N. Wilhelm, *Earthquake Taxes Capacity of Donors and Charities to Provide Relief Aid*, CHRON. OF PHILAN., Oct. 20, 2005; and C. Lynch, *Donations Slowing as Disasters Mount Worldwide*, WASH. POST, Oct. 16, 2005. Given the apparent fatigue on the part of donors, the boards of these organizations might actually need to assume a decline in contributions below historic averages as they review 2006 budgets.
23. FINANCIAL STATEMENTS OF NOT-FOR-PROFIT ORGANIZATIONS, *supra* note 12, at ¶ 6.

Unfortunately, the statement of cash flows is conceptually difficult to interpret. Each item in the statement shows how it impacted cash. Just because an item adds to cash does not mean that there has been an absolute increase in cash; another item could simultaneously reduce cash. When examining the statement of cash flows, you see each individual item on a "gross" basis, but the increase (or decrease) in cash on a "net" basis. Exhibit 5.3 is the statement of cash flows for Community Help. Those who are generally unfamiliar with the statement of cash flows will get the most out of it by examining the summary components in the statement rather than each line item. Specifically these individuals should first focus on the net cash provided by operations, net cash provided by investing activities, and the net cash provided by investing activities.

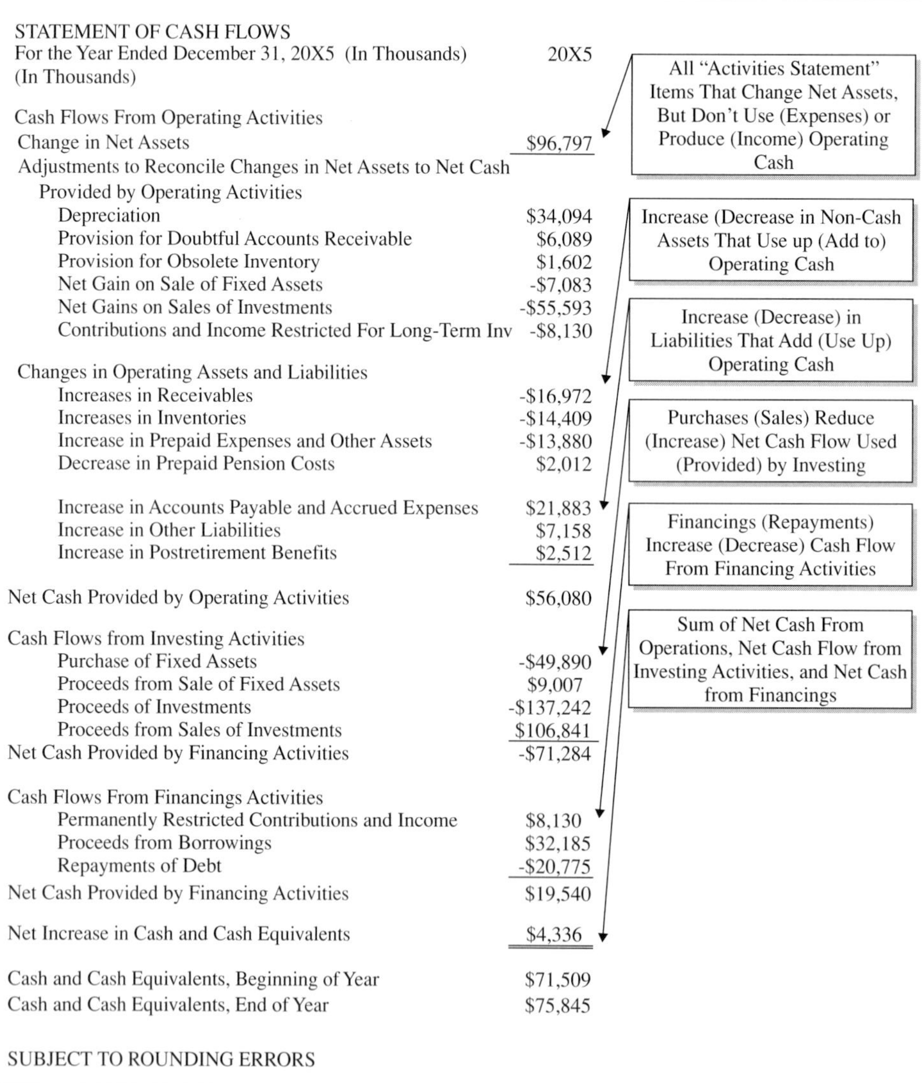

STATEMENT OF CASH FLOWS For the Year Ended December 31, 20X5 (In Thousands) (In Thousands)	20X5
Cash Flows From Operating Activities	
Change in Net Assets	$96,797
Adjustments to Reconcile Changes in Net Assets to Net Cash Provided by Operating Activities	
Depreciation	$34,094
Provision for Doubtful Accounts Receivable	$6,089
Provision for Obsolete Inventory	$1,602
Net Gain on Sale of Fixed Assets	-$7,083
Net Gains on Sales of Investments	-$55,593
Contributions and Income Restricted For Long-Term Inv	-$8,130
Changes in Operating Assets and Liabilities	
Increases in Receivables	-$16,972
Increases in Inventories	-$14,409
Increase in Prepaid Expenses and Other Assets	-$13,880
Decrease in Prepaid Pension Costs	$2,012
Increase in Accounts Payable and Accrued Expenses	$21,883
Increase in Other Liabilities	$7,158
Increase in Postretirement Benefits	$2,512
Net Cash Provided by Operating Activities	$56,080
Cash Flows from Investing Activities	
Purchase of Fixed Assets	-$49,890
Proceeds from Sale of Fixed Assets	$9,007
Proceeds of Investments	-$137,242
Proceeds from Sales of Investments	$106,841
Net Cash Provided by Financing Activities	-$71,284
Cash Flows From Financings Activities	
Permanently Restricted Contributions and Income	$8,130
Proceeds from Borrowings	$32,185
Repayments of Debt	-$20,775
Net Cash Provided by Financing Activities	$19,540
Net Increase in Cash and Cash Equivalents	$4,336
Cash and Cash Equivalents, Beginning of Year	$71,509
Cash and Cash Equivalents, End of Year	$75,845

SUBJECT TO ROUNDING ERRORS

EXHIBIT 5.3 STATEMENT OF CASH FLOWS FOR COMMUNITY HELP

As you review Community Help's statement of cash flows, pay particular attention to the starting and ending points. This statement shows a $96.7 million increase in net assets as its starting point. At the end, it shows a $4.3 million increase in cash and equivalents. In between, it shows where cash came from and where it went.

Operations provided $56 million in cash. Given the net increase of $4.3 million in net cash and equivalents, you should ask the following question: Where did all the cash from operations go? What you will see is that a significant portion of the cash went to repay debt ($20 million) and to purchase investment and fixed assets.

Community Help's statement of cash flows proves to be very revealing. Operations are generating $56 million in cash flow, but the organization's investment activities are consuming more than $56 million in cash. As a consequence, Community Help must engage in financing activities to fund the shortfall.

Should the board be concerned about this shortfall? Probably not. Community Help is purchasing only $49 million in fixed assets, which is covered by cash flow from operations. The financing activities can be viewed as financing the purchase of the remaining investment assets. Note 8 to Community Help's statement of financial position indicates that the bulk of these investments are in United States government obligations and marketable securities. These assets could be liquidated to repay the maturing debt. The board should determine whether Community Help's investment and financing activities meet its risk management criteria. This is particularly important if Community Help is using financial derivatives as part of its risk management plan.

The board might want to ask management why it invested so heavily in investments securities as opposed to program-related assets. This poses a number of philosophical issues. Should Community Help spend more today to better meet the current needs of its charitable beneficiaries, or should it build reserves to ensure that it can maintain its current levels of service for future generations of beneficiaries? These are the questions that make board meetings interesting, but they might be best left for discussion at an annual board retreat or planning session. The focus at regular periodic meetings of the board should be on assessing whether the organization's financial condition and results are in line with budget.

5.3 GUIDANCE FOR THE BOOKKEEPER

Most board members will not be directly involved in creating or maintaining the accounting system for their nonprofits. That does not mean simply ignoring the nitty-gritty. After all, the adage "garbage in, garbage out" applies to accounting systems and the financial statements that those systems produce. Whoever is responsible for creating and maintaining an organization's financial records should review *Unified Reporting System for Not-for-Profit Organizations* by

Russy D. Sumariwalla and Wilson C. Levis,[24] which explains how to develop a meaningful chart of accounts. Those authors hope that standardization among nonprofits can be achieved.

Designing a chart of accounts is not just a theoretical exercise. In February 2005, Opportunities Industrialization Center of Greater Milwaukee (OIC-GM), a major social services agency, was forced to close its doors following a year of widely reported financial scandals, including a kickback scheme that resulted in the criminal conviction of its executive director.[25] The last management letter issued by OIC-GM's auditors urged the board to "establish a standardized chart of accounts for all entities." The letter also noted that journal entries were not always supported by source or other documents and general ledgers were not analyzed and reconciled with subsidiary information on a monthly basis. The letter further noted that "[m]anagement could not provide a breakdown of expenses among program, management, and general [administration] and [those for] fund raising expenses," nor could management always provide "supporting documentation for various revenue accounts." The auditors "found the books and records of the Organization were not in the condition that we would expect for preparation of a normal audit." All of this may have been technical details, but the management letter indicated that "the financial information provided [to the board] was not an accurate reflection of the financial position or results of operations." An agency that as recently as 2004 had a $60 million budget no longer exists.[26] In short, OIC-GM paid the ultimate price, in part, because management and the board apparently did not focus on accounting details or the quality of the information that the system was generating.

That focus on detail must start with the design of the accounting system, which means that someone should focus on the chart of accounts before activities commence. If your organization's sector is represented by a trade group, someone should check with that group to determine whether there are any industry standards for a chart of accounts. Alternatively, the person charged with designing the system may want to ask the organization's outside auditors whether there are industry standards. In the next section, we briefly examine financial ratio analysis. Some of those techniques call for comparisons with other organizations engaged in similar activities. Those comparisons will be greatly enhanced if your organization's chart of accounts and financial statement presentation follow industry practice.

---

24. This excellent book is published by Jossey-Bass, a Wiley Company (2000).
25. D. Nunnally, *Jury Finds Gee Guilty in Kickback Scheme: George Associate Secretly Directed Money to Ex-Senator*, MILWAUKEE J.-SENTINEL, Aug. 19, 2004.
26. S. Schultze and L. Sykes, Jr., *Embattled OIC to Close Doors: Deep Financial Crisis Is Final Blow to Agency*, MILWAUKEE J.-SENTINEL, Feb. 10, 2005.

5.4 RATIO ANALYSIS

Financial analysts use a number of ratios to evaluate an organization's liquidity and performance. The board should have management compile a ratio analysis on a regular basis. Any report should include benchmark statistics for similar organizations as well as historical ratios for the organization so that trends can be evaluated. But do not assume that all comparisons between organizations are meaningful. Unless two organizations use the same definitions in their charts of accounts, any conclusions drawn through comparison are highly suspect. Ratios are most useful in comparing the performance of a given organization over time.

(a) SEVEN BASIC RATIOS. We examine seven commonly used ratios here, but literally dozens of ratios are available to anyone who wants to take the time to calculate them. Some will be appropriate for your organization; others will not be. Those seeking a better understanding of how to use financial ratios and what they mean should consider reviewing one or more of the following resources:

- Phil Sherman, *Analytical Procedures for Nonprofit Organizations* (American Institute of Certified Public Accountants 2005).
- *Industry Norms and Key Business Ratios* (Dun & Bradstreet 1998–99).
- Janet S. Greenlee and David Bukovinsky, "Financial Ratios in the Analytical Review of Charitable Organizations," *Ohio CPA Journal* (January–March 1998).
- Any standard finance or accounting textbook.

We now return to Community Help's financial statements to illustrate how the ratios are calculated and what they reveal.

CURRENT RATIO

Let's begin with the *current ratio*, a measure of liquidity. It is calculated as follows, with Community Help's figures in parentheses:

Current Ratio = Current Assets ($362) ÷ Current Liabilities ($165) = 2.19

An organization generally prefers this ratio to be larger (e.g., 3 ÷ 1) rather than smaller (e.g., 1 ÷ 3). However, an extremely large ratio can indicate that the organization has not appropriately deployed its assets to meet its objectives. Community Help's current ratio is 2.19, or $362 million ÷ $165 million. This calculation is limited to unrestricted assets and liabilities, which is the most meaningful approach. If large amounts of current assets are restricted, this ratio will not measure the organization's ability to cover general liabilities if it includes restricted assets. The 2.19 ratio appears to be a relatively strong number, but for a truly meaningful analysis, you need data for organizations with similar operations (and similar charts of account) as well as the organization's ratios for the prior five (or even ten years) so that trends can be evaluated. One of the issues that must be considered is the quality of the organization's receivables. The calculation assumes that the receivables are available to cover liabilities, but if the receivables are uncollectible, Community Help has a problem.

Quick Ratio

The *quick ratio* is another measure of liquidity. It is calculated as follows:

Quick Ratio = [Current Assets ($362) – Inventory ($60) – Prepaid Expenses ($7)] ÷ Current Liabilities ($165) = 1.79

This ratio is a more conservative measure of liquidity than the current ratio. It reflects the belief that receivables are much easier to convert into cash than are inventory and prepaid expenses. Community Help's quick ratio of 1.79 ($295 million ÷ $165 million) suggests a liquid organization, but the only way to judge whether this number reflects a strong or weak position is to compare Community Help's quick ratio with either the quick ratios for similar organizations or its own quick ratio calculated for a number of periods. Eliminating inventory from the consideration makes particular sense in the case of Community Help because it is not recovering the full cost of its inventory, apparently using it to further mission. Again, the focus is on unrestricted assets and liabilities. Keep in mind that some organizations will not carry meaningful inventories. In such case, using the quick ratio does not add much to the overall analysis unless the organization has significant levels of prepaid expenses.

Defensive Interval Ratio

Like the quick and current ratios, the *defensive interval ratio* is a measure of liquidity. Instead of focusing on just the balance sheet, this ratio brings the income statement into the equation. It is calculated as follows:

Defensive Interval Ratio = [Cash ($57) + Marketable Securities ($119) + Receivables ($119)] ÷ Average Monthly Expenses ($982 ÷ 12) = 3.6 Months

What would happen if Community Help received no additional revenue? The defensive interval ratio reveals that by liquidating current assets, the organization could cover 3.6 months of operating expenses. Some organizations might have included inventories when calculating the numerator. This might make sense if the organization were a museum with a gift shop. However, Community Help is selling its inventory below cost, apparently making part of it available without charge. Given that fact, including Community Help's inventory in the numerator makes less sense. Notice that the calculation is based on unrestricted accounts. This makes sense, particularly with respect to the numerator because the limitations imposed on restricted assets will often preclude their use for normal operating expenses. As usual, the 3.6 number is meaningless unless it is analyzed in terms of either Community Help's historical trends or ratios for similar organizations.

Savings Indicator

The AICPA's *Analytical Procedures for Nonprofit Organizations* offers the *savings indicator*[27] as one measurement ratio, as does a group of authors who published an article in 2002 describing factors that can be used to assess the financial vulnerability of nonprofits.[28] Those authors refer to this ratio as the *surplus margin ratio.* Obviously, if revenues exceed expenses, the organization is saving in a financial sense (but not necessarily as measured in cash). The savings indicator is calculated as follows:

Savings indicator = [Revenue ($1,029) – Expenses ($982)]
÷ Total Expenses ($982) = 4.78%

Community Help's savings indicator is 4.78 percent. This number tends to be relatively small for all charitable institutions. In one study of 20,000 charitable organizations, the savings indicator was highest for educational institutions—3.1 percent on average for those institutions in the top quartile of educational institutions—and lowest for organizations serving human needs such as the provision of food and shelter—1.5 percent for those human need organizations in the top quartile.[29] These results should not be surprising. After all, human services organizations tend to service the immediate needs of their clients. Given the study results, Community Help's number is much higher than would be expected. As noted, probably the most useful way for Community Help to use this number is to monitor it over time. Given the relatively low numbers for other organizations, the board should ask the CFO to explain why this ratio is so high.

Revenue Generation Ratio

The *revenue generation ratio* shows the relationship between an organization's revenue and assets, depicting how much revenue each dollar of assets is generating. It is calculated as follows:

Revenue Generation Ratio = Revenue ($1,029) ÷ Assets ($1,055) = 97.53%

As you can see, Community Help generates just under one dollar of revenue for each dollar of assets that it holds. That is neither good nor bad. It is just a fact and will have meaning only when the number is compared to the organization's historical trends or to the ratios for similar organizations.

This ratio could be particularly helpful in evaluating new capital projects after the fact. Let's assume a museum has $10 million of assets and $20 million of revenue. It decides to add an IMAX theater at a cost of $5 million. Having

---

27. Phil Sherman, Analytical Procedures for Nonprofit Organizations, at 4-16 (AICPA 2005).
28. J. Trussel, J. Greenlee, and T. Brady, *Predicting Financial Vulnerability in Charitable Organizations*, CPA J., June 2002.
29. J. Greenlee and D. Bukovinsky, *Financial Ratios for Use in the Analytical Review of Charitable Organizations*, Ohio CPA J., Jan.–Mar. 1998.

only $25 million of revenue following the addition suggests that the expenditure on the theater was not as productive an investment as investments in the museum's other assets. Of course, the theater may have made sense from a mission standpoint, or the theater might have been necessary to protect the existing revenue stream. As this analysis illustrates, ratios are a construct for forcing boards and executive directors to think about the impact and ramifications of their decisions.

Debt to Total Net Assets

You are probably familiar with the *debt/equity ratio*. The problem with this ratio is the absence of equity holders in the nonprofit world, but any organization can be treated as having an equity interest in its net assets, permitting a calculation that is equivalent to a debt/equity ratio. This ratio can be calculated based on all liabilities or only on long-term liabilities. Community Help's debt/equity ratio (based on just long-term liabilities) is .23, calculated as follows:

Debt/Equity Ratio = Long-Term Debt ($168) ÷ Net Assets ($721) = 23.30%

Again, the focus is on unrestricted accounts. This number suggests a strong financial position, but this conclusion is appropriate only after comparing it with the ratio for similar organizations. Lenders often require that the borrower maintain a certain debt to total net asset ratio as a condition to making a loan. If your organization has loans with such covenants, management must monitor the organization's compliance with them. In fact, you will probably want an annual report from management regarding compliance.

Times Interest Earned Ratio

The *times interest earned* ratio assesses whether an organization can service its debt. The ratio is calculated as follows:

Times Interest Earned Ratio = Operating Income ÷ Interest Expense

The higher the resulting number, the stronger an organization's ability to cover its interest expense from operations. If this number is declining over time, the organization and its board should be concerned that the nonprofit's financial health is deteriorating. Unfortunately, Community Help does not state the amount of its interest expense in its financial statements, so its times interest earned ratio cannot be determined. Community Help's board should ask management to provide this information.

(b) OTHER RATIOS. The focus here has been on ratios that measure an organization's financial health and liquidity. Other ratios should also be considered. Chapter 13 examines some common performance measurements that are often applied to charitable organizations. Those ratios focus on fundraising and management efficiency.

5.5 THE MILWAUKEE PUBLIC MUSEUM—WHAT THE FINANCIAL INFORMATION FORETOLD

To see why a regular review of an organization's financial statements by the board is important, let's consider the Milwaukee Public Museum and the financial crisis that came to light in 2005.[30] The museum is operated by a nonprofit (MPM), but Milwaukee County owns the building housing the museum[31] and many of the museum's exhibits. Both the building and the exhibits are leased to MPM on essentially a rent-free basis, with MPM responsible for various expenses such as utilities and repairs.[32] In March 2005, the county announced a new lease agreement with MPM. Under the agreement, the county was to pay MPM an annual subsidy over a 20-year period and certain capital costs, together totaling $70 million.[33] During the negotiations, count officials had been told that its operating deficit for the fiscal year ended August 31, 2004 would be in the neighborhood of $447,000.[34] Shortly after the county board approved the new subsidy package, MPM's CEO announced that MPM would have a $4.1 million operating deficit for fiscal year 2004, or 18 percent of its budget.[35] That number was revised downward to $2.4 million several days later, with the CEO indicating that he had misspoken —the $4.1 million was an estimate of the amount by which MPM's net assets had declined.[36] What appears to be a final audit for MPM's 2004 fiscal year showed a $4.3 million operating deficit and a $6.4 million decline in net assets.[37] The results for the 2005 fiscal year turned out to be much worse, with a $10.4 million decline in net assets and an $8.6 million operating deficit.[38]

---

30. With operations dating back to 1882, the Milwaukee Public Museum is considered one of the premiere natural history museums in the nation.
31. The privatization of the museum occurred in 1992. It appears that additions to the physical plant since then have been reflected in MPM's balance sheet.
32. D. Umhoefer, *Museum Reveals Huge '04 Deficit: Disclosure Could Threaten Lease with Milwaukee County*, MILWAUKEE J.-SENTINEL, May 3, 2005. *See also* MILWAUKEE PUBLIC MUSEUM, 2005 AND 2004 DRAFT CONSOLIDATED FINANCIAL STATEMENTS (DRAFT), Note 5, (2005).
33. D. Umhoefer, *Museum Contract Clears Key Hurdle: Milwaukee County Panel Recommends Proposed 20-Year Agreement*, MILWAUKEE J.-SENTINEL, May 7, 2005; and D. Umhoefer, *County, Museum Reach 20-Year Management Deal*, MILWAUKEE J.-SENTINEL, Mar. 3, 2005.
34. D. Umhoefer, *Criminal Probe Sought in Museum's $4 Million Deficit: County Board Also Wants to Know Reasons Behind Finance Official's Departure*, MILWAUKEE J.-SENTINEL, May 4, 2005.
35. *Id.*
36. D. Umhoefer and A. Link, *Museum Layoffs Expected Soon: Reserves Almost Gone, Walker Says*, MILWAUKEE J.-SENTINEL, May 10, 2005.
37. *See* MILWAUKEE PUBLIC MUSEUM, *supra* note 32. *See also* D. Umhoefer and S. Schultze, *Audit Finds More Trouble: Museum $1 Million Deeper in Debt than Previously Thought*, MILWAUKEE J.-SENTINEL, Sept. 2, 2005.
38. *See* MILWAUKEE PUBLIC MUSEUM, *supra* note 32; MILWAUKEE COUNTY DEPARTMENT OF AUDIT, AN AUDIT OF MILWAUKEE PUBLIC MUSEUM, INC. 2005 FINANCIAL CRISIS—FINAL REPORT (Dec. 2005); D. Umhoefer, S. Schultze, and A. Lank, Museum *Audit Leads to Criminal Inquiry: Report is a Damning Critique of Institution's Management*, MILWAUKEE J.-SENTINEL, Dec. 1, 2005; and D. Umhoefer, *Museum Assets in Red, Loss Greater Than Forecast*, MILWAUKEE J.-SENTINEL, Nov. 29, 2005. The November 29 article reports that people were very surprised by the numbers. The deficit for fiscal year 2005 had been estimated to be $6.2 million just two months earlier.

As might be expected, the county was not pleased with the news it received, with one county board supervisor calling for what the *Milwaukee Journal-Sentinel* characterized as a criminal probe.[39] As is often the case in these situations, many people expressed surprise over the developments.[40] Early on, part of the blame was placed on nearby freeway reconstruction project,[41] but people soon became more focused on the underlying economics, including keeping growth in line with funding.

What happened during MPM board meetings will probably never be known to the outside world, but the financial facts were clearly available to board members had they been willing to just scratch the surface of the financial statements.[42] Even a cursory review of the financial statements would have evidenced financial issues that had been on the horizon for some time. Quite apart from the board, it is difficult to imagine how county negotiators could have been surprised had they looked at MPM's financial statements.

---

39. D. Umhoefer, *Criminal Probe Sought*, *supra* note 34. At the time, the district attorney indicated that he would wait until more facts were known before proceeding with a criminal investigation. The district attorney has since commenced a probe. *See* D. Umhoefer, S. Schultze, and A. Lank, *Museum Audit Leads to Criminal Inquiry*, *supra* note 38.
40. According to the *Milwaukee Journal-Sentinel*, one county board supervisor said, "[The Museum] played us like fools, they set us up, and we want answers. This thing smells to high heaven." D. Umhoefer, *Criminal Probe Sought*, *supra* note 34. In summarizing the comments of MPM's president when the initial $4.1 million disclosure was made, the *Milwaukee Journal-Sentinel* wrote, "Surprising new information is becoming available as the museum's annual financial audit comes to a close, Stafford said." D. Umhoefer, *Museum Reveals*, *supra* note 32. The members of MPM's board of directors remained mostly silent throughout the public airing of the details. A number of comments suggest that the board was unaware of the developing crisis until at least January 2005. The Milwaukee County Department of Audit released *An Audit of the Milwaukee Public Museum, Inc. 2005 Crisis Interim Report* on June 10, 2005. In it, the auditors wrote "It does not appear, however, that the severity of the situation was ever disclosed directly by management or probed into by Directors until early in 2005. Further, presentations of any potentially negative financial results were routinely packaged with more optimistic factors to offset the concerns. The absence of any significant, detailed oversight by Directors may have been compounded by the structure of responsibilities within MPM management." One MPM board member said, "The whole community is shocked because the museum had been seen as a thriving institution." D. Umhoefer, *Week May Yield Clues on Museum's Finances: County is Pressing for Details on Big Deficit*, MILWAUKEE J.-SENTINEL, May 8, 2005. Another director said "I felt there was too little oversight," The *Journal-Sentinel* then paraphrased additional comments from this director as follows: "The museum board is mostly a fund-raising organization and is little concerned with governance of the museum's operations." A. Link and D. Umhoefer, *Museum Chief's Dedication at Issue: Critics Say He Hasn't Given Job, Crisis Sufficient Attention*, MILWAUKEE J.-SENTINEL, May 21, 2005.
41. D. Umhoefer, *Week May Yield*, *supra* note 40.
42. The MILWAUKEE JOURNAL-SENTINEL quoted MPM Chairman of the Board, David Meissner, as responding to a County Supervisor by saying "I'm embarrassed. The board is embarrassed." L. Sandler, *Top Museum Leaders Must Go, Supervisor Says: Mayo, Colleagues Recall Pension Scandal in Criticizing Officials Over Financial Problems* MILWAUKEE J.-SENTINEL, May 19, 2005. The article then reports:

    > According to board minutes, getting a quorum occasionally was difficult, and often less than two-thirds of its 27 members attended the six or so meetings a year.

    Given these statements, it is not surprising to see why some on MPM's board would be surprised. The salient question: Should they been have been surprised?

Unfortunately, MPM does not make its audited financial statements readily available on its Web site.[43] The best available alternative is the organization's IRS Forms 990 for the period from 1999 to 2003.[44] Exhibit 5.4 reveals that MPM had serious financial problems that developed over a number of years.

As already noted, nobody should have been surprised. MPM's surplus (deficit) had been declining (increasing) since 1999. It is quite apparent that revenues had at best been flat since the 1999–2000 fiscal year, and many expenses had been increasing. Notably, the numbers show that even the gift shop lost money in fiscal years 2001, 2002, and 2003.[45] Despite that reality, MPM's board apparently approved budgets that showed significant surpluses in each subsequent fiscal year. An audit completed in December 2005 contains similar discrepancies between budgeted and actual results from restaurants, concessions, and catering operations.[46] The same sort of overly optimistic budgeting was evidence in the budget for the IMAX theatre.

If you were to review an actual income statement for MPM or any other nonprofit, it would be much more complex than the data presented in Exhibit 5.4. But even to the financial neophyte, the disturbing nature of the trends reflected by the IRS Forms 990 should have been obvious.

Now let's add a summary balance sheets to the mix (see Exhibit 5.5).

MPM's net assets are trending downward. Without doing any significant financial analysis or examining budget variances, a board member who even took a cursory look at these data should have expressed alarm long before the spring of 2005.[47] In early 2005, the board had another year of data available[48]

---

43. MPM began attaching its financial statements to its IRS Form 990 for its fiscal year ending August 31, 2002. A comparison of the IRS Forms 990 with the attached financial statements indicates that much of the data presented in both formats is comparable for analytical purposes. In other words, full financial statements would be preferable, but the information provided by the tax returns is sufficient for a meaningful analysis.

44. The primary problem with the IRS Form 990 is that it does not provide for a detailed breakdown of restricted assets. Consequently, it is not clear whether the restricted assets are liquid cash or illiquid real estate.

45. The gift shop continued to lose money in fiscal year 2004 and 2005. *See* MILWAUKEE COUNTY DEPARTMENT OF AUDIT, *supra* note 38, at 46.

46. *Id.*, at 47–48. No one can fault a board if in the first year, actual results come in under budget. However, after several years of budgetary misses, the board has to start to question assumptions and demand appropriate adjustments to what are likely over-optimistic and unjustified assumptions.

47. As already noted, this financial information is taken from MPM's IRS Form 990 tax returns. Although there will be differences between the information reported on MPM's tax returns and its financial statements prepared under GAAP, IRS Form 990 calls for an explanation of key differences between an organization's IRS Form 990 and its GAAP financial statements. Specifically, lines 67 to 74 ask for information regarding unrestricted, permanently restricted, and temporarily restricted assets. Parts IV-A and IV-B ask for a reconciliation of IRS Form 990 income information with the income information reported in the organization's financial statements. Nothing in the additional information provided by MPM suggests that the information reported on IRS Form 990 presents a distorted image of MPM's financial condition relative to the GAAP financial statements.

48. Final financial statements for the fiscal year ending August 31, 2004 were unavailable even when the financial crisis first became public in May 2005. However, the board should have been demanding interim reports long before May 2005. Ideally, the board should have been receiving quarterly reports during fiscal year 2004 showing budget variances. As of October 17, 2005, MPM's IRS Form 990 for the fiscal year ending August 31, 2004 was still not posted on GuideStar's Web site.

Milwuakee Public Museum Income Statement	2003	2002	2001	2000	1999
Direct Public Support	$ 5,321,733	$ 5,398,605	$ 6,085,873	$ 6,425,028	$ 9,246,936
Indirect Public Support	$ 106,663	$ 537,610	$ 235,019	$ 379,348	$ 507,870
Government Contributions	$ 4,300,000	$ 4,300,000	$ 4,300,000	$ 4,300,000	$ 4,300,000
Direct, Indirect, Government	$ 9,728,396	$10,236,215	$10,620,892	$11,104,376	$14,054,806
Admissions	$ 2,635,489	$ 2,367,337	$ 2,597,331	$ 1,913,334	$ 846,895
Programs	$178,192	$ 397,847	$ 499,646	$ 145,446	$ 89,115
Program Services	$ 2,813,681	$ 2,765,184	$ 3,096,977	$ 2,058,780	$ 936,010
Gross Rents	$ 131,272	$ 203,178	$ 325,691	$ 234,990	$ 192,073
Less Rental Expenses	$ 257,337	$ 309,771	$ 515,453	$ 241,377	$ 235,263
Net Rental Income	($126,065)	($106,593)	($189,762)	($6,387)	($43,190)
Gross Sales—Inventory	$ 2,047,894	$ 1,937,048	$ 1,656,164	$ 1,529,679	$ 1,122,059
Cost of Good Solds	$ 2,442,998	$ 2,340,479	$ 1,911,878	$ 1,499,318	$ 1,054,885
Net Income From Gift Shop	($395,104)	($403,431)	($255,714)	$ 30,361	$ 67,174
Investment Income & Gains	$ 34,113	$ 278,221	$ 304,873	$ 46,216	$ 107,554
Catering/Beverage	$ 658,230	$ 1,055,234	$ 1,276,694	$ 1,100,797	$ 1,038,629
Civic Theatre Corp	–	–	–	$ 87,369	($24,053)
Miscellaneous	$ 67,066	–	$ 23,858	$ 67,011	$ 78,614
Restaurant/Vending	$ 1,193,729	$ 794,120	$ 960,781	$ 828,409	$ 738,390
Other Revenue	$ 1,919,025	$ 1,849,354	$ 2,261,333	$ 2,083,586	$ 1,831,580
Total Revenue	$13,974,046	$14,618,950	$15,838,599	$15,316,932	$16,953,934
Program Expenses	$12,053,558	$12,037,238	$10,492,396	$ 8,999,138	$ 9,190,479
Management Expenses	$ 2,618,449	$ 2,039,732	$ 2,095,544	$ 1,454,273	$ 1,559,134
Fundraising Expenses	$ 1,306,570	$ 1,132,341	$ 1,465,089	$ 1,377,393	$ 1,047,637
Total Expenses	$15,978,577	$15,209,311	$14,053,029	$11,830,804	$11,797,250
Surplus Deficit	($2,004,531)	($590,361)	$ 1,785,570	$ 3,486,128	$ 5,156,684

EXHIBIT 5.4 MILWAUKEE PUBLIC MUSEUM'S INCOME STATEMENT

Balance Sheet	2003	2002	2001	2000	1999
Cash/Temporary Cash Investments	$ 481,222	$ 1,475,355	$ 3,615,742	$ 4,638,603	$ 5,137,998
Net Accounts Receivable	$ 214,779	$ 256,191	$ 290,174	$ 309,595	$ 242,231
Pledges Receivable	$ 2,856,853	$ 3,267,895	$ 3,690,115	$ 5,947,709	$ 5,853,734
Inventories for Sale or Use	$ 870,873	$ 899,134	$ 576,292	$ 464,313	$ 362,483
Prepaid Expenses	$ 274,600	$ 139,133	$ 225,187	$50,172	$7,246
Investment Securities	$ 1,128,084	$ 2,804,362	$ 1,848,885	$ 602,756	$ 2,336,851
Land, Buildings, & Equipment	$23,509,075	$22,555,762	$20,894,567	$18,261,572	$ 5,788,931
Other Assets	$ 784,092	$ 329,324	$ 335,289	$ 308,026	$ 3,608,235
Total Assets	$30,119,578	$31,727,156	$31,476,251	$30,582,746	$23,337,709
Accounts Payable	$ 1,936,991	$ 1,859,445	$ 1,337,571	$ 1,518,125	$ 3,078,396
Deferred Revenue	$ 829,864	$ 953,694	$ 819,120	$ 953,187	$ 1,247,324
Tax-Exempt Bonds	$14,600,000	$15,700,000	$15,700,000	$16,700,000	$12,500,000
Other Liabilities	$ 4,776,306	$ 3,348,432	$ 2,220,514	$ 1,797,958	$ 384,641
Total Liabilities	$22,143,161	$21,861,571	$20,077,205	$20,969,270	$17,210,361
Net Assets	$ 7,976,417	$ 9,865,585	$11,399,046	$ 9,613,476	$ 6,127,348

EXHIBIT 5.5 MILWAUKEE PUBLIC MUSEUM'S SUMMARY BALANCE SHEET

which showed by all accounts that the key balances were continuing to decline.[49] Moreover, budget variances for fiscal year 2005, had anyone examined them, would have likely shown alarming trends.

The problems become very apparent when we examine a few financial ratios (Exhibit 5.6).

We defined the defensive interval ratio[50] earlier in this chapter. It now should be apparent why this is a useful ratio. In 1999, MPM had enough liquid assets on hand to cover its average monthly expenses for almost 14 months. By August 2003, the coverage had dropped to three and one-half months. The liquidity ratio also reflected the impending liquidity crisis that resulted in MPM's initial plan to cut its operating budget from $20 million[51] to $13 million, with the likelihood that more than 100[52] of 245 staff members would lose their jobs.[53] MPM's former[54] president had talked about new and innovative ways to draw the public to the museum.[55] All that talk was fine, except that the savings ratio shows that the organization was not saving any portion of its revenues.

To MPM's credit, it did maintain expenditures on program services relative to management and fundraising expenses. That is evidenced by the relatively consistent management, fundraising, and program services ratios despite deterioration in financial condition. Clearly, using ratio analysis requires somewhat more effort than just reviewing the statements of activities and financial position—but not much more.

As noted, there are some technical problems with deriving these numbers from tax return information rather than financial statements. For example, it would have been useful to make adjustments to account for restrictions on certain assets. But to a certain extent that is not a problem because the trends that are presented come from internally consistent data.

If it did not, MPM's board should have been reviewing data for peer-group museums. The CFO should have obtained financial information, developed a

49. D. Umhoefer and S. Schultze, *More Trouble*, *supra* note 42.

50. In the analysis that follows, pledges receivable are included in the numerator of this number. In all likelihood, this overstates liquidity because some of these receivables may have been due a long time in the future, meaning that some portion of the receivables may not be readily convertible into cash. This is an instance when GAAP financial statements would have been helpful, as would the ability to ask the CFO for an analysis.

51. This number has also been reported as $22 million.

52. According to one account, 118, or 44% of the staff, "left through layoffs and voluntary departures between January and September 2005." *See* D. Umhoefer, *Museum Assets in Red*, *supra* note *38*. *See also* S. Schultze and D. Umhoefer, *Museum Ran Up Credit Card Bills: As Cash Ran Low, Staffers Began Charging Travel Costs, Legal Fees*, MILWAUKEE J.-SENTINEL, Sept. 6, 2005.

53. D. Umhoefer, *Museum Board OKs $7 Million in Cuts: Directors Also Offer Support for President*, MILWAUKEE J.-SENTINEL, May 18, 2005.

54. A. Lank and D. Umhoefer, *Museum President Resigns: Departure Presents New Obstacle for Financially Challenged Institution*, MILWAUKEE J.-SENTINEL, June 3, 2005.

55. *Imagining the Museum of the Future*, U. OF WIS. LTR. AND SCI. TODAY (Spring 2005).

Financial Ratio Analysis	2003	2002	2001	2000	1999
Defensive Interval Ratio					
Cash + Marketable Securities + Receivables / Average Monthly Expenses	3.52	6.16	8.07	11.66	13.80
Liquidity Ratio					
Cash + Marketable Securities + Receivables + Inventories / Liabilities	25.07	39.81	49.91	57.05	80.96
Accounts Payable Aging Indicator					
Accounts Payable / Average Monthly Expenses	1.45	1.47	1.14	1.54	3.13
Savings Indicator					
Revenue - Expenses / Total Expenses	–12.55	–3.88	12.71	29.47	43.71
Debt Ratio					
Total Debt / Total Assets	73.52	68.90	63.79	68.57	73.74
Fundraising Efficiency Ratio					
Total Contributions (Exclude Government) / Fund Raising Expenses	4.15	5.24	4.31	4.94	9.31
Management Expense Ratio					
General & Administrative Expenses / Total Expenses	16.39	13.41	14.91	12.29	13.22
Fundraising Expense Ratio					
Fundraising Expenses / Total Expenses	8.18	7.45	10.43	11.64	8.88
Program Services Ratio					
Program Services Expenses / Total Expenses	75.44	79.14	74.66	76.07	77.90
Average Monthly Expenses	$ 1,331,548	$ 1,267,443	$ 1,171,086	$ 985,900	$ 983,104
Metropolitan Statistical Area: 2000 Population	1,500,741				

EXHIBIT 5.6 MILWAUKEE PUBLIC MUSEUM'S FINANCIAL RATIOS

comparative analysis, and presented it to the board on a regular basis. This would have given the board a better sense of whether MPM was in line with appropriate financial benchmarks for other museums. Any significant deviations should have resulted in a search for the reasons for the deviations. While a board will not be able to examine peer group data on a monthly basis, it should ask the CFO to provide comparative data on at least an annual basis.

To summarize, MPM's board should have been engaged in ongoing financial analysis. Long before the crisis first became public, the board should have been asking a number of questions in view of MPM's clearly deteriorating financial position, including the following:

- Should MPM cut research staff, possibly diminishing the museum's long-term stature?[56]
- Should MPM host more special exhibitions (e.g. it had recently sponsored two traveling shows, "Pearls: A Natural History" and "Egyptians: Quest for Immortality")?
- Should MPM conduct a major capital campaign?
- Should MPM significantly increase admission rates or would that risk making the museum inaccessible to far too many people?

The take-away point is that a board cannot address the philosophical questions without first having a firm grasp of the nonprofit's finances. That is true for all boards and all nonprofits. No matter how much you view yourself as a "mission" person, the hard fact is that you must understand the financial issues before you can adequately address mission. Not all of the facts are out, but it appears that MPM's board, which one member described as a "fundraising" board,[57] did not focus on the financial issues as much as it should have in the years leading up to the crisis. Had the board focused more on finances, it could have addressed the philosophical issues in a more considered fashion. That is why you, as a board member, should focus on the financial issues, as painful or distasteful as that might be. Mission always is a financial matter; visionaries without a grasp

56. M. Chaiklin, *Do We Really Want to Gut Our Museum?: Gutting the Museum Will Have Long-Term Implications*, MILWAUKEE J.-SENTINEL, May 21, 2005—(Op Ed Piece by the curator of Asian history at the Milwaukee Public Museum).

57. L. Sandler, *Top Museum Leaders*, *supra* note 42. *See also* A. Lank and D. Umhoefer, *Hands-Off Board Hurt Museum: Members' Lax Attendance, Cruise-Control Attitude Contributed to Financial Crisis*, MILWAUKEE J.-SENTINEL, June 25, 2005. This article discuss board attendance, meetings, and director interest in unflattering terms, although several people quoted in the article take issue with some of the criticism. MPM's board certainly does not look good as far as past practices go, but many of the comments in this and other cited articles apply equally to far too many nonprofit boards.

of the underlying finances frequently imperil institutions with their financially unrealistic expectations and proposals.[58]

A Healthy Discussion at the Corcoran Museum

* * *

In 1999, the Corcoran Museum in Washington, D.C. began a capital campaign to finance a new wing designed by famed architect Frank Gehry in the hope of revitalizing the museum and competing with the many other attractions found in Washington. By May 2005, however, the museum had failed to raise the necessary money, presenting its board a difficult choice: Push harder for additional funds for the new addition, or scrap the plans and address the more immediate concerns. The $95 million in funds that had been expected apparently included a $40 million pledge from the District of Columbia. However, the projected costs for the new addition had risen from $60 million to $200 million, with $17 million already having been spent on construction plans and $5 million on fundraising costs.[59]

The Corcoran's President, David C. Levy, believed that "this city and region can support the campaign to get that building built."[60] Other board members were not nearly so confident. On the one hand, the board and the museum had devoted considerable time and had attracted significant resources for the expansion project. On the other hand, the board and the museum still had a long way to go before the museum could finance the $200 million project. Add to that the fact that during 17 of the prior 20 years, the Corcoran has apparently operated at a deficit. The natural inclination of many would have been to push forward, ignoring the fact that sunk costs (those already expended) do not cover future ones.

What is notable about this story is that the Corcoran's board of trustees resisted the pressure to push forward with the glitzy new project. On May 23, 2005, it voted to suspend the Gehry project but agreed to reconsider it if major donors came forward in the future.[61] The board of trustees asked the right questions: Can we afford this project? Will it really increase paid attendance enough to cover the cost and the museum's existing financial needs?

Not surprising, Frank Gehry was critical of the board's move, with the *Washington Post* reporting:

> Architect Gehry, reached while traveling in Italy, said that businesspeople on museum boards sometimes overreact to financial problems "because they're used to

---

58. To alleviate the crisis, the Milwaukee County Board of Supervisors did approve a bailout plan for MPM. *See* D. Umhoefer and A. Lank, *County Board OKs Museum Bailout Deal: Loan Guarantee Comes Amid Fears for Other Institutions*, Milwaukee J.-Sentinel, June 23, 2005. MPM also hired a new president with management and budget experience. *See* D. Umhoefer and S. Schultze, *Finley Will Lead Museum: Officials Confident his Political Savvy Can Help Rebuild Institution*, Milwaukee J.-Sentinel, July 28, 2005. One of the major contributors to the museum announced its commitment to reinstate funding for the museum. *See* D. Umhoefer, *Foundation Resumes Grants to Museum: Bradley Officials Reassured on Finances*, Milwaukee J.-Sentinel, Sept. 23, 2005. A successful recovery will depend on the commitment of the Milwaukee community, as evidenced by its willingness to participate in an upcoming capital campaign, but MPM does show some signs of recovering from its 2005 debacle.
59. B. Thompson and J. Trescott, *Corcoran Could Clip Its New Wing: Chairman Says Ailing Gallery Can't Afford Frank Gehry's Showpiece*, Wash. Post, May 2005
60. *Id.*
61. Press Release, Corcoran Museum, "Board of Directors Votes on New Leadership and Agrees to Plans Addressing Strategic Planning Issues Facing the Corcoran Gallery of Art" (May 24, 2005).

keeping companies in the black, and when they see red ink, they do not understand that's the way every museum in the world is." With the push for the new wing suspended, the architect wondered, "How are they going to find another director of any significant kind?"[62]

This attitude can have an intimating effect on boards, which is why the very fact that the Corcoran board engaged in such an open discussion of difficult financial and mission issues is so refreshing.

The board's decision did not come without cost. Mr. Levy resigned in an effort to avoid a damaging internecine fight. According to the *Post,* a major benefactor withdrew a significant gift to the Corcoran because she did not like how Mr. Levy was treated. This benefactor also changed her existing plans to donate her remaining artworks as well as one-third of her residuary estate to the museum.[63]

It all came down to fiscal responsibility. Board Chairman John Hazel put it very bluntly, "If you don't have your money, you cannot build it." He and his fellow board members acted responsibly.

* * *

5.6 DONOR INSIGHTS INTO FINANCIAL INFORMATION

The GuideStar[64] Web site has received much praise as being a resource for donors to review financial information for charities before deciding to make a contribution. GuideStar makes available each charity's IRS Form 990 as part of the information that it provides. IRS Form 990 does not necessarily provide the level of detail or the format that makes for a truly meaningful assessment of how effectively a charity is using charitable contributions. Donors who are making significant commitments to a charitable organization should always base their final assessment of financial matters on audited financial statements, keeping several points in mind.

(a) USING GAAP-PREPARED STATEMENTS VERSUS IRS FORM 990. Focusing on the problems inherent in using the data on IRS Form 990, Karen Froelich, Terry Knoepfle, and Thomas Pollak[65] explain:

> Compared to the IRS 990 Return, the audited statement was often described as more tailored or specific to an individual situation; because assumptions could be stated and additional facts explained in attached notes, it was seen as more descriptive and representative of the financial situation of the organization, whereas the IRS 990 Return was seen merely as a standard government form.

62. B. Thompson, *Corcoran Director Quits; Trustees Shelve Gehry Plans*, WASH. POST, May 24, 2005.
63. *Id.*
64. http://www.guidestar.org
65. K. Froelich, T. Knoepfle, and T. Pollak, *Financial Measures in Nonprofit Organization Research: Comparing IRS Form 990 Return and Audited Financial Statement Data*, 29 NONPROFIT Q. 232, at 246 (2000). *See also* E. Keating and P. Frumkin, *Reengineering Nonprofit Financial Accountability: Toward a More Reliable Foundation for Regulation*, 63 PUB. ADMIN. REV. 1 (2003).

However, later in their article, these authors point out that the part of their survey that actually analyzed entries indicated that the perception reported may not be accurate. For the smaller contributor, GuideStar's IRS Form 990 data and summary financial statements probably are adequate, given the ease of obtaining the information and the size of the donation (e.g., $250). However, donors who are considering major donations ($10,000 and more) have the bargaining power and time to take a closer look at both the financial statements and the IRS Form 990.

(b) DISCLOSING FUNDRAISING EXPENSES. Prospective donors like to know how much of their donation will directly fund the charity's mission and how much will be used to cover administrative and fundraising expenses. Many people half-jokingly ask whether their contributions are being used entirely to create mailings to ask for additional contributions. FASB *Accounting Standard No. 117* provides that:

> a statement of activities or notes to financial statements shall provide information about expenses reported by their functional classification such as major classes of program services and supporting activities.... Supporting activities are all activities of a not-for-profit organization other than program services. Generally, they include management and general, fund-raising, and membership development activities.[66]

Under GAAP, an organization must isolate its fundraising expenses in the body of the financial statements or in accompanying footnotes.[67] If you do not see a fundraising expense category when reviewing financial statements, either you are reviewing an incomplete summary of the organization's financial statements or the financial statements have not been prepared in accordance with GAAP. At a minimum, this should cause you to ask questions. Organizations may not like to disclose this information, but they should recognize that attempts to hide or bury fundraising data may detract from their fundraising efforts, particularly when those efforts are directed toward sophisticated prospects.

(c) EXPENSING FUNDRAISING EXPENDITURES. According to the *Audit and Accounting Guide for Not-for-Profit Organizations (AAG-NPO),* prepared by the American Institute of Certified Public Accountants, a nonprofit organization must treat all fundraising costs incurred during the current period as current expenses even when the expenses represent the upfront costs of a capital campaign that may span several periods.[68] Nonprofits do not like this rule because it can bunch expenses that benefit several future periods into the current period, throwing

---

66. Financial Statements of Not-for-Profit Organizations, *supra* note 12, at ¶¶ 26 and 28.
67. *Id.*
68. AICPA, Audit and Accounting Guide for Not-for-Profit Organizations, *supra* note 18, at § 13.06.

fundraising-related measurements off. The way for the organization to deal with this is through additional disclosure.[69]

In reporting fundraising expenses, an organization must present these expenses as reductions to unrestricted net assets even if the result of the fundraising efforts gives rise to a particular expense increase the expenses of the organization's permanent endowment (permanently restricted assets).[70] You should be suspicious of any attempt to amortize fundraising expenses over more than one period, which does not comply with GAAP.

(d) ALLOCATING OVERHEAD. Donors who are opposed to having their contributions applied partially to overhead should pay careful attention to the financial statements (more likely, the footnotes and internal accounting practices) to see how the organization allocates rent, utilities, general staff salaries, and other overhead items between management, fundraising, and program functions. Organizations have leeway in making these allocations.

Quite apart from financial reporting, a donor should address the question of overhead charges in the instrument that will govern the donated funds. As a caveat, before raising too many objections to overhead ("not with my money"), donors should not expect a free ride. It takes an organization and all its accoutrements to locate, administer, and disburse money responsibly and effectively.

Just as donors should not have unrealistic expectations regarding overhead charges, organizations must consider the impact that aggressive overhead allocations may have on future contributions. The experience of the American Red Cross following September 11 illustrates this point all to well. Donors revolted at the initial attempt by the American Red Cross to allocate funds away from direct aid to September 11 victims to the organization's other long-term expenses (not necessarily overhead). The Red Cross faced a public that failed to recognize that the money the Red Cross collected was not earmarked exclusively for the victims of 9/11 despite the efforts of the Red Cross to advise the public how it planned to use the money.[71]

---

69. *Id.*

70. Financial Statements of Not-for-Profit Organizations, *supra* note 12, at Appendix B, ¶¶ 133 to 136.

71. Robert A. Katz, *A Pig in a Python: How the Charitable Response to September 11 Overwhelmed the Law of Disaster Relief*, 36 Ind. L. Rev. 251 (2003). *See generally* M. Melcher with A. Mandl, *The Philanthropic Response to 9/11: A Practical Analysis and Recommendations—A Report Commissioned by Simpson Thacher & Bartlett LLP* (Fall 2003). In testifying before Congress, the former head of the American Red Cross, Dr. Bernadine Healy, stated:

> Let me address a few issues that have been raised recently that I think should be clarified. First, the American Red Cross, to my knowledge, has never described its work as limited only to those people who were lost on September 11 and their family [*sic*], in New York, and Pennsylvania and the Pentagon. We worked with them vigorously. Everything that we thought we could do, everything that was within our mission, we did.
>
> Now, other charities have said that, that it is only for the people who were lost on that day. We heard that background noise, so we repeatedly communicated to the public our range of service, through our chapter network, through PSAs, through contacts with donors, Web sites, in numerous TV

(e) CONSIDERATION OF CONTRIBUTED SERVICES. Under FASB *Statement No. 116,*[72] a nonprofit must recognize the value of contributed services when they (1) create or enhance nonfinancial assets or (2) require specialized skills, are provided by individuals possessing those skills, and would typically need to be purchased if not provided by donation. To illustrate the first category of services, assume that Green University constructs a new student union. A local construction company donates the labor for the plumbing, valued at $100,000, which Green University must recognize as income.[73] To illustrate the second category of services, assume that Smallville Legal Aid Society has volunteer lawyers who provide legal services valued at $1 million. The society must recognize $1 million of revenue and expense $1 million for the cost of program services.[74]

The potential problem with this accounting rule is that it relies on subjective valuations rather than cash payments in recognizing revenues and expenses. To illustrate the "games people can play," assume that a particular nonprofit's financial statements show $1 million in cash contributions, $100,000 of fundraising expenses, and $900,000 of program-related expenses. That means that 10 percent of contributions are devoted to fundraising. Now let's assume that the organization receives contributed services that it must include in its statements as revenue and expense. These services have no impact on net assets because the revenue and expense amounts offset each other, but increasing the value of imputed services related to program activities makes fundraising look more efficient. Inevitably, some charities will fudge the valuations to improve their fundraising-efficiency measurements. Donors must take this possibility into account when they review nonprofit financial statements. Probably the best approach for those making comparisons is to remove the value of contributed services from the analysis.

(f) CONSOLIDATING AFFILIATED ENTITIES. Under certain circumstances, accounting rules require that two or more entities be consolidated for purposes of financial statement presentation.[75] For example, one organization (a museum) may have the power to appoint the board of a second organization that holds the first organization's endowment and raises funds on its behalf. The supporting organization's articles of incorporation often specify that the supporting organization's

---

> appearances, press releases, in several—in full-page ads in several major newspapers listing the range of services, how much money we have raised and what it was being spent for. Very much along the lines of what Attorney General Spitzer has outlined. Perhaps not everyone heard it, but we certainly have tried, and we will continue to try and get that message out.

Charitable Contributions for September 11: Protecting Against Fraud, Waste, and Abuse: Hearing Before the Subcomittee on Oversight and Investigations of the Committee on Energy and Commerce, 107th Cong. 34 (2001).

---

72. ACCOUNTING FOR CONTRIBUTIONS RECEIVED AND CONTRIBUTIONS MADE, *supra* note16, at ¶ 9.
73. *Id.*, at Appendix B, Example 11.
74. *Id.*, at Appendix B, Example 12.
75. REPORTING OF RELATED ENTITIES BY NOT-FOR-PROFIT ORGANIZATIONS, *supra* note 13.

assets are to be used exclusively for the benefit of the supported organization. As you would probably agree, one consolidated financial statement might be appropriate in such a case.

The board of each organization must be careful, however. Legally, these are two separate entities, and each board has a duty of care to its specific legal entity. The supported organization cannot simply take funds from the supporting organization. This means that each organization should have its own checking and banking accounts, assets should not be commingled, and, if possible, each organization should have different people occupying officer positions (e.g., two different treasurers).

Let's return to the Milwaukee Public Museum, which included two related entities in its consolidated financial statements, one of which held a significant portion of the museum's endowment.[76] When liquidity became a problem, MPM apparently used about $4.2 million[77] of funds designated as endowment,[78] some of which may have represented donor-restricted funds.[79] According to newspaper reports, the funds were all commingled in a MPM operating account, although that is not entirely clear.[80] The interim audit by Milwaukee County reported that MPM's board had authorized the CFO to tap the endowment fund in 2002, although MPM disputed this.[81] Here is a perfect example of why each entity included in consolidated financial statements should be operated as a separate entity despite consolidated reporting.

---

76. Milwaukee Public Museum, 2003 Consolidated Financial Statements, Footnotes, Note 1.

77. This number is consistent with interim financial statements prepared as of April 30, 2005, showing a $4.2 million receivable from MPM to its endowment fund. *See* Milwaukee County Department of Audit, *supra* note 40, at 1.

78. A. Lank and D. Umhoefer, *Museum Fund Nearly Empty*, Milwaukee J.-Sentinel, May 25, 2005. The treatment of endowment funds in the 2003 financial statements is anything but clear. Specifically, the footnotes to the 2003 financial statements state, "Net assets subject to Board-imposed stipulations which the Board has chosen to maintain as a permanent restricted asset." The accountants may have an explanation, but board-designated endowment is not considered to be permanently restricted under GAAP. The December 2005 audit describes the transaction as a loan, stating that:

    > Those [preliminary financial statements as of August 31, 2005] show MPM has borrowed $4.5 million from its Endowment Fund, including approximately $1 million in permanently restricted funds.

    See Milwaukee County Department of Audit, *supra* note 38, at page 1.

79. A. Lank and D. Umhoefer, *Museum Panel Given Bad Endowment Numbers: Misstatement in January Was Off by Nearly $4 Million*, Milwaukee J.-Sentinel, June 6, 2005.

80. A. Lank and D. Umhoefer, *Museum Fund, supra* note 78.

81. *Id. See also* Milwaukee County Department of Audit, *supra* note 40, at 2, stating:

    > The absence of any significant, detailed oversight by Directors may have been compounded by the structure of responsibilities within MPM management. Since January 2003, the same individual has served as both the Chief Operating Officer (COO) and the Chief Financial Officer (CFO). Vesting responsibility for administration, operations and finance in one person was particularly problematic given the broad power to manage MPM's funds. This authority, which included the ability to authorize the sale and disbursement of Endowment Fund assets, was granted by Board action in April 2002, without the benefit of any approval. Based on internal monthly financial statements maintained by MPM fiscal staff, the COO/CFO first accessed Endowment Fund assets to support museum operations in March 2004. As of April 30, 2005, the internal financial statements show the Endowment Fund is virtually depleted, with a balance of approximately $340,000.

5.7 AUDITOR'S REPORT

You should never read an organization's audited financial statements without reading the opinion from the independent auditor. It describes what the auditor did in performing the audit and states whether the financial statements were prepared in accordance with generally accepted accounting principles.

The audit generally involves examining the accuracy of accounts on a test basis. Consequently, an audit can never guarantee that assets have not been misused, misappropriated, or mismanaged. If the auditor issues a qualified opinion, the board should spend whatever time is necessary to address those qualifications.

> To the Organization:
>
> We have audited the accompanying consolidated statement of financial position of the Organization as of December 31, 20X5, and the related consolidated statements of activities, of functional expenses, and of cash flows for the year then ended. These consolidated financial statements are the responsibility of management of the Organization. Our responsibility is to express an opinion on these consolidated financial statements based on our audit.
>
> We conducted our audit in accordance with generally accepted auditing standards. Those standards require that we plan and perform the audit to obtain reasonable assurance about whether the financial statements are free of material misstatement. An audit includes examining, on a test basis, evidence supporting the amounts and disclosures in the consolidated financial statements. An audit also includes assessing the accounting principles used and significant estimates made by management, as well as evaluating the overall financial statement presentation. We believe that our audit provides a reasonable basis for our opinion.
>
> In our opinion, based on our audit and the reports of the other auditors, the consolidated financial statements referred to above present fairly, in all material respects, the financial position of the Organization as of December 31, 20X5, and the changes in its net assets and its cash flows for the year then ended in conformity with generally accepted accounting principles.
>
> \s\ Auditors
> March 2, 20X6

The board and the organization's management must recognize the independent auditor's limited role in the financial accounting process. Management—not the auditors—is responsible for the organization's financial statements. Management is also responsible for establishing and maintaining an adequate system of internal controls. If problems exist, the board should look to management, not to the independent auditors, to correct them. The board must be aggressive in making demands on management when it comes to the accuracy and timeliness of the financial statements that the organization's accounting system produces. These are the statements that the board uses when approving budgets and making capital commitments, making accuracy and timeliness critical to an informed decision process. Remember that the auditors are issuing an opinion with respect to *year-end* financial statements. Those are not the same statements that the board reviews at monthly or quarterly meetings, which is why the board must demand an accounting system that produces accurate information throughout the year.

As a practical matter, the audit opinion is a somewhat useless document unless it contains qualifications (which in most cases it will not). The audit opinion is simply the culminating step in a testing and review process conducted by the auditor to make sure that the financial statements produced by the nonprofit bear a reasonable relation to reality. To illustrate the problem of over-reliance on the audit opinion, consider two nonprofits of equal size. During the course of its audit, the auditor recommends 50 adjustments to the financial statements of Red Social Services, including recalculation of depreciation, inclusion of contributed service income in revenue, adjustments to accruals, and reclassification of certain assets and revenue as restricted. Yellow Social Service's audit turns out to be far less error-prone, resulting in no adjustments. All other things being equal, after the adjustments are made, the auditor will issue audit opinions that are identical (except for the organization's name). Neither opinion will say anything about reliability of budgets or interim financial statements produced by the two accounting systems, but there should be no doubt that the Red Social Services board should be far more skeptical about the interim financial statements it receives than should the Yellow Social Services board. As you will see, the boards of both these organizations should pay much closer attention to the management letter that the organizations receive from their auditors.

5.8 AUDIT COMMITTEE

Every nonprofit's board should have an *audit committee* composed of board members who are neither employees nor officers of the organization (i.e., members who are independent)—at least if the nonprofit has any significant assets or operations.[82] This committee oversees the nonprofit's financial reporting process by selecting the independent auditor, discussing the plans for the audit, reviewing the financial statements, resolving disputes between the auditor and management as to financial statement presentations and accounting policies, and considering recommendations by the auditors for improvements to the organization's system of internal controls. It is responsible for ensuring the integrity of the organization's financial statements. The audit committee should provide the full board a report at least annually.

(a) AUDIT COMMITTEE REVIEW. Being a member of the audit committee should entail more than just attending four or five meetings a year. The audit committee should review a number of issues and documents on an ongoing basis. As the committee responsible for recommending an independent auditor, the audit

82. California law now mandates an audit committee for charities with $2 million or more of revenue. *See* Cal. Gov. Code § 12586(e). This law also limits who can serve on the audit committee, with a focus on member independence.

committee should review the qualifications of the partner in charge of the audit as well as the qualifications of audit team members. At a minimum, the committee should ascertain whether these individuals (and their firm) have experience with organizations similar to the nonprofit in question. The committee should not hesitate to ask for resumes, firm brochures, and the peer reviews that are available on the American Institute of Certified Public Accountant's Web site.

The committee should examine the auditing firm's independence and any potential conflicts of interest between the organization and the auditors. Potential conflicts include consulting contracts with the nonprofit. If the value of a consulting contract exceeds the annual audit fee, the independent auditor may be more willing to "bend" its judgment on accounting issues to protect a lucrative consulting contract. Consulting contracts that put the audit firm in the position of reviewing its own work as part of a subsequent audit are also inappropriate, as are contracts that require the auditor to perform management functions.

The committee is also responsible for reviewing judgment calls and accounting estimates related to the financial statements, alternative treatments of transactions under GAAP, and material communications between management and the auditor, including the annual management letter, schedules of audit adjustments, and corrections.

Each member of the audit committee should be familiar with the organization's financial statements. As part of its work, the committee should review financial statements for nonprofits in the same industry. The independent auditor should be able to provide appropriate samples. The review should focus on approaches to financial reporting and accounting conventions. If the nonprofit is deviating from what appears to be the industry norm, committee members should determine why.

The committee should also review any material transactions, material loan and other agreements, as well as other material arrangements between officers (and employees) and the nonprofit that pose potential conflicts of interest. The committee should assess whether the financial statements properly reflect these arrangements.

Along these same lines, the audit committee should also review executive compensation arrangements and perquisites. This is particularly important in the case of contingent pay arrangements that give the executive the financial incentive to "cook" the books or metric to achieve higher levels of compensation. When one officer has the ability to decide on perquisites for other officers or employees, review is highly advisable to ensure that this ability is not being abused or the perquisites are not being granted for inappropriate actions (e.g., sexual favors or work benefiting the executive, not the organization).

As part of its routine, the audit committee should review the organization's system of internal controls in an effort to determine whether they are adequate and how they could be improved. Reviewing the independent auditor's annual management letter is an integral part of this process. This letter details deficiencies in the organization's internal controls. Each committee member should review the nonprofit's IRS Form 990 filed with the IRS. When differences exist in the information reported on the tax return and in the financial statements, the committee members should demand full explanations.

As should be apparent, responsible audit committee membership entails a great deal of additional work. Because financial statements reflect all aspects of an organization's operations and are integral to the board's oversight function, the audit committee must examine all facets of the entity's operations in ensuring that the accounting system produces accurate and reliable financial statements. Make no mistake; this enumeration of duties and responsibilities is not in any way fictional but, if anything, is abbreviated. Many publicly traded companies publish their audit committee charters on their Web sites, as do some nonprofits.[83]

(b) AUDIT COMMITTEE AND WHISTLEBLOWERS. Organizations have begun to focus on procedures for encouraging, as well as protecting, whistleblowers following the enactment of the Sarbanes-Oxley Act of 2002.[84] At the heart of every whistleblower policy is the establishment or designation of a group or person within the organization that is outside the normal reporting channels so that whistleblowers can make concerns known without fear of retaliation and with the expectation of an appropriate response. Sarbanes-Oxley requires that public companies establish procedures to respond to questionable accounting and auditing matters.[85] To the extent that nonprofits decide to adopt otherwise inapplicable portions of Sarbanes-Oxley as best practices, it makes sense for whistleblower complaints pertaining to financial abuses and fraud to be handled by the audit committee. Sarbanes-Oxley also protects whistleblowers from retaliation in the case of federal investigations. This provision applies to nonprofits. We will consider it later in this chapter and in Chapter 11.

As should be clear, the audit committee already has what are burdensome responsibilities. Consequently, in fashioning a whistleblower policy that addresses applicable legal requirements, the organization must be careful to avoid designating the audit committee as the body to respond to all matters involving whistleblowers. Specifically, employment practices, Occupational Safety and Health Administration, and other nonfinancial concerns should be handled by other bodies within the organizational hierarchy. For example, the board might designate someone in the human resources department as the contact person for employment-related concerns. Although this may appear to be a trivial point, a number of large nonprofits have already complained that their audit committees are overwhelmed by whistleblowers bringing employment practice and other

---

83. For examples, see Boeing Company's audit committee charter available at http://www.boeing.com/corp_gov/charter_audit_comittee.html, and the Ford Foundation's audit committee charter, available at http://www.fordfound.org/about/docs/committee_charters_audit.pdf

84. Pub L. 107-204, 116 Stat. 745.

85. 15 U.S.C. 78f(m)(4).

nonfinancial concerns to their attention. This is symptomatic of either a poorly designed system for responding to these complaints or a poorly articulated one.

(c) AUDIT COMMITTEE MEMBERSHIP. Each member of the board's audit committee should be independent. There is probably no universally accepted definition of independence. However, a number of factors should be considered when assessing whether committee membership is appropriate, as the following example involving the Fickle Museum demonstrates. The museum's board of directors wants to charter an audit committee. The board is considering the following individuals for committee membership: (1) Audrey Jones, a partner with Samson, Jones, and Wiley, the museum's independent auditor, (2) Bill Quarterwell, the museum's CFO, (3) Beth Rago, a local trusts and estates attorney, (4) Harry Warner, the museum's president, (5) Lyman Quawalski, a local art critic, and (6) Susan Creswell, the chairperson of the museum's fundraising committee. Several of these individuals are inappropriate candidates for committee membership.

Audrey Jones certainly is a logical candidate given her expertise in accounting and financial matters, but she is not an appropriate candidate. The audit committee oversees and reviews the museum's relationship with its independent auditor. This includes recommending who should be the independent auditor. Although it need not be hostile, the relationship between the audit committee and the independent auditor should have an adversarial aspect to it. Jones simply cannot sit on both sides of the table if she is to satisfy her obligations to each party.

Bill Quarterwell is another logical candidate. As the museum's CFO, he is the officer responsible for financial reporting and the organization's accounting system, but these responsibilities make him an inappropriate candidate. The audit committee is responsible for reviewing his work. Like Jones, Quarterwell should not be sitting on both sides of the table. This does not mean, however, that Quarterwell cannot attend audit committee meetings. This is advisable and appropriate if he attends at the invitation of the committee and the committee recognizes that there will be times when Quarterwell should not attend these meetings.

Beth Rago is an appropriate candidate. She is an attorney who is versed in financial matters. Of course, if Rago represents clients who have significant financial relationships with the museum, this conclusion might not hold true. Lyman Quawalski is also an appropriate audit committee prospect because he does not have a financial relationship with the museum, nor is he an officer, director, or employee. There is one reservation: his ability to analyze and understand financial and accounting matters. Quawalski's occupation does not require those skills.

As the museum's president, Harry Warner is not an appropriate prospect for audit committee membership. Too many people who are responsible for financial and accounting matters ultimately report to him. Susan Creswell is also an inappropriate candidate because she is in charge of fundraising, a position that mandates financial oversight by and accountability to the museum. Like Audrey Jones and Bill Quarterwell, Creswell would be sitting on both sides of the table if she were an audit committee member.

To summarize, an appropriate candidate for audit committee membership is knowledgeable about financial matters, does not have control over the accounting process or organizational assets, and will not be reviewing his own work.[86] Finding people who satisfy these requirements is difficult for many small nonprofits. One solution is to retain an expert to assist the board with the issues that would otherwise be delegated to an audit committee.

(d) CALIFORNIA'S APPROACH TO AUDIT COMMITTEE MEMBERSHIP. In 2004, California enacted legislation requiring a nonprofit board to create an audit committee if the organization receives $2 million or more in annual revenue (with certain types of revenue excluded from the computation).[87] Many charities complain that their board members lack the financial expertise necessary to make audit committee membership meaningful. The legislation addresses the concern over expertise by specifically providing that the audit committee may include individuals who are not members of the board of directors.[88]

The legislation precludes any members of the staff (including the president, CEO, treasurer, and CFO) from serving on the committee regardless of whether they are volunteers.[89] The California attorney general does make an allowance for "directors of the corporation, acting solely in their capacity as directors or officers of the board of directors."[90] This seems to draw a distinction between

---

86. Those interested in exploring the audit committee in further detail should start by examining SEC Release No. 34-47654 (Apr. 1, 2003), which contains the SEC's formulation of the audit committee for publicly traded companies (referred to in the following list as "issuer") under Sarbanes-Oxley. The SEC's requirements may be more than are necessary in the nonprofit context (although that is arguable), but these requirements could be useful in developing a charter for a nonprofit's audit committee. Specifically, the SEC requires that:

    - Each member of the audit committee of the issuer must be independent according to specified criteria.
    - The audit committee of each issuer must be directly responsible for the appointment, compensation, retention, and oversight of the work of any registered public accounting firm engaged for the purpose of preparing or issuing an audit report or performing other audit, review, or attest services for the issuer, and each such registered public accounting firm must report directly to the audit committee.
    - Each audit committee must establish procedures for the receipt, retention, and treatment of complaints regarding accounting, internal accounting controls or auditing matters, including procedures for the confidential, anonymous submission by employees of the issuer of concerns regarding questionable accounting or auditing matters.
    - Each audit committee must have the authority to engage independent counsel and other advisers, as it determines necessary to carry out its duties.
    - Each issuer must provide appropriate funding for the audit committee.

87. Cal. Gov. Code § 12586(e). The calculation excludes grants from, and contracts for services with, governmental entities for which the governmental entity requires an accounting of the funds received.
88. Cal. Gov. Code § 12586(e)(2). *See also* FAQ, Question 12, posted on the California Attorney General's Web site (viewed on Nov. 27, 2005), available at http://caag.state.ca.us/charities/faq.htm. Section 12856(e)(2) appears to be in conflict with a more general provision contained in Section 5212 of the California Nonprofit Corporation Act. Section 5212 is anything but clear, but it can be read to prohibit nonboard members from serving on board committees.
89. *Id.*
90. *Id.*

the volunteer board member who serves as the unpaid president and the paid executive director who holds the title of president. The attorney general has also indicated that *staff* includes employees "whether or not they are unpaid volunteers."[91] The California Attorney General's position is right from an *independence* standpoint, but it may not be practical in many instances.

Even though an organization can look to outsiders to serve on the audit committee, will the organization be able to find unpaid volunteers who are willing to take on the job? Yes, unpaid. The California legislation provides that members of the audit committee cannot receive any more compensation than they would be paid as directors.[92] If directors receive no compensation, then members of the audit committee can receive no compensation. This eliminates professional audit committee members. Further complicating matters is a provision that distinguishes between the audit committee and the finance committee.[93] No more than one-third of the members of the finance committee can serve on the audit committee. This requirement also makes it difficult to find the necessary expertise for the audit committee.

As a practical matter, this new requirement means that directors either need to seek some education or the audit committee needs to retain a paid outside expert (but not a member of the committee) to advise it. The bottom line: Boards of large California nonprofits will no longer be able to rely on financial ignorance as a plausible defense. The board now has a duty to create and staff a viable audit committee.

5.9 GAO AUDIT GUIDELINES

The Government Accountability Office (GAO)[94] has issued audit guidelines[95] and independence standards[96] that are relevant to nonprofits for two reasons. First, and of practical import, if a nonprofit receives federal awards[97] that equal

91. *Id.*
92. Section 12586(e)(2) of the California Government Code. There is an interpretive issue here: Can a director be paid an additional sum for taking on this task if the sum is calculated on a per-meeting basis? For example, if all directors are paid $10,000 for attending four meetings per year, can an audit committee member be paid $2,500 for each committee meeting he attends?
93. *Id.*
94. The Government Accountability Office was formerly known as the General Accounting Office.
95. United States Government Accountability Office, by the Comptroller General of the United States, Audit Standards 2003 Revision (June 2003). These standards are sometimes referred to as Generally Accepted Government Auditing Standards (GAGAS), or as the *Yellow Book* standards.
96. *Id.* The independence standards are incorporated into the Yellow book, but the GAO has also issued specific guidance regarding independence. *See* United States Government Accountability Office, Government Auditing Standards: Answers to Independence Standard Questions (July 2002).
97. *See* Office of Management and Budget, Circular A-133, Audits of States, Local Governments, and Non-Profit Organizations, § __105, defining a federal award as:

> Federal financial assistance and Federal cost-reimbursement contracts that non-Federal entities receive directly from Federal awarding agencies or indirectly from pass-through entities. It does not include procurement contracts, under grants or contracts, used to buy goods or services from vendors. Any audits of such vendors shall be covered by the terms and conditions of the contract. Contracts to operate Federal Government owned, contractor operated facilities (GOCOs) are excluded from the requirements of this part.

or exceed $500,000,[98] its independent auditors are prohibited from providing certain services under the Single Audit Act of 1984.[99] Second, these standards can serve as "best practices" for a nonprofit that is assessing the relationship with its auditors.

(a) BEST PRACTICES. A nonprofit's board of directors should want an independent auditor to review the organization's financial statements. The GAO guidelines provide an excellent framework for the board and audit committee to consider when retaining an auditor. This is true whether the nonprofit is subject to the United States Government Auditing Standards or the Single Audit Act. To be independent under the GAO definition for independence, the auditor should "be free both in fact and appearance from personal, external, and organizational impairments to independence."[100] Although the GAO standards are worth considering in assessing an organization's relationship with its outside auditor, a one-size-fits-all approach should be rejected when it comes to best practices. Nevertheless, if an organization's relationship with its auditor does not comport with the GAO standards, the board should recognize the possible risks associated with the deviation.

(b) PROHIBITED AND PERMITTED SERVICES. Under the GAO standards, auditors should not perform management functions nor make management decisions.[101] Under no circumstance should an audit firm be placed in the position of auditing its own work.[102]

The GAO standards do permit certain specific nonaudit services, but this enumeration of permitted services is always subject to the overarching independence principles.[103] Obviously, a nonprofit and its auditor that are subject to the GAO guidelines must comply with the distinction between permitted and prohibited nonaudit services. All nonprofits should review this abridged list:

PROHIBITED NONAUDIT SERVICES

- Maintaining or preparing basic accounting records.[104]
- Maintaining or taking responsibility for records that will be subject to audit.
- Providing internal audit services.[105]

---

98. *Id.*, at § _200(a).
99. Single Audit Act of 1984, Pub. L. 98-502, 98 Stat. 2327 (1984); and the Single Audit Act Amendments of 1996, Pub. L. 104-156, 110 Stat. 1396 (1996).
100. YELLOW BOOK, *supra* note 95, at ¶ 3.03.
101. *Id.*, at ¶ 3.14.
102. *Id.*, at ¶ 3.13.
103. INDEPENDENCE QUESTIONS, *supra* note 95, at 11.
104. UNITED STATES GOVERNMENT ACCOUNTABILITY OFFICE, GOVERNMENT AUDITING STANDARDS: ANSWERS TO INDEPENDENCE STANDARDS (July 2002), at Question 46. There may be some technical activities that the auditor can undertake without impairing its independence, but these assume an underlying system of books and records, as well as management assuming responsibility for the technical activities.
105. *Id.*, at Question 66.

- Supervising or operating IT services.
- Conducting executive search for significant positions.
- Preparing annual budgets or strategic plans (with certain exceptions).

PERMITTED NONAUDIT SERVICES

- Providing routine tax services such as preparing tax returns or providing advice.[106]
- Providing emergency accounting services (but subject to stringent limitations).
- Providing routine advice in establishing internal controls.[107]
- Serving on committees in an ex-offio capacity.[108]
- Answering technical questions.
- Providing training, or benchmark studies and developing audit methodologies (but with limitations).

* * *

(c) CASE: BIG FOOD BASKET AND PERSONAL IMPAIRMENTS. Let's consider a case to illustrate the potential problems posed by nonaudit services. Big Food Basket is a community food bank. Its board is in the process of selecting an auditor. Anita Brody chairs the board, and Warren Rago is the full-time executive director. Brody has proposed the Ming, Richards & Jones firm as Foodbasket's independent auditor. Most of the board supports this suggestion because the firm is willing to provide the audit services significantly below the bids of other firms. Brody has been able to obtain the lower bid through a little arm-twisting. Ming, Richards is also the auditor for Brody Meatpacking Company, one of the largest, privately held meatpackers in the county. Brody is the sole owner of Brody Meatpacking, and Big Food Basket has been her pet charity for the last 20 years. Assume that Big Food Basket receives no federal awards. The issue is whether Brody's business relationship with Ming, Richards could jeopardize the independence of Ming, Richards with respect to Big Food Basket.

This question reflects reality in the nonprofit world. Often one major contributor or moving force behind a nonprofit also is a wealthy businessperson. This person is able to induce attorneys, accountants, and other service providers to offer pro bono services to the lucky nonprofit because those providers have a lucrative relationship with that person's business. Many directors will be thrilled when these necessary services can be obtained for a significant discount, but compromising auditor independence can clearly be a downside.

In this particular case, the board might conclude that the relationship does not threaten auditor independence. Big Food Basket does have a paid executive director. But suppose Warren Rago is Brody's lackey. Or even worse, suppose

106. *Id.*, at Question 81.
107. *Id.*, at Question 27.
108. *Id.*, at Question 34.

Brody Meatpacking is a Big Food Basket supplier. Now are you disturbed or concerned?

Even if those are the facts, the board could decide to retain Ming, Richards on the theory that the financial statements are just for the board's benefit. There may be *some* merit to that argument if no lender or other outside entity relies on Big Food Basket's audited financial statements. There may be no problems for many years. However, board factions can develop over time. Sometime down the road, the board could become sharply divided over an issue rooted in Big Food Basket's financial position. The group having Brody on its side may have an advantage under those circumstances because Brody has some influence over the auditors. Consequently, Big Food Basket's directors should take care before acquiescing too quickly to Brody's offer.

If Big Food Basket receives significant federal awards, then Ming, Richards has some soul-searching to do. The firm must consider whether it can be independent under the GAO audit standards. The immediate risk that Ming, Richards runs is that the GAO or the inspector general for a governmental agency questions the firm's independence and then notifies a state accounting board, the AICPA, or a state accounting professional organization. If losses to the Big Food result from Ming Richards' lack of independence, there are obvious professional liability issues. Violations of GAO audit standards could well undercut any defense against liability the firm would offer.

5.10 INTERNAL CONTROLS

Those designing accounting systems focus on who has *custody* of assets, who *records* transactions affecting assets, and who has *decision authority* over the use of assets. The features of the accounting system that address these issues are traditionally referred to as *internal controls*. We adhere to that terminology, but you should recognize that these features are really financial controls, a subset of internal controls. The accounting profession has begun to emphasize that internal controls include nonfinancial controls such as hiring procedures, policies supporting the anonymous reporting of fraud, and outside review of executive compensation. Much of what is discussed in the other areas of this *Guide*, particularly in Chapter 11, is actually internal control by the board. Internal controls are the mechanisms by which management and the board keep their collective ear to the ground and make their wishes known to those throughout the organization. They make good governance possible.

(a) THREE BASIC INTERNAL CONTROL FUNCTIONS. The ideal accounting system is designed so that no one person (or department, if the organization is large enough) is responsible for more than one of the basic functions (custody, record keeping, and decision authority). This separation of functions is designed to prevent fraud. For example, if the same person has custody of the cash and controls decisions to spend it, that person could pocket the cash while reporting the disbursement as an organizational operating expense.

Rarely is an accounting system perfect. As part of their audit, the independent auditors report on problems they detect in the organization's system of internal controls. The board should take this report seriously, insisting that management implement recommended changes. Many of the suggested changes in the auditor's annual letter to management address situations in which two or more of the three basic accounting functions are vested in the same person or department.

(i) Custodial Function. The *custodial function* involves holding or possessing assets. A well-designed control system will place authorization for expending or using an asset and related record keeping with individuals (or departments) other than the person (or department) responsible for custody of the asset. Let's consider cash in the organization's checking account. The person authorized to write the checks (the one with custody) should not have authority to initiate expenditures or to record transactions in the financial records. Even though the check writer has apparent authority to write a check (and therefore custody of the cash), that apparent authority can be limited if someone other than the person writing the check must review and reconcile the bank statement monthly. That review should be accomplished by matching checks against written disbursement authorizations. That apparent authority can be further limited by requiring two signatures on each check when the amount of the check exceeds a certain amount.

You may ask how dividing these responsibilities prevents the person who has check-writing authority from simply writing a check to cash and absconding with $50,000. The answer is that dividing responsibilities (other than requiring two signatures) cannot prevent thefts of this nature. Proper division can, however, prevent the perpetrator from performing more subtle forms of fraud. When Lindstrom, the custodian of cash, does not show up for work and his wife says he mysteriously left for the airport with his passport, the organization knows it has a problem. (More about that shortly.) Lindstrom may be more devious, however. If he is in charge of the entire accounting system, he can prepare a purchase order for services from XYZ Company (a dummy company that he has created), write a check to XYZ company, and then record that services from XYZ Company were provided to the organization. Meanwhile, Lindstrom has the money. If someone else matches checks with purchase orders and someone else monitors whether the services were actually provided, Lindstrom must be much more creative in his efforts to defraud the organization. To provide any protection, the accounting system needs to create a *paper* or *electronic trail* that is routinely reviewed and reconciled. Creating and reviewing this trail is what internal financial controls are all about.

WHAT ABOUT OUTRIGHT THEFT?

* * *

The chief administrative officer of the American Cancer Society's Ohio Division was charged with embezzling $6.9 million from the organization.[109] According to various newspaper accounts, the officer authorized a wire transfer to a bank account in Austria in May 2000, with the proceeds ostensibly for research.[110] Fortunately for the society, the attempted fraud was quickly discovered, and the bulk of the money was recovered. The officer subsequently pled guilty to "four counts of bank fraud, mail fraud, credit card fraud, and money laundering."[111] The events giving rise to the conviction began in 1997, so the highly publicized wire transfer apparently was not an isolated incident.[112]

The Ohio Division's internal controls, as well as background checking, appear to have been lax.[113] According to an August 25, 2000, article in the *Honolulu Star-Bulletin*, the officer had been charged in 1992 with theft of $20,000 from a Hawaii food bank.[114]

To avoid similar incidents, all organizations should consider the following controls:

- *Requiring criminal background checks for all employees.* These should be performed particularly for persons who have responsibility for financial matters, although background checks may not be the panacea that many make them out to be. (See Chapter 11 for additional details regarding background checks)
- *Having strong overall controls.* A number of articles reported that in the Ohio Division situation, the chief administrative officer's activities began in 1997, involving small thefts that were perpetrated using fictitious names.[115] Had those been detected in a timely manner, the larger theft would have never happened.
- *Requiring two signatures for checks and wire transfers above certain amounts (e.g., $5,000).* One signature should be from the custodian of the funds and the other from the appropriate executive officer. It is unclear in the Ohio Division case whether two different people had to authorize the wire transfer or whether the officer had lone authority.[116] To prevent hampering day-to-day operations, set a dollar limit that provides protection against a catastrophic theft.

---

109. K. Vanderwarren, *Financial Accountability in Charitable Organizations: Mandating an Audit Committee Function*, 77 CHI.-KENT L. REV. 963 (2002).
110. K. Hoke, *Theft Claim Delivers Notice: Cancer Society Case Focuses Nonprofits on Credibility Issue*, COLUMBUS BUS. FIRST, June 9, 2000.
111. *Wiant Sentenced to 13 Years for Cancer Society Theft*, COLUMBUS BUS. FIRST, Apr. 13, 2001; and *United States v. Wiant*, 314 F.3d 826 (6th Cir. 2003).
112. *Id.*, According to that article "Wiant admitted to defrauding the Cancer Society of $923,870 from 1997 to May 2000...."
113. There apparently was some disagreement between the Cancer Society and its bank as to whether the Cancer Society had wire transfer limits that its bank exceeded. *See* M. Gallagher and V. Radcliffe, *Internal Controls in Nonprofit Organizations: The Case of the American Cancer Society, Ohio Division,* 3 NONPROFIT MGT. & LEADERSHIP (Spring 2002). *See also* T. Peske, *Embezzling Accomplices at Cancer Society May Be Known*, USA NEWS, June 5, 2000.
114. Associated Press, *Man Jailed in Hawaii Fraud Admits $7.9 Mil Cancer Society Theft*, HONOLULU STAR-BULL., Aug. 25, 2000. *See also* W. Wright, *Suspect in Ohio Theft is Hawaii Ex-Convict*, HONOLULU ADVERTISER, June 15, 2000.
115. T. Peske, *supra* note 113.
116. M. Gallagher and V. Radcliffe, *supra* note 113.

- *Notifying the executive director of wire transfers.* This assumes, of course, that the executive director is not authorized to initiate a wire transfer alone.
- *Acquiring fidelity insurance.* This allows the organization to shift a catastrophic risk to someone else.

* * *

(ii) Recording Function. The *recording function* involves the person who accounts for transactions involving assets and liabilities. This is the accounting department or, in a small nonprofit, the bookkeeper. It is important that those who have custody of assets not have responsibility for recording acquisitions or dispositions of those assets or the payment or incurrence of liabilities. Otherwise, the person who has custody of assets is, in effect, accountable to no one.

For example, the person in charge of warehouse inventory should not be in a position to authorize or record withdrawals from or additions to inventory. Otherwise, the custodian could ship goods to friends and record the transaction as a fulfillment of a customer's order. This explains the reason for the amount of paperwork in any accounting system. When an order is received, the person authorizing the sale communicates the order to warehouse personnel (custody) and the accounting department (record keeping). When the warehouse ships the goods, it notifies the accounting department. It is true that the custodian is creating a record of the shipment at that point in time. That record, however, should be compared against the original authorization to ship inventory, which was created outside the custodial function. Additions to the organization's inventory must be initiated with a purchase order that is sent to the accounting department. In other words, it is critical that there be an audit trail and that the audit trail cannot be manipulated.

Nothing prevents the custodian from stealing inventory. This is one reason that periodic physical inventory counts are taken. These counts can then be compared against purchase orders authorizing increases to inventory and shipping orders authorizing decreases to inventory. Most nonprofits do not have traditional manufacturing inventories, but their managers should not forget office supplies, gift shop inventories, hospital supplies, school books, and laptop computers. Each of these categories is subject to the inventory control just described.

(iii) Authorization (Disbursement) Function. The *authorization function* is performed by the persons who approve or authorize transactions involving the organization's assets. Those who use assets are scattered throughout the organization. It is important that asset users not be responsible for authorizing or tracking the use of assets. Consider a corporate travel system which uses cash. Every employee would like to take a trip to an expensive conference in Hawaii. In a well-designed system, each employee should lack the authority to initiate such a trip alone. Normally, employees much first obtain authorization for a trip from a supervisor. This is a first step in safeguarding the entity's assets. Because the supervisor and the employee work in the same department, there is opportunity for friendly "collusion." Why should the supervisor not give the employee a bonus of sorts?

To provide further control, all authorizations should be reviewed by the accounting department and compared against actual receipts. The organization can obtain further protection against fraud by using a corporate travel agent, establishing a prescribed list of vendors (certain identified airlines, hotels, and car rental companies), and setting policies and dollar limitations in an employee handbook. Each of these steps strengthens the control system so that even though each employee may have apparent authority to spend money while traveling, the system's controls keep each employee honest.

Another excellent control is annual budgeting. Senior management obviously does not want to review the individual travel expenses for each employee trip and relies on managers at lower levels to do so. An annual budget and a review of variances can quickly alert senior management to travel expenses that are higher than budgeted. Management can then order an investigation to determine why these expenses have increased.

The take-away point is that no one control provides absolute protection against fraud or waste. Nothing can prevent someone from simply walking away with assets. What is important is to have a system in place that catches fraud and waste, and more important, sends the message that both will be quickly detected and punished.

(b) A CLOSER LOOK AT FINANCIAL CONTROLS. The easiest way to examine financial controls is by focusing on each account category in the organization's balance sheet.

(i) Cash. Let's start with cash. The opportunity for embezzlement from nonprofits almost always can be traced back to lax financial controls. One government official recently described an override of an organization's internal controls as "clever" and "sophisticated." Such overrides could appear to people unfamiliar with controls to be clever, but more often than not, there was no override because there were not even elementary financial controls in place. Virtually every organization has some type of petty cash fund. The basic control is to keep a small amount of cash in this fund. Only the custodian should be permitted to withdraw amounts from the fund. Withdrawals might be limited to the executive director and the office manager. When any money is withdrawn, a prenumbered slip should be completed and sent to accounting. The accounting department should perform periodic reconciliations. The money should be kept in a safe or locked file cabinet. Even when the amount in petty cash is immaterial, the organization should maintain tight controls over the fund so that employees realize that controls to protect even small amounts of cash are in place.

Although thefts from petty cash funds rarely if ever make the news, larger thefts frequently do.[117] The first step is to consolidate bank and money market accounts so that the organization has as few accounts as possible. Next, although slightly inconvenient, two signatures should be required for all checks (and wire transfers) above a certain amount. The designated signatories should be in different reporting lines. Finally, the bank statement should be reconciled monthly by someone who does not report to one of the authorized signers.

Cash registers that generate receipts should be used if the organization engages in retail sales (e.g., a museum gift store or a thrift shop). A number of retail establishments post signs that state the company's offer of discounts or free goods to customers who do not receive a cash register receipt or receive one that does not match the amount shown on the register. These systems incorporate the customer in the financial control process by providing customers an incentive to check their receipts. Consider that technique in any situation involving cash registers. If there are multiple clerks, there should be multiple registers with procedures requiring separate cash drawers and checking in and out of the registers.

Whitney Museum Focuses on Art at the Expense of Internal Controls

* * *

The Whitney Museum of Art had about $880,000 stolen by two former employees from January 2002 to July 2004.[118] Fortunately one of the thieves did not spend the money but kept a significant portion of her take—$800,000—in a safe in her home. According to newspaper accounts,[119] both employees pled guilty, but neither was sentenced to jail time.

As is sadly typical in these cases, the theft could have been easily prevented had the Whitney's board and staff paid any attention to details. Both employees were cashiers at the ticket counter, and the woman was the manager of Visitor Services. They would ring up a ticket sale, void the sale, and then pocket the cash. The two employees acted independently

117. Consider these two examples: In March 2005, the Lincoln, Nebraska police reported arresting five people who allegedly stole from five seemingly unrelated non-profits. J. Swartzlander, *Nonprofit Group workers Accused of Stealing*, Lincoln J. Star, Apr. 4, 2004. Those arrested have the presumption of innocence until found guilty. Nevertheless, the clustering of allegations in one relatively small community suggests that reports of widespread fraud and abuse in the nonprofit community may have some basis in fact. It would be one thing if there were five arrests throughout the United States in one month, but five arrests in one community is quite another. As a second example, one congressional committee report listed numerous newspaper accounts of financial abuse and mismanagement in Head Start programs. *See* Majority Staff of the U.S. House Committee on Education and the Workforce, Taking Money from Children: Financial Abuse & Mismanagement in the Head Start Early Childhood Program, A Summary of Media Reports (2003–2005) (Mar. 18, 2005). This time the concentration is on one particular type of organization rather than a particular geographic region. But once again, this level of concentration suggests that the cited abuses are anything but occasional or isolated.

118. Associated Press, *Woman Admits She Stole $850G From Whitney*, N. Y. Times, Jan. 12, 2005.

119. Associated Press, *Brooklyn Woman Pleads Guilty to Stealing $850,000 from Whitney Museum*, Newsday, Jan. 13, 2005.

of each other. The museum learned of the thefts when one of the employees turned in the other one. The district attorney speculated that the informer might have decided to inform so that he could expand his own efforts.[120] The Whitney proved the existence of the scheme by installing hidden cameras, thereby catching the activities on tape.

The central question: How could the museum have prevented the theft or at least detected it before it got out of hand? Here are some thoughts.

Proof of the thefts was obtained through the use of hidden cameras—but why wait until there is an allegation of wrongdoing before installing the cameras?[121] Las Vegas casinos use cameras as part of their internal controls to protect cash—and they let everyone know that they are doing it. A video system could have been installed in the Whitney for $20,000. Of course, there are ongoing monitoring costs.[122] Those expenditures might be justifiable. However, just letting employees know that there would be random surveillance for several hours a day could serve as a less costly deterrent.

The newspaper accounts of the Whitney's experience included few details describing the ticketing process, and attempts to obtain information from the prosecutor were not successful. Assume, however, that the tickets were computer-generated on special paper. Each day the number of tickets issued (which should be recorded by the computer in a password-protected file) should have been matched against the receipts from the cash drawer. If the tickets were voided, the cashiers should have had to retain the voided copies. That way, the sum of the cash receipts divided by the ticket price plus the number of voided tickets should have equaled the recorded number of tickets issued by the computer. As the press reports seem to indicate, visitors received their tickets, and after the customer left, the employees involved in the theft voided the tickets electronically. This suggests that cash and the number of issued tickets were never reconciled. Even if this assumption is incorrect, there should have been a control (or a better one) in place to force daily reconciliations between cash and ticket sales.

The number of voided sales should have raised a red flag. When the story broke, the Whitney showed a basic admission price of $12 on its Web site. This suggests that there were somewhere between 60,000 and 70,000 voided transactions. Even if there were no theft involved, management should have focused on the number of voided tickets.[123] That

120. *2 Museum Employees Busted for In-House Theft*, 1010WINS.COM, Jan. 13, 2005.

121. Any organization considering hidden surveillance must first consider whether there are any limitations on such surveillance imposed by applicable laws and by union contracts.

122. Any organization installing video surveillance equipment should keep the following in mind. The company supplying the equipment should certify that the system produces evidence that will be acceptable in court before the system is purchased. If a perpetrator is caught in the act, the specific incident should be backed up and stored off site. Moreover, the entire hard drive should be backed up so that the perpetrator's lawyer cannot argue that the nonprofit selectively captured incidents. This can be important where there are issues pertaining to vandalism. The nonprofit should not rely on the primary system to serve as the backup device because these systems typically overwrite data on a first-in, first-out basis. The lighting should be sufficient to permit capture of clear images. If at all possible, the employees charged with operating the equipment should be certified through a training program.

In a case like the Whitney's, where the cameras were installed after the thefts had already started, the nonprofit should capture multiple incidents before having the perpetrator arrested. Establishing a pattern of criminal activity will make it easier to overcome claims that earlier, undocumented thefts, were perpetrated by someone else. Even if the nonprofit is unsuccessful in tying the perpetrator to the unrecorded incidents, obtaining multiple incidents will make it more likely that the perpetrator will be charged with a felony rather than a misdemeanor.

If the nonprofit plans to use the video evidence to obtain restitution, it should seek legal counsel before showing the video to the perpetrator or his attorneys. The nonprofit wants to avoid any claims that it was threatening criminal prosecution to extort money from the perpetrator.

123. This assumes that the voided transactions appeared in the records as such. The employees may simply have destroyed any record of the transaction or never actually created a record.

many errors should have caused management to reconsider its basic system or consider better employee training with respect to the existing system.

Many museums position an employee at the entrance to the galleries using a mechanical counter. If that had been the practice at the Whitney, the daily count should have been reconciled against the admissions tabulated at the cash registers.

The press accounts indicate that multiple employees had access to the same cash register, which is not good system design. Each employee should be assigned to a separate register with mandatory check-in and check-out procedures.

According to Line 93a of the Whitney's Fiscal Year 2003 IRS Form 990, it had $2,277,911 in admission revenue for the period beginning July 1, 2002, and ending June 30, 2003. Extrapolating, this would mean that the Whitney had roughly $5,694,777 in admission revenue over the two-plus years in which the alleged thefts were perpetrated. That at least suggests that approximately 15 percent of total admission revenue was stolen— a material number.[124] Why did the CFO or the board fail to notice this decline in revenue when they reviewed budget variances or comparisons with earlier periods? Furthermore, there were no indications of thefts of restaurant or museum gift shop revenue. Why did the CFO or the board never ask why revenue from these other operations—which are directly tied to attendance—was growing faster than (or out of line with) admission revenue? Reviewing budgets and variances is an important internal control function.

The management letter from the Whitney's auditors unfortunately is not a public document, leaving one question unanswered: Did the letter raise concerns about the internal controls designed to protect cash raised through ticket sales?

* * *

Although cash collections should be avoided, sometimes there is no way to do so. Charitable solicitations should clearly advise prospective donors not to send cash. Despite such requests, if cash is frequently received by mail, a procedure should be implemented requiring two people to open the mail and record cash receipts and a third person to immediately deposit the cash in the bank (or a secure safe until a bank deposit is feasible). This procedure should be followed whenever collections are taken from an assembled group (e.g., the Sunday collection plate). In the case of festival food and beverage service, consider a ticket system that separates those who collect cash from those serving food and beverages.

Credit cards are as a good as cash. If at all possible organizations should avoid having *corporate* credit (and debit) card accounts. Although the credit card companies promote them, corporate credit cards pose a number of serious problems for any organization. The employee who maxes out the credit limit and then disappears is most troublesome. Probably more costly is the employee who makes expenditures that are somewhat related to the organization's activities, such as buying books or entertaining a donor who is also a friend. If this employee had to pay for these expenses using a personal credit card, he might be a little more reticent before incurring an otherwise unauthorized expenditure. Employees are also less likely to travel first class if they know that their credit card expenditures

124. Obviously these are gross estimates. Whether the actual amount was 8 percent or 20 percent of actual revenue is not the relevant point for our purposes. By any measure, the amount involved was material.

will be reviewed before being reimbursed. If a business uses corporate credit cards, the bills should be reviewed by someone who does not have a corporate credit card.

(ii) Receivables. An organization that extends credit has receivables. It should run the appropriate credit checks and evaluations before providing the goods and services. These processes should be performed by someone who does not make the sale so that the credit decision is objective. In some cases, that may need to be overridden by the organization's charitable mission—for example, providing emergency services in a nonprofit hospital. Even in these cases, a system should be in place to audit the overriding process so that someone is not using the cover of an emergency to steal. That may mean periodic surveillance of overrides.

Pledges are also a type of receivable. Although most organizations do not perform credit checks on small pledges, any charity that accepts large pledges should evaluate the donor's creditworthiness. Pledges generally should be reduced to an enforceable contract.

Uncollectible accounts are to be expected any time credit is extended. The critical element in any control system is to make sure that a collection process is in place. If uncollectibles are to be written off, the decision should be made by an objective person who is not part of the credit extension process. In the case of major pledges, the board should be responsible for the decision to forgo collection.

(iii) Inventory. People normally think of factories or large retail chains when they hear the word *inventory,* but many nonprofits also carry inventories. For example, hospitals have inventories of linens, pharmaceuticals, and medical equipment. Museums and cultural organizations frequently have large gift shops. Educational institutions have inventories of textbooks. All of these assets need to be protected. To do so, the organization needs first to establish an ordering system, requiring purchases only from a preapproved list of vendors and authorized by someone who is not in day-to-day control of the inventory. A formal document such as a purchase order should be required before the order or purchase is made. When inventory is received, the invoice or shipping document should be sent to the accounting department for comparison with the purchase order. If everything is in order, authorization for payment should be sent to the persons with check-writing authority. The accounting department should maintain inventory records. Before goods can be removed from inventory, there should be appropriate authorization provided to both the custodian of the inventory and the accounting department. As noted earlier, physical counts of inventories should be taken periodically, and the results of the physical inventory should be matched against the accounting department's records. There will be discrepancies between the physical inventory and the booked inventory, which should be investigated if they are material.

(iv) Fixed Assets. Like inventories, purchases of fixed assets should be approved by someone other than the person requesting the acquisition. Purchases, particularly regularly recurring ones, should be made on a prenumbered purchase order from an authorized list of vendors. When the items arrive, the process described earlier should be followed. The items should be inventoried before being put to use. Where possible, assets should be tagged with identifying numbers. This advice is particularly apropos for laptop computers, Blackberries, and other electronic equipment that easily can be sold. If an item is assigned to an employee, some record of that fact should be added to the employee's personnel record so that if the employee resigns or is discharged, the person in charge of the exit interview will make sure the asset is returned. If vehicles play a large role in operations (e.g., Red Cross delivery or emergency vans), the vehicles should be parked in secure lots with some sort of check in and check out procedure.

Obviously, an entire book could be devoted to fixed assets. Museums must consider how they purchase art and collectibles and how they track the assets after purchase.[125] Educational institutions must track classroom furniture, lab

---

125. One newspaper reported in 1997 that one out of eight art thefts in the United States is from a museum: J.E. Kaufman, *US Museums Meet the Challenge of Theft*, ART NEWSPAPER, Sept. 1997. Mr. Kaufman describes a number of thefts that involved respected insiders, as well as one noted scholar. For stories on a theft of articles by a museum's former director, see *Official Business: Embezzlement Conviction of Former Museum Chief*, L.A. TIMES, Oct. 12, 1995; and D. Colker, *Ex-Museum Head Gets Jail, to Pay Restitution in Thefts*, L.A. TIMES, May 22, 1993. For stories on the theft of articles by a noted scholar with special access to museum collections, see P. Hartigan, *A Passion for Porcelain that Led to Theft*, BOSTON GLOBE, Dec. 27, 1991; and W. Honan, *The Trusted Museum Insider Who Turned Out to Be a Thief*, N. Y. TIMES, Dec. 19, 1991. What is interesting about these two cases is that the motivation apparently was not entirely about personal gain. The *Boston Globe* article paints a highly unusual picture of the scholar, reporting:

> But while he has been called the Robin Hood of the art world—stealing from Peter to give to Paul—his motives were not as pure as those of the renegade of Sherwood Forest. Trial records and interviews with Feller's colleagues paint a portrait of a conflicted, lonely scholar whose obsession led him to pull off one of the most bizarre series of art thefts of the century.

For a more general discussion of museum security issues, see M. Cooper, *The Walls Have Ears, and Other High-Tech Crime Gadgets*, N. Y. TIMES, Apr. 19, 2000. Thefts continue to plague the museum world. In November of 2005, the former president and CEO of the Kansas Cosmosphere and Space Center was convicted of stealing artifacts from the museum. R. Hegeman, *Ex-Head of Kansas Space Museum Convicted,* ASSOCIATED PRESS, Nov. 1, 2005.

Those concerned with authentication, security, and related issues should consider contacting the International Foundation for Art Research, which describes itself as follows:

> The International Foundation for Art Research (IFAR) is a not-for-profit educational and research organization dedicated to integrity in the visual arts. IFAR offers impartial and authoritative information on authenticity, ownership, theft, and other artistic, legal, and ethical issues concerning art objects. IFAR serves as a bridge between the public, and the scholarly and commercial art communities. We publish the quarterly IFAR Journal; organize conferences, panels, and lectures; offer a unique Art Authentication Service; and serve as an information resource. We invite all people interested in the visual arts to join our organization and help support our activities.

IFAR maintains a Web site at http://www.ifar.org. Those who experience losses should consider contacting the Art Loss Register, a well-respected organization that maintains a list of stolen objects and that assists victims of theft. They maintain a Web site at http://www.artloss.com/Default.asp.

equipment, food and beverages, office supplies, library books, maintenance equipment, and a host of other assets. Hospitals must secure expensive equipment, hospital furniture, and maintenance equipment. Each organization should focus on the particulars of protecting its fixed assets.

(v) Intangible Assets. Organizations, particularly universities and research institutions, should maintain lists of all patents, copyrights, and trademarks they own. If renewal is an issue, a system should be designed to automatically generate timely reminders to file the proper applications and notifications. Any transfers of these assets should require appropriate authorization.

Although many organizations do not hold patents or copyrights, most have investment securities. Under no circumstances should these securities ever be titled in a name other than the organization's legal name, and except for very good reasons, should not be held on the organization's premises. Paper-based securities should either be held in a safety deposit box (with the appropriate limits on access: two people required to access the box) or with a reputable broker that can offer adequate and proven protection under SIPC or through fidelity insurance or an employee bonding program.

If the organization manages its own investments, it obviously should have trade authorization procedures in place that are integrated with the organization's investment policy. There should be procedures for internal audits of adherence to decisions and policies. Under no circumstances should the person who is authorized to execute trades be authorized to withdraw funds or securities from the account. Prohibited investments (e.g., options, commodities, or short sales) should be in writing and provided to the broker. The investment accounts should be monitored by a person independent of those authorized to make investments or withdraw funds from the account.

Because of concerns regarding controls and expertise, many organizations outsource the entire investment management function. This may simplify the control process, but it does not eliminate the need for controls. Of primary importance, the organization should work with a reputable and established firm and avoid the latest fads, start-up investment management firms, and those that promise the sky through proprietary investment models that they are unwilling to disclose. Once the organization has selected an adviser, it must independently audit the adviser's performance on a monthly basis. The adviser should not have custody of the assets. This can be accomplished by establishing a trust or custody account with a corporate trustee or a brokerage firm, and then granting only trading authority to the adviser. This prevents the adviser from being able to transfer the assets to his own account. The organization should consider multiple advisors if funds will be invested with hedge funds, thereby minimizing the potential losses from asset misappropriations.[126] There is obviously no one-size-fits-all set of investment controls, but any system should separate custody of the assets from the authority to manage or "spend" the asset value.

(vi) Accounts Payable. Accounts payable can represent another significant problem area for nonprofits. Embezzlers often submit bills from fictitious payees that they create and thus control. This is one reason that the organization should develop a list of preapproved vendors. Unfortunately, unscrupulous vendors as well as insiders can take advantage of nonprofits: Vendors might submit inflated bills for goods and services and insiders might create fictitious bills. The best protection against this practice is to implement a system that compares purchase orders with invoices to verify that what was ordered is what is being paid for.

Organizations should be very careful to avoid paying phony invoices for what are actually contributed goods. As part of an alleged scheme to defraud a nonprofit, one employee allegedly submitted invoices for goods that others had contributed to the nonprofit to be given away as prizes.[127]

(vii) Payroll. Internal controls related to payroll and employee benefits are areas of concern. The organization does not want to pay fictitious employees, and it wants to make sure that it is only paying the appropriate amounts to actual employees. The organization also needs to ensure that income tax, FICA, FUTA, and other withholdings are remitted to the IRS and other appropriate government agencies in a timely manner.

As a starting point, the organization should consider using a separate payroll bank account into which the payroll is deposited and from which all payroll disbursements are made. The human resources department should maintain a master list of employees that is periodically reviewed against payroll disbursements. Only the human resources department should have authority to add or remove employees from the master list and should promptly notify the persons in charge of payroll of changes to the list

If at all possible, the system should be computerized because the various income tax withholding and employment tax rates can become very complicated. In fact, the organization may want to outsource the entire payroll system to a third-party service provider such as ADP, Paychex, or Intuit, among others.

The payroll system should be audited annually, preferably by internal auditors to ensure that pay rates match contract rates. This audit should also review withholding and tax rates.

(viii) Conclusion to Internal Controls. Pretty dull and boring? You bet—but a solid and well-thought-out system of internal controls represents the wall between your organization's assets and the potential embezzler. You want that

---

126. Nonprofits investing in hedge funds have already suffered losses due to fraud. One case involved investments in hedge funds associated with Bayou Securities. This case does not appear to have involved theft for personal gain, but a cover-up of losses. See J. Anderson, *2 at Hedge Fund Emerge to Plead Guilty to Fraud*, N.Y. TIMES, Sept. 30, 2005; J. Anderson, G. Fabrikant, and R. Atlas, *What Really Happened at Bayou*, N.Y. TIMES, Sept. 17, 2005; and J. Christoffersen, *Investors Sue Troubled Hedge Fund*, WASH. POST, Sept. 7, 2005.

127. F. Spielman, *Thefts from Charity May Have Reached $200,000*, CHICAGO SUN-TIMES, May 13, 2005.

wall to be as thick and tall as economically possible. That requires working with your organization's internal accounting staff, outside accountants and auditors, and paid consultants on an ongoing basis. For the board, this means an engaged audit committee that is willing to take the management letter from the outside auditors seriously.

(c) A CASE STUDY. Let's now consider Americans for Better Computer Software (AFBCS), a hypothetical nonprofit organization dedicated to making computer software easier to use, and Jennifer Oldroyd, its chief financial officer. AFBCS has been very successful in signing up members (five million) and raising funds ($100 million last year) with an administrative staff of only six employees. Oldroyd maintains the computers that generate financial statements and board reports. She also has signature authority over AFBCS's bank accounts and responsibility for reviewing bank statements. She has held her current position for the last eight years. The board has been satisfied with her work, including the detailed financial reports that she provides at each board meeting.

This system has obvious control lapses, the most blatant being Oldroyd's iron grip over all aspects of the accounting system. She has signature authority to write checks. What is to prevent Oldroyd from creating a phony company, authorizing purchases from it, and then writing checks to fund those purchases? The accounts payable department will not catch this fraud because Oldroyd is the accounts payable department. No one else reconciles the bank statement or will notice unusual payees because she reconciles the bank statement. The directors are unlikely to notice some unusual amounts or categories on the organization's financial statements because Oldroyd prepares the financial statements. She may be an honest person, but should the organization bet its financial security on that likelihood?

Although AFBCS is a very small organization, its directors should give serious thought to requiring two signatures on each check. The logical candidate for the other signature is the executive director. If the staff is too small, the executive director should also review the monthly bank statement. If the organization has a significant flow of assets, the board should seriously consider increasing the administrative staff. Keeping overhead costs down is laudable but not at the expense of necessary controls.

Identifying specific fixes in this situation is virtually impossible given the sketchy information. What you should recognize is that the custodial, authorization, and recordkeeping functions all reside in the same individual. This is poor design but is probably more common in the nonprofit world than most would like to admit.

(d) RECOMMENDED INTERNAL CONTROLS. Every board should consider mandating the following accounting controls. In all cases that require duplication or separation of functions, neither person participating in the process should be a subordinate of the other.

- Separate check-writing authority and bank statement reconciliation.
- Require two signatures on checks over a certain dollar amount (the lower the limit, the better).
- Require purchase orders for all purchases above a certain dollar amount and have a petty cash fund used for items below a certain amount.
- Allow accounts receivable (including pledges) to be written off only with the approval of an executive officer who is *not* charged with maintaining financial records or approving the initial extensions of credit.
- Require that physical assets be disposed of only after the receipt of written authorization from someone who does *not* have custody or record-keeping responsibility with respect to these assets.
- Make payments only to individuals and companies on an approved list.
- Require purchase orders, receipts, checks, and similar documentation to be prenumbered.
- Design a system to create a paper trail of purchase orders, checks and bank statements, fixed asset inventories, petty cash receipts, and so forth that is regularly reviewed by someone outside the process. The written record should be confirmed by taking a physical inventory, comparison with independent documentation, or other appropriate means.
- Hold marketable securities in a safe deposit box or place them with a reputable financial institution that is a member of SIPC.
- Inventory fixed assets and, when appropriate, affix identification tags to items such as laptop computers.
- Require two people to be present when cash is collected.
- Require computers used for maintaining accounting books and records to be password protected, backups to be regularly scheduled, and back-up files to be stored off site.

This is not intended as a complete list, and it must be tailored to each organization's specific circumstances. The best way to do this is to discuss proper internal controls with the organization's independent auditors. They appreciate the need for solid internal controls and have extensive experience helping organizations implement them.

(e) CONSIDERATIONS FOR ORGANIZATIONS MAKING GRANTS. Before making any grant, grant makers should thoroughly review a prospective grantee's internal controls. Although grant makers may be more interested in focusing on how innovative programs work than on internal controls, applicants with poor internal controls expose the grant maker's investment in the grantee to unacceptable risks. Grant makers can expedite their review by requesting the management letter from an applicant's outside auditors.

In reviewing grant applications, grant makers should have mechanisms to verify the information provided by the applicant. In most cases, it will be impossible to verify every piece of information, but some effort should be made to verify critical pieces of information. Without some verification, the grant maker opens itself up to third-party fraud. For example, in January 2005, there were widespread press reports[128] containing allegations that certain groups affiliated with the Boy Scouts had inflated membership numbers, possibly to increase United Way funding.[129] The Boy Scout council in question indicated that it was cooperating with the FBI and that it had commenced an internal audit.[130] Some of the disputed practices were justified on privacy grounds.[131] As a result of unrelated but similar allegations, the United Way of Metropolitan Atlanta suspended payment of grant money to the Atlanta Area Council of the Boys Scouts of America until an investigation was completed.[132] The reports with respect to the Atlanta Area Council were ultimately proven to be accurate.[133]

5.11 FINANCIAL CONTROL RECOMMENDATIONS AND REQUIREMENTS FOR RECIPIENTS OF FEDERAL FUNDS

Nonprofit organizations receiving federal grant money must pay close attention to a panoply of federal standards and requirements. Organizations that fail to comply with these rules can be cut off from federal funding, particularly as money for discretionary federal programs becomes more scarce. For example, certain members of Congress have been highly critical of several organizations running Head Start programs. Anecdotal evidence[134] regarding such organizations resulted in an audit by the GAO, which concluded that 76 percent of grantees were in noncompliance with federal financial management standards. Of those noncompliant grantees, 53 percent were characterized as repeat offenders.[135] As a consequence of the GAO study and subsequent congressional hearings, Congress considered

---

128. M. Roig-Franzia, *Boy Scouts Suspected of Inflating Rolls*, WASH. POST, Jan. 29, 2005; *Alabama Boy Scouts Accused of Padding Membership*, FOX NEWS.COM, Jan 26, 2005; S. Doyle, *FBI Investigation Shakes Up Supporters of Youth Organization*, HUNTSVILLE-TIMES, Jan. 9, 2005, V. Abrams and W. Bryant, *FBI Investigates Allegations of False Boy Scout Numbers*, BIRMINGHAM NEWS, Dec. 30, 2004.

129. J. Hansen and K. Taylor, *FBI Subpoenas Boy Scout Records from United Way*, BIRMINGHAM NEWS, Jan. 13, 2005.

130. Letter from Incoming Chairman (Jan. 26, 2005) appearing when released on the Greater Alabama Council's Web site, but no longer available on that site.

131. J. Reeves, *Boy Scouts Council Defends False Names*, WASH. POST, Feb. 12, 2005; and M. Harrison, *Fort Payne Part of Scout Controversy*, TIMES-JOURNAL, Feb. 12, 2005. It does not appear that the matter has yet been fully resolved.

132. Press Release, United Way of Metropolitan Atlanta, "Funding for Boy Scouts of America, Atlanta Area Council" (May 19, 2005).

133. *Scouts Work to Restore Withheld Funding*, ATLANTA J. CONST., Nov. 25, 2005; and D. Yee, *Probe: Boy Scouts Lied About Black Members*, ASSOCIATED PRESS, May 31, 2005; S. Reid, *United Way Says Boy Scouts Inflated Minority Figures*, ATLANTA J. CONST., May 11, 2005; and Letter from L. Tom Gay, President of the Atlanta Area Council, Boy Scouts of America (June 1, 2005).

134. MAJORITY STAFF OF THE U.S. HOUSE COMMITTEE ON EDUCATION AND THE WORKFORCE, TAKING MONEY FROM CHILDREN, *supra* note 117.

135. GOVERNMENT ACCOUNTABILITY OFFICE, REPORT NO. GAO-05-176, HEADSTART: COMPREHENSIVE APPROACH TO IDENTIFYING AND ADDRESSING RISKS COULD HELP PREVENT GRANTEE FINANCIAL MANAGEMENT WEAKNESSES (Feb. 2005).

legislation to provide the Administration of Children & Families (ACF) broader authority to terminate grantees and redirect Head Start grant money.[136] In response to the GAO audit, ACF modified its own program review guidelines to incorporate a fiscal checklist that it now uses as part of its agency review process.[137] Although this particular checklist is similar to standard internal control checklists, grantees that are subject to review would be well advised to implement the specific guidelines.

The Head Start experience is not an isolated one. Other programs that receive Community Service Block Grant funding from the federal government are being watched closely by Congress. There is little question that some in Congress have long-term plans to impose stricter financial control requirements on those running federal programs. The take-away point is that the boards of nonprofits receiving federal grants need to ensure that staff members understand these requirements and are capable of bringing the nonprofit into compliance with them.

These requirements go beyond internal controls. For example, the federal Office of Management and Budget has promulgated rules that limit what costs nonprofits can charge against federal grant money.[138] No one expects a nonprofit board to be expert in these complex and detailed accounting rules, but it must make clear to the staff that the organization will comply. Moreover, when selecting the nonprofit's independent auditors and defining the scope of the engagement, the board (or, preferably, its audit committee) should closely examine the qualifications of those under consideration to make sure that they have the relevant experience and expertise to provide meaningful services to the nonprofit.

5.12 FRAUD AND THEFT

The Association of Certified Fraud Examiners (ACFE) conducted a survey of occupational fraud in 2004.[139] The study was based on cases reported by ACFE members rather than on statistical sampling methods, meaning that the survey cannot be used to assess the overall level of fraud in the United States or the nonprofit sector. Nevertheless, the survey is based on a relatively large number of incidents that were of sufficient magnitude to warrant investigation, so its conclusions provide some insight into types of fraud and perpetrators. The conclusions certainly call into question many assumptions that people have about fraud.

Several prefatory points are in order. ACFE also conducted a 2002 survey including slightly more cases, but its findings were consistent with those of the 2004 survey. Second, in some cases, the percentages do not sum to 100 percent

---

136. School Readiness Act of 2005, H.R. 2123, 109th Cong.(2005).

137. Administration for Children & Families of the U.S. Department of Health and Human Services, Program Review Instrument for Systems Monitoring of Head Start and Early Head Start Grantees (2005)

138. Office of Management and Budget, Circular A-122, Cost Principles for Non-Profit Organizations (May 10, 2004).

139. Staff of the Association of Certified Fraud Examiners, 2004 Report to the Nation on Occupational Fraud and Abuse (2004). The complete survey is *available at* http://www.cfenet.com/pdfs/2004RttN.pdf.

because the item being measured fell into multiple categories. Third, unless the discussion indicates otherwise, the survey numbers are for all reported incidents, not just the incidents involving nonprofits.

The survey revealed 508 occupational fraud cases that resulted in $761 million in losses. Roughly 12 percent of the reported incidents involved nonprofit entities; the median loss was $100,000. The 12 percent number is not out of line with nonprofit activity relative to United States economic activity as a whole. The participants reporting incidents estimated that the losses equal somewhere around 6 percent of organizational revenue (or in the case of government, organizational budget). The survey provides a number of critical insights into financial fraud that every organization's board and officers should review.

(a) THE THREE CATEGORIES OF FRAUD. The survey divides occupational fraud into the following three categories: (1) corruption, (2) asset misappropriation, and (3) fraudulent statements. *Corruption* occurs when the perpetrator breaches his duty in order to obtain some personal benefit. Common examples include kickbacks and conflicts of interest, sales and purchase schemes, bid rigging, bribery, and illegal gratuities.

Asset misappropriation is a fancy term for theft or misuse of organizational assets. Examples include stealing inventory, check tampering, adding phony employees to payrolls, and theft of cash.

Fraudulent statements involve manipulating the nonprofit's financial statements, presenting phony employment credentials, making improper disclosures, and improperly valuing assets. When financial statements are manipulated, the perpetrator is probably attempting to inflate numbers that affect the determination of his compensation, which could be more problematic for the business community than for nonprofits because of the prevalence of stock options and other forms of contingent compensation in the for-profit world. In the nonprofit setting such manipulation may be an effort to hide theft.[140]

(b) AVOID A NARROW FOCUS. According to the survey, over 90 percent of the reported cases involved asset misappropriations. This result suggests that efforts should focus on tightening financial controls over cash and inventories (such as office supplies) and designing systems that will detect phony payees, such as fictitious employees and vendors. Certainly, these controls warrant attention, particularly when the median loss reported for this category was $93,000. Of the misappropriation cases, 93 percent involved cash and only 22 percent involved misappropriation of noncash assets.[141] Fraudulent disbursements accounted for 74.1 percent, skimming 28.2 percent, and larceny 23.9 percent of the reported cases, with fraudulent disbursements producing a $125,000 median loss.

140. For a general discussion of financial statement fraud, see CHARLES R. LUNDELIUS, FINANCIAL REPORTING FRAUD: A PRACTICAL GUIDE TO DETECTION AND INTERNAL CONTROL (AICPA 2003).

141. Given the percentages, some schemes clearly involved the misappropriation of cash and noncash assets.

At the same time, the evidence suggests that nonprofits should not ignore other types of fraud. Although corruption and fraudulent statements were present in only 30.1 percent and 7.95 percent, respectively, of the reported cases, the median dollar losses were higher. The median loss from fraudulent statements was $1 million. The median loss from corruption was $250,000. Frauds in those categories require greater sophistication or someone high in the organizational hierarchy, which probably accounts for the lower frequency of incidents.

The losses from these schemes appear to be of more serious magnitude. These conclusions are confirmed by other survey data. Although fraud perpetrated by managers accounts for roughly 34 percent of all frauds, it resulted in a median loss of $140,000, as compared to "rank and file" fraud, which accounts for 67.8 percent of the frauds but with a median loss of only $62,000. Boards should disavow any notion that executives are above suspicion. Owner/executive frauds accounted for only 12.4 percent of all frauds, but produced a median loss of $900,000.

TRUST, BUT VERIFY

* * *

When many people think about embezzlement and the nonprofit sector, they envision a small start-up charity and the loss of several thousand dollars. This is often the wrong image. Consider an embezzlement that occurred at the University of Florida Foundation (UFF). Its chief financial officer pleaded no contest to embezzling $850,000.[142] The press accounts were not entirely clear on the mechanics, but he apparently "reprinted" five checks payable to the foundation and had them deposited to his own account.[143] Does that mean he "erased" the foundation's name and substituted his own or did he just make the checks payable to himself? Several accounts describe the official's behavior as exploiting "loopholes" in the foundation's accounting procedures.[144]

All too often, newspaper articles about embezzlement contain the phrase "trusted employee whom everyone liked."[145] Nonprofits should give serious consideration to performing background checks of job applicants—this is the "verify" in the title. The chief financial officer in this case had been employed by the foundation for 15 years. Long-term

---

142. *Former UF Foundation Executive Sentenced in Embezzling Case*, ASSOCIATED PRESS, Sept. 29, 2004.

143. Nur Erenguc, *University of Florida Office of Audit & Compliance Review* at 12 (2003–04); J. Basinger, *Former Florida Fund Raiser Pleads "No Contest" to Theft*, CHRON. HIGHER EDUC., July 2, 2004; *Ex-UF Official Pleads to Crime*, TALLAHASSEE DEMOCRAT, June 24, 2004; and BOARD OF TRUSTEES, UNIVERSITY OF FLORIDA, COMMITTEE ON AUDIT & OPERATIONS REVIEWS (Dec. 4, 2003) (incident described without identification of person involved).

144. J. Basinger, *supra* note 143.

145. One newspaper article, in describing the reaction to the embezzlement at the University of Florida Foundation, reported:

> Foundation officials said last fall that they were shocked when the problems were discovered because Mr. Hillier had been trusted and well liked.

Id. This same article also reports that the employee had developed some of the accounting procedures that prosecutors charged him with exploiting.

employment does not protect against embezzlement. Internal controls are critical in the defending against fraud and embezzlement—they are the means by which an organization verifies.

* * *

(c) EMPLOYEE TIPS. More than 39.6 percent of detected frauds are uncovered through tips, placing them at the top of the list. Close to 60 percent of the tips came from employees. The 39.6 percent number rises to 48.1 percent for nonprofits only, suggesting that organizations should foster an atmosphere in which employees are comfortable about reporting suspicious behavior. When fraud hotlines exist, the median loss drops by more than 50 percent (from $135,500 to $56,500). Care must be exercised, however, when designing any program that encourages or rewards employee reporting. No organization wants to create a Stalinist work environment. Although the emphasis is often on employee reporting, the survey notes that making a reporting mechanism available to customers, vendors, and other third parties (e.g., donors) pays dividends.

Two Anonymous Tipsters Solve the Case

* * *

The *New York Times* reported in a September 6, 2004, front page story a number of accounting and financial irregularities involving the James Beard Foundation, a charity organized to honor the noted chef who died in 1985.[146] The *Times* consulted a number of nonprofit experts during its review of the foundation's records. These experts concluded that "hundreds of thousands of dollars of revenue" were unaccounted for each year.[147]

This story came to light after two anonymous callers tipped off the New York state attorney general.[148] According to a *Times* article, the former president of the Beard Foundation "could not adequately explain thousands of dollars in expenses for meals, travel and entertainment." He withdrew "several thousand dollars in cash" for payments to chefs, but apparently could not account for the payments, and made unauthorized donations of food and wine stored at the foundation's headquarters.[149] An internal audit confirmed the details.[150]

---

146. J. Moskin, *Thousands Missing In Revenue Records Of Culinary Charity*, N. Y. TIMES, Sept. 6, 2004.
147. *Id.*
148. *Id.*
149. J. Moskin, *Foundation's Ex-President Misused Funds, Chairman Says*, N.Y. TIMES, Sept. 20, 2004.
150. *See* Press Release, James Beard Foundation, "James Beard Foundation Announces Results of Independent Financial Audit" (Dec. 15, 2004), stating:

> "It is clear that the Foundation has been harmed by these actions, which led to the unsubstantiated expenditures incurred by our former President," said George Sape, Chairman of The James Beard Foundation Board of Trustees and Managing Partner of Epstein, Becker & Green. "The Foundation has rapidly grown over the last twenty years and the Board's focus was on raising money, which it did successfully. Although we were deceived and misled, in retrospect, we would have demanded better financial controls and reporting. Our former President, Len Pickell, who represented himself as a CPA, had principal responsibility for these functions. We regret that this happened and have taken immediate and appropriate action to ensure that it never happens again."

The former president initially denied any wrongdoing but subsequently pled guilty "to stealing tens of thousands of dollars from the group over the past decade," although his attorney denied that the plea was to specific charges.[151]

There is little doubt that the foundation lacked an adequate system of internal controls.[152] This is particularly troublesome given the environment in which the foundation operated. Reimbursements for food and beverages always represent an area that warrants monitoring because of the mixed personal and business components associated with these expenses. Congress has been railing against the "three-martini" lunch for years, leading to significant limitations on the deductibility of business meal expenses. The James Beard Foundation is an organization that focuses on food, fine dining, and entertainment.

The Foundation appears to have paid a heavy price for its lack of controls, although it has survived the incident, due in large part to efforts of the board chair and a number of chefs. The entire board was replaced in March 2005 by a new board initially consisting of three directors.[153] There was also a new focus on governance and internal controls.[154] Regrettably, this "new focus" all too often comes after the scandal.

* * *

5.13 INTERNAL FRAUD DETECTION

According to the ACFE survey, internal audits account for 23.8 percent and internal controls account for 18.4 percent of overall detections. External audits account for only 10.9 percent of overall detections of occupational fraud. This is not surprising because external audits are generally performed on a "statistical" or "test" basis and often rely heavily on the work of the internal auditors when that function exists. The results for nonprofits differ somewhat from overall survey results. Internal audits detected only 11.5 percent of nonprofits frauds; external audits were slightly more effective, detecting 13.5 percent of these frauds. Many nonprofits do not have internal audit functions, which may explain the low 11.5 percent discovery rate through internal audits. Internal audits may be worth their cost, however. The median loss for organizations with an internal audit function was $80,000 as compared to a $130,000 median loss for organizations without it. A disturbing fact is that 25 percent of the nonprofit frauds were detected by accident.

As stated from Note 7 of the audit report, "For the fiscal year ended March 31, 2003, the aggregate amount of the loss from unsubstantiated expenditures is being reported as $371,907, of which (i) $237,951 has been concluded in the Investigation to be improper, and (ii) $133,956 is considered likely of being deemed improper pending receipt of substantiation or other justification. The Investigation report concludes that losses of $373,251 for the fiscal year ended March 31, 2002 and $284,915 for the fiscal year ended March 31, 2004, are likely to have occurred, pending receipt of substantiation or other justification."

---

151. J. Moskin, *Beard Foundation's Ex-President Pleads Guilty to Stealing From It*, N.Y. TIMES, Jan. 25, 2005.
152. *See* Press Release, *supra* note 150.
153. J. Moskin, *Beard Foundation Restructures Board*, N. Y. TIMES, Mar. 30, 2005; and Press Release, James Beard Foundation, "James Beard Foundation Restructures Board of Trustees" (Mar. 29, 2005).
154. Press Release, "James Beard Foundation, James Beard Foundation Restructures" (Sept. 9, 2004).

The division between internal audits, external audits, and internal controls is interesting but somewhat misleading. Together, these three categories were the basis for just over 53 percent of the fraud detections, easily surpassing employee tips and other single categories of detection. The appropriate approach is to rely on all three categories because each actually complements the others. Internal controls exist in a world inhabited by internal and external auditors, who often recommend and design these controls. Internal and external auditors rely not only on internal controls but also on each other.

5.14 THE LONE PERPETRATOR ACCOUNTS FOR THE HIGHEST PERCENTAGE OF FRAUDS

According to the ACFE survey, the "lone perpetrator" accounted for roughly 65 percent of the reported frauds, with collusion accounting for the remaining 35 percent. If every organization had solid financial controls, most frauds would require some sort of collusion because a tight system of controls would require at least two people to override the system. In all likelihood, the high percentage of frauds attributable to lone perpetrators reflects the existence of opportunities resulting from poor controls. This strongly suggests that every organization should constantly review and improve its financial controls.

As has been the case in the other two observations, there is another dimension to these particular statistics. When there is collusion, the median loss to the organization is much higher ($200,000) than when there is a lone perpetrator ($58,500).

(a) BACKGROUND CHECKS MAY NOT BE THE ANSWER. Background checks are perceived as a useful tool for preventing fraud by keeping "bad" people out of the organization. This is an understandable perception, particularly given the number of newspaper articles describing frauds involving perpetrators with prior criminal records. This is obviously very embarrassing for the organization. The headlines scream, "You idiots, it was on public record! If only you had checked!" Management could be justified in mandating background checks just to avoid such embarrassments.

Unfortunately, the survey statistics strongly imply that background checks are not a fraud prevention panacea. Of those who perpetrated a financial fraud, 82.9 percent had never been charged with or convicted of a crime. The survey indicates that this is consistent with other studies.

(b) TENURE IS AN ERRONEOUS BASIS FOR TRUST. Just over 46 percent of all frauds were perpetrated by people who had worked for the organization for more than five years. Not surprising, the longer the perpetrator's tenure, the higher the median loss. The median loss for perpetrators with ten or more years of service was $171,000, while the median loss attributable to those employed for less than one year was $26,000. As already noted, many reports describe how fellow employees are shocked to learn about the fraud, often because of the perpetrator's long tenure with the nonprofit. Statistically speaking—at least based on the survey's results—no one should be surprised when the perpetrator has a long tenure.

(c) LOSS RECOVERY. The survey reported a median loss recovery in all cases of just 20 percent. In 37 percent of the cases, the organization was unable to recover any portion of its loss. Only 22 percent of the victims recovered their losses. In short, preventing a loss is the best way to avoid it. Certainly, there is value to fidelity insurance when there is a loss.

(d) THE LESSONS. When read carefully, the survey results suggest that there are no quick and easy answers to fraud prevention. The results indicate that the potential perpetrator does not fit a particular demographic profile, nor does the survey identify one pervasive type of fraud. Even though asset misappropriations led the list, a wide variety of frauds is included in that category. The survey confirms the view that solid internal controls and audits yield a high return in terms of fraud prevention. Organizations should consider creating hotlines and reward programs to encourage their employees (and third parties such as vendors and donors) to report suspicious activities, but these programs should be designed so they do not create a noxious work environment.

To reiterate, the survey is much more anecdotal than statistical. Some of the 2004 median losses differ materially from the comparable median losses reported in the ACFE's 2002 survey. This is probably due to the relatively small number of cases included in each survey. However, when comparing the 2002 and 2004 surveys, the relative findings are fairly consistent.

5.15 FRAUD AND THE CERTIFIED AUDIT

Although preventing fraud is the primary responsibility of management, the public views the independent audit as a critical element in the war against fraud. With that in mind, the AICPA's Auditing Standards Board promulgated *Statement on Auditing Standards No. 99 (SAS No. 99)*, a "beefed-up" set of procedures to improve the detection of fraud during the annual independent audit.[155] Much of *SAS No. 99* can be viewed as "inside baseball" for our purposes. Nevertheless, as a consequence of *SAS No. 99,* nonprofits should expect the following in years to come:

- Increased audit fees resulting from the laundry list of procedures that the auditor must now perform during the audit engagement.
- Specific questions to staff-level employees regarding their knowledge of fraudulent activity and opportunities to commit fraud.

155. CONSIDERATION OF FRAUD IN A FINANCIAL AUDIT, Statement of Auditing Standards No. 99, (American Institute of Certified Public Accountants 2002).

- More frequent requests of people outside the organization to confirm information provided by management.
- Surprise and unexpected audit procedures and visits from audit personnel.
- Confirmation of some account balances through review of 100 percent of the supporting material (instead of relying on statistical tests).
- More thorough and time-consuming year-end audit procedures.
- Increased skepticism on the part of outside auditors.

A typical nonprofit's first encounter with these changed procedures is likely to be a revised engagement letter from the organization's outside auditors. The board and management may be surprised by the auditor's focus on people outside the organization's accounting and finance department. People who work in human resources, the development department, and in the primary operations should expect a visit from the outside auditors. Auditors have found from discussions with people throughout the entity that there are often important gaps between what the accounting people think the procedures are and what is actually occurring throughout the organization. The auditor's goal is to see that these gaps are identified and closed.

Auditors are also asking people directly whether they know of fraud or any opportunities to commit fraud. Finally, auditors are focusing on broader governance controls. For example, they are asking whether people are comfortable reporting problems. According to one auditor, the new procedures under *SAS No. 99* have generated much greater sensitivity to governance issues among nonprofit staff. Although there may be added expense, this particular auditor believed that the benefits far outweigh that expense.

5.16 SARBANES-OXLEY REFORMS

On July 30, 2002, President George W. Bush signed into law the Sarbanes-Oxley Act[156] (sometimes referred to as *SOX)* in response to the widely publicized corporate scandals (WorldCom, Enron, Tyco). The focus of this legislation was on financial governance. It included provisions designed to improve financial reporting, auditor independence, audit committees, and internal controls.

Sarbanes-Oxley has received much discussion in nonprofit boardrooms despite the fact that its principal provisions apply only to publicly traded corporations. The reasons for this are simple: Those who are not subject to SOX view its principal provisions as potential "best practices," causing nonprofit boards to consider adopting them. Moreover, many members of nonprofit boards are officers and directors of publicly traded corporations. Having been exposed to Sarbanes-Oxley and the debate over corporate governance, these individuals are often inclined to ask whether nonprofits would benefit from similar governance

156. See *supra* note, 84.

reforms. Further fueling the fire are state regulators. New York State Attorney General Eliot Spitzer was the first to propose legislation that would apply Sarbanes-Oxley to nonprofits.[157] California, Massachusetts, and Texas have followed suit, with California actually enacting legislation.[158]

Let's examine six of the key SOX provisions in considering whether a nonprofit's board should voluntarily adopt these reforms as best practices.

(a) FINANCIAL CERTIFICATION. Section 302(a) of Sarbanes-Oxley requires the principal executive officer and the principal financial officer to certify in each annual or quarterly report that (1) the signing officer has reviewed the report, (2) based on the officer's knowledge, the report does not contain any untrue statement of a material fact or omit to state a material fact necessary in order to avoid making the statements misleading, and (3) based on such officer's knowledge, the financial statements fairly present in all material respects the issuer's financial condition and results of operations.[159] A number of disclosures regarding a company's internal controls are also required.[160] Let's consider two cases to assess whether certification of financial statements makes sense in the nonprofit context.

(i) The Artist as Executive Director—Case 1. The Far Museum wants to hire Lars Watson, the world-renowned performance artist, as its executive director. The trustees believe that Watson's presence will bring an excitement to the museum, resulting in a tenfold increase in contributions. Watson's latest performance piece, "I Don't Understand Numbers and I Don't Care," reflects his life view. The Far's endowment exceeds $4 billion, and annual admission and gift shop revenues exceed $750 million. Given those numbers, the trustees are also considering whether to require the executive director to certify that the museum's financial statements fairly represent its financial condition and operating results. The obvious questions: Does certification make sense if Lars Watson is the executive director? If not, should he be the executive director?

The board's focus on certification is largely misplaced. A nonprofit certainly will benefit from an executive director with "subject-matter" expertise. However, someone who understands financial and management issues should be in charge when a nonprofit has multiple operations, a large employee base, and significant

157. J. Jones, *N.Y. Attorney General Seeking to Apply Sarbanes-Oxley Act*, NONPROFIT TIMES, March 1, 2003. On March 9, 2005, the New York Attorney General submitted revised legislation that was far less expansive than originally proposed legislation. The revised bills would establish new conflict-of-interest validation procedures, require audit and executive committees for boards of larger organizations, but provide an opt-out procedure, and make minor changes to the New York statutes pertaining to registration of charitable organizations and fundraising.

158. *See supra* note 82.

159. *Id.*, § 302, as codified at 15 U.S.C. 7241. *See also* SEC Release No. 34-46427, Certification of Disclosure in Companies' Quarterly and Annual Reports (Aug. 28, 2002).

160. Pub. L. 107–204, *supra* note 84, § 404, as codified at 15 U.S.C. 7262.

revenues and resources.[161] If the candidate does not have the requisite knowledge to run a large operation, the board should look elsewhere for an executive director. At best, certification is a litmus test. The board is looking at the wrong person to head the organization if it believes certification is desirable, but has serious doubts whether the particular candidate is able to provide a meaningful certification. In this case, the board might consider creating an artist-in-residence position for Watson.

(ii) Minimal Financial Assets—Case 2. The New Cancer Treatment Center (NCTC) has asked Dr. Emil Bossman, a world-renowned oncologist, to serve as its president. NCTC publishes a peer-reviewed oncology quarterly, *New Cancer Treatment Journal*, which currently has 2,000 subscribers. The board believes that Dr. Bossman's reputation will triple article submissions. Mary Lambert, a Fortune 500 CEO, serves on the board. She has suggested that the board adopt a certification requirement similar to the one required by Sarbanes-Oxley. Dr. Bossman has been advised by his personal attorney not to accept the presidency if he must certify NCTC's financial statements.

In this case, the board should seriously consider rejecting the certification because it is unlikely to add any value but could cause Dr. Bossman to reject the board's offer. NCTC is a relatively small operation. It takes in subscription revenue, pays that money out to cover expenses, and distributes the journal. This is an easy operation to audit and, in all likelihood, its financial statements are fairly straightforward.

As the two cases indicate, one policy does *not* fit all organizations. Organizations must first find the right people to fill positions. Only then, should they consider certification requirements, recognizing that in some cases the requirements will be largely meaningless.

(b) AUDITOR INDEPENDENCE. Advocates for better governance have been concerned about auditor independence for years. These concerns were reflected in the GAO Audit Guidelines discussed earlier in this chapter.[162] Congress also addressed these concerns in Sarbanes-Oxley. For many years, the large accounting firms had viewed the audit function as a loss leader. Once in the door, these firms "sold" lucrative management and information-technology, tax, and other

161. Earlier in this chapter, we considered a financial analysis involving the Milwaukee Public Museum. One of the notable players in that case was MPM's president, who had been hired some eighteen months before the events erupted into a public crisis. During the crisis, he acknowledged his lack of financial experience. *See* A. Lank and D. Umhoefer, *Hands-Off Board Hurt Museum*, *supra* note 57; D. Umhoefer, *Public Museum President Stafford Resigns*, MILWAUKEE J.-SENTINEL, June 3, 2005; and A. Lank and D. Umhoefer, *Museum Chief's Dedication at Issue: Critics Say he Hasn't Given Job, Crisis Sufficient Attention*, MILWAUKEE J.-SENTINEL, May 21, 2005. The problem: An institution with what, at the time the president was hired, had apparent and significant financial issues needed a "financial man" in the top position. It is clear from the many reports that there was not good communication regarding financial issues with either MPM's board or county officials who were considering a $70 million, 20-year subsidy during this period

162. See the text accompanying footnotes 94 through 108, *supra*.

nonaudit services to their audit clients. In many cases, these same firms also provided tax and financial planning services to executive officers. In some well-publicized cases, the fees from these services accounted for a significant portion of the firm's revenue.[163]

Section 201 of Sarbanes-Oxley lists nine nonaudit services that are deemed to impair independence when provided by an organization's outside auditors.[164] The Securities and Exchange Commission has defined the prohibited services in much the same way as the GAO did in its Audit Guidelines. Suspect services include bookkeeping services, financial information system design and implementation, appraisal or valuation services, fairness opinions, actuarial services, internal audit outsourcing services, performance of management or human resource functions, investment banking services, legal services, and expert services. Is it appropriate to bar the performance of these services by a nonprofit's independent auditor?

Consider Grant Food Bank. Several of its directors are concerned about financial statement integrity. They have discovered that the external audit firm has had several minor disputes with management over certain issues. These directors question whether the firm is independent because it earns $50,000 in annual audit fees and over $500,000 in annual consulting fees. The consulting services provided include advice on improving financial controls and designing officer compensation packages. These directors want to adopt a rule ensuring auditor independence. Other directors object, arguing that the organization obtains more value for its dollar by using an audit firm that is familiar with all of its operations.

The independence problem should be apparent from the magnitude of audit fees ($50,000) relative to consulting fees ($500,000). Will the partner in charge of the Grant Food Bank audit be as willing to raise questions or object to a particular accounting treatment if he knows that his firm stands to lose significant consulting revenues? Even if the partner in charge graduated at the top of his class from Yale Divinity School (before changing career paths), he will undoubtedly feel some pressure. This is only human nature. Even if the partner in charge resists the pressure, there is still an "appearance of independence" issue.

The members of the Food Bank's board should reexamine Food Bank's relationship with its auditors. They should either find a new auditor to handle only the audit or bar the existing auditor from providing consulting services. The question is whether all consulting services should be prohibited. Interestingly,

---

163. Anyone who doubts the significance of consulting services in the audit equation need only consider the split that occurred at Arthur Andersen in 2000, when the consulting side of the firm separated from the audit firm at a cost of $1 billion. Many of Andersen's consulting partners reportedly had wanted to leave Andersen for the better part of a decade because they did not like subsidizing the audit side of Andersen's business. *See* E. MacDonald, *Andersen Worldwide Files Counterclaim for $14.5 Billion Against One of Its Units*, WALL ST. J., Nov. 22, 1999; E. MacDonald, *Andersen Consulting's Breakup Battle with Arthur Andersen Nears Showdown*, WALL ST. J., July 28, 1999; and E. MacDonald, *Andersen Consulting Tried to Thwart Arthur Andersen's Attempt to Buy Firm*, WALL ST. J., June 14, 1999.

164. Pub. L. 107–204, *supra* note 84, § 201, as codified at 15 U.S.C. 78j–1.

the SEC's rules implementing Sarbanes-Oxley focus on two prohibited classes of services. The first involves services that would result in the audit firm auditing its own work. Precluded services include bookkeeping and design of internal control systems that generate output that would be subject to the audit. The second class includes acting as a director, providing certain valuations or appraisals, and providing investment banking services. The focus here is on the conflicts that these services could generate for an auditor. Two arguments for permitting auditors to perform consulting services are frequently advanced. The first is legitimate and the second is specious. Both clients and auditors argue that performing certain consulting services helps the auditor better understand the nonprofit, its systems, and business. This is a legitimate argument, particularly when it comes to financial controls. However, this increased knowledge must be balanced against the fact that an audit firm that designs an internal control system is then auditing its own work. Some may disagree, but logic does underlie the balance struck in Sarbanes-Oxley. In cases where the Sarbanes-Oxley limitations are inapplicable, a board might legitimately strike a different balance.

The second argument is that a nonprofit saves money when its audit firm performs consulting services because the audit firm's knowledge provides economies of scale (lower overall fees). This argument has a superficial appeal given the many cash-strapped nonprofits. But the ability to pay should be irrelevant. The nonprofit's constituents who demand an audit are just as entitled to an uncompromised audit as are shareholders of a publicly traded corporation. The economies-of-scale argument does not justify relaxing standards. A large for-profit corporation can make a similar case, arguing, for example, that the potential savings from one-stop shopping can be used to provide health insurance coverage to otherwise uncovered employees.

(c) AUDITOR ROTATION. Section 203 of Sarbanes-Oxley mandates rotation of lead audit partners every five years.[165] This has caused a number of nonprofits to consider whether they should adopt auditor rotation as a best practice. There are at least two schools of thought on auditor rotation. The first school favors some form of rotation, assuming that a new set of eyes will bring new insights and analysis. There is clearly logic to that approach, but to the extent it has merit, Sarbanes-Oxley arguably did not go far enough. A rule that calls for rotation of audit firms is preferable to one that simply calls for the rotation of audit partners. As a practical matter, the replacement audit partner will come from the ranks of the junior auditors already assigned to the audit, although some SEC rules will make that a more difficult outcome to achieve. Those new eyes do not look "fresh."

Accounting firms with long-time client relationships certainly find the notion of severing those relationships unpalatable. Those firms will find support in the

165. *Id.*, § 203, as codified at 15 U.S.C. 78j-1.

second school of thought, which focuses on the expense of educating new auditors every five years. Not surprisingly, those opposed to rotation also express concern about breaking continuity. Nonprofit status alone does not support the second school of thought. Auditor rotation is a good idea for either all audits or none, but if rotation is a good idea, then nonprofit stakeholders are also entitled to more reliable audit results.

(d) AUDIT COMMITTEE MEMBER INDEPENDENCE. Sarbanes-Oxley effectively requires that covered companies have an audit committee. Its members must be members of the board of directors, and each member must be independent. Every nonprofit with any significant level of operations or assets should have an audit committee. Earlier in this chapter we considered audit committees and independence requirements. As that discussion made clear, independent audit committees should be viewed as a basic rather than a best practice.

(e) FINANCIAL EXPERTISE. Regardless of any legal requirements, the board of any nonprofit having significant financial resources and operations should have someone as a member who understands accounting and finance. This person hopefully knows how to frame and explain financial issues, so the less experienced and knowledgeable board members can participate intelligently in any deliberations.

Section 407 of Sarbanes-Oxley[166]addresses the issue of audit committee financial experts by requiring disclosures about financial experts on audit committees.[167] Although Section 407 speaks in terms of disclosure, many who focus on Section 407 view it as requiring financial experts.

To illustrate the potential issues posed by a financial expertise requirement, let's consider the New Film Society (TNFS), a nonprofit that just received a $30 million bequest. TNFS's nine directors are filmmakers, critics and film enthusiasts. The board plans to use this money to expand the society's operations with a new school and theater. Recognizing the need to better monitor TNFS's finances, two of the directors have suggested the board create an audit committee, but no one on the board has any financial expertise. Most members cannot even balance their checkbooks. Complicating matters further, the state recently imposed a "financial expert" requirement on nonprofits with assets exceeding $5 million.

In this case, state regulators are mandating that the board create an audit committee and place at least one financial expert on the committee. In some states, the members of a board committee do not have to be directors, but even when state law does contemplate nonboard committee members, it may still

166. *Id.*, § 407, as codified at 15 U.S.C. 7265.

167. Until 2005, the NYSE had an explicit requirement regarding financial experts, which was imposed through Section 303A of the NYSE Listed Company Manual. The manual appears to have been amended, specifically adopting the requirements set out in SEC Release No. 34-47654 (Apr. 1, 2003) and Exchange Act Rule 10A-3(a)(3). See SEC Release No. 34-50298, "Self-Regulatory Organizations: Notice of a Proposed Rule Change and Amendment No. 1 Thereto by the New York Stock Exchange" (Aug. 31, 2004).

limit participation on certain committees to board members.[168] Consequently, the board may not necessarily need to replace an existing director with a new one who is a financial expert (assuming the requirement does not specifically require a director to be the expert).

In looking for a financial expert, many boards are likely to look first to their outside auditor/accountant. Although this emphasis on convenience has a certain logic, convenience is unlikely to carry the day after regulators write the rules. Even if the nonprofit is voluntarily adopting a financial expert requirement, it should not ask its auditors to fulfill this role. The relationship between the audit committee and the external auditors should be one of cooperation, but some tension should exist in it. The committee should question the external auditors, monitor their work, and decide whether and when to change auditors. The auditor cannot effectively sit on both sides of the table.

The example posits a regulatory requirement. But if this is a voluntary action, the financial expert need not be a committee member. Instead, the audit committee could simply retain an outside expert or consultant to advise it on financial and auditing matters.

(f) MAKING AUDITED FINANCIAL STATEMENTS PUBLICLY AVAILABLE. Sarbanes-Oxley does not require covered companies to provide audited financial statements to their shareholders, but this has long been a requirement under federal securities law. Sarbanes-Oxley does require management of covered companies to file as part of the company's annual report certain conclusions and information regarding the company's internal controls and procedures for financial reporting.[169]

To put the issue in the nonprofit context, consider the Slick Art Museum. It has never made audited financial statements readily available to the public. However, in view of Sarbanes-Oxley, some trustees have suggested that the museum publish such statements, as well as an annual report regarding financial management and internal controls. Several trustees are adamantly opposed to this, arguing that the public will not understand the numbers. These trustees are concerned that making visible the museum's large endowment could very well result in

---

168. Surprisingly, Section 8.25 of the Revised Model Nonprofit Corporation Act (1987) does not address whether committee members must be board members. The language can be read to limit committee membership to board members. There may be some logic to such a limitation because board committees can only exercise such power as has been delegated to them by the board. At the same time, it may be possible to construe Section 8.25 as allowing nonboard members to be members of nonstanding committees. Section 108.40 of the Illinois General Not For Profit Corporation Act of 1986 specifically addresses the question of nonboard membership participation on board committees, providing:

> If the articles of incorporation or bylaws so provide, a majority of the directors may create one or more committees and appoint directors or such other persons as the board designates, to serve on the committee or committees. Each committee shall have two or more directors, a majority of its membership shall be directors, and all committee members shall serve at the pleasure of the board. However, committees appointed by the board or otherwise authorized by the bylaws relating to the election, nomination, qualification, or credentials of directors or other committees involved in the process of electing directors may be composed entirely of non-directors.

169. See *supra* note 160.

reduced contributions because some members of the public people might conclude that the museum has "enough" money. The trustees are also aware that interested parties can find the museum's IRS Form 990 filing on GuideStar.

Many museums and cultural institutions seem reluctant to make financial statements available to their donor base. Rarely do these organizations include complete financial statements in annual reports to donors or on their Web sites. Reports to donors typically contain long lists of donors by categories but little else.

Financial information should be provided to contributors and other stakeholders on an annual basis. This should be a universal practice rather than a best practice. The notion that contributors and other stakeholders could draw the wrong conclusions from these data is paternalistic. Any organization that asks the public for money should be accountable to the public. That means providing financial information that shows how public funding fits into the organization's overall financial position. If management is concerned about misunderstandings, it should also provide a letter or separate statement explaining the data.

Many donors will also find a specific report on internal controls to be particularly warranted. Those who have made restricted gifts to the organization certainly have a vested interest in knowing that the institution is safeguarding assets required to be put to specific uses. Even donors who make unrestricted donations should want to know that procedures are in place to protect their gifts from theft, fraud, and misappropriation.

(g) OTHER SARBANES-OXLEY PROVISIONS. Sarbanes-Oxley contains a number of other provisions that are worth noting, specifically provisions:

- Criminalizing document destruction, alteration, or falsification in federal investigations[170]—applicable to all organizations including nonprofits.
- Protecting whistleblowers from retaliation[171] —applicable to all employers, including nonprofits.
- Requiring attorneys to notify the board when they become aware of certain behavior and circumstances.[172]
- Requiring disclosure of certain "off-balance-sheet" arrangements so that investors understand the nature of the risks these arrangements pose.
- Requiring certain communications between audit committees and outside auditors.[173]
- Requiring disclosure as to whether the organization has implemented an ethics code for senior officers.[174]

---

170. Pub. L. 107–204, *supra* note 84, § 802, as codified at 18 U.S.C. 1519.
171. *Id.*, § 1107, as codified at 18 U.S.C. 1513(e).
172. *Id.*, § 307, as codified at 15 U.S.C. 7245.
173. *Id.*, § 204, as codified at 15 U.S.C. 78j-1.
174. *Id.*, § 404, as codified at 15 U.S.C. 7262.

No one should object if a nonprofit's board wants to consider any of these reforms as the basis for voluntary best practices. We consider the whistleblower and document destruction provisions in more detail in Chapter 11.

5.17 SUMMATION: STEPS FOR THE BOARD

If you were not familiar or comfortable with financial statements and controls before you began this chapter, you now have some new tools and insights. You should now understand why mission and finances are inextricably linked. It simply is impossible to ignore financial issues when focusing on mission because a nonprofit's finances both support and constrain mission.

The obvious question: How should a board integrate all of the material in this chapter into its governance process? There are undoubtedly many approaches. To a certain extent, each board must chart its own course, dictated, in large part, by the unique aspects of its own organization and the environment in which it operates. Recognizing that fact, the following is a list of steps that every board should consider implementing to gain control over and insight into its organization's finances:

- Each board member should be provided a complete set of financial statements (not summaries) in advance of each board meeting. These statements should be reviewed before the meeting.
- After the minutes for the last meeting have been approved, the board should discuss the organization's periodic (monthly, quarterly) financial statements.
- The board should receive an income statement that reflects budget variances so that board members can quickly isolate revenue or expenses that differ materially from budget.
- The board should receive a standard set of financial ratios analyzing the financial statements that it receives. These ratios will help the board to manage by exception. If the debt-to-gross-assets ratio has been 0.8 for the last five years and suddenly is 2, the board knows it has a crisis on its hands. If at all possible, the financial ratio analysis should contain comparative ratios for peer-group organizations. These can be developed by obtaining data from GuideStar if peer group information is not readily available.

  If the organization has different operating segments, the board should receive financial information for each operating segment. In the case of a museum, this might include information for food and vending, facilities rental, gift shop, and IMAX operations. In the case of a community service organization, it might mean information for the Head Start, adult literacy, job training, and housing programs.
- The board should review annually the management letter provided by the organization's outside auditors, and ask management to develop a plan to

address any internal control or other issues this letter identifies. The board should ask for periodic progress reports.

- The board should review internal controls on an annual basis with the appropriate officers. It also should ensure that the list of controls previously recommended in this chapter are in place.
- At least one board meeting each year should be devoted to reviewing and approving a budget for the organization.
- If the organization is receiving federal money or other specialized grants, the board should request periodic reports from the appropriate staff members that address compliance with expenditure limitations and grant overhead load factors, as well as with program and specialized audit requirements.
- The board should adopt and enforce a conflict-of-interest policy that is applicable to the board, all employees, and all third-party vendors and contractors.
- The board should adopt a set of policies and procedures to encourage and protect whistleblowers.
- The board should consider chartering audit and finance committees to filter many of the matters that are called for by this list, with those committees reporting to the board on a regular basis. However, under no circumstances should the regular review of financial statements be delegated to one of these committees. In other words, every board meeting should have a financial component.

This is not intended to be a comprehensive checklist, but if boards implement only these suggestions, they can avoid many of the problems described in this *Guide*. This may seem like a lot of work. It is, but oversight is required when money is at issue. There will be clear payoffs. If a board implements a program based on these suggested actions, it is taking a giant step toward curbing fraud and abuse and will find that its decision process and its decisions have greatly improved.

CHAPTER 6

FEDERAL TAX EXEMPTION

Joseph made it a law over the land of Egypt unto this day, that Pharaoh should have the fifth part; except that the land of the priests only, which became not Pharaoh's.

GENESIS 47:24

As already noted, nonprofit status is not the same as tax-exempt status. Federal tax-exempt status means that the entity has qualified under the provisions of the Internal Revenue Code as a tax-exempt entity. Different standards might apply for state-level tax exemption, particularly property tax exemption.

People often refer to tax-exempt entities as "Section 501(c)(3) organizations," referring to the section in the Internal Revenue Code that defines the requirements for tax-exempt status for many types of organizations. However, not all tax-exempt organizations are "Section 501(c)(3)" organizations. Other types include (1) social welfare organizations, (2) labor and agricultural organizations, (3) business leagues, (4) social clubs, (5) fraternal societies, (6) veterans' organizations, (7) employee benefit associations, and (8) political organizations. While organizations in each category are exempt from federal income taxation, federal income tax law does not necessarily bestow the same benefits or impose the same restrictions on each category. For example, generally only contributions to Section 501(c)(3) organizations (and to governmental entities and certain veterans' associations) are deductible as charitable contributions. As another example, Section 501(c)(3) organizations are prohibited from intervening in political campaigns, but several other categories of organizations can engage in such interventions on a limited basis.

6.1 TAX-EXEMPT ENTITIES

An organization must meet the requirements of Section 501(c) of the Internal Revenue Code to qualify as a tax-exempt organization for federal tax purposes. In most cases, the organization must file Form 1023 or 1024 as a first step in the formal recognition process.

According to the IRS's latest figures, more than 1.54 million tax-exempt organizations were on the IRS's Exempt Organization Master File at the end March 2004.[1] Section 501(c) has more than 25 categories of tax-exempt entities, each of which has its own individual qualification requirements. The following are nine of the most common types of organizations grouped under Section 501(c).

(a) CHARITABLE ORGANIZATIONS. To qualify as a tax-exempt charitable organization (Section 501(c)(3)), the entity must be organized and operated exclusively for religious, charitable, scientific, testing for public safety, literary, or educational purposes. The tax regulations define the word *charitable*[2] by reference to its "generally accepted legal sense." The word includes organizations that provide relief for the poor or the underprivileged or that lessen the burdens of government.

Section 501(c)(3) organizations cannot engage in political activity and are limited in the amount of lobbying activity in which they can engage. We consider both of these restrictions later in this chapter. Finally, no part of the net earnings of a Section 501(c)(3) organization can inure to the benefit of a private shareholder or individual. In other words, the earnings must be used for charitable purposes. We consider the prohibition against private inurement later in this chapter.

The advantage of being characterized as a Section 501(c)(3) organization is not only that the organization is exempt from tax (with the exception of income from certain unrelated activities) but also that a donor's charitable contributions to the organization may be tax deductible. These entities can also issue tax-exempt bonds.

(b) SOCIAL WELFARE ORGANIZATIONS. To qualify as a social welfare organization (Section 501(c)(4)), the entity must be operated exclusively for the promotion of social welfare, meaning that the organization must operate primarily to further the common good and general welfare of the community.[3] The focus must be on bettering the community as a whole as opposed to providing benefits to the organization's members. The following are examples of qualifying activities: (1) providing public bus transportation to the community during rush hours, (2) fostering industrial development to increase community employment, and (3) providing assistance to low-income families. On the other hand, a social club that operates for the benefit, pleasure, and recreation of its members will not qualify as a social welfare organization but might qualify as a social club under Section 501(c)(7).

---

1. *See* Internal Revenue Service, *Table 22 — Tax-Exempt Organizations and Other Entities Listed on the Exempt Organization Business Master File, by Type of Organization and Internal Revenue Code Section, Fiscal Years 2001-2004, reprinted in* PUBLICATION 55B, IRS DATA BOOK (FY 2004).
2. Treas. Reg. § 1.501(c)(3)-1(d)(2).
3. Treas. Reg. § 1.501(c)(4)-1(a)(2).

Some organizations might qualify for charitable organization status (Section 501(c)(3)) but for the organization's substantial lobbying activities (see the definition for "action organization"). Even a Section 501(c)(3) organization may engage in a limited amount of grassroots lobbying (e.g., urging members of the public to contact their representatives concerning particular legislative matters) or direct lobbying (e.g., contacting legislators, giving testimony, and submitting legislative language). In taking these actions, the organization can advocate specific points of view even though the views may be controversial or one sided.[4] A Section 501(c)(3) organization that has lost its tax-exempt status due to substantial lobbying activities, however, cannot then qualify for Section 501(c)(4) status.[5] An organization that desires to engage in substantial lobbying should consider seeking exemption under Section 501(c)(4) but should recognize that contributions to the organization will not be deductible.

The promotion of social welfare does not include direct or indirect participation or intervention in political campaigns on behalf of or in opposition to candidates for public office.[6] However, a Section 501(c)(4) organization can engage in some political activities, so long as those are not its primary activity.[7] Legal counsel should be consulted before any organization engages in even the slightest political activity.[8] Even if permissible under federal tax law, such activity still must run the gauntlet of federal election law.

(c) LABOR AND AGRICULTURAL ORGANIZATIONS. A labor organization (Section 501(c)(5)) is an association of workers organized to protect and promote the interests of labor in connection with employment.[9] Labor organizations often take the form of labor unions, councils, or committees. Agricultural organizations (Section 501(c)(5)) generally focus on improving methods used in forestry and farming.

Both labor and agricultural organizations can seek legislation germane to their missions. These organizations may also engage in some political activity so long as it is not their primary activity.[10] Again, any organization contemplating the slightest amount of political activity should consult with qualified legal counsel.

(d) BUSINESS LEAGUES. Trade associations and chambers of commerce can seek exemption as business leagues (Section 501(c)(6)). A *business league* is an association of persons having some common business interest, the purpose of which

---

4. Rev. Rul. 68-656, 1968-2 C.B. 216.
5. I.R.C. § 504.
6. Treas. Reg. § 1.501(c)(4)-1(a)(2)(ii).
7. *See* Rev. Rul. 2004-6, 2004-1 I.R.B. 197; Rev. Rul. 81-95, 1981-1 C.B. 332; and J. Reilly and B. Allen, *Political Campaign and Lobbying Activities of IRC 501(c)(4), (c)(5), and (c)(6) Organizations*, IRS CONTINUING EDUC. PUB. at L-3 (2003).
8. Rev. Rul. 81-95, 1981-1 C.B. 332.
9. Treas. Reg. § 1.501(c)(5)-1.
10. *See* Rev. Rul. 2004-6, 2004-1 I.R.B. 197, Marker v. Schultz, 485 F.2d 1003 (D.C. Cir. 1973), GCM 36286 (May 22, 1975), and J. Riley and B. Allen, *supra* note 7, at 5.

is to promote that commonality.[11] It cannot engage in a regular trade or business that is ordinarily carried on for profit.

Business leagues can seek legislation germane to their programs.[12] These organizations may engage in some political activity so long as it is not their primary activity.[13]

(e) SOCIAL CLUBS. Organizations that qualify for tax-exempt status as social clubs (Section 501(c)(7)) are organized for pleasure, recreation, and similar purposes.[14] The theory underlying their tax exemption is that the members are simply pooling their collective resources for their own benefit, making a social club an expense-sharing mechanism. Social clubs include country clubs, luncheon clubs, and hunting clubs. No portion of the net earnings of the club can inure to the benefit of its members or other private individuals. A club is not exempt if it provides pleasure and recreation on a commercial basis.

An organization claiming social club status will not be recognized as tax exempt if its charter, bylaws, or other relevant governing documents contain language discriminating in membership based on race, color, or religion (with the exception of a club that limits membership based on religious beliefs because the group's purpose is to further the teachings of that religion).[15]

Social clubs must derive most of their support from membership fees, dues, and assessments. However, a social club can receive up to 35 percent of its gross receipts, including investment income, from outside its membership.[16] Not more than 15 percent of the club's total gross receipts can be derived from the use of its facilities or services by the general public or from activities not furthering the social or recreational purposes for members. This special category of receipts is counted for purposes of determining whether the 35 percent limitation has been exceeded. All facts and circumstances are considered in determining whether the club is tax exempt when these limits are exceeded. In any event, the net income from nonmember sales and investments is taxable.

(f) FRATERNAL SOCIETIES. To qualify under Section 501(c)(8), a fraternal beneficiary society, order, or association must (1) be a fraternal organization, (2) operate under the lodge system or for the exclusive benefit of the members of a fraternal organization itself operating under the lodge system, and (3) provide for the payment of life, sick, accident, or other benefits to the members of such society, order, or association or their dependents.[17] All members, not only a particular class of members, must be eligible for the benefits in order to sustain

---

11. Treas. Reg. § 1.501(c)(6)-1.
12. Rev. Rul. 61-177, 1961-1 C.B. 117.
13. *See* Rev. Rul. 2004-6, 2004-1 I.R.B. 197, GCM 34233 (Dec. 3, 1969); and J. Riley and B. Allen, *supra* note 7, at 5.
14. Treas. Reg. § 1.501(c)(7)-1(a).
15. I.R.C. § 501(i).
16. S. REP. NO. 1318, 94th Cong., 2d Sess., at 4 (1976).
17. Treas. Reg. § 1.501(c)(8)-1.

exemption, but not every member must participate. Benefits must be limited to members and their dependents. Exemption will also be denied if organization members have the ability to confer benefits to individuals other than themselves and their dependents.

To qualify under Section 501(c)(10), a domestic fraternal society, order, or association must (1) be a domestic fraternal organization, (2) operate under the lodge system, and (3) devote its net earnings exclusively to religious, charitable, scientific, literary, educational, and fraternal purposes. However, it cannot provide for the payment of life, sick, accident, or other benefits to its members.[18] The organization may arrange with insurance companies to provide optional insurance to its members without jeopardizing its tax-exempt status.

(g) VETERANS' ORGANIZATIONS. A veterans' organization is exempt (Section 501(c)(19)) but only if each of the following requirements is satisfied:

- It must be a post or entity organized in the United States.[19]
- At least 75 percent of its members must be past or present members of the U.S. armed forces, and at least 97.5 percent of its members must be past or present members of the United States armed forces, cadets (including only students in college or university ROTC programs or at service academies), or spouses, widows, or widowers of any of these.[20]
- No part of the organization's net earnings may inure to the benefit of any private shareholder or individual.

In addition, the organization must be operated exclusively for one or more specified purposes, including, for example,

- To promote the social welfare of the community (that is, to promote in some way the common good and general welfare of the people of the community).
- To assist disabled and needy war veterans and members of the United States armed forces and their dependents, and the widows and orphans of deceased veterans.
- To provide entertainment, care, and assistance to hospitalized veterans or members of the United States armed forces.
- To provide social and recreational activities for its members.[21]

Contributions to these organizations qualify as charitable contributions.[22]

---

18. Treas. Reg. § 1.501(c)(10)-1(a)(1).
19. Treas. Reg. § 1.501(c)(19)-1.
20. Treas. Reg. § 1.501(c)(19)-1(b).
21. Treas. Reg. § 1.501(c)(19)-1.
22. I.R.C. § 170(c)(3).

(h) EMPLOYEES' ASSOCIATIONS. Voluntary employee benefit associations (VEBAs) can qualify for exemption from federal income tax under Section 501(c)(9). These associations pay for life, sick, accident, or other benefits to members of the association or their dependents or designated beneficiaries.[23] This is just one of several employee-benefit and pension arrangements that are governed by Section 501(c).

(i) POLITICAL ORGANIZATIONS. Political organizations are subject to a special tax regime (Section 527). A *political organization* is a party, committee, fund, or other entity organized and operated primarily for the purpose of directly or indirectly accepting contributions or making expenditures to influence the selection, nomination, election, or appointment of any individual to any public office or office in a political organization.[24]

Under this special tax regime, a political organization is required to pay tax on its "political organization taxable income" at the highest corporate tax rate (currently 35 percent) with an alternative tax if the organization has capital gains.[25] However, candidates for Congress can designate a principal campaign committee[26] that will have its political organization taxable income subject to tax at the regular corporate tax rates (meaning that the income is run through the tax brackets as opposed to subjecting all of it to the highest corporate tax rate).[27]

In calculating its political organization taxable income, a political organization is permitted to exclude contributions of money or other property, membership dues, a membership fee or assessment from a member of the political organization, proceeds from political fundraising or entertainment events, proceeds from the sale of political campaign materials (which are not received in the ordinary course of business), and proceeds from qualified bingo games.[28] This regime can be viewed as imposing a tax on an organization's investment income if the organization limits its activities to exempt functions (essentially political activity).[29]

23. Treas. Reg. § 1.501(c)(9)-1.
24. I.R.C. § 527(e)(1).
25. I.R.C. § 527(b).
26. I.R.C. § 527(h)(2).
27. I.R.C. § 527(h)(1). See J. Kindell and J. F. Reilly, *Election Year Issues*, IRS CONTINUING EDUC. PUB (2002).
28. I.R.C. § 527(c)(3).
29. I.R.C. § 501(c)(1).

6.2 THE BREAKDOWN

You might be surprised at how many organizations have gone through the exemption process to obtain tax-exempt status. The breakdown, based on 2004 data collected by the IRS, is as follows:

Title holding companies	7,144
Religious, charitable, and similar organizations	1,010,365
Social welfare organizations	138,193
Labor and agriculture organizations	62,561
Business leagues	86,054
Social and recreational clubs	70,422
Fraternal beneficiary societies	69,798
Voluntary employees' beneficiary associations	12,866
Domestic fraternal beneficiary societies	21,328
Benevolent life insurance companies	6,716
Cemetery companies	10,728
State-chartered credit unions	4,289
War veteran's organizations	36,141[30]

As you can see, the category with by far the largest number of organizations is Section 501(c)(3) charitable organizations with 1,010,365 qualified organizations in 2004. The IRS reports, however, that only 240,000 Section 501(c)(3) organizations filed tax returns for 2001, probably providing a more accurate assessment of the number organizations with material amounts of activity.[31] As of 2001, these organizations held more than $1.6 trillion in assets and reported $897 billion in revenue, 70 percent of which came from program services and activities.[32] The 240,000-plus organizations were categorized as follows among ten major categories:

Arts, culture, and humanities	26,006
Education	41,153
Environment, animals	9,413
Health	32,131
Human services	91,131
International, foreign affairs	3,360
Mutual, membership benefit	583
Public, societal benefits	21,537
Religion, related	14,989
Unknown	202

30. Internal Revenue Service, *supra* note 1.
31. P. Arnsberger, Charities and Other Tax-Exempt Organizations (2001), *available at* http://www.irs.gov/pub/irs-soi/01eochin.pdf.
32. *Id.*

In recent years, there has been a flurry of organizational activity following various disasters. For example, in the wake of the 9/11 terrorist attacks, the IRS recognized 342 organizations "that said their missions would focus on helping people recover from attacks, preventing future terrorist action, or honoring those who died."[33] The IRS received about 135 requests for exemption within the five-week period following Hurricane Katrina.[34]

Churches, their integrated auxiliaries, and conventions or associations of churches are not required to seek recognition of exemption on file returns.[35] Public charities with less than $25,000 in gross receipts are also exempt from annual filing.

Although only contributions to (c)(3) organizations (and a limited number of other organizations) [36] may be deductible by the contributor as charitable contributions, membership dues paid to a labor organization or business association may be (at least partially) deductible as business expenses.[37] Sometimes an organization qualifies for tax-exempt status under more than one category. In that case, the organization generally wants to be recognized as a Section 501(c)(3) organization.

6.3 A DETAILED LOOK AT SECTION 501(c)(3) STATUS

To qualify as charitable, the organization must be organized and operated exclusively for religious, charitable, scientific, literary, or educational purposes. The definitions of *religious, charitable, scientific, literary,* and *educational* are workable ones. Nevertheless, there has been some controversy in defining *religious* and *educational,* particularly when the organization's activities involve politics or religious beliefs that are out of the mainstream.

(a) DEFINITIONS OF *EDUCATIONAL* AND *RELIGIOUS*. Let's consider two cases that illustrate how difficult defining *educational* and *religious* can be in the Section 501(c)(3) context. The first examines the definition of *educational* and the second examines the definition of *religious.*

The National Gun Information Society is seeking recognition as a Section 501(c)(3) organization. Its membership is in favor of widespread availability of guns. The organization publishes books and holds lectures supporting its viewpoints. Although the information is presented to support the organization's viewpoint, all information is based on verified facts. The books and lectures are devoid of inflammatory language. The materials and speakers do not discuss the arguments made by those opposed to wider gun availability, nor do the materials or speakers discuss facts that might support a contrary viewpoint.

---

33. H. Lipman, *Carving Out a Role in Disaster's Wake: Some Experts Question Necessity of Charities Formed after Hurricane Katrina; Others Say They Fill a Void*, CHRON. OF PHILAN., Oct. 13, 2005.
34. *Id.*
35. I.R.C. § 508(c)(1) and 6033(a)(2).
36. See Section 170(c) for a list of the other qualifying organizations.
37. I.R.C. § 162.

Not surprising, determining whether National Gun qualifies as an educational organization is particularly difficult given its focus. The challenge to the IRS is to avoid judging the position advocated by National Gun when determining whether it is an educational organization. In response to case law holding that the IRS's original approach to defining education was unconstitutionally vague, the IRS adopted what it calls the "methodology" test.[38] Under this test, the IRS focuses on the methods the organization uses to present information rather than the substance of the information. The organization is not considered to engage in educational pursuits if its presentation (1) is of viewpoints or positions that are not supported by facts, (2) includes distorted facts in support of the organization's position, (3) uses inflammatory language or disparaging terms and expresses conclusions more on the basis of strong emotions rather than objective evaluations, or (4) is not intended to develop an understanding on the part of the intended audience because it does not consider their background or training in the subject matter. The IRS will overlook the presence of any of these factors if, based on the facts and circumstances, it determines that the organization is nevertheless engaged in educational pursuits.[39]

National Gun can make a persuasive case under the methodology test that it is engaged in educational activities. Granted, the organization advocates a specific position, but the IRS has indicated that this is permissible so long as it presents a sufficiently "full and fair exposition" of the pertinent facts, permitting the public to form an independent opinion or conclusion. The question is whether National Gun bases its presentation on facts rather than emotion and rhetoric. It clearly bases its information on verified facts.

Now let's focus on the definition of *religious.* Assume the IRS has revoked the tax-exempt Section 501(c)(3) status of Good Feelings Church. (While a church need not apply for recognition of exemption, the IRS, pursuant to special rules in the Church Audit Procedure Act,[40] may examine a church's claim to eligibility under Section 501(c)(3)). The church members hold many of the beliefs associated with other religions based on Christianity, and the church has a house of worship that looks similar to Christian churches. What makes this church different from other churches is that its members believe that they can communicate with God by taking LSD and other illegal drugs. Consequently, Good Feelings Church encourages its members to manufacture and take these drugs.

Good Feelings files a lawsuit to defend its tax-exempt status after the IRS declares that it is not a qualified charitable organization, arguing that the IRS position violates the First Amendment's prohibition against government restrictions on the free exercise of religion. Given the First Amendment's "freedom of religion" mandate, these facts present one of the more difficult issues for the IRS and the courts. The IRS has not attempted to formally define religion. However,

38. *See* Big Mama Rag, Inc. v. United States, 631 F.2d 1030 (D.C. Cir. 1980).

39. Rev. Proc. 86-43, 1986-2 C.B. 729.

40. Pub. L. 98-369, 98 Stat. 494, at § 1033(a), codified as I.R.C. § 7611.

the courts have suggested that religion deals with one's view of his relation with the creator.[41] In several instances, when confronted with the difficult issue of whether an organization qualified as a religious organization, the IRS has sidestepped the issue, asserting instead that the organization's activities would result in private benefits being conferred on its founders or members. In those instances, the IRS has denied the organization Section 501(c)(3) status but not based on a definition of *religion.* Instead, the IRS might focus on the illegal activities, using that as a basis for denying an exemption.[42]

The point is that the IRS is very reluctant to take on the task of defining what constitutes a religion. The Good Feelings case illustrates the difficulties posed by the issue. If you still cannot see the difficulties inherent in defining religion, you might want to review the Church of Scientology's history.[43] The IRS initially challenged its claim that it was tax exempt as a church but subsequently backed down.

Going Beyond Conventional Illegal Substances: Will the United States Supreme Court Settle the Issue Once and for All?

* * *

The United States Supreme Court in April 2005 agreed to consider whether a religious organization can use a substance banned under the federal controlled substances act as part of its religious services despite the illegal nature of the substance. The Tenth Circuit had ruled that the plaintiff demonstrated a likelihood of success on the merits, granting an injunction prohibiting the federal government from enforcing the federal controlled substances act with respect to the use of the substance in the plaintiff's religious services.[44]

The organization in question, Uniao Do Vegetal, a syncretic religion of Christian theology and indigenous South American beliefs, was founded in Brazil in 1961 by a rubber tapper who discovered the sacramental use of *hoasca* (the Portuguese transliteration of *ayahuasca*) in the Amazon rainforests. A highly structured organization with elected administrative and clerical officials, Uniao Do Vegetal uses hoasca, which in the Quechua Indian language means "vine of the soul," "vine of the dead," or "vision vine," as a link to the divinities, a holy communion, and a cure for ailments physical and psychological. Church doctrine dictates that members can perceive and understand God only by drinking hoasca. Brazil, in which there are about 8,000 Uniao Do Vegetal members, recognizes it as a religion and exempts sacramental use of hoasca from its prohibited controlled substances.

---

41. Davis v. Beason,133 U.S. 333 (1890); and United States v. Kuck, 288 F. Supp. 439 (D.D.C. 1968). For an extensive discussion of this complex issue, see Bruce R. Hopkins, The Law of Tax-Exempt Organizations, at 191–214 (John Wiley2003).
42. *See,* Rev. Rul. 75-384, 1975-2 C.B. 204. When one court considered this situation, it was willing to confront the issue on the "religious" merits, denying exempt status in the absence of "solid evidence of a belief in a supreme being, religious discipline, a ritual, or tenets to guide one's daily existence." Kuck, *supra* note 41.
43. Church of Scientology of California v. Commissioner, 823 F.2d 1310 (9th Cir. 1987) *aff'g* 83 T.C. 381 (1984).
44. O Centro Espirita Beneficiente Uniao Do Vegetal v. Ashcroft, 389 F.3d 973 (10th Cir. 2004).

Hoasca is ingested at least twice monthly at guided ceremonies lasting about four hours. Rituals during Uniao Do Vegetal services include the recitation of sacred law, singing of chants by the leader, question-and-answer exchanges, and religious teaching.

Uniao Do Vegetal has been in the United States officially since 1993, when its highest official visited and founded a branch in Santa Fe, New Mexico, subordinate to the Brasilia headquarters. Approximately 130 Uniao Do Vegetal members currently reside in the United States, 30 of whom are Brazilian citizens. The IRS previously granted Uniao Do Vegetal tax-exempt status.

Hoasca is made by brewing together two indigenous Brazilian plants, banisteriopsis caapi and psychotria viridis. Psychotria contains DMT; banisteriopsis contains harmala alkaloids, known as beta-carbolines, that allow DMT's hallucinogenic effects to occur by suppressing monoamine oxidase enzymes in the digestive system that otherwise would break down the DMT. Ingestion of the combination of plants allows DMT to reach the brain in levels sufficient to significantly alter consciousness.

Because the plants do not grow in the United States, hoasca is prepared in Brazil by church officials and exported to the United States. On May 21, 1999, United States Customs Service agents seized a shipment of hoasca labeled "tea extract" bound for Jeffrey Bronfman and Uniao Do Vegetal–United States. A subsequent search of Mr. Bronfman's residence resulted in the seizure of approximately 30 gallons of hoasca. Although the government has not filed any criminal charges stemming from church officials' possession of hoasca, it has threatened prosecution; accordingly, Uniao Do Vegetal has ceased using the tea in the United States.

Obviously, this is not the typical LSD or pot-smoker church, so the case should be an interesting one. The Supreme Court took the case with a one-line grant of certiorari. There is little question that regulators and commentators will be particularly interested to see whether the Supreme Court decision will have eventual impact on the definition of *religion* for tax purposes.[45]

* * *

(b) ORGANIZATIONAL TEST—THE FIRST REQUIREMENT. Section 501(c)(3) requires that the entity be "organized" for specified purposes. This is referred to as the "organizational" test. Under this test, the entity must be primarily organized for one of the designated purposes, and its organizational documents cannot expressly permit the organization to engage in activities that further nonexempt purposes (with an exception for insubstantial activities) or that are prohibited activities (such as intervention in political campaigns).

In determining whether the organizational test is satisfied, the IRS focuses on the purposes clause in the entity's articles of incorporation or other organizational document. The purposes clause can be drafted broadly ("charitable purposes") or narrowly ("to conduct a specified activity which is charitable"). Existing and proposed regulations examine the requirement that the organization serve a public purpose rather than providing a private benefit.[46]

---

45. The preceding discussion is taken in large part from the opinion in O Centro Espirita Beneficiente Unaio Do Vegetal v. Ashcroft, 342 F.3d 1170 (10th Cir. 2003).
46. Prop. Treas. Reg. § 1.501(c)(3)-1(1)(d), 70 Fed. Reg. 53,599 (Sept. 9, 2005).

(i) Specificity of the Purposes Clause. Those organizing or funding a nonprofit often relegate drafting responsibility to the lawyer. This is a mistake if the client fails to review the lawyers work. To illustrate, consider Simon Galt, who has been asked to contribute $1 million to Literacy Aid, a newly formed charitable organization that will sponsor literacy programs in inner city communities. The organizers approached Galt because he made his fortune after learning to read at age 32. Galt has publicly committed his philanthropy to literacy, having announced that he plans to leave his entire $400 million estate to organizations that support literacy efforts. Thus, the organizers of Literacy Aid thought Galt would be a perfect candidate to kick off their initial fundraising campaign.

Galt's lawyer has drafted the following four alternative purposes clauses for Literacy Aid's articles of incorporation:

- The organization can engage in any activity that is described in Section 501(c)(3) of the IRC.
- The organization can engage in any activity that a nonprofit corporation organized under the state not-for-profit corporation statute can engage in.
- The organization can only engage in literacy instruction for residents of inner city communities located in the state of Illinois.
- The organization can only engage in activities that improve the level of literacy in the United States.

Even though the focus is now on tax exemption, more general drafting considerations should never be far from consideration. From Galt's perspective, the first option is simply too broad, given his focus on literacy. Activities covered by Section 501(c)(3) go well beyond improving literacy. This purposes clause permits Literacy Aid to run a hospital or food bank. The board and officers might like this provision because it provides them a good degree of flexibility, but Galt should reject the first clause if he wants to limit the use of his money to improving literacy.

The second option will create problems during the exemption process. The IRS likely will argue that this provision permits the organization to engage in activities not described in Section 501(c)(3). For example, Literacy Aid could probably operate a country club and still satisfy its purposes clause. Galt clearly would not like that result.

The fourth option also poses a potential problem. Although the clause's focus is on literacy, the board and officers could argue that many activities well beyond Galt's narrower focus promote literacy. For example, publishing a newspaper arguably promotes literacy, but Galt clearly did not have a newspaper in mind.

Galt's preference should be for the third option because it ensures that his funds will be used for literacy instruction and will likely pass IRS scrutiny. Galt might be willing to provide the board with greater latitude, but of the four choices, this one best ensures that his objectives will be met. If he has a geographic preference, he should include the appropriate limitations here.

The purposes clause can be amended, meaning that even the most carefully drafted clause does not necessarily guarantee that the founder's objectives will be satisfied. Fred and his lawyers have several options available to address this. First, they can make sure that the procedures for amendment set a high hurdle (e.g., 80 percent of the directors must vote in favor of amending the purposes clause). Second, Fred can provide for installment payments by making a pledge instead of an outright gift. The pledge could be drafted so as to condition future payments on continued adherence to purposes that meet Fred's objectives. Finally, Fred could make a restricted gift. The terms of the gift would establish a fund that could be used only to satisfy Fred's limited objectives.

(ii) Ensuring Public Rather Than Private Benefit—Focusing on the Organization's "Death". Once assets have been transferred to a tax-exempt entity, the assets must either be used in furtherance of the organization's exempt purpose, or if the organization is dissolved, its remaining assets must be distributed to a government unit for public purposes or to another organization that will carry out the exempt purposes of the dissolved organization, usually after the parties have obtained court or attorney general approval. In other words, once the assets have been committed to an exempt purpose, they cannot find their way back into private hands for private benefit. This tax requirement is often echoed in state nonprofit corporation laws prohibiting distribution of the entity's assets to private individuals as part of the entity's dissolution, but those statutes must be read carefully.

ILLINOIS GENERAL NOT FOR PROFIT CORPORATION ACT OF 1986

* * *

DISTRIBUTION REQUIREMENTS

The assets of a corporation in the process of dissolution shall be applied and distributed as follows:

- All liabilities and obligations of the corporation shall be paid, satisfied and discharged, or adequate provision shall be made therefore;
- Assets held by the corporation upon condition requiring return, transfer or conveyance, which condition occurs by reason of the dissolution, shall be returned, transferred or conveyed in accordance with such requirements;
- Assets held for a charitable, religious, eleemosynary, benevolent, educational or similar use, but not held upon a condition requiring return, transfer or conveyance by reason of the dissolution, shall be transferred or conveyed to one or more domestic or foreign corporations, societies or organizations engaged in activities substantially similar to those of the dissolving corporation, pursuant to a plan of distribution adopted as provided in this Act;

- To the extent that the articles of incorporation or bylaws determine the distributive rights of members, or any class or classes of members, or provide distribution to others, other assets, if any, shall be distributed in accordance with such provisions;
- Any remaining assets may be distributed to such societies, organizations or domestic or foreign corporations, whether for profit or not for profit, as may be specified in a plan of distribution adopted as provided in Section 112.17 of this Act.

* * *

(c) OPERATIONAL TEST—THE SECOND REQUIREMENT. Not only must the tax-exempt entity's organizational documents specify that the entity be organized for one of the designated exempt purposes but the entity's primary activities must actually accomplish one or more of its exempt purposes. This is referred to as the *operational test.*

At one time, if an organization operated a trade or business for profit, but all income from the trade or business was destined for charitable purposes, the organization qualified for tax-exempt status.[47] In 1950, Congress did away with the "destination of income" test, focusing instead on the source of the organization's revenue. Organizations that carry on a trade or business for profit and donate the profit to a charity are referred to as *feeder organizations,* and they do not qualify for tax-exempt status.[48]

A subsequent section of this chapter considers the unrelated business income tax. The very existence of this tax implicitly recognizes that tax-exempt entities can engage in activities that do not directly contribute to the accomplishment of their exempt purposes. However, an organization will fail the operational test if more than an insubstantial part of its activities fail to further its exempt purpose.[49]

Specifically, under the operational test, a Section 501(c)(3) organization cannot be what is termed an "action organization," meaning that the organization cannot engage in any political activity, or any lobbying activity that is considered substantial in relation to its other activities. This aspect of the operational test is what created a problem for the Progress and Freedom Foundation, the organization that was closely identified with former House Speaker Newt Gingrich.[50]

Section 501(c)(4) organizations are not subject to the same "action organization" prohibitions imposed on Section 501(c)(3) organizations, but the term still has relevance for Section 501(c)(4) organizations.[51] Once a Section 501(c)(3) organization is an action organization, it cannot convert its status to Section 501(c)(4) as a means of avoiding the prohibition.[52] This rule prevents an organization from

---

47. Trinidad v. Sagrada Orden de Predicadores, 263 U.S. 578 (1924).
48. I.R.C. § 502.
49. Treas. Reg. § 1.501(c)(3)-1(c)(1).
50. *Unnumbered TAM Rules Foundation Involved with Gingrich Course Was Exempt*, TAX NOTES TODAY, Feb. 5, 1999.
51. Treas. Reg. § 1.501(c)(4)-1(a)(2)(ii).
52. *See* I.R.C. § 504(a).

building up a pool of tax-deductible funds that can then be used to engage in substantial lobbying activities.

(d) NO PRIVATE INUREMENT—THE THIRD REQUIREMENT. Under no circumstances can the entity's net earnings inure to the benefit of private persons having a personal or private interest in the activities of the organization.[53] This prohibition is designed to ensure that once assets are transferred to a Section 501(c)(3) organization, the assets (and earnings from them) cannot find their way back into private hands (as profits or dividends). Those assets now must be irrevocably devoted to charitable purposes because they have received preferential treatment under federal income tax law.

Of relatively more recent vintage is a separate prohibition against the operation of an organization for private benefit rather than public purposes.[54] This prohibition is related to the prohibition against private inurement but recognizes that more than just the siphoning off an organization's net earnings by private interests can thwart the charity's public mission. To illustrate, assume that Soledad Faber owns a for-profit teaching company that produces teaching materials and licenses them for a profit. Now assume that Faber forms a charitable organization to engage in teaching activities. The new charity licenses the teaching materials from Faber's for-profit company, paying what would be considered fair value under the license. Faber's for-profit company also provides trainers for the new charity for a fee. If the agreement is terminated, the nonprofit cannot engage in similar activities for a two-year period. This is a situation in which the IRS is likely to assert the private benefit doctrine, arguing that the arrangement serves Faber and her for-profit company rather than the public.[55]

Neither the prohibition against private inurement nor the prohibition against private benefit prevents an insider from enjoying the same benefits with respect to an entity's services or property as members of the general public or the intended class of beneficiaries. Nor do they preclude an insider from engaging in transactions with the entity if those transactions are conducted at arm's length and for fair value (and the entity is not a private foundation—such status triggers additional provisions prohibiting "self-dealing").

The prohibitions against private inurement and private benefit have been concerns for many nonprofit hospitals in the context of physician recruitment. To compete with for-profit hospitals, physician service contracts often call for a participation in revenue or profits. While not necessarily impermissible (if properly structured), these arrangements do raise inurement and self-dealing issues, as do joint ventures between Section 501(c)(3) organizations and for-profit entities.[56]

---

53. Treas. Reg. § 1.501(c)(3)-1(c)(2).
54. The "private benefit" doctrine is derived from language in Treasury Regulation Section 1.501(c)(3)-1(d)(1)(i).
55. Prop. Treas. Reg. § 1.501(c)(3)-1(d)(1)(iii), Example 3, 70 Fed. Reg. 53,599 (Sept. 9, 2005).
56. Plumbstead Theatre Society, 74 T.C. 1324 (1980), *aff'd* 675 F.2d 22 (9th Cir. 1982).

6.4 OBTAINING TAX-EXEMPT STATUS

While the IRS exemption process can be a long and involved one, if the organization is willing to dot its Is and cross its Ts, obtaining tax-exempt status is an achievable goal. Organizations usually find that the retention of an experienced lawyer is well worth the fees. This lawyer will be able to minimize time-consuming requests from the IRS, build the strongest case for exemption, and speed the process.

(a) THE EXEMPTION PROCESS—PRELIMINARIES. For purposes of this discussion, we focus on Form 1023, the application form required to be filed by charitable organizations seeking Section 501(c)(3) status. All other organizations apply on Form 1024. Before Form 1023 is filed, the organization should obtain an employer identification number, complete the organizational process, compile financial data, and execute a power of attorney.

(i) Obtain an Employer Identification Number from the IRS. Every tax-exempt organization must have an employer identification number (EIN) whether or not it has any employees. To obtain an EIN, the organization must file a completed Form SS-4, Application for Employer Identification Number. Because receiving the number can take a number of weeks if written application is made, the organization should probably use the Tele-TIN procedure to obtain the number by telephone. The organization must still file Form SS-4, but at least it has the number, so the process of obtaining exemption is not delayed.

(ii) Complete the Formal Organizational Process. For a nonprofit organization, completing the organizational process usually means formally incorporating and adopting bylaws. A charitable trust is created by a trust instrument, and it may also adopt bylaws. Each application for exemption must be accompanied by a conformed copy of the organization's articles of incorporation (and the certificate of incorporation issued by the secretary of state or other designated authority, if available) or other core organizational document. If the organization has adopted bylaws, they should be submitted with the application. The organization should wait until all organizational documents have been finalized before filing for tax-exempt status. It is also important that the organization have its officers and directors in place, as a recent denial of tax-exempt status makes clear.[57]

(iii) Compile Financial Data. As part of the application, the organization must include financial statements showing the organization's receipts and expenditures for the current year and the three preceding years (or the number of years

57. Tax Analysts, a nonprofit organization, sued under the Freedom of Information Act to force the release of IRS documents denying exempt status. At this time, there appears to be no numbering convention.

that the organization has been in existence, if less than four). For each accounting period, the organization must include the sources of its receipts and nature of its expenditures as well as a balance sheet.

If the organization has not yet begun operations or has operated for less than one year, it should include a proposed budget for two full accounting periods and a current statement of assets and liabilities. This aspect of the application process tends to be one of the more difficult because many organizers do not begin thinking about funding and financial issues until they reach the application process, making this requirement a helpful one because it forces everyone to focus on these issues.

(iv) Executing a Power of Attorney. If the organization is represented by an agent or attorney, whether in person or by correspondence, it must file a power of attorney with the exemption application. The organization can use Form 2848, Power of Attorney and Declaration of Representative, for this purpose.

(b) THE EXEMPTION PROCESS—COMPLETING AND FILING FORM 1023. Completing Form 1023 is the key to the application process. This is where the organization makes the case that it is structured and will be operated as a charitable, educational, religious, scientific, or literary organization.

The IRS significantly modified Form 1023 in November 2004 with two basic objectives in mind. First, the IRS wanted to streamline the exemption process to decrease the "back and forth" between taxpayers and the IRS. Noticing that there were predictable requests for additional information, the IRS decided to expand its request for information as part of the application. Second, and far more important, the IRS expanded the number of questions it asks, attempting to identify at the outset transactions and affiliations that tend to be problematic from a regulatory standpoint. The form now asks very specific questions about director, officer, and independent contractor compensation and qualifications, contracts, and ventures with affiliated persons and entities.

The form is now 28 pages long, with the first 12 pages applicable to all applicants. The remaining pages may or may not be applicable to a particular organization. For example, special sections apply only to churches and schools.

When completing Form 1023, the preparer should be honest but should also be an advocate for the organization. The form should be typed rather than handwritten. Better yet, the organization should consider taking advantage of the ability to complete the form electronically by using a specially coded Adobe Acrobat version. The preparer should use exhibits and attachments rather than cramming information into small spaces. All relevant questions should be answered. Finally, the preparer should anticipate questions that the examiner might have when reviewing the application. The preparer should make the decision as easy as possible for the reviewer. As was the case with the old version of Form 1023, the new version is signed under penalties of perjury. The preparer and signing officer should keep that in mind when they respond to all questions, particularly those covering compensation, affiliated parties, contracts and relationships, and conflicts of interest. The issues addressed by these questions are the same ones that the IRS focuses on during audits. Consequently, there is now a much greater chance that those engaging in deception and outright lies will be subjected to criminal prosecution.

When completing Form 1023, the preparer should recognize that the final form is a public document if the IRS approves the application. In fact, the organization must make Form 1023 and its three prior years of tax returns available to the public on request.[58] The public is becoming savvy about making requests for these documents from charities. If the organization includes trade secrets, patents, and similar confidential information in the application that would adversely affect the organization if the application were made public, it can request that this information be excluded from the public inspection process.[59] Furthermore, if it is not a private foundation, the organization need not include contributor names or addresses.[60] Confidential information does not include financial information such as salaries.

(i) Who Must File. Most organizations seeking Section 501(c)(3) status must file Form 1023 (viewed as giving the IRS notice) before they will be exempt from taxation pursuant to Section 501(c)(3).[61] However, a number of organizations are not required to file with the IRS to perfect an exemption, including churches and certain church-related organizations,[62] any organization that is not a private foundation and normally does not have gross receipts exceeding $5,000 in each taxable year,[63] and organizations covered by a group exemption.[64]

(ii) When to File IRS Form 1023. If an organization files its application within 15 months after the end of the month in which it was formed and if the IRS approves the application, the effective date of the organization's Section 501(c)(3) status is the date it was organized.[65] An automatic 12-month extension is available.[66] If an organization does not file its application (Form 1023) within 27 months after the end of the month in which it was formed, it will not qualify for exempt status as a Section 501(c)(3) organization during the period before the date of its application,[67] although it may qualify as a Section 501(c)(4)

58. I.R.C. § 6104(d).
59. I.R.C. §§ 6104(a)(1)(A) and 6104(d)(3)(B).
60. I.R.C. § 6104(d)(3)(A).
61. Treas. Reg. § 1.508-1(a).
62. Treas. Reg. § 1.508-1(a)(3)(a).
63. Treas. Reg. § 1.508-1(a)(3)(b).
64. A group exemption is issued to a central organization. It recognizes on a group basis the exemption of subordinate organizations on whose behalf the central organization has applied. *See* Treas. Reg. § 1.508-1(a)(3)(c); and Rev. Proc. 80-27, 1980-1 C.B. 677, as modified by Rev. Proc. 96-40, 1996-2 C.B. 301. For addition details see BRUCE R. HOPKINS, *supra* note 41, at § 23.7.
65. Treas. Reg. § 1.508-1(a)(2).
66. Treas. Reg. § 301.9100-2.
67. For exceptions and special rules, including automatic extensions in some cases, see Part III of Form 1023.

organization (to which contributions are not deductible). Even though a charity may view 27 months as a generous timeframe, it may find that it cannot rely on this full period because some donors insist on established Section 501(c)(3) status.

(iii) Where to File. The application must be mailed to:

Internal Revenue Service
P.O. Box 192
Covington, Kentucky 41012-0192

If the application is sent by express mail or delivery services, it should be sent to:

Internal Revenue Service
201 W. Rivercenter Blvd.
Attn: Extracting Stop 312
Covington, Kentucky 41011

These addresses come from Form 8718, and the current version should be reviewed before filing to determine whether the mailing address has changed. You should retain evidence of mailing (if by mail, send certified mail with return receipt requested).

(iv) Filing Fees. Organizations must include a user fee with Form 1023 (Part XI) before the IRS will process the application for exemption. The fee is $500 if the applicant's annual gross receipts have exceeded or will exceed $10,000 annually over a four-year period; otherwise it is $150.

(c) OTHER ORGANIZATIONS—FORM 1024. Most organizations seeking tax-exempt status under Sections 501(a) and (c) other than under Section 501(c)(3) file Form 1024 and follow the procedures outlined in its instructions. These organizations include (1) social welfare organizations, (2) labor and agricultural organizations, (3) trade associations and business leagues, (4) social clubs, (5) fraternal societies, (6) VEBAs, and (7) certain other listed organizations.

(d) APPROACHING THE EXEMPTION PROCESS. Organizers should view the exemption process as one that can be helpful to their organization. The IRS is essentially asking the organizers to submit a business plan for the organization. If Form 1023 or 1024 is difficult to complete, it could be because the organizers have not thought through what the organization is trying to accomplish. This often indicates the need to do more work or that a plan is not viable.

If you are the one preparing the application or helping an attorney complete it, remember that you are an advocate for the organization. Tell a "story." Make the application interesting and compelling. You will have succeeded if the IRS reviewer says, "Of course this organization should be exempt—look at the 'good' that it is doing." But you must be straightforward and truthful.

The IRS recently began publishing the determination letters it issues when an exemption for tax-exempt status is denied, with any identifying information redacted. Anyone who is seeking tax exemption for an organization should look at denials issued to organizations with similar missions. These letters provide a roadmap that may permit preparers to avoid repeating the mistakes of others.

(e) STATE EXEMPTION REQUIREMENTS. Under the laws of many states, exempt status under federal income tax law means automatic exempt status under state income tax law, but there are exceptions. For example, the state of Washington has a gross receipts tax. Consequently, it has a separate set of tax rules that apply to entities that are tax exempt for federal income tax purposes.[68] Even if a state accepts the federal determination, state law may still require the organization to make a notice filing. Moreover, charities are often permitted to claim exemption from state and local property tax and sales tax, but exemption again may be predicated on a filing. In summary, the organizers should check with state and local authorities to determine what needs to be done to obtain favorable exemptions under applicable state and local laws.

6.5 PRIVATE INUREMENT—THE PROHIBITION

Section 501(c)(3) status is conditioned on the absence of what lawyers call *private inurement.* This means that an organization's receipts cannot be siphoned off by an insider (generally viewed as a founder, member of the organization's board, an employee or contractor, or anyone else that could be fairly described as an insider—that is, who is the equivalent of an owner or manger).[69]

The prohibition against inurement can be viewed as another permutation of the state law requirement that a charity's assets can be used only in furtherance of its charitable purposes. In other words, once assets are committed to the charitable sector, they must remain in the charitable sector unless the charity holding them receives fair value (in kind, or through the conduct of charitable activities) for those assets.

(a) COMPENSATION. In a 2004 survey, the *Chronicle of Philanthropy* found that the median salary for the chief executive officers of the surveyed (large) charities was $291,356.[70] This is nowhere near what Wall Street tycoons, corporate executives, or many lawyers and accountants earn, but this average certainly dispels

68. Wash. Rev. Code, Chapter 82.04, § 3651, *Exemptions—Amounts Received by Nonprofit Organizations for Fund-Raising Activities*; and WASHINGTON DEPARTMENT OF REVENUE, BUSINESS & OCCUPATIONS TAX, *available at* http://dor.wa.gov/Docs/Pubs/ExciseTax/BO_PubUtil_LitterTax/BOfs.pdf.

69. See Treas. Reg. § 1.501(a)-1(c), which focuses on "persons having a personal and private interest in the activities of the organization."

70. *See* B. Gose, *Executive Pay Rises Modestly*, CHRON. OF PHILAN., Sept. 30, 2004.

the notion that all of those working in the nonprofit sector are paupers. The survey points out that compensation can be much higher in certain instances, most notably for CEOs of nonprofit hospitals, with at least one executive's compensation exceeding $1.45 million per year. The question we consider now is whether those levels of compensation are inconsistent with, and consequently jeopardize, the tax-exempt status of charitable organizations.

The IRS has said that it will generally not find inurement if the arrangement (1) is not illegal, contrary to a clearly defined and established public policy, or in conflict with express statutory restrictions, and (2) furthers the organization's exempt purpose and is reasonably related to the accomplishment of that purpose. Subsumed in the second part of this standard is the requirement that compensation reflect fair market value. By and large, the organization can avoid claims of inurement if there is no self-dealing, disloyalty, or breach of fiduciary duty on the part of the board in approving the arrangement.

To avoid problems in determining the executive director's compensation, the board should consider establishing (1) concrete performance standards, (2) a compensation committee to review salary surveys and conduct negotiations, (3) a process that removes the executive director from the process of selecting outside compensation consultants, and (4) procedures that exclude the executive director from the decision process.

(b) OTHER POTENTIAL INSTANCES OF PROHIBITED INUREMENT. Compensation is clearly an area about which boards and officers must be careful, but there are other times when inurement should be a concern. These include any contract between the organization and one of its officers, directors, or employees. Examples include building leases, investment advisory contracts, and consulting arrangements. Inurement has also been a concern when outsiders buy the assets of nonprofit organizations, particularly when members of the board or executive officers simultaneously enter into employment contracts with the organization purchasing the assets. This issue came up in the 1990s when many nonprofit hospitals sold their assets to for-profit entities.

In recent years, joint ventures between for-profit and nonprofit entities have proliferated. For example, groups of physicians own and run laboratories that provide testing services to nonprofit hospitals. The hospital often contributes capital or equipment, provides accounting and other administrative services, or leases lab space to these ventures, taking back an interest in the lab. Theaters and museums often enter into ventures with private parties that operate gift shops, festivals, food concessions, raffles, or even present concerts or performances. The IRS has indicated that if not properly structured, these ventures or revenue-sharing arrangements can result in prohibited inurement.

The IRS has also been concerned about arrangements with professional fundraisers that have resulted in a high percentage of the funds raised by the professional being paid to the fundraiser as a fee. In fact, the IRS has litigated this issue, resulting in the now infamous *United Cancer Council* case.[71] In a decisive reversal, the Seventh Circuit rejected the IRS's assertion that a high percentage paid to an unrelated fundraiser constituted private inurement. The fact that the bargain between the charity and the fundraiser might have been a bad one did not mean that the bargain was tainted. Beware, however; this case does not prevent the IRS from raising this issue in other federal circuits. Furthermore, the Seventh Circuit asked the district court to review a related basis for finding the agreement problematic.[72] The parties settled before this alternative was addressed.

6.6 INTERMEDIATE SANCTIONS

Until 1996, a finding of private inurement was a disaster because the only sanction was loss of tax-exempt status. This harsh result was not in anyone's interest because it meant that even a "foot fault" could theoretically cost an organization its exempt status. When a penalty is this harsh, it is often difficult for regulators to win cases even though the behavior should be curbed. In response to a growing perception that the IRS was either reluctant to act or any negotiated settlements were not subject to judicial scrutiny, Congress enacted legislation that created a series of "intermediate sanctions," permitting the IRS to penalize prohibited behavior without revoking exempt status. Under these new rules, the IRS can impose a penalty on the benefited insider and the representatives of the charity who sanctioned the transaction equal to a percentage of the excess benefit (e.g., compensation paid that is found to be unreasonable). These sanctions are available when a Section 501(c)(3) or 501(c)(4) organization (other than a private foundation) engages in "excess benefit transactions."

(a) EXCESS BENEFIT TRANSACTIONS. An *excess benefit transaction* is any transaction in which an economic benefit is provided by a covered organization to a Section 4958 disqualified person in which the economic benefit paid to the person exceeds the value of the services or other consideration provided to the organization.[73] The rules focus on the performance of services but also cover sales of property and joint venture arrangements, among other transactions.

The entire intermediate sanction analysis revolves around whether the transaction at issue was priced at fair value. All elements of compensation must be considered, including deferred compensation, payments to welfare benefit plans, insurance coverage, many types of fringe benefits (including certain nontaxable ones), and below-market-rate loans.[74] The rules require economic benefits provided indirectly to be considered, including compensation paid by controlled entities.[75]

---

71. United Cancer Council v. Commissioner, 165 F.3d 1173 (7th Cir. 1999).
72. *See* Preamble to Prop. Treas. Reg. § 1.501(c)(3)-1(d), 70 Fed. Reg. 53599 (Sept. 9, 2005).
73. Treas. Reg. § 53.4958-4(a).
74. Treas. Reg. §§ 53.4958-4(a)(4) and (b)(1)(ii)(B).
75. Treas. Reg. § 53.4958-4(a)(2).

Certain benefits provided to volunteers, members or donors, and charitable beneficiaries are excluded from the analysis under Section 4958.[76] With the exception of liability insurance premium payments, fringe benefits excludable from gross income under Section 132 are also excluded from the entire analysis under the intermediate sanctions,[77] as are reimbursements under accountable plans that meet the basic substantiation requirements[78] applicable to reimbursable business expenses of employees.[79]

PRIVATE INUREMENT OR VIOLATION OF THE INTERMEDIATE SANCTIONS: WHERE IS THE LINE?

* * *

The IRS recently addressed the relationship between private inurement and the intermediate sanctions in Technical Advice Memorandum (TAM) 2004-35-020.[80] The organization in question (Charity X) was a relatively new one, receiving its tax-exempt status sometime during the three or four years prior to the tax audit that generated the request for technical advice. It qualified as a church under Section 170(b)(1)(A)(i) and as a public charity (as opposed to a private foundation) under Section 509(a)(1). At this point, however, you should drop any preconceived notions of what a charity looks like. There is a heavy "family" aspect to this charity.

Charity X's bylaws are revealing, granting extraordinary powers to A, who has always been Charity X's president and a director. B, A's wife, is secretary-treasurer and a director. Their sons, C and D, are directors of Charity X. C also serves as vice president. E, who is not an employee of Charity X, is A and B's son-in-law.

The first issue discussed in the ruling is whether Property J (apparently owned by Charity X) was used by A and his family as a personal residence. The TAM notes that Charity X applied for property tax exemption for the residence but was initially denied exemption. The assessor eventually granted an exemption for the 11 percent of the property that was used for the storage of books. The ruling then goes on to describe a second house that was occupied for six months by A's two sons. This house was sold before the audit.

The ruling next examines credit card statements and charges. The agent found charges for meals, gasoline, and miscellaneous items that appeared to be unrelated to Charity X's charitable activities. The agent focused on charges incurred at about the same time as seminars that Charity X sponsored. While the TAM does not provide relative magnitudes, its tone suggests that charges that could not be traced to Charity X seminars were material.

The ruling then describes a number of vehicles owned by Charity X. The tone of the ruling suggests that they were used for personal rather than business purposes. Why does a church need a vehicle referred to as a "roadster"?

---

76. Treas. Reg. §§ 53.4958-4(a)(4)(iii), (iv), and (v).
77. Treas. Reg. § 53.4958-4(a)(4)(i).
78. Treas. Reg. § 1.62-2(c).
79. Treas. Reg. § 53.4958-4(a)(4)(ii).
80. Any guidance issued by the IRS under Section 4958 should be of interest given the current lack of precedents applying Section 4958 to actual facts.

The agent asked for policy statements regarding personal use of cars by and reimbursement to Charity X for personal expenditures incurred by employees and paid for by Charity X. There does not appear to have been formal written policy statements, but Charity X responded by saying that policies were in place to ensure that Charity X funded only charitable expenditures.

The IRS concluded that Section 4958 applied to the transactions in question. However, the IRS did not place a great deal of emphasis on whether the payments were excessive compensation, stating:

> In the instant case, A and his relatives expended funds of [Charity] X, and used [Charity] X assets, in a variety of ways described below and in separate technical advice memoranda issued to his wife, sons, and son in law. A does not contend that these expenditures and uses were intended as compensation to himself or his relatives. In any event, there is no evidence in the record that would satisfy the contemporaneous substantiation rules of section 53.4958-4(c)(3) of the regulations.

The IRS focused on whether these were properly reimbursable business expenditures, concluding that:

> It follows that unless A can satisfy the accountable plan requirements of section 1.62-2 of the regulations, or the requirements of sections 162 and (to the extent relevant) 274 and the regulations there under for ordinary and necessary business expenses, the expenditures and use of [Charity] X funds described below must qualify as automatic excess benefits.

After providing additional details regarding the excess benefits and how it computed the value of these benefits, the IRS imposed the 25 percent Tier 1 tax under Section 4958 on A, stating:

> An excise tax, as provided by section 4958(a)(1) of the Code, equal to 25 percent of the excess benefit amount, should be imposed on A. A was the founder, president, and chief executive of [Charity] X. As a practical matter, he had total control of all [Charity] X expenditures. He either approved of the excess benefit transactions by his wife, his two sons, and his son in law, or he at least acquiesced in them. If A had withdrawn funds from [Charity] X and given them to his family members, there would have been no question that such gifts would be taxable excess benefits to him. By authorizing or allowing his relatives the natural objects of his bounty to make unlimited expenditures of [Charity] X funds for personal purposes without any substantiation or evidence of an [Charity] X business purpose, he in effect improperly removed charitable assets from [Charity] X and gave them to his relatives. Accordingly, A not only is liable for the excess benefit transactions from which he personally benefited, but also is jointly and severally liable for all of the excess benefits outlined in the technical advice memoranda of today regarding B, C, D, and E. See John Marshall Law School v. United States, supra; Code Section 4958(d)(1).

The IRS then proposed that the 200 percent Tier 2 tax under Section 4958 also be imposed. This TAM ends without addressing the private inurement issue. If these facts do not at least raise the specter of private inurement, what facts do? Does this mean that when excessive and poorly documented reimbursements exist but the organization is still engaged in charitable activity, the IRS will simply force a correction of the problem through the intermediate sanctions?

* * *

(b) DISQUALIFIED PERSON—BASICS. The intermediate sanctions apply to excess benefit transactions only between a covered organization and a Section 4958 disqualified person. A *disqualified person* is any person who at any time within the five-year period ending on the date of the transaction in question (the "lookback period") was in a position to exercise substantial influence over the affairs of the organization.[81] The definition includes any individual serving on the board (or other governing body) entitled to vote, the CEO, the CFO, family members of disqualified persons, any entity in which a disqualified person is considered to control more than 35 percent of the entity, and persons who, based on a facts and circumstances test, are determined to be in a position to exercise substantial influence over the organization.

Under the *facts and circumstances test*, a person who (1) manages a discrete segment or activity of the organization that represents a substantial portion of its activities, assets, income, or expenses, as compared to the organization as a whole,[82] or (2) has or shares authority to control or determine a substantial portion of the organization's capital expenditures, operating budget, or compensation for employees[83] "tends" to have exercised substantial influence. There could, however, be cases in which this is not so. The facts and circumstances test potentially covers other significant players, including the organization's founder, substantial contributors,[84] and, among others, a person whose compensation is based on revenues derived from activities that the person controls.

Certain facts and circumstances might, on the other hand, show that the person in question does not have substantial influence over an organization. The following persons are generally not considered to be disqualified persons under the facts and circumstances test:

- A person who has taken a vow of poverty as a member of the religious group in question.
- A person who is an independent contractor, such as an attorney, accountant, or investment advisor, whose sole relationship with the organization is providing professional services and receiving commensurate fees.
- A person whose direct supervisor is not a Section 4958 disqualified person.[85]

One fact that certainly must be considered in determining whether a person exercises substantial influence over an organization is the person's salary. The higher the salary, the more likely it is that that person has some influence. The intermediate sanctions address the salary issue. If a person's compensation does not exceed a specified level for the preceding year, that person will not be

81. I.R.C. § 4958(f)(1); and Treas. Reg. § 53.4958-3.
82. Treas. Reg. § 53.4958-3(e)(2)(v).
83. Treas. Reg. § 53.4958-3(e)(2)(iv).
84. I.R.C. § 507(d)(2)(A).
85. Treas. Reg. § 53.4958-3(e)(3).

considered to be a disqualified person unless otherwise a disqualified person or a substantial contributor.[86] For 2006, that level is $100,000.[87]

Let's consider three examples that further illustrate the disqualified person concept.

(i) A Board Member—Case 1. Sylvia Strom is on the board of directors of Talk-to-Us, a nonprofit organization providing counseling services in the Tucson area. She is a real estate developer who owns significant amounts of property in the Tucson area. In need of additional office space, Talk-to-Us asks Strom about leasing space in a 200,000-square-foot office building owned by a partnership in which Strom holds a 45 percent interest. Strom and Talk-to-Us's chief executive officer negotiate a 15-year lease for 100,000 square feet of office space in the building. The partnership will receive $72 per square foot, triple net. Comparable office space in the Tucson area rents for $68 per square foot on a triple net basis.

There is absolutely no question that Strom is a disqualified person for purposes of the intermediate sanction provisions.[88] The question is whether she is in a position to exercise substantial influence over Talk-to-Us. This determination sounds as if it would require an analysis of facts, but certain individuals, including board members, are automatically deemed to be in a position to assert a substantial influence over the organization.[89] Moreover, the partnership is also a disqualified person by reason of Strom's 45 percent interest.[90]

(ii) The New Hire—Case 2. Big U wants to hire Butkus Jones as its head football coach. Football has proved critical to Big U's finances, bringing in $50 million each year in alumni contributions and $300 million in ticket and television revenue. Jones is a well-known coach, having coached winning teams for the last 20 years, and does not come cheap. He is demanding a base salary of $5 million plus 20 percent of any increase in alumni contributions during his tenure. He also wants a large mansion on Lake U and a substantial fringe benefit package. The trustees have hired an outside compensation consultant to determine what Big U should pay Jones. The consulting firm has advised Big U to "meet his demands" even though Jones will receive far more than comparable coaches.

Ignoring the contract exception discussed later, Butkus Jones is probably in a position to exercise substantial influence over Big U, subjecting the transaction to an intermediate sanctions analysis. However, Jones is not in the category of persons who are automatically classified as having substantial influence over Big U.[91] He does have managerial control over a discrete segment of Big U's

86. Treas. Reg. § 53.4958-3(d)(3).
87. IRS Notice 2005-75, 2005 I.R.B. 929.
88. Treas. Reg. § 53.4958-3(c).
89. Treas. Reg. § 53.4958-3(c)(1).
90. Treas. Reg. § 53.4958-3(b)(2)(i)(B).
91. Treas. Reg. § 53.4958-3(c).

activities, the football program.[92] Under the regulations, the question is whether the football program is a substantial portion of Big U's assets, income, or expenses. Unfortunately, the intermediate sanctions regulations do not provide a threshold percentage for making this determination. Is a "substantial portion" more than 50 percent, 33.33 percent, 20 percent, or 5 percent?

The regulations provide two examples that are marginally helpful in ascertaining what is substantial. One example[93] focuses on the dean of the law school of a large university (substantial), and the other[94] on the department head of a small department in the college of arts and sciences in the same university (insubstantial). Given the two examples, Jones will, in all likelihood, be considered a disqualified person. The revenue-based compensation arrangement supports that conclusion,[95] but there certainly is room for debate. Ask the department heads in any organization whether they wield substantial influence, and the response is likely to be laughter, but, of course, their employees may have a quite different opinion of department heads' powers.

(iii) Exercising Substantial Influence—Case 3. Professor Nadja Virhaus is head of Silicon U's computer engineering department. Silicon U is known around the world because of the engineering department's cutting-edge work. Not surprising, half of Silicon U's students and faculty are associated with this department. Virhaus recently received a patent on a new computer chip that runs four times faster than the current generation of PC chips and that can be manufactured at one-third the cost. Under her contract, Virhaus must assign her rights to the patent to Silicon U, but she is entitled to 10 percent of the net revenues generated by the chip. Assume that this arrangement and the percentage are not at all unusual for faculty members in universities throughout the United States.

Like Butkus Jones, Nadja Virhaus probably is a disqualified person for purposes of the intermediate sanctions. She is not included in any of the automatic categories, but she does have substantial influence over the affairs of Silicon U,

---

92. Treas. Reg. § 53.4958-3(e)(2)(v).
93. Treas. Reg. § 53.4958-3(g), Example 8.
94. Treas. Reg. § 53.4958-3(g), Example 9.
95. *See* Treas. Reg. § 53.4958-3(e)(2)(iii). The word "primarily" in Treasury Regulation Section 53.4958-3(e)(iii) poses the problem. In other words, a revenue-sharing arrangement does not automatically result in "disqualified person" classification. At the time the contract is signed, the board cannot determine whether Jones' revenue-sharing arrangement, by itself, makes him a disqualified person because the board doesnot know what will happen under the incentive compensation arrangement. For that reason, if the revenue-sharing arrangement is the sole basis for possible disqualified person status, the board should consider capping the amount payable under the arrangement in an effort to make valuation easier.

The "primarily" test could pose problems in certain other common situations. Celia Roady, a well-known tax lawyer in the exempt organization area, notes that many exempt organizations have salespeople who receive more than half of their total earnings from selling advertising space in periodicals on a contingent-fee basis. Ms. Roady also notes that very few people would view these individuals as exercising substantial influence over an organization, but that under the "primarily" test, they might be so viewed. C. Roady, INTERMEDIATE SANCTIONS, BNA TAX MANAGEMENT PORT. NO. 864 at A-13 (2004). She also points to university royalty-sharing agreements with inventors.

particularly when her work produces patents having significant value to the university.[96]

(c) EXCISE TAXES. The intermediate sanctions use a two-tier system to penalize disqualified persons who benefit from excess benefit transactions and organization managers who willfully and knowingly approve these transactions. Under the first tier, the disqualified person is subject to a 25 percent excise tax on any excess benefits.[97] The offending organization managers are subject to a 10 percent excise tax (up to $10,000 per excess benefit transaction).[98] If the transaction is not corrected, the disqualified person is subject to a second-tier, confiscatory excise tax equal to 200 percent of the excess benefits.[99] *Correction* means eliminating the excess benefit.[100] As noted in Chapter 4, the term *organizational manager* includes the organization's directors. Consequently, despite state statutes limiting director liability, directors who approve excess benefit transactions are potentially subject to the excise tax (although the maximum per benefit transaction on all organizational managers is $10,000).[101]

As this regime should suggest, it is the disqualified person who should be most concerned that the organization takes the actions necessary to permit the parties to rely on the rebuttable presumption and the protections afforded by contemporaneous substantiation of all benefits. The directors have an incentive to seek professional advice because relying on such advice can protect them from liability as organizational managers.[102] They also have an incentive to ask questions because negligent failures to make the necessary inquiries—inaction—is treated as participation.[103] In any case, the directors will be held liable for the tax if, among other conditions, they were aware that the transaction under the particular circumstances could violate the intermediate sanctions.[104]

(d) ABATEMENT OF TAXES. Both the first and second tier taxes can be abated. In the case of the first tier taxes, the tax will be abated if the taxpayer establishes that the payment of the excess benefit was due to reasonable cause, not to willful neglect, but only if the excess benefit is corrected within the allowable period.[105]

---

96. Treas. Reg. § 53.4958-3(e)(2)(v).
97. I.R.C. § (a)(1).
98. I.R.C. § 4958(a)(2).
99. I.R.C. § 4958(b).
100. Treas. Reg. § 53.4958-7. As a general rule, a disqualified person corrects an excess benefit through a payment of cash or its equivalent. The correction amount must also include a component for interest. In the case of nonqualified deferred compensation that has not yet been paid, the disqualified person can correct the transaction by relinquishing any right to receive the excess portion of the unpaid benefit. *See* Treas. Reg. § 53.4958-7(b)(3).
101. I.R.C. § 4958(d)(2).
102. Treas. Reg. § 53.4958-1(d)(4)(iii).
103. Treas. Reg. §§ 53.4958-1(d)(3) and (4)(C).
104. Treas. Reg. § 53.4958-1(d)(4).
105. I.R.C. § 4962(a).

The second tier tax can also be abated.[106] Because of the amount of the second tier tax, the disqualified person will most likely correct the excess benefit before the second tier tax becomes an issue.

The first tier tax poses a practical problem for the disqualified person. Without the 25 percent tax, a disqualified person would have an incentive to take his chances. He would be ahead of the game anytime an excess benefit transaction went unaudited. If, on the other hand, the transaction were audited, the disqualified person would simply return the excess benefit. The 25 percent tax serves to keep the disqualified person honest. Before the tax can be abated, the disqualified person must demonstrate that the excess benefit was truly inadvertent. Otherwise, the disqualified person will be out of pocket (the correction amount and the 25 percent tax).

(e) REBUTTABLE PRESUMPTION. Under the intermediate sanctions, a transaction between a covered organization and a disqualified person enjoys a rebuttable presumption of reasonableness if each of the following three requirements is satisfied:

- The arrangement is approved in advance by the board (or a committee of the board) composed entirely of parties without conflicts.
- The board relies on compensation or other appropriate comparables prior to reaching the decision.
- The board documents the basis for its decision concurrently with the determination.[107] Written minutes with the appropriate level of detail are advisable.

The board or compensation committee has appropriate data about comparability if, given the knowledge and expertise of its members, it has sufficient information to determine whether, under the valuation standards of the regulations, a compensation arrangement will be reasonable or a transaction is priced at fair market value. *Relevant information* includes (1) compensation levels paid by similar organizations (both for-profit and nonprofit) for functionally comparable positions in the organization's same geographic area, (2) current compensation surveys compiled by independent firms, (3) actual written offers from similar institutions competing for services of the disqualified person(s), and (4) independent appraisals of the value of property that the organization intends to purchase from or sell to the disqualified person. In setting compensation for purposes of the comparables requirement, organizations with less than $1 million in annual gross receipts (including charitable contributions) can rely on information collected from three comparable organizations in the same or similar communities for similar services.[108]

106. I.R.C. § 4961.

107. Treas. Reg. § 53.4958-6(a). This is a rebuttable presumption in favor of reasonableness of the arrangement, creating a hurdle for the IRS to overcome when challenging any arrangement in which the presumption can be invoked. *See* Treas. Reg. § 53.4958-6(b).

108. Treas. Reg. § 53.4958-6(c)(2)(iii).

A board or a committee member does not have a conflict of interest if he:

- Is not a disqualified person and is not participating in or economically benefiting from the compensation arrangement or transaction (and is not a member of the family of any such disqualified person).
- Is not in an employment relationship subject to the direction or control of any disqualified person participating in or economically benefiting from the arrangement.
- Is not receiving compensation or other payments subject to approval by any disqualified person participating in or economically benefiting from the arrangement.
- Has no material financial interest affected by the arrangement.
- Does not approve a transaction providing economic benefits to any disqualified person participating in the arrangement who in turn has approved or will approve a transaction providing economic benefits to the member.[109]

Not coincidentally, these procedures resemble safe harbors under many state nonprofit corporation statutes for approving conflict-of-interest transactions.

(f) CONTEMPORANEOUS SUBSTANTIATION. If an organization fails to provide contemporaneous written substantiation of its intent to provide compensation for services as an economic benefit, the payment automatically is treated as an excess benefit unless the payment is excludable from gross income under the Internal Revenue Code (e.g., qualified health insurance coverage)[110] or reasonable cause for such failure exists.[111] In many cases, this is not an issue because inclusion of the compensation on a timely filed Form W-2 or Form 1099 constitutes contemporaneous substantiation.[112] Organizations and recipients may run into trouble under the contemporaneous substantiation rule with executive-style fringe benefits, such as membership to a country club or use of a cell phone or Blackberry for personal purposes.

The rules provide that contemporaneous substantiation exists if the board approved the compensation before it is paid or benefit is conferred or if the compensation is part of a written employment contract approved by the board or an authorized officer.[113] Contemporaneous substantiation only keeps the compensation from automatically being classified as an excess benefit. It can still be classified as an excess benefit to the extent it is not reasonable compensation for the services provided.[114] For that purpose, the value of all benefits—regardless of whether they are taxable or exempt from taxation—is considered with the

109. Treas. Reg. § 53.4958-6(c)(1)(iii).
110. Treas. Reg. § 53.4958-4(c)(2).
111. Treas. Reg. § 53.4958-4(c)(3)(i)(B).
112. Treas. Reg. § 53.4958-4(c)(3)(i)(A).
113. Treas. Reg. § 53.4958-4(c)(3)(ii)(A).
114. Treas. Reg. § 53.4958-4(c)(2).

exception of certain fringe benefits[115] and certain expense reimbursement arrangements,[116] which are excluded from the entire analysis under the intermediate sanctions.

The contemporaneous substantiation requirement has clear implications for both nonprofit boards and executives. To prevent IRS agents from automatically classifying perks as excess benefits on audit, employment contracts should detail every benefit the executive is to receive. The regulation was obviously written to encourage just that result, thereby making it easier to determine whether compensation is reasonable.

No board should assume that the IRS will show mercy if the overall level of compensation is reasonable but the contemporaneous substantiation requirement has been ignored. A 2004 IRS training publication advises IRS agents as follows:

> However, if the organization does not satisfy the written contemporaneous substantiation requirements in Reg. § 53.4958-4(c)(1), Agents should treat the reimbursements paid under a "non-accountable plan"[117] as "automatic" excess benefit transactions without regard to whether:
>
> - The reimbursements are reasonable,
> - Any other compensation the disqualified persons may have received is reasonable, or

---

115. Treas. Reg. § 53.4958-4(a)(4)(i).
116. Treas. Reg. § 53.4958-4(a)(4)(ii).
117. INTERNAL REVENUE SERVICE, PUBLICATION 463, TRAVEL, ENTERTAINMENT, GIFT, AND CAR EXPENSES, at 28 (2005), defines an accountable reimbursement plan as follows (with slight paraphrasing):

> To be an accountable plan, the employer's reimbursement or allowance arrangement must include all of the following rules.
>
> 1. The employee's expenses must have a business connection—that is, the employee must have paid or incurred deductible expenses while performing services as an employee of his employer.
>
> 2. The employee must adequately account to his employer for these expenses within a reasonable period of time.
>
> 3. The employee must return any excess reimbursement or allowance within a reasonable period of time....
>
> The definition of reasonable period of time depends on the facts and circumstances of each employee's situation. Actions that take place within the times specified in the following list will be treated as taking place within reasonable period of time.
>
> 1. The employee receives an advance within 30 days of the time he has an expense.
>
> 2. The employee adequately accounts for his expenses within 60 days after they were paid or incurred.
>
> 3. The employee returns any excess reimbursement within 120 days after the expense was paid or incurred.
>
> 4. The employee is given a periodic statement (at least quarterly) that asks the employee to either return or adequately account for outstanding advances and he complies within 120 days of the statement.

Although Publication 463 provides a helpful summary, organization should review Treasury Regulation Section 1.62-2(c) for a full statement of the rules.

- The aggregate of the reimbursements and any other compensation the disqualified person may have received is reasonable.

Reg. § 53.4958-4(c)(1).[118]

(g) EXCEPTIONS FOR CERTAIN INCOME AND TRANSACTIONS. The intermediate sanctions contain a number of important exceptions covering special situations.

(i) Initial Written Contract Exception. Probably the most important exception to the intermediate sanctions is for initial contracts.[119] Recall the case analyzing whether Butkus Jones was a disqualified person. Because the case involved Jones's initial contract, Big U and Jones ostensibly did not have to worry about excess benefits. Under the initial contract exception, the intermediate sanctions do not apply to fixed payments to a person pursuant to an initial written contract.[120] Moreover, this exception permits contingent payments (e.g., compensation tied to increases in alumni contributions) but only if they are determined pursuant to an objective formula set out in the contract.[121] The theory underlying this exception is quite simple: A person who is not employed by an organization or otherwise disqualified cannot exert influence over the organization when it comes to the terms of his contract. The organization and the soon-to-be disqualified person should be careful if the parties contemplate a discretionary performance bonus. Although the initial contract exception applies to the fixed portion of the contract, the performance bonus (or other contingent payments) are subject to a reasonableness determination that considers all compensation, be it fixed or discretionary.[122]

As is typical, the exception contains a number of nuances. For example, if the contract is terminable at some point in time by the organization, the contract is deemed to be a new contract at the earliest date that it can be terminated.[123] The initial contract exception is a useful one, but as with many good things, the organization and the disqualified person should keep the endgame in mind. Once the contract expires, it is unlikely that the person will be willing to accept less compensation. At that time, the new contract must be analyzed under the intermediate sanctions, meaning that the organization and the disqualified person should focus on that analysis when they negotiate the initial contract if renewal is likely.

118. L. Brauer and L. Henzke, *"Automatic" Excess Benefit Transactions under IRC 4958*, IRS Continuing Educ. Pub., at 10 (2002).

119. Treas. Reg. § 53.4958-4(a)(3).

120. Treas. Reg. § 53.4958-4(a)(3)(iii). This exception will obviously not be available to "at-will" employees. The parties may not be able to avail themselves of the exception if they start work prior to signing the written contract, beginning work on a handshake. *See* C. Roady, *supra* note 95, at A-24 for additional insights into the practical realities of the exception.

121. Treas. Reg. § 53.4958-4(a)(3)(i).

122. Treas. Reg. § 53.4958-4(a)(3)(vi).

123. Treas. Reg. § 53.4958-4(a)(3)(v).

(ii) Nontaxable Fringe Benefits Exception. With several exceptions, employee fringe benefits that are excluded from gross income under Section 132[124] of the Internal Revenue Code are not considered for purposes of the intermediate sanctions—either for determining whether compensation is reasonable or whether there has been contemporaneous substantiation.[125] These benefits include qualified transportation fringe benefits, qualified employee discounts, working condition fringe benefits, and certain de minimis fringe benefits. Because fringe benefits often represent a significant aspect in employee compensation, this exception is a useful but limited one. By contrast, payments of health and dental insurance premiums, below-market-rate loans, bonuses, contributions to qualified retirement plans, and severance pay must be considered under the intermediate sanctions.[126]

Sometimes the nature of an employee's job requires him to accept meals and lodging from his employer as part of his job function. A camp counselor might be required to live in a cabin with campers as part of his duties. In such case, the value of the lodging is not taxable to the counselor.[127] Nevertheless, under the intermediate sanctions, the value of the meals and lodging must be considered for purposes of determining whether the employee received an excess benefit.[128] In other words, meals and lodging provided for the convenience of an employer

---

124. Those who are not acquainted with tax law should be very careful when considering Section 132 fringe benefits. The specific fringe benefits covered by Section 132 are significantly more limited than the phrase *fringe benefit* carries in the common vernacular.

125. Treas. Reg. § 53.4958-4(a)(4)(i). *See also* L. Brauer and L. Henzke, *supra* note 118, at 11.

126. Treas. Reg. § 53.4958-4(b)(1)(B).

127. I.R.C. § 118.

128. T.D. 8978, 67 Fed. Reg. 3076 (Jan. 23, 2002), addresses this issue, stating:

> Several comments were received requesting that lodging furnished for the convenience of the employer (i.e., meeting the requirements of section 119) be disregarded for section 4958 purposes. These comments suggested that benefits excluded from gross income under section 119 should be disregarded for purposes of section 4958 because the policy rationale underlying section 119 is the same as that underlying section 132. However, there are differences between the two sections. In general, section 132 benefits are subject to nondiscrimination rules or are de minimis in amount, which is not the case with section 119 benefits. The value of housing benefits is potentially much larger than many of the section 132 benefits, and therefore a greater potential for abuse exists in the section 119 area. Accordingly, the IRS and the Treasury Department believe it is appropriate to treat section 119 benefits differently from section 132 benefits by requiring an evaluation for reasonableness.

Organizations must be very careful when they provide meals and lodging to a disqualified person, as indicated by Example 3 to Treasury Regulation Section 53.4958-4(c)(4), which provides as follows:

> H is an applicable tax-exempt organization and J is a disqualified person with respect to H. J's written employment agreement provides for a fixed salary of $y. J's duties include soliciting funds for various programs of H. H raises a large portion of its funds in a major metropolitan area. Accordingly, H maintains an apartment there in order to provide a place to entertain potential donors. H makes the apartment available exclusively to J to assist in the fundraising. J's written employment contract does not mention the use of the apartment. H obtains the written opinion of a benefits compensation expert that the rental value of the apartment is not includable in J's income by reason of section 119, based on the expectation that the apartment will be used for fundraising activities. Consequently, H does not report the rental value of the apartment on J's Form W-2, which otherwise correctly reports J's taxable compensation. J does not report the rental value of the apartment on J's

do not qualify for the exception for nontaxable fringe benefits.[129] Although a camp counselor is unlikely to be classified as a disqualified person, a university president who lives in university-provided housing most likely will be.

(iii) Expense Reimbursement Exception. Reimbursements of employee expenses are not considered either in determining whether compensation is reasonable or whether there has been contemporaneous substantiation,[130] but only if the reimbursement is pursuant to an arrangement that satisfies certain record-keeping requirements for accountable reimbursement plans.[131] Surprisingly, a number of taxpayers have run into trouble because reimbursements of expenses were not made pursuant to an accountable plan or were not properly substantiated. In such case, if there is no contemporaneous substantiation,[132] the reimbursements will automatically be treated as excess benefits.[133] Consequently, every organization should make sure its reimbursement procedures qualify as an accountable plan.

(h) PULLING IT ALL TOGETHER—A COMPREHENSIVE EXAMPLE. The analysis under the intermediate sanctions is clearly complex and, at times, confusing. In an effort to pull the seemingly disparate parts together, let's consider the following hypothetical: Judith Mecklin is the president of Green and Blue College, a four-year undergraduate school with 5,000 students. The board of trustees is considering her pay package as part of her annual review. At this time, the board is considering the following package:

- A $200,000 base salary.
- A $50,000 bonus if the college's ranking jumps from its current 20th ranking to 15th in next year's American Academic Ratings survey.

> individual Form 1040. Later, the Internal Revenue Service correctly determines that the requirements of section 119 were not satisfied. Because of the written expert opinion, H has written evidence of its reasonable belief that use of the apartment was a nontaxable benefit as defined in paragraph (c)(2) of this section. That evidence was in existence on or before the due date of the applicable Federal tax return. Therefore, H has demonstrated its intent to treat the use of the apartment as compensation for services performed by J.

As this example demonstrates, determining whether an arrangement qualifies for Section 119 treatment is not always clear. Had the organization not obtained the opinion, the value of the benefit would have automatically been considered an excess benefit. See the second to last sentence of Treasury Regulation Section 53.4958-4(c)(1). The lesson is this: No matter how sure an organization (and the recipient) is that food or lodging qualify for Section 119 treatment, the organization should nevertheless satisfy the contemporary substantiation requirement in Treasury Regulation Section 53.4958-4(c)(1) when the recipient is a disqualified person. If the food and lodging are not covered by Section 119, the organization and the disqualified person will still have to demonstrate the reasonableness of the disqualified person's compensation (taking the food and lodging into account), but they will have avoided automatic excess benefit treatment with respect to those items.

---

129. *Id.*
130. Treas. Reg. § 53.4958-4(a)(4)(ii).
131. Treas. Reg. § 1.62-2(c).
132. Treas. Reg. § 53.4958-4(c)(3).
133. *See* L. Brauer and L. Henzke, *supra* note118, at 11.

- The payment of health insurance premiums pursuant to the college's employee health plan ($15,000 value).
- A $20,000 annual contribution to the college's qualified retirement plan.
- The reimbursement of all business-related expenses (assume $30,000).
- The use of the school's student athletic center (valued at $1,000 per year).
- A paid membership in the Green City Country Club ($15,000 annual dues; 60 percent personal use).
- The rent-free occupancy of the presidential residence on campus (valued at $30,000 per year).
- An executive chef to cook meals in the residence ($100,000 annual salary and $50,000 in material costs; 60 percent business).
- Access to a chauffeur-driven car service ($50,000 annual rental value, 60 percent business use).
- A $50,000 nonaccountable expense account for institutional gifts and other expenses.
- A retirement package that provides for an annual retirement benefit equal to 120 percent of the salary paid to the highest-paid official at Green and Blue College until President Mecklin's death.

Mecklin and the college have agreed to allocate the expenses between personal and business expense when both elements are present; when a percentage-use division is provided for, the value of the portion attributable to personal use will be included in her taxable income and not subject to reimbursement by her.

(i) Step 1—Determining Whether Each Benefit Is Included in the Overall Analysis. The starting point of the intermediate sanctions analysis is to determine which items are excluded from the analysis, although they are not necessarily excludable from Mecklin's gross income. Clearly, the $200,000 in salary and $50,000 bonus are subject to review under the intermediate sanctions.[134] The value of the health insurance coverage and the $20,000 contribution to a qualified pension plan are also subject to the analysis even though neither item is taxable.[135] Although both items are referred to as *fringe benefits,* neither is the type of fringe benefit referred to in Section 132. The right to use the athletic center could in many instances be a Section 132 benefit but in this case that is unlikely because of the substantial use of the center by nonemployees. Consequently, the value associated with the right to use these facilities will be subject to the intermediate sanctions analysis.[136] If the reimbursement of all business expenses is made pursuant to an accountable plan, those reimbursements will

134. Treas. Reg. § 43.4958-4(b)(1)(ii)(B)(*1*).

135. Treas. Reg. § 43.4958-4(b)(1)(ii)(B)(*3*).

136. I.R.C. § 132(j)(4)(B)(iii); and L. Brauer, T. Tyson, and D. Kawecki, *An Introduction to IRC 4958 (Intermediate Sanctions),* IRS CONTINUING EDUC. PUB., at 316 (2002).

also be ignored for purposes of the intermediate sanctions.[137] We will assume that is the case. The "120 percent" retirement benefit is also subject to analysis under the intermediate sanctions[138] as is the use of the presidential residence even though the amount is not taxable.[139] The chef, chauffeur, and country club pose the most difficult questions. Clearly, the amounts allocated to personal use should be included in the analysis and in the president's taxable income.[140] Assuming that the business portion of the meals and the automobile expenses is not lavish or extravagant, these amounts should be excludable from the intermediate sanctions analysis as working condition fringes under Section 132,[141] although this is not entirely without doubt.[142] Somewhat surprising and despite the normal rule disallowing deductions for any dues for social and country clubs,[143] the regulations include a special rule that appears to treat the business portion of the country club dues as a working condition fringe, and therefore, as being excludable from the analysis.[144]

137. Treas. Reg. §§ 53.4958-4(a)(4)(ii) and 1.132-5(a)(1).
138. Treas. Reg. §§ 53.4958-4(b)(1)(ii)(B)(*1*) and 53.4958-2(e)(2).
139. Treas. Reg. §§ 53.4958-4(a)(4)(i) and 53.4958-4(b)(1)(ii)(B)(*3*); and L. Brauer, T. Tyson, and D. Kawecki, *supra* note 136, at 316–318.
140. Treas. Reg. §§ 53.4958-4(a)(4)(i) and 53.4958-4(b)(1)(ii)(B)(*3*).
141. Treas. Reg. §§ 53.4958-4(a)(4)(i) and 53.4958-4(b)(1)(ii)(B)(*3*); and L. Brauer, T. Tyson, and D. Kawecki, *supra* note 136. These are considered working condition fringes, assuming that they are not lavish or extravagant.
142. If President Mecklin had incurred the meal expenses herself, she would have to seek reimbursement for them under an accountable plan before these expenses could be excluded from the entire analysis under the intermediate sanctions. A literal reading of the regulations suggests, however, that when the employer incurs the expenses directly there is no need to substantiate the benefits to qualify them as working condition fringes. But the following passage from L. Brauer, T. Tyson, and D. Kawecki, *supra* note 136, at 290, suggests that there should be parity regardless of whether the employer or employee actually incurs the cost:

> I.R.C. 132 applies only to benefits provided directly by the employer to the employee; it does not deal with reimbursements by the employer to the employee for business expenses initially paid by the employee. For example, I.R.C. 132 treats as an excludable working condition fringe the value of an airplane ticket the employer gives to the employee to make a business trip. I.R.C. 132 does not cover reimbursement paid by the employer to the employee if the employee purchases the airline ticket for the business trip. Reimbursements are technically covered by Regs. 1.62-2. However, for administrative purposes, all TE/GE administrative personnel will treat reimbursements of a business expense the same as if the expense were paid directly by the employer, as long as the employee complies with the substantiation rules of I.R.C. 62 and 274. So qualifying reimbursements will be disregarded under I.R.C. 4958, to the same extent as direct payments by the employer are disregarded under I.R.C. 132.

Alternatively, the business portion of the meal expense might be viewed as being for the convenience of the college, in which case, the expense would not be includable in President Mecklin's income but would be subject to analysis under the intermediate sanctions.
143. I.R.C. § 274(a)(3).
144. Treas. Reg. § 1.132-5(s); and L. Brauer, T. Tyson, and D. Kawecki, *supra* note 136, at 304.

To summarize:

Benefit	Includable in Analysis	Excludible from Analysis	Includable/ Excludable from Gross Income
$200,000 salary	Includable		Includable
$50,000 bonus	Includable		Includable
$20,000 contribution to pension plan	Includable		Currently excludable, but includable when distributed
$15,000 health insurance premium	Includable		Excludable (section 106)
$30,000 expense reimbursement		Excludable if accountable plan and reasonable (section 274)	Excludable if accountable plan and reasonable
$1,000 use of athletic facilities	Includable		Includable
$15,000 country club dues	$6,000 includable		Includable
		$9,000 excludable	Excludable
$30,000 rent-free use of residence	Includable		Excludable (section 119)
$150,000 chef and food cost paid by school	$60,000 includable		Possibly includable
		$90,000 excludable	Excludable (working condition fringe or section 119)
$50,000 chauffer	$20,000 includable		Includable
		$30,000 excludable	Excludable
Retirement package	Includable		Includable when received
$50,000 nonaccountable expense account	Includable		Includable

As you should see, most of the items are includable for purposes of applying the intermediate sanctions analysis. Even those items that are excludable could be reclassified for one of two reasons. First, the IRS could determine that the expenses are not reasonable and as a consequence would not be classified as working condition fringe benefits. Second, the IRS could determine that the allocation between personal and business expenses overstates the percentage allocable to business use. The intermediate sanctions regulations do not address such an arrangement. The logic of the regulations, however, strongly suggests that the university and President Mecklin should keep meticulous records and base the allocation on those records after the fact, or when they set the percentages, they should err heavily on the side of personal use. For that reason, organizations should not rely on broad allocations of the type reflected in this example. Although such rough estimates are easy to administer, from a tax and corporate standpoint, the better course of action is to require each meal to be documented and categorized as business or personal, with the tax treatment based on the actual facts.

(ii) Step 2—Contemporaneous Substantiation as Evidence of Payment for Services. The second question is whether each of these payments is considered to be made in exchange for services rendered.[145] If the IRS determines that the payments were not made in exchange for services rendered, the payments are treated as automatic excess benefits regardless of whether President Mecklin's compensation is reasonable: a draconian consequence. An easy way to avoid the problem is to list each benefit in a written employment contract that is approved by the organization's board of directors or other person or body that is authorized to approve the contract.[146] In the absence of a written contract, President Mecklin could avoid automatic adverse treatment for each item as indicated in the accompanying table.

Benefit	Method for Contemporaneous Substantiation
$200,000 salary	Included on W-2[147]
$50,000 bonus	Included on W-2[148]
$20,000 contribution to pension plan	Qualified fringe benefit—no other action required[149]
$15,000 health insurance premium	Qualified fringe benefit—no other action required[150]
$30,000 expense reimbursement	Excluded from entire analysis
$1,000 use of athletic facilities	Includable on W-2;[151] or possibly described in a handbook[152]
$15,000 country club dues	$6,000 includable on W-2[153] $9,000 excluded from entire analysis
$30,000 rent-free use of residence	Qualified fringe benefit—No other action required[154]
$150,000 chef and food cost paid by school	$60,000 includable on W-2[155] $90,000 excludable from analysis[156]
$50,000 chauffeur	$20,000 includable on W-2[157] $30,000 excludable from analysis
120 percent retirement package	Written contract[158]
$50,000 nonaccountable expense account	Includable on W-2[159]

145. Treas. Reg. § 53.4958-4(c)(3).
146. Treas. Reg. § 53.4958-4(c)(3)(ii)(A).
147. Treas. Reg. § 53.4958-4(c)(3)(i)(A)(1).
148. *Id.*
149. Treas. Reg. § 53.4958-4(c)(2).
150. *Id.*
151. Treas. Reg. § 53.4958-4(c)(3).
152. L. Brauer, T. Tyson, and D. Kawecki, *supra* note 136, at 320.
153. Treas. Reg. § 53.4958-4(c)(3)(i)(A)(1).
154. Treas. Reg. § 53.4958-4(c)(2).
155. Treas. Reg. § 53.4958-4(c)(3)(i)(A)(1).
156. The $90,000 would seem to qualify under Section 119 or be a Section 132 fringe benefit. *See* Treas. Reg. § 53.4958-4(c)(2).
157. *Id.*
158. Treas. Reg. § 53.4958-4(c)(3)(i)(A)(*1*).
159. *Id.*

The college could also rely on the opinion of an outside expert for contemporaneous substantiation of the items characterized as nontaxable. Even if the IRS disagrees with the tax treatment of an item, so long as there was contemporaneous substantiation demonstrating an intent to treat the item as paid in exchange for services rendered, the item will escape automatic classification as an excess benefit.[160]

(iii) Step 3—Determining Reasonableness of Overall Compensation. Only after these first two steps have been completed does the analysis turn to determining whether the overall compensation package is reasonable. At this point, Judith Mecklin should assert the rebuttable presumption if it is available. If the IRS rebutted the presumption, she would have to demonstrate that her compensation was reasonable in relation to the benefits she received. Under this analysis, she would not have to consider benefits that are excluded under Step 1 of the analysis or benefits that are automatically treated as excess benefits.[161]

(iv) Cautionary Note. The preceding analysis reflects a best effort to untangle the regulations. At this time, there is little guidance with respect to how the various parts of the intermediate sanctions puzzle interact with each other.

American University: The Intermediate Sanctions and Other Governance Mandates Protect Not Only the Nonprofit But Also the Chief Executive

* * *

In 2005, a major controversy erupted on the campus of American University over its president's compensation package.[162] According to the *Washington Post,* an anonymous letter sparked an investigation by the university into the president's personal and travel expenses.[163]

---

160. Treas. Reg. § 53.4958-4(c)(4), Example 3.

161. It seems appropriate to exclude these from the analysis because they are not paid in exchange for services; that is how Treasury Regulation Section 53.4958-4(c)(1) views automatic excess benefits.

162. V. Strauss and S. Kinzie, *Once-Friendly AU Board Splintered into Factions: Attorneys Hired over Ladner's Future*, WASH. POST, Sept. 28, 2005; V. Strauss and S. Kinzie, *AU Faculty Members Vote No Confidence in Ladner: Information Lacking, Suspended Leader Says*, WASH. POST, Sept. 27, 2005; P. Fain, *Troubles Deepen for American U. President as Reports of Lavish Spending Spur Trustee to Demand His Ouster*, CHRON. OF HIGHER EDUC., Sept. 26, 2005; and V. Strauss and S. Kinzie, *Federal Officials Scrutinize Ladner: Sources Say AU Received Subpoena*, WASH. POST, Sept. 20, 2005.

163. Introduction to a transcriptappearing in *American University Controversy: AU President Says He Will Consider Legal Action if He's Dismissed,* WASH. POST (Oct. 7, 2005); G. Williams, *American University Faces Legal Scrutiny over President's Spending*, CHRON. OF PHILAN., Sept. 30, 2005; and S. Jaschik, *American U. President Placed on Leave*, INSIDEHIGHER EDUC. Aug. 25, 2005.

The board commissioned an audit,[164] which was subsequently leaked to the press.[165] Stories about elaborate dinners,[166] a personal chef,[167] and extravagant travel[168] began to circulate.

Then American University President Benjamin Ladner mounted a strong defense of his expenses, strongly denying any wrongdoing,[169] but admitting that several personal expenses had been improperly accounted for.[170] President Ladner wrote a check to correct those errors.[171] Ultimately, the governing board removed him from his office.[172] The parties subsequently reached an agreement over severance[173] but not before several board members resigned as a direct consequence of the controversy.[174] The Senate Finance Committee has decided to conduct an investigation into the matter, making a formal request for documents and other information from American University.[175] While members of the board of trustees probably hoped they were bringing the matter to a close when they reached a severance agreement with President Ladner,[176] the Finance Committee's request will keep this controversy alive for sometime to come.

Whether President Ladner was right or wrong, the entire incident has a number of important lessons for those holding executive positions with tax-exempt organizations. First, and most important, although President Ladner's contract apparently provided for reimbursement of "first class" travel expenditures,[177] this does not mean that the executive has carte blanche authority to engage in extravagance. Some trustees, faculty members, and students were outraged by what they read in the press.[178] Even if some of the alleged expenditures that generated the outrage were technically permissible under President Ladner's contract, he apparently ignored the fact that perceptions count,[179] affecting an executive's creditability and ability to get things done.[180]

Second, President Ladner gave a number of interviews during the course of the controversy.[181] It is unclear whether he really understood the significance of the intermediate

164. V. Strauss, *AU Calls in Lawyers, Auditors to Investigate Finances*, WASH. POST, July 30, 2005.

165. *See* P. Fain, *Troubles Deepen, supra*note 162.

166. *Controversy on the Menu*, WASH. POST, Sept. 25, 2005.

167. S. Kinzie and V. Strauss, *Layoff Amid Probe of AU Head's Spending*, WASH. POST, Sept. 16, 2005.

168. S. Kinzie and V. Strauss, *$500,000 in Ladner Spending Itemized: Trustees at AU Deeply Divided*, WASH. POST, Sept. 22, 2005.

169. S. Kinzie and V. Strauss, *Attorneys Challenge AU Trustees' Leadership*, WASH. POST, Oct. 8, 2005.

170. *In His Own Words, supra* note 170. CHRON. OF HIGHER EDUC., Sept. 29, 2005; S. Kinzie and V. Strauss, *AU's Ladner Defends His Spending: Suspended President Says Trustees Have Treated Him Unfairly*, WASH. POST, Sept. 24, 2005.

171. M. Janofsky, *Suspended College President Offers to Accept Lesser Pact*, N.Y. TIMES, Sept. 24, 2005.

172. M. Janofsky, *American University Dismisses Its President over Spending*, N.Y. TIMES, Oct. 12, 2005.

173. S. Kinzie and V. Strauss, *Ladner's $3.75 Million Deal Severs Ties to American U.: Ex-President Allowed to Resign Rather Than Be Fired*, WASH. POST, Oct. 25, 2005.

174. *Id. See also* L. Bains, G. Collins, L. Jaskol, and P Wolff, *An Open Letter to the American University Community* (undated).This document was *available at* http://www.benladner.com. on December 18, 2005.

175. S. Kinzie and V. Strauss, *Senate Panel Requests Records from AU on Ladner and Board*, WASH. POST, Oct. 28, 2005.

176. S. Kinzie and V. Strauss, *Ladner's $3.75 Million Deal Severs Ties to American U.: Ex-President Allowed to Resign Rather than Be Fired*, WASH. POST, Oct. 25, 2005.

177. S. Kinzie and V. Strauss, *American U. Board Split on Keeping President: Some Negotiating New Deal for Ladner*, WASH. POST, Sept. 25, 2005.

178. Press Release, Concerned AU Students, American University Organizing to Oppose Ladner, Oct. 10, 2005; S. Kinzie and V. Strauss, *Majority of Trustees Say Ladner Must Leave: Some Board Members Seek Generous Deal*, WASH. POST, Sept. 30, 2005; and S. Kinzie and V. Strauss, *Ladner Memo in 2004 Sought $5 Million Boost: AU Students Demonstrate against President*, WASH. POST, Sept. 29, 2005.

179. Editorial, *Mr. Ladner's "Mistakes,"* WASH. POST, Oct. 8, 2005.

180. L. Romano, *AU Scandal Atypical in Post-Enron Era, College Presidents Say*, WASH. POST, Oct. 9, 2005.

181. *In His Own Words, supra* note 170; and *American University Controversy, supra* note 163.

sanctions when he entered into the controversial contract. But by the time the controversy had run its course, President Ladner clearly understood that he, not American University, stood to benefit the most from the rebuttable presumption under the sanctions, as well as compliance with all minutia in the regulations.[182]

While every board should obviously be concerned about setting appropriate compensation for the organization's personnel, the executives should be the ones who demand that the board obtain comparables, consult with lawyers, accountants, and compensation professionals, and utilize written employment contracts. Executives should also be sticklers about substantiating their expenses under accountable reimbursement plans. While the directors can be subject to penalties, the executives are the ones who must return any excess benefits—that is, real money.

Third, President Ladner claimed that he submitted appropriate reimbursements for many expenses but that the university had a record retention policy that resulted in the destruction of those records after a one-year period of time.[183] According to President Ladner, this led the auditors to recharacterize many business expenditures as personal when in fact they had been business related.[184] This record retention practice could also have implications if the IRS decides to audit the compensation arrangement. As is true with the intermediate sanctions, a document retention policy does not just protect the institution. Given the fact that a six-year statute of limitations could apply in the case of the intermediate sanctions,[185] executives should insist on lengthy record retention policies when it comes to expense reimbursements.

Fourth, whether the 1997 contract was valid was controversial. Those defending President Ladner argued that the entire board had the opportunity to review its terms if members so desired.[186] Others said that some of the board members had not seen the contract.[187] Newspaper accounts were unclear as to whether the contract was approved by an executive committee, a compensation committee, or the chair of the board. For present purposes, the facts of that particular situation are largely irrelevant. The lesson is this: While the chief executive might prefer negotiating a contract with the chair of the board or the compensation committee, the safer course of action is to seek a decision of the full board following full disclosure of the contract's terms.

Fifth and last, President Ladner seemed to suggest that concerns over better governance in the nonprofit sector were rooted in the 2002 Sarbanes-Oxely Act,[188] applicable for the most part to large publicly traded corporations but influencing those serving on nonprofit boards.[189] There is no doubt that Sarbanes-Oxley is impacting nonprofit governance, but the intermediate sanctions predate Sarbanes-Oxley by six years. Although the regulations are mired in technicalities, at their core, the sanctions are directed at conflicts of interest and director decision making. Consequently, those regulating tax-exempt operations were actually at the forefront concerning governance.

* * *

---

182. *In His Own Words*, *supra* note 170; and G. Williams, *Embattled President of American U. Says Changing Legal Landscape Should Concern Other College Leaders*, CHRON. OF HIGHER EDUC., Sept. 29, 2005.

183. *In His Own Words*, *supra* note 170.

184. *Id.*

185. Treas. Reg. § 301.6501(e)-1(c)(3)(ii); and E. Brody, *Administrative Troubles for the Intermediate Sanctions Regime*, TAX NOTES, July 16, 2001.

186. S. Kinzie and V. Strauss, *Lawyers' Report Says Ladner Should Repay AU $115,000: Study Raises Doubts on Validity of Contract*, WASH. POST, Oct. 7, 2005. President Ladner described the process in an interview, indicating that he was told that the board was informed of the "actual ingredients or elements of the contract." See *In His Own Words*, *supra* note 170.

187. *Id.*

188. Sarbanes-Oxley Act of 2002, Pub. L. 107–204, 116 Stat. 745.

189. *In His Own Words*, *supra* note 170.

(i) ADDITIONAL PUNISHMENT FOR EVILDOERS. Chapter 5 discussed fraud and embezzlement. If an organization suffers a loss due to an employee theft, it may be able to make the employee's life miserable by asking the IRS to invoke the intermediate sanctions. The regulations treat the booty from a theft or embezzlement as something other than compensation in exchange services.[190] This means the payment is per se unreasonable, and therefore, the recipient is subject to the intermediate sanctions.[191] There are no reported cases that the IRS has invoked the sanctions in such a case, but that does not mean that under the right circumstances it would not invoke them.

(j) WHAT IS REALLY GOING ON. The intermediate sanctions represent an attempt to federalize the duties of care and loyalty imposed on directors by the states with respect to financial transactions with organizational insiders. Apparently Congress was not satisfied with state enforcement action in the wake of scandals involving United Way of America,[192] Adelphi University,[193] and the Bishop estate.[194] The effect of these rules is to force directors to take a serious look at compensation (and other financial transactions involving conflicts of interest) and document their decisions. Whether this is appropriate or not is certainly open to question, but it is now the price of tax exemption under Sections 501(c)(3) and (c)(4).

The Staff of the Senate Finance Committee Is Unhappy with the Lack of Impact from the Intermediate Sanctions

* * *

The staff of Senate Committee on Finance issued a staff discussion document on June 22, 2004, stating a wide range of proposals for regulating nonprofits at the federal level.[195] The

190. Treas. Reg. § 53.4958-4(c)(1)—last sentence.

191. *See* C. Roady, *supra* note 95, at A-23. Ms. Roady points out that the disclosure requirements on Form 990 may require a carefully worded explanation. *See also,* L. Brauer & L. Henzke, *Intermediate Sanctions* (IRC 4958) Update, IRS Continuing Educ. Pub., at E-19, providing that a judicial determination of a crime is not necessary.

192. See, John S. Glaser, The United Way Scandal: An Insider's Account of What Went Wrong and Why (John Wiley 1994).

193. G. Judson, *Inquiry Faults Trustees' Acts at Adelphi U.*, N.Y. Times, Apr. 18, 1996; L. Sheppard, *Exempt Organizations: A Tale of Guyland Greed*, 72 Tax Notes 797 (1996); and Panel of New York State of Regents, Report of Recommendations after Hearing to the Full Board of Regents, at 26–33; Vaco v. Diamandopolous, 715 N.Y.S.2d 269 (N.Y. App. Div. 1998); and In the Matter of Adelphi University v. Board of Regents of State of New York, 229 A.D.2d 36 (N.Y. App. Div. 1997).

194. See, E. Brody, *Administrative Troubles for the Intermediate Sanctions*, Tax Notes (July 16, 2001); and *Symposium Issue on the Bishop Estate Controversy*, U. of Hawaii L. Rev. (Winter 1999).

195. This document is *available at* http://finance.senate.gov.

proposals suggest that the staff is at least dissatisfied with the impact of the intermediate sanctions as well as the performance of state regulators. Specific proposals include these:

- Reviewing each organization's exempt status every five years.
- Providing for revocation of exempt status if a tax-exempt organization serves as an accommodation party in a tax shelter.
- Requiring additional disclosures by tax-exempt organizations on the annual tax returns filed (Form 990) with the IRS.
- Limiting the compensation paid to private foundation directors and trustees.
- Expanding the strict private foundation self-dealing prohibitions to cover public charities.
- Imposing federal liability for directors' breaches of their duties.
- Granting the IRS the power to remove directors of tax-exempt organizations.
- Providing the United States Tax Court with jurisdiction over tax-exempt organizations and their directors.
- Granting private individuals the right to trigger a regulatory action against tax-exempt organizations through a complaint process.

Separately, in January 2005, the staff of the Joint Committee on Taxation proposed that the rebuttable presumption be eliminated. The current standards for invoking the presumption would become minimum standards for conduct under the staff's proposal.[196] Is more regulation needed, or do the IRS and state regulators need to start enforcing the current regulatory regulations?

* * *

(k) COMPLIANCE PROCEDURES. Every organization that is covered by intermediate sanctions should implement or at least consider implementing the following procedures:

- Adopt and enforce a comprehensive conflict-of-interest policy.
- Adopt procedures for identifying transactions potentially subject to intermediate sanctions.
- Develop a list of disqualified persons and organization managers, and require them to sign the conflict-of-interest policy and make annual reports.
- Report compensation to disqualified persons on Forms 990, W-2, or 1099 as required.
- Have transactions with disqualified persons approved only by members of the board (or authorized committee) who do not have conflicts of interest (and use the definitions and concepts in the regulations).
- When entering into arrangements with disqualified persons, obtain comparables or appraisals.
- Contemporaneously document the decisions leading to arrangements with disqualified persons.

---

196. STAFF OF THE JOINT COMMITTEE ON TAXATION, OPTIONS TO IMPROVE TAX COMPLIANCE AND REFORM TAX EXPENDITURES, at 265 (Jan. 27, 2005).

(l) COMPARABLES: JUSTIFYING COMPENSATION. A number of compensation consulting firms conduct reasonable compensation studies for nonprofits. The Economic Research Institute, a private, for-profit concern, has assembled a database that includes compensation statistics for more than 150,000 nonprofit organizations. Licensing their software may be a relatively inexpensive way for small organizations to develop appropriate comparables.[197]

(m) IRS DIRECTION TO AGENTS CONDUCTING AUDITS. The IRS is actively conducting intermediate sanctions reviews of compensation arrangements between insiders and charities. Agents have been instructed to review employment, deferred compensation, bonus, retirement, and severance agreements.[198] Agents have also been directed to closely examine expense reimbursement agreements to determine whether they constitute accountable plans.

Beyond Museums, Hospitals, and Universities: Small Social Service Agencies Must Watch Out, Too

* * *

Like other nonprofits, social service agencies are clearly concerned about governance issues, but the intermediate sanctions may not be at the top of their list of immediate concerns. That is not surprising given two basic facts: First, the people running social service agencies are clearly scrambling for funding. Obviously, that is their top priority. Second, the very lexicon used to describe the sanctions makes them somewhat mysterious, something only a tax lawyer could love. "Intermediate sanctions?"

When tax lawyers discuss these sanctions, they often speak in terms of large dollar amounts and juicy fringes, such as $500,000 salaries, memberships in country clubs, and the right to use a luxury car owned by the institution. Not surprising, they think of large universities and hospitals first (and the large legal fees that these institutions pay them). Rarely does an executive director of a local food bank or advocacy group for the homeless receive anywhere near $150,000 in annual salary, even though the long hours and hard work might justify such a salary. This could explain why the social services crowd touches on the intermediate sanctions at their conferences but does not dwell on them. That may be a mistake.

Consider a recent tax controversy between a small social service agency and the IRS. The agency in question was started many years ago by a dedicated gentleman who had served as the agency's executive since its inception. Being dedicated, he was quite satisfied with very low pay for years, presumably so the agency would have the funds to grow. In fact, so dedicated was this executive director that he never asked the board to make contributions to a qualified retirement plan on his behalf.

As happens to all, this executive director reached retirement age. The board decided to continue his salary at a reduced rate of $25,000 per year, no work required—a very

---

197. This is a suggestion for consideration, not an endorsement of this software. Before any organization considers licensing this software, it should obtain a demonstration copy and discuss the software's adequacy with its counsel.

198. L. Brauer andL. Henzke, *supra* note 191, at 13.

understandable gesture. The IRS did not see it quite the same way, nor did the disgruntled employee who decided to tip the IRS off.

To make a long story short, the agency's directors, the retired executive director, and the IRS entered into the following settlement: The retired executive director would return all retirement payments that he had received, but the IRS would waive the 25 percent excise tax that would have normally been imposed on him, as well as the 10 percent penalty that would have applied to the board members who knowingly approved the payments. There may not yet be many court cases that flush out the hidden meanings in the regulations under the intermediate sanctions, but the IRS is apparently willing to apply them when confronted with what it perceives to be an abusive arrangement.

Many might say, "But these were retirement benefits, clearly reasonable in the normal course of business." That might be true, and the attorney for the organization made that argument. The problem was that labels matter, and these payments were labeled as salary payments for no work.

In a discussion of this case, the question arose as to whether the board considered re-designating future payments as severance or retirement benefits and whether the IRS auditors gave any indication whether such redesignation would eliminate the issue. Apparently, the retired executive director was so embarrassed and horrified by all the trouble he had caused his former agency that he said he did not even want to reconsider restructuring the arrangement. He had been reluctant to accept the payments in the first place.

Assuming that the executive director's compensation was very low throughout the years, a qualified retirement plan that would have provided him with $25,000 in defined benefits each year would seem to be reasonable. The regulations under the intermediate sanctions certainly anticipate qualified retirement plans.[199]

The obvious question is whether this agency could have avoided the problem by labeling the payments a severance benefit when the board approved them. The regulations mention severance benefits, but must those benefits be accrued over the term of the employment to have any chance to be considered reasonable benefits? Under the general law of reasonable compensation—with its thousands of case law decisions over the years—there are surely cases involving retroactive payments intended as "make-ups" for what everybody now views as unfair levels of historical compensation. The answers may lie in that case law.

The lessons in this case for others are clear. First, even small social service agencies and other small charities (or more appropriately, their directors and key employees) can become snarled in the intermediate sanctions. Second, although not raised by this case, the most likely way that the small agency will run into trouble is with expense reimbursements that are considered to have been made pursuant to nonaccountable plans. This is particularly a problematic area because the sanctions will be imposed automatically and without the opportunity to raise a "reasonableness" defense. Third, as is always true, all organizations must watch out for the disgruntled former employee.

* * *

6.7 PRIVATE FOUNDATIONS

A second aspect to the Section 501(c)(3) exemption process is often just as important as obtaining tax-exempt status. This is avoiding classification as a *private foundation,*[200] a term (although not entirely the concept) coined by the Tax

199. Treas. Reg. §§ 53.4958-4(b)(1)(ii)(B)(I) and 53.4958-1(e)(2).

200. See I.R.C. § 509 for the definition of *private foundation*.

Reform Act of 1969 when Congress created a comprehensive regulatory regime for private foundations.

This legislation resulted in part from the activities of the Ford Foundation that came to light such as establishing fellowships for aides to the then recently assassinated Robert Kennedy, providing funds to the Cleveland chapter of the Congress for Racial Equality that allegedly found their way into the Cleveland mayoral race, and funding activities to decentralize public schools in New York that met opposition from the teachers' union.[201]

As you will see, private foundation status carries a number of burdens, including compliance with onerous limitations on self-dealing, excess business holdings, and jeopardy investments. Separately, a donor to a private foundation faces tighter limits on deductibility than apply to donors to a public charity (see Chapter 7).

(a) PUBLIC CHARITIES VERSUS PRIVATE FOUNDATIONS—WORKABLE DEFINITIONS. Literary thousands of pages of commentary have been written distinguishing between private foundations and nonprivate foundations ("public charities"). The process of distinguishing between the two has been called "almost frighteningly complex and difficult."[202] For our purposes, an organization is generally excluded from private foundation classification if it (1) performs functions traditionally viewed as religious, educational, or charitable, (2) has broad public support, or (3) actively functions in a supporting relationship to the first two categories of organizations. All Section 501(c)(3) organizations are presumed to be *private foundations* until otherwise demonstrated.

As part of the exemption process, new organizations must request either an advanced or a definitive ruling regarding their status as public charities. Those charities seeking to avoid private foundation status based on the financial tests described here will most likely apply for what is termed an advanced ruling. It gives the charity a five-year period to obtain the financial support that will qualify it as a public charity. To receive an advanced ruling, the charity must agree to extend the statute of limitations for each of the five tax years in the advanced ruling period. Before the IRS will consider issuing an advanced ruling, the organization must demonstrate that its structure and plan of operation can be reasonably expected to satisfy the tests.[203] If the organization has completed its first taxable year that consisted of at least eight months, it has the option to apply for a definitive ruling. Organizations that qualify as public charities because they are a church, school, or hospital or are supporting organizations apply for a definitive ruling when they apply for tax-exempt status.

---

201. K Bird, The Color of Truth, at 376-95 (Simon & Schuster 1998).

202. Friends of the Society of Servants of God, 75 T.C. 209 (1980). Another court has said that "the IRS has drafted fantastically intricate and detailed regulations to thwart the fantastically intricate and detailed efforts of taxpayers...." *See* Windsor Foundation v. United States 77-2 USTC 9709 (E.D. Va. 1977).

203. Treas. Reg. § 1.170A-9(e)(5)(ii); and Treas. Reg. § 1.509(a)-3(d)(2).

(i) Category 1—Absolutes and Publicly Supported. Certain types of charities are automatically excluded from classification as private foundations.[204] These including the following:

- Churches.
- Schools if they maintain a regular faculty and curriculum and normally have a regular body of enrolled students.
- Hospitals and certain other medical research and care organizations.
- State, federal, and several other governmental entities.

This category also includes what are termed *publicly supported* organizations.[205] They are charitable organizations that normally receive a substantial part of their support (exclusive of income received from activities that are the basis for their exemption) from a governmental entity or from contributions from the general public. The focus is on levels of donations, which should be clear from the parenthetical language excluding exempt function income from the analysis.[206]

Publicly supported organizations generally include museums, libraries, community centers, arts groups, and organizations that provide direct services to the public such as the American Red Cross.[207] To qualify as publicly supported, the organization must *normally* receive at least one-third of its total support from the following sources: (1) governmental units, (2) direct and indirect contributions from the general public, and (3) other public charities.[208]

An alternative test for qualification as a publicly supported organization considers facts and circumstances but only if at least 10 percent of the organization's qualifying support comes from the three sources just named.[209] Among the facts and circumstances considered are whether (1) the organization's board is widely representative,[210] (2) the organization actively seeks public funds,[211] and (3) the organization makes its facilities available to the public on a continuous basis (such as a library or museum).[212] To illustrate a situation where the facts and circumstances test could be helpful, consider a museum that receives a significant portion of its support in the form of investment income from a large endowment (that resulted from contributions from the general public rather than a few individuals)[213] but that actively solicits funds from the general public and has a board that is representative of the community[214] rather than a small number of donors.

---

204. See I.R.C. § 509(a)(1), referring to organizations described in I.R.C. § 170(b)(1)(A).
205. I.R.C. § 170(b)(1)(A)(vi).
206. Treas. Reg. § 1.170A-9(e)(7)(i)(a).
207. Treas. Reg. § 1.170A-9(e)(1).
208. Treas. Reg. § 1.170A-9(e)(2).
209. Treas. Reg. § 1.170A-9(e)(3).
210. Treas. Reg. § 1.170A-9(e)(3)(v).
211. Treas. Reg. § 1.170A-9(e)(3)(ii).
212. Treas. Reg. § 1.170A-9(e)(3)(vi).
213. Treas. Reg. § 1.170A-9(e)(3)(iii).
214. Treas. Reg. § 1.170A-9(e)(3)(iv).

In calculating the support fraction, income from the performance of exempt functions is excluded from both the numerator and the denominator.[215] Consequently, a museum that charges an admission fee must exclude the fees from the calculation. Membership fees are excluded to the extent they represent admission fees.[216] If a portion of the membership is for general support of the museum, however, it is included in both the numerator and the denominator. Gross investment income[217] is included in the numerator but excluded from the denominator, as is net income from an unrelated trade or business. Capital gains are not treated as gross investment income or as support.

Contributions from each person or entity[218] are included in the denominator in full but are included in the numerator only to the extent of 2 percent of the contributions made during the applicable testing period.[219] This means that relatively large contributions could have a negative impact on the likelihood that either the 33 percent or 10 percent tests will be satisfied. For that reason, there is an allowance for "unusual grants." These can be excluded from both the numerator and the denominator.[220]

The specifics can be quite complicated, but the "normally" received requirement referred to earlier generally means that the 33 percent and 10 percent tests must be met based on the support during the four-year period immediately preceding the current tax year[221] (with a shorter test period for new organizations).[222] The calculations are made on an aggregate basis.

The following example illustrates the basic calculations. During a four-year period, an organization receives the following support: (1) $80,000 of interest and dividends, (2) $20,000 from unrelated business activities, (3) $200,000 from gifts and contributions from the general public, (4) $5,000 in capital gains, and (5) $5,000 in admission fees from an exempt function.[223] The organization's support denominator includes the interest and dividends (but not capital gains), the net income from the unrelated business activity, and the gifts and contributions from the public—$300,000. Its support numerator is limited to the $200,000 in charitable contributions. As a consequence, more than one-third of its support is attributable to "public support," meaning that the organization escapes private foundation status.[224] Notice that income from the performance of related functions is excluded from both the numerator and denominator of the

215. Treas. Reg. § 1.170A-9(e)(7)(i)(a).
216. Treas. Reg. § 1.170A-9(e)(iii).
217. I.R.C. § 509(e).
218. The 2 percent rule does not apply to support from governmental units or to contributions from other publicly supported organizations, with a special exception that is outlined in Treasury Regulation Section 1.170A-9(e)(6)(v) for certain earmarked contributions.
219. Treas. Reg. § 1.170A-9(e)(6)(i).
220. Treas. Reg. § 1.170A-9(e)(6)(ii).
221. Treas. Reg. § 1.170A-9(e)(4)(ii).
222. V. Richardson and J. F. Reilly, *Public Charity or Private Foundation Status Issues under IRC 509(a)(1)-(4), 4942(j)(3), and 507*, IRS CONTINUING EDUC. PUB., at 70 (2003).
223. Treas. Reg. § 1.170A-9(e)(7)(a).
224. V. Richardson and J.F. Reilly, *supra* note 223, at 54.

support fraction. That revenue should be viewed as "good" income—as we will see shortly when we consider Category 2—but this category focuses exclusively on public support.

Now suppose that $120,000 of the contributions comes from one individual; that contribution exceeds more than $6,000—2 percent of total support. The full amount is included in the support fraction's denominator, but only $6,000 is included in the numerator of the fraction.[225] As a consequence, the organization now fails the more than one-third support test: $86,000/$300,000 (28.66 percent). This is admittedly an extreme example, relying on just one contributor to "blow" the test, but it is easy to imagine a situation in which ten people each contribute relatively equal and large amounts to seed an organization but find that they are unable to generate much support from the general public. In appropriate circumstances, relief is available: The regulations permit an organization to exclude "extraordinary grants,"[226] and there is always the 10 percent/facts and circumstances test.

(ii) Category 2—Broadly Supported/Service Organization. Certain broadly supported organizations are excluded from private foundation status.[227] Organizations that fall within this category must satisfy two tests. Under the first test, the organization must normally receive more than one-third of its support each taxable year from (1) gifts, grants, contributions, or membership fees and (2) gross receipts from admissions, sales of merchandise, or performance of services or the use of facilities in activities that do not constitute unrelated trades or businesses.[228] Qualifying support (the numerator) excludes support from disqualified persons.[229] There is also a "greater of $5,000 or 1 percent of total support" limit on related-activity gross receipts from any person or from any bureau or similar agency of a governmental unit.[230] Under the second test, the organization cannot normally receive more than one-third of its support each taxable year from (1) gross investment income and (2) taxable income from unrelated trades or businesses (reduced by related taxes).[231]

To qualify as a public charity, these two tests require that an organization be broadly supported and not rely heavily on investment income or unrelated trade or business income for support. The test is similar in overall spirit to the public support test discussed under Section 170(b)(1)(A)(vi) earlier, but this test differs from the public support test because it brings income from the provision of exempt functions into the analysis.

---

225. Treas. Reg. § 1.170A-9(e)(9)(1), Example 1.
226. Treas. Reg. § 1.170A-9(e)(6)(ii).
227. I.R.C. § 509(a)(2).
228. Treas. Reg. § 1.509(a)-3(a)(2).
229. The term *disqualified person* is defined in Section 4946. It includes directors, certain officers, other foundation managers, substantial contributors, and certain carefully defined related parties.
230. Treas. Reg. § 1.509(a)-3(b).
231. Treas. Reg. § 1.509(a)-(a)(3).

The following example illustrates the basic calculations. During the four-year period, an organization received $600,000 in total support from the following sources: (1) $10,000 each from two government bureaus[232] for the performance of exempt function services, (2) $150,000 from the general public for exempt function services, (3) $40,000 in contributions from the general public, (4) $150,000 in gross investment income, and (5) $240,000 from substantial contributors (classified as disqualified persons). The full $600,000 comprises the denominator of the support fraction. Only $6,000 of each $10,000 in receipts from each government bureau is included in the numerator of the fraction (the greater of $5,000 or 1 percent of $600,000). The $150,000 and the $40,000 from the general public are also included in the numerator, but the $150,000 in investment income and the $240,000 from substantial contributors are excluded. As a consequence, the organization meets the "more than one-third" test, but just barely: $202,000/$600,000, or 33.667 percent.[233] The organization also satisfies the "not more than one-third" test: It has $150,000 in investment income and no unrelated business income, representing 25 percent of its total support ($600,000).

Although we will not go into the details, the tests for Category 2 organizations devote a significant amount of effort to distinguishing between gross receipts and other types of support such as contributions, grants, and investment income. Although certainly not intuitive, the distinction between "any bureau or similar agency of a government unit" and a government can also be critical.

The mathematical tests in Categories 1 and 2 are extraordinarily complicated, at times requiring a spreadsheet to calculate and analyze the required four-year moving averages. The analysis is often also complicated by ambiguities in defined terms as well as the formulas for crunching numbers, meaning that the organization may need to undertake the analysis using different interpretations of what are often ambiguous regulations so that the organization can adequately assess whether there would be a problem if the IRS adversely interpreted an ambiguity. This can be particularly important when the organization and related parties have financial relationships and dealings. These dealings may be perfectly appropriate if the charity is classified as a public charity but could result in confiscatory excise taxes on self-dealing if the organization unexpectedly finds itself classified as a private foundation.

The board of any charity that is relying on the two mathematically based tests for public charity status should demand an annual analysis regarding the organization's ability to continue to maintain its status as a public charity. The focus should be on the moving averages and the trends those averages reflect. Furthermore, the organization should negotiate contracts with clauses that would permit

---

232. For purposes of this *Guide*, you do not need to focus on what a government bureau is exactly or why one might be important. At the same time, the fact that this level of detail has found its way into an example should give you some sense of just how complex these tests really are.

233. Treas. Reg. § 1.509(a)-3(b)(2), Example 1.

the organization to terminate the contract if a change in status would result in the imposition of various excise taxes.

(iii) Category 3—Supporting Organizations. Certain organizations are formed to support other public charities.[234] Although these organizations often would be classified as private foundations if they were tested under the mathematically based tests for Category 2 and certain Category 1 organizations, the tax law is nevertheless willing to remove them from private foundation status. In a sense, their public charity status is derivative because it depends on their relationship to an organization that is a public charity. The regulations defining this third category of public charities devote many pages to examining the relationships between the supporting and supported organization. The following three requirements must be satisfied before an organization can be classified as Category 3 supporting organization: (1) it must be organized and operated exclusively "for the benefit of, to perform the functions of, or to carry out the purposes of" one or more Category 1 or 2 organizations,[235] (2) the organization must be operated, supervised, or controlled by or in connection with one or more Category 1 or 2 organizations,[236] and (3) the organization cannot be controlled directly or indirectly by one or more disqualified persons other than foundation managers.[237]

Under the organizational prong of the first requirement, the organization's purposes must be limited to permissible purposes and the organization's activities must be limited to specified purposes, and two other requirements must be satisfied.[238] Under the operational prong of the first requirement, the supporting organization must either make payments to permissible beneficiaries or conduct an independent activity or program in support of permissible beneficiaries.[239] Permissible beneficiaries include the supported organization as well as members of a charitable class benefited by the supported organization. Of the three requirements, the second is viewed as the most important,[240] requiring that the relationship between the supporting organization and the supported organization either (1) resemble a parent-subsidiary relationship[241] or (2) a brother-sister relationship[242] or (3) satisfy tests for responsiveness and integral part.[243]

To grossly overly simplify the characteristics of those organizations qualifying for Category 3 status, the supporting organization's activities must further the supported organization's mission, the link between the supporting and supported organization in terms of governance must be strong, and large donors to

234. I.R.C. § 509(a)(3).
235. I.R.C. § 509(a)(3)(A); and Treas. Reg. §§ 1.509(a)-4(b)-(e).
236. I.R.C. § 509(a)(3)(B); and Treas. Reg. §§ 1.509(a)-4(f)-(i).
237. I.R.C. § 509(a)(3)(C); and Treas. Reg. §§ 1.509(a)-4(j).
238. Treas. Reg. §§ 1.509(a)-4(c) and (d).
239. Treas. Reg. §§ 1.509(a)-4(e)(1) and (2).
240. V. Richardson and J.F. Reilly, *supra*note 223, at 117.
241. Treas. Reg. § 1.509(a)-4(g).
242. Treas. Reg. § 1.509(a)-4(h).
243. Treas. Reg. § 1.509(a)-4 (i).

the supported organization cannot exercise control over the supporting organization. Rather than bogging down in further details, consider the following examples:

- *Home for the Aged Supporting a Church's Mission.* A church forms a nonprofit corporation to operate a home for the aged. Under the new corporation's articles of incorporation, each of the directors must be a high-ranking church official. One of the church's long-standing missions is the care of the aged. This new corporation will in all likelihood be treated as a supporting organization, thereby removing it from the private foundation category without regard to its number of donors (here only the church) or patrons.[244]
- *Alumni Association Supporting a University's Alumni, Faculty, and Students.* Boosters, Inc., a Section 501(c)(3) organization, operates as an alumni association for Big Red University. Boosters' articles of incorporation give the university no powers to appoint directors to its board but identify Big Red University as the sole beneficiary of Boosters' support. Boosters uses all of its dues and income to support its own educational programs for alumni, faculty, and students of Big Red University but makes no financial contributions to it. Boosters will probably be treated as a supporting organization, although it could also qualify as a nonprivate foundation based on its broad sources of donative support.[245]
- *University Press Supporting a University's Research Efforts.* Cowford Press is a university press organized and operated as a nonprofit organization to provide publishing and printing for Cowford University, a publicly supported educational institution. Control of the Cowford Press board is vested in the Cowford University board. In all likelihood, Cowford Press will be treated as a supporting organization rather than as a private foundation.[246]

Notice that the conclusions concerning each of these organizations are couched in terms of *likely* outcomes because these determinations depend on specific facts and circumstances. Consequently, there can be no certainty in the absence of an actual IRS determination. Unlike charities that derive their public charity status as publicly supported or broadly supported organizations, once a supporting organization has been designated as such, it will always be considered

244. Treas. Reg. § 1.509(a)-(4)(d)(2)(iii), Example 2. In this and the next two cases, the example is taken from a section of the regulations that address one aspect of the three requirements. These examples do not specifically address the other requirements, but examples are written in such away to at least suggest that the organizations in question would satisfy those other requirements.

245. Treas. Reg. § 1.509(a)-(4)(e)(3), Example 1.

246. Treas. Reg. § 1.509(a)-(4)(g)(2), Example 1.

a supporting organization (assuming the relationship does not change) so long as the supported organization is a public charity.[247]

During 2004 and 2005, one type of supporting organization received considerable criticism from certain members of Congress who were concerned that particular individuals were using these organizations to skirt the various limitations imposed on private foundations although such organizations had the characteristics of family foundations. Specifically, critics pointed to what are referred to as *Type III support organizations* (a subset of Category 3 organizations), which had the least burdensome requirements in defining the relationship between the public charity and the supported organization. These organizations are characterized by a relationship to the supported organization that satisfies the responsiveness and integral part tests mentioned earlier. Initially, the staff of the Senate Finance Committee proposed completely eliminating Type III supporting organizations, but that was clearly too radical a proposal because many of these organizations were established for bona fide reasons. Until Congress definitively acts, any organization seeking public charity status as a Type III supporting organization must be willing to undergo special IRS scrutiny.

(b) TYPICAL PRIVATE FOUNDATION. You probably are familiar with the typical private foundation. This is an organization that is created by one individual or family or is a publicly held corporation to facilitate charitable giving. It is not unusual for a family to create a foundation following the sale of a large closely held business. Doing so permits the family to set aside a portion of the proceeds for charitable purposes in the year of sale when a large taxable gain occurs but to actually distribute the funds through the foundation in subsequent years. Next time you visit a museum or attend a symphony, look at the donor plaques or listings in the program. Some of the donors (e.g., the Smith Family Foundation) will be private foundations.

(c) REASONS TO AVOID PRIVATE FOUNDATION STATUS. While many people like seeing their names associated with a foundation, most operating charities avoid private foundation status if at all possible because of some onerous consequences that flow from private foundation status. These consequences include (1) a 2 percent tax on net investment income, (2) prohibitions on self-dealing between the charity and its significant contributors and other designated insiders, (3) minimum annual distribution requirements, (4) restrictions on certain business holdings, (5) limitations on "jeopardizing" investments, and (6) more involved reporting requirements.

(i) Tax on Net Investment Income. When Congress decided to tighten the controls on private foundations in 1969, it realized that administering these regulations would be an added cost for the IRS. To fund those costs, Congress

247. Under certain circumstances, a supporting organization can support an exempt organization other than a Section 501(c)(3) organization. *See* Treas. Reg. § 1.509(a)-4(k).

imposed a 2 percent excise tax (now reduced to 1 percent in certain circumstances)[248] on the net investment income of most domestic tax-exempt private foundations, including private operating foundations.[249] Congress has never actually allocated this revenue stream to fund the IRS's exempt-organization function despite the persistence of the tax. The tax must be reported on Form 990-PF, Return of Private Foundations. Payment of the tax is subject to estimated tax requirements. In determining its net investment income, a private foundation can deduct from its gross investment income ordinary and necessary expenses paid or incurred in producing or collecting such income and for managing, conserving, or maintaining property that is held for the production of income subject to certain modifications.[250]

(ii) Tax on Self-Dealing. The tax rules impose an excise tax on acts of self-dealing between a private foundation and disqualified persons. The most important exception is for reasonable compensation for personal services[251]—clearly, an important exception because it permits a foundation to obtain vital services from people who would normally be considered disqualified persons, including directors and officers, substantial contributors, and their family members. To qualify for this exception, the services provided must be "reasonable and necessary to carry out the exempt purpose of the private foundation."[252]

The excise tax is designed to discourage related-party transactions by imposing tax at confiscatory rates; that is, the tax is not a revenue-raising measure. Self-dealing transactions include (1) sales, exchanges, and leasing property, (2) loans and other extensions of credit, (3) provision of goods, services, or facilities, (4) payment of compensation or reimbursing expenses incurred by a disqualified person (except to the extent the payment falls within the exception discussed earlier), and (5) certain other transactions. The fact that the transaction is priced at fair market value is irrelevant.[253] Just to be clear, *the fact that the transaction is priced at fair market value is irrelevant.*

A tax is imposed (at the rate of 5 percent of the amount involved) not only on the disqualified person[254] but also (at the rate of 2.5 percent of the amount involved) on a foundation manager who knowingly participates in the act of

---

248. I.R.C. § 4940(e).

249. Joint Committee on Taxation, Rep. No. JCS 16-70, *General Explanation of the Tax Reform Act of 1969* (Dec. 3, 1970). The tax was originally set at 4 percent but reduced to 2 percent in 1978. *See* Revenue Act of 1978, Pub. L. No. 95-600, 92 Stat. 2763, at § 520 (1978). The reduction took place because of evidence that more money was being raised by the tax than being used to finance the regulation of tax-exempt entities by the IRS. In an October 25, 2004, speech at the annual NAAG-NASCO public session in Washington, D.C., Dorothy Ridings, then president and CEO of the Council of Foundations, expressed concern that the tax on investment income was still collecting much more revenue than was being used to regulate tax-exempt entities. She was not proposing a reduction to the tax but increased levels of enforcement funded by the amounts collected.

250. I.R.C. § 4940(c)(3).

251. I.R.C. § 4941(d)(2)(E).

252. Treas. Reg. § 53.4941(d)-3(c)(1).

253. Treas. Reg. § 53.4941(d)-1(a).

254. Treas. Reg. § 53.4941(a)-1(a).

self-dealing[255] (both of which are referred to as *Tier 1 taxes*). Foundation managers can knowingly participate by silence or inaction. Legal counsel is important in this process because individuals who act after obtaining the advice of counsel have a defense if they reasonably rely on it.

As noted, these taxes seek to influence behavior rather than collect revenue. Consequently, the opportunity to avoid the confiscatory portion (*Tier 2*) tax, imposed at 200 percent of the amount involved, exists if the transaction is corrected within a specified period of time.[256]

As previously mentioned, self-dealing can apply to all substantial contributors and foundation managers, as well as affiliated entities and family members, among others. A *foundation manager* is a foundation officer, director, trustee, or, in the case of specific acts, any employee who has final authority over the act. Let's consider the following cases to illustrate the workings of the prohibition against self-dealing.

TRANSACTION PRICED AT FAIR MARKET VALUE—CASE 1

Malcolm Sullivan, a computer mogul, set up Good Deeds Foundation, a Section 501(c)(3) charitable organization, as a private foundation. He is its sole contributor and has donated $100 million to the foundation since its inception. Good Deeds has a staff of ten. Sullivan wants to keep his eyes on their activities. Consequently, he decides to have Good Deeds rent office space from Macrohard, Inc., which is the source of his enormous wealth. He currently owns 40 percent of its outstanding stock. Sullivan's common sense tells him to avoid the appearance of any impropriety with respect to his dealings with Good Deeds Foundation. Consequently, he retains three independent appraisers to determine the fair rental value for the office space. They arrive at three different but close numbers. Sullivan subtracts 10 percent from the lowest number and sets that as the rent.

The law provides that leases between a disqualified person and a private foundation constitute self-dealing.[257] Macrohard is considered a disqualified person because Sullivan owns more than 35 percent of the combined voting power of its stock and is a substantial contributor to the foundation. *There is no exception for transactions entered into at fair market value.* In fact, the transaction would be considered self-dealing even if Macrohard leased the property to the foundation at a bargain rate. To be very clear, neither multiple appraisals, independent determinations, formula prices, nor ten bishops attesting to the fairness of the transaction will eliminate the taint of self-dealing from it.[258] There is one important exception to this rule: If the lease requires no payments by the private foundation, the transaction will not be treated as an act of self-dealing.[259]

---

255. Treas. Reg. § 53.4941(a)-1(b).
256. Treas. Reg. § 53.4941(b)-1.
257. Treas. Reg. § 53.4941(d)-2(b).
258. For another example, see Rev. Rul. 76-18, 1978-1 C.B. 355, involving the sale by a private foundation of art at an auction.
259. Treas. Reg. § 53.4941(d)-2(b)(2).

Acquisition of Director and Officer Insurance—Case 2

Katherine Janson is employed by Benevolent Givers, as its investment manager, and is in charge of investing its $500 million endowment. Benevolent Givers is a Section 501(c)(3) charitable organization that is a private foundation. Janson is a conservative portfolio manager, using a 45/55 mix of stocks and bonds. The stock portfolio she manages is well diversified consisting of blue chip stocks with international coverage. The bond portfolio is composed of high-quality corporate bonds. Janson has read several articles written by leading academics arguing that investment managers should simply invest the stock portion of their portfolio in index funds. These academics argue that any manager who does not take this course of action should be held personally liable for any losses experienced by the portfolio. Janson would like Benevolent Givers to purchase insurance protecting her from suits alleging that she has mismanaged Benevolent's investment funds, but both she and Benevolent are concerned about the self-dealing rules.

In all likelihood, Benevolent and Janson have not engaged in an act of self-dealing if Benevolent pays the insurance premium for Janson's professional liability coverage. Chapter 12 examines directors' and officers' (D & O) insurance as well as indemnification payments. At that time, we consider the tax consequences flowing from such insurance and indemnification payments. In this situation, the insurance is unlikely to be a problem, but some portion of the payment may have to be classified as compensatory, meaning that it will be considered in determining whether Janson's compensation is reasonable for purposes of the prohibition on self-dealing. Whether the payment should be included in her income is a separate question. The board should review state law to determine to what extent indemnification and D & O insurance are permitted.

Undoing an Act of Self-Dealing—Case 3

Harry Lowe is a wealthy industrialist said to be worth $700 million. His holdings primarily comprise illiquid real estate and interests in closely held businesses. As a consequence, he was a little short of cash for his Christmas shopping last year. Lowe likes to buy only the most expensive gifts and only from the Neiman-Marcus Christmas catalog. To fund his purchases, he borrowed $500,000 from Harry's Charities, a private foundation that he created a number of years ago. As usual, Lowe did not consult with Wynona Zimmerman, his long-standing corporate attorney and personal advisor. When Zimmerman heard about this loan, she hit the ceiling because this was an act of self-dealing. She knew that Lowe wanted to sell a parcel of real estate worth $600,000. Zimmerman suggested that Lowe repay the loan by transferring the parcel of real estate to Harry's Charities. Lowe thought this was a splendid idea and told her to draft the transfer deed.

It is difficult to argue with Zimmerman's logic, but the rules are clear: An act that is otherwise an act of self-dealing is not rendered a permissible act because it is priced at or below fair market value. Nor do "noble" motivations eliminate the self-dealing taint. Rather than correcting the act of self-dealing, Lowe engaged in a second act of self-dealing when he transferred the real estate to Harry's Charities.[260] The only way for him to correct the first act of self-dealing is to return the cash plus interest (in cash).

Incidental Benefit—Case 4

Electrical Design Corp is a large multinational, publicly held corporation that designs and manufactures high-tech electrical equipment. It formed a private foundation several years ago to manage its corporate charitable giving. Mary Horvath, the chair of Electrical Design Corp's board of directors, knows that a shortage of electrical engineers is adversely affecting Electrical Design Corp's business. She proposes that the foundation donate $1 million to Green University's electrical engineering department in an effort to improve and expand the department's programs. The hope is that an expanded program will produce more engineers for Electrical Design Corp. Green's president is so pleased with the proposal that he has indicated that he will instruct the university's placement office to give Electrical Design the opportunity to contact seniors two weeks before other employers.

The foundation's grant to Green University could be viewed as an act of self-dealing because Electrical Design will undoubtedly benefit from the increase in electrical engineering graduates. The transaction could be recategorized as a transfer from the foundation to Electrical Design. The IRS has considered such situations and concluded that although the employer could benefit from them, the benefit was too incidental or tenuous to warrant treating the contribution as an act of self-dealing.[261] The key fact in that ruling was the absence of preferential treatment for the corporate employer that had created and funded the contributing foundation.

In the present situation, Electrical Design will receive preferential treatment. Based on the tenor of the published guidance, the IRS is likely to treat the foundation's contribution as producing more than an incidental benefit for Electrical Design Corp, resulting in a finding of self-dealing. However, if Electrical Design Corp is willing to forgo the preferential treatment, the donation should not be a problem.

Using Foundation Property—Case 5

Maureen Brody is the managing director and curator of the High Art and Culture Foundation (HACF), a private foundation created by Karen Barnett, the heiress to the Bruce Barnett fortune. Barnett donated her extensive art collection (including more than 1,000 French Impressionist paintings) to HACF. The collection is housed on Bruce Barnett's estate located along the Hudson River, just north of New York City. Although Mr. Barnett was very wealthy, his mansion is not large enough to display even half of the paintings at any given time. Paintings not displayed are

260. Anyone who finds this difficult to believe should look at Rev. Rul. 81-40, 1981-1 C.B. 508.
261. Rev. Rul. 80-310, 1980-2 C.B. 319.

stored in the mansion's basement vault. Brody is distressed that all those beautiful Renoirs are sitting in a musty vault. She decides to take two paintings home. Everyone knows that Brody has borrowed the two Renoirs. In fact, she has even agreed to pay the insurance premium for them.

Brody is a foundation manager, so she needs to be careful in her dealings with HACF. Self-dealing includes transfers of foundation assets by a foundation for the use by a disqualified person. In this case, HACF and Brody engaged in an act of self-dealing when it permitted her to borrow the paintings.[262] This transaction is beneficial to HACF, because it cannot display all the paintings although it must insure them. When Brody borrowed the paintings and agreed to pay the insurance, she actually reduced the foundation's insurance premiums. The self-dealing rules, however, are not so logical or forgiving. That is the point of this and the other cases.

I Hear You Knocking: Will the IRS Compound the Problems Facing Former Managers of a Texas Foundation?

* * *

Carl Yeckel, the grandson of the founders, was the CEO of the Carl B. and Florence E. King Foundation until 2003, when the Texas attorney general obtained his resignation.[263] The attorney general was concerned that Yeckel's compensation was excessive, and a good case can be made for that concern. Between 1993 and sometime in 2002 or 2003, Yeckel received more than $5.4 million in cash compensation.[264] One newspaper reported that the Foundation spent more than twice as much on salaries and expenses ($2.6 million) in 2001 than it made in charitable grants.[265]

As is typical in unreasonable compensation disputes, the people "structuring" the compensation arrangement were just plain stupid in how they "dressed-up" the compensation. It is one thing to pay yourself a large dollar amount, but there had been $748,000 in undocumented credit charges over a six-year period.[266] This amount included charges by Yeckel and the foundation's former secretary, Thomas Vett. According to the *Austin-American*

---

262. Rev. Rul. 74-600, 1974-2 C.B. 385.
263. M. Davis and B. Weiss, *When Bad Things Happened to a Good Foundation*, FOUNDATION NEWS & COMMENTARY (Sept./Oct. 2004); and R. Williamson, *Charitable Funds Going to Least in Need—Foundation Board Members*, NONPROFIT TIMES, Mar. 15, 2003.
264. DAVIS AND WEISS, *supra* note 263. Carl Yeckel resigned in 2003. The article does not provide an ending date for payments. According to one newspaper account, the jury required Yeckel to pay back $4.1 million in excess salary for the period from 1993 to 2002. *See* C. Osborn, *Two Must Pay Charity $14 Million: Damages Are to Punish Former King Foundation Executives for Bloated Salaries, Credit Card Use*, AMERICAN-STATESMAN, June 15, 2004.
265. A. Price, *2 Tapped Charity Coffers: Former Execs Face Trial for Lavish Salaries, Perks*, AMERICAN-STATESMAN, May 25, 2004.
266. DAVIS AND WEISS, *supra* note 263.

Statesmen, in 2001, the two spent $6,531 in health club membership charges.[267] There were also $41,634 for hotels and rental cars, $15,229 on doctors, and $23,036 in retail shopping.[268] These expenditures just do not pass the "smell" test. A Texas jury agreed, delivering a stunning verdict on June 11, 2004, requiring Yeckel and Vett to repay more than $6 million to the foundation.[269] The jury then added $14 million in punitive damages.[270]

Executives of nonprofits, particularly private foundations, should view this decision as an important milestone. Over the last several years, a number of private foundations have received criticism about what some view as excessive compensation and perks. You can expect other state charity officials to be inspired by the King Foundation decision.

The abuses at the King Foundation were detailed in a *Boston Globe* series in 2003, which also revealed that Paul C. Cabot Jr. of Needham, Massachusetts, had been taking at least $1 million in annual salary (since 2000) from his family foundation, whose assets had dwindled from a high of approximately $14 million in the mid-1990s to $3.8 million by 2003.[271] Massachusetts Attorney General Thomas F. Reilly subsequently investigated the Cabot Trust.[272] Cabot entered into an agreement with the attorney general to repay more than $4 million to the trust.[273]

The facts in executive compensation cases make for eye-catching headlines, particularly when the salaries and perks are large. One must wonder whether the King Foundation or Cabot Trust headlines caught the eyes of the IRS.

* * *

(iii) Tax on Failure to Make a 5 Percent Distribution. Private foundations (other than private operating foundations) are required annually to make a minimum distribution to charities or pay an initial tax of 15 percent on the undistributed income.[274] The formula for determining the required distribution (the "5 percent distribution") is complex but can be summarized as requiring a distribution equal to 5 percent of the value of assets that are *not* used to further the foundation's exempt purpose (with the taxable base including investment assets such as stocks, bonds, and rental real estate).[275]

Distribution does not refer to payments to "shareholders" but to expenditures that further the foundation's tax-exempt purpose (grants, expenditures to acquire charitable assets, the investment excise tax, and reasonable administrative expenses). Certain amounts set aside for charitable purposes are treated as qualifying distributions when certain conditions are satisfied,[276] with the focus

---

267. 2 Tapped Charity, *supra* note 265.
268. *Id.*
269. C. Osborn, *Jury Decides Ex-Officials of Nonprofit Owe Millions*, American-Statesman, June 12, 2004.
270. B. Healy, *Ex-Officers Ordered to Pay $14m in Texas Charity Fraud*, Boston Globe, June 15, 2004.
271. W. Robinson and M. Rezendes, *Foundation Chief Agrees to Repay Over $4 Million*, Boston Globe, Dec. 16, 2004.
272. *Id.*
273. *Id.*
274. I.R.C. § 4942(a).
275. *See* I.R.C. § 4942(d), defining *distributable amount*, and I.R.C. § 4942(e), defining *minimum investment return.*
276. I.R.C. § 4942(g)(2).

on specific projects to be completed within five years or less. A 100 percent tax is imposed on any required distributions that remain undistributed as of the end of the designated measurement period.[277]

Congress recently considered a provision to limit the amount of administrative expenses that a private foundation can treat as distributions for purposes of satisfying the 5 percent distribution requirement.[278] Lawmakers have been disturbed by a number of newspaper accounts of excessive compensation paid to substantial contributors and their children.[279]

(iv) Tax on Excess Business Holdings. Congress did not want private foundations to hold significant interests in operating businesses that are unrelated to the foundations' exempt activities (e.g., a business corporation). As a consequence, a private foundation is generally limited to holding no more than 20 percent of the voting stock of a corporation reduced by the percentage of voting stock actually or constructively owned by disqualified persons. Any holdings in excess of that amount are referred to as *excess business holdings,* which are subject to a two-tier excise tax.[280] The rules also cover holdings in other business entities, such as partnerships and limited liability companies.[281]

The 20 percent limit has four exceptions. The first involves businesses in which those unconnected with the foundation effectively take control of the company from the foundation[282]; in this case, the private foundation and disqualified persons may own up to a 35 percent interest of the business. The second applies to corporations that engage in activities that are functionally related to the exempt purposes of the foundation.[283] The third involves a trade or business at least 95 percent of whose gross income is derived from passive sources (for example, dividends and investment income).[284] The fourth involves program investments.

Foundations can unexpectedly find themselves with excess business holdings. In certain circumstances, the law provides the foundation with specific periods of time to reduce its holdings to permissible levels. The classic example involves a foundation that receives stock as a charitable bequest.

277. I.R.C. § 4942(b).

278. *See* Section 105 of the Charitable Giving Act of 2003, H.R. No. 7, 108th Cong 1st Sess. (2003).

279. For an example, see *Some Officers of Charities Steer Assets to Selves*, BOSTON GLOBE, Oct. 9, 2003, the first in a series of occasional articles that earned the *Globe* national attention.

280. I.R.C. § 4943.

281. I.R.C. § 4943(c)(3).

282. I.R.C. § 4943(c)(2)(B), raising the limit to 35 percent.

283. I.R.C. § 4943(d)(3)(A).

284. I.R.C. § 4943(d)(3)(B); and Treas. Reg. § 53.4943-10.

THE MADDOX FOUNDATION: THE COMING TOGETHER OF STATE LAW AND PRIVATE FOUNDATION EXCISE TAXES

* * *

In 2004, the State of Tennessee filed suit against the Maddox Foundation and its president (who also is a foundation director) in which the state made numerous allegations regarding its management.[285] The suit was further complicated when the Mississippi Attorney General intervened, arguing that the foundation was subject to Mississippi jurisdiction.[286]

One of the more interesting allegations in Tennessee's complaint involves the foundation's purchase of the Memphis RiverKings, a professional hockey team, and the Memphis Xplorers, a professional arena football team.[287] According to the complaint, the foundation spent $1,760,000 on these purchases and has continued to fund significant operating losses.[288] Tennessee has taken the position that these were not appropriate investments.[289]

The allegations raise an interesting tax issue: Do the foundation's investments in the two teams constitute excess business holdings under Section 4943 of the Internal Revenue Code and, therefore, potentially subject the foundation to confiscatory taxes, or do these holdings qualify as either functionally related businesses within the meaning of Section 4942(j)(4) or as program-related investments, thereby removing them from the grasps of the excess business holding rules?[290]

Tennessee's lawsuit also alleges in a highly critical fashion that the foundation did not obtain a private letter ruling from the IRS blessing the transaction prior to the acquisition.[291] It is not at all clear why the excess business holding rules do not pose a problem. In all likelihood, the foundation is taking the position that the investment is program related, specifically that it serves some community development purpose. The problem with that argument is that applies equally to just about any investment in a business that employs local people.

In 1995, the IRS issued a series of rulings that addressed the prohibition against excess business holdings when a community foundation bought the Kansas City Royals baseball team in an effort to keep the team in Kansas City.[292] It may be that the Maddox Foundation is relying on these rulings, which specifically concluded that there was not a problem under the prohibition against excess business holdings. Such reliance may be misplaced because the complex structure involving the community foundation's investment in the Royals not only placed voting control with private interests but also was intended to result in the eventual sale

285. Complaint, Victor S. Johnson III, District Attorney General and Tommye Maddox Working v. Robin G. Costa and the Maddox Foundation (7th Cir. Ct. Davidson County, Tenn. filed on or about August 31, 2004); and Associated Press, *State Sues Trustee for Mismanaging Charitable Foundation*, SUN-HERALD, Sept. 1, 2004.

286. S. Strom, *After Donor Dies, Battle Erupts over Charity's Vision and Venue*, N. Y. TIMES, Feb. 16, 2005; and Temporary Restraining Order (Ch. Ct. DeSoto County, Ms. Nov. 18, 2004).

287. Complaint, *supra* note 285, at § I, ¶¶ 60 to 70.

288. *Id.*, at ¶ 60.

289. *Id.*, at § I, ¶¶ 68 to 69.

290. Treas. Reg. § 53.4943-10(b).

291. Complaint, *supra* note 285, at § I, ¶ 69.

292. *See* Priv. Let. Rul. 95-30-024 (July 28, 1995); Priv. Let. Rul. 93-53-0025 (July 28, 1995); and Priv. Let. Rul. 95-30-026 (July 28, 1995), as well as an astute analysis by P. Streckfuss, *Rulings in Search of a Rationale*, 68 TAX NOTES 891 (1995).

of the Royals to private interests. The Maddox Foundation, on the other hand, has voting control over the two teams and apparently has no plans to sell them.

It will therefore be interesting to see whether the state of Tennessee and the IRS find themselves in partnership in policing what the state views as inappropriate behavior.

* * *

(v) Tax on Jeopardizing Investments. If a private foundation makes any investments that would financially jeopardize conducting its exempt purposes, both the foundation and its individual managers may be liable for taxes on such investments under a two-tier excise tax structure.[293] This excise tax can be viewed as the "federalization" of the prudent investor standard applied to investment decisions made by fiduciaries. What is a bit puzzling is why only private foundations were singled out for regulation.

Jeopardizing investments generally are those that reflect a lack of reasonable business care and prudence in providing for the long- and short-term financial needs of the foundation to perform its exempt function.[294] No single factor determines whether an investment is a jeopardizing investment, but the following investments are carefully scrutinized:

- Securities purchased on margin.
- Commodity futures.
- Working interests in oil and gas wells.
- Puts, calls, and straddles.
- Warrants.
- Short sales.

Whether an investment jeopardizes the foundation's exempt purposes is determined when the investment is made. The determination considers the foundation's portfolio as a whole. Foundation managers may consider expected returns, risks of rising and falling prices, and the need for diversification within the investment portfolio. To avoid the tax on jeopardizing investments, however, a careful analysis of potential investments must be made and good business judgment exercised.

Some foundations make what are termed *program-related investments.*[295] For example, a foundation may make below-market loans to inner city housing developers to further its exempt purpose of increasing housing available to the poor. Such investments are not treated as jeopardizing investments.

(vi) Tax on Taxable Expenditures. Private foundations that engage in certain activities are subject to excise taxes on expenditures used to finance those

293. I.R.C. § 4944.

294. Treas. Reg. § 53.4944-1(a)(2)(i).

295. I.R.C. § 4944(c).

activities.[296] The intent is to deter private foundations from engaging in the specified activities, including:

- Efforts to influence legislation.
- Efforts to influence the outcome of a specific election or conduct a voter registration drive (with an exception for certain nonpartisan activities).
- Making grants to individuals for travel, study, or similar purposes unless the grant is awarded on an objective and nondiscriminatory basis, meets certain other requirements, and the procedure for awarding the grant is approved in advance by the IRS.
- Making grants to other private foundations unless the granting foundation exercises expenditure responsibility (with an exception for certain operating foundations).
- Making expenditures for noncharitable purposes with exceptions for investment activity, payments of taxes, and several other designated expenditures.[297]

Like the other private foundation excise taxes, the tax on taxable expenditures is applied in tiers. The first tier is imposed on the foundation at a rate of 10 percent of the expenditure.[298] As part of the first-tier, a 2.5 percent tax is imposed on any agreement by a foundation manager to make a taxable expenditure if the foundation manager willfully and knowingly entered into the agreement to make the expenditure.[299] Under the second tier, the foundation is subject to confiscatory excise taxes unless the expenditure is corrected within the designated time period.[300] As part of the two-tier system, a foundation manager who refuses to a make correction is subject to a tax equal to 50 percent of the taxable expenditures.

Each of these prohibited expenditures is important to note, but one of the most important is the prohibition against grants to individuals for travel and study unless certain requirements are satisfied. The applicable rules are particularly important for corporate foundations that want to create scholarship funds. To avoid being a taxable expenditure, the foundation must demonstrate that the scholarships will be awarded on an objective and nondiscriminatory basis and that the grant is either (1) for study at an educational institution that normally maintains a regular faculty and curriculum, (2) a prize or award made to a member of the general public, or (3) used to produce a report or similar product, or to improve or enhance a literary, artistic, musical, scientific, or teaching skill or talent of the grantee.[301] The foundation must submit its grant-making procedure to

---

296. I.R.C. § 4945(d).
297. Treas. Reg. § 53.4945-6(b).
298. I.R.C. § 4945(a)(1).
299. I.R.C. § 4945(a)(2).
300. I.R.C. § 4945(b).
301. Treas. Reg. § 53.4945-4(a)(3).

the IRS for advanced approval. As part of the process, the foundation must generally show that the class of potential recipients is large enough to constitute a charitable class; the required IRS approval is of the grant-making procedures, not the individual grants themselves.

Company foundations can give preference in awarding scholarships to employees or the children or relatives of employees, assuming that the program satisfies all other requirements, including the advanced approval procedures. However, scholarship grants that essentially provide extra pay, fringe benefits, or employment incentives do not qualify. For a company scholarship program to qualify, it must satisfy each of the following requirements:

- The preferential treatment must not have any significance beyond that of an initial qualifier.
- The selection process must be controlled by an independent committee, and selection must be based on nonemployment-related factors.
- The probability that qualified employees or their children will receive scholarship grants must be limited.[302]

(d) ALTERNATIVES TO PRIVATE FOUNDATIONS. There are a number of viable alternatives to private foundations, each alternative eliminating the need to worry about the complex rules embodied in the private foundation excise taxes. Here are three of the alternatives:

(i) Community Foundations. Wealthy donors should consider contributing to a community foundation in lieu of creating a private foundation. A *community foundation* is an entity (often a trust or corporation) established to attract large pools of capital for the benefit of a particular community or geographic area.[303] The donor typically creates a separate fund that is treated as part of the community foundation. The donor can impose restrictions on how the income and assets from the fund are to be utilized, but these restrictions must be subject to a variance power[304] held by the foundation when the foundation is set up as a trust and cannot be material.[305] This structure can accommodate donor-advised funds, in which the donor offers advice as to how the income and assets from his fund are utilized. Final decision authority for distribution of the funds must reside with the trustees or directors of the community foundation if the contribution is to be deductible as a charitable contribution and the fund is to be aggregated with other such funds in determining the public support of the community foundation. Community foundations permit donors to make large one-time donations (often one with the proceeds from the sale of a business or a highly appreciated asset)

---

302. Rev. Proc. 76-47, 1976-2 C.B. 670. See Rev. Proc. 80-39, 1980-2 C.B. 772, *mod. by* Rev. Proc. 83-36, 1983-1 C.B. 763, for a set of similar requirements for educational loans.
303. Treas. Reg. §. 1.170A-9(e)(11)(i).
304. Treas. Reg. § 1.170A-9(e)(11)(v)(B)(1).
305. Treas. Reg. § 1.507-2(a)(8).

and to offer advice as to how principal and income from the fund are to be directed in subsequent years.

(ii) Funds Sponsored by Commercial Entities. In recent years, commercial entities such as large mutual fund companies have established donor-advised funds that offer another alternative to private foundations. These funds are classified as Section 501(c)(3) organizations and can qualify as public charities. Under the typical structure, a donor creates a fund that becomes part of the "umbrella" organization, receiving a charitable contribution deduction for the donor's contribution. The donor directs the fund's investment of the contributions and, most important, advises the umbrella organization on how to disburse the income and assets from the fund among qualified charities. Although developed as commercial vehicles, these funds must satisfy certain income tax requirements. Of particular note is the requirement that the umbrella organization retain the power to reject the donor's suggested charities.

Some argue that donor-advised funds sponsored and administered by commercial entities tend to be more donor centric than those at community foundations. Many in the community foundation circle allege that the sponsors of donor-advised funds do not adequately monitor the donor's designation and that these funds are designed to circumvent the private foundation rules. This controversy should come as no surprise. Community foundations focus on the community and are operated by community representatives. On the other hand, the commercial vehicles are formed by entities motivated by fees generated by investment activity. These entities view their constituency as the funders rather than the charitable beneficiaries.

(iii) Supporting Organizations. Supporting organizations were briefly considered earlier. They are simply Section 501(c)(3) organizations that escape private foundation status by establishing a "close" relationship to a public charity. Individuals seeking to avoid private foundation status generally use supporting organizations to hold endowments set aside to support one or more specifically designated charitable entities[306] (which can include a community foundation, thus providing additional flexibility).[307]

Establishing the relationship between a Type III supporting organization (defined earlier) and a public charity is not always easy but generally is achievable. In addition to requiring a relationship with the public charity, the tax regulations require that the donor or disqualified persons (i.e., persons and entities related to the donor) not control the supporting organization.[308] This requirement

306. Treas. Reg. § 1.509(a)-4(d)(4)(i)(a).

307. *See* J. Davine, *Everything You Ever Wanted to Know About Type 3 Supporting Organizations*, PLANNED GIVING DESIGN CENTER (June 28, 2000). The article is *available* at *http://*www.pgdc.com/usa/item/?itemID=26561.

308. I.R.C. § 509(a)(3)(C); and Treas. Reg. § 1.509(a)-4(j).

does not preclude some involvement by the donor, but it does prevent the donor from naming only himself and family members as the trustees. In many cases, this limitation poses the greatest difficulties. Congress is in the process of reviewing both donor-advised funds and Type III supporting organizations. New limitations on both types of vehicles are expected.

(e) TERMINATION OF STATUS. By now you should have the sense that Congress does not particularly trust those running private foundations to exercise good judgment without the application of several statutory cattle prods. Consequently, it should come as no surprise that Congress would be suspicious of anyone who wants to get out of the private foundation pen after enduring repeated electric shocks.

Briefly, a private foundation can most easily terminate its status by transferring its assets to an organization described in Section 170(b)(1)(A) other than a private operating foundation and certain supporting and other organizations. In other words, it can a transfer the assets to a church, college or university, hospital, or publicly supported charity described in Section 170(b)(1)(A)(vi).[309] The recipient must have held its qualifying status for at least 60 months before it receives the foundation's assets. Similarly, the private foundation may covert to public charity status after qualifying as a public charity during a 60-month seasoning period.[310]

The private foundation (the transferor) can also terminate[311] its status by transferring all of its assets to another private foundation.[312] For the transferor, this is easy enough—figuratively speaking, because nothing is easy when it comes to the termination of private foundation status—but the recipient foundation should make sure that the transfer is not a Trojan horse. The recipient foundation inherits certain tax attributes and tax obligations of the transferor. The details of this process are beyond the scope of this *Guide,* but the consequences have important implications for the recipient. Before the board of directors of the potential recipient foundation agrees to accept assets from another private foundation, it should retain tax counsel experienced in this process to advise the board whether to accept or reject the offer. The recipient should also undertake due diligence including obtaining various representations from the transferor foundation and its managers.

The three alternatives just discussed will result in the foundation's assets being held by another Section 501(c)(3) organization. If the assets are transferred to any organization—assuming this is even permissible under the organization's governing documents or state law—the transferor foundation is subject

---

309. I.R.C. § 507(b)(1)(A).

310. I.R.C. § 507(b)(1)(B).

311. The foundation is still technically a private foundation after the transfer, but that is more a technical matter-with no material consequences, assuming that the foundation then goes out of existence.

312. I.R.C. § 507(b)(2).

to a termination tax.[313] This tax is referred to as the *ringer tax*. It seeks to collect the value of all prior tax benefits or, if less, all of the foundation's assets. This tax generally is abated if the transfer is to other Section 501(c)(3) organizations, but specific notifications and requirements must be satisfied.[314]

Finally, the IRS can involuntary terminate a private foundation[315] if the foundation engages in willful, flagrant, or repeated acts or failures to act that result in the imposition of the various excise taxes previously enumerated. Even if the IRS does not terminate the status, prohibited acts (or failures to act) can preclude a private foundation from availing itself of the voluntary termination procedures, meaning that it may be subject to the termination tax if it otherwise attempts such voluntary procedures.

(f) CONCLUSIONS. There is no advantage to being a private foundation, but there are plenty of disadvantages. Consequently, every effort should be made to avoid private foundation status, but that is not always possible. Any time a corporation or a wealthy individual creates a foundation, everyone involved must focus on the private foundation rules, particularly the various excise taxes. While the complexities and burdens resulting from private foundation status often outweigh the benefits, if the decision is made to proceed with the organization of a charitable entity that will be classified as a private foundation, the resulting organization needs qualified legal counsel to help it, the insiders, and managers avoid trouble.

6.8 POLITICAL ACTIVITIES

Tax-exempt organizations must proceed cautiously before participating in political activities and campaigns. Such activities can cost them their exempt status. In considering questions of political activity, the distinction between Section 501(c)(3) organizations and other Section 501(c) organizations is the key to staying on the right side of the line.

The message to Section 501(c)(3) organizations is clear: Stay out of political campaigns (including the publication or distribution of statements). However, this does not mean that these organizations cannot express their views with respect to policy issues that are in the political arena.

(a) CHARITABLE ORGANIZATIONS. Organizations that are exempt from taxation under Section 501(c)(3) cannot participate or intervene in any political campaign on behalf of (or in opposition to) any candidate for office.[316] This is an *absolute prohibition* on political activity. Its rationale is quite simple: Campaign contributions are not deductible, so people should not be able to do indirectly (make a

---

313. I.R.C. § 507(c).
314. I.R.C. § 507(g).
315. I.R.C. § 507(a)(2).
316. I.R.C. § 501(c)(3); and Treas. Reg. § 1.501(c)(3)-1(c)(3)(iii).

tax-deductible charitable contribution that is used for political purposes) what they cannot do directly (make a deductible political contribution). Not so surprising, Lyndon Johnson first put forward this limitation in 1954 when he was a senator to help thwart his opponent's fundraising efforts.[317] Failure to abide by this prohibition can result in the imposition of excise taxes on the organization and its managers as well as its loss of tax-exempt status.[318]

(i) Education or Politics? Tax exemption under Section 501(c)(3) can be predicated on educational purposes, but, as discussed earlier, where does an organization draw the line between fulfilling its educational purposes and engaging in political activity?[319] For example, an organization might want to hold a candidate forum, disseminate legislative voting records, or provide written information about candidates for public office. The determination as to whether any of these activities is permissible is based on facts and circumstances.[320] No organization should engage in these activities without first consulting legal counsel.

What is important to keep in mind is how people and organizations that play close to the line (or overstep it) are detected. Push the limits, and the political opposition or a watchdog group[321] is likely to inform major media outlets and the IRS about the potential violation. Then Congress or the IRS begins to investigate. The IRS does not need to constantly monitor every organization because the opposition and watchdogs are watching and have every incentive to let the world know about questionable political activities.

---

317. See P. Daniel, *More Honored in the Breach: A Historical Perspective of the Permeable IRS Prohibition on Campaigning by Churches*, 42 Bost. Col. L. Rev. 733 (2001). Lyndon Johnson was opposed in the 1954 Senate primary race by Dudley Dougherty. Suspicious that Dougherty's campaign was being financed by two private foundations (the Facts Forum and the Committee for Constitutional Government), Johnson proposed the prohibition against intervention in political campaigns to thwart his opponent. Of course, this raises the age-old question: Is it good politics or good policy?

318. I.R.C. § 4955.

319. See Rev. Rul. 66-256, 1966-2 C.B. 210, granting Section 501(c)(3) status to an organization that planned to conduct public forums at which lectures and debates on social, political, and international matters would be presented even though some of its programs would include controversial speakers or subjects. This organization's charter provided that it was to have no institutional point of view.

320. See Rev. Rul. 76-456, 1976-2 C.B. 151, where the IRS granted Section 501(c)(3) status to an organization that collected, collated, and disseminated, on a nonpartisan basis, information concerning general campaign practices, through the press, radio, television, mail, and public speeches. It qualified as an educational organization because it instructed and encouraged the public about political campaigns, a subject useful to the individual and beneficial to the community. *See also* American Campaign Academy, 92 T.C. 1053 (1989), where the IRS successfully contested the Section 501(c)(3) status of an organization that trained campaign managers but on a partisan basis.

321. A good example of such a group is Americans United for Separation of Church and State. A review of the press releases on their Web site (http://www.au.org) shows just how active this group has been in identifying what it claims to be prohibited political activity. Of particular note is a May 9, 2005, press release announcing that the organization had written a letter to the IRS asking it to investigate "a North Carolina church whose pastor garnered national headlines after he expelled several Democrats from the congregation."

Permitted Activity or Crossing the Line?

* * *

Brian Ross of ABC News reported that a number of charities were conducting fundraising events at the same time the 2004 Republican National Convention was held in New York City.[322]

In his report, Mr. Ross focused on an event sponsored by World of Hope, an AIDS organization that had recently been formed. The organization sponsored a fundraising concert at Rockefeller Center during the convention.[323] Patrons who gave $250,000 or more were given access to a VIP lounge where they could meet Senate Majority Leader Bill Frist. Mr. Ross reported that the concert/party was heavily attended by corporate executives and lobbyists. Outsiders whom Mr. Ross interviewed claimed that the event was used to sell access to Senator Frist.

Just how closely connected is World of Hope to the Republican Party? Mr. Ross reported that the person who "registered" the charity with the IRS was listed on a GOP Web site as general counsel to the Republican National Party.[324]

This is the reflexive reaction to Brian Ross's story: The named charity does not qualify as a Section 501(c)(3) organization because it is engaging in political activity. On further reflection, however, this is not so clear. This could have been some very clever and perfectly legitimate tax planning.

Recall that under Section 501(c)(3), an organization is prohibited from engaging in political activity. There is no allowance for even de minimis political activity. But were any of the contributions to World of Hope used for political activity? It is impossible to determine for sure because GuideStar's Web site has no Form 990 for World of Hope.[325] Given the involvement of Senator Frist, it is highly unlikely that the charitable contributions were actually used for political expenditures. In fact, there are reports that World of Hope did make contributions of at least $3 million to AIDS charities.[326]

In another context, the IRS has indicated that the opportunity to meet celebrities in exchange for certain levels of contributions is not a problem, specifically stating that the value attributable to meeting the celebrity does not reduce the charitable contribution deduction (meals or goods provided may still require reduction to the charitable contribution deduction).[327] The fact that meeting a politician may not have value for tax purposes may not be a complete defense against a charge that a charitable organization engaged in

322. B. Ross, R. Schwartz, and D. Scott, *Charitable Donations Can Win Access: Donating to Win Access and Tax Benefits*, ABC News (Transcript dated Sept. 30, 2004). See also Press Release, National Center for Responsive Philanthropy, Frist's RNC Charity Fundraiser Really a Political Fundraiser in Disguise, Philanthropic Watchdogs Charges (Aug. 31, 2004); and S. Lowenberg, *Party Favors*, Mother Jones (July/Aug. 2004).

323. B. Ross, R. Schwartz, and D. Scott, *supra* note 322.

324. *Id.*

325. The Guide Star site was last checked on October 3, 2005.

326. Press Release, Africacare, Senator Bill Frist's "World of Hope" Charity Awards Africare for Its Fights Against HIV/AIDS (Sept. 2004).

327. Treas. Reg. § 1.6115-1(a)(2), Example 3. While this regulation specifically pertains to disclosure by the charity, it appears to be consistent with the IRS position on the valuation question, particularly given the reference to Treasury Regulation Section 1.170A-1(c)(2).

prohibited political activity. In other words, the valuation of the contributions and the prohibition against political activity do not necessarily represent the same issue, but an advocate could certainly use the IRS's disclosure and valuation position to attempt to cleanse the "meet and greet" of any political taint.

Where is the line when it comes to defining *celebrity*? Is meeting a famous political figure really any different from meeting Luciano Pavarotti, Bob Dylan, Jasper Johns, or J.D. Salinger? Some people will want to meet Bob Dylan simply to shake his hand and tell him how his songs have had such a great influence on their lives. Other people will want to meet President George W. Bush simply to shake his hand and tell him how his speeches and policies have had a great influence on their lives. If that is all that is happening, has the charity engaged in political activity?

Now let's follow the money. If the $250,000 had gone to World of Hope that in turn had contributed it to the Republican Party, the IRS would certainly be justified in revoking World of Hope's Section 501(c)(3) status. That would be a clear violation of the prohibition against political intervention. But what is the harm if every last dollar of the $250,000 goes to fund a university professor's AIDS research activities? The money will be used for charitable purposes, and, as a consequence, it should be deductible under Section 170 as a qualifying charitable contribution.

Where there might be a problem is if $10,000 of the $250,000 was used by the charity to cover its costs in sponsoring the event. While meeting Senator Frist might have no value for purposes of valuing the charitable contribution deduction, the event may still have political taint. One can only wonder whether any campaign-related comments like "Four More Years" were chanted by the performers from the stage.

So far, the discussion has focused on violations resulting from prohibited political activity. It could be instead that this is not political activity on the part of the charities in question but lobbying activity. Section 501(c)(3) organizations are permitted to engage in a limited amount of lobbying activity without jeopardizing their tax-exempt status. Senator Frist is a doctor and an influential member of Congress, so why would an organization that focuses on a disease not want to involve Senator Frist in an activity to meet its supporters?

The ABC News report could disturb you. Like it or not, however, our entire economic and political system is driven by elites with access. The old adage "It's who you know, not what you know" still holds true. At least in this case, it appears that the money went to a good cause rather than to Washington lobbyists who then used it to buy country club memberships, luxury cars, and Gucci loafers, or so the stereotype goes.

* * *

(ii) Permitted Activities. A Section 501(c)(3) organization can distribute certain newsletters and engage in certain types of voter education. The IRS has permitted organizations to distribute newsletters that report on legislators' views on issues that are of particular interest to the organization when the information is not distributed in connection with a campaign,[328] but the IRS has not approved all newsletters. In one instance, the IRS indicated that a fundraising newsletter constituted prohibited political activity because the timing of the newsletter

328. *See* Rev. Rul. 80-282, 1980-2 C.B. 178. In this ruling, the information was distributed through a newsletter in which the organization indicated whether it agreed or disagreed with the position. The saving grace was the absence of a political campaign. The IRS listed nine factors that it considered in concluding that the newsletter did not constitute involvement in a political campaign.

coincided with a political campaign.[329] Advisors have a difficult task when counseling organizations that want to distribute newsletters that express the organization's opinions with respect to office-holder positions; this task is made even more difficult by ever-lengthening campaigns.

The IRS has ruled that Section 501(c)(3) organizations may engage in voter education under certain circumstances. The watchwords are *neutrality* and *non-partisan*. For example, an organization may conduct public forums for political candidates so long as the forums are fair and impartial.[330] Organizations can also prepare and disseminate voting records of candidates so long as there is no editorial bias and the issues are not limited to those only of particular interest to the organization.[331]

(iii) Prohibited Activities. A Section 501(c)(3) organization cannot (1) endorse a candidate in writing or orally,[332] (2) rate candidates,[333] (3) distribute partisan campaign literature, (4) provide or solicit financial support for a candidate, (5) or form a political action committee. These rules have been strictly construed, as the New York City Bar Association learned when it attempted to rate judges who were running for office.[334]

There has always been a question as to whether the IRS will actually revoke Section 501(c)(3) status if an organization engages in a very small amount of prohibited activity through a foot fault or rogue operator. Tax-exempt organizations should avoid testing the limits,[335] but the IRS did show some mercy in a

329. Tech. Adv. Mem. 96-09-007 (Mar. 1, 1996).
330. Rev. Rul. 86-95, 1986-1 C.B. 332.
331. Rev. Rul. 78-248, 1978-1 C.B. 154.
332. *Id.*
333. *Id.*
334. *Id.*
335. *See* United States v. Dykema, 666 F.2d 1096, 1101 (7th Cir. 1981). However, the legislative history underlying Section 4955 suggests that Congress believed the IRS has some discretion under the provision, providing as follows:

> The committee believes that the penalty excise tax structure applicable under present law if a private foundation makes a prohibited political expenditure should also apply in the case of prohibited political expenditures made by a public charity. As the Congress concluded in adopting the two-tier foundation excise tax structure in 1969, the Internal Revenue Service may hesitate to revoke the exempt status of a charitable organization for engaging in political campaign activities in circumstances where that penalty may seem to be disproportionate—i.e., where the expenditure was unintentional and involved only a small amount and where the organization subsequently had adopted procedures to assure that similar expenditures would not be made in the future, particularly where the managers responsible for the prohibited expenditure are no longer associated with the organization. At the same time, where an organization claiming status as a charity engages in significant, uncorrected violations of the prohibition on political campaign activities, revocation of exempt status may be ineffective as penalty or as a deterrent, particularly if the organization ceases operations after it has diverted all its assets to improper purposes.
>
> The committee believes that the additional, two-tier excise tax structure applicable under present law to private foundations operates in a fair and effective manner and hence appropriately should be extended to public charities. The adoption of the excise tax sanction does not modify the present-law rule that an organization does not qualify for tax-exempt status as a charitable organization, and

ruling pertaining to a religious organization.[336] In this case, a minister had made several statements during religious broadcasts, including a claim that if the candidate were elected, it would be "dangerous to be an American" and that the minister "would go into exile." The IRS concluded that these statements represented prohibited political intervention in a political campaign. The church argued that this was a statement by the minister, not by the church. The IRS rejected that argument, saying that the church could only distance itself from the statements if it had a clear policy that its ministers were not to make such statements. No such policy existed at the time the statements were made. However, the IRS decided not to revoke the organization's exempt status, citing legislative history giving it some discretion,[337] but it did impose excise taxes on political expenditures associated with the otherwise prohibited statements.[338] The IRS and the courts have not always been so merciful,[339] so charities should not count on being able to negotiate away the problem. Following the 2004 election, 131 charities (including some churches) were audited for this type of activity.[340]

(iv) Attribution of Individual Positions to the Organization. The prohibition on political campaign activity applies to Section 501(c)(3) organizations, not to the activities of individuals associated with the organization when those individuals are not acting in their official capacity. Consequently, an individual associated with a Section 501(c)(3) organization can engage in private political activity "so long as that official does not in any way utilize the organization's financial resources, facilities, or personnel, and clearly and unambiguously indicates that the actions taken or the statements made are those of the individual and not of the organization."[341]

The IRS looks to the facts and circumstances to determine whether to attribute an individual's acts to the organization. Although a facts and circumstances test is never particularly helpful in providing clear lines, the test does prohibit an official from engaging in political activity at the organization's official functions or through its official publications. It also prohibits the official from using the

---

is not eligible to receive tax-deductible contributions, unless the organization does not participate in, or intervene in, any political campaign on behalf of or in opposition to any candidate for public office (secs. 501(c)(3), 170(c)(2).

H.R. Rep. No. 100-391, 100th Cong., 1st Sess. 1623-1624 (1987). *See also* Treasury Decision 8628, 60 Fed. Reg. 62,209 (Dec. 5, 1995).

---

336. Tech. Adv. Mem. 2004-37-040 (Sept. 10, 2004).

337. H.R. Rep. No. 100-391, 100th Cong. 1st Sess. 1623-1624 (1987)

338. I.R.C. § 4955.

339. *See* Branch Ministries v. Commissioner, 40 F. Supp. 2d 15 (D.D.C. 1999), *aff'd* 221 F.3d 137 (D.C. Cir. 2000); and Tech. Adv. Mem. 1999-07-021 (May 20, 1998).

340. Treasury Inspector General for Tax Administration, (Reference No. 2005-10-035) Review of the Exempt Organizations Function for Reviewing Alleged Political Campaign Intervention by Tax-Exempt Organizations (Feb. 2005).

341. J. Kindell and J.F. Reilly, *supra* note 27.

organization's financial resources, facilities, or personnel. According to the IRS, "officials acting in their individual capacity may be identified as officials of the organization so long as they make it clear that they are acting in their individual capacity, that they are not acting on behalf of the organization, and that their association with the organization is given for identification purposes only."[342] The IRS goes on to provide that:

> when an official of an IRC 501(c)(3) organization endorses a candidate somewhere other than in the organization's publications or at its official functions, and the organization is mentioned, it should be made clear that such endorsement is being made by the individual in his or her private capacity and not on the organization's behalf. The following language would serve as a sufficient disclaimer: "Organization shown for identification purposes only; no endorsement by the organization is implied." However, as stated earlier, if the endorsement occurs in the organization's publication or at its official function, such a disclaimer is insufficient to avoid attribution of the endorsement to the organization.[343]

Boards should adopt a policy prohibiting political activity by their employees, contractors, and agents when acting in their organizational capacities. Obviously, the terms of any given policy statement will depend on specific exempt activities and circumstances.

NAACP Defies the IRS: Express Advocacy, Coded Language, or Policy Discussion?

* * *

On July 11, 2004, Julian Bond, the NAACP's chair, gave what turned out to be a very controversial speech,[344] although there was nothing particularly radical about it.[345] No doubt the intended audience enjoyed it, applauded throughout, and then went home. Then the IRS entered the picture, beginning an investigation as to whether Mr. Bond's speech constituted a prohibited intervention into the 2004 presidential campaign. Contrary to some news reports, the IRS did not single out the NAACP[346] but was acting under authority granted by Congress,[347] relying on a "fast-track" procedure to respond quickly to referrals of potential political intervention in order to prevent recurring violations by the same organizations.[348]

---

342. *Id.*

343. *Id.*

344. M. Allen, *NAACP Faces IRS Investigation*, Wash. Post, Oct. 29, 2004; Press Release, NAACP, NAACP Questions Timing of IRS Examination of Tax Exempt Status: Internal Revenue Service Claims Speech by Chairman Bond Critical of Bush Was Partisan (Oct. 29, 2004); and Letter from IRS Agent Kathleen D. Krawczyk to the NAACP notifying the NAACP of the investigation (Oct. 8, 2004).

345. Julian Bond, Transcript of Speech at NAACP Annual Convention (July 11, 2004).

346. S. Strom, *Nonprofit Groups Question Motive for Federal Actions*, N.Y. Times, Mar. 21, 2005.

347. I.R.C. § 6852 (termination assessments for flagrant violations); and I.R.C. § 7409 (injunctions to enjoin flagrant violations).

348. Treasury Inspector General for Tax Administration, *supra* note 340.

From July 30, 2004, through November 22, 2004, the IRS reviewed 131 information items alleging potential political activities by tax-exempt organizations.[349] The Treasury Inspector General for Tax Administration audited the IRS's Exempt Organization Division's activity, sampling 40 of the cases that the IRS reviewed.[350] Of the 40 cases, 18 involved organizations with pro-Republican leanings, 12 with pro-Democratic leanings, and 9 whose leanings could not be ascertained for one reason or another. Although the Treasury Inspector General's report noted the need for certain improvements in the IRS procedures, the report provided a favorable assessment of the IRS's objectivity in administering the program. Notwithstanding this apparent objectivity, the NAACP issued a press release on January 31, 2005, indicating that it would refuse to reply with a request for information from the IRS.[351]

Nowhere in the text of his speech does Mr. Bond say "I hereby endorse John Kerry for President of the United States," or "Do not vote for George Bush for President of the United States." The speech was 29 pages long,[352] began with a discussion of Dr. W. E. B. DuBois and moved on to *Plessy* v. *Ferguson, Brown* v. *Board of Education,* Rosa Parks, the 1964 Civil Rights Act, Emmett Till, President Lyndon Johnson, and Dr. Martin Luther King, Jr. Along the way, it provided some personal history.[353] Toward the end of the speech, Mr. Bond discussed the current climate. But there was a clear subtext running throughout the speech, particularly the last third of it. The speech criticized President George W. Bush, Vice President Dick Cheney, and Attorney General John Ashcroft. It also criticized the war in Iraq, federal budget deficits, current health care policies, current environmental policies, and various other Bush Administration policies. At several points in the speech, Mr. Bond emphasized the need to vote and register voters. At the outset, he said "The race is on! The gloves are off! We are in a fight for our lives, and we are here to commit to winning it!"

So was Mr. Bond permitted to say anything he wanted so long as he did not utter the magic phrase "Vote for John Kerry"? Such an utterance is termed "express advocacy," and the IRS has taken the position that although this standard is written into federal election campaign law,[354] it differs from the prohibition in Section 501(c)(3).[355] Representatives of the IRS have stated:

> ....No situation better illustrates the principle that all the facts and circumstances must be considered than the problem of when issue advocacy becomes participation or intervention in a political campaign. On the one hand, the Service is not going to tell IRC 501(c)(3) organizations that they cannot talk about issues of morality or of social or economic problems at particular times of the year, simply because there is a campaign occurring. As the 1995 ABA Comments state:
>
>> Nothing in Section 501(c)(3) prohibits a charity from purchasing media time for a discussion of issues in furtherance of its exempt purposes, whether or not such discussion coincides with an election. A charity's issue based message should be no more limited during an election campaign than it is during any other time of the year. The fact that candidates have aligned themselves on one or another side of an issue should not impact a charity's ability to reach the public with a pure issue message, particularly in view of

349. *Id.*
350. *Id.*
351. Press Release, NAACP, NAACP Says No to Internal Revenue Request for Documents (Jan. 31, 2005).
352. Julian Bond, *supra* note 345.
353. *Id.*
354. 2 U.S.C. 431(17).
355. J. Kindell and J.F. Reilly, *supra* note 27, at 346.

the fact that the candidate's position is an external factor beyond the charity's control. The independent actions or positions of candidates should not be imputed to exempt organizations.

In contrast to the "pure issue message" an IRC 501(c)(3) organization may avail itself of the opportunity to intervene in a political campaign in a rather surreptitious manner. The concern is that an IRC 501(c)(3) organization may support or oppose a particular candidate in a political campaign without specifically naming the candidate by using code words to substitute for the candidate's name in its messages, such as "conservative," "liberal," "pro-life," "pro-choice," "anti-choice," "Republican," "Democrat," etc., coupled with a discussion of the candidacy or the election. When this occurs, it is quite evident what is happening—an intervention is taking place. See Technical Advice Memorandum 9117001 (Sept. 5, 1990) for an example of coded language constituting political campaign intervention....

Therefore, the fundamental test that the Service uses to decide whether an IRC 501(c)(3) organization has engaged in political campaign intervention while advocating an issue is whether support for or opposition to a candidate is mentioned or indicated by a particular label used as a stand-in for a candidate. Accordingly, the appropriate focus is on whether the organization, in fact, is commenting on a candidate rather than speaking about an issue.

Only time will tell whether the NAACP will be sanctioned for Mr. Bond's speech. If the matter ends up in litigation and the IRS view of what constitutes intervention in a political campaign is correct, it will be up to the trier of fact to determine whether Mr. Bond was using code words to substitute for the candidate's name in his message.

Boards that want their organizations to steer clear of disputes with the IRS over prohibited political intervention should develop a policy for officers and employees on what speech is and is not permitted. This does not mean that the organization's officers and employees should be precluded from speaking out in favor of a candidate. No one questions the right of every American to engage in the political process, but officers and employees cannot engage in these activities on "company time" or while using "company resources."

Organizations that want to play close to the line should pay particular attention to the report of the Treasury Inspector General of Tax Administration,[356] which makes clear that the IRS intends to continue with its "fast-track" program during national political campaigns. Both the IRS and the public are used to thinking of the IRS as the agency that audits tax returns. The fast-track program represents a movement away from enforcement powers tied to tax returns. This movement away from return-centric tax administration should be kept in mind by those who want the IRS to focus on corporate governance.

* * *

(v) Excise Taxes on Political Activity. The Internal Revenue Code imposes a two-tier excise tax[357] on Section 501(c)(3) organizations[358] that engage in prohibited political activity. Under Tier 1, the organization is subject to a 10 percent

356. Inspector General Report, *supra* note 345.

357. I.R.C. § 4955.

358. Section 4955(d)(2) expands the list of prohibited expenditures in the case of an organization that is formed primarily to promote the candidacy (or prospective candidacy) of an individual for public office or that is effectively controlled by a candidate or prospective candidate and that is availed of primarily for such purposes.

tax on these expenditures. A separate 2.5 percent tax (up to $5,000) is imposed on organization managers who "authorize" the expenditure knowing that it is an impermissible one. If the expenditure is not corrected within a specified period of time, a Tier 2 tax equal to 100 percent of the expenditure is imposed on the organization and an additional 50 percent tax is imposed on the knowing manager (up to $10,000).[359]

(b) PRIVATE FOUNDATIONS. Section 501(c)(3) organizations that are private foundations will also want to be particularly careful in avoiding political activities. In addition to losing their tax-exempt status, private foundations (and their managers) are subject to an initial 10 percent (2.5 percent on the manager who agreed to make the expenditure) excise tax on expenditures to influence the outcome of any specific public election or to carry on any voter registration drive (with limited exceptions for certain nonpartisan activities).[360] If the offending expenditure is not reversed within the specified time, additional confiscatory taxes will be imposed on the parties.[361]

(c) OTHER ORGANIZATIONS. As discussed, Section 501(c)(3) organizations cannot intervene in political campaigns. However, certain other tax-exempt organizations can participate in such activity on a limited basis. Specifically, trade associations and labor unions can engage in limited political activities so long as these activities are not their "primary" activities. Political intervention is not considered to further their exempt purposes.[362] Labor and trade associations should review any proposed activities with qualified legal counsel before proceeding.

Social welfare organizations can attempt to influence legislation and take positions on controversial issues, but they cannot participate in the campaigns of candidates for public office as part of their primary social welfare activities, although there is limited room for some participation.[363] Before proceeding, a social welfare organization should seek the advice of qualified legal counsel.

(i) Tax on Political Expenditures or Net Investment Income. When these other Section 501(c) organizations do engage in political activities, they are subject to a tax under Section 527 on their expenditures with respect to political activities.[364] The taxable amount is equal to the lesser of (1) the organization's net investment income and (2) the aggregate amount of political expenditures.[365]

---

359. For additional details, see I.R.C. § 4955.
360. For additional details, see I.R.C. § 4945(a).
361. For additional details, see I.R.C. §§ 4945(b) and (c)(2).
362. Gen. Couns. Mem. 34233 (Dec. 3, 1969)
363. Rev. Rul. 81-95, 1981-1 C.B. 332.
364. I.R.C. § 527(f).
365. I.R.C. § 527(f).

(ii) Deductible Dues: The Proxy Tax or Disclosure. Amounts paid to trade associations, labor unions, and various other tax-exempt organizations are not deductible as charitable contributions but may be deductible as business expenses.[366] When amounts are specifically earmarked for political expenditures by the organization, those amounts are not deductible as business expenses.[367] When a trade association or labor union's political activities are substantial in relation to its other activities, someone paying membership dues is permitted to deduct only the portion of the dues for nonpolitical activities.[368] While those making the payments must reduce their deductions, the question of substantiality focuses on the entity. To bridge the gap, Congress shifted responsibility for determining the amount deductible to the organization. Under the resulting regulations, the organization has the option either to undertake the calculations and then notify its members of the amount by which any deduction must be reduced or to pay a proxy tax on the amount by which the organization's members would otherwise have to reduce their deductions.[369] As a practical matter, this system will have the most significant impact on trade associations because their corporate members will be able to deduct dues without regard to limitations that apply to labor union members. Consequently, the IRS, acting pursuant to statutory authority,[370] has exempted labor unions and certain veterans' organizations from the regulations.[371] The IRS has also created safe harbor requirements that will exempt certain other organizations from the system when they can satisfy the requirements. Finally, the present discussion focuses on political expenditures, but this regulation extends to certain other expenditures, including certain lobbying expenditures.

(d) POLITICS AND THE INTERNET. Section 501(c)(3) organizations should be careful when using the Internet to communicate with their members and the public to avoid running afoul of the prohibition on political intervention. The IRS has recognized this as a potential problem area; it has requested comments regarding this and other Internet-related issues.[372] While the IRS has not yet addressed the issue, organizations should keep a number of guidelines in mind when engaging in Internet communications, including the following:

- *Look to the Paper-Based Analogue.* If an organization cannot do something in the paper-based world, it should assume that similar actions on the Internet are also prohibited. For example, posting information supporting a candidate for president of the United States to a Section

366. I.R.C. § 162. In the case of labor union dues, the amount is subject to the 2 percent limitation on miscellaneous itemized deductions.
367. I.R.C. § 162(e)(1).
368. Treas. Reg. § 1.162-20(c)(3).
369. I.R.C. §§ 162(e)(3) and 6033(e).
370. I.R.C. § 6033(e)(3).
371. Rev. Proc. 98-19, 1998-1 C.B. 547.
372. Ann. 2000-84, 42 I.R.B. 385.

501(c)(3) organization's Web site does *not* somehow cleanse the communication.

- *Monitor Internet Links.* Hyperlinks to other Web sites pose potential problems for Section 501(c)(3) organizations because organizations cannot control the content posted on third-party Web sites. For example, the IRS could construe hyperlinks from a Section 501(c)(3) organization's Web site to those maintained by other organizations that contain political campaign material to be a prohibited intervention. As a precautionary measure, organizations should review the content contained on any Web site before linking to it. In addition, organizations should periodically review linked Web sites to make sure that content has not changed.
- *Moderate Listservs.* Section 501(c)(3) organizations should be careful when they sponsor blogs, listservs, or other Web-discussion forums. Although an organization can certainly control what it posts to that forum, participants outside the organization may make statements that are inconsistent with the prohibition on political activities. Organizations should strongly consider using moderated forums, possibly prescreening comments before they are posted.
- *Make Cost Allocations.* If an organization is engaging in permitted political activity that is subject to tax under Section 527, it should develop a scheme for allocating Web site costs between taxable and nontaxable expenditures.

(e) POLITICAL ACTIVITY: THE OTHER REGULATORY REGIME. Up to this point, we have focused on political activity from a tax perspective. Every organization engaging in political activity must also keep in mind federal election law, as well as state counterparts. These laws are highly specialized and quite Byzantine. Consequently, this *Guide* makes no effort to address them. Suffice it to say that a tax-exempt organization that determines under federal tax law that it can engage in activity that touches the political realm must then address an entirely separate body of law.

6.9 LOBBYING

A Section 501(c)(3) organization will lose its exempt status if a substantial part of its activities involve attempting to influence legislation ("lobbying").[373] While these organizations are prohibited from engaging in any political activity, they can engage in some amount of lobbying so long as such activity is not "substantial." Organizations that engage in substantial lobbying activities are referred to as *action organizations*.

---

373. Treas. Reg. § 1.501(c)(3)-1(c)(3)(ii).

Congress recognized that defining the point where insubstantial activities become substantial is virtually impossible. Congress responded by enacting the elective safe harbor of Section 501(h) to provide certainty to organizations that are interested in engaging in some lobbying.[374]

(a) *LOBBYING* DEFINED. An organization engages in *lobbying* if it contacts, or urges the public to contact, members of a legislative body for the purpose of proposing, supporting, or opposing legislation, or if the organization advocates the adoption or rejection of legislation. The IRS has identified a number of actions that it does not consider to be lobbying. It is important to note that an organization may try to influence action by the executive branch of government or an action by an independent regulatory agency without being deemed to be engaging in lobbying.[375]

Legislation includes action by Congress, any state legislature, any local council or similar governing body, or by the public in a referendum, initiative, constitutional amendment, or similar procedure.[376] The term applies to legislation not only in the United States but also in a foreign country.[377]

(b) EXCLUDED ACTIVITIES. An organization is not considered to be engaged in lobbying when it (1) makes available the results of nonpartisan analysis, study, or research, (2) examines and discusses broad social, economic, and similar problems, (3) provides technical advice or assistance (when the advice would otherwise constitute the influencing of legislation) to a governmental body or to a committee or other subdivision thereof in response to a written request by that body or subdivision, or (4) appears before or communicates with any legislative body about a possible decision of that body that might affect the existence of the organization, its powers and duties, its tax-exempt status, or the deduction of contributions to the organization.[378]

---

374. See Treas. Reg. § 1.501(c)(3)-1(c)(3)(ii)
375. Treasury Regulation Section 56.4911-2(d)(3) provides that "a 'legislative body' does not include executive, judicial, or administrative bodies."
376. Treas. Reg. § 1.501(c)(3)-1(c)(3).
377. Rev. Rul. 73-440, 1973-2 C.B. 177.
378. Treas. Reg. § 1.501(c)(3)-1(c)(3)(iv). *See also*STAFF OF THE JOINT COMMITTEE ON TAXATION, DESCRIPTION OF PRESENT-LAW RULES RELATING TO POLITICAL AND OTHER ACTIVITIES OF ORGANIZATIONS DESCRIBED IN SECTION 501(C)(3) AND PROPOSALS REGARDING CHURCHES SCHEDULES FOR A HEARING BEFORE THE SUBCOMMITTEE ON OVERSIGHT OF THE HOUSE WAYS & MEANS COMMITTEE ON MAY 14, 2002 at fn. 35 (May 14, 2002), which provides:

> Although there is no precedential ruling from the IRS applying the section 4945 exceptions to lobbying for private foundations to nonelecting public charities, the IRS has stated that the section 4945 definitions and exceptions apply to section 501(c)(3) because of a statement in the legislative history that section 4945 intended no change to the substantive law of lobbying other than the substantial part rule. GCM 34289 (May 8, 1970). See Haswell v.United States, 500 F.2d 1133, 1141-44 (Ct. Cl.), *cert. denied,* 419 U.S. 1107 (1974) (using the section 4945 regulations to clarify the section 501(c)(3) lobbying provisions); and J. Kindell and J.F. Reilly, *Lobbying Issues* in IRS CONTINUING EDUC. PUB. at 277 n.20 (1996).

Also excluded from the definition of *lobbying* are communications between an organization and its bona fide members about legislation or proposed legislation of direct interest to the organization and its members[379] unless the communications directly encourage the members to attempt to influence legislation or directly encourage the members to urge nonmembers to attempt to influence legislation.

(c) "INSUBSTANTIAL" LEVEL OF ACTIVITY. The courts and taxpayers have struggled to define what level of lobbying activity constitutes a "substantial" level. As anyone who has any experience with the development of the law through judicial decisions knows, relying on court formulations produces anything but a clear answer to what is insubstantial. One court carved out a safe harbor that permitted an organization to avoid trouble when the organization kept its lobbying activities below 5 percent of its total activities,[380] but other courts have rejected such approach.[381] The authors of a 1997 IRS continuing education document point out that some courts have looked to the 5 percent limit as a safe harbor. These same authors also indicate that activities exceeding 16 percent to 20 percent of total activities are "generally considered to be substantial." Is this determination made on the basis of time, expenditures, visibility, or some combination of these factors?

(d) THE ELECTION UNDER SECTION 501(h)—ELIMINATING UNCERTAINTY. As part of the Tax Reform Act of 1976, Congress gave most, but not all, Section 501(c)(3) organizations the opportunity to elect into a system that would provide more certainty as to whether their lobbying activities jeopardize their exempt status. Private foundations, churches, and certain church affiliates, auxiliaries, and associations cannot take advantage of this election.[382]

An organization can make lobbying expenditures without losing its exempt status so long as its expenditures do not normally exceed an amount determined pursuant to a complex formula. Organizations that engage in lobbying activity should review the formula, which is contained in Sections 501(h) and 4911.

To elect Section 501(h), the organization must file Form 5768. The election remains in effect for all taxable years that end after the date of the election and begin before a notice of revocation is filed.[383] If an organization is a calendar year taxpayer and files Form 5768 on December 31, 20X5, it is governed by Section 501(h) for the taxable year beginning January 1, 20X5. If the organization files a notice of revocation on July 1, 20X7, the election remains in effect for the full taxable year beginning January 1, 20X7. If an election under Section 501(h) is in

379. I.R.C.§4911(d)(2)(D).

380. Seasongood v. Commissioner of Internal Revenue, 227 F.2d 907 (6th Cir. 1955)

381. *See* Christian Echoes National Ministry v. United States, 470 F.2d 849 (10th Cir. 1972), *cert denied*, 414 U.S. 864 (1973), where the court took a "balancing" approach.

382. I.R.C. § 501(h)(5).

383. Treas. Reg. § 1.501(h)-2.

effect and an organization exceeds the expenditure limits for the year, a 25 percent excise tax on the excess lobbying expenditures is imposed on the organization.[384] The tax is imposed on the greater of the excess lobbying or excess grass roots expenditures.[385]

The question arises whether repeated excess expenditures pose a problem for the organization. In this case, the "normally" standard comes into play. The organization is required to calculate a four-year moving average[386]; the results of this calculation determine whether the organization loses its tax-exempt status.

(e) LOBBYING BY OTHER TAX-EXEMPTS. Some other types of tax-exempt organizations can engage in lobbying activities on a less restrictive basis than Section 501(c)(3) organizations. For example, a Section 501(c)(4) social welfare organization can engage in unlimited lobbying activities so long as the lobbying advances its tax-exempt purpose.[387] Consider a social welfare organization formed to promote education. It could devote all of its resources to lobbying Congress for education tax breaks. However, it would run into trouble if it devoted all resources to lobbying for a larger military budget. Moreover, as mentioned earlier, a Section 501(c)(3) organization that loses its exemption because of excessive lobbying cannot claim exemption under Section 501(c)(4).[388] Trade associations and labor unions[389] can also engage in extensive lobbying activities that promote the interests of their members.

The requirements for exempt status imposed under the various subparagraphs of Section 501(c) differ greatly. Consequently, an organization other than a Section 501(c)(3) organization attempting to assess how much lobbying it can engage in without jeopardizing its exempt status must closely examine the specific rules that apply to it.

6.10 UBIT—NOT ALL INCOME IS TAX EXEMPT

A tax-exempt organization is not taxed on its income from activities that are substantially related to the charitable, educational, or other purposes that are the basis for the organization's exemption.[390] Such income is exempt even if the activity constitutes a trade or business. If, however, an exempt organization

---

384. I.R.C. § 4911(a).
385. I.R.C. § 4911(b).
386. Treas. Reg. § 1.501(h)-3(b)(1) and (c)(7).
387. Treas. Reg. § 1.501(c)(4)-(a)(2)(ii).
388. I.R.C. § 501(c)(4).
389. Rev. Rul. 61-177, 1961-2 C.B. 117.
390. The focus of the inquiry is the source of the income and its relation to exempt activities rather than the use or destination of the income generated by the activity. This focus reverses the "destination" test originally set out by the United States Supreme Court in Trinidad v. Sagrada Orden, *supra* note 47. Section 502 specifically provides that organizations that carry on a trade or business are not exempt from tax simply because all of their income is payable to an exempt organization—a rejection of the Supreme Court's destination of income test. Such an organization is referred to as a *feeder* organization.

regularly conducts a trade or business that is *not* substantially related to its exempt purpose except that it provides funds to carry out that purpose, the organization is subject to tax on its income from the unrelated trade or business.[391] This tax is referred to as the *unrelated business income tax,* or UBIT.

Examples of "related" (exempt) businesses include colleges that charge tuition, hospitals that charge for medical services, theaters that sell tickets, and art museums that sell reproductions of artwork that they own. Note that both ticket sales and broadcast revenue for a college athletic event are viewed as related, but leasing a college athletic stadium to a promoter for a rock concert is considered to be an unrelated activity.[392] A tax-exempt organization must file Form 990-T when the organization's gross income from unrelated businesses is $1,000 or more. This form accompanies the Form 990 but is not subject to public disclosure.

(a) ORGANIZATIONS SUBJECT TO THE TAX. Although our focus is Section 501(c)(3) organizations, which are clearly subject to the tax, UBIT is generally applicable to all tax-exempt organizations, with a special rule including state colleges and universities.[393] Various types of organizations have specialized exemptions within the structure of this tax. For example, charities, social welfare organizations, trade associations/business leagues,[394] labor unions, and agriculture and horticultural organizations can take advantage of a special exemption for certain convention and trade show activities, but other organizations cannot.[395] Another exemption for certain entertainment activities is available to those same entities with the exception of trade associations and business leagues.[396]

The IRC contains a number of special rules applicable to different types of tax-exempt organizations, including foreign organizations,[397] social clubs, VEBAs, certain life insurance associations, and title-holding companies.[398]

(b) REASON FOR THE TAX. UBIT, the tax on unrelated business activities, is designed in part to prevent tax-exempt entities from unfairly competing with commercial entities.[399] Without this tax, exempt entities could, in theory, charge lower prices for their goods and services (vis-à-vis commercial entities) because they would not otherwise be required to pay tax on the income. While some argue that this is not the case, travel industry representatives, for example, were

391. I.R.C. § 511.
392. Rev. Rul. 80-298, 1980-2 C.B. 197.
393. I.R.C. § 511(a)(2).
394. In other words, organizations that are described in Section 501(c)(6).
395. I.R.C. §§ 513(d)(3)(A) and (C).
396. I.R.C. § 513(d)(2).
397. I.R.C. § 512(a)(2).
398. I.R.C. § 512(a)(3)(C).
399. *Hearings before the Subcommittee on Oversight, Ways and Means Committee, June 22,* Serial 100-26 (1987); and Revenue Act of 1950, Pub. L. No. 81-814, 64 Stat. 906 (1950).

quite vocal in arguing that college- and university-sponsored travel tours pose unfair competition to the commercial tour industry.[400]

Not surprising, the tax on unrelated business income has generated a great deal of controversy and litigation. By and large, the tax-exempt community has been very successful in advocating positions favorable to it. In fact, it has been so successful that it has defeated frequent calls for reform of the tax on unrelated business income.

(c) TAX RATE. Organizations subject to the tax on unrelated business income are generally taxable at corporate rates on that income.[401] Under the current rate structure, this means that the income can be subject to tax at a 35 percent maximum rate. Obviously, organizations would prefer that their income not be characterized as being unrelated to their exempt function.

(d) TRIGGERING THE TAX: THE THREE CRITICAL CONDITIONS. For income to be subject to UBIT, each of the following three conditions must exist with respect to the activity generating that income: (1) it must be regularly carried on, (2) it must constitute a trade or business, and (3) its conduct \must be not be substantially related to the conduct of the organization's exempt function. Let's explore each of these conditions now. In doing so, we will consider income attributable to advertising because it provides an excellent way to demonstrate why each condition is important to the overall determination as to whether income is taxable.

(i) "Regularly Carried On." The organization must regularly carry on an activity from an unrelated trade or business before the associated income can be characterized as unrelated business income. If commercial organizations normally conduct a particular activity on a year-round basis, an exempt organization's conduct of a similar activity for a few days or weeks a year will not be considered to be "regularly carrying on" that activity.[402] An excellent example is a food concession stand at a state fair or street festival. Restaurants normally sell food year round. Consequently, sale of food at a weekend street festival held over the July 4 holiday weekend is not considered regularly carrying on an unrelated trade or business.[403] However, if the comparable commercial activity is seasonal, such as the sale of Christmas trees, the conduct of the activity by the exempt organization for a significant portion of the season is considered "regular."[404]

---

400. M. Carson, *Nonprofits' Travel Offerings Are "Bad Trips," Say For-Profit Firms,* TAX ANALYSTS BULL., July 29, 1996; and Letter from Jere W. Glover, Chief Counsel, Small Business Administration to Charles Rossotti, Commissioner of Internal Revenue (Sept. 21, 1998).

401. I.R.C. § 511(a)(1).

402. Treas. Reg. § 1.513-1(c).

403. Treas. Reg. § 1.513-1(c)(2)(i).

404. For a discussion of arguments for the contrary position, see Veterans of Foreign Wars, 89 T.C. 7 (1987).

The law generally treats "intermittent" conduct of activities as something other than regular conduct, but this is generally conditioned on the activities being conducted "without the competitive and promotional efforts typical of commercial endeavors."[405] Probably the most important aspect of the intermittent rule is embodied in the following passage from the regulations:

> Certain intermittent income producing activities occur so infrequently that neither their recurrence nor the manner of their conduct will cause them to be regarded as trade or business regularly carried on. For example, income producing or fund raising activities lasting only a short period of time will not ordinarily be treated as regularly carried on if they recur only occasionally or sporadically. Furthermore, such activities will not be regarded as regularly carried on merely because they are conducted on an annually recurrent basis. Accordingly, income derived from the conduct of an annual dance or similar fund raising event for charity would not be income from trade or business regularly carried on.[406]

It is this provision that explains why an annual fundraising event with entertainment does not generate UBIT even though the patrons may pay an admission and the event is widely advertised. It also explains why food sales at a free annual concert or street festival do not generate UBIT. In a practical sense, this may be the single most significant paragraph in all of the UBIT regulations.

Unfortunately, the IRS has muddied the waters by occasionally taking the position that preparatory activities must be considered in determining whether an income should be excluded under the intermittent rule.[407] The IRS position is arguably inconsistent with its own regulations and their examples, which say absolutely nothing about preparatory activity. Moreover, the courts have shown a tendency to reject this activity.[408] Do not be surprised, however, if it is raised on audit because the IRS apparently persists on occasion.

This same section of the regulations addresses advertising, providing as follows:

> For example, the publication of advertising in programs for sports events or music or drama performances will not ordinarily be deemed the regular carrying of business.[409]

Despite this apparently plain language, the IRS has asserted that in ascertaining the length of time that an activity is carried on, the organization must consider the period during which advertising sales take place rather than the time period for the actual event (an evening or a weekend).[410] The IRS has raised

---

405. Treas. Reg. § 1.513-1(c)(2)(ii).

406. Treas. Reg. § 1.513-1(c)(iii).

407. Tech. Adv. Mem. 91-47-007 (Nov. 30, 1990); and Priv. Let. Rul. 91-37-002 (Apr. 29, 1991). *See also* BRUCE R. HOPKINS, *supra* note 41, at 662–63.

408. For examples, see National Athletic Collegiate Ass'n v. Commissioner, 914 F.2d 1417 (10th Cir 1990), and Suffolk County Patrolmen's Benevolent Ass'n, 77 T.C. 1313 (1981).

409. Treas. Reg. § 1.513-1(c)(ii).

410. C. Freitag, UNRELATED BUSINESS INCOME TAX, BNA TAX MANAGEMENT. PORT. NO. 874-2nd at A-39.

sales periods in determining whether advertising sales relating to yearbooks[411], programs,[412] and seasonal publications are regularly carried on. As is typical in this area, there is a lot of hair splitting. One commentator summarizes the case law as follows:

> It appears that, if an exempt organization distributes a publication containing advertising in conjunction with an annual or less frequent fundraising or other special event, the preparatory activity in soliciting advertising is less likely to be taken into account in determining whether the unrelated business activity is regularly carried on and the advertising is more likely to escape taxation. Conversely, when a publication is disseminated outside the context of an annual or other special fundraising event, the preparatory activity is more likely to be considered and the advertising income is therefore more likely to be taxed.[413]

This commentator then notes that the IRS has continued to challenge the exclusion of preparatory time in the case of annual or less frequent events.[414] When deciding how to structure its advertising activities, any organization selling advertising for programs should look closely at the case law applicable to it or obtain legal counsel. However, there is a more significant point: This dispute nicely illustrates how the first condition of the previously enumerated three conditions can by itself eliminate the entire UBIT issue.

(ii) "Trade or Business." The term *trade or business* generally includes any activity carried on for the production of income from selling goods or performing services.[415] An activity does not lose its identity as a trade or business merely because it is carried on within a larger group of similar activities that may or may not be related to the exempt purposes of the organization. For example, a hospital pharmacy that regularly sells pharmaceutical supplies to the general public does not lose its identity as a trade or business, even though the pharmacy also furnishes supplies to the hospital and its patients in accordance with its exempt purpose.[416]

Soliciting, selling, and publishing commercial advertising is a trade or business.[417] This is true even though the advertisement is published in an exempt organization's periodical that contains editorial matter related to the organization's exempt purpose. Note that we are now addressing whether advertising constitutes a "trade or business," whereas we previously considered whether an advertising activity was "regularly carried on." This is a critical point. Recall that before an activity is subject to tax, the organization must be a (1) trade or business (2) that is

---

411. Rev. Rul. 73-424, 1973-2 C.B. 190.
412. Rev. Rul. 75-200, 1975-1 C.B. 163.
413. C. Freitag, *supra* note 410, at A-40.
414. National Collegiate Athletic Ass'n v. Commissioner, 914 F.2d 1417 (10th Cir. 1990), *nonacq. See also* Tech. Adv. Mem. 97-12-001 (Oct. 17, 1996).
415. Treas. Reg. § 1.513-1(b).
416. Treas. Reg. § 1.513-1(b).
417. Treas. Reg. § 1.513-1(b).

regularly carried on and (3) not substantially related to the particular organization's exempt purpose. For example, carrying on an annual street festival probably constitutes a trade or business, but it is not regularly carried on. Consequently, the income, even though from the trade or business, is not taxable.

(iii) "Unrelated." A trade or business is considered *unrelated* if its conduct is not substantially related to the organization's exempt function (aside from providing money to support that function).[418] The regulations do not add much to this initial gloss. They do note that the distribution of goods or the performance of the services must contribute importantly to the accomplishment of the exempt organization's exempt purposes. These regulations also indicate that if the conduct of the activity is larger than necessary to accomplish those exempt purposes, the income from the excess portion of the activity will be treated as unrelated income.[419] Clearly, the provision of medical services by a nonprofit hospital is substantially related to its exempt function, meaning that any fees the hospital receives are related. The same would hold true for a legal service clinic providing deeply discounted legal services to low-income people. A nonprofit music school that received fees from performances by its students at a school-sponsored recital could treat the fees as substantially related to its exempt function because participation in performances is an essential aspect of the students' training.[420] A trade association would also be able to treat fee income from renting booths at a trade show designed to showcase industry products as substantially related to its exempt function, assuming the show was not a sales facility for individual exhibitors.[421]

Now let's return to advertising. While getting their message out is very important, many nonprofits also use their newsletters to raise revenue from ad sales. Whether the revenue is taxable depends largely on the advertising content. Consider the Port Jazz Society (PJS), a Section 501(c)(3) organization dedicated to educating the public about traditional jazz through concerts and lectures. PJS sells advertising space to local bars, restaurants, and assorted retailers in its concert programs. These programs are published throughout the course of the year every two weeks. For the just-completed year, PJS received $20,000 in advertising revenue.

As a general rule, advertising revenue that a tax-exempt entity receives is subject to the tax as unrelated business income.[422] In this situation, the ads do not relate in any way to PJS's exempt purpose,[423] but there are cases in which

418. Treas. Reg. § 1.513-1(a).

419. Treas. Reg. § 1.513-1(c)(3).

420. Treas. Reg. § 1.513-1(c)(4), Example 1.

421. Treas. Reg. § 1.513-1(c)(4), Example 2. It is not clear from this example whether the absence of sales activity was a critical factor in the conclusion reached. Note that this example involves a Section 501(c)(6) organization.

422. I.R.C. § 513(c).

423. Rev. Rul. 75-200, 1975-1 C.B. 163.

advertising revenue is not subject to UBIT. For example, if PJS puts on only one concert per year, it could arguably treat advertising revenues received from sale of ads in the program as exempt from UBIT because the activity is not "regularly carried on"[424]; see the earlier discussion.

The United States Supreme Court has held that in some instances, advertising activities are substantially related to the organization's exempt purposes,[425] stating that the test is whether the organization uses the advertising "to provide its readers a comprehensive or systematic presentation of any aspect of the goods and services advertised." The Court then went on to state that the organization can accomplish this "[b]y coordinating the content of the advertisements with the editorial content of the issue...." One can certainly envision situations in which PJS could meet this standard. For example, a quarterly publication could include advertising from used record dealers from around the world that handled traditional jazz recordings, providing PJS members a comprehensive list of dealers of recordings that are of interest to the members. However, the burden of proof is on PJS to demonstrate that these ads "contribute importantly to its exempt purpose."[426] If the list is not comprehensive and is repeated quarterly, the readers may not be obtaining new information that arguably contributes to furthering an educational mission. Again, any organization in a similar position is well advised to consult qualified tax counsel before assuming the income is exempt from UBIT.

(e) EXCEPTIONS FROM TAX. Certain income from what would be considered unrelated activities is exempted from the unrelated business income tax under a number of important exceptions to the normal rule. We will refer to these as *exceptions for types of income.* In actuality, the favorable tax treatment may result from a specific exclusion of income from tax, a rule that provides that a certain activity is not an unrelated trade or business, or some other mechanism.

(i) Exception for Investment Income. The most important of these exceptions is for income from interest, dividends, royalties, rents from real property, and gains or losses from the sale of capital assets (passive income).[427] This exception is often referred to as the one for "investment" or "passive" income, but no blanket exemption for all investment income exists. Instead the Internal Revenue Code provides that in calculating the amount of unrelated business taxable income, a modification excluding certain types of investment income can be made. This provision is very important to all charitable organizations, particularly organizations with large endowments.

---

424. Rev. Rul. 75-201, 1975-1 C.B. 164.

425. United States v. American College of Physicians, 475 U.S. 834 (1986).

426. Specifically, PJS must be prepared to show that the advertising "provide[s] its readers a comprehensive or systematic presentation of any aspect of the goods or services publicized." *Id.*, at 849.

427. I.R.C. §§ 512(b)(1), (2), (3), and (5).

Income that would otherwise be excluded may be subject to unrelated business income tax if and to the extent that it is derived from "debt-financed property,"[428] which refers to any property held to produce income and for which there is acquisition indebtedness at any time during the tax year (or 12-month period before the disposition date of that property). If substantially all (85 percent or more) of the use of any property is significantly related to an organization's exempt purposes, the property is not treated as debt-financed property.[429] "Related use" does not include a use related solely to the organization's need for income or its use of the profits. The extent to which property is used for a particular purpose is determined on the basis of all facts.

(ii) Exception for Activities Involving Volunteer Labor. Income derived from an activity that relies exclusively on volunteer labor is not subject to the tax on unrelated business income.[430] For example, assume that an orphanage runs a retail store operated by an all-volunteer workforce. The income from the sales is not subject to the unrelated trade or business tax because the workforce is composed entirely of volunteers. As a second example, assume that a volunteer fire company conducts weekly public dances. Holding public dances and charging admission on a regular basis may, given the facts and circumstances of a particular case, be considered an unrelated trade or business, but because the work at the dances is performed by unpaid volunteers, the income from the dances is not taxable as unrelated business income.

(iii) Exception for Activities Operated for the Convenience of Employees, Members, and Others. Income derived from an activity operated for the convenience of the organization's members, students, patients, officers, or employees is not subject to the tax on unrelated business income.[431] For example, assume that Bedsheet University, a liberal arts college, operates a laundry for dormitory linens and students' clothing. This is not considered to be an unrelated trade or business.[432]

(iv) Exception for Income from the Sale of Donated Goods. Income derived from the sale of donated goods is not subject to the tax on unrelated business income even if the goods are sold by paid employees.[433] For example, consider Community Help, a Section 501(c)(3) organization, that runs an annual book and record fair in November where it sells books and records donated throughout the year. Community Help hires 100 high school students to assist its members during this very popular fair. It pays each student $8 per hour. Although Community

---

428. I.R.C. §§ 512(b)(4) and 514.
429. Treas. Reg. § 1.514(b)-1(b)(1)(ii).
430. I.R.C. § 513(a)(1).
431. I.R.C. § 513(a)(2).
432. Treas. Reg. § 1.513-1(e).
433. I.R.C. § 513(a)(3).

Help uses paid labor to assist with the book fair, the fair does not constitute an unrelated trade or business because all books and records are donated.[434]

(v) Exception for Sponsorship Payments. Income received by an organization for the use or acknowledgement of the sponsor's name or logo (but not advertising) escapes the tax on unrelated business income if the income constitutes a "qualified sponsorship payment."[435] A *qualified sponsorship payment* is any payment by a commercial enterprise if there is no arrangement or expectation that the enterprise will receive any substantial return benefit other than the use or acknowledgement of the enterprise's name or logo (or product lines) in connection with the exempt organization's activities. This exception was added to the litany of exceptions after the IRS ruled that a corporation's payments to sponsor a college bowl football game constituted unrelated business income.[436] As is often the case, Congress created this exception to reverse a decision by the IRS, but the resulting statutory language and regulations create a formal framework for analyzing a wide variety of sponsorship payments.

The framework for sponsorship payments uses the concept "substantial return benefit" to determine whether a payment is taxable or not.[437] If the sponsor receives only an acknowledgment, there is no substantial return benefit. However, advertising itself is considered to be a substantial return benefit, requiring taxpayers to distinguish between acknowledgments and advertising. The regulations also classify the receipt of goods, facilities, services, or other privileges, exclusive provider arrangements, and certain exclusive and nonexclusive rights with respect to intangible assets as substantial return benefits.[438] There is a de minimis rule which provides that items that would otherwise be benefits will be disregarded if the aggregate value of benefits provided to the sponsor does not exceed 2 percent of the sponsorship payment.[439] As a consequence, even though these may be return benefits, they will not result in the sponsorship payment constituting unrelated business income.

When a sponsor receives both an acknowledgement and substantial return benefits, the exempt organization must allocate the payments from the "sponsor" between qualified sponsorship payments and benefits for purposes of determining what portion of the overall payment constitutes unrelated business income.[440] The rule provides that only the fair market value of the payment in excess of the benefits meet the requirements as qualified sponsorship payments.

As noted, these rules were inspired by college football bowl sponsorships, but their scope goes well beyond them. The regulations contain examples involving

---

434. I.R.C. § 513(a)(3); and Rev. Rul. 71-581, 1971-2 C.B. 236.
435. I.R.C. § 513(i); and Rev. Rul. 71-581, 1971-2 C.B. 236.
436. Priv. Ltr. Rul. 91-47-007 (Nov. 30, 1990).
437. Treas. Reg. § 1.513-4(c)(2).
438. Treas. Reg. § 1.513-4(c)(2)(iii).
439. Treas. Reg. §1.513-4(c)(2)(ii).
440. Treas. Reg. § 1.513-4(d).

sponsorship of a walkathon,[441] an art museum exhibit,[442] and a sports tournament.[443] They also illustrate exclusive provider arrangements with an example involving a school that enters into a contract making a soft drink manufacturer the exclusive provider of soft drinks on campus.[444] Not surprising, the regulations also contain an example involving public television station sponsorship.[445] Example 8 addresses sponsorship payments when the sponsor receives complimentary advertising space in a program guide, making it one of the more relevant examples for many organizations. The example requires that the value of the advertising and complimentary tickets be treated as UBIT but excludes the remainder of the sponsorship payment.[446] If you ever want to fully understand how an acknowledgement differs from advertising, just watch your local public television station while reading the regulations. In an ironic twist, the example in the regulations addressing college bowl sponsorship concludes that the sponsorship in question does not produce unrelated business income.[447]

(vi) Exception for Low-Cost Items. Contributions received from donors are not subject to the tax on unrelated business income even though a Section 501(c)(3) organization gives the donors a premium but only if the premium is a "low-cost item."[448] To qualify as *low-cost,* the cost of the item to the charity cannot exceed $8.60 for 2006.[449] For example, the Be-Humane-to-Cats Society sends potential contributors address labels with the contributors' addresses. Each year the label contains an image of a different breed of cat. The cost of the labels is $2.45 per contributor. No portion of any resulting contribution will be subject to UBIT if (1) the contributor did not request the labels, (2) the gift is made without the contributor's express consent, (3) the item is accompanied by a solicitation for a charitable contribution, and (4) a statement is enclosed explaining that the potential contributor can keep the item without making a contribution.

(vii) Exception for Mailing List Rentals. The Internal Revenue Code provides that income received by Section 501(c)(3) organizations from renting donor or membership lists is excludible from UBIT if the list is rented to another Section 501(c)(3) organization.[450] There was some controversy between taxpayers and the IRS over whether the rental of mailing lists to other organizations is a taxable activity. The Tax Court held that the income is royalty income and, as a

441. Treas. Reg. § 1.514-4(f), Example 1.
442. Treas. Reg. § 1.514-4(f), Example 2.
443. Treas. Reg. § 1.514-4(f), Example 3.
444. Treas. Reg. § 1.514-4(f), Example 6.
445. Treas. Reg. § 1.514-4(f), Example 7.
446. Treas. Reg. § 1.514-4(f), Example 8.
447. Treas. Reg. § 1.5413-4(f), Example 4.
448. I.R.C. § 513(h).
449. Rev. Proc. 2005-70, 2005-47 I.R.B. 979.
450. I.R.C. § 513(h)(1)(B).

consequence, is excludible regardless of who leases the lists.[451] Under the resulting law, the treatment turns on whether the organization is performing services (UBIT) or receiving a royalty for the use of intangible property (not UBIT). The IRS now appears to have conceded the core issue with respect to mailing lists and affinity credit cards. However, an organization should expect the IRS to continue to challenge excludability if the organization is in substance providing services rather than renting property.

Consider Citizens for a Pure Environment, a Section 501(c)(3) organization devoted to protecting the environment. It decides to use its membership list to produce additional revenue. It contracts with Lists-for-Rent, a for-profit entity, to market its list. Under the contract, Lists is responsible for maintaining and marketing Citizens' membership list. The only control that Citizens maintains over the list is its right to use the list and to veto its sale to any given entity. The concern is that the list not be sold to an organization that opposes Citizens' views or would be offensive to Citizens' contributors or members (e.g., an Internet pornography site). In all likelihood, Citizens will prevail if it excludes the income from UBIT.[452]

(viii) Exception for Bingo Games. Income received from certain bingo games is not income from an unrelated trade or business. This is a very limited exception.[453] To qualify, each of the following requirements must be satisfied:

- The game must be legal under both state and local law.[454] The fact that a state or local authority does not enforce laws making bingo illegal does not cause the games to be considered to be legal under state law.
- The game must not directly compete with bingo games conducted by commercial entities.[455] This can be a complicated determination but generally means that commercial bingo games are not permitted in the jurisdiction.
- The gaming process (placing bets, determining the winners, and paying prizes) must take place in the presence of all participants.

The IRS defines *bingo* "as a game of chance played with cards that are generally printed with five rows of five squares each. Participants place markers over randomly called numbers on the cards in an attempt to form a pre-selected

451. Disabled American Veterans, 94 T.C. 60 (1990), but this decision was reversed, 942 F.2d 309 (6th Cir. 1991), on procedural grounds.

452. Oregon State University Alumni Association v. Commissioner, 193 F.3d 1098 (9th Cir. 1999); Sierra Club, Inc. v. Commissioner, 86 F.3d 1526 (9th Cir. 1996); Common Cause, 112 T.C. 332 (1999); and Planned Parenthood Federation of America, T.C. Memo 1999-206. All of these cases resulted in taxpayer-favorable decisions.

453. I.R.C. § 513(f).

454. Treas. Reg. § 1.513-5(c)(1).

455. Treas. Reg. § 1.513-5(c)(2)

pattern such as a horizontal, vertical, or diagonal line, or all four corners. The first participant to form the pre-selected pattern wins the game."[456]

The exception does not apply to *pull-tab games,* which the IRS defines as games in which (1) an individual places a wager by purchasing preprinted cards covered with pull tabs, (2) the winner is determined when an individual pulls back the sealed tabs on the front of the card to reveal a pattern that matches the winning pattern preprinted on the back of the card, and (3) winners normally collect their prizes from the pull-tab seller cashier. Instant-Bingo and Mini-Bingo are considered pull-tab games.[457]

Just because gambling income does not qualify for this exception does not mean that it is automatically subject to UBIT. The presumption is in favor of taxation because there is nothing inherently charitable about gaming. Nevertheless, if only volunteers conduct the activity, its income should be exempt under the exception for volunteer labor.[458] If the event is a one-night fundraiser, the organization should be able to take the position that it is not regularly carrying on the activity. The activity might also qualify for the exception if it is a certain qualified entertainment activity, which will be discussed shortly. Finally, certain activities conducted in North Dakota have a special exception.

(ix) Exception for Qualified Convention and Trade Show Activities. Because of the importance of trade shows and conventions, Congress has provided that the conduct of qualified trade show activities does not constitute an unrelated trade or business.[459] To qualify, the trade show must be part of an international, national, state, regional, or local convention, annual meeting, or show conducted by a qualified organization that promotes the industry and its products or educates attendees about new products or laws regulating the industry. As noted earlier, qualifying organizations include charities, social welfare organizations, labor unions, agricultural and horticultural organizations, and trade associations, provided that one of the purposes is to sponsor the convention or trade show activity. Income derived from the rental of exhibition space to exhibitors (including those who supply products to the industry) is exempt income even when sales are made to members of the industry. Consequently, the organization sponsoring an annual convention for heavy equipment manufacturers could exclude fees paid by the following exhibitors: (1) an association member who displayed its latest heavy earth mover, (2) an association member who took orders for its heavy earth mover, and (3) a computer supplier who explains

456. Treas. Reg. § 1.513-5(d).

457. Julius M. Israel Lodge of B'nai B'rith No. 2113, T.C.Memo 1995-439, *aff'd*, 98 F.3d 190 (5th Cir. 1996).

458. Any organization relying on the volunteer exception should make sure that the volunteers do not receive tips. *See* Executive Network Club, Inc., 69 T.C.M 1680 (1995).

459. I.R.C. § 513(d).

how members of the industry can use computers to design equipment and takes orders at the show for computers.[460]

(x) Exception for Qualified Entertainment Activity. Congress has also provided a special exemption for income derived from qualified public entertainment activities conducted in conjunction with an agricultural and education fair or exposition.[461] The focus of this exclusion is on state and local agricultural fairs. By contrast, the typical tax-exempt organization can rely on the intermittent rule described earlier to exclude income from the annual entertainment fundraiser.

(f) SOME COMMON TYPES OF INCOME. Let's consider some common types of income that tax-exempt organizations receive by examining several cases.

(i) Income from Museum Gift Shops and Other Activities.[462] One could be tempted to refer to museum gift shops as "UBIT shops" with tongue in cheek, but these shops actually should be referred to as the "Anything-But-UBIT" shops as the case of American Bauhaus Movement Museum's on-site gift shop aptly demonstrates. The shop sells the following items:

- Reproductions of works in the museum's own collection.
- Reproductions of works in other museum collections (e.g., postcards).
- Metal, wood, and ceramic copies of Bauhaus objects from other museum collections.
- Instructional literature and scientific books and souvenir items concerning the history and development of art.
- Scientific books and souvenir items representing the city in which the museum is located (e.g., sales of red apple trinkets in an art museum located in New York City).

Under the "full fragmentation" rule,[463] the UBIT determination is made on an item-by-item basis. There is a great deal of authority concerning whether sales of particular categories of goods by museum gift shops constitute an unrelated trade or business. Many museums probably come very close to crossing the line but stay on the nontaxable side. With the exception of the scientific books and city souvenir items, none of the items sold by American Bauhaus Movement Museum's gift shop generates taxable income.[464] The IRS has basically said that sales of any art-related items by an art museum are exempt from the UBIT even

460. Treas. Reg. § 1.513-3(d)(1) and (2); and Treas. Reg. § 1.513-3(e), Examples 1 and 3. Some nuisances, particularly with respect to suppliers, should be explored by an organization seeking to avail itself of this exclusion.
461. I.R.C. § 513(d)(2).
462. Internal Revenue Service, *Museum Retailing—UBIT*, IRS Continuing Educ. Pub. (1979).
463. Treas. Reg. § 1.513-1(b).
464. Rev. Rul. 73-105, 1973-1 C.B. 264.

though the merchandise relates to art located in other museums or includes everyday items (e.g., postcards depicting art).[465]

There are some nuances in this area, so museums should consult an attorney or accountant before embarking on an aggressive sales campaign. For example, inexpensive clothing with the museum's logo may not be considered to be a taxable sale, but more expensive clothing might cause the sale to be taxable. If the museum is selling furniture that does not relate to its collection or displays, its sale may be taxable if the furniture is considered "utilitarian."

Museums also derive revenues from certain common activities. Specifically, fees from parking and museum restaurants are not considered to be taxable so long as the services are provided for the convenience of the museum patrons.[466] However, if a museum were to provide monthly parking for office workers in the museum's vicinity, those revenues would be taxable. Museums have also become active in *renting* space for corporate meetings, social celebrations, and community events. It is difficult to enunciate a general rule as to taxability of the income because the following issues can come into play: (1) Is a significant level of services provided?[467] (2) Is the activity substantially related to the museum's exempt function? (3) Does the museum regularly engage in this type of activity? (4) Is the facility debt financed? The IRS has taken the position in at least one case that rentals of museum facilities are subject to UBIT,[468] but the Tax Court in another case concluded that some aspects of the rental activity were subject to UBIT but some were not.[469]

(ii) Income from Travel Tours. Anyone who is a college graduate or a member of a professional association has received literature for travel tours to exotic lands. These tours are big fundraisers for their organizations, raising the obvious question concerning whether the income is unrelated business income. To illustrate the issues surrounding this question, consider Big U, a large university offering undergraduate and graduate degrees in a wide variety of fields. Each year Big U and various alumni associations sponsor a number of tours. Some of these tours are for college credit and attract mostly students. Others are for pleasure but have a very small educational component. Still others are directed at alumni and are not for college credit but are led by Big U professors. The professors conduct lectures that relate to the tour's attractions. In some cases, Big U or the alumni association organizes and operates the tour. In other cases, they contract with third-party operators.

The IRS has issued regulations in an effort to bring some consistency to the treatment of travel tours sponsored by tax-exempt institutions.[470] The issue is

465. Rev. Rul. 73-104, 1973-1 C.B. 263.
466. Rev. Rul. 74-399, 1974-2 C.B. 172.
467. Treas. Reg. § 1.512(b)-1(c)(5).
468. Tech. Adv. Mem. 97-02-003 (Aug. 28, 1996).
469. John W. Madden, Jr., T.C. Memo. 1997-395.
470. Treas. Reg. § 1.513-7.

whether the tour is sufficiently related to the organization's exempt purposes to be exempt from UBIT. Under these regulations and prior guidance, there is no absolute rule with respect to alumni association or educational institutions.

In one example in the regulations, an alumni association offers regular travel tours to its members.[471] Although a faculty member of the university is invited on the trip, the person offers no scheduled instruction. Consequently, the regulation concludes that the tour income was subject to UBIT.[472] On the other hand, if the alumni association can demonstrate that the tour is substantially related to its exempt functions (in all likelihood, meaning a significant educational aspect), the income should not be subject to tax.

In a second example in the regulations, the organization offers travel tour programs to students and other interested parties.[473] Those taking the tour receive academic credit for their efforts. In exchange for that credit, the participants are required to attend five to six hours of organized study per day and to prepare reports and engage in discussion. Given the heavy emphasis on education, the regulation concludes that the income from these tours is not subject to UBIT.

These issues also apply to museums that sponsor art tours and organizations that sponsor pilgrimages and retreats. Each case must be considered on its own merits.

(iii) Income from Insurance Activities. Congress has established special rules that pertain to Section 501(c)(3) and (c)(4) organizations that provide commercial-type insurance.[474] Basically, these rules provide that this activity is an unrelated trade or business and that it cannot constitute a substantial part of the organization's activities. There are exceptions for insurance provided to further the organization's charitable mission (e.g., subsidies for low-income individuals), certain property and casualty insurance provided by a church or convention of churches, and charitable gift annuities. Although the provision of insurance by (c)(3)s and (c)(4)s is an unrelated trade or business, these organizations are taxed on this income under the provisions of the tax law that apply to insurance companies.

The tax law contemplates that certain other types of tax-exempt organizations will provide insurance-related products to their members. For example, veterans' organizations described in Section 501(c)(19) will not be taxed on their income from certain insurance activities benefiting their members.[475] An organization that acts as a group insurance policyholder for its members and collects a fee for performing administrative services is normally carrying on an unrelated trade or

471. Treas. Reg. § 1.513-7(b), Example 1.
472. Rev. Rul. 78-43, 1978-1 C.B. 164, for another, more detailed example.
473. Treas. Reg. § 1.513-7(b), Example 2.
474. I.R.C. § 501(m)(1).
475. I.R.C. § 512(a)(4).

business. Organizations such as fraternal beneficiary societies, voluntary employee beneficiary associations, and labor organizations whose exempt activities may include the provision of insurance benefits are generally excepted from this rule, however.[476]

Insurance activities are a highly specialized area. Any organization contemplating providing insurance or insurance services should consult with legal counsel before doing so, particularly because state insurance laws can be an issue. To the extent the organization is relying on a third-party program to provide these services, it should be able to obtain basic tax information from the program sponsor and trade associations.

(iv) Income from Partnerships. An organization that holds an interest in a partnership may have unrelated trade or business income from the partnership's activities if those activities would produce unrelated trade or business income if the organization conducted them directly.[477] This is true regardless of whether the organization is a general or limited partner. Persons responsible for acquiring the interest in the partnership on behalf of the organization must be particularly careful in ensuring that the partnership either receives a cash distribution from the partnership or has sufficient cash to pay any taxes attributable to the portion of the partnership's income that the organization must treat as unrelated trade or business income. This is necessary because under the tax regulations applicable to partnerships and partners, taxation of partnership income and distribution of that income are separate events.

If a Section 501(c)(3) organization owns an interest in a limited liability company (LLC), the following apply. If the organization is the single member, the LLC is generally "disregarded" for tax purposes, and its income will be viewed as being earned directly by the member.[478] If the LLC has more than one member, one of two possible regimes applies. If the LLC is treated for tax purposes as a partnership, the rules in the previous paragraph apply. If instead the LLC elects to be treated as a corporation and all of the LLC's members are Section 501(c)(3) organizations, the LLC itself may apply for recognition of tax exemption under Section 501(c)(3).[479] Because the use of LLCs by exempt organizations is a recent phenomenon, professional counsel is essential.

(v) Income from Online Activities. Internet-related activities certainly have UBIT implications. Consider the Medical Education Foundation (MEF), an exempt organization that educates the public about health and medical matters. To further

476. Internal Revenue Service, Publication 598, Tax on Unrelated Business Income of Tax-Exempt Organizations, at 5 (Mar. 2005).
477. I.R.C. § 512(c).
478. Ann. 99-102, 1999-43 I.R.B. 545.
479. See R. McCray and W. Thomas, *Limited Liability Companies as Exempt Organizations*, IRS Continuing Educ. Pub. (2001), setting out 12 conditions that must be satisfied.

its objectives, MEF has created an elaborate Web site with thousands of articles on health and medical matters.

To raise revenue, MEF registers as an Amazon.com associate. It lists a number of books on its own Web site that pertain to health and medical matters. Each listing includes a hypertext link to Amazon.com's Web site. If a user purchases a book listed on MEF's Web site by following the link to Amazon.com's site, Amazon.com pays MEF a commission. Last year, MEF earned $200,000 in such commissions.

This is currently uncharted territory, but the IRS promised guidance sometime during 2005. The $200,000 revenue could be viewed as advertising revenue, subject to the tax on unrelated business income. In commenting on the subject, one IRS official has suggested characterization as advertising revenue.[480]

MEF, however, could make a very good argument that the revenue is substantially related to its exempt function if the organization is viewed as a retailer and Amazon.com as its wholesaler. MEF is performing an editorial function, much like a specialty bookstore. It selects books related to its exempt purpose and provides a description of the book to its constituency. This is more than just advertising for Amazon.com. If MEF were to open a "bricks and mortar" bookstore to sell health-related books, no one would argue that the resulting income is subject to taxation as unrelated business income. Is this so different?

It is worth noting that the IRS has issued guidance on revenue derived from on-line activities ancillary to qualified trade show activities.[481]

(g) DEDUCTIONS IN COMPUTING UNRELATED BUSINESS TAXABLE INCOME. As previously noted, a tax is computed on unrelated business taxable income. Not surprising, taxpayers may deduct certain expenses in computing unrelated business taxable income.[482] To be deductible, the expenses must be directly connected with producing the unrelated income. To be directly connected with the conduct of an unrelated business, deductions must have a proximate and primary relationship to carrying on that business. When a dual use of facilities and personnel by exempt and taxable functions exists, the organization must make reasonable allocations of the related expenses between the activities.[483] These computations and the related issues can become very complicated and, therefore, should be discussed by each organization with its accounting staff and outside advisor.

We previously considered the issue of advertising when discussing the basic concepts. For that reason, note that some special and detailed rules apply to deductibility of expenses associated with taxable advertising revenue, but these rules are beyond the scope of this *Guide*.[484]

---

480. The Internal Revenue Service recognized this as an issue when it issued IRS Announcement 2000-84, 42 I.R.B. 385, requesting comments regarding this and other issues.
481. Rev. Rul. 2004-112, 2004-51 I.R.B.
482. Treas. Reg. § 1.512(a)-1(a).
483. Treas. Reg. § 1.512(a)-1(c).
484. Treas. Reg. § 1.512(a)-1(f).

For an organization engaged in an unrelated trade or business, the crucial point is the importance of documenting and retaining records to support the organization's deductions and allocations. Moreover, even if the organization claims that it has no unrelated business income, it should maintain adequate records, particularly with respect to activities that could be reclassified as unrelated businesses.

(h) A WORKABLE APPROACH TO UBIT. At this point, you should be ready to throw your hands up in despair. That is reasonable given the conditions, exceptions, and myriad definitions that permeate this area. It is difficult to rationalize the area with any coherent theory. The only thing that can be said with certainty is that exempt organizations keep coming up with creative and successful arguments for avoiding the tax. With that in mind, if your organization has income that is not clearly related to its exempt function, it should take the following steps to assess whether that income is taxable:

- Begin by considering the three basic conditions that must be satisfied before income is taxable: (1) trade or business, (2) regularly carried on, and (3) unrelated to exempt purpose.
- If your organization has a question, someone else has likely encountered the same question. Call the relevant trade association and see whether your industry has faced the problem and how the majority in the industry handles the problem.
- If you do decide to undertake legal research, begin by looking for similar factual situations and then worry about the technical definitions and exceptions. Thus, if you are reviewing a treatise on UBIT, look at the index and see whether there is a section devoted to credit card affinity programs, advertising, gift shops, or Internet sales.
- If the index proves unhelpful, look for exceptions. Typically, statutory exceptions come about when a particular industry that is subject to tax on a particular type of income is able to convince Congress that an exception is warranted.
- In any event, if the amount of income involved is material, your organization should discuss the matter with its tax counsel or CPA. As should be apparent, changing one or two minor facts can make a difference. Consequently, obtaining the advice of someone who regularly structures arrangements to achieve favorable tax results can be well worth the expense. In fact, a good case could be made that this should be the first step in the process, with a tax professional undertaking the remaining steps.
- If the organization decides to take an aggressive, but legitimate, position that certain revenue is not subject to UBIT, it should make sure that it has sufficient resources set aside so that if the IRS should prevail, it can pay the resulting taxes on a timely basis.

Given all the exceptions-within-exceptions and nuances, every organization should examine each source of revenue to determine which is taxable and which is exempt. Keep in mind that the slightest variation in facts can be the deciding element. If you want to obtain a better sense of just how situational the law can be, take time to review IRS Publication 598, "Tax on Unrelated Business Income of Exempt Organizations."

6.11 REPORTING REQUIREMENTS

Tax-exempt organizations must provide the IRS certain information on a regular basis. Our focus is the annual information return. When applicable, however, all organizations must file employment tax, unrelated business income tax, and political activity returns, among others. Tax-exempt organizations also must comply with state tax reporting requirements.

(a) INFORMATION RETURNS—THE FORM 990 SERIES. Although tax-exempt organizations *generally* do not pay taxes, they must file information returns with the IRS annually. The basic return is Form 990. Smaller organizations are permitted to file a shorter version, Form 990-EZ, if they meet both of the following requirements:

- Gross receipts during the year are less than $100,000.
- Total assets at the end of the year are less than $250,000.

Private foundations are required to file Form 990-PF. This form resembles Form 990, but it also requires the organization to make disclosures that will permit the IRS to determine whether any of the private foundation excise taxes are applicable.

Certain organizations are exempt from the basic filing requirements. Probably the most important of these exemptions is the one for exempt organizations (other than a private foundation) with gross receipts in each tax year that normally do not exceed $25,000. This exemption is most useful to the small organization that is not well counseled and, as a consequence, is unaware of the filing requirements. The local garden club is a good example. Any organization that qualifies for this exemption should at least consider filing an information return because it starts the statute of limitations running for the year in question. This may seem like a "technical" reason for filing, but it means that if the organization has overlooked an issue, the IRS will be barred from raising the issue for the year in question after a specified period of time (generally after three years). The law specifically excuses churches, their integrated auxiliaries, and conventions or associations of churches from filing returns.[485]

---

485. I.R.C. § 6033(a)(2).

(i) IRS Form 990 Content. If you have not reviewed Form 990, you should. Somewhat surprising, it is longer and requests more detailed information than the Form 1040 with which most taxpayers are all too familiar. Specifically, Form 990 requires the organization to provide the following information to the IRS:

- A complete accounting of its revenue, expenses, and changes in net asset or fund balances.
- A complete accounting of its functional expenses (those that further its exempt purpose).
- A detailed balance sheet.
- A list of officers, directors, trustees, and key employees and information regarding their compensation.
- Responses to questions asking whether the organization has unrelated business income, has engaged in political activities, is affiliated with certain other entities, or has engaged in other activities that the IRS polices.
- An analysis of the organization's revenues for purposes of ascertaining whether the unrelated business income tax is applicable.

(ii) Preparation of IRS Form 990. An accountant asked to serve on a board for his accounting expertise should be careful about "getting roped into" preparing the Form 990 unless he is already knowledgeable about exempt organizations and Form 990. Preparation of Form 990 is not a "Sunday Afternoon in Front of the TV" venture. In fact, the form asks many Yes/No questions about suspect activity. These questions often are phrased using references to Internal Revenue Code sections, so it is not clear to the untrained person what the question is driving at. Placing responsibility for answering these questions in the hands of someone who is not willing to take the time to interpret the question could have disastrous consequences. This is particularly true in the case of Form 990-PF, the return prepared by private foundations. In short, every organization should retain an experienced accountant or lawyer to prepare Form 990.[486]

WATCH OUT FOR QUESTION 89B

* * *

The IRS is now closely examining the compensation of high-ranking nonprofit officers and employees, looking for instances of excessive levels of compensation and abusive arrangements. Form 990 is one of the IRS's primary tools in this effort.

---

486. Even this may not be sufficient. See. M. Fremont-Smith, GOVERNING NONPROFIT ORGANIZATIONS: FEDERAL AND STATE LAW REGULATION (Belknap Press 2004), indicating that there appears to be a higherror rate even in returns prepared by CPAs.

Question 89b of Form 990 asks whether the organization has engaged in any excess benefit transactions during the year. As the name implies, an *excess benefit transaction* is one in which an insider received more than fair consideration for services or other consideration.

One IRS official indicated that several thousand organizations ignore Question 89b each year, leaving the Yes/No space blank. It is not surprising that this official indicated that the IRS no longer tolerates this noncompliance in view of its focus on excess compensation.

The IRS is also developing special audit tools and measures to apply to the information reported on Form 990. They will examine the relationship between compensation and other reported information. The IRS will also be looking at loans and payments to related parties or affiliates.

* * *

Any organization that has the good fortune to have both knowledgeable lawyers and accountants working for it (either on staff or as outside professionals) should make sure that both groups of professionals review the Form 990 before it is filed. The lawyers and the accountants bring different skills and insights to its preparation.

(iii) Filing IRS Form 990. Form 990 must be filed on or before the 15th day of the fifth month following the close of the organization's taxable year. Organizations with a calendar year tax year must file Form 990 on or before May 15. The organization can obtain an extension of time for filing, including an automatic three-month extension (but the organization must file Form 8868 to obtain an automatic extension). This filing date is designed to provide relief to accountants affected by the annual April 15 crush from their clients who file as individuals.

(iv) Review by the Board. At least one member of the board of directors, if not the entire board, should review the organization's Form 990 before it is filed with the IRS. Because of its importance, Form 990 is filed under penalties of perjury, so the officers who prepare and sign it are likely to provide a "less rosy" assessment of the organization's position than they present at board meetings. (This is not meant as a criticism of nonprofit officers and staff but as a realistic assessment of human nature.) The Form 990 is likely to provide an early indication of organizational financial troubles or activities that, if ignored, could cost the organization its exempt status. Moreover, as described next, the board should appreciate the fact that Form 990 is now the public face of the organization, particularly because GuideStar makes these returns availible on the Internet.

(v) Disclosure Now Required. Since 1987, each tax-exempt organization has been required to make its Forms 990s available for inspection at its office (and regional offices that have three or more employees).[487] To comply, the organization

487. I.R.C. § 6104(d)(1)(A).

must permit the requesting party to take notes while inspecting the return. In 1996, Congress expanded the disclosure requirements, mandating that exempt organizations provide a copy of their Forms 990 for the three previous years and their exemption application to anyone who requests them.[488] Disclosure of Form 990-T is not required. Each organization is entitled to be reimbursed for its costs from the requester.

An exempt organization is not required to furnish copies of the required information if that information is widely available.[489] The rule defining *widely available* focuses exclusively on the posting of documents on the Internet.[490] To satisfy this requirement, the posting must satisfy each of the following requirements:

- The information must be available on the Internet as part of a Web page (suggesting that access through a bulletin board or FTP does not satisfy the requirement).
- The documents, when viewed and printed, must exactly reproduce their images. In other words, the information cannot be reformatted (but information not required to be disclosed can be withheld). Given this requirement, most organizations taking advantage of Internet disclosure will in all likelihood utilize the Adobe Acrobat PDF file format, particularly because the IRS has sanctioned its use.[491]
- The organization has the option to post the documents on its own Web site or as part of a database of similar documents of other tax-exempt organizations maintained by another organization on the Web.

Note: The 2003 IRS CPE publication *Disclosure, FOIA, and the Privacy Act*[492] specifically states that simply providing GuideStar's Web site address does not make the documents widely available because of GuideStar's redaction of the signature lines.

Not all tax-exempt entities engage in activities or hold views that are widely accepted or supported, posing concerns that the mandatory disclosure requirements open them to harassment. The disclosure rules provide procedures that organizations can follow if they believe requests for documents are part of a harassment campaign.[493] Under these procedures, the organization can suspend compliance with the rules by filing an application for determination with the designated IRS official within ten business days of suspending compliance. Responsible organizations need to be careful about asserting that there is a harassment campaign against them because they can be penalized if in fact there is not such a campaign but they nevertheless suspended compliance. The easiest way to

488. I.R.C. § 6104(d)(1)(B).
489. I.R.C. § 6104(d)(4).
490. Treas. Reg. § 301.6104(d)-2.
491. Ann. 99-62, 1999-25 I.R.B. 13.
492. S. Paul and B. Brockner, *Disclosure, FOIA and the Privacy Act*, IRS Continuing Educ. Pub. (2003).
493. Treas. Reg. § 301.6104(d)-3.

eliminate the whole harassment issue is for the organization to post its application for recognition and its annual information returns on the Internet in a manner that satisfies the widely available requirement.

Obviously, certain information included on the returns and application is sensitive. The regulations make allowance for this by permitting organizations to redact certain information, including contributor names and addresses,[494] when making disclosure, but the organization cannot avoid making the required disclosures regarding compensation. Whoever is in charge of making the information available to the public should be aware of the redaction rules. Quite a few stories are circulating about organizations that disclosed donor information because someone did not know what could be redacted or just pulled the copy from the file and copied it.

(vi) The Implications Flowing from Disclosure. The new disclosure requirements have serious implications for tax-exempt organizations. As just noted, some of the information included in Form 990 is sensitive. In many cases, organizations would probably prefer that certain information not be known by employees, donors, or other stakeholders. A good example is the compensation paid to the organization's five highest paid employees. However, prospective donors and employees will have access to this information, so organizations should consider the fundraising implications and employee morale issues associated with disclosure of this information. This is one more reason the board should review Form 990.

Instead of just posting their "raw" documents, organizations that make Internet disclosure should also consider posting information in a summary form that emphasizes the facts in a light that is most favorable. In doing so, they can take advantage of the public's interest in Form 990 to market themselves to potential donors. Moreover, organizations should consider adding schedules that provide more detailed breakdowns as either part of the Form 990 or as supplementary material. For example, Form 990 requires a reconciliation between the organization's tax and its financial statement balance sheets, with a breakdown between restricted and unrestricted assets. Regrettably, the form does not require a detailed analysis of assets within the restricted assets category. Consequently, someone relying on Form 990 will be in a better position to draw fair conclusions if a supplemental schedule clarifies what assets are restricted (e.g., land or accounts receivable).

Form 990 asks the organization to split its basic revenue into various categories, including direct public support, indirect public support, and government contributions. The person completing Form 990 should not guess what items are included in each category but should first read the instructions to Form 990 and then attempt to ascertain whether similar organizations have developed reporting

---

494. Treas. Reg. § 301.6104(b)-1(b).

practices. This extra effort could prevent your organization's numbers from appearing out of line when someone undertakes a comparative financial analysis.

Along these same lines, the organization should not adhere strictly to the labels it places on a revenue stream. Membership dues may constitute direct public support (line 1a) if they are only for benefits of nominal value, they may be for membership benefits having more than a nominal value (line 3), or some combination of the two. Again, providing a detailed schedule can eliminate confusion and save the organization from a "best-efforts" independent analysis by a newspaper reporter who can only guess whether amounts that should be split between two categories have been inappropriately lumped together.

(b) OTHER REPORTING REQUIREMENTS. Although the basic tax-exempt information is the main focus here, tax-exempt organizations must file other returns. An organization may be required to file the following federal tax returns, among others:

- Form 990-T if the organization has unrelated business income (gross income in excess of $1,000 from unrelated businesses). If the organization expects its tax for the year to be $500 or more, it must also make quarterly estimated tax payments.
- Employment tax returns if the organization pays wages to employees.
- Form 1120-POL if the organization expends any amount to influence the selection, nomination, election, or appointment of any individual to any federal, state, or local public office or office in a political organization or the election of presidential and vice presidential electors (whether or not those individuals or electors are selected, nominated, elected, or appointed) and your organization has political organization taxable income.
- Form 8282 if the organization receives a contribution of property and sells, exchanges, or otherwise disposes of the property within two years after its receipt. However, this is not required if the property is valued at $500 or less or is distributed for charitable purposes.

6.12 REPORTING AND WITHHOLDING FOR GAMBLING ACTIVITIES

Gambling activities can trigger rather involved reporting and withholding requirements. IRS Publication 3079[495] details these rule.

(a) REPORTING REQUIREMENTS. Organizations must complete Form W-2G when someone wins certain specified amounts from a wager. Copy A of the form must be submitted to the IRS by February 28 of the following year. Copies B and

495. Internal Revenue Service, Publication 3079, Gaming Publications for Tax-Exempt Organizations (Apr. 1998).

C must be given to the prize winner. As a general rule, gambling winnings are reportable if the amount paid reduced, at the option of the payer, by the wager is (1) $600 or more and (2) at least 300 times the amount of the wager. In the case of bingo winnings, an organization must complete a Form W-2G for each bingo winner who wins $1,200 or more (calculated without reduction for the wager).[496] Different thresholds apply to instant bingo, pull-tab,[497] and keno games.

The organization must also file Form 1096, Annual Summary and Transmittal of U.S. Information Returns. Form 5754 must be filed when winnings are paid to the members of a group of winners or someone who is not the actual winner.

(b) WITHHOLDING REQUIREMENTS. As a general rule, an organization must withhold at the rate of 25 percent if the winnings are more than $5,000 and are from (1) sweepstakes, (2) wagering pools, (3) lotteries, or (4) other wagering transactions if the winnings are at least 300 times the amount wagered.[498] No withholding is required in the case of bingo, keno, or slot machine winnings.[499] Regular gambling withholding applies to the total amount of the gross proceeds (the amount of the winnings reduced by the amount wagered),[500] not merely the amount in excess of $5,000.[501] A noncash payment (e.g., an automobile) must be valued at fair market value for both reporting and withholding purposes.[502] If the winner pays the withholding tax to the payer, the withholding amount is equal to 25 percent of the fair market value of the noncash payment after reduction for the amount wagered. If the payer pays the withholding tax, the withholding amount is equal to 33.33 percent of the fair market value of the noncash payment after subtracting the amount wagered. Special withholding forms are required if the winner is a nonresident alien.

(c) BACKUP WITHHOLDING REQUIREMENTS. An organization may be required to withhold 28 percent of gambling winnings (including those from bingo, keno, and slot machines) for federal income tax. This is referred to as *backup withholding,* which applies to the total amount of the wager reduced, at the option of the payer, by the amount of the wager. An organization must backup withhold if (1) the winner does not furnish a correct taxpayer identification number and (2) 25 percent has not been withheld or the winnings are from bingo, keno, or slot machines. If the organization is not required to report the winnings on a form W2-G, it is not required to backup withhold.[503] Both the withholding and backup withholding rates should be reviewed annually.

---

496. *Id.* at 12. *See* Treas. Reg. § 7.6041-1(a).
497. These games are not considered to be bingo. *See* Julius Israel, *supra* note 457.
498. I.R.C. § 3402(q)(3)(A). The withholding rate is equal to the third lowest tax rate under Section 1(c).
499. I.R.C. § 3402(q)(5).
500. I.R.C. § 3402(q)(4)(A).
501. 2005 Instructions for Form W-2G.
502. I.R.C. § 3402(q)(4)(B).
503. 2005 Instructions, *supra* note 501; and I.R.C. § 3406(a)(1).

(d) PROTECTING THE ORGANIZATION IN THE CASE OF NONCASH PAYMENTS. As noted, if an organization raffles a car, vacation, or other big-ticket item, it must withhold and backup withhold a certain percent if the value of the prize exceeds specified amounts. An organization that fails to withhold is liable for the amount that was subject to withholding or backup withholding. Consequently, organizations awarding noncash prizes should take the following steps:

- Add language to all publicity and tickets for the event clearly stating that the prizes are subject to withholding and that the winner will be required to make a cash payment to the organization.
- Condition winning on the payment of the amount required to be withheld.
- Prohibit the transfer of any noncash winnings until the winner has paid the required withholding.

(e) EXCISE TAXES TRIGGERED BY WAGERING. Section 4401 of the Internal Revenue Code imposes an excise tax on persons in the business of accepting wagers. It also imposes an occupational tax on each person who is liable for the Section 4401 excise tax on wagering. This tax is part of a registration process. The workings of Sections 4401 and 4411 are largely beyond the scope of this *Guide*. However, bingo,[504] card games, dice games, or roulette[505] do not trigger these taxes, but lotteries, which include raffles, do.[506] Section 4401 taxes do not apply, however, to the extent that the lottery is conducted by an organization exempt from taxes under Sections 501 or 521 but *only* if no part of the net proceeds from the lottery inure to the benefit of any private shareholder or individual.[507]

The regulations provide that drawing or lottery proceeds used for general operating expenses of an organization constitute inurement to its members.[508] Although it is not entirely clear, the exclusion for lotteries apparently applies to those conducted by Section 501(c)(3) organizations, but the "general operating expense" language in the prior sentence could subject lottery wagers to tax if they are members in organizations such as fraternal organizations, social clubs, and trade associations. To the extent that the proceeds go to the general operating fund in the case of non-Section 501(c)(3) organizations, the proceeds reduce future membership dues, creating inurement.[509] Those organizations conducting wagering activities not clearly excluded from these taxes should contact the IRS for clarification or seek appropriate legal counsel.

---

504. Treas. Reg. § 44.4421-1(b)(2).
505. *Id.*
506. Internal Revenue Service, *supra* note 495, at 21.
507. Treas. Reg. § 44.4421-1(b)(2)(ii).
508. Internal Revenue Service, *supra* note 495, at 21; and Treas. Reg. § 44.4421-(b)(4).
509. *Id.*, at 21, Example 21.

6.13 TERRORISM AND THE NONPROFIT SECTOR

In response to the September 11, 2001 terrorist attack on the United States, President George W. Bush issued Executive Order 13224 (September 21, 2001) that, among other things, prohibits every citizen of the United States from making or receiving any contribution of funds, goods, or services to or for the benefit of those persons listed on the Annex to the order. The Annex includes a long list of terrorist organizations.

Although all Americans, including charitable organizations, want to do everything possible to fight terrorists, Executive Order 13224 has presented problems for some United States charities. This order probably doesn't pose much of a problem for a charity that is running a foodbank in a United States city or providing literacy training in the United States, but even these charities must be vigilant, because there have been instances of terrorists infiltrating United States-based charities and grantees.

Executive Order 13224 should be of paramount concern to United States colleges and universities that give scholarships to foreign students and United States charities that operate overseas by offering medical assistance to earthquake victims, food to rural tribes of people, or agricultural training to residents of remote villages. Such charities do not always know where the money, goods, or services that they provide go, particularly when the charities work through an intermediary such as a village chief. A number of nonprofit organizations have asked how they can continue to provide such humanitarian services and benefits without running afoul of the otherwise understandable prohibitions in Executive Order 13224. These concerns are particularly germane given the fact that violation of Executive Order 13224 can result in criminal prosecution.

In response to these concerns, the United States Treasury issued "Voluntary Best Practices for United States-Based Charities" in November 2002. On December 5, 2005 the United States Treasury revised that document with a much more detailed set of best practices.[510] The first half of the revision focuses on governance. The second half focuses more specifically on financial controls designed to prevent the charity's assets from falling into the hands of terrorists. As of this writing, a great deal of uncertainty exists regarding the exact meaning and significance of these and other suggested best practices. Nevertheless, organizations that could be taken advantage of by terrorist organizations should actively address the terrorism issue.

510. Press Release, United States Treasury, Treasury Seeks Comment on Updated Guidelines to Help Protect Charitable Giving from Illicit Abuse (Dec. 5, 2005).

THE 2004 TSUNAMIS AND TERRORISM

* * *

Everyone remembers the pictures of the complete devastation in Banda Aceh, Indonesia, Sri Lanka, and other locales in South Asia following the December 26, 2004, earthquake and subsequent tsunamis. United States relief organizations were primarily concerned with providing humanitarian relief as quickly as possible, but they also needed to worry about complying with Executive Order 13224[511] when they provided relief through local organizations? The *Wall Street Journal* reported that the United States Treasury Department's Office of Terrorism and Financial Intelligence "is closely watching tsunami-relief organizations"[512] because of legitimate concern regarding terrorism.

Sri Lanka expatriates coordinated relief efforts for portions of Sri Lanka under control of the Tamil Tigers through the Tamils Rehabilitation Organization, a group with offices in 14 countries including the United States, according to the *Wall Street Journal*.[513] The Tigers are listed as a terrorist organization in Executive Order 13224. Tamils Rehabilitation claimed that it was independent of the Tamil Tigers, but it risked trouble with the United States government if its money or materials found their way into the hands of the Tamil Tigers. This posed a difficult problem for this organization, given the fact that the Tamil Tigers controlled territory where the aid was being directed. One person affiliated with the organization was quoted by the *Journal* as saying, "We simply do not have time to debate at this time. There are too many lives at stake."[514]

To put the question of terrorism in sharper perspective, consider the following report that was posted on the Sri Lankan army's Web site:

> Situation Report as at UTC 0730 (1330) 07 February 2005
>
> [Web updated at UTC 0851 on 07 February 2005]
>
> COLOMBO. TRO gets steel balls as tsunami relief items. A consignment of seventy-six metal pots, earmarked for Tamil Rehabilitation Organization (TRO), said to have been engaged in relief work in un-cleared areas of the north & east, has contained a stock of stainless steel balls (bicycle balls) hidden inside.
>
> COLOMBO port authorities with naval troops on 05 February 2005 during their routine custom checks on relief items sent for tsunami victims had come across a consignment of 148 metal pots made of steel and copper, earmarked for TRO which were unusually weighty. However, authorities on suspicion opened one of the metal pots from a point close to its neck and recovered a total of 150 steel balls that could be used for production of bombs or explosives.
>
> The stock, addressed to the consignee, Mr. RAMANADAN, Tamil Rehabilitation Organization (TRO) of No 410 – 112, Bauddhaloka Mawatha, Colombo 07, has been retained at the port warehouse for further investigations after detection of those hidden steel balls. Those pots were believed to have been shipped from a port in United Kingdom.

---

511. Executive Order No. 13224, *Executive Order on Terrorist Financing*, 66 Fed. Reg. 49,079 (Sept. 25, 2001).
512. J. Hookway and J. Solomon, *Fragile State in Sri Lanka, Aid to Tamils Deepens Political Tensions: Officials Worry Expats' Efforts May Spark Rebels' Resolve and Test Tenuous Truce*, WALL STREET J., Jan. 11, 2005.
513. *Id.*
514. *Id.*

Further investigations are on.[515]

In a February 7, 2005, article, the *Scotsman* reported that the British government had distanced itself from this report and that a number of international relief agencies claimed to have no knowledge of it.[516] Was the Sri Lankan army report factual or propaganda? That question will inevitably come up when two sides are engaged in a battle and charities try to provide humanitarian relief. That is the reason that Executive Order 13224 poses particular issues for relief organizations working in countries with large Muslim populations such as Indonesia, particularly when these organizations partner with local NGOs.

* * *

During the last several years, a number of grant makers have added language to their grant contracts requiring grantees to take efforts to prevent grant money from finding its way into the hands of terrorists. The Charles Stewart Mott Foundation requires grantees who re-grant funds "to check the terrorism watch lists issued by the United States government, the European Union, and the United Nations, and to refrain from providing financial or material support to any listed individual or organizations."[517] The Mott Foundation's Web site contains a discussion of these requirements, as well as forms. The Ford Foundation now requires grantees to agree that "By countersigning this grant letter, you agree that your organization will not promote or engage in violence, terrorism, bigotry or the destruction of any state, nor will it make sub-grants to any entity that engages in these activities."[518] The Combined Federal Campaign has also imposed a certification requirement before a charity can participate in the federal government's workplace fundraising campaign.[519] Other grant makers have also responded to the grant-making community's struggle to arrive at workable solutions. This is a fast-moving area, but those who ignore these issues risk losing their tax-exempt status, having their assets frozen, and possibly facing criminal prosecution.

---

515. The press release was last viewed on April 5, 2005, at http://www.army.lk/Sitrep/2005/02/07_0730.htm

516. C. Gammell, *Bomb Equipment Found Inside Tsunami Aid Supplies*, SCOTSMAN, Feb. 7, 2005.

517. http://toolbox.mott.org/patriotact.asp (June 12, 2005).

518. FORD FOUNDATION, MEMORANDUM FROM THE FORD FOUNDATION TO GRANTEES (Jan. 8, 2004), *available at* http://fordfound.org.

519. G. Williams, *Government Overhauls Antiterrorism Rule for Charities in Federal Drive*, CHRON. OF PHILAN., Nov. 24, 2005. The government's original approach required that employee names be checked against two lists. That proved highly controversial, resulting in a lawsuit by the American Civil Liberties Union and 12 other nonprofit organizations.

An area of the Council of Foundations' Web site is devoted to these issues. All organizations would be wise to check it on a regular basis[520] and monitor the United States Treasury's Web site. Any organization that has any inkling that it may be dealing with terrorists is well advised to seek legal counsel immediately. Organizations making international grants should retain qualified counsel for ongoing advice and consultation.

---

520. Of particular note are the following two publications: EDGARDO RAMOS, TIMOTHY LYMAN, PATRICIA CANAVAN, AND CLIFFORD NICHOLS III, HANDBOOK ON COUNTER-TERRORISM MEASURES: WHAT U.S. NON-PROFITS AND GRANT MAKERS NEED TO KNOW (Day, Berry & Howard 2004); and JANNE GALLAGHER, LEGAL DIMENSIONS OF INTERNATIONAL GRANTMAKING: GRANTMAKING IN AN AGE OF TERRORISM: SOME THOUGHTS ABOUTCOMPLIANCE STRATEGIES (Council on Foundations 2004). These publications are *available at* http://www.cof.org. See also, M. Schniederman, *Seeking a Safe Harbor*, FOUNDATION NEWS & COMMENTARY (May/June 2004).

CHAPTER 7

TAX ASPECTS OF CHARITABLE GIVING

Anyway they already expect you just to give a check to tax-deductible charity organizations.

BOB DYLAN[1]

When you help others, You can't help helping yourself!

AVENUE Q[2]

---

1. *Ballad of a Thin Man*, *on* HIGHWAY 61 REVISITED (Columbia 1965).
2. *The Money Song*, *on* AVENUE Q (2003 ORIGINAL BROADWAY CAST) (RCA 2003).

Chapter 6 considered the tax aspects of organizing and operating a tax-exempt organization. Let's now move from the entity to the donor level, primarily considering the tax benefits that donors receive when they make charitable contributions to qualified charitable organizations.

This topic should be of interest to you both as a potential donor and as a director or officer. The deduction for charitable contributions certainly reduces the cost of giving by reducing the donor's tax liability. Everyone has a self-interest in understanding these rules, but as a director or officer, you should also consider how the rules can be used to maximize the funds generated from donors.

7.1 DEDUCTION BASICS

Contributions to Section 501(c)(3) organizations are deductible for federal income tax purposes as charitable contributions. We would all like to believe that donors are motivated by the good that these organizations do. That is often the case, but the tax deduction can also be a significant motivating factor.

The charitable contribution deduction is available only as an itemized deduction, meaning that taxpayers who claim the standard deduction gain no tax benefit from having made a charitable contribution.[3] Taxpayers who do itemize their deductions may not receive the full benefit from the deduction because

3. Congress has given serious consideration to providing a tax benefit for charitable contributions by individuals who otherwise claim the standard deduction. *See, e.g.*, Tax Relief Act of 2005, S. 2020, 109th Cong. (2005), as passed by the Senate on November 18, 2005.

their deductions may be limited by the 3 percent floor on itemized deductions, applicable to higher income taxpayers.[4] An itemizer's deduction may also be limited, depending on the type of property given, the recipient's status as a private foundation, and the taxpayer's income level.

(a) OVERVIEW. A donor can generally deduct the amount of money and the fair market value of property contributed *to or for the use*[5] of a Section 501(c)(3) organization. To be deductible, contributions must be made to a qualified organization rather than being set aside for use by a specific person. A donor who receives a benefit as a result of making a contribution to a qualified organization can deduct only the amount of the contribution that exceeds the value of the benefit received. The donor's deduction for charitable contributions is generally limited to 50 percent of his adjusted gross income,[6] but in some cases 30 percent and 20 percent limits (with those limits being based on a different base amount) apply.

(b) THE DEDUCTION'S VALUE. For some reason, many people believe that the government pays the entire cost of a charitable contribution because it is deductible. Nothing could be further from the truth. The tax benefit from a charitable contribution is equal to the tax savings produced by it. To illustrate, assume that Assad Hussein's taxable income (before contributions) is $100,000, that he is in a flat 35 percent tax bracket, and that he gives $20,000 to a qualified charity. To make the example simple, we ignore the 3 percent floor on itemized deductions.[7] Hussein has given $20,000 away, but the tax savings are only $7,000. In other words, the contribution costs Hussein $13,000.

As should be apparent, the government does *not* bear the full burden of the contribution. Hussein would be $13,000 wealthier if he had not made the charitable contribution. Deductibility shifts only $7,000 of the cost of the contribution to the government. The price of giving falls as the taxpayer's marginal tax rate increases. Consequently, if charitable giving were entirely tax driven, the level of

4. I.R.C. § 68(c).
5. The phrase "for use of" is a highly technical one. A taxpayer who permits a charity to use property rent-free might be viewed as permitting the charity to "use" the property in common parlance, but the "for use of" phrase does not include such use. In other words, that sort of use does not generate a deductible contribution. Those wanting additional information should review BRUCE HOPKINS, THE LAW OF CHARITABLE GIVING, § 10.3 (John Wiley 2005), as well as Davis v. U.S., 495 U.S. 472 (1990); Rockefeller v. Commissioner, 676 F.2d 35 (2nd Cir. 1982); and Treas. Reg. 1.170A-8(a)(2).
6. The percentage limitations are actually measured against the taxpayer's *contribution base*, which is defined in Section 170(b)(1)(F) as the taxpayer's adjusted gross income computed without regard to any net operating loss carryback to the taxable year. For purposes of this *Guide*, the reference will be to adjusted gross income because that in most cases will be the number used to determine the limit.
7. I.R.C. § 68(a).

contributions in recent years should have declined as federal tax rates have been reduced.[8]

(c) QUALIFIED ORGANIZATIONS. To be deductible, the contribution must be to a *qualified organization,*[9] which generally means a Section 501(c)(3) organization and a limited number of other clearly defined organizations (e.g., certain veterans' organizations).[10] Business leagues, social clubs, and political organizations are all tax-exempt organizations, but contributions to these organizations are *not* deductible as charitable contributions.

A donor cannot deduct contributions to foreign organizations (unless permitted by a tax treaty),[11] but donors can claim deductions to United States organizations that spend the funds abroad. In the latter case, the question of deductibility comes down to the degree of control that the United States charity has over the donated funds.[12] If the donor has earmarked the funds for use by a foreign charity, the fact that the funds pass momentarily through a United States charity will not preserve the charitable contribution deduction.[13] However, a deduction will be allowed if the United States charity has discretion over how funds are spent even if the donor suggests that they be spent abroad.[14]

To better understand the concept of qualified organization, consider the following cases.

(i) Business or Charitable Organization. Sometimes contributions are deductible but not because the recipient is a qualifying organization. Consider Jen

8. Economists have determined that charitable contributions are not entirely tax driven. One study estimates that in the absence of tax deductibility, charitable contributions would decline by about 30 percent. This study further estimates that the resources available to the charitable sector would decline by somewhere between 0.5 percent and 20 percent, because charities are not 100 percent donor supported. E. Brody and J. Cordes, *Tax Treatment of Nonprofit Organizations: A Two-Edged Sword? in* NONPROFITS & GOVERNMENT: COLLABORATION AND CONFLICT (Elizabeth Boris and Eugene Steurerle ed).
9. I.R.C. § 170(c).
10. I.R.C. § 170(c)(3).
11. I.R.C. § 170(c)(2)(A).
12. *See* Rev. Rul. 63-252, 1963-2 C.B. 101. For a general discussion of this issue, see BRUCE HOPKINS, *supra* note 5, at § 18.3.
13. *See* Bilingual Montessori School of Paris, 75 T.C. 480 (1980); S.E. Thomason, 2 T.C. 441 (1943); Rev. Rul. 75-65, 1975-1 C.B. 79; Rev. Rul. 66-79, 1966-1 C.B. 48; and Rev. Rul. 63-252, 1963-2 C.B. 101. *See also* B. Kirschten and C. Neeley, CHARITABLE CONTRIBUTIONS: INCOME TAX ASPECTS, BNA TAX MANAGEMENT. PORT. NO. 281-3rd, at A16-17.
14. There are really two issues at play. The first is whether the contribution is to a United States. domestic charity. That issue raises the question of earmarking. The second is whether a United States charity can engage in charitable activities abroad. Both Rev. Rul. 63-252, 1963-2 C.B. 101, and Rev. Rul. 71-460, 1971-2 C.B. 231, address the second issue, with Rev. Rul. 63-252 providing:

> At the outset, it should be noted that section 170(c)(2) (A) of the Code relates only to the place of creation of the charitable organization to which deductible contributions may be made and does not restrict the area in which deductible contributions may be used. Compare the last sentence in section 170(c)(2) of the Code, which requires that certain corporate contributions be used within the United States. Accordingly, the following discussion should not be construed as limiting in any way the geographical areas in which deductible contributions by individuals may be used.

Stevenson, who is a partner with Green & Blue, a large law firm. She is a member of the American Bar Association (ABA), a Section 501(c)(6) organization. On May 27, 20X5, Stevenson pays her $325 in annual dues. She also gives $1,000 to the American Bar Association Foundation, a Section 501(c)(3) organization. Finally, she gives the ABA an additional $3,000 for its activities.

To be deductible as a charitable contribution, the donation must be to a qualified organization. The ABA is a trade association and as such, it is not a qualified organization, meaning that Stevenson's $325 dues payment is not a charitable contribution. As a partner in a law firm, Stevenson can deduct this expense as an ordinary and necessary business expense. If she were an employee of the law firm, she could deduct the payment as a miscellaneous itemized deduction. As such, the deduction would be subject to the 2 percent floor on miscellaneous itemized deductions.[15] The deductibility of a portion of the dues payment is further limited if the payment is attributable to certain lobbying and political expenditures by the American Bar Association.[16]

By contrast, the American Bar Association Foundation is a Section 501(c)(3) organization, and as such, it is a qualified organization. Consequently, Stevenson's $1,000 contribution to the American Bar Association Foundation is deductible as a charitable contribution. The $3,000 "contribution" is clearly not deductible as a charitable contribution because the ABA is not a qualified charitable organization. The donation is probably not deductible as an ordinary and necessary business expense because Stevenson is not required to make it and receives nothing tangible for it.

Two lessons can be learned from this example. First, to be deductible as charitable contributions, donations must be made to qualified organizations. Second, even though a payment is not deductible as a charitable contribution, it may nevertheless be deductible under another section of the Internal Revenue Code.

(ii) Individuals. Private gifts are not deductible, and individuals are never qualified organizations. To illustrate, consider David Edwards. While walking down the street, he encounters a homeless person. Edwards gives the homeless person $100 for food. Although Edwards should be commended for his generosity, he is not entitled to a charitable contribution deduction. A homeless person is simply not a qualified organization.

(iii) Widows and Orphans. For many people, the example involving a homeless person is understandable, but when the recipients are widows and orphans, perceptions become clouded. Consider Joe Jones, a police officer, who was killed in the line of duty by a gang of teenage drug dealers. Jones leaves behind a wife and one young child. A local bank sets up a fund for the benefit of

---

15. I.R.C. § 162.
16. I.R.C. § 162(e).

the child's college education. Allison Albert, a concerned and caring citizen, decides to contribute $1,000 to the fund.

As noted, individuals are not qualified organizations. So the short and technically correct answer is that Albert's gift is not deductible as a charitable contribution because the Jones family is not a qualified organization. Moreover, even if the community tried to create a qualified charitable organization to help the Jones family, the IRS would in all likelihood not recognize it as a Section 501(c)(3) organization because the Jones family is not what the IRS terms a *charitable class.*[17] If the death of Officer Jones resulted in members of the community establishing an organization to help the children of municipal employees injured or killed while in the line of duty, the IRS likely would recognize the organization as a charitable one. To qualify, however, it would have to meet certain requirements, and gifts could not be earmarked for particular beneficiaries.[18] Despite these rules, there can be little doubt that many people are deducting these contributions as a matter of practice. That practice is neither right nor legal, but people have their own sense of "rough justice."

This issue has had even more relevance following the September 11 terrorist attacks on New York City, Washington, D.C., and the airplane above Pennsylvania. Charities are not permitted just to give money to individuals.[19] Instead, gifts to individuals must be based on need or some other charitable standard. Without such limitation, taxpayers could use charities to do indirectly (make deductible gifts to individuals by using the charity as a "disbursement" agent) what they cannot do directly (make deductible gifts to individuals). As a consequence of this limitation, a number of charities were initially concerned that they might lose their tax-exempt status if they gave money to September 11 survivors who had independent means.

In light of the extraordinary distress caused by the September 11 attacks and subsequent incidents involving anthrax, Congress enacted a special rule allowing charitable organizations to disburse aid to victims of these attacks and their families without the charities' assessing need.[20] This special statute provides that the organization must make the payments in good faith using a reasonable and objective formula that is consistently applied. While a specific need assessment is not required, September 11 relief assistance must serve a charitable class that is large or indefinite in size.[21]

(d) CHARITABLE CLASS—DISASTER RELIEF. In a post–September 11 publication,[22] the IRS gave examples that illustrate the basic rules regarding assistance to victims

---

17. Internal Revenue Service, Publication 3833, Disaster Relief, at 5 (Mar. 2002).
18. *Id. See also* Tripp v. Commissioner, 337 F.2d 432 (7th Cir. 1964); Rev. Rul. 79-81, 1979-1 C.B. 107; Rev. Rul. 68-484, 1968-2 C.B. 105; and Rev. Rul. 57-188, 1957-1 C.B. 97.
19. Internal Revenue Service, *supra* note 17, at 7.
20. Victims of Terrorism Tax Relief Act of 2001, Pub. L. No 107-134, 115 Stat. 2467 (2002).
21. Internal Revenue Service, *supra* note 17, at 10-11.
22. Internal Revenue Service, *supra* note 17.

of disasters and tragic events (other than the victims of the September 11 events who receive special treatment). We touched on the first example in the publication when we considered Joe Jones and his survivors. The remaining examples focus on what constitutes a suitable group of recipients for charitable relief.

In Example 2, a hurricane causes widespread damage to property and loss of life in several counties of a coastal state. More than 100,000 homes are damaged or destroyed by high winds and floods. The group of people affected by the disaster is large enough so that providing aid to it benefits the public as a whole. Therefore, a charitable organization can be formed to assist persons in this group because the eligible recipients compose a charitable class.[23]

Finally, in Example 3, a hurricane causes widespread damage to property and loss of life in several counties of a coastal state. In one of the affected counties, an existing charitable organization has an ongoing program that provides emergency assistance to county residents A small number of this county's residents suffered significant injury or property damage as a result of the storm. The organization provided assistance to some of them. The organization's assistance was provided to a charitable class because the group of potential recipients is indefinite, including other victims of future disasters in the county.[24]

(e) PAYMENTS FOR SERVICES. People sometimes confuse charitable contributions with payments for services. Consider Warren Taylor, who decides to help his nephew, Marshall, by paying his $10,000 tuition to Pariser College. Warren is not entitled to a charitable contribution deduction. His tuition payment is a gift to Marshall, who in turn is purchasing educational benefits from Pariser College.

PUSHING THE LIMITS CAN RESULT IN JAIL TIME

* * *

On June 20, 2003, the United States Attorney's Office for the Northern District of California announced that a resident of San Rafael, California, had been sentenced on June 19, 2003, to five months in prison followed by five months of home detention and two years of supervised release.[25] United States District Court Judge Martin J. Jenkins handed down the sentence following a guilty plea on all six counts of the Information filed October 23, 2001, which charged this person with tax evasion.[26]

According to an earlier press release issued by the United States Attorney's Office:

> In 1995, the taxpayer created a foundation at the National Heritage Foundation (NHF) called The Taxpayer Family Foundation (Family Foundation). In each of the

---

23. Id., at 6–7.
24. Id., at 7.
25. Press Release, U.S. Attorney's Office for the Northern District of California (June 20, 2003). The quoted portion of the press release has been modified, replacing the particular taxpayer's name with the phrase "the taxpayer" or its equivalent.
26. *Id.*

years 1995 through 1999, the taxpayer sent payments to NHF and earmarked them for the account of the family foundation. The taxpayer informed his return preparer that the payments to NHF were charitable donations. Rather than being bona fide charitable contributions to NHF, however, the taxpayer admitted using the proceeds of the family foundation account to pay for the school tuition for his children at the San Domenico Primary School in San Anselmo, California.

To make it appear that the tuition payments were bona fide charitable contributions, the taxpayer made payments to NHF, which credited the payments to his account under the name of the Taxpayer Family Foundation. Thereafter, pursuant to his instructions, NHF issued checks to San Domenico Convent, which were used, not as donations, but to pay for the tuition of his children at the Primary School.

Despite the fact that the NHF payments were ultimately used to pay for his children's tuition, the taxpayer improperly claimed as a charitable contribution deduction in each year the payments he made to the NHF. In addition, for the years 1996 through 1999, the taxpayer admitted claiming false business expenses on his Forms 1040, Schedules C and the corporate return of Taxpayer Associates, Ltd., for the year 1999.

The government requested at the sentencing hearing that the defendant be ordered to pay restitution to the United States in the amount of $274,326.57, which included $165,326.57 in interest and penalties. The defendant paid $109,000 to the United States IRS on the eve of sentencing. The Court will decide on July 31, 2003 whether the defendant shall be ordered to pay as restitution the additional interest and penalties. [27]

* * *

(f) QUID PRO QUO CONTRIBUTIONS. When a donor receives a benefit as a consequence of making a contribution to a qualified organization, the donor can deduct only the amount of the contribution that is more than the value of the benefit he received.[28] If a donor pays more than the fair market value to a qualified organization for merchandise, goods, or services, only the amount that is more than the value of the item is deductible as a charitable contribution if the donor intends to make a gift of the excess.

To illustrate, consider the following two examples. Benjamin Burt purchases a ticket to a dinner dance sponsored by a local charity for $250. The value of the dinner is $100. He is entitled to claim a $150 charitable contribution deduction.[29] The donor can deduct only the amount by which the payment exceeds the value of goods and services that the donor received from the charitable organization.

This type of transaction is referred to as a *quid pro quo contribution* because it is in part a contribution and in part a purchase from the charity. A charity receiving a quid pro quo contribution that exceeds $75 must disclose to the donor that only a portion of the contribution is deductible and provide a good faith estimate

27. *Id.*
28. United States v. American Bar Endowment, 477 U.S. 105 (1986); Treas. Reg. § 1.170A-1(h)(2); and Rev. Rul. 67-246, 1967-2 C.B. 104.
29. *Id.*

of the value (not just the cost to the charity) of the goods and services provided to the donor.[30]

Now let's consider Nell Jayroe, who was watching her local public TV station during its quarterly membership campaign. She phoned to donate $250 to the station. That level of contribution entitled Nell to a "premium" in the form of a one-year subscription to a cooking newsletter published by the host of a popular cooking show that ordinarily costs $85. Nell can deduct $165 of the $250 payment as a charitable contribution. There is logic to this approach. She should receive a deduction only to the extent that her payment exceeds the value of the goods and services that she receives.[31] When the amount of the contribution equals or exceeds $250, the taxpayer must receive a contemporaneous written acknowledgment from the charity before he can claim a charitable contribution deduction.[32]

(g) WHEN TO CLAIM A DEDUCTION—TIMING. A donor can deduct a charitable contribution only in the year the contribution is actually made in cash or other property (or in a succeeding carryover year). This is true whether the donor uses the cash or accrual method (usually used by businesses) of accounting.[33] The donor is generally deemed to make a contribution at the time he unconditionally delivers the property, but the form of payment can alter the timing of the deduction. Specifically, contributions

- By check are deductible in the year the donor mails the check.[34]
- By credit card are deductible in the year that the cardholder initiates the charge.[35]
- By pledge are not deductible as charitable contributions until the pledge is fulfilled.[36]
- By a properly endorsed stock certificate are completed on the date of mailing or other delivery to the charity or to the charity's agent. However, if the donor gives a stock certificate to his agent or to the issuing corporation for transfer to the name of the charity, the gift is not completed until the date the stock is transferred on the books of the corporation.[37] In other words, form and structure matter.

30. I.R.C. § 6115.
31. Rev. Rul. 67-246, 1967-2 C.B. 104.
32. I.R.C. § 170(f)(8)(A). Rev. Proc. 92-49, 1992-1 C.B. 987, and Rev. Proc. 90-12, 1990-1 C.B. 471, provide detailed rules regarding the treatment of premiums.
33. I.R.C. § 170(a)(1).
34. Treas. Reg. § 1.170A-1(b).
35. Rev. Rul. 78-38, 1978-1 C.B. 67. The IRS reversed its prior position in this ruling, concluding that the donor created a debt to the credit card company, not the charity, and therefore the donor was simply borrowing funds from a third party to make a charitable contribution.
36. Treas. Reg. § 1.170A-1(a)(1); and Rev. Rul. 55-410, 1955-1 C.B. 297.
37. Treas. Reg. § 1.170A-1(b).

- A donor whose contribution is a conditional gift that depends on a future act or event that may not take place, cannot take a deduction until the uncertainty as to whether there will be a gift is resolved and the gift is actually made. If there is only a negligible chance that the act or event will not take place, the donor can claim a deduction when the money or property is transferred to the charity.[38] To illustrate, assume that Larry Macleod donates $1,000 to Large City Opera but is entitled to receive it back if the opera does not raise $200,000 as part of the current fundraising campaign. Macleod cannot deduct the contribution until Large City Opera raises $200,000 as part of its current fundraising campaign. On the other hand, if he gives a parcel of land to a city for a public park but requires the gift to revert in the event the city does not use the land for this purpose, he will be entitled to a charitable contribution deduction if, on the date he transfers the land to the city, the city plans to use it as a public park and the likelihood that the city will someday convert the land to another use is so remote that it is negligible.[39]

As we will see in Chapter 10, donors often make gifts to charities that restrict how the gift can be used. For example, a donor might contribute funds to a college for a scholarship fund. Or, a donor might contribute a painting to an art museum, requiring that the museum display it, but not lend it to other institutions.[40] These restrictions generally do not impair the deductibility of the contribution, but they could reduce the fair market value of the gift (and consequently, the amount of the deduction). The deductibility of the contribution could be jeopardized if the terms of the gift instrument provide for the return of the gift if the restrictions are violated. For this reason, some donors provide for what is termed a "gift over" to another charity in the event the restrictions are violated.

Corporations using the accrual method can elect to deduct a contribution in the year the corporation makes the commitment if the board of directors authorizes the contribution in that year and the corporation pays it on or before the 15th day of the third month following the end of that tax year.[41]

(h) AMOUNT OF THE DEDUCTION. Assuming that a contribution is otherwise deductible, the donor is permitted to deduct the amount of cash or, with certain notable exceptions, the fair market value of property that he contributes to the

38. Treas. Reg. § 1.170A-1(e); and Mitzi S. Briggs, 72 T.C. 646 (1979); Rev. Rul. 2003-28, 2003-11 I.R.B. 594; Rev. Rul. 79-249, 1979-2 C.B. 104. This regulation distinguishes between *conditions precedent* and *conditions subsequent*. However, the effect of either on deductibility is the same. The deduction will only be allowable if the possibility that the condition will preclude (condition precedent) or reverse (condition subsequent) the contribution "is so remote as to be negligible."
39. Treas. Reg. § 1.170A-1(e). *See also* BRUCE HOPKINS, *supra* note 5, at 374.
40. See A. Rothchild, *The Dos and Don'ts of Donor Control*, ACTEC J. (Spring 2005); Priv. Let. Rul. 2002-02-032 (Jan. 11, 2002); and Priv. Let. Rul. 2002-03-013 (Jan. 18, 2002).
41. I.R.C. § 170(a)(2).

qualified organization. A volunteer cannot deduct the value of his services provided to a qualified organization. Nor can someone deduct the rental value of property that he permits a qualified organization to use rent free.

A taxpayer may be required to reduce the amount of his otherwise deductible contribution (1) if his annual contributions exceed certain amounts, (2) he gives certain types of property, or (3) he makes a donation to certain categories of organizations.

The general rule permitting taxpayers to deduct the fair market value of property donated to a charity has a number of exceptions. These exceptions either limit the taxpayer's deduction to the property's adjusted basis (often cost reduced by depreciation deductions) or to an amount, as determined by formula, which will below fair market value.[42] Although this is nominally the donor's problem, the charity may bear the brunt of a donor's anger if he is unable to claim an anticipated deduction. Charities should not give legal advice to potential donors, and boards should adopt policies to make sure that they do not. At the same time, the charity's fundraisers should be aware of the basic rules so that they are in a position to discuss the benefits with potential donors (but always advising donors to seek professional advice).

The following are the major exceptions to the basic rule that donors can deduct the fair market value of property donated to qualified charities.

(i) Donor-Created Property. If the donor creates the property being donated to the charity, he can deduct only the costs he incurred in creating the property.[43] Consider Hillary Youst, a famous artist, who painted an abstract oil painting that she believes would look great in the lobby of the new performing arts center located in her hometown. She decides to donate the painting to the center, a Section 501(c)(3) organization.

Youst uses expensive materials in executing her works of art. This particular painting cost her $20,000 in paint and other material. At the time of the donation, the painting is worth $15 million. She is entitled to claim only a $20,000 charitable contribution deduction.[44] Does this seem unfair? Maybe so, but keep in mind that Youst has never paid tax on the appreciation that represents the value of her work and creative efforts.[45]

(ii) Ordinary Income Property. If the donor contributes property that would generate ordinary income if sold, he must reduce the amount of the contribution

42. Treas. Reg. § 1.170A-4A.
43. Treas. Reg. § 1.170A-4(b)(1). See note 50, *infra*, for an example.
44. I.R.C. §§ 170(e)(1)(A) and 170(b)(1)(C)(iv); and Treas. Reg. § 1.170-4(b)(1).
45. Congress has given serious consideration to providing greater tax benefits to artists who make charitable contributions of their artworks. *See*, e.g., Tax Relief Act of 2005, *supra* note 3, which, if enacted, would permit a fair market value deduction for a qualified artistic contribution.

(fair market value) by the amount of the ordinary income component.[46] The unstated focus of this rule is inventory. Consider Jeremy Liccione, who runs a small bookstore. The local chapter of Unplanned Grandparenthood, a Section 501(c)(3) organization, holds an annual charity auction. Liccione donates children's books from the bookstore's inventory that were valued at $5,000 to Unplanned Grandparenthood for the auction. He paid his supplier $3,000 for the books. If Liccione sold these books in the ordinary course of his business, the resulting income would be ordinary income. As a consequence, he can deduct only $3,000 as his contribution. Does this also seem unfair? Maybe so, but keep in mind that Liccione has never been required to pay tax on the $2,000 component that represents his potential profit.

There is a partial exception to the "ordinary income" reduction rule in the case of donations of certain scientific equipment to certain charities.[47] There is also a partial exception for certain contributions of computer technology or equipment for educational purposes.[48] Finally, there is a special rule applicable to contributions by corporations (other than S corporations) of certain inventory and other property.[49] This provision has been used by pharmaceutical companies to provide medicines for disaster relief and restaurants to provide food to homeless shelters. Generally speaking, it permits qualified donors to deduct the cost of the goods plus a limited portion of the markup.[50]

(iii) Short-Term Capital Gain Property. A donor who contributes property that would generate short-term capital gain if sold must reduce the amount of the contribution (fair market value) by the portion of the gain that represents short-term capital gain.[51] For example, on April 15, 20X5, Sam Baldwin purchased 1,000 shares of Intel for $120,000. He is not a day trader but does turn his stocks quickly. He guessed right with respect to Intel. On May 1, 20X5, Baldwin's Intel

---

46. I.R.C. § 170(e)(1)(A).
47. I.R.C. § 170(e)(4).
48. I.R.C. § 170(e)(6). Congress has given serious consideration to expanding these sort of exceptions. *See, e.g.*, Tax Relief Act of 2005, *supra* note 3.
49. I.R.C. § 170(e)(3).
50. Example 1 of Treas. Reg. § 1.170A-4A(c)(4) offers the following illustration of the computations:

> During 1978 corporation X, a calendar year taxpayer, makes a qualified contribution of women's coats which was [inventory] property. The fair market value of the property at the date of contribution is $1,000, and the basis of the property is $200. The amount of the charitable contribution which would be taken into account under section 170(a) is the fair market value ($1,000). The amount of gain which would not have been long-term capital gain if the property had been sold is $800 ($1,000 – $200). The amount of the contribution is reduced by one-half the amount which would not have been capital gain if the property had been sold ($800/2 = $400).
>
> After this reduction, the amount of the contribution thatmay be considered is $600 ($1,000 – $400). A second reduction is made in the amount of the charitable contribution because this amount (as first reduced to $600) is more than $400, which is an amount equal to twice the basis of the property. The amount of the further reduction is $200 [$600 – (2 × $200)], and the amount of the contribution as finally reduced is $400 [$1,000 – ($400 + $200)].

51. I.R.C. § 170(e)(1)(A).

stock was worth $240,000. He has been having a pretty good year in the market, so he decides to donate his Intel stock to Watson Broadcasters Hall of Fame, a Section 501(c)(3) organization. Baldwin can claim only a $120,000 charitable contribution deduction for this contribution. He has not held the stock for more than one year, meaning that the stock is short-term capital gain property. Does this seem unfair? Maybe so, but keep in mind that Baldwin is never required to pay tax on the $120,000 of built-in gain.

(iv) Tangible Personal Property Unrelated to the Charity's Exempt Purpose. If a donor contributes appreciated tangible personal property to a charity that does not use the property in a function that is related to the charity's exempt purpose, the donor must reduce the amount of the charitable contribution deduction by any built-in gain.[52] For example, Julian Hughes owns a Picasso oil painting worth $10 million. He decides to contribute it to the local chapter of the Red Cross, which sells it to raise cash for operations. Hughes originally paid $300,000 for the painting and so can deduct only that $300,000 cost. The Red Cross is a Section 501(c)(3) organization but does not use the painting as part of its exempt function. Hughes is entitled to a full fair market value deduction only if he had given the painting to the local art museum to hang as part of its permanent collection.[53]

(v) Long-Term Capital Gain Property Contributed to Certain Private Foundations. As you have already seen, the general rule requires taxpayers to reduce the amount of charitable contributions by the amount of gain that is not a long-term capital gain. This rule is extended to the portion of gain that is a long-term capital gain when the associated property is contributed to a private foundation other than a private operating private foundation, private conduit foundation, or a common fund, as defined in the Internal Revenue Code.[54] There is an important exception to this rule in the case of a contribution of stock to a private foundation if the gain is long-term and market quotations for the stock are readily available on an established securities market;[55] then the donor is entitled to a deduction at fair market value. There are limitations on this exception in case of donations involving more than 10 percent of the stock of the corporation.

(vi) Property Eligible for a Special Election. The tax law gives the donor the option to elect to reduce the deduction by the amount of any built-in gain in exchange for subjecting the deduction to the 50 percent limitation on charitable contributions[56] rather than the 30 percent limitation.[57] Under certain circumstances,

52. I.R.C. § 170(e)(1)(B)(i); and Treas. Reg. § 1.170A-4(b)(3)(i).
53. Treas. Reg. § 1.170A-4(b)(3)(i).
54. I.R.C. § 170(e)(1)(B)(ii) and 170(b)(1)(E).
55. I.R.C. § 170(e)(5).
56. We will conisder this and the 30 percent limitation shortly.
57. I.R.C. § 170(b)(1)(C)(iii).

the taxpayer may decide that it is better to claim a deduction equal to the adjusted basis in the property to be contributed rather than its fair market value. This may seem counterintuitive, but the decision is based on an interaction between annual percentage limitations on charitable contributions, carryover rules, tax rates, and time of value of money considerations. To illustrate, Laura Michael paid $98,000 for stock in 19X1 and decides to give it to her synagogue as a contribution. The stock is now worth $100,000. This is her only charitable contribution in 20X5. Her adjusted gross income for 20X5 is $200,000. Under the 30 percent limitation on charitable contributions, Michael can deduct only $60,000 of the contribution (assume that she has no net operating loss carrybacks).[58] This strikes Michael as unfair because even though this is "capital gain" property, she has only a $2,000 unrealized gain. Michael can elect to subject this contribution to the 50 percent limitation, but her contribution will be reduced by the $2,000 of appreciation. Based on these facts, making the election probably makes sense. The election applies to all capital gain property contributed to 50 percent limit organizations during a tax year.[59] This rule has implications for carryovers to the year of the election.[60]

(i) BARGAIN SALES TO CHARITIES. Special rules apply when someone sells property to a charity below its fair market value, referred to as a *bargain sale*. Under these rules, the seller is treated as having engaged in two transactions: (1) the donation of a charitable gift and (2) the sale of property. The basic rule is best illustrated by an example. Assume that Maggie Sattler owns a Picasso oil painting valued at $5 million. She wants it to be part of Big Art Museum's collection, but she simply cannot afford to give away a $5 million painting. To induce Big Art to buy it, she offers it at a bargain price of $2 million, which the museum agrees to pay. Sattler's adjusted basis in the painting is $3 million. For tax purposes, she has made a $3 million charitable contribution and has sold a portion of the painting for $2 million. She must allocate her adjusted basis for purposes of calculating her gain on the sale portion of the transaction.[61] She does this based on relative fair market value. In others words, two-fifths of her basis is attributable to sale: $1.2 million. That means that Sattler has an $800,000 gain on the sale. In this case, Sattler does not need to know her adjusted basis in the portion of the property she gave to the museum. If, however, Sattler had engaged in the bargain sale with a social services agency, she would also need to know her adjusted basis for the gift portion of the transaction so that she could apply the reduction rules.

---

58. I.R.C. § 170(b)(1)(C)(i).
59. INTERNAL REVENUE SERVICE, PUBLICATION 526, CHARITABLE CONTRIBUTIONS, at 12 (Dec. 2003).
60. See Treas. Reg. § 1.170A-8(d)(2)(i)(b). For a general discussion of the election and its impact on surrounding tax years, see BRUCE HOPKINS, *supra* note 5, at § 7.7
61. Treas. Reg. § 1.1011-2.

(j) CONTRIBUTIONS OF ENCUMBERED PROPERTY. Contributions of property subject to debt do not produce as intuitive result as might be expected. To illustrate, suppose that Harry Stone owns real estate with a $2 million fair market value, but it is encumbered by a $500,000 debt. If Stone gives the property subject to the $500,000 debt to a charity, he is entitled to a $1.5 million charitable contribution deduction (assume that no reduction is required). However, the bargain sale to charity rules come into play.[62] If Stone has a $700,000 adjusted basis in the property, he must compute his gain on the sale portion of the transaction.[63] In other words, Stone has a $325,000 taxable gain. His basis allocable to the sale portion of the transaction is equal to $175,000, or his total adjusted basis ($700,000) multiplied by a fraction having as its numerator $500,000 (the assumed debt) and as its denominator $2 million (the property's value). These rules can also apply when a limited partner tries to escape a phantom gain associated with a burned-out tax shelter.[64] As anyone who is familiar with the tax laws knows, transactions involving debt can pose complex tax questions. Persons considering making a contribution of encumbered property to a charity should seek qualified tax counsel. The charity on the other side of a transaction involving indebtedness will want to take a very close look at the unrelated debt-finance income rules[65] to make sure that it has considered the UBIT implications associated with the gift.

(k) LIMITS ON INDIVIDUAL CONTRIBUTIONS. A taxpayer's total charitable contribution deduction for the year is limited by three factors: (1) the form of property involved, (2) the taxpayer's adjusted gross income, and (3) the type of charity receiving the gift. When the charitable contributions for the year exceed the applicable income limits, the excess amounts can be carried forward for five years.[66]

As a general rule, an individual cannot deduct charitable contributions to the extent that the deductions exceed 50 percent of the donor's adjusted gross income.[67] Donors also need to be cognizant of three other limitations, all of which are applied after the reductions discussed earlier.

To understand how the percentage limitations on charitable contributions work, it is first necessary to distinguish between two types of charities: 50 percent-limit charities and 30 percent-limit charities. To generalize, *50 percent-limit charities* include public charities (e.g., the Red Cross, the American Cancer Society), private operating foundations, private conduit foundations, and common funds that satisfy certain requirements, and *30 percent-limit* charities include traditional corporate and family foundations, as well as certain veterans',

---

62. Treas. Reg. § 1.1011-2(a)(3).
63. Rev. Rul. 81-163, 1981-1 C.B. 433.
64. *See, e.g.*, Rev. Rul. 75-194, 1975-1 C.B. 80.
65. I.R.C. § 514(a).
66. I.R.C. §§ 170(d) and 170(b)(1)(B), flush language.
67. I.R.C. §§ 170(b)(1)(A) and 170(d). See note 6 *supra*.

fraternal, and cemetery organizations.[68] The various limits favor 50 percent-limit charities.

To greatly oversimplify, gifts to public charities are allowed up to 50 percent of adjusted gross income for cash gifts and up to 30 percent for gifts of capital gain property eligible for deduction at fair market value.[69] Gifts to private foundations are allowed up to 30 percent for cash gifts[70] and 20 percent for gifts of capital gain property.[71] The various interactions between these limitations could easily take several more pages to describe, but that technical discussion is beyond this *Guide's* scope.

(l) CARRYFORWARDS. As noted in the preceding discussion, when the 50 percent and 30 percent income limitations reduce a taxpayer's otherwise allowable charitable contribution deduction for the current year, the amounts that are *not* deductible can be carried forward to each of the next five years.[72] Such contributions are subject to the same limitations in the year to which they are carried. In other words, contributions that are carried forward as 30 percent-limit contributions retain the 30 percent taint for purposes of the limitations in the subsequent year.

For each category of contributions, the taxpayer must deduct current year contributions before the carryforward amounts.[73] In other words, a taxpayer with a carryforward should plan carefully with respect to future contributions to ensure that carryforwards do not needlessly expire. If a taxpayer has carryforwards from two or more prior tax years, those from the earliest year are used first.[74]

(m) GUIDELINES FOR WORKING WITH THE REDUCTION AND LIMITATION RULES. Even the most sophisticated tax professionals have trouble working with the four tiers of limits applicable to charitable contributions by individuals. This regime is extremely complex. Here are three simple rules that most donors can use to avoid unexpectedly running afoul of the reduction requirements and income limits: Donors should consult with qualified legal counsel or an accountant when:

- The donation involves property rather than cash.
- The donation is to a private foundation (as opposed to a public charity).
- The donor's total donations for the year exceed 20 percent of his adjusted gross income.

(n) LIMITS ON CORPORATE CHARITABLE CONTRIBUTION DEDUCTIONS. A taxable corporation can deduct charitable contributions only to the extent that its contributions for the year do not exceed 10 percent of the corporation's taxable

68. B. Kirschten and C. Neeley, *supra* note 13, at A-122-23.
69. I.R.C. § 170(b)(1)(C).
70. I.R.C. § 170(b)(1)(B).
71. I.R.C. § 170(b)(1)(D).
72. Internal Revenue Service, *supra* note 59, at 12.
73. I.R.C. § 170(d)(A)(i).
74. *Id.*

income, determined without regard to the charitable contributions deduction, certain carrybacks, and certain other deductions.[75] Many large corporations attempt to consolidate their gift giving and maximize the tax benefits by creating a private foundation. Before soliciting a large corporation for a charitable contribution, a charity should first determine whether the corporation has created a foundation to administer its philanthropic activities.

(o) VOLUNTEERS. Although volunteers cannot deduct the value of their contributed services,[76] volunteer directors and officers may be able to deduct certain expenses as charitable contributions if the organization is a qualified charity. As is the case with all deductions, volunteer directors and officers must be able to substantiate the deduction with the appropriate written documentation.[77] To be deductible, the amounts must be (1) unreimbursed, (2) directly connected with the services provided to the charity, and (3) incurred only because of the services rendered. Under no circumstances can the expenses be personal, living, or family expenses. Allowed expenses can include the cost of special uniforms, car and other transportation expenses, out-of-pocket expenses for entertaining underprivileged youth if the charity selects the youth,[78] travel and related expenses when selected to represent an organization at a convention, and certain expenses incurred as a foster parent.[79]

(p) CONCLUDING THOUGHTS. The deduction for charitable contributions permits taxpayers to shift part of the cost of making charitable contributions to the government. However, taxpayers who think that a charitable contribution reduces their taxes without a cost to them are wrong.

When considering whether to make a charitable contribution, the donor must be cognizant of various deduction limitations. In particular, a prospective donor must consider whether the donation will be limited because it exceeds a certain amount that is determined in relation to his adjusted gross income. A prospective donor considering contributing property must focus on whether he will receive a charitable contribution deduction for the full fair market value of the property or a lower amount.

Charities should focus on accepting assets that make charitable giving less costly to donors. In particular, a charity should consider suggesting gifts of appreciated stock when the built-in gain is characterized as long-term capital gain; by contrast, a donor considering a gift of stock with a built-in loss should be encouraged to sell the stock instead (claiming the loss on his tax return) and donate the cash proceeds.

---

75. I.R.C. §§ 170(b)(2) and (d)(2).
76. Treas. Reg. § 1.170A-1(g).
77. Treas. Reg. § 1.170A-13(f)(10).
78. Rev. Rul. 70-519, 1970-2 C.B. 62.
79. INTERNAL REVENUE SERVICE, *supra* note 59, at 4–5.

7.2 DISCLOSURES AND NOTICES BY CHARITIES

In recent years, the United States Treasury and Congress have been concerned that taxpayers are claiming charitable deductions for payments to charities that actually represent payments for goods and services or are claiming charitable deductions for nonexistent contributions. Congress has responded to these abuses by enacting laws that require charities to make certain written disclosures to the contributor regarding charitable contributions. Failure on the part of the charity to comply can cost the donor his deduction, obviously pressuring charities to comply. Without compliance with these laws, the likelihood for repeat contributions is greatly reduced, particularly by a donor who is audited.

(a) QUID PRO QUO CONTRIBUTIONS. Charities must make certain disclosures when a donor makes a quid pro quo contribution that exceeds $75 (determined without reduction for the value of the goods or services provided to the taxpayer).[80] As previously defined, a *quid pro quo contribution* is a payment made partly as a contribution and partly as payment for goods or services provided to the donor. Celebrity value is generally disregarded.[81]

A charity provides goods or services in consideration for a contributor's payment if, at the time of the payment, the contributor receives or expects to receive them in exchange for that payment, including those provided in a year other than the one in which the contributor made the payment. For example, on December 20, 20X5, a contributor provides Washington Opera, a Section 501(c)(3) organization, $100 in consideration for a dinner ticket with a fair market value of $60. The dinner is to take place January 21, 20X6. Washington Opera must give the contributor a timely disclosure statement indicating, among other things, that the value of the dinner is $60. The contributor may claim the $40 as a charitable deduction on his 20X5 tax return. Note that in determining whether the $75 threshold is met, the charity considers the entire amount involved ($100 in this case), not the portion deductible by the donor ($40 in this case).

The required written statement from the charity must do the following:

- State that the amount of the contribution the donor may deduct for federal income tax purposes is limited to the amount that exceeds the value of the goods or services provided by the charity in the exchange.
- Provide a good faith estimate of the fair market value of the goods or services (which is not necessarily the charity's cost).[82]

Charities must furnish the disclosure statements in a timely manner—with either the solicitation of the quid pro quo contribution or the receipt of it.[83] If the

80. I.R.C. § 6115(a).
81. Treas. Reg. § 1.16115-1(a)(3), Example 3.
82. INTERNAL REVENUE SERVICE, PUBLICATION 1771, CHARITABLE CONTRIBUTIONS—SUBSTANTIATION AND DISCLOSURE REQUIREMENTS, at 11 (July 2005).
83. *Id.*, at 12.

disclosure statements are furnished in connection with a particular solicitation, it is not necessary for charities to provide additional statements when contributions are actually received.

Disclosure statements are not required in any of the following circumstances:

- *When goods or services given to contributors by a charity have an insubstantial or de minimis value.*[84] For example, as part of its 2006 fundraising campaign, the March of Quarters provides a plastic bookmark bearing its logo to any contributor donating $75 or more. The cost of each bookmark is twenty-five cents. The IRS has published guidelines for determining whether an item is de minimis. If the contribution for 2006 is more than $43 and the items provided bear the organization's name or logo (e.g., calendars, mugs, or posters), the items are considered de minimis if their cost does not exceed $8.60.[85] Alternatively, the items will be considered de minimis if their fair market value does not exceed 2 percent of the contribution, or $86, whichever is less.[86] These thresholds are indexed for inflation, so each year the thresholds should be reviewed. Not surprisingly, each bookmark is considered a low-cost or de minimis article.
- *When no donative or gift element exists in a particular transaction.* A typical museum gift shop sale is an example of a transaction without a donative element. Another example is a payment to a hospital for medical services.
- *When only an intangible religious benefit is provided to contributors.*[87] Admission to a religious ceremony is not considered to be a quid pro quo contribution. Consequently, amounts paid for tickets to Rosh Hashanah or Yom Kippur services are not considered quid pro quo contributions. The exception also includes de minimis tangible benefits, such as wine or a wafer provided in connection with a religious ceremony. However, the intangible religious benefit exception does not apply to such items as payments for tuition for education leading to a recognized degree or for travel services or consumer goods.
- *When certain membership benefits are involved.*[88] Members receiving a discounted admission to a museum are not considered to have received a quid quo pro benefit. Benefits include free or discounted admission to the organization's facilities, events, or parking; preferred access to goods or services; and discounts on the purchase of goods or services. The following example from the regulations under Section 170 illustrates the exception:

> Membership benefits disregarded. Performing Arts Center E is an organization described in section 170(c). In return for a payment of $75, E offers a package of

84. Treas. Reg. §§ 1.6115-1(b) and 1.170A-13(f)(8)(i)(A).
85. Rev. Proc. 2005-70, I.R.B. 2004-47 (Nov. 21, 2004). See Rev. Proc. 90-12, 1990-1 C.B. 471 (as amplified and modified).
86. *Id.*
87. I.R.C. § 6115(b).
88. Treas. Reg. §§ 1.6115-1(b) and 1.170A-13(f)(8)(i)(B).

basic membership benefits that includes the right to purchase tickets to performances one week before they go on sale to the general public, free parking in E's garage during evening and weekend performances, and a 10 percent discount on merchandise sold in E's gift shop. In return for a payment of $150, E offers a package of preferred membership benefits that includes all of the benefits in the $75 package as well as a poster that is sold in E's gift shop for $20. The basic membership and the preferred membership are each valid for twelve months, and there are approximately 50 performances of various productions at E during a twelve-month period. E's gift shop is open for several hours each week and at performance times. F, a patron of the arts, is solicited by E to make a contribution. E offers F the preferred membership benefits in return for a payment of $150 or more. F makes a payment of $300 to E. F can satisfy the substantiation requirement of section 170(f)(8) by obtaining a contemporaneous written acknowledgment from E that includes a description of the poster and a good faith estimate of its fair market value ($20) and disregards the remaining membership benefits.[89]

A charity that fails to make the appropriate disclosures for quid pro quo contributions is subject to a penalty of $10 per contribution, not to exceed $5,000 per fundraising event or mailing.[90] Charities can avoid this penalty by demonstrating that the failure was due to reasonable cause, dependent on the particular facts and circumstances. This, however, is the type of argument that no charity ever wants to find itself making.

(b) SUBSTANTIATION REQUIREMENTS. No charitable contribution deduction is allowed for a contribution of $250 or more, whether in cash or property, unless the contributor receives and retains a contemporaneous written acknowledgment from the charity.[91] The donor cannot rely on canceled checks alone to substantiate the contribution. It is the contributor's responsibility to obtain the written statement, so a charity should not be surprised when contributors ask for an acknowledgements if it fails to provide them promptly. In calculating the $250 amount, separate contributions of less than $250 are not aggregated.[92] To illustrate, a church would not be required to provide a written acknowledgement to a congregant who dropped $10 dollars in the collection plate each Sunday. However, the congregant should either use a check or ask for a receipt each week so that he can substantiate the individual contributions.

(i) Content. The written statement must include sufficient information to substantiate the deduction. If the contribution form is cash, the amount must be

89. Treas. Reg. § 1.170A-13(f)(8)(ii), Example 1. Keep in mind that this regulation applies to contributions of $75 or less, which makes little sense in the context of Section 6115 because the amount that triggers the disclosure requirement is a contribution in excess of $75. However, the reference in the regulations under Section 6115 are to the type of benefits described in the regulations under Section 170.

90. I.R.C. § 6714.

91. I.R.C. § 170(f)(8).

92. Treas. Reg. § 1.170A-13(f)(1).

in the written statement.[93] If the form is property, the written statement must describe the property but need not value it.[94] In other words, charities are not required to attest to property value that they receive; this is very important and controversial. The statement must also indicate whether the charity provided any goods or services in consideration for the contribution. If so, the statement must provide a description and a good faith estimate of the fair market value of the goods or services.[95] If the donor received nothing in return for the contribution, the written statement must say so. The statement should *not* include the contributor's Social Security or tax identification numbers.

(ii) Sample Substantiation Language. Every charity should work with its legal counsel to develop appropriate substantiation language. Here is an example on which a charity's legal counsel can base a draft.

> The Good Deeds Foundation, Inc. ("Good Deeds") gratefully acknowledges the payment by personal check (dated April 15, 20X6) of Five Hundred Dollars ($500) during the year ended December 31, 20X6. Except as indicated herein, Good Deeds provided no goods or services in return for these contributions. PLEASE RETAIN THIS RECEIPT since the Internal Revenue Service requires that you substantiate your charitable gifts.

No goods or services were provided by Good Deeds to the donor.

The written statement must be contemporaneous and provided to the donor by the earlier of (1) the date on which the donor actually files his return or (2) the due date (including extensions) of the return.[96] As a practical matter, this means that these statements should be mailed no later than December 31 of the year of the contribution (but no later than the end of January of the following year).

(iii) A Cautionary Tale about Social Security Numbers. A nationally recognized nonprofit attorney relayed the following story at a conference: Sometime shortly after September 11, 2001, some high-income individuals noticed mysterious charges on their credit cards. In fact, one individual was startled to receive a statement because he did not even have the type of credit card in question. After a series of phone calls and investigation, someone realized that all of the victims of this particular fraud had given money to a particular charity. This charity routinely collected Social Security numbers from its donors (why they willingly gave this information is a mystery). Apparently, an insider obtained access to the numbers, which became the "key" for the insider (or a relative) to apply for and receive the charge cards. By the way, the charges were apparently for one-way airplane tickets to Middle Eastern countries. **There is no need to collect Social Security numbers from donors, so do not.**

---

93. Treas. Reg. § 1.170A-13(f)(2)(i).
94. *Id.*
95. Treas. Reg. § §1.170A-13(f)(2)(ii) and (iii).
96. Treas. Reg. § 1.170A-13(f)(3).

(c) THE BOARD'S ROLE. Nobody expects the board to actually prepare the necessary disclosure and substantiation statements. It should make sure, however, that procedures are in place to ensure that appropriate disclosures and statements are provided on a timely basis. The directors should take these requirements very seriously because failure to comply will jeopardize the organization's future cash flow from charitable contributions.

APPRAISALS ARE THE DONOR'S RESPONSIBILITY, BUT CHARITIES SHOULD BE CAREFUL, TOO

* * *

In 2004, both the *New York Times* and the *New Jersey Star Ledger* ran articles describing a transaction between Herbert R. Axelrod and the New Jersey Symphony Orchestra involving the orchestra's purchase of rare violins from Mr. Axelrod for a reported $17 million.[97] Both articles indicated that Mr. Axelrod claimed the violins were worth $50 million, which if true, would have entitled him to a charitable contribution deduction under the bargain sale rules.[98] Some questioned the $50 million valuation.[99]

The stories also indicated that Mr. Axelrod had fled the United States. He subsequently pled guilty in an unrelated tax fraud case, and the IRS agreed to drop other charges.[100] As part of the plea agreement, Mr. Axelrod agreed to file a 2003 tax return that did not claim a charitable contribution deduction for the violins.[101]

In December 2004, an independent committee created by the orchestra's board of trustees issued a report.[102] Couched in diplomatic language, its substance included stinging criticisms of the decision process that led to the orchestra's acquisition of the violin collection. The report indicates that unfavorable information about the value and authenticity of the collection was withheld from the full board as was information about federal investigations of Mr. Axelrod.[103] Specifically, the report concludes:

> Given the size of the transaction, there was too much concern to avoid conflict with the seller—understandable given his great generosity to the Orchestra in the past—and not enough to ensure that the Board understood what it was getting for the money it was investing. The NJSO Board of Trustees is characterized by having a small group of a dozen or so members who are actively involved in the running of the Orchestra and who regularly attend Board and Committee meetings. The remaining members have significantly less involvement.

---

97. P. McGlone and M. Mueller, *FBI Probes Symphony Purchase of Violins: Fugitive Philanthropist Got $17M for Rare Strings*, STAR LEDGER, May 13, 2004; and R. Jones, D.C. Johnston, and A. Kozinn, *A Violin's Value, And What to Pay The I.R.S. Fiddler*, N.Y. TIMES, May 2, 2004. This number was confirmed by NEW JERSEY SYMPHONY ORCHESTRA, REPORT OF TRUSTEE REVIEW PANEL, at 9–11 (Dec. 16, 2004).
98. Treas. Reg. § 1.1011-2.
99. P. McGlone and M. Mueller, *supra* note 97; R. Jones, D.C. Johnston, and A. Kozinn, *supra* note 97; and M. Mueller, *False Notes*, STAR LEDGER, Aug. 2, 2004. The *False Notes* article is a very lengthy, in-depth article on the entire series of events surrounding the orchestra's purchase of the violins.
100. JJ. Linkous, *Philanthropist Admits Tax Fraud*, PHIL. INQ., Dec. 9, 2004.
101. *Id.*; and D. Wakin, *The Dark Side of a Windfall*, N.Y. TIMES, Dec. 11, 2004.
102. NEW JERSEY SYMPHONY ORCHESTRA, *supra* note 97, at 3-5.
103. *Id.*; and D. Wakin, *Report Faults Orchestra Officials on Deal for Rare Instruments*, N.Y. TIMES, Dec. 18, 2004.

> It is understandable that the Orchestra did not publicly challenge the seller's $50 million valuation. But that number was used by the NJSO in the press release and in the 2004–2005 season brochure, further exacerbating the problem. The Orchestra clearly wanted publicity to put itself "on the map" but should have refrained from use of the $50 million number....
>
> The independent opinions obtained by the Instrument Committee revealed concerns with the authenticity of parts of several of the instruments, but this information was not provided to the full Board. By not informing the Board of the existence of questions of authenticity of the instruments, the Instrument Committee did not meet its obligation to the Board for a thorough presentation of the proposed transaction.[104]

While the report concludes that the acquisition price was fair, clearly the governance failures and questionable claims regarding value made by Mr. Axelrod exposed the orchestra to unnecessary risk. Certainly, the orchestra did not like this publicity.

The lesson from this story is that a charity should know whom it is dealing with when it accepts in-kind contributions or participates in a bargain sale. Although the donor is the one who bears the liability if he is overly aggressive when claiming a charitable contribution deduction, any resulting fallout can reflect poorly on the charity, potentially damaging its reputation. The charity should also remember that someone who is willing to commit tax fraud may also be willing to defraud the charity with a counterfeit item.

* * *

7.3 SUBSTANTIATION BY THE DONOR AND APPRAISALS

Before being able to claim a charitable contribution deduction, the donor must be able to substantiate its value. If the donation involves property whose value exceeds $500,[105] the donor must also be able to support the valuation for the claimed deduction. The easiest way to explain these rules is through a chart.[106]

Donation Type	Amount	Rule
Cash	Less than $250	Retain (1) canceled check, (2) receipt from charity (with its name, date of contribution, and amount contributed), or (3) other comparable evidence.[107]
	$250 or more	Obtain a written acknowledgement from the charity (1) stating the amount of cash contributed, (2) stating whether it gave the donor consideration in exchange for the contribution (exclusive of certain token and membership benefits), and (3) including a description and good faith estimate of any consideration received in exchange for the contribution.[108]

104. NEW JERSEY SYMPHONY ORCHESTRA, *supra* note 81, at 4. What is notable about this passage is its implicit view that board committees have an obligation to keep the board fully informed. Unfortunately, the passage does not go far enough by acknowledging the full board's duty to ask probing questions. The passage also implicitly acknowledges the problem of large boards—that being the tendency for an inner circle of directors to develop a type of de facto executive committee.

105. Treas. Reg. §§ 1.170A-13(b)(2)(ii) and (3).

106. This chart is based on information in INTERNAL REVENUE SERVICE, *supra* note 59.

107. Treas. Reg. § 1.170A-13(a)(1).

108. I.R.C. § 170(f)(8).

Donation Type	Amount	Rule
	Less than $250	Obtain a receipt from the charity showing (1) its name, (2) the date and location of the contribution, and (3) a reasonably detailed description of the property. This is not required if obtaining the receipt is not feasible under the circumstances (e.g., leaving property at an untended drop site).[109] The taxpayer is required to have records that show the fair market value of the property and how that value was determined.
	At least $250 but less than $500	Obtain a receipt that meets the requirements for a property gift of $250 or less indicating whether the donor received consideration in exchange for the donation (with the exception of certain intangible religious benefits); the receipt also must contain a good faith estimate for the value of any consideration received by the donor.[110]
PROPERTY	At least $500 but not more than $5,000	Obtain a receipt that meets the requirements for a property gift of at least $250 but less than $500. The donor's records must reflect how and the date when the taxpayer obtained the contributed property, its adjusted basis if held 12 months or less, and if available, the adjusted basis of property held more than 12 months.[111]
	More than $5,000	Satisfy the same requirements for property contributions that have a value at least equal to $500 but not more than $5,000, obtain a qualified written appraisal, and include the appraisal as an attachment to the tax return.[112]

(a) APPRAISALS. Generally, if the claimed charitable deduction for an item or group of similar items of donated property other than money and publicly traded securities is more than $5,000, the donor must obtain an appraisal made by a qualified appraiser and must attach an appraisal summary (Section B of Form 8283 and instructions) to his tax return.[113] The donor should keep the appraiser's report with his written records.

A *qualified appraisal* (1) is an appraisal made not earlier than 60 days prior to the date of contribution of the appraised property, (2) does not involve a prohibited appraisal fee, (3) includes certain required information, and (4) is prepared, signed, and dated by a qualified appraiser.[114]

(i) Qualified Appraiser. A qualified appraiser is an individual who declares on the appraisal summary that he (1) holds himself out to the public as an appraiser or performs appraisals on a regular basis, (2) is qualified to make appraisals of the type of property being valued because of his qualifications described in the

109. Treas. Reg. § 1.170A-13(b)(1).
110. I.R.C. § 170(f)(8)(B).
111. Treas. Reg. § 1.170A-13(b)(3)(i).
112. Treas. Reg. § 1.170A-13(c).
113. Treas. Reg. § 1.170A-13(c)(2).
114. Treas. Reg. § 1.170A-13(c)(3).

appraisal, (3) is not an excluded individual, and (4) understands that an intentionally false overstatement of the value of property may subject him to the penalty for aiding and abetting an understatement of tax liability.[115] An appraiser must complete Part III of Section B of Form 8283 to be considered a qualified appraiser. The following persons cannot be qualified appraisers with respect to particular property:

- The donor of the property or the taxpayer who claims the deduction.
- The donee of the property.
- A party to the transaction in which the donor acquired the property being appraised unless the property is donated within two months of the date of acquisition and its appraised value does not exceed its acquisition price. This applies to the person who sold, exchanged, or gave the property to the donor or any person who acted as an agent for the transferor or donor in the transaction.

There are related-party antiabuse rules.[116]

(ii) Prohibited Appraisal Fees. Generally, no part of the fee arrangement for a qualified appraisal can be based on a percentage of the appraised value of the property.[117] If a fee arrangement is based on what is allowed as a deduction, after IRS examination or otherwise, it is treated as a fee based on a percentage of appraised value. However, appraisals are not disqualified when an otherwise prohibited fee is paid to a generally recognized association that regulates appraisers if (1) the association is not organized for profit and no part of its net earnings benefits any private shareholder or individual, (2) the appraiser does not receive any compensation from the association or any other persons for making the appraisal, and (3) the fee arrangement is not based in whole or in part on the amount of the appraised value that is allowed as a deduction after an IRS examination or otherwise.[118]

(iii) Required Information. A qualified appraisal must provide the following information:

- A description of the property in sufficient detail for a person not generally familiar with the type of property to determine that the property appraised is the property that was (or will be) contributed.
- The physical condition of any tangible property.
- The date (or expected date) of contribution.

115. Treas. Reg. § 1.170A-13(c)(5).
116. Treas. Reg. § 1.170A-13(c)(5)(iv)(E).
117. Treas. Reg. § 1.170A-13(c)(6)(i).
118. Treas. Reg. § 1.170A-13(c)(6)(ii).

- The terms of any agreement or understanding entered into (or expected to be entered into) by or on behalf of the donor that relates to the use, sale, or other disposition of the donated property.
- The name, address, and taxpayer identification number of the qualified appraiser and, if the appraiser is a partner, an employee, or an independent contractor engaged by a person other than the donor, the name, address, and taxpayer identification number of the partnership or the person who employs or engages the appraiser.
- The qualifications of the qualified appraiser who signs the appraisal, including the appraiser's background, experience, education, and any membership in professional appraisal associations.
- A statement that the appraisal was prepared for income tax purposes.
- The date (or dates) on which the property was valued.
- The appraised fair market value on the date (or expected date) of contribution.
- The method of valuation used to determine fair market value, such as the income approach, the comparable sales or market data approach, or the replacement cost less depreciation approach.
- The specific basis for the valuation, such as any specific comparable sales transaction.[119]

(iv) Artwork. Special rules apply to charitable contributions of artworks. When claiming a deduction of $20,000 or more for donations of art, the donor must attach a complete copy of the signed appraisal to his tax return. For individual objects valued at $20,000 or more, a photograph of a size and quality fully showing the object, preferably an 8 × 10-inch color photograph or a color transparency no smaller than 4 × 5 inches, must be provided upon request.[120] If the artwork is valued at $50,000 or more, the donor can request a Statement of Value from the IRS.[121] The resulting process is intended to resolve valuation disputes and provide certainty regarding the amount of the contribution. The Statement of Value must be requested before filing the tax return that reports the donation.

(v) Tax Treatment of Appraisal Fees. Appraisal fees are not deductible as charitable contributions but may be deducted as miscellaneous itemized deductions subject to the 2 percent limitation on itemized deductions.[122]

---

119. Treas. Reg. § 1.170A-13(c)(3)(ii).
120. Internal Revenue Service, Publication 561, Determining the Value of Donated Property, at 4 (Feb. 2000).
121. For additional details, see Internal Revenue Service, Publication 561, Determining the Value of Donated Property (rev. 10/05).
122. Internal Revenue Service, Publication 529, Miscellaneous Itemized Deductions, at 9 (2004).

(vi) Postgift Sale. Finally, the donee organization must file a Form 8282 if it sells the donated property (valued at more than $500 at the time of the gift) within two years. Presumably, the IRS will challenge a deduction for an amount far in excess of what the charity realized in cash from the subsequent sale.

(b) SPECIAL RULE FOR AUTOMOBILES, BOATS, AND AIRPLANES. To curb what were perceived as widespread valuation abuses, Congress enacted special rules applicable to gifts of automobiles, boats, and airplanes to charitable organizations.[123] Under these special rules, a taxpayer cannot claim a deduction for the contribution of a qualified vehicle whose claimed value exceeds $500 unless the taxpayer substantiates the contribution by a contemporaneous written acknowledgement from the charity.[124] More significant, the deduction is limited to the gross proceeds realized by the charity if it sells the vehicle without any significant intervening use or material improvement.[125] To be contemporaneous, the acknowledgement must be given within 30 days of the sale of the qualified vehicle.[126] It must include this information:

- The donor's name and taxpayer identification number.
- The vehicle identification number.
- A certification that the vehicle was sold in an arm's-length transaction between unrelated parties.
- The amount of gross proceeds from the sale.
- A statement that the deduction may not exceed the amount of the gross proceeds from the sale.

There are alternative certifications if the charity improves or uses the car. Charities should be reluctant to play games with the acknowledgements because the penalties are stiff, calculated on a car-by-car basis, and based on the product of the highest individual income tax rate and the gross proceeds from the sale of the vehicle.[127]

7.4 PLANNED GIVING

You may have noticed references to sophisticated investment arrangements referred to as *planned giving* in fundraising literature from charities. In recent years, charities have become very aggressive in making high net worth donors aware of these arrangements; in fact, some charities have special departments that work with donors and their advisers to implement planned gifts.

123. I.R.C. § 170(f)(12).
124. IRS Notice 2005-44, I.R.B. 2005-25, at § 3.03.
125. I.R.C. § 170(f)(12)(A)(ii).
126. I.R.C. § 170(f)(12)(C).
127. I.R.C. § 6720.

Charities have taken advantage of the Web to promote their planned giving programs. These Web sites are excellent places to look for information about such programs. The following sites are representative:

- Greenpeace: http://www.greenpeaceusa.org/support/planned.htm.
- Shriners Hospitals: http://www.shrinershq.org/Hospitals/help.html.
- Harvard Law School Baker House Alumni Center: http://www.fas.harvard.edu/~dtang/HLSAlumniCenter/giving.html

A complete discussion of these programs is well beyond the scope of this *Guide,* but directors and executive officers should have some familiarity with these arrangements so that they can determine whether offering planned giving opportunities to donors might prove beneficial.

The five basic categories of arrangements that fall within the planned giving rubric are (1) pooled income funds, (2) charitable remainder trusts, (3) charitable lead trusts, (4) charitable gift annuities, and (5) remainder interests in property. These all involve gifts of partial interests in property. Donors can use planned giving vehicles to facilitate lifetime and postmortem giving programs. If it is structured as a lifetime gift, the donor generally gives the property to a charity, retains an interest in the property, and claims a charitable contribution for its value. If structured as a postmortem gift, the donor's will or other testamentary instrument will provide for the gift following the donor's death. We will limit our focus to lifetime gifts.

(a) POOLED INCOME FUNDS. A *pooled income fund* is created by a public charity to invest funds contributed to the fund by donors.[128] The donors are entitled to a proportionate share of the income for their lives. The charity holds the remainder interest.[129] The donor can also specify that the life interest be created for one or more other beneficiaries.

The donor can transfer assets to the fund without triggering tax liability (with the exception of property encumbered by debt or transferred in exchange for property other than a qualifying interest in the fund).[130] The donor is entitled to claim a charitable contribution in the year of the transfer for the actuarially determined value of the remainder interest.[131]

(i) Pooled Income Funds from the Donor's Perspective. Under federal securities laws and SEC policy, pooled income funds must provide prospective donors a disclosure statement.[132] It goes without saying that every prospective donor should review the disclosure statement to become familiar with the particular

128. I.R.C. § 642(c)(5).
129. Treas. Reg. §§ 1.642(c)-5(b)(2), (7), and (c).
130. Treas. Reg. § 1.642(c)-5(a)(3).
131. I.R.C. § 170(f)(2)(A); and Treas. Reg. § 1.642(c)-5(a)(4).
132. SEC Release 33-6175 (1980).

fund's investment objectives and policies, distribution procedures, management, and general operation.

A pooled income fund is similar to a mutual fund. The donor receives a proportionate share of income each year. There is no guaranteed or minimum distribution. In short, the donor is relying on the performance of the fund managers, so he should review their track record. Unlike mutual funds, the donor cannot simply sell his interest in a pooled income fund and then reinvest the proceeds in another one.

The capital gains of a typical pooled income fund are added to the trust principal, meaning that they are not distributed to the donor-participants.[133] Donors considering a pooled income fund must recognize that their distributions will therefore come from dividends, interest, rents, and royalties rather than directly from capital gains. As a consequence, donors often will be foregoing the higher returns that have been associated with capital appreciation in recent years.

Pooled income funds are probably the simplest of all the planned giving tools from a donor's perspective. Nevertheless, the donor probably should retain a lawyer to review the documents but does not need one to draft custom trust documents. Although the donor bears the cost of administering the fund, this cost is often spread over many participants. The donor does not have to create the administrative apparatus.

Furthermore, the donor is able to diversify his holdings by transferring existing assets without incurring a tax liability in exchange for an interest in a diversified pool of assets.[134]

(ii) Pooled Income Funds from the Charity's Perspective. Pooled income funds (as well as other planned giving programs) permit charities to "lock in" donors. The donor could give a small amount of capital each year to a charity and use the income from the remaining capital for his personal needs. The charity hopes that the donor to a pooled income fund will turn over a larger portion

---

133. Federal income tax law requires that all income be distributed to the pool of donors participating in a pooled income fund each year. However, federal tax law looks to state law for the definition for income. *See* I.R.C. §643(b). Traditionally, state law—which obviously varies from state to state—has excluded capital gains from the definition of income, but in recent years there has been some movement away from treating capital gains as additions to principal rather than income. Although pooled income funds might, as a theoretical matter, be able to distribute long-term capital gains to donor participants, the tax rules appear to create disincentives to structures contemplating such a result. *See* Tres. Reg. 1.642(c)-2(c). *See also* Planned Giving Design Center, Pooled Income Fund Technical Details *available at* http://www.pgdc.com/usa/itemID=60848; and Bruce Hopkins, *supra* note 5, at § 13.8. A search of the Web did not reveal any pooled income funds that provided for distributions of long-term capital gains.

If capital gains are retained by the pooled income fund, it will not be required to pay tax with respect to such gains. This makes sense because the beneficiary of those gains will be the charitable remainder interest. The tax law accomplishes this result by providing a deduction for long-term capital gains that are permanently set aside for charitable purposes. *See* I.R.C. § 642(c)(3). A pooled income fund that does not treat short-term capital gains as income therefore faces a tax liability with respect to those gains.

134. Treas. Reg. 1,642(c)-5(a)(3).

of capital at the outset in exchange for a larger charitable contribution deduction in the year of the contribution and a continuing income stream. This provides the charity more certainty than an unenforceable pattern of annual giving.

Charities relying on pooled income funds need to make sure (but not guarantee) that donors receive what they are promised. Although it may be locking in more capital through a pooled income fund, a charity is unlikely to receive additional contributions from a particular donor should that donor have a bad experience with the fund.

Pooled income funds are subject to many of the same excise taxes that apply to private foundations,[135] meaning that their sponsors must focus on the rules against self-dealing, jeopardy investments, and excess business holdings, but the jeopardy investment and excess business holding rules apply in only certain circumstances.[136]

(iii) Pooled Income Fund Example. Consider Fran Wiley, a 72-year-old retired advertising executive, who owns shares of Intel with a fair market value of $250,000 and a cost basis of $100,000. Wiley would like to make a contribution to the Ross School of Design, her alma mater, but she will require some of the income from the value represented by her investment in Intel to live on. The development officer for the Ross School of Design has suggested that she consider an investment in the school's pooled income fund. He has suggested that she contribute her Intel stock to the fund. Assume the fund is currently earning a 7 percent return and the applicable discount rate is also 7 percent.

Transfer date	June 1, 20X5
Section 7520 discount rate	7%
Wiley's age	72
Payout Schedule	Quarterly

Wiley will receive $17,500 of income in the first year following her investment. After that, her income from the fund will be dependent on the fund's income. She will receive a $116,890 charitable contribution deduction. Finally, she will pay no tax on the transfer of the Intel stock to the pooled income fund.[137] She will pay tax on the distributions from the fund.

Pooled income funds are not black boxes that create wealth. If Wiley decides to contribute to the school's fund, she will have the satisfaction that she made a charitable contribution to a worthy organization, but her overall net worth will be reduced. The anticipated tax benefits and income stream will not fully compensate her for the $250,000 contribution.

135. I.R.C. § 4947(a)(2).

136. I.R.C. §§ 4947(a)(2) and (b)(3).

137. Treas. Reg. § 1.642(c)-5(a)(3).

(iv) Pooled Income Fund Statistics. According to IRS statistics, pooled income funds represent one of the least popular planned giving programs. In 2002, the IRS received 1,675 returns for pooled income funds reporting just over $1.5 billion in net asset value. This pales in comparison to the IRS's estimates of asset values for charitable remainder trusts ($94 billion) and charitable lead trusts ($12.2 billion). Charities certainly are free to consider a pooled income fund, but the statistics suggest that other areas may produce better results for them.[138]

(b) CHARITABLE REMAINDER TRUSTS. A *charitable remainder trust* is established by a donor to provide for specified periodic distributions to one or more beneficiaries for life or a specific number of years; the assets remaining at the end of the specified term are distributed to a named charity.[139] The donor, not the charity, creates the trust, although a charity certainly can recommend it.

Charitable remainder trusts are similar to pooled income funds, but without the pooling of investments by multiple donors. A prospective donor who sells or plans to sell a major asset that will trigger a large taxable gain might consider creating a charitable remainder trust. The trust would permit the donor to reduce his tax liability in the year of sale through a charitable contribution deduction and will provide him with income for a specified term of years or until his death. Charitable remainder trusts can be structured as either unitrusts or annuity trusts. A unitrust makes payments to the donor based on a percentage of the trust's value. An annuity trust provides for a level periodic payment. Tax lawyers have developed a number of variations on these two basic formats, having acronyms like SCRUT, FLIPCRUT, and NICRUT. In other words, these devises can be tailored to address specific issues, but those efforts add complexity.

(i) Charitable Remainder Trusts from the Donor's Perspective. Donors should consider several issues before implementing a charitable remainder trust. Most important, they must understand the inverse relationship between the term of the income interest they "retain" and the size of the charitable contribution deduction. The relative size of the charitable contribution deduction declines as the term of the trust grows longer, but the longer the trust's term, the more future income the donors will receive.

No appraisal is necessary if the transferred property is cash or publicly traded securities. Donors must otherwise obtain a qualified appraisal to substantiate the deduction when the claimed deduction exceeds $5,000 ($10,000 if closely held stock).

---

138. L. Schreiber, *Spit-Interest Trusts, 2002*, IRS STAT. ON INC. BUL. (Winter 2004-05)
139. I.R.C. § 664.

Donors should carefully consider selecting the trustee, who can be a professional corporate trustee, the charity (if it is willing to accommodate the donor), or, under certain circumstances, the donor.[140] Donors must recognize that a charity has a potential conflict of interest when it acts as trustee. Donors also need to evaluate the trustee's investment performance, fee structure, accounting and reporting system, and specific experience with charitable remainder trusts.

The trust instrument of a charitable remainder trust cannot contain a provision restricting the trustee from investing the trust assets in a manner that could result in the realization of a reasonable amount of income or gain from the disposition of trust assets.[141] According to one commentator, this limitation is designed to prevent the invasion of the trust corpus to the detriment of the charity.[142]

Donors can transfer appreciated property to a charitable remainder trust without triggering a tax, thereby deferring the built-in tax liability. If, however, the charity immediately sells the asset in a prearranged sale, the IRS may attribute the gain to the donor, resulting in tax liability. There are ways to avoid this problem but these require planning well before sale negotiations begin.[143]

(ii) Charitable Remainder Trusts from the Charity's Perspective. Charities have few concerns with charitable remainder trusts. In fact, many charitable remainder trusts are created without the charity's knowledge.[144] In many instances, the charity is not the trustee and, consequently, has nothing to do with the trust's administration. When a donor approaches a charity about establishing a charitable remainder trust, the charity should consider these points. First, as the prospective recipient of the remainder interest in the trust, the charity should consider whether it is creating a potential conflict of interest with the income beneficiaries if it serves as trustee.

Second, if a charity advises a donor to select a corporate trustee, the charity should recognize that many large corporate trustees handle charitable remainder trusts only if the initial contribution exceeds a certain amount. If the amount involved is too small, the charity might suggest a charitable gift annuity or a pooled income fund instead.

Third, the charity should assess the type of property used to fund the trust. Publicly traded securities involve few issues. If the donor is proposing real estate, however, the charity should consider environmental liabilities. It may be able to disclaim the interest in the property when the trust terminates, but it does not want to lose the value represented by the remainder interest if it can avoid doing so by recommending a more suitable asset to fund the trust. Charities

---

140. Rev. Rul. 77-285, 1977-2 C.B. 213

141. Treas. Reg. § 1.664-1(a)(3). See Rev. Rul. 73-610, 1973-2 C.B. 213.

142. M. Hoffman, *The Charitable Remainder Trust*, Planned Giving Design Center, http://www.pgdc.com.

143. Rev. Rul. 60-370, 1960-2 C.B. 203.

144. But see, for example,Illinois Statutes, Title 14, Subtitle B, Chapter II, Part 480, which imposes registration requirements on certain charitable remainder trusts.

should also steer donors away from using property that will create unrelated business income for the charity.

(iii) Charitable Remainder Trust Example. Consider John and Evelyn Clay, who are happily married. John is 65 and Evelyn is 63; they have no children. In 1985, they invested $200,000 in General Electric. That investment is now valued at $2 million. They have an additional $7 million in financial assets and a $1 million home. The assets generate $700,000 of taxable income each year.

Both John and Evelyn are patrons of Chicago Belini Opera Company (Belini). They have always planned to leave the bulk of their estate to it. They now view their General Electric investment as too risky for their portfolio. Consequently, they decide to establish a charitable remainder unitrust, funding it with the General Electric stock. The Five Spot Bank will act as trustee, and Belini will be entitled to receive the trust assets upon the death of the survivor. Following the contribution, the trust will sell the General Electric stock, realizing a $1 million gain. Under the terms of the trust, John and Evelyn will be entitled to receive annual distributions equal to 6 percent of the trust's fair market value. The trust assets will be invested in high-grade corporate bonds. Here is a summary of the assumptions:

Transfer date	June 1, 20X5
Section 7520 discount rate	5%
John's age	65
Evelyn's age	63
Unitrust payments	Annually
Unitrust payout rate	6%
Date of first payment	January 1, 2006
Last to die	Yes
Life trust	Yes

The calculations indicate that John and Evelyn's retained interest is worth $1,469,340, meaning that they will be entitled to an immediate income tax deduction of $530,660 (recognizing that the percentage limitations may apply). Upon the death of the survivor, the remaining trust assets will pass to Belini.

(iv) Charitable Remainder Trusts Are Not Black Boxes. As noted at the outset of this discussion, planned giving devices are not black boxes. Consider Harold Williams, a person "who earned it and wants to spend it all." A charitable remainder trust is not a suitable investment vehicle for Williams. It is a legitimate way to accelerate charitable contributions into a year when the donor is in a high income tax bracket and to defer capital gains taxes, but the rules governing charitable remainder trusts are designed to prevent the donor from having 110 percent of his pregift value after establishing a trust. Williams may be retaining an interest in the donated asset, but he is actually making a gift to a charity.

Although there will be tax savings and investment income, Williams is parting with asset value. If Williams is not charitably inclined, he should avoid charitable remainder trusts.

(v) Charitable Remainder Trusts Represent Fertile Ground for Fundraisers. According to IRS statistics, charitable remainder trusts are popular giving vehicles.[145] Just over 114,000 tax returns were filed for charitable remainder trusts for the 2002 taxable year. By far the most popular format (91,371 returns) is the unitrust format. The IRS estimates that charitable remainder trusts held somewhere around $94 billion in assets,[146] with about 97,000 of the returns reporting assets with a book value of $1 million or less.

(c) CHARITABLE LEAD TRUSTS. A *charitable lead trust* is the exact opposite of a charitable remainder trust, but it is not a tax-exempt entity. The donor designates a term of years (or the life or lives of certain persons) as the period during which the charity will receive the income from the trust assets.[147] At the end of this term, the assets pass to the donor or his designee, free of any further claim by the charity. Donors are typically attracted to lead trusts because they permit donors to shift appreciation from their estates while making a current gift to a charity. As with a charitable remainder trust, the income interest must be paid at least annually based either on a fixed sum (annuity trust) or a percentage of the trust's fair market value (unitrust) before a donor may, depending on the structure of the trust, receive a charitable contribution deduction for the initial transfer to the trust.[148]

(i) Charitable Lead Trusts from the Donor's Perspective. Unlike a charitable remainder trust, a charitable lead trust does not necessarily provide the donor a charitable income tax deduction for the value of the interest given to the charity. There are two possible outcomes, with the result depending on the donor's desires and the trust's structure.

GRANTOR TRUST

If the donor structures the trust as a *grantor trust* under federal income tax law,[149] the donor will receive a charitable contribution income tax deduction equal to the discounted value of the income interest, but the donor will be required to include the trust's taxable income in his gross income each year during the trust's term, thereby preventing the donor from receiving a "double dip" in the form of an income tax deduction and an exclusion of the income earned on the trust assets. Although this reduces the tax benefits, a donor who is currently in a high tax bracket and expects to be in a lower tax bracket during the term of

145. L. Schreiber, *supra* note 138.

146. Unitrusts reported $84 billion in assets based on fair market value, and annuity trusts reported $10 billion in assets determined based on book value.

147. I.R.C. §170(f)(2)(B).

148. Treas. Reg. §§ 1.170A-6(c)(2)(i) and (ii).

149. Treas. Reg. § 1.170A-6(c)(1).

the trust is a good candidate for a grantor trust, all other things being equal and assuming that phantom taxable income will not pose a problem. As an alternative, the trust could be funded with tax-exempt bonds; as a result, the donor still receives a charitable contribution deduction but has little income to include in his gross income over the term of the income interest.[150]

A NONGRANTOR TRUST

If the donor structures the lead trust as a *nongrantor trust,* the donor forgoes a charitable contribution income tax deduction when he funds the trust, but the income is attributed to the trust rather than the donor. These trusts are particularly appropriate for shifting taxable value to a child or grandchild on a tax-favored basis. Special rules apply if the trust receives unrelated business taxable income. Once again, lead trusts only make sense if the donor is charitably inclined.

(ii) Estate and Gift Tax Consequences. Establishing a charitable lead trust clearly has significant gift and estate tax implications. It often makes sense to fund the trust with property that the donor expects to appreciate because he may be able to shift that appreciation to the remainder beneficiaries on a tax-advantaged basis. If the remainder beneficiary is a grandchild (or other "skip" person), the donor and his estate planner must also consider whether the generation-skipping tax applies to the transaction. In 2001, President George W. Bush signed into law tax legislation that repeals the estate tax in 2010. That change has implications for charitable lead trusts that are best left to an experienced tax planner.

(iii) Private Foundation Excise Taxes. Although a charitable lead trust is not a private foundation, it is subject to a number of the excise taxes imposed on private foundations.[151] These trusts are generally subject to the self-dealing excise tax and, under certain circumstances, to the excise taxes pertaining to excess business holdings and jeopardizing investments.[152]

(iv) Charitable Lead Trust Example. Consider Malcolm Hiken, a widower with one grandchild, Patty Milford. Hiken has a sizable estate and is in the 35 percent income tax bracket. He would like to leave money to Milford, but he does not want her to have access to the money until she is 30 years old and has solid values. Hiken realizes that his estate is growing at a very fast rate and that the appreciation will be subject to an assumed 50 percent estate tax.

---

150. A. Grumet, *Choosing the Best Charitable Lead Trust to Meet a Client's Needs*, PLANNED GIVING DESIGN CENTER (Mar. 19, 2003). This article indicates that tax-exempt bonds are a permissible investment. However, it does suggest that if the donor is charitably inclined, his paying taxes on the trust's income attributed to him may be a benefit. This sort of planning is beyond the scope of this *Guide*. The article originally appeared in ESTATE PLANNING.

151. I.R.C. § 4947.

152. I.R.C. § 4947(a)(2).

Hiken's wife, Julie, was a supporter of Red Bird House Society, a Section 501(c)(3) organization. He would like to honor Julie by making a significant contribution to the Society. Gertrude Spitzer, Hiken's estate planner, suggests a charitable lead trust as a way to honor Julie and leave money for Milford without spoiling her values.

Transfer date	June 1, 20X5
Section 7520 discount rate	6.4%
Beginning principal amount	$3,000,000
Unitrust payments	Annually
Unitrust payout rate	5%
Term	20 Years
Date of first payment	January 1, 2006

The remainder interest that will pass to Milford has a value of $1,075,458. That means that Malcolm could receive a $1,942,542 charitable contribution deduction if the trust is structured as a grantor trust. In that case, Malcolm will also be required to include the trust's taxable income in his gross income over the time that Red Bird House Society receives income from the trust. He also has a potential gift tax on the transfer of the remainder interest. Incurring that tax may not make sense because of recent and proposed changes in the federal gift and estate tax. That is something each potential donor should discuss with his estate planner.

(v) Charitable Lead Trust Statistics. According to IRS statistics, charitable lead trusts are far less popular than charitable remainder trusts, with just over 5,480 returns reporting the use of charitable lead trusts in 2002.[153] However, the IRS estimated that these trusts held just over $12.2 billion dollars in assets. These statistics are a bit surprising because a quick search of the Web leaves the impression that hundreds if not thousands of charities and advisers are willing to advise charitably inclined individuals about the benefits of charitable lead trusts—apparently wishful thinking on their part.

(d) CHARITABLE GIFT ANNUITIES. *Charitable gift annuities* are exactly what the name implies. The donor transfers property (most likely appreciated property but it can be cash) to a charity in exchange for its promise to pay the donor an annuity for his life or the joint lives of two persons (usually the donor and spouse, with payments continuing until the death of the survivor). The annuity payout rate is fixed so that the annuity's present value is less than the value of the property transferred, making the transfer in part a sale to the charity and in part a gift to which the bargain sale rules apply.[154]

153. L. Schreiber, *supra* note 138.
154. Treas. Reg. § 1.170A-1(d)(3).

(i) Charitable Gift Annuity from the Donor's Perspective. A charitable gift annuity is a general obligation of the charitable organization issuing it. As a consequence, donors should ascertain whether the charity has the financial wherewithal to satisfy its obligations, not only next year but also over the annuity's entire term. One large charitable organization filed bankruptcy, probably making the holders of its gift annuities nervous. Fortunately for those holders, the bankruptcy court authorized a plan that permitted payments under the annuities to continue.[155] Holders of gift annuities issued by other charities might not be so fortunate.

Donors should recognize that although the charity is issuing an annuity contract, its contract differs economically from those issued by life insurers and other commercial issuers. Under a charitable gift annuity, the donor is entitled to a stream of payments that has a present value significantly less than the amount the donor is transferring to the charity. This should not come as a surprise because the donor is making a charitable contribution as part of the charitable gift annuity transaction.

Charities do not offer fixed-term annuities because doing so would either jeopardize their exempt status or result in tax.[156] The annuity's terms can provide a deferred starting date,[157] which has the effect of increasing the size of the charitable contribution deduction that the donor receives.

The bargain sale to charity rules apply if the donor funds the annuity with a transfer of appreciated to the charity,[158] meaning that to calculate the taxpayer's gain on the sale, he must allocate his adjusted basis in the property between the sale portion and the charitable portion. This allocation is based on the relative fair market values of the investment in the contract and the value of the property transferred to the charity. If appreciated property is transferred in exchange for the annuity, the taxpayer can report the gain over his life expectancy[159] if the arrangement satisfies each of the following requirements: (1) a charitable contribution deduction is allowable, (2) the annuity is either nonassignable or assignable only to the charitable organization to which the property is sold, and (3) the taxpayer is the only annuitant or the taxpayer and a designated survivor annuitant or annuitants are the only annuitants.[160]

A donor who receives an annuity payment is required to determine the amount of the payment that must be included in gross income. The taxpayer must determine the "investment in the contract," "expected return," and "exclusion ratio." The *investment in the contract* is best thought of as what the donor paid for the contract; it equals the annuity's present value. This amount will not include the

155. Press Release, National Benevolent Association (May 7, 2004), stating that "[t]he order on gift annuities authorizes the uninterrupted payment of all gift annuities written prior to NBA's Chapter 11 filing Feb. 16."
156. I.R.C. §§ 501(m) and 514(c)(5).
157. BRUCE HOPKINS, *supra* note 1575.
158. Treas. Reg. § 1.1011-2.
159. *Id.;* and Example 8 for an illustration of the calculations.
160. Treas. Reg. § 1.1011-2(a)(4)(ii). See BRUCE HOPKINS, *supra* note 1575, at 498-99.

full value of the property that the donor transferred to the charity because a part of that value represents a donation. The *expected return* is the amount that the donor expects to receive under the contract over its term. This amount is determined using tables provided by the IRS. The *exclusion ratio* is the investment in the contract divided by the expected return. The resulting percentage is multiplied by each payment to determine the amount of the payment that is excluded from the taxpayer's gross income, but the total amount excluded over the life of the contract can never exceed the investment in the contract. The remaining portion of each payment is taxable as ordinary income. The best way to understand these and the preceding calculations is to review Example 8 in Treasury Regulation Section 1.1011-2(c), keeping in mind that the format set out in the regulations is correct but that the tables used for the calculations have since been revised.

As already noted, charitable gift annuities involve a bargain element. The IRS has issued a series of tables that permit the donor to calculate the amount of charitable contribution deduction generated by the bargain element. The resulting income tax deduction is subject to the various limitations on charitable contribution deductions.

(ii) Charitable Gift Annuity from the Charity's Perspective. Charities love charitable gift annuities because they are relatively simple to implement and inexpensive to administer. In fact, they can be lucrative for a charity even when the gift is as low as $5,000.[161] A charity must recognize, however, that its obligations to pay the annuity is a general obligation. In other words, the obligation to the annuitant is a claim against all of the charity's assets. This differs from charitable remainder and lead trusts whose only claim for distributions is against the assets held in the trust.

Like commercial annuities, charitable annuities are an insurance product and, as such, can be subject to state regulation. Any charity implementing a charitable gift annuity program should check with the appropriate state insurance or comparable regulators to determine whether it or its annuity plans must be registered or reserves must be maintained.[162]

Charities typically describe charitable gift annuities using payout rates pegged to various ages. The payout rate is stated as a percentage (e.g., 7.1 percent) at a specified age (e.g., 50) and, when multiplied by the value transferred (e.g., $10,000) to the charity, determines the annual annuity payment (e.g., $710). This rate is *not* set by the tax law but by market forces. Charities were concerned that competition would lead to high payout rates and thus a corresponding reduction in the value of the actual contribution to them. In response to that concern, a number of charities formed the American Council on Gift Annuities (the Council). It established payout rates designed to ensure that the charities received benefits

161. A search of the Web identified dozens of charities that have set the minimum gift at $5,000 or $10,000.

162. *See, e.g.*, Wis. Stat., Chapter 615, §§ 615.03 through 615.15, regulating charitable gift annuities. The American Council on Gift Annuities maintains a Web site that describes the regulatory provisions in each state.

from these transactions. These rates reflect the following assumptions: (1) at the expiration of the annuity, (2) the charity will receive approximately 50 percent of the amount originally donated; the charity will incur expenses equal to 1 percent of its gift annuity reserves, and (3) the charity's annual expected rate of return will equal 6 percent of its gift annuity reserves.[163]

In 1995, a donor sued the council, arguing that its activities violated antitrust laws. The suit was successful,[164] but Congress subsequently enacted legislation providing that the council's activities do not violate antitrust laws.[165] Many charities use the council's payout rates to calculate annuity payments. Others choose to set their own rates.

Unless properly structured, a charitable gift annuity can generate unrelated business income to the charity, resulting in a tax liability. To avoid that result, (1) the annuity must be the sole consideration issued for the transfer of the property, (2) the value of the annuity when the property is transferred to the charity must be less than 90 percent of the value of the property the charity receives, (3) the annuity must be payable over the life of one individual who is alive when the annuity is issued or over the lives of two individuals who are alive at that time, and (4) the annuity cannot guarantee a minimum amount of payments or specify a maximum amount of payments or adjust the annuity payment amount by reference to the income received from the transferred property.[166] On occasion, donors transfer property subject to liabilities. These transfers also have unrelated business income tax implications.

In setting up a gift annuity program, the charity, like an insurance company, must focus on appropriate investments and donor mortality rates so that it has the funds available to pay the annuity.[167] Typically, donors making charitable gift annuities are wealthy, meaning that their mortality rates can differ from those of the general population. Even within this category of donors, there may be adverse selection (from the charity's standpoint). People who are attracted to life annuities are likely to be healthier than the average member of the population—at least that is a good hypothesis. The following question illustrates that point: Why would someone with terminal cancer opt for a gift annuity?

(iii) Charitable Gift Annuity Example. Consider Claire Jones, who on June 1, 20X5, transfers real estate that she has held for investment to Good Deeds Charity in exchange for a charitable gift annuity. Jones purchased the real estate in 1996 and has used the straight-line method of depreciation for tax purposes.

---

163. F. Minton, *Maximizing the Benefits from Your Gift Annuity Program*, PLANNED GIVING DESIGN CENTER (July 8, 2004).

164. Richie v. American Council on Gift Annuities, 943 F. Supp. 685 (N.D. Tex. 1996).

165. Charitable Gift Annuity Antitrust Relief Act of 1995, Pub. L. 104-63, 109 Stat. 687 (1995), *codified at* 15 U.S.C. 37, et. seq. This act was subsequently amended by the Charitable Donation Antitrust Immunity Act of 1997, Pub. L. 105-26, 111 Stat. 241 (1997), to clarify its broad scope.

166. I.R.C. § 514(c)(5).

167. F. Minton, *supra* note 163.

At the time of the transfer, the real estate was valued at $500,000 and had a $50,000 adjusted basis. In exchange for the transfer, Good Deeds has agreed to pay Jones an annual annuity for the remainder of her life. The payout rate is equal to 7 percent, resulting in a $35,000 annual payment. Jones is 65 years of age.

Transfer date	June 1, 20X5
Section 7520 discount rate	6.4%
Land value	$500,000
Payments	Annually
Annuity rate	7%
Date of first payment	January 1, 2006
Type	End of period
Lives	Single life
Age	65

Under the formula for valuing charitable gift annuities, Jones will be entitled to a $170,566 charitable contribution deduction and a $35,000 annual payment. For the first 19.5 years, $15,205 of the payment will be taxed as capital gain, $18,095 of it will be taxed as ordinary income, and $1,700 will be nontaxable. After that period, the entire payment will be taxed as ordinary income.

(e) OTHER PARTIAL INTERESTS IN PROPERTY. As a general rule, taxpayers cannot deduct gifts of partial interests in property to charities.[168] For example, if an individual permits a local food bank to lease space rent free in a building that he owns, he is not permitted to deduct the rental value as a charitable contribution. That's the classic example. Charitable remainder trusts, charitable lead trusts, and pooled income funds are all exceptions to the general rule prohibiting charitable contribution deductions for gifts of partial interests.

More recently, the IRS and corporate taxpayers have had disputes over whether certain contributions of patents and other intellectual property are deductible as charitable contributions.[169] Corporations generate far more patentable ideas than they can commercially exploit. To recoup some of the cost of developing patents that will not be exploited, a corporation may enter into an agreement to contribute one or more of these patents to a university. Problems arise if the corporation imposes limitations on the university's use or transfer of the patent. The question is whether the corporation has donated the patent outright or retained an interest in it (eliminating the basis for a charitable contribution deduction).[170] Recent legislation has curbed some of the valuation abuses

168. I.R.C. § 170(f)(3).
169. Rev. Rul. 2003-28, 2003-11 I.R.B.
170. IRS Notice 2004-7, 2004-3 I.R.B. 1.

when it comes to intellectual property,[171] but the partial interest question is still an issue.

Let's consider three specific types of transactions that can generate a charitable contribution deduction even though the donor retains an interest in the property.

(i) Partial Interests in Personal Residences and Farms. One well-developed exception to the basic partial interest rule involves gifts of remainder interests in personal residences and farms.[172] The term *personal residence* includes more than just a taxpayer's principal residence. For example, it includes a vacation home [173] but not its furnishings.[174]

As a general rule, parties should obtain a qualified appraisal of a residence or farm because the charitable contribution deduction exceeds $5,000. In valuing the remainder interest, the taxpayer must determine the estimated useful life and salvage value of the improvements so that depreciation can be factored into the valuation.[175] As with other valuations, the taxpayer must use prescribed discount rates and mortality tables to determine a value for the remainder interest and the associated deduction.[176]

The IRS has not provided taxpayers any language for transfers of personal residence and farm remainders, so taxpayers are on their own. The transfer of the remainder interest must be irrevocable. The agreement should address insurance, maintenance, property leases, proceeds from involuntary conversions (e.g., insurance proceeds paid as a result of a casualty), and how to handle the sale proceeds and other decisions.

A charity should consider at least two issues before accepting a remainder interest in a personal residence or farm. First, the charity should address the property's rental. Although it may have to wait until the death of the donor to receive its interest in the personal residence or farm, the donor may choose or be forced by health problems to move out of the residence or farm. In such event, the donor may want to rent the property to a third party and retain the rent. If the donor conditions the gift on such a provision, the charity will certainly have an interest in knowing to whom the property can be rented and under what terms.

Second, and of even more importance, a charity should consider environmental liabilities. The Comprehensive Environmental Response, Compensation and Liability Act now provides charities some relief under specific circumstances from potential liability for environmental cleanup so long as the charity is not

---

171. I.R.C. § 170(e)(1)(B)(iii), as added by the American Jobs Creation Act of 2004, Pub. L. 108-357, 118 Stat. 1418 (2004). See IRS Notice 2005-41, 2005-23 I.R.B.
172. I.R.C. § 170(f)(3)(B)(i).
173. Treas. Reg. § 1.170A-7(b)(3).
174. Rev. Rul. 76-165, 1976-1 C.B. 279.
175. I.R.C. 170(f)(4).
176. Treas. Reg. § 1.170A-12.

responsible for the contamination.[177] Nevertheless, the charity should undertake an appropriate environmental study because other federal and state laws may not be so lenient. Furthermore, if the charity plans to sell the property, associated environmental problems could depress its sales price. Finally, the charity does not want to build anything on a contaminated site. The charity could be forced to incur substantial costs to alleviate the problem. Moreover, there could be adverse publicity.

(ii) Conservation Easements. Taxpayers can claim a charitable contribution deduction for *qualified conservation contributions*,[178] which are contributions of a qualified real property interest to a qualified organization to be used only for conservation purposes. For these purposes, a qualified organization is (1) a governmental unit, (2) a publicly supported charitable, religious, scientific, literary, or educational organization, and (3) other specified organizations.[179] Therefore a large universe of potential recipients exists.[180] The organization receiving the otherwise deductible contribution must have a commitment to protect the conservation purposes underlying the donation and the resources available to enforce the restrictions.[181]

The contribution must be made for only one of the following conservation purposes: (1) preservation of land areas for outdoor recreation by, or for the education of, the general public, (2) protection of a relatively natural habitat of fish, wildlife, or plants, or a similar ecosystem, (3) preservation of open space, including farmland and forest land, or (4) preservation of an historically important land area or a certified historic structure.[182] The preservation of open space must yield a significant public benefit. It must be either for the scenic enjoyment of the general public or under a clearly delineated federal, state, or local governmental conservation policy.[183] To be deductible, the interest in the real property must either be (1) the entire interest in real estate other than a qualified mineral interest (subsurface oil, gas, or other minerals, and the right of access to these minerals), (2) a remainder interest, or (3) a restriction (granted in perpetuity) on the use of the real property.[184]

Probably the most difficult aspect of a conservation easement or surface rights (with reserved mineral rights) contribution is the valuation of the contribution. In determining the value of the restrictions, the donor should consider

---

177. Small Business Liability Relief and Brownfields Revitalization Act, Pub. L. 107-118, 115 Stat. 2356 (2002), but the scope of these rules is not immediately clear. A number of law firm newsletters available on the Web describe this legislation as providing very limited relief. Consequently, any charity considering any transaction involving real estate should consult an environmental law specialist rather than relying on this text.

178. *Id.*

179. I.R.C. § 170(h)(3).

180. *Id.*

181. Treas. Reg. § 1.170A-14(c)(1).

182. I.R.C. § 170(h)(4).

183. Treas. Reg. § 1.170A-14(d)(4).

184. I.R.C. § 170(h)(2).

the selling price of other properties with comparable restriction in arm's-length transactions.[185] If there are no qualified sales, the restrictions are valued indirectly as the difference between the fair market value of the property involved before and after the grant of the restriction.[186] The fair market value of the property *before* contribution of the restriction should consider not only current use but also the likelihood that, without the restriction, it would be developed. The donor must also consider any zoning, conservation, or historical preservation laws that would restrict development. Granting an easement may increase, rather than reduce, the value of property, and in such case, no deduction is allowed.

To illustrate a situation where someone might grant a conservation easement, consider Helen Kaplan, a CEO experiencing many pressures. She owns 100,000 acres of land in Montana. She likes to retreat to her Montana home for fly fishing, horseback riding, and cross-country skiing. Kaplan received a $6 million bonus this past July and is quite concerned about the income tax implications. She might consider granting a conservation easement with respect to her Montana land to the federal government or the Sierra Club. Under the law, even though she would be granting a partial interest in her property, she would be eligible to claim a charitable contribution deduction if the easement is properly structured.

(iii) Partial Interests in Works of Art. A donor can qualify a gift of a partial interest in property for a charitable contribution deduction by contributing a fraction of all aspects of his interest in a particular piece of property.[187] The best example is a piece of artwork.[188]

Consider Elizabeth Lima, who lives on Chicago's Gold Coast. Her fabulous art collection is worth in excess of $100 million. Each year when Lima travels to her Palm Beach winter home for three months, she is concerned about theft of the collection. The insurance company requires an additional premium for the extra risk associated with her three-month absence from her Chicago apartment.

Lima plans to leave her collection at her death to the Chicago Art Institute. Her attorney has asked her to consider making an immediate gift of a one-fourth interest in the collection to the institute. The attorney's proposal gives the institute the right to display the collection during the three-month period in which Lima is in Florida. The institute would pay for the insurance during that period. If Lima should sell the collection, the institute would be entitled to one-fourth of the proceeds.

185. Treas. Reg. § 1.170A-14(h)(3)(i).
186. Treas. Reg. § 1.170A-14(h)(3)(ii).
187. Treas. Reg. § 1.170A-7(b)(1).
188. James Winokur, 90 T.C. 733 (1988).

Lima should be intrigued.[189] This example is frequently used to demonstrate how a donor can contribute a partial interest in property and achieve a current income tax deduction. Lima is creating a *tenancy in common* with the institute.[190] If she lends the painting for five years, she is *not* entitled to a deduction. Likewise, she is not entitled to a current deduction if she gives the institute a remainder interest in her collection whose possession she retains but will pass to the museum at her death.[191]

In the example, if Lima agrees to the proposal, she grants the institute the right to possess the collection equal to its proportionate interest in the property, as well as the right to an interest in the sale proceeds equal to the institute's proportionate interest in the collection. Generally speaking, this should be enough, at least as far as the traditional example goes in terms of describing the terms of the gift.[192] From a technical standpoint, Lima must grant an undivided portion of her entire interest in the artworks before she can claim a current charitable contribution deduction for the contribution.[193] An *undivided portion* of someone's entire interest in property consists of a fraction or a percentage of each interest or right that the person has in the property, and it must extend over the entire term of that person's interest in that property or in other property into which the donated property is converted. Consequently, the transfer agreement probably will spell out more rights in terms of the grant. For example, it may include a provision that the institute will receive its share of insurance proceeds should the collection or any part be stolen or destroyed or that expenses such as cleaning costs will be allocated to Lima and the institute in proportion to their relative interests in the collection.[194]

The institute should require some assurance from Lima that she will transfer the remaining 75 percent interest in the collection to the museum at her death. Otherwise, Lima's heirs could pose problems.

(f) NEW DEVICES ARE PROPOSED ALL THE TIME. In recent years, a number of articles discussing charitable limited partnerships and split-dollar life insurance used in connection with a charitable gift planning have appeared in the *Wall*

189. *See* Priv. Let. Ruls. 2002-02-032 (Jan. 11, 2002) and 92-18-067 (Jan. 31, 1992) for two examples that raise issues regarding partial interests in artworks.
190. Treas. Reg. § 1.170A-5(a)(2).
191. Treas. Reg. § 1.170-5(b), Example 2.
192. I.R.C. § 170(f)(3)(B)(ii); and Rev. Rul. 57-293, 1957-2 C.B. 153.
193. For additional considerations, see Treas. Reg. § 1.170A-7(a)(3); Winokur, *supra* note 189; *Briggs*, 72 T.C. 646 (1979); Priv. Let. Rul. 2004-2-001 (Jan. 9, 2004); Priv. Let. Rul. 93-03-007 (Oct. 20, 1992); Priv. Let. Rul. 91-52-036 (Sept. 30, 1991); and Priv. Let. Rul. 8008105 (Nov. 29, 1979).
194. How do the parties allocate management rights? Is it permissible to let Lima have the right to determine whether the collection can be sold? Or does the fact that Lima has a 75 percent interest give her majority control, making such a right irrelevant? Under the present facts there is not a difference, but suppose that Lima vacations in Europe eight months each year. If the institute had a 75 percent interest, could Lima retain the right to sell the collection (with the proceeds being split based on relative interests) without jeopardizing the current income tax deduction?

Street Journal and the *New York Times*. The IRS has issued a notice prohibiting the split-dollar, life insurance–giving arrangements and is now considering whether to prohibit charitable limited partnerships.[195] For a number of reasons, charities should proceed cautiously before using or recommending newly engineered tax-planning devices. For one reason, the IRS could determine to treat these devices as abusive tax shelters and levy penalties on charities that promote them.[196] Second, if the arrangements do not work as described, the charity could have unhappy donors. Third, if the IRS recharacterizes such arrangements, the charity could have unexpected tax consequences, such as unrelated business income. In short, your organization should first consider whether it should adopt a planned giving program for donors. If it decides to implement one, it should select a tried-and-true vehicles, which are complex enough.

195. IRS Notice 99-36, 1999-26 I.R.B. 3. *See* Bruce Hopkins, *supra* note 5, at § 9.24 for a discussion of charitable family limited partnerships.

196. Form 8886, Listed Transactions.

CHAPTER 8

OTHER BENEFITS

I really don't deserve this [award], but I have arthritis and I don't deserve that either.

JACK BENNY

Nonprofit organizations receive a number of benefits in addition to possible federal tax exemption and the right to receive tax-deductible contributions (assuming they are charities). These benefits hinge on meeting the qualification requirements for the particular benefit. As some nonprofits have gravitated toward what are perceived as commercial activities, those granting benefits to nonprofits have begun to question the basis for these benefits (which are really subsidies). This is particularly true in the area of property tax exemptions, as you will see. Before rejoicing over a particular subsidy, an organization must first confirm that it qualifies for the benefit. Moreover, the organization must be prepared to undergo audits, file reports, and comply with assorted other requirements.

8.1 PROPERTY TAXES

Most if not all states provide some exemption from property taxes to charitable organizations. This is a significant subsidy. State laws also often extend exemption to certain benevolent organizations but not to all nonprofit organizations generally. One estimate places the savings to charities from these exemptions at somewhere between $8 and $13 billion per year.[1] In some cases, these exemptions are written right into the state constitution. Others are found in state statutes.

ILLINOIS STATE CONSTITUTION AND STATUTES

* * *

Section 6, Article IX of the Illinois Constitution provides as follows:

> The General Assembly by law may exempt from taxation only...property used exclusively for agricultural and horticultural societies, and for school, religious, cemetery and charitable purposes.

Section 15-65 of the Illinois Property Tax Code provides as follows:

> All property of the following is exempt when actually and exclusively used for charitable or beneficent purposes, and not leased or otherwise used with a view to profit:
>
> **a)** Institutions of public charity.
>
> **b)** Beneficent and charitable organizations incorporated in any state of the United States, including organizations whose owner, and no other person, uses the property exclusively for the distribution, sale, or resale of donated goods and related activities and uses all the income from those activities to support the charitable, religious or beneficent activities of the owner, whether or not such activities occur on the property....

* * *

The two major sources of controversy have been whether the entity asserting the exemption is an included entity and whether the property in question is used for exempt purposes. These two questions actually address the same concern: Is the property used for charitable purposes?

(a) THREE CASES. Let's take a look at three cases to help focus on the recurring issues faced by nonprofits seeking property tax exemptions.

(i) Exclusive Use—Case 1. Under many exemption provisions, an organization's use of the property must be "exclusively" for charitable purposes. Consider the Fifth Congregational Church (FCC), whose cathedral and religious school facility are in a major downtown metropolitan area. FCC also owns three

---

1. Joseph Cordes, Marie Gantz, and Thomas Pollak, *What Is the Property-Tax Exemption Worth? in* PROPERTY-TAX EXEMPTION FOR CHARITIES (Evelyn Brody ed., 2002).

square blocks of vacant land valued at $30 million and located two blocks from the cathedral and school. It currently operates three commercial parking lots on this land. It hopes some day to build a hospital on the land to serve only poor people. State X's constitution provides that property used exclusively for religious or charitable purposes is exempt from ad valorem real property taxes. Property tax statutes generally require examination of a charity's use on an annual basis. In this case, FCC is using the vacant land as a public parking lot. This does not further its religious purpose; consequently in many, if not most, jurisdictions, FCC's land will be subject to the property tax regardless of FCC's future plans. For example, under Illinois law, the property must be "actually and exclusively used for charitable purposes."[2] There is little question that the FCC would fail this test because the actual use is not charitable.[3] Several jurisdictions tax real property during the construction period even though the building under construction would clearly be used for tax-exempt purposes upon completion. These jurisdictions would likely refuse to grant FCC an exemption for the commercial parking lot, assuming the law did not specifically address parking lots.

(ii) Exempt Use—Case 2. Even when the organization uses the property to further its charitable mission, the taxing authority may still challenge whether the use is exempt. To illustrate, consider Secure Shelter, a Section 501(c)(3) organization that provides assistance to the elderly.[4] It decides to build and operate a new assisted living facility on land that it owns. Secure Shelter owns and operates a number of facilities for the elderly. Several of these facilities serve indigent elderly people; others provide luxury accommodations whose residents pay their way. The city assessor is seeking to levy property taxes with respect to these units.

As is the case with all property tax questions, the answer to this one depends on the state in which the assisted living facility is located. In Utah and Idaho, the courts have denied a property tax exemption, despite the fact that the facility was operated by a federally tax-exempt entity, if the housing is provided only to persons who can pay their own way.[5] In Wisconsin, the courts had interpreted the property tax exemption for housing much more leniently,[6] but these precedents may have been overruled by a 2003 case[7] involving a tax-exempt entity that leased apartments to low-income individuals. The court concluded that an apartment

2. Illinois Property Tax Code § 15-65.
3. Note that Illinois has a special statute that addresses exemptions for religious organization and parking lots, but the property would not be considered exempt under that provision because it is operated with a view toward profit. *See* Illinois Property Tax Code §§ 15-40 and 15-125.
4. For an excellent discussion of the issues surrounding elderly housing and property tax exemption, see G. Hagopian, *"Nonprofit" Senior Housing and Property Tax Exemptions*, 7 ASSESSMENT J. 6, at 31 (2000).
5. Friendship Manor Corp v. Commission, 487 P.2d 1272 (Utah 1971); and Evangelical Lutheran Good Samaritan Society v. Board of Equalization, 804 P.2d 299 (Idaho 1990).
6. Friendship Village of Greater Milwaukee, Inc. v. City of Milwaukee, 511 N.W.2d 345 (Wis. Ct. App. 1993); and Milwaukee Protestant Home v. City of Milwaukee, 164 N.W.2d 289 (Wisconsin 1969).
7. Columbus Park Housing Corporation v. City of Kenosha, 267 Wis. 2d 59, 761 N.W. 2d 633 (2003).

project did not qualify for property tax exemption because the property would not have been exempt from property taxation had the tenant-lessees owned their apartments outright. According to the court, the hypothetical ownership analysis required by the statute is applied to the tenants, not to the tax-exempt entity.[8]

This case created an uproar in Wisconsin as a number of nonprofit providers of affordable housing anticipated the decision's impact on them.[9] The protests were successful, and the Wisconsin legislature overrode the Wisconsin Supreme Court's decision with a legislative fix.[10] This is a perfect example of why nonprofits and their boards must monitor developments in this area, which can be radical and occur quickly.

THESE DISPUTES OCCUR IN THE REAL WORLD

* * *

The Ohio Supreme Court reviewed a claim to a property tax exemption by Bethesda Healthcare (Bethesda).[11] The case involved an athletic club operated by Bethesda. Bethesda's specific purposes as set forth in its articles of incorporation, are (1) "[t]o benefit and carry out the purposes of Bethesda Hospital, Inc., through the provision of ambulatory care and other health care services" and (2) "[t]o engage in any and all activities consistent with or in furtherance of the above purposes."

The facility in question was a 110,477-square-foot, three-story building, which is known as the TriHealth Fitness and Health Pavilion (Pavilion). The Fitness Center, which advertises itself on its Web site as "Cincinnati's premier fitness center," contains a multitude of state-of-the-art exercise facilities.

The Ohio Supreme Court considered how the facility was used. It noted that the nonprofit provided scholarships to eight individuals who could not afford membership. But with over 5,400 members, the court concluded, eight was not enough to qualify the portions of the building used as a health club for exemption. However, the court did agree that certain portions of the facility were exempt because they were sufficiently connected with Bethesda Hospital's rehabilitation and other charitable activities.

---

8. D. Blinka and T. Hammer, *Supreme Court Digest: Taxation*, 77 WIS. BAR J. (Feb. 2004).
9. An Internet search demonstrates just how controversial the Wisconsin Supreme Court's decision was. The Wisconsin Association of Homes and Services for the Aged sent a February 18, 2004, memorandum to "Interested Legislators," stating in relevant part,

> WAHSA members respectfully request your support for passage of legislation this session that would not allow this to happen. That legislation could simply grandfather those residential property owners who would have qualified for a property tax exemption under s.70.11(4), Wis. Stats., as of January 1, 2003, the tax year of the 11/19/03 Columbus Park decision. If further discussion is warranted on whether certain low income or senior housing providers should pay property taxes, we would suggest this legislation include the creation of a Legislative Council special committee to give this issue the thorough scrutiny it deserves.

10. *See* revised language in Section 70.11 (intro) of Chapter 70 of the Wisconsin Statutes, following an amendment by Act 195 of the Wisconsin Legislature (2004).
11. Bethesda Healthcare, Inc. v. Wilkins, 101 Ohio St.3d 420 (2000).

The lesson for directors: Monitor the legal environment as it pertains to property tax exemptions. This is particularly important when deciding whether to pursue a capital project. Directors should not assume that the project will be exempt from property taxation just because the entity that owns the facility is a charity.

* * *

(iii) Commercial Competition—Case 3. Frequently, commercial entities complain about unfair competition by a nonprofit with a property tax exemption. Take YMIA, a nonprofit organization devoted to promoting the Islamic faith and values. It recognizes that a fit and healthy body is an integral part of Islamic values. To promote fitness, it opens a health club in Greenville that has a running track, aerobics workout room, various exercise machines, sauna, basketball courts, prayer and study facilities, library, meeting rooms, and eating facilities. Membership is $100 per month. Comparable downtown health clubs charge, on average, a membership fee of $120 per month. At the urging of HotBod Center, a for-profit health club, the Greenville assessor is considering assessing property taxes on the YMIA facility. The potential hurdle to exemption for YMIA is the fact that the facility provides mixed activities, some commercial and others religious or educational. It should not come as a surprise that a local for-profit athletic club is objecting to the exemption.

HotBod's objection focuses on the means or specific activities. If the state constitution or relevant statute focuses exclusively on the means or activity, YMIA likely will fail to qualify for exemption. If the standard requires an analysis of whether the activity furthers the charity's objectives, YMIA is much more likely to succeed. In the case of YMCAs, the long-standing practice in many states has been specifically to exempt the "health clublike" facilities from property taxes (when the state constitutions or statutes have basic exemption provisions). One wonders whether these exemptions would be granted if policymakers were writing on a clean slate. With that in mind, note that this issue has been litigated in recent years in at least two jurisdictions.[12]

Stepping back from the specifics of this particular situation, nonprofits that engage in activities that could be considered as competitive with for-profit ventures can learn several lessons here. First, they should build a record that shows how the potentially competitive activity furthers the nonprofit's charitable mission. Second, they should consider whether the tax savings are large enough to support the potential ill will generated. Finally, they should consider structuring the activity so that if the related property is determined not to qualify for an exemption, this determination does not taint the property that has qualified for exemption. In the case of the YMIA, if it has strictly religious or educational facilities, the YMIA might want to place the health club facility in a separate facility.

---

12. Dynamic Sports Fitness Corporation of America v. Community YMCA of Eastern Delaware County, 768 A.2d 375 (Pa. Commw. 2001); and Clubs of California for Fair Competition v. Kroger, 7 Cal. App.4th 709 (1992).

"It's So Elementary, It's Almost Embarrassing"

* * *

The Milwaukee Police Athletic Association (MPAA), a Section 501(c)(3) organization, failed to file the necessary forms with the city of Milwaukee to perfect an exemption from property taxes on its new facility,[13] leaving the MPAA in debt to the city for $286,000 in back property taxes, penalties, and interest. In the MPAA case, there apparently was no challenge to the exemption, but the failure to perfect the exemption is the equivalent. And an article that appeared in the *Milwaukee Journal-Sentinel* reported that the MPAA had serious financial issues.[14]

The members of the board should not complete the forms to perfect a property tax exemption, but when a board discusses the organization's finances, the board should ask whether property tax exemptions have been filed. These exemptions can be a significant source of "revenue" because they free cash flow that otherwise would be paid to the taxing authority. Some organizations can obtain $286,000 from a large donor with just a phone call, but most cannot. That is why a board, even one that wrongly focuses on fundraising to the exclusion of governance, should ask questions about property tax exemptions.

No board would want to see its chair quoted in the press as was the MPAA chair:

> "We never asked the city to give us tax-exempt status," Pochowski sheepishly admitted Wednesday. "And then you say, 'God almighty, that's the most basic thing,' and I say, 'Yeah, it is,' and you say, 'How could we be so dumb?' and I say, 'I don't know. It's so elementary—it's almost embarrassing.' "[15]

Was this disclosure surprising? Not really. The MPAA was the victim of a widely publicized kickback scandal. One attorney pled guilty to a charge related to the scandal and a Wisconsin state senator was charged in the scandal but pled guilty to an unrelated (but similar) charge involving another nonprofit.[16] As a consequence, contributions dropped, the MPAA temporarily stopped selling memberships, and its staff was cut from eight to three people.[17] Two foundations stepped in to fill the gap, but there apparently continued to be fiscal problems.

The *Milwaukee Journal-Sentinel* published an article[18] indicating that MPAA was a poorly governed organization. According to the article, MPAA lacked an experienced financial officer, did not adequately delineate responsibilities, and was plagued by poor record-keeping. The board brought in the senator to help with funding matters. He became MPAA's chairman. One board member (also the MPAA's founder) says the senator "screamed and hollered, and there were certain things he wanted done, and he was a powerful guy."[19] According to the article, the senator "drove out the treasurer, fired the development director

---

13. C Spivak and D. Bice, *Debts Threaten Athletic League Facing Bankruptcy, PAL May Have to Sell Building*, Milwaukee J.-Sentinel, Feb. 10, 2005.
14. *Id.*
15. *Id.*
16. G. Zielinski, *Sostarich Pleads Guilty in George Scandal: He Admits to Kicking Back Legal Fees to Ex-Senator*, Milwaukee J.-Sentinel, Jan. 30, 2004.
17. L. Sykes, *PAL Slowly Arises from Ashes of Scandal*, Milwaukee J.-Sentinel, Dec. 19, 2004.
18. J. McBride, *With George at Helm, Athletic League's Financial Health Deteriorated*, Milwaukee J.-Sentinel, Dec. 2, 2003.
19. *Id.*

and wound up the only person allowed to write the league's checks...."[20] A gymnasium was named after the senator's parents.[21] He also brought in people affiliated with him, according to the article, including the attorney who was involved in the kickback scandal.

Is it surprising that important forms were not timely filed?

* * *

(b) PILOTs. While state law often is the basis for exemptions from property taxes for nonprofits, local municipalities (particularly those in urban areas with large concentrations of universities, museums, and hospitals) bear the burden of forgone tax revenue. To reduce this burden, some municipalities have sought voluntary "payments in lieu of taxes" (PILOTs) from nonprofit organizations. For example, in June 2003, the City of Providence, Rhode Island, entered into a highly publicized agreement with four local colleges.[22] PILOTs are intended to cover municipal services that directly benefit the nonprofit, including police and fire protection, and garbage collection.

(i) Philadelphia's PILOT Experience. The Pennsylvania Supreme Court handed down a decision in 1985 holding that a charitable organization had to provide a substantial amount of gratuitous service before it could qualify for exemption from property taxes.[23] This decision spawned a great deal of consternation and litigation because many nonprofits (particularly schools and hospitals) appeared unable to satisfy the stringent standards in the court's decision for property tax exemption. In 1994, the City of Philadelphia, through a mayoral executive order, created the Voluntary Contribution Program. As a result, many nonprofits entered into PILOTs in exchange for agreements not to challenge their property tax exemptions. It has been reported that in 1994 nonprofits that did not qualify as "purely public charities" were asked to make a voluntary contribution equal to 40 percent of what they would have owed had they been taxable. Early adopters were permitted to drop the percentage to 33 percent.[24]

In 1997, the Pennsylvania legislature passed Act 55, the Institutions of Purely Public Charity Act.[25] It was designed to bring uniformity to the practical application of property tax exemptions throughout the state. One of Act 55's goals was to encourage nonprofits to enter into voluntary agreements to make some payments to local governments.[26]

---

20. *Id.*
21. *Id.*
22. *See* Memorandum of Understanding with Respect to Voluntary Payments to Be Paid to the City of Providence, Rhode Island by Brown University, Rhode Island School of Design, Providence College, and Johnson & Wales University (June 5, 2003); and S. Greene, *Taxing Times for Charity: More Municipalities Seek Revenue from Nonprofit Groups*, CHRON. OF PHILAN., Sept. 18, 2003.
23. Hospital Utilization Project v. Commonwealth, 507 Pa. 1, 487 A.2d 1306 (1985).
24. D. Glancey, *PILOTs: Philadelphia and Pennsylvania* at 216–217 in PROPERTY-TAX EXEMPTION, *supra* note 1.
25. Act of November 26, 1997, Pub. L. 508, 10 P.S. §§ 371–385.
26. For additional information, see various chapters in PROPERTY-TAX EXEMPTION, *supra* note 1, particularly chapter 9.

(ii) Benefits of PILOTs to Nonprofits. Why should a nonprofit make a voluntary PILOT payment? One reason is to maintain goodwill with the community, but there are two very pragmatic reasons why nonprofits make these payments. First, the municipality may "condition" zoning changes on such payments. Although a direct link may be illegal, there is no question that delays and other subtle actions can be incorporated into the zoning approval process to coerce an agreement.[27]

The second pragmatic reason is that there is often uncertainty whether the property tax exemption applies to a particular nonprofit itself or to a specific activity that it provides. Consequently, some municipalities use "graymail" to obtain voluntary payments: The city will not contest an exemption if the nonprofit will make a "voluntary" payment of an amount that is less than the tax would be.

TAKING THE OFFENSIVE WITH PILOTS

* * *

Milwaukee-based Aurora Health Care, a large health care system, proposed construction of a new $85 million hospital and physician clinic in the Town of Summit, west of Milwaukee.[28] Before construction could begin, Summit had to amend its master zoning plan from "business" to "institutional."[29] Although a portion of the Aurora project would be subject to property tax, the portion related to the hospital would have been exempt. Everybody acknowledged that the new project would require Summit to expend additional funds on municipal services, including police and fire protection.

Then ProHealth Care Inc., owner and operator of the Oconomowoc Memorial and Waukesha Memorial Hospitals, entered the picture. Aurora's proposed project was approximately three miles from Oconomowoc Memorial Hospital. ProHealth opposed the zoning change, arguing that the Aurora project would drive up health care costs by duplicating medical services already available to the community.[30] The question was whether that argument was an appropriate one in the context of a land use decision.

Several newspaper reports indicate that this had became a bitter battle, the *Business Journal of Milwaukee,* quoted Evan Zeppos, a well-known public relations executive, as saying:

> If the campaign continues like this, the greater Waukesha County community is the loser.... It's bitter, and people will lose friendships over this."[31]

---

27. *See* Pacer v. City of Middleton, 217 AD.2d 47, 635 N.Y.S.2d 704 (1995).
28. A. Rinard and L, Unterberger, *1,000-Plus People Square Off at Hospital Hearing in Summit: Aurora Health's Plans Draw Praise, Condemnation*, MILWAUKEE J.-SENTINEL, July 29, 2004.
29. *Id.*
30. J. Sneider, *Campaign Signals Heated Debate Over Hospital*, BUS. J. OF WIS., Aug. 16, 2004.
31. *Id.*

This is where the story really begins. In an effort to take the property tax issue off the table, Aurora Health Care proposed entering into a PILOT agreement.[32] Summit estimated that it would have to incur $2.2 million in costs following the new hospital's opening.[33] Aurora proposed initial annual $350,000 payments for 12 years. However, the first six payments would be paid in a $1.5 million lump sum when Summit issued the building permit for the new hospitai, and the last six payments would be paid as a $1.2 million lump sum when Summit issued an occupancy permit. The lump-sum payments obviously included a discount factor. Aurora's proposal then included a $200,000 annual payment in Years 13 through 29 and a $250,000 annual payment thereafter. Just to put things in perspective, Summit levied $1,254,343 in property taxes in 2003.[34]

Aurora's sweetener apparently did the trick at the town level. Summit's board voted to make the zoning change that would permit Aurora to move to the next step in the process, which was Waukesha County Board's approval.[35] At that point, Aurora's proposal ran into trouble; the Waukesha County Board denied approval.[36] Litigation then ensued.[37]

PILOTs are often viewed as "blackmail" payments. One could certainly argue that Aurora would not have made its generous offer had the project not been so controversial. Like everyone else, however, Aurora and other nonprofits must respond to the environment in which they operate. The Aurora proposal was a very creative use of a PILOT. It apparently succeeded in neutralizing the property tax issue at the initial stage of the approval process.

* * *

(iii) PILOT Targets. Currently, PILOTs are primarily aimed at hospitals and universities, although there have been suggestions of expanding them to museum and performing arts groups to tax people who live in suburban areas but participate in activities in the city (the taxing municipality).[38]

PILOTs are becoming increasingly popular, so do not be surprised if your organization's board is asked to consider a PILOT proposal from the municipality in which the organization owns property. In doing long-term budgeting, every tax-exempt organization that owns real property should be cognizant of the PILOT environment in its locale. As the long-standing dispute between the city of Evanston, Illinois, and Northwestern University demonstrates, property tax disputes and PILOT proposals can become heated. Cities have been more than

---

32. A. Rinard, *Aurora Has Payment Plan for Hospital—Lump Sum Would Help Summit with Site's Expenses*, MILWAUKEE J.-SENTINEL, Sept. 21, 2004.
33. *Id.*
34. *Id.*
35. A. Rinard, *Summit Board Backs New Hospital: Vote Sends Aurora Project to County Level*, MILWAUKEE J.-SENTINEL, Dec. 2, 2004; and A. Rinard, *Plan Commission Urges Changes to Allow Hospital: 4-2 Summit Vote Recommends Approval of Land Use Revision*, MILWAUKEE J.-SENTINEL, Sept. 22, 2004.
36. S. Williams, *New Hospital Rejected: Waukesha County Thwarts Aurora's Efforts to Expand West*, MILWAUKEE J.-SENTINEL, Apr. 26, 2005.
37. S. Williams, *Aurora Sues over Hospital Denial: Town of Summit Joins Challenge to County*, MILWAUKEE J.-SENTINEL, May 23, 2005.
38. Evelyn Brody and Joseph Cordes, *Tax Treatment of Nonprofit Organizations: A Two-Edged Sword? in* NONPROFITS AND GOVERNMENT: COLLABORATION AND CONFLICT (Elizabeth Borris and Eugene Steuerle eds. 1998).

willing to play hardball with nonprofits but have run into legal problems when they attempt to link PILOTs to zoning and other approvals.[39]

PILOTs: Playing Hardball

* * *

Northwestern University (NWU) is the largest landowner in the city of Evanston, Illinois. NWU has a special property tax exemption in its 19th-century charter that cannot be amended, making the NWU situation somewhat unique. In the summer of 2000, more than 80 percent of Evanston voters supported a nonbinding referendum calling on the city to take measures to require NWU to pay its "fair share."[40] This is just one chapter in the long-standing dispute between Evanston and NWU over the exemption.

Over the years, the city has continually requested voluntary payments from NWU, some of which NWU has agreed to (for water, building permits, and other services estimated as exceeding $2.2 million annually in 2000),[41] but some city alderpersons demanded more. At one time, the city even proposed a tuition tax on students (which the then mayor and the state legislature vetoed).[42]

In 2000, Evanston proposed a per head tax on entities that employ more than 1,000 people in the city.[43] That tax would have affected three employers, all nonprofits. NWU was one of them.

In that same year, Evanston also created a historic district that included 42 of NWU's buildings.[44] The restrictions on owners of properties in the district would clearly have placed a heavy burden on NWU. This matter was settled[45] but not without a trip to federal court.[46]

Disputes over property tax exemptions often turn into warfare. Nonprofits should avoid such conflicts because, at a minimum, they are distractions and produce negative publicity. PILOTs are one way to reduce the potential for open conflict.

* * *

---

39. *See* Pacer, *supra* note 27, involving denial of zoning approval; and Emerson College v. City of Boston, 391 Mass. 415 (1984), involving a tax disguised as a fee.
40. D. Theriault, *Timeline of Development of City's Historic District*, Daily Northwestern, Nov. 21, 2000.
41. L. Black, *Evanston, NU Tussle over Head Tax; Monthly Levy Would Affect University, 2 Hospitals*, Chi. Trib., Nov. 19, 2000.
42. Complaint, Northwestern University v. City of Evanston, 2002 U.S. Dist. LEXIS 17104 (ND Il. September 11, 2002).
43. Black, *Evanston, NU Tussle*, *supra* note 41.
44. L. Austin, *NU Sues Evanston Citing Discrimination, University Asks federal Court to Invalidate Historic District*, Daily Northwestern, Nov. 21, 2000.
45. City of Evanston, *Minutes from February 10, 2004, City Council Meeting*; M. Lopas, *Town-Gown Relations Rest on Issues of Power Money: Evanston-NU Settlement Puts an End to the Lawsuit, But It Is Just Step One on the Long Road Toward Full Reconciliation*, Daily Northwestern, Feb. 13, 2004.
46. *See* note 42 *supra*.

(c) CHECKLIST. The following checklist should help your organization focus on property tax exemptions and PILOTs:

Leasing to other exempt entities	An organization may have excess capacity that it considers leasing to other charitable organizations. Do *not* assume that a property tax exemption will still be available if your organization leases a portion of its property to another exempt entity. This is true even if the other entity would qualify for an exemption if it owned the property outright.
Leasing property to nonexempt entities	An organization may decide to lease property to a nonexempt entity; for example, a hospital might lease office space to physician practice groups. The board should take property tax consequences into account when pricing the lease.
Expanding class of users	If an organization plans to expand the class of individuals that it serves, the board should consider whether the new class of users will adversely impact the organization's property tax exemption.
Entering into commercial ventures	Before a nonprofit engages in an activity that will produce unrelated business taxable income under federal income tax law, its should consider the property tax implications.
Seeking other payments and subsidies	Before an organization apples for new subsidies for its services, its board should ensure that those subsidies do not somehow preclude it from claiming an otherwise available property tax exemption.

8.2 SALES TAXES—PURCHASES BY NONPROFITS

Many states exempt purchases by nonprofits from retail sales taxes. Some states base the exemption on Section 501(c)(3) status, but as is the case with property tax exemptions, there is not a uniform approach. A nonprofit should not assume that exemptions are the general rule. For example, California ties a number of "nonprofit" exemptions to specific activities or circumstances.[47] Iowa law provides that as a general rule, there is *no* nonprofit exemption but that sales to certain types of institutions may be exempt.[48]

47. *See* California Board of Equalization, Publication 61, *Sales and Use Taxes: Exemptions and Exclusions* (May 2003).

48. Iowa Department of Revenue, *Iowa Tax Issues for Nonprofit Entities available at* http://www.state.ia.us/tax/educate/78595.html (as viewed on Oct. 28, 2005).

Iowa Department of Revenue: Iowa Tax Issues for Nonprofit Entities

* * *

SALES TO NONPROFITS

The Iowa Department of Revenue provides the following information to nonprofits on its Web site:[49]

> Nonprofit entities, churches and religious organizations are not automatically exempt from paying state sales taxes on taxable goods and services. This is true even if these entities are exempt from the payment of state and federal income taxes. State sales tax must be paid unless some other general sales tax exemption applies. Local option sales taxes must also be paid on purchases made in jurisdictions which impose the taxes.
>
> Purchases made for resale are exempt from all sales tax. In other words, a nonprofit corporation, church or other religious organization is treated the same as any other private citizen for sales and use tax purposes when purchasing goods and taxable services at retail.
>
> Examples:
>
> A church purchases hymn books from a local merchant. The hymn books are used only by its congregation. The sales tax applies.
>
> A nonprofit corporation purchases heating oil and electricity from a local utility. The sales tax applies.
>
> A local nonprofit animal shelter that provides shelter, medical care, socialization, and adoption services for homeless animals sells T-shirts and sweatshirts depicting rescued animals as a fund raiser. Items purchased by the shelter for resale are exempt from sales tax. Items purchased by the shelter that are not for resale, such as dog or cat food that will be used by the shelter, is subject to sales tax.
>
> The church purchases canned goods and meat from a local grocery store to feed the homeless. The sales tax does not apply since this type of food qualifies to be purchased with Food Stamps.
>
> A nonprofit corporation pays to have its monthly newsletter printed at a local printer. The sales tax applies.
>
> A church purchases Bibles from a local book publisher to resell to its members. Since the purchase is for resale, sales tax does not apply.

This publication then points out some specific exemptions, including one for certain sales of tangible personal property to parochial schools. Iowa nonprofits should review the relevant statute and regulations rather than relying on this summary.

* * *

Even when an organization qualifies for exemption, most exemption statutes require that the organization file an application with the state to perfect that exemption. Typically, a state providing an exemption issues the organization a number that it must provide sellers to prove that it is entitled to the exemption.

---

49. *Id.*

A nonprofit receiving an exemption should have a clear policy regarding its use and monitor it carefully. The *New York Times* reported that someone at a local chapter of the Disabled Veterans of America had allegedly been using a chapter credit card to make personal purchases and take advantage of the chapter's exemption.[50] On a best-case basis, this can prove to be embarrassing. For the local chapter, it is proving to be worse; this and other activity (at other local chapters) is under investigation by the state attorney general.[51]

8.3 SALES TAXES—SALES BY NONPROFITS

There are always two sides to the sales tax equation. Nonprofits can sell goods and services that are subject to sales taxes. Nonprofits should assume that their sales are subject to sales tax unless they find a specific exemption. Taxability is the rule, although some states provide special exemptions for certain sales by nonprofits. For example, Iowa provides an exemption that is tied to how the proceeds from the sale are used.[52] Every nonprofit should determine whether exemptions in the relevant jurisdictions are available.

IOWA DEPARTMENT OF REVENUE: IOWA TAX ISSUES FOR NONPROFIT ENTITIES

* * *

SALES BY NONPROFITS

The Iowa Department of Revenue provides the following information to nonprofits on its Web site[53]:

> When are sales exempt? Sales made by entities or organizations engaged in educational, religious, or charitable activities are exempt based on the following criteria:
>
> - The gross receipts must be from a retail sale or rental of tangible personal property or taxable services;
> - The profits from the sale must be used by or donated to one of the following:
>   - **An entity that is exempt from federal income tax under Internal Revenue Code Section 501(c)(3);**
>   - **A government entity; or**
>   - **A private nonprofit educational institution**
> - The profits must be expended on educational, religious, or charitable activities (see definitions)
> - An exemption from sales tax is allowed to the extent net proceeds are expended for qualifying educational, religious, or charitable purposes.

---

50. K. Semple, *Veterans' Charity Chapters Are Investigated*, N.Y. TIMES, Oct. 24, 2004. Mr. Semple did not specifically refer to sales taxes, but he did refer to the credit card as a "tax-exempt" credit card.
51. *Id.*
52. Iowa Department of Revenue, *Iowa Tax Issues*, *supra* note 48.
53. *Id.*

Example: A local Jaycees chapter raises $10,000 from a haunted house fund raiser. The chapter gives $9,000 to the United Way and retains the other $1,000 for a pizza party for the chapter members and for others who helped with the event. The Jaycees can receive an exemption on the $9,000, but must remit sales tax on the remaining $1,000.

Current Iowa law does not focus on the nonprofit status of an organization as a qualification for exemption from sales tax under Internal Revenue Code 501(c)(3). Instead, Iowa law focuses on the manner and the extent that net proceeds are expended for a defined exempt activity. (Note: The June 2002 version of this publication said Iowa law does focus on nonprofit status as qualification for exemption; this is not true. We regret the error.)

Is gambling taxable? All receipts from gambling activities are subject to the sales tax, regardless of the ultimate use of the proceeds.

Iowa nonprofits should review the relevant statute and regulations rather than relying on this summary.

* * *

8.4 POSTAL NONPROFIT STANDARD MAILING RATE

The United States Postal Service (USPS) offers reduced rates. That rate had been 16.5 cents for nonprofit standard mail,[54] but was increased to 17.0 cents starting January 8, 2006[55] for certain nonprofits with respect to certain types of mail. This rate represents a roughly 40 percent reduction over the commercial rate that would otherwise apply. The basic 17.0-cent rate can be reduced further, depending on how much an organization is willing to do in terms of presorting, addressing, and other tasks that ease USPS's burden. Although 17.0 cents is the base rate that everyone refers to, the actual rate depends on the weight of the mailed piece. If it weights 3.3 ounces or less, the rate is the 17.0-cents per piece rate.[56] Even then, the rate schedule distinguishes between letters and flats.[57] When the piece's weight exceeds 3.3 ounces, the rate is based on a combination of the number of pieces and weight,[58] but there is no longer a distinction between flats and letters. To qualify for the nonprofit standard mail rate, the piece must be under 16 ounces.[59] Special rates apply to parcels because they are not machine readable.

---

54. UNITED STATES POSTAL SERVICE, DOMESTIC MAIL MANUAL, Part 242, § 1.4 (as posted on the USPS Web site on July 25, 2005); and USPS Notice 123, Ratefold (effective June 30, 2002)
55. On April 8, 2005, the USPS filed a rate case with the Postal Rate Commission seeking an expedited recommended decision to raise rates 5.4 percent for almost all categories. The United States Postal Service Board of Governors approved a plan in November 2005 that increased the basic rate by 3 percent. Those nonprofits using discounts for the "nonprofit enhanced carrier route" category saw their rates increase by slightly more than 12 percent. According to industry sources, the USPS already is planning to submit a new rate case with its proposed rates to be effective sometime in 2007. *See* C. Preston, *New Postal Rates for Charities to Take Effect in January*, CHRON. OF PHILAN., Nov. 24, 2005. Those increases are expected to be significant.
56. *Id.*
57. The terms *letter, flat,* and *parcel* are defined terms. For definitions, see DOMESTIC MAIL MANUAL, *supra* note 54, at §§ 243.2, 343.2, and 443.2.
58. *Id.*
59. *See* UNITED STATES POSTAL SERVICE, QUICK SERVICE GUIDE 703: STANDARD MAIL—NONPROFIT ELIGIBILITY AT ELIGIBILITY OVERVIEW (May 2005), referring to the general standards for letters, flats, and parcels.

Nonprofits that want to take advantage of the special rates should contact a direct marking professional for assistance. As too often is the case when dealing with subsidies, an entire industry has developed around compliance with complex requirements that must be satisfied for nonprofit standard rate eligibility.

Organizations that typically are eligible for nonprofit rates include (1) agricultural, (2) educational, (3) fraternal, (4) labor, (5) philanthropic, (6) religious, (7) scientific, (8) veterans, and (9) some political committees.[60] Individuals are *not* eligible for nonprofit rates, nor are business leagues, chambers of commerce, social and hobby clubs, and certain political organizations.[61]

An authorization to mail at the nonprofit standard mail rates is a privilege reserved by law to authorized organizations. Civil and criminal penalties apply to false, fictitious, or fraudulent statements made in connection with a nonprofit standard mailing.

(a) BASIC RULES. Nonprofit standard mail includes printed matter such as pamphlets, newsletters, direct mail, and merchandise that weighs less than 16 ounces.[62] It excludes material that is typed (as opposed to printed) or handwritten.[63] To constitute standard mail, the piece must be part of at least 200 identical pieces of mail or a mailing that exceeds 50 pounds. In other words, standard mail is bulk mail; thus, the organization's routine mail (e.g., payments to vendors and correspondence with attorneys and accountants) are subject to regular first-class mailing rates.

The rules draw a distinction between advertisements for products and the products themselves.[64] It is clearly possible for a product to be eligible for the nonprofit standard mailing rate while the advertisement is not.[65]

(i) Products. A *product* may be mailed at nonprofit standard mail rates only if it is (1) a low-cost item, (2) a periodical publication of a nonprofit organization that meets certain requirements regarding advertising content, or (3) a gift or donation obtained by the organization at no cost.[66] A product need not be substantially related to the purposes of the organization to otherwise qualify for nonprofit standard mail rates. For 2006, any item that costs no more than $8.60 is considered to be a low-cost item. This threshold is linked to the determination of low-cost items under Section 513 of the Internal Revenue Code (see Chapter 6), so it changes annually.[67]

---

60. DOMESTIC MAIL MANUAL, *supra* note 54, at Part E670, § 2.0; and UNITED STATES POSTAL SERVICE, PUBLICATION 417, NONPROFIT STANDARD MAIL ELIGIBILITY, at 8 (Oct. 1996).
61. DOMESTIC MAIL MANUAL, *supra* note 54, at Part E670, § 4.0.
62. QUICK SERVICE GUIDE *703*, *supra* note 59, *Frequently Asked Questions*, Question 1; and PUBLICATION 417, *supra* note 60, at § 4-3.
63. DOMESTIC MAIL MANUAL, *supra* note 54, at Part 430, § 3.3.
64. PUBLICATION 417, *supra* note 60, at § 6-1.
65. *Id.*, at § 6-1.4.
66. QUICK SERVICE GUIDE, *supra* note 59, Question 2; and PUBLICATION 417, *supra* note 60, at § 6-3.
67. PUBLICATION 417, *supra* note 60, at § 6-3.2.3; and Rev. Proc. 2005-70, 2005-47, I.R.B. 979, at § 3.24.

To constitute a product, a periodical publication must be sold or have a listed price or represented value.[68] In addition, it must satisfy each of these requirements: (1) have a title, (2) be published at regular intervals of at least four times a year, (3) be formed of printed sheets, (4) have an identification statement, (5) have a known office of publication, (6) meet the eligibility requirements for one of the periodical categories (for example, a general publication, a requester publication, or a publication of an institution or society), and (7) be eligible for mailing as Standard Mail(A) matter.[69]

To illustrate the most important relationship between the three product categories, let's consider Greenview Cancer Society, a Section 501(c)(3) organization. Twice a year, it sends to subscribers a publication with articles describing its research activities and covering different aspects of cancer prevention. An annual subscription costs $20. Each copy is produced at a cost of $2. Finally, the publication contains no advertising. The publication qualifies for nonprofit standard mail rates, but not because it is a periodical. To be considered a periodical, it must be published at regular intervals at least four times a year.[70] Instead, the publication qualifies for the favorable rate because it qualifies as a low-cost item.

As another example, consider Maple Tree College, a four-year undergraduate college. The chair of its economics department has been appointed to head the President's Council of Economic Advisers. To remind its alumni of the quality education they received at Maple Tree, the college purchases 10,000 copies of the chair's latest book for $20 each and sends one to each alum. The book is not a periodical publication because it is not published at least four times per year. It was not donated, nor is it a product. Consequently, the mailing does not qualify for the nonprofit standard mailing rates.[71] If Joe Whitman, a Maple Tree alum, had donated the 10,000 copies to Maple Tree, the mailing would qualify for nonprofit standard rates as a donated product. This example is a taken from a USPS publication with the facts slightly embellished.[72] Although the donated textbooks may be eligible products, it is unlikely that each weighs less than 16 ounces, so this mailing probably would not qualify for nonprofit standard mail rates.

All products, regardless of whether they are periodicals, low-cost items, or donated items, must meet certain additional requirements if they contain advertising.[73] We consider those requirements now.

(ii) Advertising Content. Advertising is generally not eligible for reduced nonprofit mailing rates unless the mailpiece meets certain periodical content requirements,[74] or all advertised products or services are substantially related to

---

68. *Id.*, at § 6-3.2.5.
69. DOMESTIC MAIL MANUAL, *supra* note 54, at Part 707, § 6.0.
70. PUBLICATION 417, *supra* note 60, at § 6-3.2.5.
71. *Id.*, § 6-3.2.2, Example 2.
72. *Id.*, at § 6-3.2.4.
73. *Id.*, at § 6-3.3.
74. *Id.*, at § 6-3.5.

the organization's exempt purpose.[75] Solicitations for donations are generally not considered to be advertisements.[76] The following types of advertising are ineligible for the nonprofit standard rates:

- Advertisements that promote credit, debit, or charge cards.[77]
- Advertising that promotes or offers any insurance policy unless it is promoted to members, donors, supporters, or beneficiaries of the authorized mailer and the policy coverage is not otherwise generally commercially available.[78]
- Advertising or announcements that promote the availability of any travel arrangement are ineligible unless the arrangement is promoted to members, donors, and supporters of the organization, and the reason for the travel contributes substantially to the organization's qualifying purpose.[79]
- Advertisements for products or services that are not substantially related to one or more of the organization's qualifying purposes.[80]

If a mailpiece qualifies for standard mail rates under the product rules, it will nevertheless be ineligible for the favorable rates if it contains any ineligible advertising.[81] Returning to Greenville Cancer Society, assume its semiannual publication contains an ad for an affinity credit card or an ad for a trip to Disney World. Clearly, the ad for the credit card prevents qualification for nonprofit standard mail rates. This is likely also true of the Disney World ad because the reason for the travel probably does not contribute substantially to Greenville's purpose.

The USPS has interpreted what constitutes prohibited advertising very broadly. For example, it has concluded that a mailing soliciting new members fails to qualify for nonprofit standard mail rates if it simply lists membership benefits and one of those benefits is a "no annual fee affinity credit card."[82] The publication is somewhat internally inconsistent. At another point, it states that "references to membership benefits of an authorized nonprofit organization" are not considered advertising.[83] Apparently, the phrase "no annual fee" is considered promotional, which results in classification as advertising. What this really means is that nonprofits must either work with experienced consultants or mailers or seek legal counsel when putting their mailings together. A mailing may acknowledge sponsors, donors, or contributors without being considered

75. *Id.*, at § 6-3.6.
76. *Id.*, at § 6-3.3.3.
77. Domestic Mail Manual, *supra* note 54, at Part E670, § 5.4(a).
78. *Id.*, at Part E670, § 5.4(b).
79. *Id.*, at Part E670, § 5.4(c).
80. *Id.*, at Part E670, § 5.4(d).
81. Publication 417, *supra* note 60, Appendix A, Case Study 1, Step 4, and § 6.3.4.
82. *Id.*, at § 6-3.3.3, second example under "Listings Considered as Advertising."
83. *Id.*, at § 6-3.3.7.

advertising, but there are once again limitations (e.g., the rules draw a distinction between "Acme Ice Cream Parlor, Our City's Favorite Ice Cream Parlor"—problematic—and "Acme Ice Cream Parlor"—permissible).[84]

Even if the advertising is not outright ineligible, it may still be problematic. This depends on whether the mailpiece satisfies what are termed *content requirements*. If it includes a title, is formed of printed sheets, contains identification of specified information, and consists of at least 25 percent nonadvertising matter, it satisfies the content requirements.[85] This means that any advertising need not be substantially related to the organization's purposes.[86] If, on the other hand, the mailpiece fails the content requirements, all advertising must be substantially related to the organization's purposes.[87] In either case, none of the advertising can be ineligible advertising (e.g., an ad for a credit card or an unrelated travel program).

What can be confusing about the "content requirement" is how it applies to products. Even when a product qualifies for nonprofit standard rates, it still must undergo an analysis under the "content requirements."[88] For example, assume that Greenville Cancer Prevention converts its semiannual publication to a quarterly publication, qualifying it as a periodical publication. If the publication contains only 10 percent editorial content, it fails the content requirement; that is, to be eligible for nonprofit standard rates, all advertising must be eligible advertising and must be substantially related to the Greenville's purposes.[89] If the publication contains 40 percent editorial content and otherwise meets the content requirements, all advertising must be eligible advertising, but it need not be substantially related to Greenville's purposes.

The USPS provides a flowchart as part of Publication 417 to help summarize the steps that must be applied when focusing on advertising content: It is reproduced in Exhibit 8.1.

(iii) Personal Information. Mail that contains personal information even if the communication relates to the organization's mission is not eligible for nonprofit standard rates[90] unless (1) it contains explicit advertising for a product or service for sale or lease or an explicit solicitation for a donation, (2) all personal information is directly related to the advertising or solicitation, and (3) the

84. *Id.*, at § 6-3.3.8.
85. *Id.*, at § 6-3.5.2.
86. *Id.*, at § 6-3.5.3.
87. *Id.*
88. *Id.*, Appendix A, Case Study 1, Step 5, and § 6.3.4
89. *Id.*, at § 6-3.6.2, first example.
90. See 69 Fed. Reg. 62,578 (Oct. 27, 2004). Under this rule, organizations can still send solicitations and fundraising materials that are personalized to the recipient (e.g., listing past contributions) using the favorable rates so long as the use of the personal information is to "support the advertising or solicitation in the mailpiece."

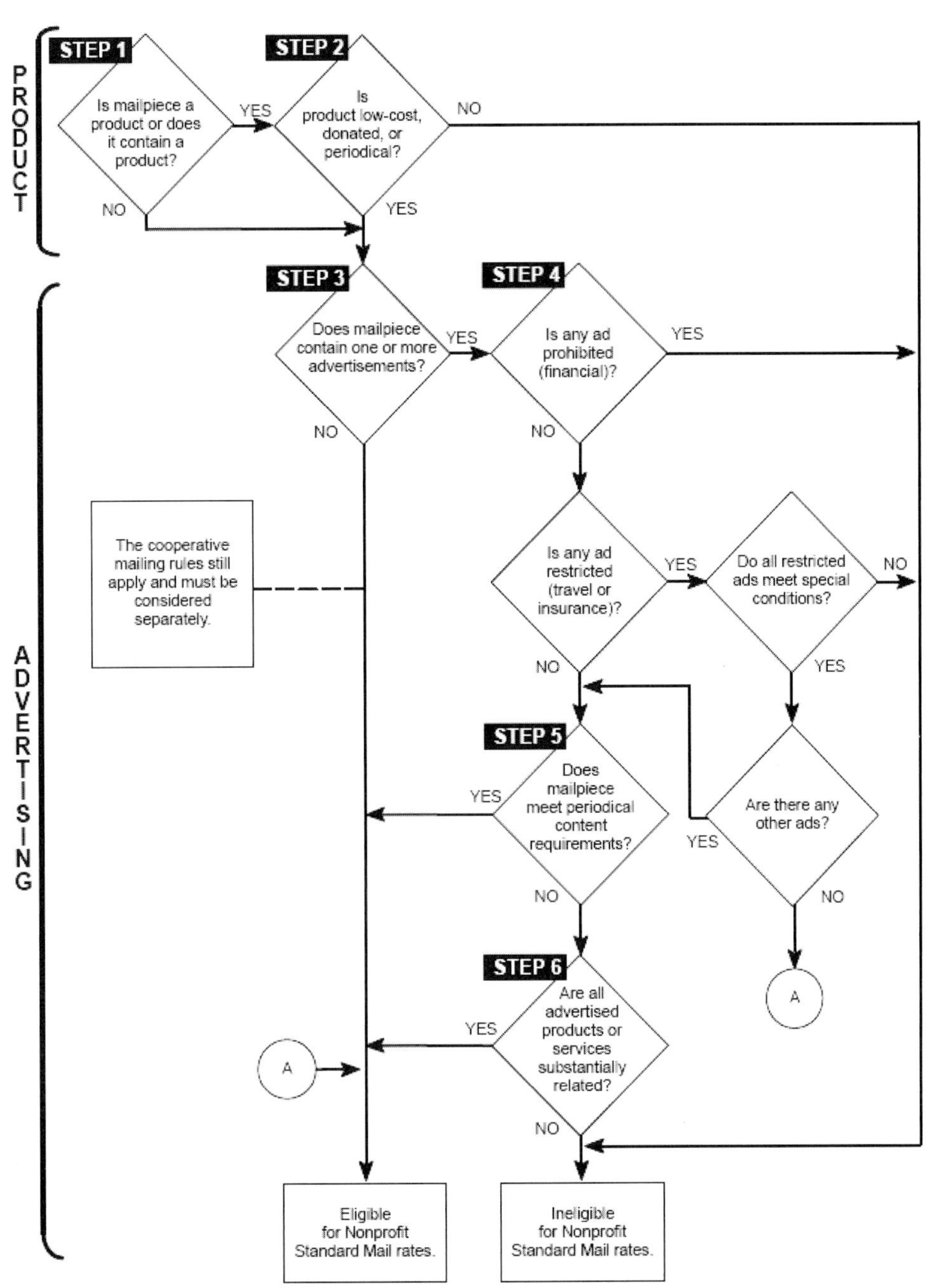

EXHIBIT 8.1 USPS DIAGRAM

exclusive reason to include all of the personal information is to support the advertising or solicitation in the piece.[91] The nonprofit sector was very concerned about how the "personal information" rule would be applied to solicitations and membership materials. As a consequence, the sector requested and received special guidance from the USPS, which any organization should review before it makes personal solicitations or acknowledges prior contributions.[92] Parts of this guidance are very formalistic and should be read carefully.

While these rules were an irritant to the sector when proposed in 2004, the basic concept makes sense once one recognizes that the nonprofit standard mailing rate applies to *bulk mailings*. If each mailing is highly personalized, can it still be considered a bulk mailing? The USPS guidance provides that although the name and address of a recipient are clearly "personal" information in everyday parlance, for purpose of the rule, they are not considered personal.[93] On the other hand, the recipient's prior contributions, duration of membership (e.g., "Class of 1973" or "member since 1956"), birth date, and medical condition, are considered to be personal information.[94]

As noted, personal information may be used if the use satisfies three conditions. First, the mailpiece must contain an explicit advertisement for a product or service or an explicit solicitation for a donation. Both a request for a contribution and a request that the recipient join the organization (or renew a membership) are considered to be explicit requests of the type required,[95] as are requests that the recipient contribute volunteer services and complete and mail an opinion survey, feedback or evaluation form, petition, or open letter (e.g., "Please sign the enclosed letter and send it to your representative in Congress").[96]

Under the second requirement, the personal information must relate directly to the permitted advertising or solicitation.[97] For example, including the expiration date of the recipient's membership in the organization is permissible use of personal information if the mailing asks the person to renew the membership. Although the guidance does not offer this example, indicating that information from a diabetic-focused medical organization might be helpful because the recipient is a diabetic appears to be permissible, as does a solicitation to members of the "Class of 1973" for a class gift.

Under the third and final requirement, the use of the personal information must be exclusively related to supporting the advertising or solicitation.[98] The

---

91. DOMESTIC MAIL MANUAL, *supra* note 54, at Part 343, § 2.2.
92. UNITED STATES POSTAL SERVICE, PS-323 COMPUTER-PREPARED MAILPIECES ENTERED BY NONPROFIT ORGANIZATIONS, CUSTOMER SUPPORT RULING MAILING STANDARDS HEADQUARTERS (May 2005).
93. *Id.*, at § 1, Enumeration 2(b).
94. *Id.*, at § 1, Enumeration 1.
95. *Id.*, at § 2.
96. *Id.*, at §§ 2(c) and (f). One would initially suspect that such communications would have to be accompanied by a solicitation to qualify. However, the text at the end of this section suggests not. It refers to all of these "solicitations" and refers to the phrase "please read."
97. *Id.*, at § 3.
98. *Id.*, at § 4.

guidance does not provide much in the way of specific examples, with one important exception. Mailpieces that constitute receipts or acknowledgements for charitable contributions and that contain information about the amount of a prior donation are ineligible for the nonprofit standard mailing rate even if the mailpiece contains a new solicitation. On the other hand, simply stating that "Your contribution may be tax deductible," "No goods or services were provided in exchange for this gift," or "The IRS requires written substantiation of charitable gifts of $250 or more" will not, alone, make a mailing ineligible.

(b) COMPREHENSIVE EXAMPLE. To illustrate the analysis required to determine eligibility for nonprofit standard rates, let's consider Albertsville Cancer Society's monthly newsletter, mailed on behalf of the society by EZ Printers, a commercial printer. The issue is whether the society is treated as mailing the newsletter for purposes of the obtaining the favorable postage rates. If the commercial entity (EZ Printers) is acting on behalf of the nonprofit (as its agent), the mailing should qualify for nonprofit standard mail rates, assuming that it otherwise qualifies.[99] A monthly newsletter should qualify for these rates, assuming it has no advertising. Advertising does not necessarily preclude the use of the rates, but it does require a special analysis. If EZ Printers receives a share of the proceeds or profits, the mailing becomes ineligible.[100]

Consider now Albertsville Cancer Society's monthly magazine, which sells for $1.50 on the newsstand. The magazine is mailed to its members. For mailing purposes, the magazine likely qualifies as a periodical product or a low-cost item.[101] The next necessary determination is whether there is any advertising in the publication. Ten percent of the magazine's content includes commercial advertising. To qualify for favorable rates, it can contain no advertising for credit cards, unrelated travel, or readily available insurance.[102] Assuming the magazine does not contain any prohibited advertising content, no more than 75 percent of its content can be advertising.[103] Note that even if the 75 percent requirement is not satisfied (but the other requirements are satisfied), the mailing may still qualify for favorable rates if the advertising is substantially related to one or more of the organization's nonprofit purposes.[104] In this case, the monthly newsletter contains 90 percent editorial content, so the advertising could include ads for cars or potato chips. If the editorial content only were 20 percent of the content, such ads would be problematic because they are not substantially related to the society's purposes.

---

99. *Id.*, at § 5-2.2.

100. PUBLICATION 417, *supra* note 60, at § 5.3. This section and other authorities should be reviewed to determine what are and what are not permissible arrangements. Ineligible publications of this nature are referred to as "cooperative mailings."

101. *Id.*, at § 6-3.

102. *Id.*, at § 6-3.4.

103. *Id.*, at § 6-3.5.

104. *Id.*, at § 6-3.6.

Issues can also arise when solicitations are accompanied by premium offers. For example, assume the Albertsville Cancer Society offers people who donate more than $200 a free skin cancer home screening kit valued at $10. This is referred to as a *back-end premium*. Somewhat surprising, the request for donations is considered a product advertisement because of the home screening kit.[105] Because the screening kit appears to be substantially related to the society's purposes, the initial solicitation should qualify for the nonprofit standard mailing rates.[106] When the society mails the screening kit to those donors making contributions in excess of $200, it will be able to take advantage of the favorable rates only if the kit is considered to be a low-cost item or was donated by someone.[107] Even then, if the kit weighs 16 ounces or more, it will not qualify for the nonprofit standard mailing rate.

Changing the facts, assume the society sends a box of greeting cards with no written content but pictures of various flowers to people who donate more than $200. In this case, the mailing does not qualify for the nonprofit standard rate because it is viewed as an advertisement and is not substantially related to the organization's purposes. However, if the cards qualify as a low-cost item and weigh less than 16 ounces, the subsequent mailing of the cards will qualify for nonprofit standard mailing rates.[108]

(c) APPLYING FOR FAVORABLE RATES. An organization that qualifies for favorable nonprofit standard mail rates *cannot* simply start applying reduced postage to qualifying mail. It must first apply by filing PS Form 3624 with the USPS.[109] The organization can start taking advantage of the nonprofit standard mail rates only after it has been approved.

Once an organization has received USPS status as a qualified nonprofit, it can then submit PS Form 3533 to request a refund of amounts it has paid for postage that exceeded the nonprofit standard mail rates since the application date. Specific rules define what amounts are refundable.[110] For example, no refund will be made for pieces mailed at first-class or priority rates.[111] Anyone planning to seek a refund should carefully review the specific rules.

(d) PRACTICAL ISSUE. Clearly, the nonprofit standard mail rate is a benefit that nonprofit organizations should consider. They should not be blinded, though, by the potential benefits. To take advantage of this rate, it could be necessary to retain consultants or fundraising firms to assist in assembling a mailing so that it is eligible. Consultants can be costly. The organization should consider such

105. *Id.*, at § 6-3.1.3.
106. *Id.*, Appendix A, Case Study 2.
107. *Id.*, at § 6-3.1.3, second example.
108. *Id.*
109. *Id.*, at § 3-1.
110. DOMESTIC MAIL MANUAL, *supra* note 54, Part 343, § 1.9.0.
111. *Id.*, at Part 343, § 1.9.3.

costs before take advantage of the nonprofit standard mail rates. If the mailing consists of tens of thousands of pieces, the fees charged by others to assist the nonprofit will probably not exceed the rate benefits. As the size of the mailing diminishes, the organization may find that first-class mail or media mail rates are more economical.

8.5 SECURITIES OFFERINGS

People do not normally think of nonprofit organizations as issuing securities, particularly because the word *securities* brings to mind stocks. However, schools, hospitals, and other organizations that have large tangible assets (buildings and equipment) or that take advantage of governmental programs (e.g., low-income housing tax credits and packaging collateralized securities such as student or mortgage loans) can sell partnership interests, debt, and collateralized securities.

Normally, an organization that sells securities is subject to certain registration and disclosure requirements under federal and state securities laws. If the organization is a nonprofit, its offering may be exempt from certain of these registration requirements. For example, the federal Securities Act of 1933 specifically exempts tax-exempt securities[112] and those issued by the equivalent of Section 501(c)(3) organizations[113] from registration.

Disclosure is still an issue, however. The SEC has issued special disclosure requirements for municipal issuers, which could include tax-exempt organizations.[114] The specifics of those rules are beyond the scope of this *Guide*. Remember, however, that disclosure requirements ensure that investors receive all material information necessary to make an informed investment decision.

Section 3(a)(4) of the Securities Act of 1933

* * *

Exempted Securities. Except as hereinafter expressly provided, the provisions of this subchapter shall not apply to any of the following classes of securities:...

Any security issued by a person organized and operated exclusively for religious, educational, benevolent, fraternal, charitable, or reformatory purposes and not for pecuniary profit, and no part of the net earnings of which inures to the benefit of any person, private stockholder, or individual; or any security of a fund that is excluded from the definition of an investment company under section 3(c)(10)(B) of the Investment Company Act of 1940.

* * *

---

112. Securities Act of 1933, § 3(a)(2), as codified at 15 U.S.C. 77c(a)(4).
113. Securities Act of 1933, § 3(a)(4), as codified at 15 U.S.C. 77c(a)(4).
114. Securities Exchange Act of 1934, Rule 15c2-12.

8.6 TAX-EXEMPT FINANCING

Under the federal tax law, Section 501(c)(3) organizations can issue tax-exempt bonds to finance the acquisition of facilities, equipment, and real property.[115] Universities and hospitals frequently issue such bonds. The advantage to a tax-exempt financing is lower interest costs because the interest on the bonds is exempt from federal (and possibly state and local) income tax. An even abbreviated discussion of the rules pertaining to tax-exempt financing is beyond the scope of these materials. Organizations that plan debt financing for a major capital project should contact a reputable bond lawyer for assistance in determining whether tax-exempt financing is viable. Typically, this means contacting a large corporate law firm. Potential issuers can also review *The Bond Buyer's Municipal Marketplace,* referred to in the trade as the *Red Book,* for listings of the "players." It is now published by LexisNexis and is available online.

When an organization decides that tax-exempt financing would be beneficial, it may need to go through an approval process to undertake the financing. In certain instances, there are volume-cap limitations on the amount of bonds that can be issued, meaning that the organization and the proposed project will need to compete for an allocation under the volume cap from a governmental authority.[116]

Tax-exempt financing can have disadvantages. First, and most important, the organization must maintain its status as a Section 501(c)(3) organization throughout the term of the bonds.[117] Normally, maintaining this status is desirable to the organization, but this requirement could result in bond covenants that prevent it from taking certain actions without first obtaining legal opinions that the action will not jeopardize its exempt status. This can be cumbersome.

Second, the facilities financed with tax-exempt financing are subject to restrictions on private use.[118] These restrictions could prevent the organization from permitting private use of the facility. For example, a private college might normally rent its stadium to a professional football team for several weeks during

---

115. I.R.C. § 145. The IRS has issued three publications that explain the ins and outs of tax-exempt financing: (1) PUBLICATION 4077, TAX-EXEMPT BONDS FOR 501(C)(3) CHARITABLE ORGANIZATIONS (Jan. 2004), (2) PUBLICATION 4078, TAX-EXEMPT PRIVATE ACTIVITY BONDS (May 2004), and (3) PUBLICATION 4079, TAX-EXEMPT GOVERNMENT BONDS (Apr. 2003). All three publications provide an overview of the opportunities and issues associated with tax-exempt financing. Although plain-language writing in this area is an oxymoron, these publications come as close to being clear, concise, and understandable, given the subject matter, as any publication could.

116. These limitations apparently do not apply to Section 145 bonds. *See* I.R.C. § 146(g)(2). However, under other Internal Revenue Code provisions, Section 501(c)(3) organizations can issue tax-exempt bonds.

117. Treas. Reg. § 1.145-2(a). See Tech. Adv. Mem. 2000-06-049 (Oct. 22, 1999), which discusses how the loss of Section 501(c)(3) status impacts the tax-exempt status of the interest paid on the bonds issued by the entity.

118. Treas. Reg. § 1.145-2, making reference to Treas. Reg. §§ 1.141-0 through 1.141-15.

the summer for practice. If the stadium was financed with tax-exempt bonds, however, this may not be possible. The organization must also carefully analyze management and service contracts with third parties to ensure that these contracts will not result in prohibited private use of the facilities.[119]

Third, the organization must be particularly careful in conducting its activities so that the facilities are not used in an unrelated trade or business activity (see Chapter 6).[120] Note that the question is whether the activity is an unrelated trade or business, not whether it generates income that is ultimately taxable as unrelated business taxable income.[121]

Finally, tax-exempt financing can have significant transaction costs. As a consequence, conventional bank financing could be more economical when the amount to be financed is relatively small or the difference between taxable and tax-exempt interest rates is small.

As part of its review of financial forecast related to the project to be bond financed, the board must ask probing questions. Consider the Umberto Film Society (UFS), a recently formed Section 501(c)(3) organization, which is seeking financing for a new film center to show foreign films to United States audiences. UFS's goal is to inspire an audience to turn from the banality of Hollywood blockbusters to the pathos offered by art films. The financial projections and budgets show that a state-of-the-art film center must gross $5 million a year in ticket and concession stand revenue to break even. Assume that if the construction costs could be financed with tax-exempt bonds, the breakeven point would drop to $4.7 million due to a $300,000 annual reduction in financing costs.

UFS's directors would be remiss if they did not seriously consider obtaining tax-exempt financing, assuming the society and its project are eligible. The decision, however, should not be automatic. Foreign films seldom garner large audiences in the United States. This absence of an audience poses significant risk that UFS's hopes and goal may not be realized. If the audience for foreign films cannot be built, UFS might need to exhibit commercial films or lease the theater to for-profit producers (e.g., Broadway touring companies) or to businesses for meeting and presentation space. Leasing the space, however, could violate the terms of its bond covenants. From a technical standpoint, the bond terms will be designed to ensure that the bonds are *not* private activity bonds (which do not qualify as tax-exempt bonds). In other words, tax-exempt financing will limit

---

119. See Rev. Proc. 97-13, 1977-1 C.B. 632, for safe harbors.

120. I.R.C. § 145(a)(2)(A).

121. *See* IRS TE/GE Division, Module 1, IRC § 145 Qualified 501(c) (3) Bonds, Example 6, at I-10 (Rev. Sept. 2003), *available at* http://www.irs.gov/pub/irs-tege/tebph1i.pdf.

UFS's flexibility.[122] The board must decide whether a $300,000 saving per year is worth the loss of flexibility.

8.7 GRANTS

State and federal governments as well as nonprofits and foundations offer grants that often require the recipient to be a Section 501(c)(3) or other specified type of organization. Such grants are the reason that some ad hoc groups decide to formalize their activities by incorporating and applying for Section 501(c)(3) status.

Obviously, the requirements for a particular grant are somewhat unique. Those in the organization who apply for grants on its behalf must research the requirements for each grant. Many organizations waste time applying to every private foundation or corporate program in a particular state or region for grant money. The far more productive approach is to identify those organizations that make grants to groups having specific programs and objectives.

If significant amounts of money are available, the organization, especially if it is a start up, should consider hiring a consultant to write the grant application.

8.8 "DO NOT CALL" REGISTRY AND OTHER FTC LIMITATIONS

By now, just about everyone who has a telephone is aware of the Federal Trade Commission's Do Not Call Registry. However, the rules applicable to telemarketing, including telemarketing on behalf of charities, go well beyond the "Do Not Call List."[123] These rules are issued by the FTC, and apply to interstate telephone calls. Even though the FTC's Telemarketing Sales Rule (the "TSR") does not apply to charitable organizations,[124] these groups must still focus on this rule, as well as state and local rules.

(a) TWO RULES. Neither charities nor those acting on behalf of charities (telefunders) are covered by the National Do Not Call Registry when soliciting charitable contributions.[125] A *telefunder*[126] is a paid telemarketer who solicits charitable contributions. However, "entity-specific" rules require a telefunder to honor a consumer's request during a permitted phone solicitation to refrain from further solicitations on behalf of the charity.[127] Even though a paid solicitor cannot ignore the rule, the rule's phrasing appears to permit the charity itself to

---

122. Priv. Ltr. Rul. 96-23-032 (March 7, 1996).
123. 16 C.F.R. 310.
124. National Federation of the Blind v. FTC, 303 F. Supp. 2d 707 (D. Md. 2004), *aff'd* 420 F.3d 331 (4th Cir. 2005).
125. 16 C.F.R. 310.6(a), which makes specific reference to Section 310.4(b)(1)(iii)(B), the portion of the FTC's telemarketing sales rule that prohibits calls to the people listed on the FTC's National Do Not Call Registry. This exemption does not focus on charities but on "solicitations to induce charitable contributions."
126. 16 C.F.R. 310.29(bb), which defines *telemarketer,* but in other publications, the Federal Trade Commission refers to *telefunders*.
127. 16 C.F.R. 310.4(b)(1)(iii)(A).

continue to make charitable solicitation calls despite the consumer's request to add his name to the charity's do not call list.[128]

The solicitation rule, as applied to charities that use telefunders, provides a charity "one free bite at the apple." Even though commercial entities may be precluded from placing phone calls to someone listed on the FTC's National Do Not Call Registry, a telefunder acting on behalf of a charity can make that first call soliciting a contribution despite the fact that the call recipient's name is on the registry. The telefunder must cease calling on behalf of that charity if the consumer requests that the charity not call again.[129] The following examples provided by the FTC are instructive:

> Charity A is a non-profit charitable organization not covered by the TSR. Charity A engages Telefunder 1, a for-profit service bureau subject to the TSR, to conduct fundraising telephone campaigns on its behalf. Charity A uses Telefunder 1 to conduct a fundraising campaign for six months, then uses Telefunder 2, another for-profit service bureau, for the next six months. It will violate the Rule for Telefunder 2 to initiate an outbound telephone call on behalf of Charity A to a person who has already asked not to be called on behalf of Charity A. It is the responsibility of Telefunder 2 to get the Do Not Call list relating to Charity A compiled and maintained by Telefunder 1, and to keep from placing calls to anyone on that list when calling on behalf of Charity A.
>
> If Telefunder 2 also conducts a fundraising campaign for Charity B, Telefunder 2 may call potential donors on behalf of Charity B even if they're on Charity A's Do Not Call list. But when calling on behalf of Charity B, Telefunder 2 may not call potential donors on Charity B's Do Not Call list.[130]

Charities negotiating contracts with telefunders should require not only that the telefunder maintain an accurate entity-level do not call list but also that the telefunder turn over the list when the charity requests so it can give the list to a replacement telefunder. Failure to obtain the list could make it difficult for the charity to retain a replacement telefunder that charges lower fees or has higher success rates.

Many charities view the less restrictive "do not call" limitations as another benefit that flows from being engaged in charitable activity. These less restrictive

---

128. This conclusion is supported by language in National Federation of the Blind, *supra* note 124, which provides as follows:

> The plain language of the USA PATRIOT Act undermines Plaintiffs' contention. The Act expanded the definition of "telemarketing" to include solicitation of "charitable contributions." 15 U.S.C. § 6106(4). At the same time, the FTC's jurisdiction remained unchanged—that is, nonprofit organizations were still exempt from FTC regulation. 15 U.S.C. § 6105(a); 67 Fed. Reg. at 4496. The only logical conclusion that can be drawn from reading these two provisions together is that charitable solicitations by nonprofits themselves remain exempt, but charitable solicitations by professional representatives fall within the FTC's jurisdiction. If that were not the case, the addition of charitable contribution solicitations to the definition of telemarketing would have been meaningless.

129. Federal Trade Commission, Complying with Telemarketing Sales Rule, at 34-35 (undated, but reviewed on the FTC's Web site on July 26, 2005).

130. *Id.*, at 35.

rules may, in fact, be a benefit, but every charity should first consider this cautionary note. Although a particular organization may have the right to continue soliciting contributions by phone, people on the list have expressly told the world that they do not like telephone calls from solicitors. Exercising the right to contact these people could create a great deal of ill will. Consequently, every organization's board should consider whether exercising the group's rights is truly in its best interests.

As a final note, the exemption from compliance with the National Do Not Call Registry is limited to solicitations to induce charitable contributions. Given that limitation, can a telemarketer acting on behalf of a Section 501(c)(3) opera company or symphony ignore the registry when calling to ask whether the consumer wants to purchase season tickets?

(b) ADDITIONAL RULES APPLICABLE TO TELEPHONE SOLICITATIONS. The FTC's TSR[131] contains a number of provisions that go beyond do not call limitations. When placing a call, a telefunder must disclose the identity of the charity on whose behalf the solicitation is being made and that the purpose of the call is to solicit a contribution.[132] A series of very specific prohibitions has been designed to protect consumers from fraud and deceptive practices in responding to charitable solicitations.[133] Finally, telefunders must comply with limitations on "abandoned calls,"[134] times when calls can be made,[135] and transmitting caller ID information.[136] An organization's board and officers should make sure that any telefunders retained by the organization are complying with the FTC's rules. This means retaining only reputable firms, adding compliance language to appropriate contracts, and policing the process.

(c) STATE-LEVEL RULES. This discussion has focused on FTC rules. Most states have consumer protection laws that may include state "do not call" registries and special regulation regarding charitable solicitations, all of which may apply not only to telemarketers but also to charities. An effort is under way to make the requirements uniform among the various jurisdictions.

---

131. 16 C.F.R. 310.3 covering deceptive telemarketing acts or practices; and 16 C.F.R. 310.4 covering abusive telemarketing acts or practices
132. 16 C.F.R. 310.4(e).
133. 16 C.F.R. 310.3(d), making it a deceptive practice to misrepresent (1) the nature, purpose, or mission of any entity on behalf of which a charitable contribution is being requested, (2) that any charitable contribution is tax deductible in whole or in part, (3) the purpose for which any charitable contribution will be used, (4) the percentage or amount of any charitable contribution that will go to a charitable organization or to any particular charitable program, (5) any material aspect of a prize promotion including, but not limited to: the odds of being able to receive a prize, the nature or value of a prize, or that a charitable contribution is required to win a prize or to participate in a prize promotion, or (6) a charitable organization's or telemarketer's affiliation with, or endorsement or sponsorship by, any person or government entity.
134. 16 C.F.R. 310.4(b)(1)(iv).
135. 16 C.F.R. 310.4(c).
136. 16 C.F.R. 310.4(a)(7).

8.9 FEDERAL FUNDING FOR FAITH-BASED ORGANIZATIONS

At the outset of his administration, President George W. Bush created the White House Office of Faith-Based and Community Initiatives (OFBCI) to establish policies, priorities, and objectives for the federal government's effort to enlist, expand, equip, empower, and enable the work of faith-based and community service groups. As part of its mission, the OFBCI identifies and acts to remedy statutory, regulatory, and bureaucratic barriers that stand in the way of effective faith-based and community social programs. The OFBCI also ensures that, consistent with the law, faith-based programs have equal opportunity to compete for federal funding and other support.

Faith-based initiatives are not new to the federal government. In 1996, President Bill Clinton signed into law welfare reform legislation that contained "charitable choice" provisions.[137] These provisions permitted states to contract with religious organizations on the same basis they do with other organizations to provide services under welfare-to-work programs. This legislation protected religious organizations by permitting them to provide the services directly rather than through separate organizations or facilities. However, the legislation prohibited religious organizations from discriminating against beneficiaries on the basis of religious belief or the refusal to participate in a religious practice. It also required that the programs be conducted in a manner consistent with the Establishment Clause of the United States Constitution, which means that the funds cannot be used to promote religion or to fund religious activities. Finally, the legislation required that a state provide an alternative provider if the recipient objects to religious character of the otherwise designated service provider—hence the term "charitable choice."

President Bush's faith-based initiatives have expanded the range of programs well beyond welfare-to-work programs. Like the 1996 legislation, his initiatives are not designed to provide additional benefits to religious organizations just because of their status as religious organizations. Instead, these initiatives are intended to make federal money available for social services while ensuring that religious status alone does not preclude access to those funds. The initiatives of both President Clinton and President Bush have been controversial because the prohibition against bringing religious teaching into social service programs runs counter to the natural inclinations of religious organizations and their belief in the power of religion to transform people's lives. In other words, those who have opposed charitable choice and faith-based initiatives believe that the limitations on religious organizations will be honored in the breach.

---

137. Personal Responsibility and Work Opportunity Reconciliation Act of 1996, Pub. L. 104-193, 110 Stat. 2105. The specific provisions relating to charitable choice are codified at 42 U.S.C. 604a.

Pursuant to legislation, on December 12, 2002, President Bush issued an executive order that affects faith-based organizations providing social services funded by federal financial assistance by:

- Prohibiting discrimination on the basis of religion or religious belief in administering or distributing federal financial assistance under social service programs.
- Prohibiting discrimination based on religion or religious belief against beneficiaries of social services programs.
- Permitting organizations to continue engaging in inherently religious activities but requiring them to offer the social services separately in time or location from the religious activities (and that any participation in religious activities by service recipients be voluntary).
- Permitting these organizations to provide such services without being required to remove or alter religious art, icons, scriptures, or other symbols from their facilities. In addition, a faith-based organization that applies for or participates in a social service program supported with federal financial assistance may retain religious terms in its organization's name, select its board members on a religious basis, and include religious references in its organization's mission statements and other chartering or governing documents.[138]

President Bush has also earmarked federal assistance for faith-based and community organizations that provide services through soup kitchens, homeless shelters, drug treatment centers (e.g., Access to Recovery), job training programs, and programs to aid children at risk. The availability of this money is not limited to faith-based organizations, but they can seek funding through these and other federal programs.

According to a March 1, 2005, White House report, $2 billion in competitive grants were awarded to faith-based organizations during fiscal year 2004 through 151 programs and 17 program areas.[139] During that same period, Health and Human Services, HUD, the Justice Department, the Department of Labor, and the Department of Education awarded 334 grants to faith-based organizations, up 20 percent from the prior year. Clearly, President Bush's faith-based initiative is growing and provides an important source of funds for such organizations.

Faith-based social service agencies accepting federal grants must be careful how they use federal grant money. If the award is made directly to the organization,

---

138. Exec. Order No.13,279, *Equal Protection of the Laws for Faith-Based and Community Organizations*, 67 Fed. Reg. 77,141 (Dec. 12, 2002).

139. White House Office of Faith-Based and Community Initiatives, Grants to Faith-Based Organizations FY 2004 (Mar. 1, 2005), *available at* http://www.whitehouse.gov/government/fbci/final-report.pdf.

it must separate the social service aspects of its program from the religious aspects as the preceding guidelines require.[140] As stated earlier, participation in the program cannot be limited to individuals subscribing to a particular religious persuasion, nor can federal funds be used to purchase religious textbooks or articles or to pay the salaries of employees engaged in religious activities, including religious worship, instruction, and proselytization.[141]

In a March 1, 2005, speech to a White House-sponsored conference, Rebecca Dummermuth, associate director for Legal Affairs (White House Office of Faith-Based and Community Initiatives), described the "dos and don'ts" when a faith-based organization accepts a direct federal grant. She was explicit: Religious teachings must be kept separate from the social services component. For example, a faith-based social services agency conducting an anger management program for prison inmates cannot introduce God into the discussion. It can, however, invite the inmates to participate in a voluntary religious program at a different time, provided no federal funds are used to finance it.[142] This separation must be maintained even when there are alternative secular providers of comparable social services available to program participants.[143]

The rules differ when federal funding is made available in the form of program vouchers granted to participants. This is referred to as *indirect federal funding*. A faith-based organization permitted to accept vouchers from program participants can integrate religion into its program, according to Ms. Dummermuth.[144] There is support for this position in a 2002 Supreme Court decision

---

140. *See* Mitchell v. Helms, 530 U.S. 793 (2000); and Agostini v. Felton, 521 U.S. 203 (1997). *See also* White House Office of Faith-Based and Community Initiatives, Guidance to Faith-Based and Community Organizations Partnering with the Federal Government, at 10-11 (Nov. 2003).

141. *Id.*, at 11-12.

142. *Id.*

143. *Id.*, at 13, stating:

> If you take Federal money you may not discriminate against a person seeking help who is eligible for the service. For example, if you are a religious organization and receive public money to run an emergency food distribution program, you may not serve only persons of your faith and turn away others. In addition, and as discussed above, you may not require those you serve to profess a certain faith or participate in religious activities, in order to receive the service you provide for the Federal government.

144. *Id.*, at 11, stating:

> This rule of thumb is different if your organization receives Federal money that comes in the form of "vouchers" or other so-called "indirect aid." In simple terms, an indirect aid program is one that gives funds or certificates to individuals in need, which can be used to obtain services from a number of qualified organizations. A good example of indirect aid is a child-care certificate that a parent can use for daycare at any participating child-care center. School vouchers are another example of indirect aid. Recently, the United States Supreme Court upheld a school voucher program in Cleveland where the vouchers were used for education at religious schools. However, the vast majority of programs affected by President Bush's Faith-Based and Community Initiative involve direct aid to organizations (that is, money that goes directly to the organizations themselves), not vouchers or indirect aid.

> You should note that this statement is a bit tentative, suggesting that this is still not entirely settled law.

involving school vouchers,[145] but some caution is warranted before relying too heavily on that decision. Specifically, that case involved a school that conducted secular classes (reading, writing, and arithmetic) with religious instruction. There can be little doubt that those who oppose faith-based programs would challenge a voucher-financed program that provided religious teachings but no secular social services. At this time, the vast majority of federal faith-based funding is direct rather than voucher-based, so there has been little opportunity to test the constitutionality of voucher-based programs in the social services context.

President Bush's faith-based initiative also seeks to protect faith-based organizations from requirements that would strip them of their religious artifacts and elements. Consequently, the organization can provide the services in the same space that it provides religious instruction or worship opportunities, just not at the same time that the social services are provided.[146] The organization can require that staff members who are paid with federal grant money be of a particular religious persuasion, but the federal funds cannot fund salaries of people to the extent their activities are inherently religious.[147] There are certain federal grant programs (e.g., Community Service Block Grants) that do require an organization's board of directors to be comprised of certain government officials and other specified categories of individuals. A faith-based organization must comply with these requirements.[148] If the organization uses its religious facilities to house its social services programs, it need not remove religious symbols or artifacts.

Many federal programs impose audit and documentation requirements on agency participants, as well as specifications on what goods and services can be procured with federal funds. Any faith-based organization receiving federal funds must be prepared to comply with these requirements and specifications. As a practical matter, faith-based service providers may want to create a separate Section 501(c)(3) organization to ease compliance burdens and ensure that federal funds are not used for inherently religious activities, but this clearly is not required.[149]

---

145. Zelman v. Simon Harris, 536 U.S. 639 (2002).

146. *Id.*, at 11.

147. *Id.*, at 12.

148. *Id.*, at 14.

149. *Id.*, at 13, stating:

> There is no general Federal requirement that an organization incorporate or operate as a nonprofit or obtain tax-exempt status under section 501(c)(3) of the Internal Revenue Code in order to receive Federal funds. However, some Federal, State, or local programs may impose such a requirement.
>
> Although it will take some time and cost some money, a faith-based organization may wish to establish a separate nonprofit organization to use the government funds it receives. Taking this step can make it easier for a faith-based organization to keep track of the public funds that it receives and spends. It will also be easier for the government to monitor the group's use of grant funds without intruding on the group's internal affairs, in the event that an audit is conducted.

Boards of Faith-Based Organizations Receiving Government Funding Should Closely Monitor Organizational Activity to Avoid Lawsuits

* * *

Opponents of charitable choice have commenced litigation now that charitable choice has been federally mandated for several years and has a track record. For example, the Freedom from Religion Foundation filed suit against a number of federal government officials over the administration of certain programs run by federal agencies that make federal funds available to nonprofits, including faith-based charities. In a January 11, 2005, decision,[150] a federal court (Western District of Wisconsin) addressed the concerns raised by the Freedom from Religion Foundation with respect to a program that had been operated by MentorKids USA, a mentoring organization located in Phoenix, Arizona. MentorKids applied for and received a three-year Mentoring Children of Prisoners grant in 2003. Here are some of the salient facts taken from the district court's opinion:

> MentorKids' articles of incorporation state that it was created for specific purposes that include:
>
> > To exalt the Lord Jesus Christ as the Son of God, the Savior of the World and the head of his church. (Matthew 16:13-18; Romans 10:8-11; Ephesians 5:23l Col. 1:15-19;
> >
> > [and]
> >
> > To propagate the gospel of the Lord Jesus Christ, as outlined in the Bible, at home and abroad, by way of operating and maintaining missions, parsonages, and Christian educational institutions which may offer both religious and secular subjects, Christian camps, and Christian recreational facilities; MentorKids recruits and hires only Christians as mentors.
>
> The MentorKids' mentor application requires an essay entitled "Personal Testimony," which "should include your life before Christ, your conversion, and what your life is like now. Your life now should include who Jesus is for you, and how He affects your daily life." The essay also inquires: "Briefly describe how you might be able to share your Christian faith with a youth." Potential mentors receive a "fact sheet" stating that "mentors introduce children to the gospel of Jesus Christ, allowing them to build their lives on the solid foundation of God's love." Mentors are required to provide monthly reports to their coordinator that assess whether their mentee "seems to be progressing in relationship with God." The monthly report also asks mentors to address whether their mentee has "discussed God;" "participated in Bible Study;" "Attended Church;" or "accepted Christ this month."
>
> In a 2003 memo to case managers, MentorKids' President John Gibson labeled the year as the "year of intentionality." Gibson described MentorKids' mission for the year as follows:
>
> > As the ministry moves forward to a new era of excellence we plan to be much more intentional about introducing the kids in the program to Christ and nurturing their growth and foundation in Him. Note the Miniseries [sic] new

150. Freedom from Religion Foundation v. Towey, Memorandum and Order 04-C-381-S (W.D. Wis., Jan. 11, 2005).

> Mission Statement: Our mission is to locate, train and empower mentors to be the presence of Christ to kids facing tough life challenges through one-on-one relationships. We pledge to provide the tools for you and your mentors to be equipped to maximize the possibility of the child developing an authentic lifechanging relationship with Christ, through relevant bible disciplining interphased with life skills. The mentor relationship will only last a season—the relationship between the child and their Savior will guide and comfort them every day, and last for eternity.
>
> Similar references permeate MentorKids' Web site, board meeting minutes (e.g., MentorKids' "number one priority" is "to share the gospel of Jesus Christ with MatchKids so that they have an opportunity to know him"), and newsletters (e.g., "we want to be an intentional ministry; intentionally bringing kids into healthy maturity and a relationship with Jesus Christ").

In view of these facts, the Department of Health and Human Services suspended funding for the program. Nevertheless, the district court refused to dismiss the lawsuit. It ruled in favor of Freedom from Religion, ordering that the Mentoring Children of Prisoners grant to MentorKids USA to be vacated and denying any further funding to it under its existing structure. The court did not address whether MentorKids USA could be forced to repay the grant.

The issue of damages in such cases was raised in a 2002 lawsuit brought by the American Jewish Congress and Texas Civil Rights Project against the Texas Department of Human Services and the Jobs Partnership of Washington County on the ground that "Protestant evangelical Christianity permeate[d]" the program.[151] The program maintained that "change [could] only be accomplished through a relationship with Jesus Christ." The original complaint asked the district court to invalidate the rules under which Texas had operated the program. The case was dismissed as moot because the program had ended, but on appeal, the United States Court of Appeals for the Fifth Circuit, in an unpublished opinion, remanded the case for a determination as to whether Texas officials were liable for damages.[152] One of the litigants has indicated that the case was eventually terminated because the total grant in dispute was relatively small—$18,000, segregating the funds that had been used unconstitutionally was difficult, and the program had no assets. In other words, there was no decision on the merits because of the circumstances.

The American Civil Liberties Union has also filed a lawsuit alleging that an organization running a job training program for prisoners overstepped the bounds of permissible activity.[153] One of the defendants, The Firm Foundation of America, is alleged to have received federal, state, and local government funding to operate a vocational training program for inmates in the Bradford County, Pennsylvania, Correctional Facility. The suit alleges that a significant proportion of inmates' time in the program was spent on religious discussions, religious lectures, and prayer.

According to a court filing, the Firm Foundation describes its program as "a prison ministry." Program staff are required to be "believer[s] in Christ and Christian Life today" and to "shar[e] these ideals when opportunity arises." Program staff proselytize inmates in the specific religious beliefs of the Firm Foundation. Inmates are pressured to take part in prayer.... The Firm Foundation makes no effort to segregate government funds for solely secular uses; nor, as a practical matter, could it do so, given the nature of the Firm Foundation program. The

---

151. Press Release, American Jewish Congress AJC Congress Hails Victory as Federal Appeals Court Reinstates Challenge to Charitable Choice Program Permeated by Christianity (May 20, 2002), describing the unpublished decision in American Jewish Congress and Texas Civil Rights Project v. Bost (5th Cir. 2002).

152. *Id.*

153. Complaint, Moeller v. Bradford County (M.D. Penn., filed Feb. 17, 2005).

government is thus financing religious activity and instruction. And because government funds are being used to pay the salaries of Firm Foundation employees, who must meet a religious test to be hired, the government is also financing religious discrimination in employment.[154]

There is also the question of whether the religious organization can discriminate on the basis of religious belief when hiring employees who will staff the social service activities. President Bush takes the position that such discrimination is permissible,[155] and a brief review of the law finds support for his position,[156] but that does not mean that those opposed to faith-based initiatives will not mount a challenge to that position. In fact, in September 2005, the United States District Court for the Southern District of New York rejected a claim made by the plaintiffs (current and former employees) against the Salvation Army for religious discrimination but permitted the plaintiffs to proceed with a retaliation claim pursuant to state and local law. No federal funding was involved,[157] but there was some $50 million in state and local funding.[158] There is every reason to believe that those opposing faith-based initiatives will continue to raise similar objections regarding discrimination in favor of religious adherents, particularly in instances involving federal funding. The judge in the *Lown* case did not dismiss a claim that some of the government funding was being diverted for religious purposes.[159]

Undoubtedly, more suits will make similar allegations with respect to faith-based organizations. Given the current climate, the boards of faith-based organizations should consider taking the following steps to protect their organizations and their ability to use government funds to finance social services programs:

- Governing documents (articles of incorporation, bylaws, director resolutions and minutes) should not mandate religious teaching or religious activity as part of the social services operations.
- If at all possible, the government-funded activities should be conducted through separate corporate entities.
- Until there is a definitive court ruling, program staff should not be required to subscribe to particular religious views—although this may be overcautious given the White House position on this issue.[160] Those who want to take a different position should seek legal counsel.

---

154. *Id.* at ¶¶ 1 and 2.

155. White House Office of Faith-Based and Community Initiatives, Protecting the Civil Rights and Religious Liberty of Faith-Based Organizations: Why Religious Hiring Rights Must Be Preserved (Jun. 2003).

156. *See* Church of Jesus Christ of Latter-Day Saints v. Amos, 481 U.S. 327 (1987); and 42 U.S.C. 2000e-1(a), which provides as follows:

> This subchapter shall not apply to an employer with respect to ... a religious corporation, association, educational institution, or society with respect to the employment of individuals of particular religion to perform work connected with the carrying on by such corporation, association, educational institution, or society of its activities.

157. Lown v. Salvation Army, Inc., 393 F. Supp. 2d 223 (S.D.N.Y 2005).

158. I. Lupu and R. Tuttle, *Lown (and others) vs. The Salvation Army, Inc; Commissioner, New York City Administration for Children's Services (and Others)*, Roundtable on Religion & Social Welfare Policy (June 21, 2004).

159. B. Jackson, *Federal District Court Ruling Seen as Victory for Faith-Based Initiative*, Roundtable on Religion & Social Welfare Policy (Oct. 4, 2005).

160. White House Office of Faith-Based and Community Initiatives, Guidance to Faith-Based and Community Organizations Partnering with the Federal Government, *supra* note 140, at 12.

- Participation in the program should not be conditioned on participation in religious services, ceremonies, discussions, or classes.
- There should be no pressure on participants to participate in religious programs or activities.

Most important, boards should be honest with themselves. An organization should not seek federal funding for a program if it truly believes that participation in religious activities is a necessary and integral part of achieving the program's objectives. Subterfuge will likely lead to trouble because entities that oppose faith-based funding are monitoring the faith-based organizations.

Some faith-based organizations will inevitably test the limits of permissible activity. Their boards should keep in mind the American Jewish Congress lawsuit. At some point, a plaintiff will ask that the faith-based organization repay government funding that was misapplied. That could be disastrous, potentially putting an organization out of business. In other words, an organization that loses a case could suffer consequences that go well beyond a court-administered slap on the wrist.

* * *

8.10 VENDOR PROGRAMS

So far the focus has been almost exclusively on a number of governmental subsidies available to various categories of nonprofits. Nonprofits should also determine whether vendors offer discounts to them. A number of insurance and software companies offer significant discounts to qualified nonprofits. In addition, several companies that offer background checks and whistle-blowing programs provide discounts to qualified nonprofits.

8.11 CONCLUSIONS

This chapter examined some of the more significant benefits that can accrue to nonprofit or Section 501(c)(3) organizations, including property tax exemptions, favorable postage rates, exemptions from state retail sales taxes, availability of tax-exempt financing, exemption from security registration, and the availability of grants. As with federal tax exemption, obtaining these benefits often depends on carefully structuring activities so the activities qualify for a particular benefit. One way to determine whether benefits are available is for the organization to join a trade group of similar organizations. Trade groups generally monitor the availability of the "freebies."

CHAPTER 9

REGISTRATION AND REPORTING BY CHARITABLE ORGANIZATIONS

Morality cannot be legislated but behavior can be regulated.

MARTIN LUTHER KING, JR.

As should be quite apparent by now, federal income tax law is not the only law regulating nonprofit organizations. State corporate and trust laws also dictate the formation and governance of nonprofit corporations. Motivated by consumer protection concerns, many states have enacted additional laws that require charitable organizations to register with and make annual reports to the appropriate state agency.

9.1 REGISTRATION: THE BASICS

Registration requirements vary from state to state, but two approaches are common. Some states require registration if the organization has been incorporated under a particular statute or holds charitable assets.[1] Other states link registration to solicitation of charitable contributions. These laws often extend beyond charitable organizations, subjecting paid fundraisers and other members of the public who solicit charitable funds to registration. Compliance with these laws is relatively easy for most organizations. Except in the case of outright fraud, compliance failures are most likely due to a lack of knowledge.

Most state registration statutes include exemptions from registration. These typically apply to religious organizations, hospitals, and colleges, among others. Different rationales underlie the various exemptions. In the case of exemptions for religious organizations, legislatures have traditionally been concerned with constitutional limits on regulation. In the case of hospitals, legislatures have granted the exemption because they have placed reliance on another state agency to regulate these institutions. In some cases, certain charities are exempted from registration because they do not seek public support, such as membership organizations.

Many states provide an exemption from registration for small organizations, with the threshold based on the level of contributions. For example, in Pennsylvania, if contributions do not exceed $25,000 nationally, the organization need not register unless it utilizes a professional solicitor.[2] It is difficult to imagine charitable organizations turning down funds, but the costs that can be associated with registration could actually cause organizations near a filing threshold to refuse contributions (or defer them) to avoid having to register.

Obviously, charities formed under the laws of a particular state must adhere to that state's registration requirements in their capacity as domestic corporations. If a charity located in one state decides to solicit contributions in a second state or engage in business in that state, it must also ascertain whether it must register in the second state. It is conceivable that the charity may not only have to register under a state charitable registration regime in the second state, but also under a separate and more general "doing business" registration requirement. That

1. *See, e.g.*, Cal. Gov't Code, Title 2, Div.3, Part 2, Chapter 6, Art. 7, § 12580 *et. seq.* California's attorney general provides guidance through the following Q & A (July 31, 2005) appearing on its Web site:

> When is an organization required to register with the Attorney General's Office?
>
> As of January 1, 2005, registration is required within 30 days after receiving assets. To register, an organization must submit Articles of Incorporation and By-laws and pay an initial registration fee of $25. The initial registration fee applies to all charities registering with the Attorney General's Registry of Charitable Trusts for the first time regardless of gross revenue or assets. Use the Initial Registration Checklist on the Charities Forms Web page.
>
> If already registered, a charity must submit the Annual Registration Renewal Fee Report along with the appropriate fee. Charities renewing their registration also must submit a copy of the IRS Form 990, if applicable.

For a more in-depth discussion of registration requirements, see MARION FREMONT-SMITH, GOVERNING NONPROFIT ORGANIZATIONS: FEDERAL AND STATE LAW REGULATION, at 351-61 (Belknap Press 2004).

2. This conclusion is based on a chart located on the Web site of the Pennsylvania Department of State (as viewed on March 21, 2005) summarizing the Pennsylvania Solicitation of Funds for Charitable Purposes Act. Even if an organization is exempt from the registration requirements under this act, if it is located in Pennsylvania, it is still required to file an Institutions of Purely Public Charity Registration Statement required annually by the Institutions of Purely Public Charity Act.

corporation is referred to as a *foreign* corporation. The triggering event requiring registration by a foreign corporation may be different than the event requiring a domestic corporation to register. Any nonprofit deciding to cross state borders should consult with local counsel in each state in which it contemplates activity before engaging in that activity.[3]

Organizations also should be sure to check county and city registration requirements because some local governments separately regulate charitable solicitation.[4]

9.2 REGISTRATION IS CONSTITUTIONAL

Some have argued that attempts to regulate charitable solicitation abridge rights to freedom of religion and speech. States can require most charities to register and file annual reports. States do face constitutional constraints on their ability to set limits on how funds raised through solicitation are used. For example, the Supreme Court held that a municipal ordinance could not mandate that a specific percentage of the funds raised through solicitation be used for charitable purposes.[5] In another case, the Supreme Court invalidated a municipal ordinance that prohibited paid solicitors from receiving more than 25 percent of the fees raised.[6] However, states can prohibit charities from engaging in deceptive or misleading practices when they solicit funds.[7] If a prospective donor asks about how funds will be used or what percentage of contributions is paid to fundraisers, the charity can choose not to answer the question. But if it does answer, the answer cannot be deceptive or misleading.

(a) EASING THE BURDEN. To reduce the burden on organizations operating in multiple states, the National Association of States Attorneys General and the

---

3. The National Association of State Charity Officials maintains a Web site that contains directory information for state offices that regulate charitable organizations and solicitation. It is *available at* http://www.nasconet.org/agencies/document_view. That same organization and the National Association of State Attorneys General maintains a Web site detailing the registration requirements for each state requiring registration. It is *available at* http://www.multistatefiling.org.
4. For litigation over a Los Angeles municipal ordinance, see Gospel Missions of America v. City of Los Angeles, 419 F.3d 1042 (9th Cir. 2005).
5. Schaumburg v. Citizens for a Better Environment, 444 U.S. 620 (1980).
6. Maryland v. Joseph H. Munson Co., 467 U.S. 947 (1984). *See also* Riley v. National Federation for the Blind, 487 U.S. 781 (1988), prohibiting required disclosures regarding fundraising fees.
7. Madigan v. Telemarketing Associates, Inc., 538 U.S. 600 (2003). Justice Ruth Bader Ginsberg wrote for a unanimous court:

   > The First Amendment protects the right to engage in charitable solicitation. See Schaumburg, 444 U. S., at 632 ("charitable appeals for funds . . . involve a variety of speech interests—communication of information, the dissemination and propagation of views and ideas, and the advocacy of causes—that are within the protection of the First Amendment"); *Riley*, 487 U. S., at 788–789. But the First Amendment does not shield fraud. See, e.g., Donaldson v. Read Magazine, Inc., 333 U. S. 178, 190 (1948) (the government's power "to protect people against fraud" has "always been recognized in this country and is firmly established")....

   Id., at 611-12.

National Association of State Charity Officials (NAAG-NASCO) have developed a standardized registration form (the Uniform Registration Statement). This form is now accepted by 35 of the 39 states requiring registration; Alaska, Colorado, the District of Columbia, Florida, and Oklahoma require special forms.[8] The Uniform Registration Statement can eliminate retyping information, but it must be filed in each jurisdiction in which the charity solicits funds. Complicating matters, many of the participating states require specialized attachments to the Uniform Registration Statement.

NASCO and the National Center for Charitable Statistics have been working to place the state registration process online.[9] Pennsylvania was the first state to allow organizations subject to registration to complete and register online. Unfortunately, registering organizations still must pay the fees with checks and file various exhibits on paper. Eventually, the regulators hope to permit centralized electronic filing of all required documents as well as centralized electronic payment of fees, but that is at least five years into the future.

(b) DISCOVERING FAILURES TO REGISTER. In July 1999, an alleged former member of the World Church of the Creator went on a shooting spree apparently motivated by hatred of certain minorities.[10] The story received widespread coverage in the national media. Following the incident, Illinois's attorney general filed suit against the World Church, asserting that it had not complied with requirements that it register with and file reports with the state. The Illinois Supreme Court subsequently upheld the constitutionality of Illinois's charitable solicitation statute.[11] The facts in this case are highly unusual, but they demonstrate that unregistered charities are often detected either by adverse publicity or notification by someone with opposing views.

In February 2005, the Florida Department of Agriculture and Consumer Services filed an administrative complaint against the Terri Schindler-Schiavo Foundation for failing to register with the state.[12] As you will undoubtedly remember, Terri Schiavo was the Florida woman who was the subject of a highly controversial state and national debate over whether her feeding tube should have been removed. A Florida official indicated that the department initiated the investigation only after it received several phone calls regarding the foundation.[13]

---

8. *Id.*
9. It is not entirely clear where this project currently stands. Information is *available at* http://efile.form990.org.
10. M. O'Connor, *Hale Held in Plot to Kill Judge*, CHI. TRIB., Jan. 9, 2003. For clarification purposes, Mr. Hale was the head of the church, but he was not the alleged shooter.
11. People ex rel Ryan v. World Church of the Creator, 760 N.W.2d 953 (Ill. 2001).
12. M. Stacy, *State Fines Terri Schiavo Charity: Fund Was Started to Help Her Parents Pay Legal Costs in Fight to Keep Her Alive*, LAKELAND LEDGER, Feb. 9, 2005; and D. Kam, *State Investigating Schiavo Foundation*, PALM BEACH POST, Feb. 8, 2005.
13. The official made this disclosure during a telephone conversation with the author. The foundation has since registered with the state of Florida.

Florida Statutes Chapter 496 Solicitation of Contributions Act

* * *

Section 496.404. Definitions.

(20) "Solicitation" means a request, directly or indirectly, for money, property, financial assistance, or any other thing of value on the plea or representation that such money, property, financial assistance, or other thing of value or a portion of it will be used for a charitable or sponsor purpose or will benefit a charitable organization or sponsor. "Solicitation" includes, but is not limited to, the following methods of requesting or securing the promise, pledge, or grant of money, property, financial assistance, or any other thing of value:

- (a) Any oral or written request;
- (b) Making any announcement to the press, on radio or television, by telephone or telegraph, or by any other communication device concerning an appeal or campaign by or for any charitable organization or sponsor or for any charitable or sponsor purpose;
- (c) Distributing, circulating, posting, or publishing any handbill, written advertisement, or other publication that directly or by implication seeks to obtain any contribution; or
- (d) Selling or offering or attempting to sell any advertisement, advertising space, book, card, coupon, chance, device, magazine, membership, merchandise, subscription, sponsorship, flower, admission, ticket, food, or other service or tangible good, item, or thing of value, or any right of any description in connection with which any appeal is made for any charitable organization or sponsor or charitable or sponsor purpose, or when the name of any charitable organization or sponsor is used or referred to in any such appeal as an inducement or reason for making the sale or when, in connection with the sale or offer or attempt to sell, any statement is made that all or part of the proceeds from the sale will be used for any charitable or sponsor purpose or will benefit any charitable organization or sponsor.

A solicitation is considered as having taken place whether or not the person making the solicitation receives any contribution. A solicitation does not occur when a person applies for a grant or an award to the government or to an organization that is exempt from federal income taxation under s. 501(a) of the Internal Revenue Code and described in s. 501(c) of the Internal Revenue Code and is duly registered with the department.

* * *

Even more recently, Missouri's attorney general filed a lawsuit against a controversial organization that was soliciting contributions over the Internet for Hurricane Katrina relief.[14] Although some of the attorney general's allegations involved misrepresentations, the complaint also focused on the failure to register under Missouri's Merchandising Practices Act, which requires registration with

14. Complaint, State of Missouri v. Internet Donations, Inc. and Frank Weltner (filed Sept. 7, 2005); Press Release, Missouri Attorney General, Nixon Sues Author of Racist Internet Web site for Deceptively Soliciting Funds in the Name of Hurricane Relief (Sept. 7, 2005); and T. Zellner, Jr., *Storm and Crisis: The Come-ons; After the Storm, the Swindlers*, N.Y. Times, Sept. 8, 2005.

the attorney general.[15] According to the *New York Times*, the attorney general was granted a temporary restraining order against the corporate entity.[16]

The lesson from these three cases should be quite clear: If a charity is engaged in controversial activities, it should take the registration requirement quite seriously. Regulators desiring to shutdown the charity will have another avenue in the case of noncompliant charities. If the charity is controversial, its opposition may use noncompliance to temporarily impede the activities of the charity. This could be a problem if the charity is on the eve of a major fundraising event.

(c) ANNUAL FINANCIAL REPORTS. If an organization is required to register, it often also must file an annual financial report or a renewal registration with the state. This report often includes information that updates the initial registration. However, even when an organization is not required to file because it does not engage in solicitation activities, it can still be required to file annual financial or other reports because it holds "charitable" assets.

Not all states require that the annual report include audited financial statements, but many do. Whether an audit is required often depends on the magnitude of the organization's revenue. For example, Illinois requires an audit if the organization's gross revenue exceeds $150,000 or if the charity uses a professional fundraiser who raises more than $25,000.[17] California recently amended its solicitation statute to require an audit if revenue (excluding certain revenue from services) equals or exceeds $2 million.[18] In some cases, an audit is not required, but a CPA must review the report. For example, New York requires a review if revenue is between $100,000 and $250,000 and an audit when revenue exceeds $250,000.[19]

Typically, these annual reports are due within some period of time following the end of the organization's fiscal year, but some states have a fixed due date for all reporting organizations. In many states, reporting organizations must include the IRS Form 990 as part of the report.

(d) THE INTERNET RAISES DIFFICULT QUESTIONS. Like everyone else, charities are looking to the Internet as a new source for revenue. The question is whether solicitation by a charity that is physically located in one state constitutes solicitation in the other 49 states (and the District of Columbia). If so, must that charity comply with the registration and reporting requirements in each state requiring registration? In theory, a charity soliciting contributions over the Internet is subject to registration in multiple jurisdictions because the statutes tend to be

15. Complaint, *supra* note 14.
16. T. Zellner, *supra* note 11.
17. Illinois Solicitation for Charity Act § 4. See Instructions to Illinois Form AG990-IL.INS (rev. March 2005).
18. Cal. Gov't Code, Title 2, Div.3, Chapter 6, Art. 7, § 12586(e)(1).
19. N.Y. Consol. L., Exec. L., Art. 7-A, §§ 172-b-1 and 172-b-2.

phrased broadly, arguably encompassing Internet solicitation.[20] However, some people dispute whether a state has jurisdiction solely because of Internet solicitations.

There has been much discussion among state officials regarding Internet solicitation, culminating in the promulgation of the Charleston Principles,[21] a nonbinding set of guidelines to help state charity officials determine when registration should be required because of Internet activities. Consider two hypothetical cases that the National Association of State Charity Officials has posted on its Web site.

(i) Smallville Children's Theatre—Case 1. The first hypothetical focuses on the following facts:

The Smallville Children's Theatre (SCT), a small nonprofit organization located in the state of Lincoln, provides after-school drama classes for children between the ages of 5 and 12. The children enrolled in the classes perform four plays a year for local audiences. The program is partly funded by fees paid by children who enroll, but SCT requires a steady flow of donations. The fees do not cover the entire cost of the program, and children whose parents are unable to afford to pay are allowed to participate at no cost. SCT's promotional materials, distributed locally within the community, stress the charitable nature of the program, emphasizing that they teach kids important life skills, the ability to work together on difficult projects, and that they keep kids off drugs.

In order to increase their contributor base, SCT launches a Web site touting the benefits of the program. The site includes the ability to make contributions by inputting credit card information onto a secure Web server. The site clearly explains that SCT operates only in Smallville, but does not otherwise say anything about who should contribute.

Lesley lives in the state of Jefferson and was one of the first kids to enroll in SCT when it was first founded. At age 4 she played a duck in "Peter and the Wolf," caught the theatre bug, and eventually majored in drama in college. She is now an adult, and a star in a soap opera on network television. She sees the SCT

---

20. National Association of State Charity Officials (NASCO), The Charleston Principles: Guidelines on Charitable Solicitation Using the Internet, General Principles 1D (Mar. 14, 2001), which provides as follows:

> The basic premise of these Principles is this: Although existing state laws govern charitable solicitations on the Internet, in many instances the use of the Internet raises new questions that state charity officials must answer in order to effectively carry out their statutory missions. Therefore, state charity officials should require registration of those over whom their state courts could constitutionally assert personal jurisdiction to enforce a registration requirement. State charity officials and those who solicit contributions using the Internet should note that in actions to enforce state laws against deceptive charitable solicitations, including fraud and misuse of charitable funds, jurisdiction typically exists over some organizations not required to register in the state.

21. *Id.*

Web site, and for old time's sake, uses her credit card to make a contribution.[22] The state of Jefferson Charitable Solicitation Statute defines a solicitation as follows:

> (c) A solicitation for charitable purposes, or a sale, offer or attempt to sell for charitable purposes, shall include the making or disseminating or causing to be made or disseminated before the public in this state, in any newspaper or other publication, or any advertising device, or by public outcry or proclamation, or in any other manner or means whatsoever any such solicitation.

Under the Charleston Principles, SCT must register in the state of Lincoln, although this may not be necessary if SCT is otherwise exempt from registration.[23]

The issue as it applies to registration in other states, such as the state of Jefferson, is simple to identify: What does *solicitation* mean as it is used in the state of Jefferson's statute? The state official charged with enforcing the law can easily argue that the statute requires SCT to register. The plain language of the statute contemplates registration in the absence of physical presence. If the Charleston Principles are read into the term "solicitation," registration might not be required if this is an isolated contribution and SCT does not specifically target persons physically located in the state of Jefferson.[24] Even though registration may not be required under the Charleston Principles, the state regulator is not bound by those principles and could well interpret the statute to mandate registration.

Whether such an assertion would withstand constitutional muster is open to question, particularly if there are no contributions from residents of the state of Jefferson. If SCT did not want to register, it could argue that it had no expectation of contributions from people outside the state of Lincoln, given the localized nature of SCT's activities. Taking this reasoning one step further, SCT could also argue that until there is a contribution from a Jefferson resident, it cannot be required to register with Jefferson. Following Lesley's contribution, SCT has a more difficult argument against registration, but it could still assert that her contribution is an isolated one that makes registration too burdensome to withstand constitutional scrutiny.

---

22. The actual hypothetical is longer, but this condensed version captures the basic facts and is used with the permission of the National Association of State Charity Officials.

23. *See* NATIONAL ASSOCIATION OF STATE CHARITY OFFICIALS, *supra* note 20, at § IIIA-1 This particular principle does not address the question of other exemptions in the state of domicile that may be applicable.

24. NATIONAL ASSOCIATION OF STATE CHARITY OFFICIALS, *supra* note 20, at § IIIB-2, which would require registration if the Web site specifically targets residents of the state of Jefferson or the charity "receives contributions from the state [the state of Jefferson] on a repeated and ongoing basis or a substantial basis through its Web site."

(ii) Save the Bay—Case 2. The second hypothetical[25] focuses on the following facts:

Save the Bay, a tax-exempt organization located in the state of Lincoln, is organized to promote clean water in the Lincoln Bay. Because the bay is physically located in both the state of Lincoln and the state of Jefferson, the charity provides program services in its home state and in the state of Jefferson.

Although the quality of the water in the bay is improving, the charity believes that additional funding sources will be required for its efforts to continue to make a difference in the Lincoln Bay. In the past, the efforts of the charity have been sustained by a small number of loyal contributors in the state of Lincoln. The charity views the Internet as a way to promote its organization and mission and receive additional contributions from individuals concerned about the water quality of the Lincoln Bay. As a result, the charity contracts with a Web designer to design the content and layout of the Web site, and uses Rapid and Reliable Internet as its Internet service provider and Quick and Easy E-payments as its credit card processor.

The Web site describes the charity's mission and specific programs in the states of Lincoln and Jefferson instituted to improve the quality of water in the Lincoln Bay, and invites visitors to contribute to the charity. The "make a contribution" portion of the site provides a mailing address for donors to mail a donation and allows the donor to make an online credit card contribution. A donor that wishes to make an online contribution is required to provide the donor's name, billing address for the credit card, and the credit card number.

As a result of the Web site, the charity receives online contributions from residents of states of Lincoln, Jefferson, and Adams. Although the Lincoln Bay is not located in the state of Adams, the charity receives funds from residents of the state of Adams. About 25 donors contributed during the first fiscal year of the Web site a total of about $30,000.

Because the charity was able to attract donors from the state of Adams, where the charity does not have program services, the executive director brainstormed about how the charity could get more donors from the state of Adams. He decided that the charity could include program services on the Web site about the charity's efforts to clean up the Quincy River in the state of Adams, even though the charity had no intention of trying to clean up the Quincy River. Within six months of including a description of the efforts to improve the water quality of the Quincy River, the charity had received over $20,000 in donations from the state of Adams.

---

25. This hypothetical is used with the permission of the National Association of State Charity Officials.

The states of Lincoln, Jefferson, and Adams have enacted the Model Charitable Solicitations Act, which provides as follows:

> (c) "Solicit" and "solicitation" mean the request directly or indirectly for money, credit, property, financial assistance, or other thing of any kind or value on the plea or representation that such money, credit, property, financial assistance, or other thing of any kind or value, or any portion thereof, will be used for a charitable purpose or benefit a charitable organization. Without limiting the scope of the foregoing, these words shall include the following methods of requesting or securing such money, credit, property, financial assistance or other thing of value:
>
> 1. Any oral or written request;
> 2. The making of any announcement to the press, over the radio or television or by telephone or telegraph concerning an appeal or campaign by or for any charitable organization or purpose;
> 3. The distribution, circulation, posting or publishing of any handbill, written advertisement or other publication which directly or by implication seeks to obtain public support;
> 4. The sale of, offer or attempt to sell, any advertisement, advertising space, book, card, tag, coupon, device, magazine, membership, merchandise, subscription, flower, ticket, candy, cookies or other tangible item in connection with which any appeal is made for any charitable organization or purpose, or where the name of any charitable organization is used or referred to in any such appeal as an inducement or reason for making any such sale, or when or where in connection with any such sale, any statement is made that the whole or any part of the proceeds from any such sale will be used for any charitable purpose or benefit any charitable organization.
>
> A solicitation shall be deemed to have taken place whether or not the person making the same receives any contribution.
>
> In addition to the registration authority, the designated state agencies also have enforcement authority over misrepresentation and fraudulent solicitations.

More than anything, this hypothetical could reflect a problem with the Model Charitable Solicitations Act. Its language is clearly outdated, making no reference to the Internet even though other means of electronic communication (e.g., television, radio, and telegraph) are enumerated. This could lead an unscrupulous Internet solicitor to argue that each legislature believed that imposing registration requirements on any Web site located anywhere posed an undue burden on charities that maintained Web sites.

The state of Adams has a legitimate interest in regulating Save the Bay's solicitation activities for two reasons. First, Save the Bay is receiving contributions from Adams residents. The level of contributions ($30,000) is not insignificant, and contributions appear to be regular and continuous. Second, Save the Bay has decided to modify its Web site to address state of Adams environmental issues. This created the implication that some of the contributed funds will be used to address these problems. If the Charleston Principles are applicable, Save the Bay must register in the state of Adams.[26]

A court forced to consider the registration requirements could take one of two approaches. As noted, it could conclude that the exclusion of the Internet from the list was intentional, or that the legislature did not find the need to amend the statute because it contains language referring to "direct or indirect" means of solicitation. Although the statute enumerates various types of solicitation, that part of the statute is prefaced with the phrase "Without limiting the scope of the foregoing." Because of Save the Bay's own action in modifying the Web site to address state of Adams issues, a court could reasonably conclude that Adams has a legitimate interest in requiring the organization to register.

In September 2005, some unconfirmed reports indicated that several states were preparing to formally reject the nonbinding Charleston Principles. Moreover, the reports indicated that these states were planning to require out of state charities soliciting only through the Internet to register. Clearly, those charities using the Internet to expand the reach of their appeals should watch future developments closely.

(e) PROFESSIONAL FUNDRAISERS GENERALLY MUST REGISTER. Many charities choose to use professionals to plan and conduct fundraising campaigns. This often makes sense for charities that have limited resources and fundraising knowledge and skills. Many states require professional fundraisers,[27] professional

---

26. NATIONAL ASSOCIATION OF STATE CHARITY OFFICIALS, *supra* note 20, at § IIIB-2, which would require registration because the Web site specifically targets residents of the state of Adams, and Save the Bay is arguably "receiving contributions from the state [of Adams] on a repeated and ongoing basis or a substantial basis through its Web site."

27. As just one example, New York defines a professional fundraiser as:

> Any person who directly or indirectly, by contract, including but not limited to subcontract, letter or other agreement or other engagement on any basis, for compensation or other consideration (a) plans, manages, conducts, carries on or assists in connection with a charitable solicitation or who employs or otherwise engages on any basis another person to solicit from persons in this state for or on behalf of any charitable organization or any other person, or who engages in the business of, or holds himself out to persons in this state as independently engaged in the business of soliciting for such purpose; (b) solicits on behalf of a charitable organization or any other person; or (c) who advertises that the purchase or use of goods, services, entertainment or any other thing of value will benefit a charitable organization but is not a commercial co-venturer. A bona fide director, trustee, officer, volunteer, or employee of a charitable organization or a fund raising counsel shall not be deemed a PFR.

A professional fundraiser must pay an $800 annual fee, post a $10,000 bond, and file a closing statement. NEW YORK ATTORNEY GENERAL, SUMMARY OF REGISTRATION AND FILING REQUIREMENTS FOR PROFESSIONAL FUND RAISERS, PROFESSIONAL SOLICITORS, FUND RAISING COUNSEL & COMMERCIAL CO-VENTURERS (ARTICLE 7-A OF THE EXECUTIVE LAW & NYCRR TITLE 13, CHAPTER V, PARTS 110 - 115.1), *available at* http://www.oag.state.ny.us/charities/forms/char009.pdf.

solicitors,[28] fundraising counsel,[29] and commercial co-venturers (CCVs)[30] to register with the state for consumer protection reasons and to ensure disclosure of the fees relative to total amounts raised. Some states require certain service providers to post surety bonds or other security. It is not at all unusual for state law to impose certain contract terms. For example, New York law requires all fundraising contracts to include the following provisions:

- If funds are to be received by the fund raiser, within five days of receipt all funds solicited by a fund raiser must be deposited in a bank account exclusively controlled by the charity.
- The charity must have the right to cancel the contract without cost, penalty, or liability within 15 days after the fund raiser has filed it with the attorney general.
- The services to be provided by the professional fund raiser and the financial terms of the contract must be clearly described.
- Names, addresses, and registration numbers of both parties to the contract, as well as the dated signatures of the fundraiser and the charity, must be included.[31]

---

28. As just one example, New York defines a professional solicitor as:

> Any person who is employed or retained for compensation by a professional fund raiser to solicit contributions for charitable purposes or for the purposes of any law enforcement support organization from persons in this state.

Id.

29. As just one example, New York defines a fund raising counsel as:

> Any person who for compensation consults with a charitable organization or who plans, manages, advises or assists with respect to the solicitation in this state of contributions for or on behalf of a charitable organization, but who does not have access to contributions or other receipts from a solicitation or authority to pay expenses associated with a solicitation and who does not solicit. A bona fide officer, volunteer, or employee of a charitable organization or an attorney at law retained by a charitable organization, shall not be deemed a FRC.

A fund raising counsel must pay an $800 annual fee and file a FRC Registration Statement. *Id.*

30. As just one example, New York defines a commercial co-venturer as:

> Any person who for profit is regularly and primarily engaged in trade or commerce other than in connection with the raising of funds or any other thing of value for a charitable organization and who advertises that the purchase or use of goods, services, entertainment, or any other thing of value will benefit a charitable organization.

Within 90 days after the termination of a sales promotion advertised to benefit a charitable organization, a CCV must provide the charitable organization with an accounting stating the number of items sold, the dollar amount of each sale and the amount paid or to be paid to the charitable organization. In the event that any such sales promotion is longer than a one-year period, the CCV must provide the charitable organization with an interim report at least annually.

Any charitable organization that enters into a contract with a CCV must file a statement with the organization's next annual financial report, on forms prescribed by the attorney general, signed by an officer of the organization under penalties for perjury, that includes:

> a list of the names and addresses of all CCVs authorized to use its name during the year covered by the financial report; (b) a statement of the financial terms and conditions of each contract and (c) whether the CCV has provided an accounting as prescribed.

Id.

31. N.Y. Consol. L., Exec. L., Art. 7-A, §§ 173-a and 174-a.

Before a charity uses a paid professional for a fundraising program or plan, it should ensure that the professional has complied with applicable registration and reporting requirements. In fact, some states impose an affirmative legal duty on the charity to obtain a certificate of compliance.

If an organization is negotiating a percentage fee arrangement with a professional fundraiser, it should check published information to determine what terms other charities are receiving. The organization should also keep in mind that fees based on a percentage of the amount raised are controversial as an ethical matter. More important, the board should know the professional fundraiser and its reputation. This is important in maintaining goodwill with the public and because state regulators are becoming much more vigilant in policing fraud in this area.

(f) USING A CHARITY'S NAME. Charities spend a great deal of time and money developing a favorable public identity. Naturally, charities want to protect their reputations. This can be a problem if a less reputable organization adopts a name similar to that of a well-established charity, or if someone makes unauthorized solicitations on a charity's behalf. A well-established charity will object when the upstart engages in fraudulent, deceptive, or criminal solicitations. Every charity also has legitimate reasons for wanting to control even well-intentioned appeals by a freelance supporter acting on the charity's behalf.

In many states, a charity plagued by someone using its or a similar name can look to state regulators for assistance. For example, Washington prohibits people from using an "identical or deceptively similar name, symbol, or emblem for any other entity for the purpose of soliciting contributions from persons."[32] Washington's secretary of state has the authority to request anyone using this information to provide written consent from the established charity before registering the upstart. The secretary of state also has the authority to revoke the upstart's registration if it does not comply.

In addition to relying on the state for assistance, a charity may have rights under trademark or other intellectual property laws. Although suing to defend

32. Wash. Rev. Code, Title 19, Chapter 1.09, § 19.09.230, which provides as follows:

> No charitable organization, commercial fund raiser, or other entity may knowingly use the identical or deceptively similar name, symbol, or emblem of any other entity for the purpose of soliciting contributions from persons in this state without the written consent of such other entity. If the official name or the "doing business name" being registered is the same or deceptively similar as that of another entity, the secretary may request that a copy of the written consent from that entity be filed with the registration. Such consent may be deemed to have been given by anyone who is a director, trustee, or other authorized officer of that entity. A copy of the written consent must be kept on file by the charitable organization or commercial fund raiser and made available to the secretary, attorney general, or county prosecutor upon demand.
>
> A person may be deemed to have used the name of another person for the purpose of soliciting contributions if such latter person's name is listed on any stationery, advertisement, brochure, or correspondence of the charitable organization or person or if such name is listed or represented to any one who has contributed to, sponsored, or endorsed the charitable organization or person, or its or his activities.
>
> The secretary may revoke or deny any application for registration that violates this section.

these rights can be expensive, often just the threat is sufficient to cause the upstart to cease and desist. Of course, such hardball tactics should be avoided if the solicitor is just a good-natured person who truly wants to help the charity. This is someone the charity may want to bring into its formal solicitation process.

(g) SOME CONCLUDING THOUGHTS. Every charitable organization that will solicit contributions should comply with applicable state registration requirements. For most, this will mean registering in the state in which it is physically located. If it is solicits in other states, it must also comply with the registration laws of those states. If it has an Internet site, the organization should discuss with its counsel whether it should register in states in which it does not otherwise have a physical presence. Some organizations have turned registration into a constitutional issue. This may be warranted in extreme cases, but registration is simply a fact of life for most organizations.

9.3 LOBBYING

A nonprofit that engages in lobbying activities may be required to register its staff or employees as lobbyists under federal and state laws. This is obviously a very specialized area of the law, but because many nonprofits engage in certain activities that could require registration, let's focus on the federal requirements imposed by the Lobbying Disclosure Act of 1995 (and subsequent amendments to it),[33] but do not forget the limitations on lobbying imposed by federal tax law discussed in Chapter 6.

The Lobbying Disclosure Act of 1995 requires a nonprofit to register its in-house lobbyists and to report semiannually on issues it lobbied for and on lobbying expenses incurred by in-house lobbyists and third parties lobbying on the nonprofit's behalf. These reporting requirements are triggered when certain thresholds are satisfied.

The Lobbying Disclosure Act is filled with lengthy definitions. Fortunately, both the Senate and House Web sites have helpful explanations, so organizations that need additional information may want to start with the congressional guides.

(a) LOBBYING DISCLOSURE ACT OF 1995. Under the Lobbying Disclosure Act of 1995, a *lobbyist* is (1) an employee of a nonprofit[34] who engages in lobbying or someone who works on his own or for a lobbying firm and is retained by the nonprofit or entity to lobby on its behalf, (2) who makes more than one "lobbying contact," and (3) who spends at least 20 percent of his total time for that

33. Lobbying Disclosure Act of 1995, Pub. L. 104-65, 109 Stat. 691 (1995), as subsequently amended by the Lobbying Disclosure Technical Amendments act of 1998, Pub. L. 105-166, 112 Stat. 38 (1998).

34. *Id.* The Lobbying Disclosure Act applies to all organizations, but the term *nonprofit* is used throughout this discussion to focus your attention on nonprofits.

employer or client on "lobbying activities" over a six-month period.[35] "More than one" lobbying contact means more than one communication to a "covered official."[36]

(i) Two Basic Categories of Lobbyists. Employees of the nonprofit who are compensated, at least in part, to lobby on its behalf are referred to as *in-house lobbyists*. A nonprofit is exempt from registration if its total expenses for lobbying activities (including payments to outside lobbyists)[37] do not exceed or not are expected to exceed $24,500 during a semiannual period.[38] The registration requirement applies to the nonprofit rather than to its in-house lobbyists, but costs attributable to an in-house lobbyist are counted for purposes of determining whether the reporting threshold is exceeded.

Members of a lobbying firm, partnership, or sole proprietorship that engage in lobbying for outside clients are referred to as *outside lobbyists*. A lobbying firm is required to file a separate registration for a particular client if its total income from that client for lobbying activities exceeds or is expected to exceed $6,000[39] during a semiannual period.[40]

For purposes of determining whether the $24,500 and $6,000 thresholds are met, Section 501(c)(3) organizations may base their determination of lobbying expenses on tax law definitions rather than on the basic definitions set out in the Lobbying Disclosure Act of 1995.

(ii) Basic Registration Requirements. An organization is required to register with the clerk of the House and the secretary of the Senate on Form LD-1 no later than 45 days after it employs or retains a lobbyist to make more than one lobbying contact on behalf of the client or the date a lobbyist in fact makes a second contact.[41] For example, Lobbying Firm A is retained to monitor an issue, but whether it makes lobbying contacts depends on future legislative developments. In another example, Corporation B knows that its in-house lobbyist will make contacts but reasonably expects that its lobbying expenditures will not amount to $24,500 in a semiannual period. As the facts evolve, the issues of interest to B turn out to be more controversial than expected, and it exceeds the $24,500 threshold in two months. Lobbying Firm A has no registration requirement at the present time. The requirement is triggered when and if the firm makes

35. *Id.* § 3(10) of Lobbying Disclosure Act of 1995.
36. This language is taken from the United States Senate Web site at http://www.senate.gov/legislative/common/briefing/lobby_disc_briefing.htm#4 (viewed July 31, 2005) under the section "More than One Lobbying Contact."
37. *Id.*, under the section entitled "Relationship Between 20 percent of Time and Monetary Threshold, Example 3."
38. This amount is periodically adjusted for inflation. See Section 4(a)(3)(B) of Lobbying Disclosure Act of 1995, *supra* note 33.
39. *Id.*
40. United States Senate Web site, *supra* note 36, under the section entitled "Who Must Register and When."
41. *Id.*, under the section entitled "Timing."

or reasonably expects to make contacts. Corporation B was required to register as soon as it knew, or reasonably expected, that its lobbying expenditures would exceed $24,500; it needs to register immediately.[42]

Each registrant must file a semiannual report on Form LD-2 no later than 45 days after the end of the semiannual period beginning on the first day of January and the first day of July of each year in which it is registered.[43] Lobbying firms must file separate reports for each client for each semiannual reporting period. Organizations employing in-house lobbyists file one report covering their lobbying activities each semiannual reporting period. The clerk and secretary consider reports to be filed in time if they are postmarked by February 14 or August 14. In the event that either of these dates occurs on a weekend or a federal holiday, the next business day postmark is also considered timely.

(iii) Compliance. An organization that is required to register but does not is subject to a civil fine of up to $50,000.[44] The United States Attorney General begins proceedings when organizations or lobbyists subject to the registration requirements fail to register or report. Complying with this law is relatively painless. Consequently, organizations that are in doubt about registration or reporting issues because of ambiguities in the law should choose to register and report. In other words, unless unusual circumstances exist, organizations should be very reluctant to pay a lawyer $500 an hour to look for ways to avoid registration and reporting.

(iv) Expense and Time Allocations. A difficult issue for nonprofits that use in-house personnel to conduct lobbying activities is determining whether an employee is a lobbyist and whether the organization has incurred the threshold level of expense that triggers reporting. Determining whether one person is a lobbyist should not be a problem for an organization that has one person who devotes all of his time to lobbying activities, but what about the organization's CEO, who periodically meets with staff to develop background materials for lobbying and then acts as the organization's front person on Capitol Hill? This person must keep detailed time records and salary allocations related to these activities. Furthermore, overhead allocation can be an issue. For example, what percentage of the office rent paid by the organization constitutes expenses for lobbying?

(v) Optional Reporting. Certain organizations that are subject to the Lobbying Disclosure Act of 1995 are given the option to report their activities based on definitions in the Internal Revenue Code.[45] For example, Section 501(c)(3)

---

42. *Id.*
43. *Id.*, under the section entitled "When and Why a Report Is Needed."
44. *Id.*, under the section entitled "Penalties."
45. *Id.*, under the section entitled "Organizations Reporting Expenses under Section 15 'Optional IRC Reporting Methods.'"

organizations can elect to characterize the amounts they incur for "influencing legislation," a term that is defined under the Internal Revenue Code as lobbying expenses for purposes of the Lobbying Disclosure Act of 1995. The intent is to eliminate the need to keep two sets of records regarding lobbying expenses. However, the definitions in the Internal Revenue Code and the Lobbying Disclosure Act of 1995 are not harmonized in terms of expense reporting. As a consequence, organizations that elect to use the Internal Revenue Code definition are required to take into account grassroots and state and local lobbying expenses for purposes of the registration and reporting thresholds and the amounts to be reported.[46]

(vi) Two Common Scenarios. Let's consider two examples that illustrate common issues.

THE VOLUNTEER WHO GOES TO WASHINGTON, D.C.—CASE 1

In the first example, Betsy Landau serves as a volunteer director on the board of Open Pathways, a Wisconsin nonprofit dedicated to reclaiming abandoned railroad lines for bicycle paths. From January through May, Landau makes ten trips to Washington, D.C., to lobby Congress regarding four abandoned railroad lines that she would like Congress to set aside and reconstruct as bicycle paths.

Assume that Landau's travel and lodging expenses exceed $15,000. She also spends another $25,000 to research and write a study detailing the Open Pathways program and proposal. The organization does not reimburse her for these expenses. All of this activity consumes 60 percent of Landau's time.

Neither Betsy Landau nor Open Pathways is required to register as a lobbyist or file semiannual reports with the clerk of the United States House of Representatives or the secretary of the United States Senate. The facts indicate that Landau satisfies the 20 percent time and dollar expenditure conditions that would normally trigger an obligation to compliance. However, the Lobbying Disclosure Act focuses on employees and other compensated individuals, specifically excluding "volunteers who receive no financial or other compensation from the person or entity for their services" from the definition for "employee." Consequently, Landau's activities do not trigger registration or reporting obligations.[47]

THE VOLUNTEER WHO GOES TO WASHINGTON, D.C.—CASE 2

The facts in the second example are same as those in the first, but Landau's efforts are successful, and as a consequence, Open Pathways reimburses all of her expenses. The facts indicate that Landau satisfies the 20 percent time and dollar expenditure conditions that normally trigger the obligation to register, but the Lobbying Disclosure Act focuses on employees and other compensated

46. *Id.*
47. This conclusion was confirmed by a staff member of the Clerk of the United States House of Representatives who handles lobbying matters.

individuals; it specifically excludes from the definition of *employee* "volunteers who receive no financial or other compensation from the person or entity for their services." Nevertheless, a staff member of the Clerk of the United States House of Representatives who handles lobbying matters indicated that the reimbursement constitutes compensation; consequently, registration and reporting are mandated. Unless Open Pathways obtained advice from legal counsel with lobbying law experience, Landau and Open Pathways should comply with the registration and reporting requirements, which should be easy.

(b) COMPLIANCE WITH STATE LAW. Many states have their own laws addressing lobbying contacts of state and local legislative bodies, as well as the governor and executive agencies. If Landau also needed to contact Wisconsin legislators regarding state law that affects Open Pathways, she should be cognizant of Wisconsin lobbying law.

(c) REGISTRATION PROVIDES USEFUL INFORMATION. Nonprofits now have access to the filings made by organizations subject to the Lobbying Disclosure Act of 1995. To view filings beginning in 1998, go to http://sopr.senate.gov. An organization may find this information useful if its mission focuses on controversial issues that are subject to legislative and executive branch actions. For example, a trade association of manufacturers may want to monitor the lobbying activities of environmental groups so that it can plan counter strategies. No doubt those environmental groups will, in turn, want to monitor the lobbying activities of that association.

CHAPTER 10

FUNDRAISING, PLEDGES, GIFT POLICIES, AND RESTRICTED GIFTS

Those who beg in silence, starve in silence.

RUDYARD KIPLING[1]

I am deeply touched—not as deeply touched as you have been by coming to this dinner, but nevertheless, it is a sentimental occasion.

JOHN F. KENNEDY[2]

---

1. KIM, 15 (Mod. Lib. 2004) (1901)
2. Senator John F. Kennedy, Remarks at a Fundraising Dinner in Salt Lake City, Utah (Sept. 23, 1960).

This chapter considers a number of issues pertaining to fundraising activities. As Chapter 9 made clear, many states require charities to register with a designated authority before they can solicit charitable contributions. Board members should consider a number of other fundraising issues as part of their oversight duties.

10.1 TRUTH IN SOLICITATION

Until the al Qaeda attacks on September 11, 2001, most people simply assumed that charitable organizations used donations for charitable purposes. Something very interesting happened in the aftermath of those attacks. Some September 11 survivors, as well as state and federal regulators, questioned the fundraising practices of once venerable organizations, most notably the American Red Cross (Red Cross). The concern was that these charities raised hundreds of millions of dollars to assist the survivors of the attacks but were spending the funds for other charitable purposes.

The Red Cross raised more than $1 billion in response to the September 11 attacks,[3] but that event was just one of about 70,000 disasters[4] that the Red Cross responds to each year. In response to the September 11 attacks, the Red Cross decided to create a separate fund designated as the Liberty Fund.[5] Although the Red Cross never expressly indicated that all of the funds it raised would go directly to victims of the attacks, the public made that assumption. In fact, the press release announcing the Liberty Fund was clear in stating that the fund would be used to support a number of programs to respond to the future terrorist attacks.[6] Unfortunately, being right did not insulate the Red Cross from widespread criticism.

---

3. *Red Cross Defends Handling of September 11 Donations*, CNN.COM, Nov. 6, 2001.
4. In its *America's Disasters 2004: Meeting the Challenge*, the American Red Cross reported that it responded to just under 70,000 disasters in 2004, 92 percent of which were fires.
5. Press Release, American Red Cross, Preserving America's Spirit: The Liberty Disaster Fund (Oct. 10, 2001), stating:

> The Liberty Disaster Relief Fund will support the immediate and emerging efforts of the American Red Cross....The work of the American Red Cross in the aftermath and as a consequence of September 11 will not just be about supporting "disaster relief services for victims of this and other disasters." Rather, the Liberty Disaster Fund will support our integrated response that involves virtually all of our lines of service....

6. *Id.*

The approach of the Red Cross was not at all inconsistent with its prior practices. When a major disaster occurred, all of the funds raised immediately following it did not go to the disaster's victims. The Red Cross used "poster-child" disasters to help fund its response to ones that receive little or no publicity (such as house fires). This was probably an impression that the Red Cross did not want to change. In the case of September 11, the public was keenly aware of the victims and their families.

Now add to the mix an ambitious state attorney general (New York Attorney General Eliot Spitzer), several congressional committees, and TV commentators. The Red Cross had a public relations nightmare on its hands. In an effort to regain the high ground, the Red Cross channeled more money to the victims and their families, expanded its services to those victims and families, and even offered refunds to some contributors.[7] The Red Cross also made cash awards to family members of victims without means testing.

The long-term effect has been a change in the way the Red Cross solicits money, which it refers to as Donor DIRECT (Donor Intent Recognition Confirmation and Trust). The new procedures are intended to educate donors as to how the Red Cross uses their funds, clarify each donor's individual intent, and set clear standards for how much money needs to be raised and channeled to high-profile disasters.[8] The program continues to use high-profile disasters as poster children for raising disaster relief funds, but it now permits donors to designate that their contributions will be used to fund relief directed to the particular disaster generating the contributions. Under the new standards, the Red Cross is no longer required to find superfluous ways to spend money on the victims of a particular disaster.

The lesson that every charity and its board should draw from the September 11 experience of the Red Cross is that any organization raising funds should avoid creating the impression that every last dollar raised will be directed to popular program services as they exist at a particular moment in time. Organizations need the flexibility to expand, contract, and modify the programs they use to further their mission. Moreover, every organization has administrative, fundraising, and other overhead costs.

---

7. American Red Cross, Liberty Disaster Relief Fund Distribution Plan (Jan. 31, 2002); and Press Release, American Red Cross, American Red Cross News Conference "Major Changes in Liberty Fund" (Nov. 14, 2001).
8. Press Relief, American Red Cross, Donor DIRECT Program to Revolutionize Red Cross Disaster Fundraising (June 5, 2002).

Honoring Donor Intent: Direct Relief International Sets an Example for Other Relief Organizations to Follow When it Comes to Transparency

* * *

Direct Relief International was a frequently mentioned disaster relief organization providing aid to the victims of the South Asia/Indian Ocean earthquake and tsunami. Immediately following the tsunami, Direct Relief's online donation form did not specifically provide for earmarking of funds for the tsunami disaster.[9] Later, however, Direct Relief International did address the issue. Its policy had no ambiguities; the relevant portion of it follows.

> Statement Regarding Contributions Designated for Tsunami Relief
>
> [B]ecause of the outpouring of generosity and contributions that Direct Relief and it appears many other organizations are receiving, we think it necessary to state very clearly our policy with regard to specifically designated contributions and what we will do with money that we receive that is designated for the tsunami relief efforts.
>
> First, Direct Relief has never used a specific tragedy as a general fundraising opportunity. We will not do so in this instance.
>
> Second, we will establish a separate bank account into which specifically designated funds will be deposited.
>
> Third, we consider the funds that contributed specifically for this disaster to be entrusted to us for the benefit of people whose lives have been tragically affected. The people who have called us, many grieving and emotional about the tragedy, have made it clear that they want their money to assist these victims—not others in other places that we assist who also face extraordinary challenges and are vulnerable. We understand this, and we will honor that intent.
>
> Fourth, although all of our worldwide activities are compelling and extremely important on a humanitarian basis, we will not redirect any funds that we receive for this tragedy to any other tragedy. We have no fine print or qualification in our accepting of a donation for this tragedy. We will use this money solely to pay for expenses directly related to assisting people in the affected areas.
>
> Fifth, if the type of medical material assistance that Direct Relief provides at some point becomes less important than another type of assistance that the victims need, we will make cash grants to the health facilities that will have a long, hard road in the future or to other organizations who we are convinced will spend the money wisely and efficiently to assist the victims.
>
> Sixth, we will spend money from this account only when it is clearly related to the tsunami relief effort. These expenses will include such things as air-cargo transportation, procurement of medicines, supplies, medical equipment, or other health-related items (such as water purification equipment) that are not donated, packaging material, travel costs for professional staff or contract experts to go disaster areas to ensure efficient distribution and use of material, or cash grants to organizations providing on-site relief. We will not pay the salaries of our current professional staff from

---

9. Review by the author, which the organization confirmed in a subsequent e-mail pointing out a change that had been made to the organization's Web site.

> the tsunami-relief contributions, even though many of us will spend a significant amount of our time on this disaster effort.
>
> Seventh, our organization has ongoing expenses that we need to raise from friends and supporters each year. To conduct our assistance programs we need to maintain our warehouse, biomedical and pharmacy operations, obtain medical material contributions or buy essential products, pay for overseas shipping, and pay our staff of 29 persons. We typically operate at a deficit for 50 out of 52 weeks, and this tragedy occurred during the last week of the year, which is when we learn whether we made our budget for the year. We still need to raise funds to cover our general operating expenses, but we will not use tsunami-relief contributions for this purpose.
>
> Eighth, we will not allocate any percentage of general administration, fundraising, existing warehouse space costs, or general overhead to the tsunami relief fund....

While Direct Relief International's transparency and willingness to honor donor intentions serve as a model for other organizations, its policy is not entirely sound. This policy arguably placed Direct Relief in the position of "burning down its house to stay warm." Donors need to be realistic about charities. As noted in a subsequent chapter, the people who work full-time for charities are entitled to be paid. Why should some of the tsunami relief funds not have gone to pay people who were directly engaged in the relief efforts? For those same reasons, can anyone really object to a reasonable overhead allocation? It costs money to run a charity efficiently.

Doctors Without Borders took a different, but equally laudable, approach to donor intent. When it had raised the money necessary to fund its commitment to tsunami relief, it refused any further earmarked contributions. In fact, it actually offered to return somewhere around $500,000 to donors.[10]

* * *

10.2 FUNDRAISING AND MISSION

All too often the drive for revenue supplants an institution's core mission. To illustrate, consider the Smithsonian Institution's National Museum of American History, which faced a dilemma in 2001 when it discovered that it had two donors (one contributing $38 million and another $20 million) for permanent exhibitions that would have had significant program overlaps and, together, would have taken up 10 percent of exhibition space. According to Ivan Selin, then chair of the museum, the problem occurred because the negotiations "[with one of the two donors], particularly in the early stages, were largely carried out by [two officials] with little input from the museum staff and its board."[11] This donor eventually withdrew the gift in the face of objections from a number of museum curators and scholars.[12]

The museum has a separate board, which raises the question of why it was not more engaged in the oversight that should have prevented any confusion and miscommunication. While board members should not negotiate contracts or

---

10. Associated Press, *Some Aid Groups Stop Seeking Tsunami Donations*, CNN.Com, Mar. 16, 2005.
11. E. Sciolino, *Smithsonian Must Exhibit Ingenuity in the Face of Overlapping Gifts*, N.Y. Times, Aug. 6, 2001.
12. D. Rosenbaum, *Museum Insisted on Control of $38 Million Gift*, N.Y. Times, Feb. 6, 2002.

make specific curatorial judgments, they should have a general sense of what the staff is doing. More important, the staff should report to the board before committing an institution to major projects. Although the decision to forgo the gifts spawned no known lawsuits, it is not difficult to envision a legal dispute if a museum or other institution "sold" the same space or naming rights twice. Every board should set a tone that discourages maverick fundraisers and uncoordinated fundraising campaigns.

The other lesson to be learned is the need to keep the institution's mission clearly in sight. Many asserted that the proposed gifts focused on celebrity rather than science, natural history, and United States history and culture. Obviously, drawing clear lines is difficult in the case of an institution with as broad a reach as the museum, but the consensus in the press was that the exhibits in question were clearly outside the museum's traditional focus. Other institutions have had to make decisions regarding their core missions when faced with donor demands linked to donor money. In 1995, Yale University returned[13] a $20 million gift earmarked for a new Western civilization program when the donor and the university failed to reach agreement regarding its use.[14] For four years, the Yale community debated whether the focus should be on Western civilization as traditionally taught or Western civilization through a more multicultural prism. When the donor became concerned over the direction of the program to be funded with his gift, he asked to have input into the faculty appointment process for the funded program, something that Yale said it could not allow.[15] The president of Yale was widely criticized for letting the "big one get away," but at least the institution addressed the potential impact of a donor's conditions on its core mission and its independence.[16]

More recently, the New York Historical Society received a significant gift from two donors who apparently wanted the society to focus more on American history than New York City history; the two donors "dangled" a possible gift of a prized collection of documents in front of the society's trustees.[17] Some believed that the society should not change its mission just because someone offered needed support. That is certainly a legitimate position, but should an organization strictly adhere to a mission that is not receiving sufficient support from the public at large?

---

13. K. Srinivasan, *University Returns $20M Bass Monies*, YALE DAILY NEWS, Mar. 20, 1995. It is not entirely clear whether Yale rejected the gift and returned the money or whether Mr. Bass withdrew the gift once his conditions were not satisfied. Various newspaper accounts offer different characterizations.
14. J. Kaylin, *Bass, Yale, and West. Civ.*, YALE ALUMNI MAG., Summer 1995.
15. R. Smith, *The Bass Grant: Why Yale Gave $20 Million Back*, YALE HERALD, Mar. 24, 1995
16. Editorial, *Moolah, Moolah*, BOSTON GLOBE, Mar. 16, 2005; Editorial, *How the West Was Lost*, TIMES OF LONDON, Mar. 20, 1995; G. Pieler, *When Money Doesn't Talk: Yale's Never-Ending Story*, PHILAN. MAG., Nov. 1998. Both the *New York Times* and the *San Francisco Chronicle* ran editorials praising Yale's decision. Yale initiated an independent investigation following the return of the money, promising a full report. When the investigation was completed, Yale officials then refused to release the report, arguing that Yale was under no obligation to do so. While Yale certainly was not obligated to conduct an investigation or promise public release of the findings, once it had made the promise, it was foolish to refuse to release the report.
17. R. Pogrebin and G. Collins, *Shift at Historical Society Raises Concerns*, N.Y. TIMES, July 19, 2004.

This *Guide* certainly cannot resolve the philosophical questions that the Smithsonian, Yale University, or the New York City Historical Society faced. These are questions for the boards of institutions to debate. Although boards do not deserve criticism when they make a difficult decision regarding mission, they do when they let others make important decisions regarding an institution's mission.

10.3 PLEDGES

Unfulfilled pledges can be the source of trouble. Charities are very reluctant to sue donors over the terms of a gift for fear of adverse publicity. Requiring that all pledges be in written form, with detailed payment terms, is the best way to avoid disputes. In the case of a married donor, the charity should ask that the donor's spouse be made a party to the pledge agreement.

BEWARE OF THE BIG MAN ON CAMPUS

* * *

Beginning in 1997, Saint Mary's College, located in Moraga, California, received a series of pledges totaling $121[18] million from an anonymous donor[19] for the construction of a new science building—the J.C. Gatehouse Science Building. The building was completed in 2000.[20] In anticipation of payment under the pledges, the college had tapped its reserves and borrowed money to finance the construction of the building and placed a number of other planned capital improvements on hold.[21]

On August 13, 2004, Nicholas Moore, chair of the board of trustees, and Brother Craig J. Franz, president of the college, issued a letter announcing that the anonymous donor was unable to pay the pledge.[22] The funding underlying the pledge was tangled in a fraudulent real estate scheme.[23] Newspaper articles described an 84-year-old man as the prime suspect behind the fraud.[24] Officials believe that he fled the country, possibly with millions of dollars of funds obtained through the scheme. The investors were apparently told that the

---

18. This number has been subject to some slight variation over time. The basic pledge was for $112.5 million. Then several additional pledges were made and at times were included in the aggregate number and at other times were not included. *See* D. Brown, R. Freed, and R. Larkin, *Report by the Special Committee Regarding the Failed Anonymous Pledges*, Oct. 14, 2004.
19. *Id.* It has never been entirely clear whether there was a second anonymous donor. This article indicated that the principal donor expected a second person to fund a portion of the pledge. Without the underlying documents, it is impossible to assess the relationship between the two individuals or the nature of any agreement.
20. D. Murphy, *$112 Million Promised to College Turns Out to Be All Promise and No Cash*, N.Y. TIMES, Sept. 26, 2004; and J. Burrell and S. Donaldson, *St. Mary's President Steps Down*, CONTRACOSTA TIMES, Sept. 22, 2004.
21. D. Brown, R. Freed, and R. Larkin, *supra* note 18.
22. Saint Mary's College of California, Office of the President, *Letter to the Community from Board Chair Nicholas Moore and Brother Craig Franz*, Aug. 13, 2004.
23. D. Murphy, *supra* note 20.
24. C. Sturrock, *Scam Suspect Tied to St. Mary's Pledge*, SAN FRAN. CHRON. (Aug. 25, 2004); and D. Brown, R. Freed, and R. Larkin, *supra* note 18. Just to be clear, no allegations have been made against the anonymous donor, who apparently was a victim of the scheme.

investment properties were the sites of fast-food restaurants owned by PepsiCo and that PepsiCo would lease the underlying land back from the investors.[25] The anonymous donor, who was one of the investors, apparently had been looking to future profits from the real estate investment to fund the pledge.

Since the story broke, the president of the college has resigned,[26] and the identity of the anonymous donor has been revealed. He had no prior affiliation with the college at the time of the pledge. Not surprising, he was appointed to the college's board of regents following the pledge. The donor[27] had nowhere near the $121 million in assets needed to fulfill the pledge, and as a consequence, the college wrote it off.

Saint Mary's board of trustees authorized an investigation, which was completed in October 2004. As is usual with highly publicized governance failures, this report proposed a number of what have become standard governance reforms.[28]

Although ultimate blame rests with the once anonymous donor, Saint Mary's board of trustees did not perform adequate due diligence and should not have authorized commencement of construction until some tangible payments had been made pursuant to the pledge. The board does not appear to have paid close enough attention to the college's financial statements, which reported the pledge as a contingent asset rather than a receivable. The report noted that very little information was known about the real estate investment supporting the pledge. Newspaper reports indicated Saint Mary's chief financial officer was uncomfortable with the pledge, particularly when construction began without any pledged payments having been made.[29]

A number of colleges and experts have indicated that colleges should not begin construction until they have at least some of the pledge money in hand.[30] In short, Saint Mary's board of trustees exercised very poor judgment when it relied on an anonymous pledge to fund a major construction project.

* * *

(a) ENFORCEABILITY OF PLEDGES. One recurring question concerning pledges is whether they are legally enforceable. This is strictly a matter of state law, so the answer is jurisdiction dependent. The modern judicial trend is to enforce pledges, particularly when the charity has relied on them.[31] Even given this trend,

---

25. D. Brown, R. Freed, and R. Larkin, *supra* note 18.
26. E. Strout, *College President Resigns After $112-Million Pledge Evaporates*, CHRON. HIGH. EDUC., Sept. 23, 2004.
27. It is not entirely clear whether the principal donor was the only one making a pledge. The Special Committee's report, *supra* note 18, indicated that the principal donor was authorized to make a pledge on behalf of the person allegedly behind the fraudulent real estate scheme. For our purposes, this is largely irrelevant because our focus is on the governance failure, not on the specifics of the pledges and who was making them.
28. D. Brown, R. Freed, and R. Larkin, *supra* note 18.
29. C. Sturrock, *Decision to Go Ahead with Building Unusual*, SAN FRAN. CHRON., Sept. 7, 2004; and E. Strout, *supra* note 26.
30. *Id.*
31. *See generally* M. Butig, G. Butler, and L. Murphy, *Pledges to Nonprofit Organizations: Are They Enforceable and Must They be Enforced,* U. SAN FRAN. L. REV., at 47-147. *See* Woodmere Academy v. Saul P. Steinberg, 53 A.D.2d 156 (1976) enforcing a pledge when the school had built the library and named it after the donor's wife; and Congregation B'Nai Shalom v. Martin, 382 MICH. 659 (1969) (also holding a charitable subscription enforceable). *But see* Maryland National Bank v. United Jewish Appeal Federation of Greater Washington, 286 Md. 274 (1979) in which the court refused to enforce a pledge against the widow of the donor.

enforceability is often open to question, with intent being the critical factor. If a charity wants to be in a position to successfully enforce a pledge, it should avoid labeling the document as a "letter of intent." That label may be more palatable from the donor's perspective, but the charity is engaging in an act of self-deception if the only way it can obtain a commitment is by calling it a letter of intent rather than a binding contract.

To illustrate the problem with letters of intent, consider a $5 million pledge made by Paul Oliver-Hoffman to Chicago's Museum of Contemporary Art (MCA) in April 1990.[32] At the time of the pledge, Mr. Hoffman was chair of MCA's board of trustees. In 1997, MCA filed a lawsuit in Cook County Court to collect the $5 million pledge.[33] The suit was settled in July 1998 when Mrs. Hoffman agreed to transfer two artworks to the museum.[34]

Mr. Hoffman's pledge provided as follows:

> Letter of Intent: To assist the Chicago Contemporary Campaign for the Museum of Contemporary Art (MCA) and in consideration of the gifts of others for the same purpose I/we Paul and Camille Hoffman hereby subscribe and agree to pay to the MCA the amount indicated below in accordance with the schedule noted. I/we agree that the commitment will be binding on my/our estate in the event I/we do not complete the pledge during my/our lifetime(s).
>
> $5,000,000.00 Total Pledge. Preferred Payment Schedule: From time to time over a period of seven years, beginning June 30, 1990. Amount: Variable each payment.
>
> Herewith: $0.

Whoever drafted the MCA pledge expected that the document would be treated as a legally binding contract. If that were not so, the drafter would not have used the phrase "in consideration of gifts of others" or have made any unpaid amounts a liability of the donor's estate. The drafter probably would have preferred even more legalese, but many development officers resist clearer language to get the deal done.[35]

There is no question: A pledge agreement should read like a contract, specifically stating that the parties are creating legally binding obligations. Charities are asking for trouble when they cower before prospective donors. Charities relying on ambiguity to entice a commitment deserve the disappointment that sometimes follows. Charities should always demand a clear and unambiguous commitment

---

32. A. Artner, *$5 Million MCA Pledge Foundered in Power Feud: Ex-Chairman, Wife Reportedly at Odds With Museum*, CHI. TRIB., Jan. 11, 1998
33. A. Artner, *MCA Sues Ex-Chairman over $5 Million Pledge: Museum Targets Collector and Wife*, CHI. TRIB., Jan. 1, 1998.
34. A. Artner, *Museum Settles Suit over Reneged Pledge: Chairman's Widow Agrees to Donate 2 Paintings*, CHI. TRIB., July 10, 1998.
35. Whether that was the case with the Hoffman pledge is not known.

whenever a donor receives public recognition as well as sought-after perks in exchange for a pledge. Ideally, every pledge should do the following:

- Avoid using the phrase "letter of intent."
- Specifically refer to the benefits that the donor is receiving as a result of making the pledge.
- Specify a payment schedule, with stated payment dates and amounts.
- Describe the damages that the organization will suffer if the pledge is not fulfilled.
- Provide for the spouse's signature.
- State that the pledge is enforceable against the donor's estate.[36]
- Include some indication of the donor's financial wherewithal.

The pledge should also contain a "bad boy" clause if the charity is naming a building or other significant object, grant, or program in honor of the donor. In recent years, some large donors have been convicted of serious crimes. In such cases, the nonprofits would probably prefer to remove the name. While not involving a nonprofit, the Enron debacle offers an excellent example of why "bad boy" clauses are advisable: The Houston Astros wanted to drop the name "Enron Field" after Enron became the image of corporate crime.[37]

(b) HIGH-PRESSURE TACTICS. Charities should also give second thought to the use of high-pressure tactics. To illustrate, consider Zak Hamilton, who reluctantly attended a meeting at his church in early 20X5. At the meeting, he and 12 other members agreed to make a pilgrimage to Bethlehem. Hamilton was very nervous about this meeting because he had heard of past pressure tactics to extract pledges for the church from those making the pilgrimage. Events validated Hamilton's suspicions. After the slide shows and speeches, Hamilton signed a written $200,000 pledge to the church's general fund. When he got home, his wife Ethel asked how he could have done that without asking her. Hamilton told Ethel that ten of his buddies all pledged like amounts, so he could not say no. Sadly, Hamilton never made the pilgrimage to Bethlehem. He died on October 12, 20X5, after paying just $20,000 of the agreed amount. Ethel was never as religious as Hamilton. When the church filed a $180,000 claim against Hamilton's estate, she instructed the estate's lawyer to dispute the claim.

---

36. For an interesting discussion of the distinction between binding pledges and nonbinding letters of intent, *see* J. Lyons, *Pledges vs. Letters of Intent*, EXEMPT ORG. TAX REV., at 347 (Dec. 2003). Mr. Lyon provides a number of reasons (some of which are rooted in the private foundation excise tax provisions) that the parties might want a nonbinding agreement. His thinking is understandable, but in the vast majority of cases, charities should still seek binding agreements when they can.
37. For a naming dispute in the nonprofit context, see Stock v. Augsburg College, 2002 Minn. App. LEXIS 421 (2002); the dispute was resolved largely on procedural grounds. In this case, the donor had mailed what the college viewed as inappropriate letters to certain individuals. As a consequence, the college did not want such a visible association between itself and the donor.

The courts in some jurisdictions would enforce Hamilton's pledge, but the circumstances surrounding this pledge are just the type that can lead a court to invalidate the pledge despite modern case law to the contrary. One potential problem with Hamilton's pledge is its focus on the general fund. Had the pledge been for the construction of new Sunday school classrooms and construction had begun, the church would be able to argue detrimental reliance as a basis for enforcement. Based on the facts in Hamilton's case, the church will have much more difficulty arguing that it changed its position based on the pledge.

A second problem with Hamilton's pledge is that Ethel did not agree to it. In many states, this is probably not "legally" relevant because the donor has capacity to enter into contracts. In this case, however, the widow never agreed to what appears to be a relatively large pledge. An old legal adage is to be very careful when a "widow, orphan, or sailor" is the defendant.

The terms of the pledge (which were not described) could also pose a problem for the church. If the pledge says nothing about consideration and the court wants to protect Ethel, it can invalidate the pledge with relative ease. More likely, the pledge states that it was made in consideration of and as inducement to the others to make similar pledges. Some courts will enforce a pledge when they find such language. This example was inspired by a case in which a Maryland court held that a pledge made under similar circumstances was *not* enforceable.[38] In that case, the pledge failed to even recite that it was made in consideration of other pledges.

The Maryland case provides one other lesson. Some testimony suggested that the charity may have used high-pressure tactics to obtain the pledge. Such tactics may work in the short run, but they often create resentment and ill will. People do have second thoughts and may try to escape what they believe to be a coerced promise.

(c) PLEDGES CAN SERVE USEFUL FUNCTIONS FOR DONORS. Later in this chapter, you will see that courts do not always permit donors to bring lawsuits to enforce restrictions that they impose when they make charitable gifts. For this reason, some donors who have specific projects in mind may view an "unenforceable" or conditional pledge agreement to be a valuable "stick" to make sure that a charity fulfills its side of the agreement. For example, a donor might want to donate $10 million to a university for cancer research but want to see how the university uses a portion of the money before contributing the full $10 million. In this case, the donor may purposely want to make an $8 million pledge to be paid in four equal installments but only if the university spends an initial $2 contribution (and each subsequent installment) in accordance with the standards specified by the donor. In this case, although the university would like the certainty associated with a legally binding commitment with no contingencies, it had better be willing to accept what could be viewed as a conditional pledge. The trick for the

38. Maryland National Bank, *supra* note 31.

university's counsel is to have what the donor may consider as a pledge or a letter of intent (and the all ambiguities associated with those terms) be treated as a legally enforceable contract if the institution satisfies the various conditions. The institution's counsel should make sure that the conditions are phrased using clearly ascertainable standards and benchmarks.

Quite apart from providing control to a donor, an unenforceable pledge can have certain tax advantages when used as part of a sophisticated tax planning strategy. If the donor plans to have a private foundation satisfy a binding pledge, the satisfaction will be deemed to be an act of self-dealing if the person is a disqualified person.[39] This may not be the case if the pledge is nonbinding, but the issue has not been entirely settled.[40] A similar issue arises in the case of charitable remainder trusts.[41] Tax issues may favor a nonbinding pledge when the planned giving strategy involves a charitable gift annuity or a donor-advised fund.[42] As a side note, a binding pledge could potentially raise issues under intermediate sanctions if the donor is a disqualified person and fails to satisfy the pledge.[43] Obviously, all of these issues arise in the context of some very sophisticated philanthropy, requiring that tax advisers be consulted before the prospective donor makes the pledge.

(d) FINANCIAL STATEMENT TREATMENT. Under the financial accounting rules, contributions received, including unconditional promises, must be recognized as revenues in the period received.[44] Pledges are treated as temporarily restricted assets[45] unless they are subject to a contingency. Conditional pledges are recorded as revenue only in the period that the condition is satisfied, but they should be reflected in the notes to the financial statements if the amounts are material. These rules apply equally to pledges of dollar amounts and pledges of property.[46] In recording the revenue attributable to a pledge, the organization is required to apply an appropriate discount rate to determine the present value of the pledge.[47] This discount rate should take collection risk into account.

---

39. Treas. Reg. § 53.4941(d)-2(f).
40. For an excellent discussion of this and other tax-related issues involving binding and nonbinding pledges, see J. Lyons, *supra* note 36.
41. Priv. Let. Rul. 97-14-010 (Dec. 20, 1996).
42. J. Lyons, *supra* note 36.
43. *Id.*
44. ACCOUNTING FOR CONTRIBUTIONS RECEIVED AND CONTRIBUTIONS MADE, Statement of Fin. Accounting Standards No. 116, ¶¶ 15 and 18, (Fin. Accounting Standards Bd. 1993).
45. *Id.*, at ¶ 15.
46. *Id.* at ¶ 3. *But see* ¶ 11, which provides that an organization is not required to recognize contributions of art, historical treasures, and similar items that are added to collections and meet all of the following conditions: (1) The items are held for public exhibition, education, or research in furtherance of public service rather than financial gain, (ii) The items are protected, kept unencumbered, cared for, and preserved, and (iii) The items are subject to an organizational policy that requires the proceeds from sales of collection items to be used to acquire other items for collection.
47. *Id.*, ¶ 20.

Accounting rules governing pledges have significant implications for nonprofits. Depending on the governing state law and the specific facts, some people fear that a board could be required to initiate a lawsuit for delinquent pledge payments. The logic for this goes something like this: Pledges are assets, and the directors have a duty of care with respect to the organization's assets. Failing to bring suit to enforce a pledge could constitute a breach of their duty to protect the nonprofit's assets. The accounting rules now force the directors to acknowledge that pledges are assets rather than some less tangible item. However, if state law requires the directors to exercise reason and prudence, they should apply a balancing analysis, taking into account the impact that a lawsuit will have on other donors, for instance. No standard should or does mandate a lawsuit in every case. For example, if the donor has no assets, a lawsuit is simply a waste of time and money. At the same time, no board can or should, as a matter of routine, decide to ignore or write off all delinquent pledges.

Accounting rules have implications for fundraisers. Potential donors could be more reluctant to contribute to an organization after reviewing its balance sheet and seeing that it is flush with assets.[48] A charity's fundraisers should be prepared to explain that not all of the contributions shown on the charity's income statement represent available cash. This is where the distinction between restricted and unrestricted assets is helpful.

10.4 RESTRICTED GIFTS

As noted earlier, donors who make large cash and property contributions often impose conditions and restrictions with respect to the assets represented by those contributions. The following are among the typical restrictions that donors impose: A painting must be displayed as part of a particular collection or cannot be lent to other institutions; a scholarship fund must be used to fund the study of certain subjects; a building or garden must be named after the donor; and an investment asset (e.g., stock of a particular company) must be held in perpetuity. Although boards and development officers are often reluctant to turn down restricted gifts, they should review the proposed restrictions carefully before accepting gifts that, in some cases, could turn out to be white elephants.

(a) EXAMPLES. Consider the following examples of restricted gifts:

- A gift of a Van Gogh painting that must be hung in a particular museum wing.
- A $2 million contribution to a university in the form of a scholarship fund for the members of Delta fraternity with B+ or better grade point averages.

48. For an example, see D. Brown, R. Freed, and R. Larkin, *supra* note 18, at 70.

- A $40 million contribution to a university from Ronen Corporation to build a new building to be named the Ronen School of Commerce.
- A $1,000 contribution to a community theater with the donor's name engraved on a seat.

Each of these gifts poses potential problems for the recipient that can be eliminated if the restrictions are addressed up front. As noted, charities are often reluctant to raise any issues that might discourage a donor from making a gift, but often that discussion is in everybody's best interests. A donor's attorney may initially object to nonnegotiatable policies and terms, but may be impressed on further reflection with the organization's precautions and attention to detail. To illustrate, let's consider the gifts described in the preceding list.

The first donor demands that the Van Gogh be hung in a particular location in the museum. There is nothing wrong with this. As all development officers quickly learn, emotions and unusual experiences motivate many donations. Both the donor and the museum should agree, however, on what happens when the museum's facilities are redesigned or are replaced with new ones. The massive stone structures housing New York's Metropolitan Museum of Art and the Art of Institute of Chicago give the illusion of permanence through the ages. However, New York's Museum of Modern Art recently shattered such an illusion with its second major renovation in 25 years. If the gallery displaying the Van Gogh becomes a restaurant as a result of renovation, is the Van Gogh supposed to hang in the restaurant, subjected to splashes from pasta sauces and the odors seeping from the kitchen? On a less extreme note, does the restriction prevent the museum from ever lending the Van Gogh to another museum for a special exhibit? A museum should address such questions before accepting the gift.

Do these questions pose insurmountable problems? Probably not. The museum and the donor could agree on a standard to be applied in the event the museum is renovated or relocated. Or the museum might grant the donor (and descendents) the right to approve a new location for a term of 50 years, with the museum able to decide on the location (in the event of changed circumstances) after this period but subject to an agreed-upon standard. Whatever the case, both the museum and the donor should recognize that circumstances change.

Without a doubt, the university and its students will greatly appreciate the second donor's scholarship fund given ever-increasing tuition. Suppose, however, that fraternity membership declines, and Delta fraternity is forced to dissolve or merge with another fraternity. Can the scholarship fund then be used to fund scholarships for students living in other fraternities on campus? Even if Delta continues into perpetuity, what happens if the university changes its grading system to a numerical one? What then is considered B+ or better? All of these issues should be addressed when the gift is made.

The university must address any number of questions when the third donor requests naming rights. The obvious one is what happens if the donor's name subsequently carries negative connotations. For example, what happens if Ronen

Corporation is convicted of illegal activities that led to thousands of deaths? Or suppose the building is named after an individual who subsequently is involved in a horrendous scandal. At that point, the university will undoubtedly want to change the name. More benignly, what happens if the corporation merges or changes its name? Separately, buildings do not last forever. Suppose in 30 years the Ronen School of Business is torn down and replaced with a new building funded by another donor. Must the new building be named after Ronen Corporation? These are issues that the university and the donor should address before the university accepts the gift.

Buy a brick in the sidewalk or name a seat in the theatre. This is a popular gimmick that nonprofit marketing departments have developed to fund new facilities. These devices raise many of the same issues posed by the previous example. Given the fact that the contributions in question tend to be relatively small, the nonprofit should utilize an agreement that clearly spells out the rules. Entity-favorable rules are unlikely to deter the fourth donor who just likes the thrill of seeing his name on a chair.

The Name Game Leads to a Lawsuit: "How Would You Feel if They Changed the Name on an Ancestor's Tombstone?"

* * *

Naming rights represent a sensitive issue to donors. During a dispute over the naming of a cancer center in Detroit, Michigan, the relative of one deceased donor exclaimed, "How would you feel if they changed the name on an ancestor's tombstone? It was meant to memorialize the name of Meyer L. Prentis."[49] Charities need to be cautious in conferring these rights. Charities should ensure that they are receiving maximum value for the much sought-after honor of naming rights and that the transaction is adequately documented.

So what was the hullabaloo about in Detroit? The story began in 1985 when the Meyer and Anna Prentis Family Foundation gave $1.5 million to the Michigan Cancer Foundation. The gift was memorialized with a written contract that provided:

The fund is established according to the following provisions:

1. In recognition of the significant and long-standing commitment of and leadership and support by the Prentis Foundation in the fields of cancer education, detection and research and the generous financial contributions made over many years by the Prentis Foundation in furtherance thereof
2. and in further recognition of and appreciation to the Prentis Foundation for the fund it is hereby creating, the University, Center and the Michigan Cancer Foundation ("Foundation") do hereby agree that Center shall be renamed and henceforth be known as the Meyer L. Prentis Comprehensive Cancer Center of Metropolitan Detroit.

---

49. D. Barkholz, *Karmanos Institute Name Disputed; Cancer Center Should Bear Prentis Moniker*, Crain's Detroit Bus., Aug. 21, 2000.

The law firm that represented the Institute apparently failed to file papers with the state of Michigan to change the name of the entity.[50]

Now fast forward to 1994 when the Michigan Cancer Foundation was merged with the Prentis Center, the cancer programs of Wayne State University, and the Detroit Medical Center to create a new institute.[51] Then in 1995, Peter Karmanos gave $15 million to what appears to be the merged entity, at which time it was renamed the Barbara Ann Karmanos Cancer Institute in honor of Mr. Karmanos' late wife, Barbara.

Mr. Prentis' heirs were not pleased to see the Prentis name become overshadowed by the Karmanos name over the ensuing years—although the institute still used the Prentis name in what it claimed to be a prominent manner. As you can guess, the resulting dispute resulted in a lawsuit and a court decision that was anything but Solomon like.[52]

The appeals court ruled in favor of the Karmanos Institute, rejecting the claim by the Prentis heirs. The court's analysis is interesting but technical and wooden. To briefly summarize, the court first ruled that the naming rights were not contractual but a "recognition of and appreciation to." At this point, the court could have stopped, particularly because its reasoning could have easily led to the conclusion that the Prentis heirs lacked standing.[53] The Michigan court continued, however, concluding that there was not a contract because the parties had not used the magic phrase "in consideration for." The court said it would not attempt to ascertain the subjective intent of each party.

The problem with the court's reasoning is that both parties had manifested their clear intent with respect to naming rights. In all likelihood, the court was actually troubled by the fact that the complaining party had waited five years to assert its objections to the Karmanos name despite the presence of a Prentis representative as a board member at the time of the merger.

The Technical Lesson: A lawyer representing a donor should add the phrase "in consideration for" to agreements granting naming rights. Actually, the lawyer should go further, providing very clear language that both parties believe they are entering into a binding contract, assuming that doing so is desirable.

When a donor expects something in return for his charitable gift, his legal counsel should be sure that there is a written agreement containing whatever language is necessary to create a legally binding contract. Of course, courts do not seem to have much trouble ignoring contracts when they want to, so the advisor should consider some other practical protection, including the following:

- Creating an express right of reverter (or a gift over to an alternative charity) in case the benefits are not forthcoming or as negotiated.
- In the case of building naming rights, opting for chiseled names rather than easily replaced signage.
- In the case of building naming rights, filing an appropriate deed that requires any building associated with the land to carry the specified name.

---

50. P. Anstett, *Battle to Rename Cancer Institute Leads to Lawsuit: At Stake Is the Legacy of 2 Prominent Families*, DETROIT FREE PRESS, Sept. 9, 2000. A Michigan appeals court opinion contains one line referring to a failure to change the name of the center but does not go into any detail. *See* Prentis Family Foundation v. Barbara Ann Karmanos Cancer Institute, 266 Mich App 39 (Mich. C.A. 2005). In fact, it does not specifically mention who failed to change the name.
51. D. Barkholz, *supra* note 49.
52. Prentis Family Foundation, *supra* note 50.
53. The court suggests that the Prentis Family Foundation could have used reverter language had it wanted an enforceable contract. That reference strongly implies that it is the state attorney general who now has exclusive standing with respect to the charitable assets in question.

- Holding back a portion of the contribution and making that portion contingent on compliance with the terms of the gift.
- Addressing merger and asset sales in the agreement. Although a building may have an air of permanence to it, institutions can change hands.
- Retaining separate legal counsel rather than relying on the charity's legal counsel to document the transaction.
- Undertaking post transfer due diligence to ensure that required acts have been properly completed.

Contractual provisions pertaining to naming rights of the type in question here should not jeopardize the deductibility of the contribution, but the specific legal authority addressing this question is scant at best.[54] Consequently, before proceeding with any major gift, a tax lawyer should review the arrangement.

That the dispute ended in a lawsuit is not surprising given the characterization of the cancer center as an "ancestor's tombstone." Any institution that disappoints a donor's expectations to the degree that the cancer center apparently did should not expect future major contributions. Being in the legal right does not always make good business sense. A significant issue in the litigation was whether the law firm that represented the institution had breached a duty to the donor. Apparently, one of the Prentis heirs viewed the law firm as the donor's counsel. Consequently, charities should never permit a donor to rely on the institution's legal counsel but should insist that separate counsel represent the donor.

* * *

(b) LEGAL ACTION. Donors are increasingly demonstrating the willingness to bring lawsuits against charities that do not adhere to the terms of restricted gifts. Under the common law, once a donor makes a gift, he has no continuing interest in the property but may sue for its return if the donor retained a right of *reverter*. Traditionally, only the state attorney general had standing to maintain a suit to enforce gift restrictions unless the donor specifically reserved rights to police the restrictions. Recent litigation is chipping away at that paradigm, however.[55]

Permitting donors to bring lawsuits has some policy justification. Donors possessing these rights are more likely to monitor compliance than state attorneys

54. For a relatively recent discussion of how contracts are being used by donors, see D. Blum, *Ties That Bind: More Donors Specify Terms for Their Gifts to Charity*, CHRON OF PHILAN., Mar. 21, 2002. For relevant authority, see Treas. Reg. § 53.4941(d)-2(f)(2), Example 4; and Rev. Rul. 73-407, 1973-2 C.B. 383. These two authorities refer to naming rights as an "incidental and tenuous" benefit. The issue becomes more difficult when the naming rights or recognition have a commercial or advertising element associated with them. *See* Tech. Adv. Mem. 91-47-007 (Aug. 16, 1991) involving corporate sponsorship of a college bowl football game. In that situation, the question is not so much deductibility but whether the payment constitutes unrelated trade or business income. Although the United States Treasury has issued regulations to address the UBIT issues, these regulations distinguish between advertising (potentially problematic) and a mere acknowledgement (not problematic). *See* Treas. Reg. § 1.513-4; and Announcement 92-15, 1992-5 I.R.B. 51. *See also* C. Roady, *Planning Corporate Sponsorship and Affinity Programs*, Fifth Annual Western Conference on Tax-Exempt Organizations (Nov. 2001).
55. See, for example, L.B. Research and Education Foundation v. UCLA Foundation,130 Cal. App. 4th 171 (June 14, 2005), in which the court held that a gift created a conditional contract that provided the donor standing to enforce the terms of the gift.

general because donors are much closer to the situation (both in terms of following developments and emotional involvement). On the other hand, broad grants of standing can pose problems, particularly when a now-deceased donor's rights are asserted derivatively by a member of a subsequent generation who is not as enchanted with the charity. Consider the following cases that bear out these observations.

- "Representatives of a Texas oil heiress regarded as the Metropolitan Opera's greatest individual donor [sued] the Met to recover millions of dollars that they say were used against the woman's artistic wishes" according to a report in the *New York Times*.[56] In a 1987 pledge agreement, Sybil Harrington required that her $20 million pledge be used to stage "at least one new production each Metropolitan Opera season by composers such as Verdi, Puccini, Bizet, Wagner, Strauss and others whose works have been the core of the repertory of the Metropolitan Opera during its first century, with each new production to be staged and performed in a traditional manner that is generally faithful to the intentions of the composer and librettist." The dispute arose when the Met contacted the Amarillo Area Foundation seeking permission to use apparently restricted funds to telecast an opera that was "not a traditional staging of the opera."[57] The suit sought the return of $5 million that was to be used for televising traditional grand opera, as well as an accounting for funds that may have been inappropriately spent. The *Times* article quoted a Metropolitan Opera spokesperson as saying that he was confident that "at the end of this affair, the name of the Metropolitan Opera will remain unsullied." The parties entered into a confidential settlement in April 2004.[58]
- Paul Glenn sued the University of Southern California (USC) over a $1.6 million grant that he made to fund a professorship in cellular and molecular gerontology, alleging that USC did not award the professorship. In September 2002, a California appeals court ruled that Mr. Glenn could proceed with his legal action,[59] but the matter was settled out of court in 2004.[60] The technical question was whether Mr. Glenn had made a gift (not enforceable by the donor) or had entered into an enforceable contract.

---

56. R. Pogrebin, *Donor's Estate Sues Metropolitan Opera*, N.Y. TIMES, July 24, 2004.
57. *Id.*
58. Associated Press, *Settlement Reached in Opera Dispute*, STAR-TELEGRAM, Apr. 13, 2004
59. Paul F. Glenn v. University of Southern California, 2002 Cal. App. Unpub. LEXIS 8508.
60. G. Winter and J. Cheng, *Givers and Colleges Clash on Spending*, N.Y. TIMES, Nov. 27, 2004. In discussing how this experience changed the giving experience, Mr. Glenn said:

> We were assuming the honestly and integrity of everyone involved. We now know that there's got be a quid pro quo here. This is not a donation. It's a contract, and both parties have to live up to it.

- Members of the Searle family brought suit against the Chicago Community Trust over the control of a $280 million fund.[61] Family members contended that the Chicago Community Trust had stopped listening to their recommendations over the distribution of money held in the fund.[62] The family members also alleged that administration fees being charged by the Chicago Community Trust with respect to management of the fund may have been excessive.[63] The Chicago Community Trust filed a countersuit. The *Chicago Tribune* reported that the parties reached a settlement under which the Chicago Community Trust will continue to administer the fund and Searle family representatives will share responsibility for grant making.[64]
- In 1961, Mr. and Mrs. Charles Robertson donated approximately $35 million in stock to fund the annual operating budget of the Woodrow Wilson School of Public and International Affairs at Princeton University.[65] By 2002, the endowment had grown to roughly $560 million, providing about 75 percent of the school's annual operating budget.[66] Robertson descendants filed suit in July 2002 seeking the return of the funds, alleging that Princeton University had disenfranchised family members from participation in the administration of the fund, had commingled funds, and had failed to fulfill the fund's mission.[67] In February 2005, Princeton filed for a judicial declaration that Princeton University and the Woodrow Wilson School are and will continue to be the sole beneficiary. In that filing, Princeton went back to various documents that were apparently submitted in support of ruling requests from the IRS that demonstrate that the original gift was for the sole benefit of Princeton University.[68] The dispute has not yet been resolved.
- R. Brinkley Smithers gave $10 million between 1971 and 1983 to fund an alcohol treatment center at St. Luke's-Roosevelt Hospital.[69] The facts in the court opinion are not entirely clear, but it appears that the hospital wanted to sell the building that housed the center and use some of the proceeds for general purposes rather than as specified by the Smithers gift.[70]

61. J. Yates and L. Cohen, *Community Trust Grants in Dispute*, CHI. TRIB., May 25, 2002. The value of the trust has been reported as $280 million, $300 million, and $350 million.
62. *Id.*
63. S. Greene, *Seeking Control in Court: Disgruntled Donors Sue over Use of Their Gifts*, CHRON. OF PHILAN., Nov. 28, 2002.
64. J. Yates, *Accord Frees Millions for Charity; Searle Family, Trust Will End 3-Year Dispute*, CHI. TRIB., Apr. 6, 2004.
65. M. Newman, *Princeton University Is Sued over Control of Foundation*, N.Y. TIMES, July 18, 2002.
66. *Id.*
67. Complaint, Robertson v. Princeton University (filed July 17, 2002 in Sup. Ct. of N.J.).
68. Press Release, Princeton University, University Seeks Resolution of Key Issues in Robertson Lawsuit (Feb. 2, 2005).
69. Smithers v. St. Luke's Roosevelt Hospital, N.Y.S.2d 426 (2001).
70. S. Greene, *N.Y. Hospital Settles Case Filed by Donor's Widow*, CHRON. OF PHILAN. Oct. 30, 2003; and S. Strom, *Donors Add Watchdog Role to Relations with Charities*, N.Y. TIMES, Mar. 29, 2003.

After the donor's death, the New York State Attorney General attempted to negotiate a settlement between the hospital and the donor's widow (acting as his personal administrator). When the attorney general and the hospital reached an agreement that Mrs. Smithers-Fornaci did not like, she brought her own suit. In 2001, a New York appellate court ruled that Mrs. Smithers-Fornaci had standing to bring her suit as a representative of the donor's estate.[71] The parties finally reached an out-of-court settlement in 2003 that transferred the funds for the treatment center back to the Smithers endowment fund to underwrite substance abuse programs.[72]

- In an unusual move, businessman and philanthropist Peter B. Lewis told the Cleveland nonprofit community that he would not make any more donations to local nonprofits until the governance of Case Western Reserve University is improved to his satisfaction. He described Case Western as "a diseased university that is collapsing and sucking Cleveland into a hole with it."[73] Mr. Lewis apparently hoped that by putting funding pressure on other charities, he could enlist their aid in improving Case Western Reserve University by encouraging some of the university trustees to resign.[74] This is a clear recognition of the interlocking directorships (some might say, inbreeding) among major nonprofit organizations in many communities. Mr. Lewis had donated more than $36 million to fund a new building to house Case Western Reserve's business school.[75] Mr. Lewis, also a contributor to the Solomon R. Guggenheim Museum, told the director of the museum to either clean up the museum's finances or lose his job.[76] Mr. Lewis has since resigned as chairman of the Guggenheim.[77]

A practical technique available to donors to police gift restrictions is to provide for a "gift over" in the gift instrument; if the original donee charity cannot carry out the donor's restrictions, an alternative charitable beneficiary is given standing to sue for the transfer of the assets, with the understanding that the alternative beneficiary will carry out the restrictions. That appears to be what was provided for in the Sybil Harrington gift to the Metropolitan Opera.

(c) RESTRICTIONS, CONTRACTS, AND TAXES: DOES GOOD PLANNING CREATE TAX ISSUES? As should be apparent from the examples in the last section, donors who make restricted gifts to charities are often willing to sue to ensure that a charity adheres to the restrictions. Some of these suits have been successful. A

71. Smithers, *supra* note 69.
72. S. Greene, *supra* note 70.
73. S. Litt, *Lewis 'Sad, Shocked' by Rampage inside Namesake Building*, CLEVELAND PLAIN DEALER, May 13, 2003.
74. J. Pulley, *Money Talks, More So When It Walks*, CHRON. OF HIGHER EDUC., Oct. 25, 2002.
75. *Id.*
76. R. Pogrebin, *Behind the Guggenheim Struggle*, INTERNATIONAL HERALD TRIB., Jan. 24, 2005.
77. C. Vogel, *Guggenheim Loses Top Donor in Rift on Spending and Vision*, N.Y. TIMES, Jan. 20, 2005.

donor certainly will not hurt his position from a legal standpoint by couching the terms of a restricted gift in language that is clearly designed to create a contract. Donors should consider specifying that the "deed of gift" is a contract, the terms of the restrictions, any rights that the donor will receive as a consequence of having made the gift (e.g., naming rights), and the donor's right to enforce the terms of the gift. Although donors must recognize that some courts are not willing to enforce such a contract on public policy grounds (because the state's attorney general has the responsibility to enforce the terms of a restricted gift after the gift is made), donors certainly are no worse off for having tried to clarify and specify their rights. The risks of litigation cut both ways: A charity faced with clear and unambiguous language is more likely to listen to an angry donor's demands before forcing the donor to seek redress through the courts.

As previously noted, every donor who wants to build contractual rights into the terms of a gift should discuss the matter with a tax attorney before finalizing the gift. To a certain extent, any tax risk depends on the specific terms of the arrangement. For example, any arrangement that provides for a reversion of a gift to a donor[78] if certain conditions are not satisfied carries tax risks. Under the tax rules, a donor will lose his deduction if there is more than a negligible likelihood that a reversion will occur.[79] On the other hand, if the donor imposes restrictions on how the funds are to be used and that use is charitable, there should be no tax risk if the donor provides for a gift over to another charity in the event that the original recipient fails or is unable to honor the restrictions.

As also noted earlier, although there seems to be little authority specifically concerning the tax treatment of honorariums such as naming rights, practical everyday experience undercuts most concerns, particularly in the case of naming rights and the right to direct charitable efforts through restrictions.[80] These are common arrangements, yet there does not appear to be meaningful case law disallowing deductions when donors are granted these sorts of rights. Many of these transactions are based on a handshake or a simple understanding that the donor will have a hall or building named after his family. However, when the amounts involved are in the millions of dollars, some donors require that the understanding be in writing. Some of these "understandings" may be unenforceable as a matter of contract law, but given the latitude of the courts, a finding of contractual rights is clearly possible although the parties may have never considered that they were entering into a contract. Consequently, any rule that would deny classifying a charitable contribution as a deduction because the gift was found to be contractual would be highly formalistic and create quite unpredictable outcomes.

Moreover, when confronted with the question of naming rights from the charity's perspective, Congress has enacted legislation providing that such rights do not create unrelated business income when there is no substantial return benefit

78. The focus is on individuals rather than foundations.

79. Treas. Reg. § 1.170A-1(e).

80. See note 54 *supra*.

(such as significant levels of product advertising) flowing to the donor.[81] Most tax lawyers would agree that whether a payment is taxable has little bearing on whether the payment is deductible to the other party. In the case of naming rights, however, the IRS has determined that such payments do not jeopardize exempt status because "such benefits are merely incidental to the benefits flowing to the general public."[82] The quoted language suggests that the IRS does not view the donor as receiving something of tangible value, thereby suggesting that the affect of these rights on exemption may have some bearing on the question of deductibility.

In sum, there does not appear to be much of a tax issue if the focus is on traditional naming rights (e.g., scholarship funds or building names), but each taxpayer should address the issue with his tax counsel.

(d) LOANS, PLEDGES, AND SALES. Nonprofits that have endowment funds often wonder whether they can pledge the endowed assets as collateral for loans or borrow from the endowed funds for general operations.[83] The first step any organization asking these questions should do is consult qualified legal counsel. The following introduces some of the issues that a board must consider before engaging in intraorganizational loans, pledges, or sales of restricted endowment assets.

(i) Intraorganizational Loans. "Intraorganizational" loans from restricted funds to unrestricted operations appear to be more troublesome than other types of loans, assuming that the restrictions even permit such loans. At a minimum, a loan must be structured as a bona fide, arm's-length arrangement. Under the laws of most, if not all, states, the board of a charitable organization must demonstrate that a loan (an investment transaction from the standpoint of the restricted fund) is prudent. In many cases, the board will have trouble doing so, particularly when the loan will fund operating shortfalls or other needs, which reflect the organization's financial difficulties. Finally, such loans carry the taint associated with duality of interests. The charity's unrestricted operations and the endowment funds can be viewed as two distinct entities. Can the directors be objective when they are responsible for each of these entities and they are simultaneously serving both sides?

To illustrate, consider Greensville Humane Society, an organization that has recently seen a significant drop in its contributions from the public. This decline could not have come at a worse time: It just completed construction of a new $20 million shelter. Bill Russert, the CFO, has been scrambling to make the monthly debt service payments while keeping the doors open. If the shelter is closed even two days a week, hundreds of animals that would have otherwise

81. I.R.C. § 513(i). The regulations distinguish between mere acknowledgements and "substantial return benefits." *See* Treas. Reg. § 1.513-4(c)(2).

82. Rev. Rul. 77-367, 1977-2 C.B. 193.

83. For an excellent article discussing these issues in far greater detail, see M. Peregrine and J. Schwartz, *A General Counsel's Guide to Assessing Restricted Gifts*, 29 EXEMPT ORG. TAX REV. 27 (July 2000)

been adopted will be euthanized. To avoid that result, Russert decides to "borrow" $100,000 from three restricted funds that finance specific educational programs to service the society's existing debt. Sadly, contributions do not increase, and the society files for bankruptcy.

Civil liability for breach of fiduciary duties may not be the only worry for directors and officers. In a highly publicized case, the Pennsylvania attorney general filed criminal charges against the chief executive officer of Allegheny Health Education and Research Foundation.[84] The CEO was charged with "allegedly raid[ing] more than 350 charitable endowments to prop up the ailing health system."[85] In an unusual 12-page opinion, the judge concluded that the prosecutors had established that monies paid to 353 endowments were "for definite purposes and the defendant Abdelhak directed these monies be used for general operating purposes."[86] The amounts involved almost $35 million.[87] According to the grand jury presentment, Abdelhak characterized the transactions "as a loan, for your cash needs." Nevertheless, after pleading guilty to a single misdemeanor, he was subsequently sentenced to a prison term of 11½ to 23 months.[88] The judge in the case dismissed more severe charges because Mr. Abdelhak did not personally benefit from the money in question.[89]

The Pennsylvania attorney general's efforts may be an aberration, or they may reflect a new trend toward stronger enforcement action in the wake of some well-publicized scandals that have plagued the charitable sector in recent years. Whether Bill Russert would be prosecuted for his action is certainly open to debate, particularly given the relatively small amount involved and his charitable motives. Any prosecutor would at least have to consider exercising prosecutorial discretion, given the likely reluctance of a jury to convict Russert on these facts. Nevertheless, most lawyers would spend a great deal of time trying to dissuade a person in Russert's position from borrowing the funds. Note that Russert acted unilaterally without bothering to obtain board approval.

The Greensville Humane Society case illustrates the truly well-intentioned "loan," but what if the board had ulterior motives in authorizing an intraorganizational loan? Consider Ruth Schoenberg, who in 1970 made a $5 million restricted gift to Alpha Opera Company to be invested in stocks and bonds. The resulting income was to be used to stage a Wagner opera whenever the fund's accumulated income was sufficient to defray half of the costs of a production.

---

84. Press Release, Penn. Att'y Gen., AG Fisher Says Former AHERF Chief Abdelhak to Face Trial That He Raided Hundreds of Charitable Endowments (May 10, 2001).

85. *Id.*

86. State of Pennsylvania v. Abdelhak, Penn. Ct. Com. Pleas, Alleghany County, Crim. Division (May 10, 2001).

87. Press Release, *supra* note 84.

88. *Id. See also* Editorial, *AHERF Whimper/Its Former CEO Is Sentenced on a Single Count*, PITTSBURGH POST-GAZETTE, Sept. 8, 2002. This editorial is critical of both the Pennsylvania attorney general and Mr. Abdelhak. It also placed some blame for the organization's failure on its board of directors.

89. Press Release, Penn. Att'y Gen., Press Release: Former AHERF Official Pleads Guilty to Raiding Endowment (Aug. 29, 2002).

Being tediously long, Wagner operas require vast sums to stage. The current Alpha board would much prefer to stage operas by Puccini and Verdi. Consequently, the board has voted to make short-term loans from the Wagner fund to the company at a 4 percent market rate (well below the expected 7 percent return from investments in long-term debt and stocks). The company's investment adviser has indicated that the loan will not jeopardize the fund's principal given the company's strong balance sheet.

This transaction can be viewed in one of two ways. In a "positive light," the loan is simply a legitimate investment by the Wagner fund. Although it is true that the fund is receiving only a 4 percent return, a bank making a similar short-term loan would receive only 4 percent.[90] In other words, the risk/reward ratio of this investment is in line with what would be expected. Because the company is in good shape financially, the fund's capital is not at risk.

This transaction also can be viewed far less favorably. The Alpha board apparently does not like Wagner (and who can blame the board?). By investing in a low-return investment, the board is effectively reducing the number of Wagner operas that the company will be required to stage. Money is fungible, so by funding the company's short-term financial needs with the Wagner fund assets, the board is "freeing up" other unrestricted assets to be used either to reduce longer term borrowing (and the related higher interest expenses) or to be invested in higher return unrestricted investments. Arguably, there is an economic transfer of income from the restricted fund to the unrestricted assets of the company. The net effect could be viewed as an effort by the Alpha board to defeat the fund's objectives.

The state's attorney general could very easily question this transaction. Even though the investment is prudent from a safety standpoint, it may not be considered prudent when measured against the fund's objectives of staging Wagner operas over the long term. Someone really trying to satisfy the donor's intentions would invest in longer term debt and equities.

In the late 1970s, California's attorney general took action against Hastings College of Law for the investment of certain restricted funds. These funds were required to be expended on student financial aid for distinct classes of students. The college used them to purchase real estate for the college's expansion that produced no income, apparently taking the position that this was a prudent investment. Not surprisingly, the California attorney general objected to this use of funds, arguing that it defeated the charitable purposes underlying the trusts. While there was no court decision in the matter, the college and the attorney general entered into a consent decree that resulted in the college's return of all principal and imputed interest that would have been earned on the trust funds.[91]

---

90. This rate is predicated on a low-interest rate environment that has existed for the last several years.

91. Complaint for Declaratory Relief, Van de Kamp v. Hastings College of Law (Apr. 28, 1998); and M. Peregrine and J. Schwartz, *supra* note 83, at 27.

(ii) Asset Pledges. Assuming that state law and an organization's governing documents grant the organization the power to pledge its assets as security for loans, the board must review the specific terms of each restricted fund to determine whether pledges are permitted. Even then, the board must also determine whether such action would be considered a prudent use of those assets under the Uniform Management of Institutional Funds Act (UMIFA) or other relevant state law. At least two commentators view pledges as permissible under certain circumstances.[92]

To illustrate the potential problems a pledge can pose, consider Middlemain Art Museum, a member of the American Association of Museums, which recently needed $5 million to meet cost overruns arising from the construction of a new sculpture garden. Unable to raise the money from additional contributions from its long-standing donors, the museum was forced to borrow the funds from the Five Spot Bank.

The Five Spot Bank agreed to the loan, but only if the museum pledged the following assets as collateral for the loan:

- A Picasso painting valued at $2 million. Olivia Reinhardt had donated the painting with the proviso that it could be transferred only to another art museum.
- $3 million of restricted funds whose income the museum can use for general operations but whose principal must be held in perpetuity.
- $2 million of restricted funds whose income the museum must use for educational purposes only but whose principal must be held in perpetuity.

The Revised Model Nonprofit Corporation Act (Revised Model Act) permits nonprofits to pledge assets,[93] but it does not specifically address pledges of restricted assets, thus possibly implying that the drafters did not attempt to single out restricted assets for special treatment. Several cases suggest that pledging certain restricted assets may be consistent with a donor's general intent to support the institution when the donor imposed no specific limitations regarding pledges.[94]

Notwithstanding the Revised Model Act, the three restricted assets in this case highlight some of the issues that must be considered before pledging assets. The most problematic pledge in this case is the Picasso painting. Olivia Reinhardt has allowed the transfer of the painting only if it will continue to be on public display.

92. *See* M. Peregrine and J. Schwartz, *supra* note 83. As a general proposition, the authors appear to view such pledges as being permissible, citing Attorney General v. President and Fellows of Harvard College, 213 N.E.2d 840 (1966).

93. Revised Model Nonprofit Corporation Act (1987) § 12.01.

94. *See In re* Winstead Memorial Hospital, 249 B.R. 588 (Bankr. D. Conn. 2000), subjecting income, but principal to creditor claims; In the Matter of the Estate of Donald Othmer 185 Misc. 2c 122 (N.Y. 2000), permitting reformation to invade principal; Matter of St. Charles Hospital, N.Y.L.J. (Aug. 4, 1995); Freme v. Maher, 480 A.2d 783 (Me. 1984); and Knickerbocker Hospital v. Goldstein, 41 N.Y.S. 2d 32 (N.Y 1943). These cases are cited in the excellent outline entitled *The End of the Road: When a Charity Goes Bankrupt* presented at the ABA Section of Taxation, Exempt Organizations Committee (Sept. 12, 2003).

By pledging the painting, the museum is opening the possibility that the painting could end up in the hands of a private collector. This pledge is arguably inconsistent with Reinhardt's intent. As a member of the American Association of Museums, Middlemain Art Museum should also review the Association's Code of Ethics, which provides:

> Thus, the museum ensures that disposal of collections through sale is solely for the advancement of the museum's mission. Proceeds from the sale of nonliving collections are to be used consistent with the established standards of the museum's discipline, but in no event shall they be used for anything other than acquisitions or direct care of collections.

This language is a bit ambiguous, but Reinhardt could certainly argue that her restricted gift should not allow Middlemain Art Museum to place the Picasso in jeopardy of being sold other than for the acquisition of another object of art or the care of an object of art.

The $3 million restricted fund is less troubling but still does not necessarily lend itself to an easy decision from a legal standpoint. The donor arguably expressed a general charitable intent with respect to Middlemain Art Museum. The income from the pledged assets is being used for general operations. Nevertheless, a donor could still object to the pledge, arguing that this jeopardizes his intent that the gift benefit the museum in perpetuity. After all, the donor's funds are being placed at risk, albeit for the museum's long-term benefit.

The $2 million restricted fund poses more difficult issues. These restrictions are much closer to the ones applicable to the Picasso painting, requiring the principal to be held in perpetuity, with income being used only for specific purposes. In the case of these funds, if a foreclosure occurs, the principal that supported educational activities will have been used for other (albeit charitable) purposes.

This discussion has been phrased in terms of donor objections because the focus of the discussion is donor intent. Unless the donor specifically reserves rights permitting him to object, state law grants the donor rights, or there is a "gift over," the state's attorney general or comparable official is the party to object to the pledge. The charity may also seek court instruction to resolve any legal ambiguity.

Institutions considering a pledge of restricted funds should closely review the terms of each fund. An institution's legal counsel could be pressured to advise the lender that the institution has legal authority to pledge the assets. That can be a very difficult legal opinion to provide.

The experience of the Milwaukee Art Museum is instructive. In April 2002, the museum's board apparently discussed the possibly of using artwork to secure the financing for the museum's Calatrava expansion project.[95] When rumors about a possible pledge of artwork made headlines, museum officials quickly

95. B. Murphy, *Art Museum Hits Snag in Financing Debt: Banks Have Raised Concerns about Collateral, Switch to Long-Term Loan*, MILWAUKEE J.-SENTINEL, May 28, 2002.

clarified that the artworks would never be pledged.[96] The museum apparently did find it necessary to pledge a number of restricted funds to finance its debt.[97] According to the *Milwaukee Journal-Sentinel*, the museum did not pledge funds that had been designated by donors for acquisitions but apparently did pledge funds with no restrictions on their use as well as funds with restrictions "such as [for] exhibitions, education and conservation of artworks."[98] A spokesperson for the Wisconsin attorney general indicated that "just looking at the statute, it does not seem there's any direct authority for the attorney general to take action."[99] Somewhat surprisingly, the spokesperson did note that there could be a private right of action. The museum's executive director indicated that there was very little to be concerned about because "there is no risk [of a default]."[100] That assessment may have been accurate, but one must wonder what the reaction would have been had there been a default. As events turned out, the museum was able to obtain longer term financing that did not require it to pledge endowments or artwork.[101]

There is a lesson here for all nonprofits: When accepting a restricted gift, organizations should address the question of pledging assets subject to restrictions. Unfortunately, most institutions will not heed this advice, and understandably so. When a donor makes a gift to an institution that is to survive in perpetuity, he is implicitly indicating that he believes the institution will survive in perpetuity. Nothing could jeopardize a charitable gift more than for the fundraising director to start discussing the possible financial disasters that could befall an institution—yet the courts have been faced with nonprofit bankruptcies.[102]

(iii) Asset Sales. On occasion, donors fund an endowment using a specific asset and stipulate that the asset be held in perpetuity. The organization must be careful not to inadvertently sell the asset in question. In one instance, an organization sold such an asset (many years after the gift when the restriction had long been forgotten) and the donor forced the institution to buy it back. The board should ensure that the organization catalogs restricted gifts and notes any limitations.

---

96. The rumor first made headlines in B. Murphy and M. L. Schumacher, *Art Museum in a Cash Crunch: With Shortfall of at Least $20 Million, Collection May Be Used as Collateral for Loan*, MILWAUKEE J.-SENTINEL, May 18, 2002. A day later, the matter was clarified, with Milwaukee Art Museum officials indicating that the artwork would not be pledged to secure the loan. *See* M.L. Schumacher and B. Murphy, *Artwork Is Safe, Museum Says: Officials Insist It Is Off-Limits as Collateral for Loan But Won't Say What Assets They'd Use*, MILWAUKEE J.-SENTINEL, May 20, 2002.

97. B. Murphy, *Art Museum Used Gifts for Collateral*, MILWAUKEE J.-SENTINEL, July 2, 2002.

98. *Id.* The *Journal-Sentinel* appears to have reviewed documents that one of the lenders had filed with the Wisconsin Department of Financial Institutions to arrive at its conclusions about the pledges. The problem is that the documents in question were filed in April 2001, but the article was written in July 2001, shortly after the *Journal-Sentinel* carried articles about efforts to obtain long-term financing.

99. *Id.*

100. *Id.*

101. P. Gores, *Art Museum Gains Financial Reprieve: Group of Banks Shares Risk in 5-Year Loan*, MILWAUKEE J.-SENTINEL, Oct. 22, 2002.

102. E. Brody, *The Charity in Bankruptcy and Ghosts of Donors Past, Present, and Future*, part of the Symposium Issue on Bankruptcy in the Religious Non-Profit Context, 29 SETON HALL J. ON LEG. 471(2005).

10.5 DONOR-RESTRICTED ENDOWMENTS

Many charities receive gifts that must be set aside as part of the institution's endowment. The preceding section focused on restricted gifts in general. This section considers funds held as part of charitable endowments. The focus shifts from honoring restrictions to how funds can be invested, how income can be utilized, and how endowments are treated for financial accounting purposes. Despite this change in focus, you should never lose sight of the basic requirement that donor restrictions must be honored.

For present purposes, the word *endowment* refers to funds (money or property) contributed by donors that the organization cannot currently spend at will because of donors' designations or restrictions. This form of endowment should be distinguished from "board-designated endowments," which represent otherwise unrestricted assets that a board has designated as being unavailable for general operations. There is nothing wrong with such designations. In fact, the sentiment underlying this designation or reservation may reflect prudent stewardship by the organization's directors, but board-designated endowments are not irrevocably binding.

Donor restrictions take many forms. The principal may be permanently set aside as part of the endowment, but the annual income may be required either to be added to principal, spent for specified purposes, or made available for general use. Alternatively, the principal may be restricted for a specified period of time, and following that period, made available for general purposes.

When accepting a monetary gift to endowment, the board (or gift-acceptance committee) should ascertain whether the income generated from it must be added to the organization's endowment or can be used without restriction. Finally, the board should also determine whether the funds will be subject to the Uniform Management of Institutional Funds Act (UMIFA), which is likely because almost all states have adopted it, and if so, whether the terms of the gift restrict the organization's powers under UMIFA.

The challenge for many institutions is that their "endowments" actually comprise many pools of assets, each carrying its own restriction(s). Even though the board is often permitted under state law and the terms of the separate endowment funds to commingle assets for investment purposes, it must nevertheless make sure that it adheres to the spending restrictions in each separate fund. This means that the board should mandate that the officers implement an appropriate inventory and audit program to test compliance. There should be periodic reports to the board regarding compliance with applicable restrictions. The board can delegate the management of this process to its audit, finance, or investment committees. Each year, the designated committee should report to the full board regarding compliance with restrictions.

(a) UMIFA BASICS. Historically, charitable institutions viewed interest and dividend income from endowment funds as "spendable" but capital appreciation as remaining part of the endowment. During the last 30 years, the investment community has developed a "total return" measure that considers realized and unrealized capital gains and losses in measuring return on investment. UMIFA incorporates this concept, permitting charities to treat capital appreciation on endowed funds as unrestricted or temporarily restricted income (assuming the donor has not specifically restricted the use of the appreciation or that state law does not impose other restrictions).

While UMIFA allows net appreciation from restricted assets to be appropriated, this does not mean that this appreciation is there just for the taking. This is true even though the financial statements may classify this appreciation as unrestricted income. The board must first determine that appropriating this appreciation is prudent. Several states have explicitly addressed this issue; New York's attorney general clearly has stated that a prudence standard applies to expenditures of the net appreciation.[103]

Massachusetts law creates a presumption that appropriations of net appreciation in excess of 7 percent of value are imprudent.[104] Rhode Island requires that fiduciaries consider inflation,[105] and Pennsylvania, a non-UMIFA state, has a prudence rule that uses a minimum of 2 percent and a maximum of 7 percent of the value of assets as its baseline for corporations that elect into the regime.[106] Other states do not set percentage thresholds but require the board to act prudently. Ascertaining where the line is drawn can result in some heated board discussions followed by feelings of uncertainty and ambivalence. The National Conference of Commissioners on Uniform State Laws is currently revising UMIFA to address some of these ambiguities. After the drafting is complete, state legislatures still must enact the revision.

(b) DONOR RESTRICTIONS. Donor-restricted endowments pose a number of problems for charities. Although UMIFA endorses total return concepts to determine a restricted fund's income, it and related state laws still require that the money be spent only in accordance with the restrictions imposed by the donor.

To illustrate, consider the following facts: In 1980, Waycliff Hospital received a $1 million gift from Victor Count. The terms of the gift provide that the principal is to be held in perpetuity, but the income is to be used for the benefit of the hospital. The Victor Count Fund is currently valued at $3 million, $2 million of which represents unrealized appreciation in fund assets. Due to changes in Medicare reimbursement rates, the hospital is running what it expects will be a one-time $500,000 operating deficit. The obvious question is whether Waycliff Hospital's board can appropriate $500,000 of the net appreciation in the Victor Count Fund to cover its operating deficit.

---

103. N. Y. Att'y Gen., New York State Attorney General Eliot Spitzer Advises Not-for-Profit Corporations on the Appropriation of Endowment Fund Appreciation (rev. July 2003).

104. Gen. L. Mass., Part I, Title XXII, Chapter 180A, § 2.

105. R.I. Stat., Title 18, Chapter 18-12, § 18-12-6.

106. Penn. Stat. § 5548.

As noted, UMIFA contemplates applying a "total return" spending approach to donor-restricted endowment funds.[107] In other words, donor endowments that provide for the expenditure of "income" can consider capital appreciation when determining the amount available for expenditure. Assuming that a board determines an expenditure to be prudent, it can authorize the use of the net investment appreciation to cover an operating deficit or other organizational needs. The analysis does not end there, however, as our example demonstrates. The Waycliff Hospital board must still comply with restrictions on the use of that income. In this case, the Victor Count Fund clearly contemplates using income for general operations. Using the appreciation to fund an operating deficit is consistent with that restriction.

Section 6 of UMIFA requires the Waycliff board to consider a number of factors before expending the appreciation, including the rate of inflation, the organization's long- and short-term needs, and general economic conditions. Waycliff Hospital apparently did not adjust its pricing soon enough to account for Medicare reductions. This suggests that the deficit is a one-time event. Covering the deficit from the appreciation on the investments held in the Victor Count Fund is arguably a responsible way to address the hospital's short-term needs.

UMIFA does not require income in the form of net asset appreciation to be replenished or repaid once the board appropriates it. Net appreciation is no different than interest or dividend income. It can be tapped so long as express restrictions do not preclude its diversion to the desired use and that use is prudent.

One of the most common restrictions that donors impose on endowments is the use of related income, requiring that it be used only for a specified purpose such as an annual scholarship, research, or acquisitions of particular artwork. When the use of income is so restricted, the organization cannot use the net asset appreciation for other purposes. Consider the Waycliff Hospital example, but assume that Victor Count provided that all of the fund's income is to be used to fund cancer research. Even though UMIFA permits nonprofits to tap net appreciation from their endowments, the Waycliff Hospital board must still comply with restrictions on the use of that income. In this case, the Victor Count Fund permits its income to be used only for cancer research. Therefore, no matter how worthy or logical the proposed alternative use, the Waycliff board cannot appropriate any of the Victor Count Fund's income for anything but cancer research.

If the organization is also funding the specified activity with its own funds, the obvious question is whether it can divert that income to other uses. Unless the gift creating the endowment contains some requirement precluding such a shift, there is no reason that the organization cannot divert unrestricted income to other uses. For example, whether Waycliff Hospital can reduce its own contribution to cancer

107. UMIFA §§ 2 and 6.

research depends on the specific terms of the Victor Count Fund. Some donors recognize that money is fungible, specifically requiring that the income from the funds increase levels of the funded activity. If the Victor Count Fund is subject to such a restriction, Waycliff Hospital cannot adjust how it expends its unrestricted income.[108] Barring such a provision, diversion of other resources should be possible—but recognize that donors may still object.

Sometimes the easy approach to troublesome restrictions is to ask the donor to consent to a change. After all, the donor made the gift because he likes what the organization is doing. Many donors may agree to a change after the issues have been adequately explained. UMIFA permits a donor to consent to a complete or partial release of restrictions even though the gift has been completed.[109] Many disputes, as well as much hand wringing, could be avoided if organizations would simply talk with their benefactors about problems as they arise. If the donor is dead, UMIFA allows the organization to request a court-ordered release of the restrictions. UMIFA requires that the state's attorney general be notified.[110] Most important, UMIFA does not require the organization to seek a waiver from the donor's descendents, eliminating one potentially large stumbling block to change. Returning to the example, if Victor Count is still alive, the Waycliff board should seriously consider asking him about the use of $500,000 of appreciation in the Victor Count Fund.

So far we have considered an endowment funded with marketable securities. Suppose, however, that the investment assets comprise nonmarketable securities such as limited partnership interests or interests in hedge funds. New York law prohibits a board from appropriating unrealized appreciation with respect to nonmarketable investments.[111] The New York legislature was apparently concerned with valuation issues. This prohibition demonstrates why simply adhering to UMIFA is not sufficient. A board must always consider governing state law. Although most states have adopted UMIFA in some form, many of them made changes to it. Assume in the Waycliff Hospital example that the Victor Count Fund is currently valued at $3 million, represented by the following assets: (1) $1 million in marketable securities, with $300,000 attributable to unrealized appreciation ($700,000 historical value), and (2) $2 million in hedge fund investments, with $100,000 attributable to realized appreciation and $1.6 million

108. Mid-Iowa Council of Boy Scouts v. Norwest Banks, 641 N.W.2d 771 (Iowa 2002).

109. UMIFA § 7(a).

110. UMIFA § 7(b).

111. N.Y. Con. L., Chapter 35, § 513(c), which provides as follows:

> Administration of Assets Received for Specific Purposes.
>
> (c) The governing board may appropriate for expenditure for the uses and purposes for which an endowment fund is established so much of the net appreciation, realized (with respect to all assets) and unrealized (with respect only to readily marketable assets), in the fair value of the assets of an endowment fund over the historic dollar value of the fund as is prudent under the standard established by section 717 (Duty of Directors and Officers). This section is not intended to restrict the authority of the governing board to expend funds as permitted under other law, the terms of the applicable gift instrument or the certificate of incorporation of the corporation.

attributable to unrealized appreciation ($300,000 historical value). Under New York law, the Waycliff board could appropriate only $400,000 of the appreciation (the $300,000 of unrealized appreciation with respect to the marketable securities and the $100,000 of realized appreciation with respect to the hedge fund investments). Even then, the decision would be subject to the overarching requirement that it be prudent.

When boards review an organization's financial statements and budgets, they may see references to an endowment. They should keep in mind that an endowment is not a monolith, as financial statement presentation or board discussions sometimes imply. The endowment for a large hospital, museum, or university typically comprises many small funds created by individual donors. The terms of each of individual fund must be respected, and the board must act prudently with respect to each fund. If the board had determined that making annual withdrawals equal to some percentage of the asset value of its overall endowment is appropriate, it must first determine whether such withdrawals are prudent on a fund-by-fund basis. To illustrate, assume that the Waycliff Hospital endowment is composed of the following two funds:

	Historic Value	Current Value
Victor Count	$1 million	$2 million
Lars Franke	$2 million	$2 million

Assume that the only income is from capital appreciation. Each fund provides that it is to be held in perpetuity, with all income being for the benefit of the hospital. In prior years (when each fund had appreciation), the Waycliff board determined that it was prudent to use 5 percent of the fund's value for general operations. This year the board would like to appropriate $200,000 (5 percent of the $4 million combined value of the two funds) from the Count Fund (10 percent of its value) for general operations. Apparently, the board views the 5 percent threshold as the maximum prudent appropriation. If New York law were applicable, the board could not authorize a 10 percent withdrawal from the Victor Count Fund because the state's attorney general requires application of the rules on a fund-by-fund basis.[112] If the board truly believes that the 5 percent number is a maximum, the 10 percent withdrawal from the Victor Count Fund raises prudence issues. As noted, some states effectively cap the amount that can be withdrawn. The Waycliff board's appropriation in this case would violate the law to the extent that any caps apply on a fund-by-fund basis.

Following the precipitous decline in the stock market in early 2001, many nonprofits had "underwater endowments": Their value had dropped below the amounts initially contributed. Boards wanted to know whether they were obligated to restore the funds to their initial values before they could spend any more

112. N. Y. Att'y Gen, *supra* note 103.

income from the endowments. Section 2 of UMIFA addresses appropriation of appreciation, but neither the plain text of the statute nor the accompanying commentary addresses restoration of declines below historic value. This suggests that there is no legal obligation to restore an underwater fund to its historic value before making additional distributions of income (unless the donor has specifically provided otherwise).

Underlying UMIFA is the goal to permit distributions and grants limited to endowment income to be based on total return rather than only interest and dividend income. Applying total return principles when values are rising but ignoring those principles when values are declining is problematic. A donor could certainly argue that he wanted only income expended, and therefore, his intent was that any interest and dividend income first be used to restore the fund to its historic dollar value. Of course, a donor has the ability to address this issue by clearly stating his intentions in the deed of gift.

Janne G. Gallagher, general counsel for the Council on Foundations, has stated:

> Before UMIFA, charities could expend the actual income they received from assets held in endowed funds. Most lawyers who have looked at this question have concluded that UMIFA did not displace this rule. In other words, community foundations may still use a fund's [interest, dividend, and royalty income] to make grants, even if the fund is below historic dollar value.[113]

This conclusion appears to be supported (at least for purposes of New York law) by a statement (Paragraph 2) on the New York attorney general's Web site pertaining to appropriation of appreciation. This issue and the uncertainty surrounding it represent one reason that the National Conference of Commissioners is revising UMIFA and apparently considering whether to drop historic dollar value in favor of a generalized "prudence" approach to spending fund income (including capital appreciation).

To illustrate the issue, assume that the Victor Count Fund is currently valued at \$4.5 million (with a \$5 million historic value). This year, the fund will receive \$300,000 in dividend and interest income. Barring specific state law to the contrary, Waycliff Hospital should be able to spend \$300,000 even though the fund's value has dropped below its historic value.

To summarize, organizations that are subject to UMIFA-styled statutes have a great deal of latitude in appropriating capital appreciation so long as the donor does not expressly restrict the use of such appreciation. Although the adoption of a spending policy based on a set percentage of asset values is a temptation, the board's decision to spend otherwise unrestricted income must always be prudent.

(c) ACCOUNTING FOR ENDOWMENTS. The accounting profession has added to the confusion surrounding UMIFA, admittedly a poorly drafted and cryptic statutory regime. This confusion stems from the accounting profession's desire for

---

113. J. Gallagher, *Been Down So Long, It Looks Like UMIFA to Me*, FOUNDATION NEWS & COMMENTARY (Mar./Apr. 2003).

certainty. Although state law may limit a board's ability to appropriate unrealized capital appreciation due to prudence standards, accountants insist on what can be viewed as misleading reclassifications.

Financial Accounting Standards Board *Statement 124* defines the accounting treatment for endowments.[114] Unless gains and losses from an endowment fund are temporarily or permanently restricted by a donor's explicit stipulation or by a law that extends a donor's restrictions to them, gains and losses on investments of a donor-restricted endowment fund represent changes in unrestricted net assets.[115] If losses reduce the assets of a donor-restricted endowment fund below the level required by the donor or law (under UMIFA, historic dollar value), gains that restore the fair value of assets of the endowment fund to the required level are classified as increases in unrestricted net assets.[116]

The best and only way to understand the accounting issues associated with endowment funds is to examine a number of examples. To do that, let's focus on the Huntsville Museum, which is located in a jurisdiction that has adopted UMIFA. As you consider the examples, do not focus on the rules but on the questions that should be asked when reviewing financial statements. The basic facts are as follows:

> Alberta Parsons donated $1 million in marketable securities to the Huntsville Museum on January 2, 20X5, establishing the Alberta Parsons Fund. The fund is to be held in perpetuity, but the income from it is to be used for the museum's general benefit. On December 31, 20X5, the fund comprises securities valued at $1.2 million and cash representing dividend income of $20,000. The museum's board appropriates no dividend income or unrealized appreciation from the Fund in 20X5.

Under FASB *Statement 124*, securities with readily determinable fair values are included in the financial statements at their fair market value.[117] In other words, FASB *Statement 124* adopts mark-to-market accounting with respect to securities with readily determinable fair market values. It then requires that net asset appreciation be reclassified as an unrestricted asset in the absence of any limitations imposed by the donor.[118] In the Huntsville example, the $200,000 of net appreciation is reclassified as unrestricted income because Alberta Parsons did not explicitly restrict the use of those funds. Huntsville Museum is also free to spend the dividend income from the Alberta Parsons Fund; the result is that the dividend income is also classified as unrestricted income. This is the simple case, but it already produces a misleading result. A director or prospective donor might easily conclude that the museum now has $200,000 in additional unrestricted net assets. However, it is not at all clear that the museum is free to spend

---

114. ACCOUNTING FOR CERTAIN INVESTMENTS HELD BY NOT-FOR-PROFIT ORGANIZATIONS, Statement of Fin. Accounting Standards No. 124, ¶ 11-13 (Fin. Accounting Standards Bd. 1995).
115. *Id.*, at ¶ 11B.
116. *Id.*, at ¶ 13.
117. *Id.*, at ¶ 7.
118. *Id.*, at ¶ 11.

this $200,000. This largely depends on the governing state law. Assuming that UMIFA is the governing law, the museum's board must still act prudently before expending these additional amounts.

Let's change the facts slightly. In 20X5, the Parsons Fund receives no dividend income, but the value of the securities it holds increases to $1.4 million. The Huntsville Museum board authorizes the expenditure of $100,000 of the $400,000 in appreciation (requiring the sale of $100,000 in securities). Originally, the board wanted to expend the full $400,000 of appreciation, but its legal counsel advised in a formal legal opinion (that was blessed by four bishops) that expending more than $100,000 of the appreciation would be imprudent under state law. Doing so would subject the directors to liability for breach of their duties.

Unfortunately, FASB *Statement 124* mandates that the full $300,000 of remaining appreciation ($400,000 gross appreciation reduced by the $100,000 expenditure) be reported as an increase in unrestricted assets despite the legal opinion that such funds are not available for expenditure. The American Institute of Certified Public Accountants' *Audit and Accounting Guide for Not-For-Profit Organizations* (2001) states:

> Legal limitations that require the governing board to act to appropriate net appreciation for expenditure under a statutorily prescribed standard of ordinary business care and prudence do not extend donor restrictions to net appreciation. Accordingly, unless the donor has explicitly restricted the net appreciation on an endowment, net appreciation subject to such limitations should be reported as a change in unrestricted net assets.[119]

The bottom line is that even though expenditure of some portion of the $300,000 of unexpended appreciation would be imprudent, FASB *Statement 124* still requires the financial statements to show that the $300,000 is expendable without limitation. This is an extremely misleading presentation because it overstates the assets available to the Huntsville Museum board for expenditure. Assume that the board wants to maintain the purchasing power of the Parsons Fund and that the inflation rate is at a 5 percent. The board should add at least $50,000 of the appreciation to "historic value" in 20X5, but the accountants will not sanction doing so.

The accounting treatment creates both management and fundraising problems. Potential donors reviewing the financial statements could conclude that Huntsville Museum has more unrestricted assets than it actually does, possibly leading some donors to shift their future contributions to an organization with "greater need." This same phenomenon could influence foundations or government entities considering grant requests.

Donors desiring to limit the use of income from their restricted gifts or to protect the purchasing power of the fund are well advised to explicitly set out their

---

119. AICPA, Audit and Accounting Guide for Not-for Profit Organizations, at § AAG-NPO 8.15, fn. 9 (2001).

intentions in writing when they make the gift. Donors are in a position to prevent the accounting profession from mischaracterizing the income attributable to the donor's restricted gift. Nonprofits should encourage this specificity.

FASB *Statement 124* does not produce any clearer results concerning a decline in fund value. The rules require that the reduction in asset value be reflected as a reduction in unrestricted net assets[120] rather than as a reduction to net restricted assets. The apparent logic is that at some point, the restricted fund must be restored to its historic dollar value, making a reduction to the fund's historic dollar value inappropriate. This characterization arguably understates the organization's assets available for general operations. This could mislead potential donors and grant makers, creating the mistaken impression that the organization has fewer unrestricted resources than it actually has.

Going back to the example, assume that the Parsons Fund experiences a \$200,000 loss in net value in 20X5, resulting in a decline of its balance from \$1 million to \$800,000. Under FASB *Statement 124*, this loss would be charged against Huntsville Museum's unrestricted net assets. This understates those assets, creating the impression that the museum's general operations are worse off than they really are.

Some accountants have even recommended that the financial statements show a liability from the unrestricted assets to the restricted fund. This mischaracterizes the legal status of the unrestricted assets vis-à-vis the restricted fund. Under UMIFA, if the board acts prudently with respect to the restricted fund, there is no legal claim by that fund against the organization's unrestricted assets. A disgruntled donor might even argue that a nonprofit organization has an obligation to restore a fund he created to its historic dollar value, supporting his argument by pointing to the financial statement treatment. If the use of income from the fund is restricted and the donor did prevail in having the organization restore the fund, the organization would be using unrestricted assets to restore the fund. Management should hotly contest booking intracompany loans before conceding the issue. If the accountant prevails in requiring an intrafund payable-receivable, management should at least insist on a footnote clarification.[121]

These accounting issues have implications that go far beyond misleading donors and grantmakers. They could affect nonprofits that have engaged in long-term bond financing that have covenants requiring that certain liquidity and debt/net worth ratios be maintained. The distortions created by the accounting profession's unwillingness to adequately address the treatment of capital appreciation could throw the ratio analysis into havoc, possibly resulting in a technical default under the covenants. If a nonprofit does have financial difficulties, economically inaccurate financial statements could also become a problem in a bankruptcy setting.

---

120. ACCOUNTING FOR CERTAIN INVESTMENTS HELD BY NOT-FOR-PROFIT ORGANIZATIONS, *supra* note 114, at ¶ 12.

121. For additional insight, see S. Riley and J. McCarthy *Understanding Underwater Endowment Funds* (PRICEWATERHOUSECOOPERS 2003). The discussion includes sample entries, but with no intrafund receivables-payables called for in the sample entries. The paper is available on the Web.

FASB *Statement 124* does a good job of tracking the economics with respect to endowments whose donors restrict the use of the income. If the restricted income is not expended during the current period, the organization must report it as an increase in temporarily restricted assets, reflecting the fact that the income is not available for general operations. To put this treatment in the context of the Parsons Fund, assume that Alberta Parsons requires that any income be used to purchase paintings by Gerhard Richter. If the Parsons Fund earns $50,000 in dividend income but does not buy a painting, the $50,000 will be reflected on the balance sheet as an increase in temporarily restricted assets.

Let's now focus on board-designated endowments. It is not at all unusual to find a resolution like the following one in the minutes for a board meeting:

> BE IT RESOLVED, that to ensure that the Museum has sufficient funds to acquire art work, the Board hereby directs that $1 million of general contributions received during 20X5 be designated as an endowment, with the principal amount being held in perpetuity and the income being devoted for the acquisition of artwork. Said assets shall be invested in a diversified portfolio of large-cap equity securities and investment-grade debt securities.

This resolution will *not* result in the reclassification of the unrestricted contributions. In other words, those contributions will continue to be reflected as unrestricted net assets and income. FASB *Statement 124*'s reclassification applies only to donor-restricted endowment funds. In fact, the definition of *endowment fund* in FASB *Statement 12* specifically provides:

> An organization's governing board may earmark a portion of its unrestricted net assets as a board-designated endowment to be invested to provide income for a long but unspecified period. A board-designated endowment, which results from an internal designation, is not a donor restricted fund and is classified as unrestricted net assets.

There certainly is nothing wrong with a board making such a designation, but it is not recognized for financial accounting purposes because under the law, the board can reverse the designation.

Much tougher accounting questions arise for nonprofits located in states that have adopted modified versions of UMIFA. For example, in Rhode Island, are nonprofits required to add a certain portion of unrealized and realized appreciation to permanently restricted assets to reflect inflation? The financial statements of one Rhode Island nonprofit recognize this inflation adjustment. That treatment seems to be mandated by the definition of "historic dollar value" in the Rhode Island statutes.[122] In Massachusetts, must institutions add any appreciation above 7 percent to permanently or temporarily restricted assets because the statute[123] implies that it would not be prudent to spend that money? The

---

122. R. I. Stat., Title 18, Chapter 18-12, § 1, which provides, in part, that "the historic dollar value of an endowment fund shall be prudently adjusted from time to time to reflect the change, if any, in the purchasing power of the historic dollar value of the fund."

123. See Mass. Stat., Part 1, Title XXII, Chapter 180A, § 2, particularly the proviso.

financial statements of one Massachusetts school apply the specifics of Massachusetts law. Similar issues exist outside UMIFA, as reflected in the Pennsylvania statutes.[124]

This discussion should reinforce the importance of reading the footnotes to financial statements because the footnotes should discuss the specifics of how the asset and revenue classifications were determined. Ultimately, the solution for both donors and charities is *not* to rely on UMIFA or other state statutes to govern the charity's rights and duties with respect to donor-restricted endowments. Gift instruments should affirmatively address how asset appreciation is to be utilized, whether the charity must use income from a restricted fund first to restore losses in the value of that fund, and whether the charity is restricted as to how it can invest endowed funds, among other issues.

Such clarity would minimize the likelihood that the charity and its directors will be deemed to have acted imprudently. This clarity would also minimize the possibility that the charity could be forced to restore depreciated endowments with funds from general operations. Most important, this clarity should permit the charity to prepare financial statements that reflect actual legal limitations on the use of assets.

10.6 CHANGED CIRCUMSTANCES—CY PRES AND EQUITABLE DEVIATION

What happens when changed circumstances make it impossible to comply with gift restrictions? For example, suppose a 1925 restricted gift to a medical research foundation provided that all income must be used to find a cure for polio. Once the cure was discovered in 1954, what happened to the continuing income? Did the entire fund revert back to the donor or surviving heirs, or was the medical foundation allowed to use the income to help those who still bore the scars of polio or for other charitable purposes?

Two basic legal doctrines, cy pres and equitable deviation, have evolved to address these issues. *Cy pres* is a trust law doctrine that the courts apply to a restricted gift when the designated charitable purpose becomes unlawful, impractical, or impossible to carry out, or it becomes wasteful to continue to apply the property to the designated charitable purpose. The doctrine can be invoked only if the terms of the gift instrument do not provide instructions on how to proceed when the gift's purpose can no longer be achieved. Under cy pres, the gift will not fail, but the court will direct the application of the property or an appropriate portion of it to a charitable purpose that reasonably approximates the designated purpose.[125] In other words, the doctrine permits the courts

124. Pennsylvania Statute Section 5548 allows an election to be made to pay out a percentage of a fund's assets value with the percentage being no less than 2 percent and no more than 7 percent. The percentage must be consistent with preserving the real value of the fund.

125. RESTATEMENT (THIRD) OF TRUSTS (2003), § 67.

to alter the charitable purpose if the donor's original ones are no longer possible to achieve.[126] At one time, the donor had to have expressed a general charitable intent before the doctrine could be invoked,[127] but that requirement has diminished in importance under the laws of some states.[128]

A relatively recent case involving a hospital that had run into financial difficulty provides an excellent example of the use of the cy pres doctrine. Two very wealthy donors had made a large restricted gift (in excess of $134 million) to the hospital. The hospital asked the court to permit it to pledge a portion of the gift fund to secure new financing and use another portion to acquire, renovate, and improve a medical treatment facility. The court permitted the funds to be so used after it had been convinced that, because of changes in the hospital's economic circumstances, the hospital would otherwise have to close its doors. That would make the donors' original purposes for the gift impossible to achieve; you cannot apply income for the benefit of a hospital if there is no hospital.[129]

The doctrine of *equitable deviation* addresses what happens when the means for carrying out a gift's purposes becomes impossible, impracticable, illegal, obsolete, ineffective, or prejudicial to the public interest to carry out.[130] The focus is on the restricted gift's administrative provisions rather than its purposes.

Probably the best example of the application of the doctrine of *equitable deviation* is the recent dispute over whether the famous Barnes Foundation collection of Impressionistic paintings could be relocated from the foundation's suburban Mainline location to a new museum to be constructed on Philadelphia's famed Benjamin Franklin Parkway, home to the city's many museums. Dr. Barnes had placed numerous restrictions on the public's access to the collection in an effort to preserve the collection for the benefit of art students and their education. Those restrictions were bankrupting the foundation, placing the priceless collection at risk.

In January 2004 the Orphans' Court of Montgomery County, Pennsylvania, decided that Dr. Barnes's will was not "sacrosanct" and indicated that it would consider alternatives to the status quo. The expectation was that the court would approve the alternative that deviated the least from the current administration of the assets.[131] A number of experts provided testimony to the court, with some favoring the move to downtown Philadelphia and others favoring sales of the assets ("redundant Renoirs," was one expert's term of art) to shore up the endowment for the current facilities. In December 2004, the court decided that the

---

126. *Id.* This definition is based on the definition of cy pres in § 67.

127. Evans v. Abney, 396 U.S. 435 (1970).

128. *But see* N.Y. Con. L., Chapter 17, Art. 8, § 8-1.1(c), where the "general charitable intent" requirement has been preserved.

129. In the Matter of Estate of Donald F. Othmer, 710 N.Y.S.2d 848 (2000).

130. Restatement (Third) Trusts, *supra* note 125, § 66.

131. *In re* Barnes Foundation, 24 Fiduc. Rep. 94 (Ct. Com. Pl. Mont. County, Pa., Orphans' Ct. 2004).

move to downtown Philadelphia resulted in the least deviation.[132] The court's ruling was challenged in 2005, but the Pennsylvania Supreme Court upheld it.[133]

Both the doctrines of cy pres and of equitable deviation are useful when donors do not adequately provide for changed circumstances that inevitably arise with the passage of time. However, the court-administered process is often expensive. For example, the fact finding in the Barnes case took over 11 months, costing more than $1 million. In other words, charities should encourage their donors to focus carefully on the restrictions that they impose on gifts. Here are a few points to keep in mind when negotiating a restricted gift:

- Anticipate future developments.
- Specify what happens in the event that the restrictions no longer can be satisfied because of changed circumstances. The terms of the gift might provide for a transfer to the charity's unrestricted fund or to another charity, or reversion to the donor's survivors (which has potential tax implications).
- Consider setting a time when the restrictions lapse, recognizing that those living 100 years from now can best make decisions regarding resource allocation.
- Consider an arbitration clause or private resolution procedure to avoid an expensive lawsuit in the event that all possibilities are not anticipated.

There is also a lesson for prospective donors in the *Barnes Foundation* case: Immortality is great, but do not try to achieve it with your gift. Society will move forward after your death. In making a restricted gift, provide future generations the opportunity to enjoy and benefit from your generosity. That means providing the flexibility to deal with social and technological changes that you cannot anticipate while you are alive. Whatever you do, do not burden the world with endless litigation over inflexible restrictions.

10.7 GIFT-ACCEPTANCE POLICIES

One of the best ways for an organization to coordinate its management of restricted gifts (and other gifts, for that matter) is to develop a gift-acceptance policy. This policy outlines what types of property the organization will accept, due diligence procedures to be followed before accepting various types of gifts, what commitments the organization will make to donors, and whose approval must be obtained before the organization can accept a particular type or size of gift. A gift-acceptance policy should address different types of property, the circumstances requiring board approval, and the actions that must be taken before a gift is accepted.

---

132. *In re* Barnes Foundation, 69 Pa. D. & C.4th 129 (Ct. Com. Pl. Mont. County, Pa., Orphans' Ct. 2004).
133. *In re* Barnes Foundation, 871 A.2d 792 (2005).

(a) TYPES OF ASSETS. At a minimum, a gift acceptance policy for any sizable organization should address the asset classes discussed in the following sections.

(i) Cash and Equivalents. As a general rule, cash is the most prevalent and straightforward of gifts. Nevertheless, these gifts can pose problems. First and foremost, the organization should implement policies to ensure that its employees or other agents not misappropriate the cash. This means using receipts and having independent audits. The policy should also establish procedures for handling online, credit card, wire-transfers, and payroll deduction plans. The policy should also set procedures to be followed to ascertain whether the donor is making an unrestricted or restricted gift.

(ii) Publicly Traded Securities. Publicly traded or marketable securities represent another popular gift form. A gift-acceptance policy should outline the procedures to be followed when the donor owns the shares in his own name or in a street name or with a brokerage firm or holds them in a mutual fund. If the securities are being transferred by the estate of a deceased donor, the policy should require the estate's executor or administrator to provide a certificate indicating that all debts, taxes, and claims of or against the estate have been paid or provided for. The policy should indicate whether the organization will hold the securities or immediately dispose of them.

(iii) Real Estate. The gift-acceptance policy concerning real estate should require an appropriate title search to make sure that the donor has clear and unencumbered title. The policy should then require appropriate environmental testing. Before the board even considers the gift, a Phase I environmental audit (nonintrusive review of the property) should be conducted. If the board decides tentatively to accept the gift, a Phase II environmental audit (physical sampling) should be completed. Except in very unusual circumstances, the policy should require an environmental indemnification from the donor. The terms of that indemnification should be based on a standard form agreement that is drafted to favor the organization.

The organization should also have a predefined standard in place for determining whether to sell or hold donated real estate. For example, some universities sell real property as a matter of course unless the particular property fits into the campus plan. If the property is to be taken subject to indebtedness, the policy should require a thorough analysis of the unrelated business taxable income implications.

(iv) Other Assets. Donors contribute many types of assets to charitable organizations. Examples include stock in closely held businesses, restricted stock, patents, stock options, general or limited partnership interests, interests in limited liability companies, copyrights, gas and mineral interests, installment notes, tangible personal property such as medical or educational equipment, and collectibles such as manuscripts, artwork, stamps and coins, and memorabilia. A gift-acceptance policy should require the organization's legal counsel, tax counsel, and gift-acceptance committee to review gifts of these assets. The policy should address how the organization will respond to and handle gifts of any of these types of property. At a minimum, the policy should do the following:

- Set minimum dollar values on property before assets will be accepted.
- Require the organization to ascertain the costs of maintaining the asset should the gift be accepted, to thoroughly analyze whether the asset will produce unrelated business income, and to identify and assess any restrictions on the transfer or use of the asset (e.g., a patent or restricted stock).

If the organization has a planned giving program, the policy should state what types of assets are not appropriate for transfer to a pooled income fund, charitable remainder trust, or other planned giving device.

(b) SPECIFIC FORMS. At a minimum, a gift-acceptance policy for any sizable organization should address the following types of transactions.

(i) Bargain Sales. The gift-acceptance policy should require an appraisal by an independent appraiser satisfactory to the organization if an asset is being transferred to it as part of a bargain sale. The policy should also require that the authenticity of collectibles and similar assets be verified, either in conjunction with or as part of the appraisal. Finally, the policy should specify whether the organization will accept an appraisal paid for by the donor.

(ii) Pledges. The gift-acceptance policy should specify how to handle pledges to make future gifts. At a minimum, the policy should contain a standard form pledge agreement that meets the requirements discussed earlier. The policy should state how to handle overdue obligations under pledges. If distinctions will be drawn between small and large pledges, the policy should reflect those distinctions.

(iii) Restricted Gifts to Endowment. As already noted, many donors prefer to make restricted gifts. There is nothing wrong with this. However, the gift-acceptance policy should address gifts that are to be set aside for specific purposes, as opposed to for general endowment. Among other issues, the policy should specify (1) whether and when the organization has a right to invade the principal, (2) whether the organization can spend the gift's annual income and, if so, how much (e.g., a fixed dollar amount or a percentage of fund value), (3) whether distributions can be made if the fund's value drops below its initial value (4) how to define *income*, (5) what happens to the fund if the institution's charitable mission changes or the purposes for which the fund was established are no longer meaningful or achievable, (6) how to invest the fund's assets, (7) whether the institution can use investment mangers to mange fund assets, and (8) whether the organization is entitled to charge an administrative fee to cover the expenses of maintaining the fund. Although UMIFA addresses some of these issues, it does not do so clearly or satisfactorily. By ensuring that the organization and donors explicitly address these issues, the gift-acceptance policy can eliminate much of the uncertainty associated with restricted gifts to endowment.

(iv) Scholarship Funds and Special Programs. Some donors want to establish a scholarship or other special-purpose funds or programs. The gift-acceptance policy should require a thorough review at the appropriate organizational level to ensure that such fund or program is feasible and consistent with the organization's mission. For example, if the gift is to endow a subscription service for a law library, the librarian may be the only one who needs to review the gift from a feasibility or need standpoint. In contrast, if the gift is to a museum to build a new wing that would double its exhibition space, the full board should be involved.

As is the case with all restricted gifts, the policy should specify exactly what happens when carrying out the donor's intentions no longer is possible for whatever reason. This situation has been addressed in earlier sections.

(c) DONOR BENEFITS. At a minimum, a gift-acceptance policy for any sizable organization should address the following benefits to donors.

(i) Tax Consequences. Obviously, the organization does not provide tax benefits directly to its donors. However, fundraisers inevitability discuss those benefits with potential donors. If most attorneys had their druthers, such conversations would not take place. However, any policy that mandated silence would be honored in the breach. Given that fact, the gift-acceptance policy should outline the tax consequences of various types of gifts and gift-related transactions with the expectation that development officers and other fundraisers will stick to the script. The policy should require the discussion always to end with the admonition that the donor should not rely on the discussion but should seek tax advice from legal counsel or an accountant. The policy should cover the 50 percent, 30 percent, and 20 percent limitations, the fair market value reduction rules, the consequences of prearranged sales by charities, the requirements under the tax law for appraisals, and other relevant issues (see Chapter 7). The policy should clearly prohibit the organization and its representatives from offering any assessments of specific values for purposes of determining a deductible amount. Finally, the policy should set out the procedures and content for satisfying the notice, substantiation, and appraisal requirements imposed by the Internal Revenue Code on charities.

(ii) Naming Opportunities. As discussed earlier in detail, those who make significant gifts often want to name a scholarship fund, building, or other public manifestation of their gift after them or someone else. The gift-acceptance policy should contain guidelines for how the organization will handle naming requests and opportunities. The policy should do the following:

- Specify the circumstances or standards to be met before a donor is granted a naming opportunity.
- Specify what happens when the named asset is replaced, renovated, or becomes obsolete.
- Require an agreement memorializing the transaction.
- Require a "bad boy" provision in the naming agreement.
- Specify any control over the named asset, fund, or program retained by the donor, with the understanding that, as a general matter, control resides with the organization, not the donor (except for those items specifically reserved).
- Outline any publicity or ceremonies that will accompany the naming.

(iii) Planned Giving Programs. Chapter 7 addressed the mechanics for planned giving programs. The gift-acceptance policy should contain a detailed set of rules and guidelines that apply to such gifts and how to administer the programs. The policy should require that planned giving gifts be coordinated with the organization's tax counsel and should specify any assets that will not be accepted for funding various planned giving vehicles. The policy should also require the donor to be represented by separate legal counsel in structuring a planned giving investment. Finally, the policy should specify the circumstances under which the organization will serve as a trustee and those that will require an independent trustee.

(iv) Donor Expenses. On occasion, donors ask the organization to pay all or some of the expenses associated with their gifts. These expenses can include naming plaques, dedication ceremonies, appraisals, ongoing costs associated with gifts, transportation, and insurance premiums. The gift-acceptance policy should establish standards and policies for these expenses.

(v) Quid Pro Quo. The gift-acceptance policy should address quid pro quo contributions from a tax perspective. Most important, the policy should establish procedures for providing required IRS notifications to donors. The policy should also include procedures for establishing the value of the benefits conferred on the donor (see Chapter 7).

(d) GIFT-ACCEPTANCE COMMITTEE. Institutions that have the good fortune to receive a wide variety of gifts on a regular basis should consider a gift-acceptance committee. It does not necessarily have to be a committee composed of directors, although it should have some director representation. The committee, which should meet on a periodic basis, should include the organization's chief development officer, treasurer, general counsel, and tax counsel, or their designees.

10.8 BINGO AND RAFFLES

Many nonprofits raise funds through raffles, bingo, and other forms of gambling. Whether this is permissible depends on applicable state law. Consequently, before starting to sell tickets for a raffle, or even advertising one, a charity should check with the state's secretary of state, attorney general, or other agency charged with regulating such events. The board should assume that any form of gambling is illegal and require the officers to clearly demonstrate that the proposed activity is legal and that all applicable licenses have been obtained.

In many states, only certain nonprofits are entitled to sponsor bingo games and raffles. Often, these will be Section 501(c)(3) organizations. Even though the local garden club or school auxiliary may be a worthy organization, if it does not meet the statutory requirements, it *cannot* engage in this sort of activity. Before proceeding, the organization should ask the following questions:

- Are raffles or bingo games permitted in the state in which the organization is located?
- Is the organization within the class of organizations permitted to hold such events? The focus should not be limited to whether the organization is a Section 501(c)(3) or other type of permitted organization. At least one state requires the organization to have been in existence for a minimum period of time.
- Is the organization required to register with the state or local authorities or pay a licensing or registration fee?
- When can the organization begin advertising the event and selling tickets to it? It may be illegal to advertise or sell tickets unless the organization has registered or obtained a license.
- Are there limitations on who can sell tickets or conduct the event? Some states permit only unpaid volunteers to sell tickets.
- Must tickets be printed in a specific form and manner? Is consecutive numbering required? What information must be displayed on the ticket?
- Is registration or licensing required on a per event basis or for all events during a particular time period?
- After the event, is the organization required to file a report with the regulating authority?
- Is the income taxable? See the discussion of the unrelated business income tax in Chapter 6.

Our discussion has focused on bingo and raffles, the traditional games of choice for charitable fundraising. In recent years, there has been widespread interest in poker, which has led some charities to consider sponsoring poker tournaments as fundraisers. Poker is particularly perilous from a legal standpoint. As a consequence, there often are no clearly defined rules concerning poker tournaments. Charities that are interested in exploring such events should begin by contacting the appropriate regulator. In Massachusetts, the attorney general's office has issued an advisory regarding charity-sponsored poker tournaments.[134] Other states are probably wrestling with this issue.

10.9 FEDERAL GRANTS

Many examples in this chapter involved cultural and educational institutions. Typically, these organizations are the recipients of restricted gifts that constitute their endowments. Social service agencies also can accumulate endowments, but many simply do not have significant endowments, so they must rely on service revenue and grant money to support their programs and operations.

A *grant* is nothing more than a contract. It is similar to a restricted gift. In a sense, the law of grants is quite simple: The organization must do what it has agreed to do. That is true whether the grant comes from a private foundation or the federal government. The terms of a grant can be quite complex. In the case of federal, state, and local government grants, the terms are often not explicitly set within the grant but in an extensive set of regulations and circulars. This is particularly true of grants from the federal government, which we now consider in some detail. Consider this one caveat: Federal grant and procurement law is a world unto itself, with extremely complex rules that are often hidden in agency regulations, congressional appropriation and authorization legislation, and Office of Management and Budget (OMB) circulars. The following brief discussion highlights major issues and concerns. The intent is to sensitize you to the issues, not make you an expert in grant compliance, cost allocation, or procurement requirements.

(a) TYPES OF FEDERAL GRANTS. Currently, more than 26 federal grant-making agencies offer 900 different grant programs.[135] The federal government has developed two Web sites that explain available grants and how to apply for them. The first is the Catalog of Federal Domestic Assistance and the second is Grants.gov. Both sites permit the user to search the inventory of available grants. Of the two sites, Grants.gov provides more direct access to federal grant programs; it groups available programs into 21 categories, including grants for agriculture, education, food and nutrition, community development, arts, health, social services, and regional development.

134. Mass. Att'y Gen., Advisory on Poker Tournaments (June 30, 2005).
135. http://www.grants.gov (as viewed on Aug. 8, 2005).

Federal grants take a variety of forms. Formula grants allocate money to state and political subdivisions on a formula basis for activities of a continuing basis that are not confined to specific projects. Grants for specific projects can advance money or provide for reimbursement of specified costs. Obviously, advances are preferable to reimbursements. Some grants provide that state grant-making rules apply; others rely on federal rules. Grants also can take hybrid forms. For example, Community Service Block Grant money is distributed to the states on a formula basis, but the states are required to distribute at least 90 percent of the money to federally defined eligible entities and the program is subject to federal administrative guidelines.

(b) OMB CIRCULARS. As a general rule, the administration of federal grants is explained in a series of federal Office of Management and Budget circulars. For nonprofits, the three most relevant circulars are Circular A-110, which pertains to general administration; Circular A-122, which addresses permissible costs and cost allocations; and Circular A-133, which pertains to auditing requirements. Other circulars apply to specific types of institutions. For example, nonprofit educational institutions are governed by Circular A-87. Moreover, the terms of a specific grant may provide that all or some of the terms in a circular of general application are inapplicable to the grant. This should hardly be surprising because in authorizing legislation, Congress can tailor the grant requirements through overrides of and exceptions to administrative rules.

As a general rule, the board of a nonprofit need not be concerned with the specific details of grant administration. On the other hand, the organization's executive director and CFO should review relevant circulars to familiarize themselves with the issues and requirements even if other people on staff have responsibility for grant compliance. As is always the case, the board should require periodic reports on procedures for and compliance with grants that the nonprofit has been awarded. When a grant will have a material impact on general operations, either through significant limitations or additional requirements, the board should be apprised of the relevant details so that it can perform its general oversight function.

(i) OMB Circular No. A-110, "General Administration." Unless the terms of a grant provide otherwise, OMB Circular A-110 (revised September 30, 1999) is applicable to all federal agencies making grants and their grant recipients.[136] It establishes uniform administrative requirements for hospitals, institutions of higher education, and other nonprofits awarded federal grant money. Circular A-110 not surprisingly requires grant recipients to have adequate financial management

136. OFFICE OF MANAGEMENT AND BUDGET, CIRCULAR A-110, UNIFORM ADMINISTRATIVE REQUIREMENTS FOR GRANTS AND AGREEMENTS WITH INSTITUTIONS OF HIGHER EDUCATION, HOSPITALS, AND OTHER NON-PROFIT ORGANIZATIONS, 64 Fed. Reg. 54,926, at ¶ 3 (Sept. 30, 1999)

systems.[137] Specifically, the grantee must be able to track the source and application of federal funds. It must also have effective control over and accountability for all its funds, property, and other assets and have adequate safeguards to ensure that grant assets are used only for authorized purposes. The grantee must also monitor actual expenditures in terms of program budgets. Circular A-110 established procedures for advancing grant funds in anticipation of expenditures,[138] but if the grantee's accounting system does not satisfy the basic requirements imposed by Circular A-110, the federal agency can make the grant on a monthly reimbursement basis.[139] This could be a problem for many cash-strapped nonprofits, which is why Circular A-110 provides for working capital advances in an attempt to avoid the need for third-party financing.[140] Circular A-110 provides that agencies awarding grants should not require separate bank accounts for awarded funds provided that the nonprofit is able to adequately account for and track the specific funds.[141]

Some federal grants are made on a *matching* (also referred to as *cost-sharing*) *basis*. For example, the awarding agency covers only 60 percent of eligible costs, requiring the nonprofit to obtain the remaining 40 percent elsewhere. Precise rules govern what funds count toward the nonprofit's portion.[142] The match may be satisfied with cash and third-party in-kind contributions. This puts a premium on tracking and adequately valuing volunteer time and donated property. When funds are included as part of the match for one federal program, they may not be counted again for another federal grant's match.[143] Likewise, funds received under another federal grant may not be counted toward a matching requirement in a different federal grant (unless specifically permitted).[144] For volunteer service to count toward a matching requirement, it must be an integral and necessary part of an approved project or program.[145]

Typically, nonprofits are required to submit a budget during the application process to the federal agency making the grant. Before they can deviate from this budget, nonprofits must obtain the agency's prior approval if the deviation results, for example, in changes in project scope, key personnel, or the relationship between direct and indirect costs or a subaward, or transfers of any work to another agency.[146]

As Chapter 5 noted, nonprofits that receive federal awards of $500,000 or more are subject to the Single Audit Act, requiring them to undergo an independent

---

137. *Id.*, at ¶ 21.
138. *Id.*, 136, at ¶ 22(b).
139. *Id.*, at ¶ 21.22(e).
140. *Id.*, at ¶ 21.22(f).
141. *Id.*, at ¶ 21.22(i)(1).
142. *Id.*, at ¶ 21.23.
143. *Id.*, at ¶ 21.23(a)(2).
144. *Id.*, at ¶ 21.23(a)(5).
145. *Id.*, at ¶ 21.23(d).
146. *Id.*, at ¶ 21.25.

audit that complies with Yellow Book standards, including auditor independence requirements.[147]

Nonprofits receiving federal grants must comply with Circular A-110's procurement standards applicable to the acquisition of property, equipment, real property, and other services.[148] These standards require a written code of conduct applicable to those involved in the procurement process, which includes limitations on "real or apparent" conflicts of interest. This is another reason that a conflict-of-interest policy is a warranted control.[149] The procurement process contemplates competitive bidding by the recipient of a grant, but price is not the sole determining factor in awarding a contract.[150] Whenever possible, the nonprofit is required to utilize small businesses, minority-owned firms, and women's business enterprises.[151]

As should be expected, Circular A-110 has various reporting requirements for nonprofits receiving federal grants.[152] These requirements include providing performance and financial reports. The financial reports are generally made on standardized OMB forms.[153] Circular A-110 contains its own set of record retention requirements.[154] As a general rule, financial records, supporting documents, statistical records, and all other documents pertinent to a grant, including cash advances, must be retained for a period of three years from the date of the submission of the final expenditure report. Different rules apply to grants that are renewed quarterly or annually.[155] Moreover, some circumstances (e.g., litigation) require extension of the retention period.

Circular A-110 also contains "close-out" procedures, which specify what happens when the program or activity supported by the federal grant is completed.[156] This section provides for prompt payment of costs covered by the grant, refunds of unused funds by the nonprofit, and an accounting for property acquired with federal funds.

Federal grants are subject to "cross-cutting" requirements, so named because they cut across all federal grants. In a sense, Circular A-110 is a cross-cutting requirement, but the reference to such requirements is to assorted legislation with separate objectives.[157] The following are examples of cross-cutting requirements:

- *Disbarment and Suspension—Executive Orders 12549 and 12689.* Individuals and entities that violate various requirements under federal programs

---

147. *Id.*, at ¶ 26.
148. *Id.*, at ¶ 40, et. seq.
149. *Id.*, at ¶ 42.
150. *Id.*, at ¶ 43.
151. *Id.*, at ¶ 44(b).
152. *Id.*, at ¶ 50 et. seq.
153. *Id.*, at ¶ 52.
154. *Id.*, at ¶ 53.
155. *Id.*, at ¶ 53(b).
156. *Id.*, at ¶ 71.
157. *Id.*, at Appendix A.

can be disbarred or suspended from further participation. This can apply to recipients of benefits as well as those providing goods and services paid for with federal funds.[158] An individual or entity disbarred or suspended from participation by a federal agency cannot participate in any federal programs The General Services Administration maintains a list of individuals and entities that are either barred or suspended from receiving payments for goods or services with federal funds. Nonprofits contracting for goods and services must comply with the requirements of Executive Orders 12549 and 12689 in their procurement process, which means not using federal funds to pay for goods or services provided by disbarred or suspended individuals or entities. A list of disbarred and suspended individuals and entities is maintained at http://www.epls.gov.

- *Davis-Bacon Act.* Nonprofit grant recipients must comply with the terms of the Davis-Bacon Act,[159] which requires that a contract over $2,000 for the construction, alteration, or repair of public buildings or public works contain a clause setting forth the minimum wages to be paid to various classes of laborers and mechanics employed under the contract, but only if the United States or the District of Columbia is a party. Under the act's provisions, contractors or their subcontractors are to pay workers employed directly on the work site no less than the locally prevailing wages and fringe benefits paid on similar projects. In addition to the Davis-Bacon Act itself, Congress has added prevailing wage provisions to approximately 60 statutes that affect construction projects through grants, loans, loan guarantees, and insurance. These "related acts" involve construction in areas such as transportation, housing, air and water pollution reduction, and health. If a construction project is funded or assisted under more than one federal statute, the Davis-Bacon prevailing wage provisions apply to the project if any of the applicable statutes require payment of Davis-Bacon wage rates.[160]
- *Drug-Free Workplace of 1988.* Under this act,[161] a nonprofit receiving a federal grant must make a good faith effort, on a continuing basis, to maintain a drug-free workplace. Implementing regulations describe in detail the specific measures that the organization must take in this regard.[162] Briefly, those measures require that the organization (1) publish

---

158. *Id.*, at Appendix A, Item 8.

159. 40 U.S.C. 276a.

160. U.S. DEPART. LAB. EMPL. STANDARDS ADMIN., WAGE AND HOUR DIVISION, GENERAL WAGE DETERMINATIONS ISSUED UNDER THE DAVIS-BACON AND RELATED ACTS: DAVIS-BACON WAGE DETERMINATION REFERENCE MATERIAL, *available at* http://www.gpo.gov/davisbacon/referencemat.html (viewed June 18, 2005). This Web site also provides information about prevailing wage rates throughout the country.

161. 41 U.S.C. 701.

162. 45 C.F.R. 630.

a drug-free workplace statement and establish a drug-free awareness program for its employees and (2) take actions concerning employees convicted of violating drug statutes in the workplace.

- *Civil Rights Act of 1964, Title VI.* Under the Civil Rights Act of 1964,[163] a nonprofit cannot discriminate on the basis of race, national origin, or color with respect to the administration of any program funded with federal funds. Clearly, employment laws protect employees and job applicants. This provision extends the requirement to program beneficiaries as well as potential volunteers who want to provide services in connection with the program.[164]
- *Byrd Anti-Lobbying Amendment.* This amendment[165] prohibits contractors who receive an award of $100,000 or more from using federal appropriated funds to pay any person or organization for influencing or attempting to influence an officer or employee of any agency, a member of Congress, officer or employee of Congress, or an employee of a member of Congress in connection with obtaining any federal contract, grant, or any other award covered by amendment. Nonprofits are required to obtain a certification from the contractor. Disclosures are also required regarding the use of nonfederal funds to lobby for a federal award.

Appendix A to Circular A-110 contains additional cross-cutting requirements that any nonprofit that receives federal grant money should review.

(ii) OMB Circular No. A-122, "Cost Principles for Non-Nonprofit Organizations." OMB Circular A-122 (May 10, 2004) establishes the principles for determining costs of grants with the federal government. The principles are generally applicable to nonprofit organizations, with the exception of colleges and universities, which are subject to OMB Circular A-21, "Cost Principles for Educational Institutions."

Circular A-122 focuses on determining which costs can (and cannot) be reimbursed from federal grants. It draws an important distinction between direct and indirect costs.[166] *Direct* costs can be identified specifically with a particular grant.[167] *Indirect* costs are incurred for common or joint objectives and cannot be readily identified with a particular grant. Indirect costs typically include depreciation or use allowances, the cost of operating and maintaining facilities, and general expenses for executive officers, personnel administration, and accounting

163. 42 U.S.C. 2000d-2000d-4.
164. 28 C.F.R. 42.104(b)(1)(vi) and (vii).
165. 31 U.S.C. 1352.
166. Office of Management and Budget, Circular A-122, Cost Principles for Non-profit Organizations, 69 Fed. Reg. 25,970, at Attachment A, Section A (May 10, 2004).
167. *Id.*, at Attachment A, Section B.

personnel.[168] Circular A-122 recognizes that there are variations in how organizations distinguish between direct and indirect costs. Both direct and indirect costs can be reimbursed; an allocation is required to determine the amount of indirect costs that are subject to reimbursement. In any event, to be allowable against a federal grant, costs must be reasonable, not be excludible, be determined in accordance with generally accepted accounting principles, and be adequately documented.[169]

Attachment B to Circular A-122 lists 52 categories of specific costs and identifies whether they are allowable against a federal grant. Included in the list are costs for advertising, alcoholic beverages, bad debts, lobbying, professional service costs, taxes, training costs, and travel costs. Just to provide a sense of how Attachment B approaches various costs, consider these two excerpts:

> 17. Fund raising and investment management costs.
>
> Costs of organized fund raising, including financial campaigns, endowment drives, solicitation of gifts and bequests, and similar expenses incurred solely to raise capital or obtain contributions are unallowable.
>
> Costs of investment counsel and staff and similar expenses incurred solely to enhance income from investments are unallowable.
>
> Fund raising and investment activities shall be allocated an appropriate share of indirect costs under the conditions described....
>
> 28. Materials and supplies costs.
>
> Costs incurred for materials, supplies, and fabricated parts necessary to carry out a federal award are allowable.
>
> Purchased materials and supplies shall be charged at their actual prices, net of applicable credits. Withdrawals from general stores or stockrooms should be charged at their actual net cost under any recognized method of pricing inventory withdrawals, consistently applied. Incoming transportation charges are a proper part of materials and supplies costs.
>
> Only materials and supplies actually used for the performance of a federal award may be charged as direct costs.
>
> Where federally donated or furnished materials are used in performing the federal award, such materials will be used without charge.

Professional and technical personnel, consultants, and other skilled and unskilled labor may furnish donated or volunteer services to an organization,[170] but the value of these services is not reimbursable either as a direct or indirect cost. However, the value of donated services may be used to meet cost-sharing or matching requirements.[171] When material in amount, the value of donated services utilized in performing a direct cost activity will be considered in determining

168. *Id.*, at Attachment A, Section C.

169. *Id.*, at ¶ A(2).

170. *Id.*, at Attachment B, Item 12.

171. *Id.*, at Attachment B, Item 12(5).

the nonprofit organization's indirect costs or rate(s). Accordingly, these services will be allocated a proportionate share of applicable indirect costs when the following conditions are satisfied: (1) the aggregate value of the services is material, (2) the services are supported by a significant amount of the indirect costs incurred by the nonprofit organization, and (3) the grant activity is not pursued primarily for the benefit of the federal government.[172] When donated services directly benefit a project supported by an award, the indirect costs allocated to the volunteer services will be considered a part of the total costs of the project.[173]

To illustrate, a nonprofit that receives $200,000 in volunteer services cannot recover the cost of those services against the grant, but if $20,000 of indirect costs are allocable to those services, the organization can recover that $20,000 from the grant. This makes perfect sense. To understand why, assume that a private school runs an adult literacy program funded by a federal grant. The school's administration manages the program, which requires 1,000 square feet of the school's building. Community volunteers provide the actual literacy training. Their services are valued at $200,000. The school cannot seek reimbursement of the $200,000 in services because it is not out of pocket. However, the $20,000 of indirect costs (janitorial services and school administrator time) is an actual cost.

Circular A-122 provides a number of methods for allocating indirect costs to grant activities. Under the simplified allocation method, if an organization's major functions benefit from its indirect costs to the same degree, the allocation of indirect costs can be made by separating the organization's costs into direct and indirect costs and then dividing the total allowable indirect costs by an equitable distribution base.[174] So, for example, if Green Social Services Agencies had two federal grants, one for counseling homeless people and another for counseling at-risk teenagers, its cost allocation schedule might be as follows:[175]

172. *Id.*, at Attachment B, Item 12(2).

173. *Id.*, at Attachment B, Item 12(4).

174. *Id.*, at Attachment A, ¶ D(2).

175. The author is not an expert in these calculations. This example represents a reasonable effort to illustrate the rules, but actual allocations should be prepared by an experienced professional. Unlike tax regulations, these administrative rules do not contain illustrative calculations, a true deficiency.

	Overhead	Homeless Grant	At-Risk Grant	Fundraising	Direct Labor Costs	Recoverable Indirect Cost as a Percent of Direct Labor Costs
Direct cost: Salary of homeless counselor		$40,000			$ 40,000	
Direct cost: Salary of at-risk counselor			$60,000		$ 60,000	$ 15,000 $105,000
Direct cost: Fundraising expenses				$5,000	$ 5,000	
Agency overhead not directly allocable to either program	$15,000 in salaries for general activities					
Total					$105,000	14.285%
Allocation of allowable indirect costs		$5,714 ($40,000 × 14.285%)	$8,571 ($60,000 × 14.285%)	$714 ($5,000 × 14.285%)		rate to be applied to direct labor costs

The allowable indirect costs are $15,000. The $5,000 of fundraising expenses is not recoverable,[176] yet this activity must bear its appropriate burden of the overhead or indirect costs.[177] Consequently, of the $15,000 in indirect costs, only $14,285 is recoverable from the federal grants. Of the $15,000 of eligible indirect expenses, $714 must be allocated to the fundraising function. Notice that the allocation is based on personnel costs, which is appropriate. However, the agency rented its facility and had a janitor and maintenance crew, so allocating the related costs on the basis of square footage occupied by each function could be appropriate. In fact, if Green Social Services received more than $10 million in federal awards for direct costs per annum, it would have to break its indirect costs into two categories—administration and facilities—and develop appropriate allocation rates for each of the two categories of indirect costs.[178]

176. *Id.*, at Attachment B, Item 17.

177. *Id.*, at Attachment A, ¶ B(3).

178. *Id.*, at Attachment A, ¶ D(2)(e). This assumes that the simplified allocation method is applicable. There is also a "Multiple Base Allocation Method" that applies when an organization's indirect costs benefit different functions in varying degrees.

In the preceding example, if the homeless counseling function utilized volunteer labor valued at $50,000, the value of that labor could not be reimbursed under the general reimbursement rules. However, instead of including $40,000 of direct labor costs in the allocation base, the agency would include $90,000 of costs for allocating indirect costs.[179] The effect would be to increase the overall indirect costs that are recoverable from federal grants and to significantly increase the proportion of these costs that are recoverable from the grant for homeless counseling.

If the organization has indirect costs that benefit its major functions in varying degrees, it must engage in a more complex series of allocations. It would first assign its indirect costs into the following indirect cost pools: (1) depreciation and use allowances, (2) interest, (3) operations and maintenance expenses, and (4) general administration and general expenses.[180] It would then determine an appropriate, equitable base on which to allocate the costs in a particular pool to the organization's different functions.

Circular A-122 contains many additional details and approaches to allocating costs. These computations can become very complex. Most important, allocation rates are subject to negotiation and approval by the federal agencies making the grants.[181] Accordingly, administrative practices must be treated as part Circular A-122. Fortunately, Circular A-122 anticipates nonprofits receiving grants from multiple agencies. To minimize the administrative burden on all involved, it designates the agency making the largest grant as the *cognizant agency,* which takes the lead in the negotiation so that only one set of allocation rates must be established.[182]

As previously noted, the board of directors need not and should not be involved in the details of this process. However, the board must ensure that someone who understands and has experience in cost recovery is involved in the process when the organization prepares the grant application, the grant contract is negotiated, and the grant is administered.

(iii) OMB Circular No. A-133, "Audits of States, Local Governments, and Non-Nonprofit Organizations." Any organization accepting federal grant money must be prepared to deal with the Single Audit Act, as well as OMB Circular A-133 (June 27, 2003), both of which were discussed in Chapter 5.

(c) FEDERAL FALSE CLAIMS ACT. The federal government has an obvious interest in ensuring that those receiving grants receive only what they are entitled to under the terms of the grants. Congress enacted the Federal False Claims Act to punish those who make false claims against the federal government. Specifically,

---

179. *Id.*, at Attachment B, Item 12(2).
180. *Id.*, at Attachment A, § D(3).
181. *Id.*, at Attachment A, § E.
182. *Id.*

Section 3729 of Title 31 of the United States Code provides as follows:

> Any person who
>
> 1. knowingly presents, or causes to be presented, to an officer or employee of the United States Government or a member of the Armed Forces of the United States a false or fraudulent claim for payment or approval;
> 2. knowingly makes, uses, or causes to be made or used, a false record or statement to get a false or fraudulent claim paid or approved by the Government;
> 3. conspires to defraud the Government by getting a false or fraudulent claim allowed or paid....
> 4. is liable to the United States Government for a civil penalty of not less than $5,000 and not more than $10,000, plus 3 times the amount of damages which the Government sustains because of the act of that person.

People who manage agencies should think long and hard before they submit a false claim or anything that could be construed as one because this statute permits private individuals to initiate actions on behalf of the federal government, acting as *qui tam*. If an individual's *qui tam* suit is successful, he participates in the government's financial recovery. There is an active bar supporting those wanting to act as *qui tam*. If there is any doubt about that, just search "Federal False Claims Act" in Google. The Federal False Claims Act also includes criminal sanctions.

If for no other reason, the Federal False Claims Act should cause a nonprofit's managers to take care when it applies for grants and makes required reports. There is no question that the organization must have qualified and experienced people involved in all phases of the grant process. The watchwords should be cooperation and full disclosure when dealing with the federal government.

(d) STATE AND LOCAL GRANTS. Nonprofits can and should seek funding from state and local governments that have grant programs. Obviously, the multitude of state and local jurisdictions and grant programs makes an in-depth analysis of these programs impossible. As noted earlier, a grant is nothing but a contract, so a nonprofit need only understand the various requirements and rules applicable to the grant in question. Fortunately, many jurisdictions refer to the various OMB circulars in formulating their grant programs. The result is that nonprofits can participate in many state and local grant programs without necessarily reinventing their compliance systems or maintaining multiple sets of books.

(e) FUNDRAISING THROUGH THE INTERNET. Charities have been quick to take advantage of the Internet for fundraising. Like entities that use the Internet for commercial activities, charities must comply with the Controlling the Assault of Non-Solicited Pornography and Marketing Act of 2003 (CAN-SPAM).[183] It limits commercial e-mail messages, including a requirement that commercial e-mail

183. Pub. L. 108-187, 117 Stat. 2699 (2003).

solicitations provide the recipient an opt-out option.[184] It also (1) requires that address and sender information be accurate,[185] (2) prohibits deceptive subject lines,[186] (3) requires that commercial e-mail be identified as an advertisement or solicitation,[187] and (4) requires that e-mail classified as commercial mail contain a physical postal address.[188]

There is really very little reason for legitimate entities, be they commercial or charitable, to object to any of these requirements, including the opt-out provision. As a matter of good practice and member relations, nonprofits would be better served by complying with the requirements instead of looking for loopholes in them. For example, the FTC received a fair number of comments arguing that communication by associations to their members should not be considered commercial but should qualify for the transactional exemption provided by the statute. Rather than endlessly debating the issue, why not just provide the opt-out? If the communication is really useful to the recipients, they will not opt out. On the other hand, if 90 percent of the recipients opt out, the organization has gained valuable information—communications to its members are not effective and need to be improved. But any notion that organizations should have the right to force information on people who do not want it is misguided and counter productive.

CAN-SPAM could appear to have little relevance to nonprofits for two basic reasons. First, the Federal Trade Commission has primary administrative responsibilities with respect to CAN-SPAM, and as we have seen, the FTC has no regulatory authority over nonprofits.[189] Second, charitable solicitations are arguably noncommercial and are not subject to the rule.[190] As is often the case, however, the devil is in the details. Although the FTC has no jurisdiction with respect to nonprofits, CAN-SPAM provides enforcement mechanisms to Internet

184. 15 U.S.C. 7704(a)(4).
185. 15 U.S.C. 7704(a)(1).
186. 15 U.S.C. 7704(a)(2).
187. 15 U.S.C. 7704(a)(5).
188. *Id.*
189. 15 U.S.C. 7706(d) provides that the FTC cannot initiate enforcement action against anyone whom the FTC does not have basic jurisdiction over. The FTC does not have jurisdiction over any entity that is not "organized to carry on business for its own profit or that of its members." 15 U.S.C. 44. For a general discussion, see Definitions, Implementations, and Reporting Requirements Under the CAN-SPAM Act, 69 Fed. Reg. 50,091 (proposed Aug. 13, 2004).
190. Whether something is commercial or not is arguably in the eyes of the beholder. Unfortunately, CAN-SPAM does not specifically address whether charitable solicitations are commercial, nor do the FTC regulations. However, Definitions, Implementations, and Reporting Requirements Under the CAN-SPAM Act, *supra* note 189, does provide as follows:

> Some nonprofit entities argued that the multiple references to the word "commercial" in the definition of "commercial electronic mail message" reflect an intent to distinguish between for-profit and nonprofit messages. The Commission is not persuaded by this argument. CANSPAM does not set up a dichotomy between "commercial" and "nonprofit" messages. Rather, it focuses on messages whose primary purpose is to sell something, as distinguished from "transactional or relationship messages," informational and editorial messages, and (relevant to nonprofit entities) messages seeking a charitable contribution.

service providers (ISPs)[191] and state attorneys general.[192] As is the case with the FTC's telemarketing rule, the focus is not on who is acting (e.g., a nonprofit or a commercial entity) but the action (e.g., making a phone call or sending an e-mail). Consequently, nonprofits sending commercial e-mail messages may not need to worry about the FTC, but they should recognize that CAN-SPAM gives ISPs and state attorneys general certain enforcement options. Moreover, charitable solicitations may not be considered "commercial," but nonprofits send other types of e-mail, including those promoting products and services.

As noted, the rules apply to commercial communications. Probably the most important exception in the rule is the one for transactional and relationship messages (the "transactional exception").[193] The FTC refused to expand this exception to cover all communications between associations and their members, but the FTC acknowledges that many types of e-mail communications between an organization's members will be exempt under the transaction exception. Common understanding of the meaning of *commercial* suggests that newsletters without advertising, surveys, and announcements about upcoming noncommercial programs for members (e.g., free recitals, member annual meetings, and elections) would be excluded from the opt-out provision in CAN-SPAM because they are noncommercial.

At least one commentator has suggested that e-mails promoting products and services that are related to an organization's exempt function should not be considered commercial messages.[194] The regulations do not explicitly support this position, so organizations should not be lulled by the intuitive appeal of this interpretation unless the FTC issues specific guidance sanctioning it.

The statutory structure also requires an organization to focus on the primary purpose of a message that contains mixed content.[195] Even if some of the content would qualify for the transactional exception, if the primary purpose of the e-mail is commercial, the e-mail must comply with the requirements imposed by

---

So pure charitable solicitations appear to be outside the rule. But this is a lousy regulatory approach to addressing basic issues posed by the statutory scheme. The FTC should have promulgated a specific rule that dealt with charitable and "product" solicitations by nonprofits. For example, can a Section 501(c)(3) symphony orchestra solicit members of the public for subscriptions to its concert series? This is clearly not a charitable solicitation and involves the sale of a product (tickets), albeit one that is in furtherance of the symphony's exempt function. In the absence of a specific rule, this sort of e-mail would appear to be commercial, subjecting it to the rule. Posing even more difficult questions is the "quid pro quo" charitable solicitation. For example, a public television station might send an e-mail soliciting a contribution, but offer a DVD valued at $100 for a contribution in excess of $300.

---

191. 15 U.S.C. 7706(g).
192. 15 U.S.C. 7706(f).
193. 15 U.S.C. 7702(17); and 16 C.F.R. 316.3(c).
194. S. Coffman, *Staying on the E-mail Up and Up: What Nonprofits Need to Know about CAN-SPAM*, GUIDESTAR NEWSLETTER (Jan. 2005). This article is apparently based on a conversation with an intellectual property attorney and may reflect that attorney's conclusions rather than Ms. Coffman's conclusions.
195. 16 C.F.R. 316.3

CAN-SPAM. If an e-mail contains both the commercial content as well as content that qualifies under the transactional exception, the message's primary purpose will be deemed commercial if (1) the subject line would lead the recipient to reasonably conclude that the message is commercial or (2) the content qualifying for the transactional or relational exception does not appear, in whole or in substantial part, at the beginning of the body of the message.[196]

If the e-mail message contains both commercial and noncommercial content (other than content falling into the transactional exception), the e-mail's primary purpose will be deemed commercial if a recipient reasonably interpreting (1) the subject line of the e-mail would likely conclude that the message contains the commercial advertisement or promotion of a commercial product or service or (2) the body of the e-mail would likely conclude that the primary purpose of the message is the commercial advertisement or promotion of a commercial product or service.[197] Factors include (1) the placement of content that is the commercial advertisement or promotion of a commercial product or service, in whole or in substantial part, at the beginning of the body of the message, (2) the proportion of the message dedicated to such content, and (3) how color, graphics, type size, and style are used to highlight commercial content.

As should be apparent from this discussion, CAN-SPAM rules are relatively new and the law has not been fully developed. Consequently, nonprofits that do not want to provide opt-out options or otherwise comply should be alert for additional regulations, FTC industry-specific guidance, and pronouncements from industry associations. Even when CAN-SPAM does not impose limitations, individual states may have done so.

---

196. 16 U.S.C. 316(a)(2); and 16 C.F.R. 316.3(a)(2).
197. 16 U.S.C. 316(a)(3); and 16 C.F.R. 316(a)(3).

CHAPTER 11

AVOIDING OPERATIONAL LIABILITIES

Let the world, then, take notice, when Fortune has the will to ruin a man, how many divers ways she takes!

BENVENUTO CELLINI[1]

1. AUTOBIOGRAPHY, at Chapter 113 (Harvard Classics 1909-14).

Many nonprofit organizations demonstrate a willingness to "cut corners" when conducting business. This does not mean that the directors, officers, or employees are evil people, but instead doing so is usually a sign of inadequate financial and management resources and controls. It sometimes reflects the underlying belief that no one will take issue because the organization is "just doing good." But ignoring certain legal requirements can be costly, embarrassing, and can even result in criminal liability.

11.1 AVOIDING OPERATIONAL LIABILITIES FROM THE INTERACTION OF CORE ACTIVITIES WITH ORGANIZATIONAL CULTURE

The biggest challenge facing any board is implementing incentives and controls to protect the organization from the "big liability" and organizational self-destruction. This is also the most difficult challenge because organizational self-destruction rarely is attributable to poor financial controls. To put names behind this assertion, consider Merck, Royal Dutch Shell Oil, and Marsh & McLennan. Each of these companies was the bluest of the blue-chip companies. Yet, each recently found itself embroiled in a major scandal that reduced its market value by billions of dollars, destroyed goodwill and credibility with the public, consumers, and investors, and will distract management from the its core mission for years to come. In each instance, the scandal centered on the core business.

Consider Merck, whose mission is to sell safe pharmaceuticals. The company allegedly obtained research results that showed its drug Vioxx might increase the risk of heart attacks four years before it withdrew Vioxx from the market. The investigation is ongoing, but the *Wall Street Journal* reported that Merck's chief of research was aware of the research results and apparently chose to discount them.[2] The *Wall Street Journal* also described one training document that apparently instructed Merck salespeople to dodge questions from physicians about cardiovascular safety. At this time, one jury has determined that Vioxx was responsible for one death and required Merck to pay $253 million in damages.[3] Merck will appeal that verdict, but thousands of other suits are pending.

The *Wall Street Journal* has also offered extensive coverage of the insurance industry scandal centered on Marsh & McLennan, the world's largest insurance broker, accused by New York State Attorney General Eliot Spitzer of bid rigging.[4] At least three Marsh (or affiliated) employees have pled guilty to criminal charges,[5] the CEO resigned,[6] and the company entered into an $850 million settlement with Attorney General Spitzer[7] in which Marsh apologized for "unlawful" and "shameful" conduct.[8] This scandal also involved the company's core business activity; it was not a question of failing to reconcile bank accounts or

2. A. Mathews and B. Martinez, *E-Mails Suggest Merck Knew Vioxx's Dangers at Early Stage*, WALL ST. J., Nov. 1, 2004.
3. E. Rosenthal, *For Merck, Global Legal Woes*, N.Y. TIMES, Aug. 26, 2005.
4. T. Francis, *Spitzer Charges Bid Rigging in Insurance: Top Broker, Major Firms Named in Legal Action; 'Trust Me: This Is Day One'*, WALL ST. J., Oct. 15, 2004.
5. Press Release, New York Attorney General, Broker Enters Guilty Plea in Ongoing Insurance Probe (Feb. 24, 2005); Press Release, New York Attorney General, Three More Guilty Pleas Obtained in Insurance Industry Probe (Feb. 15, 2005); *AIG, Marsh Execs Plead Guilty in NY AG Spitzer Probe*, INSUR. J., Feb. 15, 2005; and I. McDonald, *Marsh Ex-Broker Enters Guilty Plea in Bid-Rig Case*, WALL ST. J., Jan. 7, 2005.
6. M. Langley and I. McDonald, *Marsh Averts Criminal Case with New CEO*, WALL. ST. J., Oct. 25, 2004.
7. I. McDonald, *Marsh's Results Are Hurt by Loss of Commissions*, WALL. ST. J., Aug. 3, 2005.
8. Press Release, New York Attorney General, Insurance Broker Agrees to Sweeping Reforms, Marsh to Pay $850 Million in Restitution and Ban Contingent Commissions (Jan. 31, 2005).

require that purchases above $500 be authorized by a vice president but one of culture and compensation.

Finally, consider Dutch Royal Shell, the large international oil, energy, and petrochemical company. In 2004, the company was required to restate its proven hydrocarbon reserves by 23 percent,[9] a very significant step because these reserves are the key factor in how the market values an integrated oil company. This story sparked an SEC investigation,[10] key executive ousters,[11] and a major restructuring of the company.[12]

Undoubtedly, lengthy business school case studies will be written about each of these incidents. Time will tell, but the focus of these cases is likely to be company culture, incentives, and governance. Even if the specific incidents caught the respective boards by surprise, it is certainly fair to ask whether these boards (1) placed sufficient checks on incentive compensation to ensure that incentive pay did not produce a culture in which the ends justified any means, (2) employed people with the appropriate values, and (3) adequately monitored the cultures that developed in these organizations.

This chapter lists a number of actions that a nonprofit should take to reduce its exposure to liabilities. Unfortunately, the issues facing companies like Merck, Marsh & McLennan, and Dutch Royal Shell do not lend themselves to simple checklists. The issues that the management of each of these companies faced are one of the reasons their executives are so highly compensated. Addressing these issues is what business is about: Management must design strategies and procedures that consider incentives, the regulatory environment, the marketplace, and cumulative industry and company experience. Although responsibility for design and implementation of these systems rests with senior management, the board is responsible for providing management with the direction and ensuring that management continually focuses on these and other macro issues. Those holding senior positions can sometimes be a significant contributing factor when major systems break down, making board efforts to monitor senior management critical.

The obvious retort is that these three examples involve for-profit businesses. That is true, but each provides a stark reminder of how management and board failures to adequately control core business processes can diminish value, goodwill, and businesses. Major disasters can befall any nonprofit with significant operations, as the following two examples illustrate.

---

9. Press Release 2004-116, Securities and Exchange Commission, Royal Dutch Petroleum Company and "Shell" Transport and Trading Company, P.L.C. Pay $120 Million to Settle SEC Fraud Case Involving Massive Overstatement of Proved Hydrocarbon Reserves (Aug. 24, 2004).

10. C. Cummins and A. Latour, *Changing Drill: How Shell's Move to Revamp Culture Ended in Scandal*, WALL ST. J., Nov. 2, 2004; and Complaint H-04-3359 Securities and Exchange Commission, filed in the United States District Court for the Southern District of Texas, Houston Division.

11. Business Week Online, *Philip Watts,* Jan. 10, 2005; *Shell Games at Royal Dutch/Shell: Will They Affect Corporate Governance in Europe*, SRI MEDIA, July 30, 2004; and T. Maclister, *Shell Gains L1Bn as Watts Is Axed,* GUARDIAN UNLIMITED, Mar. 4, 2004.

12. C. Cummins, *Shell Shakes Up Corporate Structure*, WALL ST. J., Oct. 4, 2004.

(a) NATURE CONSERVANCY. In May 2003, the *Washington Post* ran a four-part series examining the Nature Conservancy, a leading environmental nonprofit organization.[13] The series questioned whether the Conservancy's seemingly close ties and affiliations with the business community had corrupted the organization's pursuit of its core mission. The first article in the series noted that the conservancy had been late in taking a position on Alaska oil drilling and global warming, raising the possibility that its silence was attributable to the Conservancy's relationships with ExxonMobil, GM, and Phillips Alaska.[14] These and other large industrial corporations had contributed large amounts of cash to the Conservancy, joined its leadership council, and assisted in fundraising activities.[15] The series then detailed failed business ventures,[16] transactions with board members,[17] movement away from the science that normally underpins positions taken by environmental organizations,[18] underreported executive compensation,[19] questionable business practices that led to a lawsuit that was eventually settled at a cost to the Conservancy of $5.6 million,[20] and possible abuses involving conservation easements.[21]

As is typical in situations involving "establishment" nonprofits that run into public relations problems, the Conservancy appointed an independent panel of governance experts, who then issued a report making recommending reforms.[22] The Nature Conservancy's president and CEO also published a reply to the *Washington Post*'s series. The reply first enumerated the many accomplishments of the Conservancy in an effort to counter what the president referred to as a "distorted picture of our organization ... misrepresented our motives and methods, took quotations our of context and omitted key details (such as our mission) and differing points of view."[23] At the end of the response, the president reported that the Conservancy had temporarily suspended certain activities until the board of trustees could review them at its June 2003 meeting. On June 13, 2003, the Conservancy's board prohibited the organization from buying or selling land in transactions with related parties, required all charitable gifts associated with certain conservation transactions to be legally documented, prohibited new loans to

13. J. Stephens and D. Ottaway, *Nonprofit Land Bank Amasses Billions*, WASH. POST, May 4, 2003, the first article in the series.
14. *Id.*
15. *Id.*
16. D. Ottaway and J. Stephens, *On Eastern Shore, For-Profit "Flagship" Hits Shoals: Local Ventures Launched, Foundered and Failed*, WASH. POST, May 5, 2003.
17. J. Stephens and D. Ottaway, *supra* note 13.
18. *Id.*
19. J. Stephens and D. Ottaway, *$420,000 a Year and No Strings Fund: Conservancy Underreported President's Pay and Perks of Office*, WASH. POST, May 4, 2003.
20. J. Stephens and D. Ottaway, *How a Bid to Save a Species Came to Grief*, WASH. POST, May 5, 2003.
21. J. Stephens and D. Ottaway, *Developers Find Payoff in Preservation: Donors Reap Tax Benefits by Giving to Land Trusts, but Critics Fear Abuse of System*, WASH. POST, Dec. 21, 2003.
22. REPORT OF THE GOVERNANCE ADVISORY PANEL TO THE EXECUTIVE COMMITTEE AND THE BOARD OF GOVERNORS OF THE NATURE CONSERVANCY (Mar. 19, 2004).
23. S. McCormick, *Balancing the Story*, WASH. POST, May 13, 2003.

employees, prohibited the organization from initiating new oil and gas drilling or mining, and adopted additional internal policies to govern cause-related marketing.[24] As should be apparent, these reforms focused on some of the central activities highlighted in the *Washington Post* series.

Based on comments in the series, the Nature Conservancy will apparently move away from for-profit business ventures, although the June 13 board meeting did not specifically address such ventures. In apparent response to the *Post's* series, the IRS commenced an unprecedented audit[25] of the Conservancy, and the Senate Finance Committee requested information about the audit.[26]

There is no doubt that the Nature Conservancy has been successful in carrying out its core mission (conservation and preservation of natural and open spaces), something its supporters are undoubtedly proud of but that those charged with the organization's governance lost control of it. The board of trustees and senior officers did not properly assess the implications of its efforts to partner with corporate America, to enter into transactions with wealthy individuals and companies that in some cases had affiliations with the Conservancy, and to engage in commercial activities. Although some affiliated with the Nature Conservancy may disagree with this last statement, the facts that an independent group of governance experts recommended significant reforms in direct response to the *Post*'s series and that the Conservancy's board of governors adopted resolutions prohibiting some of the activities described in the series undercuts any such disagreement.[27]

The Nature Conservancy is on a course that should enable it to survive, although as this is written, both the Senate Finance Committee and the IRS are considering tightening the rules governing charitable contribution deductions for conservation easements, which could devalue the "currency" that the Nature Conservancy has used to further its mission.[28] The bigger lesson from the Nature Conservancy's recent experience is the need for those governing an organization to constantly assess its mission and the means used to achieve it. Poor financial controls can be costly, resulting in fraud and theft. Failure to adequately control employment practices, workplace safety, fundraising events, tax reporting, and various other operational functions can result in liability. The methods for avoiding liabilities arising from such lapses, however, are fairly straightforward. But when a board loses control over the core mission, as apparently was the case with the Nature Conservancy, the organization can suffer intangible losses that are not recoverable through insurance. In sum, an organization's goodwill can be substantially diminished. That has significant implications in terms of fundraising

---

24. Press Release, Nature Conservancy, Actions Taken by the Board of Governors (June 13, 2003).
25. J. Stephens and D. Ottaway, *IRS to Audit Nature Conservancy from Inside*, WASH. POST, Jan. 17, 2004.
26. Press Release, Nature Conservancy, Statement from the Nature Conservancy: Senate Finance Committee Letter (Nov. 7, 2003).
27. Governance Advisory Panel, *supra* note 22.
28. SENATE FINANCE COMMITTEE, REPORT ON OF THE STAFF INVESTIGATIONS OF THE NATURE CONSERVANCY, S. Print 109-26 (June 8, 2005).

capacity, government relations, employee morale, and the ability to move the mission forward.

(b) OPPORTUNITIES INDUSTRIALIZATION CENTER OF GREATER MILWAUKEE. Opportunities Industrialization Center of Greater Milwaukee (OIC-GM) was a nonprofit organization established in 1967[29] that operated a broad range of programs and services that fell into the following two basic categories: (1) comprehensive job training and skills development programs for low-income people, and (2) economic and neighborhood development initiatives targeted at Milwaukee's central city community.[30] In 1997, the Wisconsin Department of Workforce Development selected OIC-GM to deliver services in Milwaukee County under the state's then newly created Wisconsin Works (W-2) program, its innovative effort to replace its traditional welfare program (Aid to Dependent Families with Children) with one that links work and subsistence payments. During the ensuing years, OIC-GM entered into contracts with the state of Wisconsin valued at $231.5 million.[31] By 2004, OIC-GM was responsible for providing services to approximately 50 percent of the W-2 participants in Milwaukee County, which represented approximately 40 percent of the caseload in Wisconsin. In short, OIC-GM's funding and activities were tightly linked to the state of Wisconsin.

Naturally, given OIC-GM's prominence, news that some people associated with it were the subject of a criminal investigation related to a kickback scheme grabbed the headlines of the *Milwaukee Journal-Sentinel.* The details are a bit murky because of plea agreements, but when the dust settled, a Wisconsin state senator had been indicted on charges of participating in a kickback scheme involving a prominent attorney representing OIC-GM. According to a January 22, 2004, article in the *Journal-Sentinel*, the state senator pled guilty to "a single count of conspiracy to accept kickbacks of legal fees paid by the [OIC-GM]," but four unrelated counts were dismissed.[32]

If that were the end, the story would hold little interest. However, in August 2004, a jury convicted OIC-GM's long-time head of committing conspiracy for his involvement in the same kickback scheme.[33] The conspiracy also involved the purchase by OIC-GM of an interest in a Virgin Islands television station controlled by the state senator's family.[34] OIC-GM never received the stock

29. Wisconsin Legislative Audit Bureau, Review of OIC-GM (Nov. 9, 2004).
30. Part III of OIC-GM's 2002 IRS Form 990.
31. Wisconsin Legislative Audit Bureau, *supra* note 29.
32. G. Zielinski, *George Pleads Guilty to Fraud: Four Other Counts Dismissed; Ex-Senator to Cooperate*, Milwaukee J.-Sentinel, Jan. 22, 2004.
33. G. Barton, *Gee Receives 2-Year Prison Term for Role in OIC Kickback Scheme: Former Director Knew of Illegal Payments to George, U.S. Said*, Milwaukee J.-Sentinel, Jan. 25, 2005; L. Sykes, Jr., *OIC Dream May Have Been Nothing More Than a Mirage: Gee's Legacy at Agency Unravels Under Scandal, State Audits*, Milwaukee J.-Sentinel, Dec. 5, 2004; and D. Nunnally, *Jury Finds Gee Guilty in Kickback Scheme*, Milwaukee J.-Sentinel, Aug. 19, 2004.
34. G. Barton, *Gee Receives 2-Year Prison Term*, *supra* note 33; and B. Murphy, *Investment Leads to Legal Troubles*, Milwaukee J.-Sentinel, May 30, 2004.

certificates evidencing its ownership interest.[35] Following the conviction, two OIC-GM affiliates were indicted by the federal prosecutor,[36] allegations circulated about a questionable real estate transaction,[37] and other allegations were made about misuse of W-2 funds.[38]

During 2003 and 2004, numerous stories in the *Milwaukee Journal-Sentinel* portrayed OIC-GM (and its affiliates) as a deeply troubled organization with poor governance. The criminal prosecution did not reflect the depth of the problems, which is often the case, and relied on plea bargains that effectively curtailed a full airing of the facts. However, headlines in the *Journal-Sentinel* toward the end of 2004 and beginning of 2005 provided insight into the public relations problems that followed after a year of scandal. The headlines included these: *OIC May Not Receive New Funds for '05: Common Council Advised to Withhold Block Grant Money; Incomplete Projects Cited* (October 29, 2004); *George Kin Aboard OIC Gravy Train* (October 13, 2004); *OIC Loses More of Its W-2 Contract: State Takes Away Another $10.3 Million and 2,000 Clients* (December 9, 2004); *OIC Attempts to Steady Itself Amid Whirlwind of Scandal: Agency Struggles with Big Deficit, Poor Morale and Criminal Probes* (December 12, 2004); *OIC Laying Off 130: Third of Staff to Go as Agency's Funding Slashed* (December 20, 2004); *OIC Board Resigns as Affiliations End* (January 14, 2005); *Subcontractors Say OIC Owes $655,000 Plus for Weatherization* (January 7, 2005); *OIC Draws More Fire: Agency Should Lose W-2 Deal, Republicans Say* (January 28, 2005); and *Audit Uncovers Widespread Problems at OIC* (February 1, 2005). The company's latest audit is particularly interesting because it details internal control lapses, including one deficiency that permitted an employee to allegedly continue paying aid to W-2 program beneficiaries after they had left the program.[39] Several of the articles contained critical comments from elected representatives and calls for investigations.

On February 10, 2005, the *Journal-Sentinel* reported that the OIC-GM board had voted to shut the agency down.[40] Subsequent articles have indicated that the state of Wisconsin essentially took over the agency to protect state interests.

---

35. B. Murphy, *supra* note 34.
36. G. Barton, *2 Former Affiliates of OIC Sentenced: Case Prompted Investigation of County Board Chairman*, MILWAUKEE J.-SENTINEL, July 21, 2005.
37. D. Umhoefer & G. Pabst, *Ethics Board Charges Holloway: Supervisor Accused of Violating OIC Real Estate Dealings*, MILWAUKEE J.-SENTINEL, June 14, 2005; D. Umhoeffer, *Ethics Inquiry to Focus on Holloway-OIC Deal: Preliminary Findings Expected by March*, MILWAUKEE J.-SENTINEL, Jan. 31, 2005; and L. Sandler, *Ethics Inquiry Sought on Holloway: 8 Supervisors Say OIC Paid for Building He Retains*, MILWAUKEE J.-SENTINEL, Dec. 23, 2004.
38. S. Schultze, *Former Welfare Execs' Pay Total in Millions*, MILWAUKEE J.-SENTINEL, Nov. 12, 2004; S. Schultze, *W-2 Money Went to Radio Host McGee: State Audit Faults OIC for Those, Other Payments; Overnight Added*, MILWAUKEE J.-SENTINEL, Nov. 9, 2004; Editorial, *Little Time Left for OIC*, MILWAUKEE J.-SENTINEL, Nov. 10, 2004, in which the *Journal-Sentinel* writes, "As a story in Wednesday's *Journal-Sentinel* revealed, OIC has come under justifiable fire by state auditors for spending millions of dollars in welfare reform money in recent years on its own subsidiaries and executives."
39. S. Schultze, *Ex-Clients Kept Getting OIC Payments, Audits Find*, MILWAUKEE J.-SENTINEL, Feb. 1, 2005.
40. S. Schultze and L. Sykes, Jr., *Embattled OIC to Close Its Doors: Deep Financial Crisis Is Final Blow to Agency*, MILWAUKEE J.-SENTINEL, Feb. 10, 2005.

A February 14, 2005, article in the *Journal-Sentinel* is headlined *At OIC, Who to Blame Is All That Remains: Politicians, Insiders Are All under Scrutiny.* Surprisingly, the article never mentioned the organization's board of directors, nor do many of the other articles.

The types of problems that plagued OIC-GM are not easily addressed by a controls checklist. How then does a board protect against a long-standing executive officer from engaging in illegal activity? The board cannot look to Item 11 on the controls checklist to prevent that type of moral lapse. Nevertheless, OIC-GM had to face the consequences of its board's failure to control those running the organization. Why was a social services agency in Milwaukee, Wisconsin, investing in a television station in the Virgin Islands? Why was a social services agency spending tens of thousands of dollars on advertising for one radio show?[41] Why did a social services agency need so many affiliated entities when virtually everyone describing the corporate structure referred to it as very complex and hard to understand? What work was actually being performed by all of the lawyers and consultants?[42] What controls were in place to make sure that state W-2 money was properly spent? Why did the board or finance committee apparently receive only written financial summaries at monthly meetings rather than complete financial statements?[43] Why did the organization have more than 30 checking accounts? How were transactions between affiliates being valued? These are the questions the board should have been asking; only board members know what really happened at board meetings.

No matter how many controls organizations implement, there unfortunately will be the case of the bookkeeper who steals $100,000 or $200,000. It is difficult to be too critical if the board had implemented financial controls, put surety bonds or fidelity insurance in place, and listened to its auditors. There is only so much a board can do. But the problems at both the Nature Conservancy and OIC-GM went well beyond a dishonest employee. In the end, both organizations lost their long-standing goodwill. In both cases, that loss came about because the board lost control of core aspects of operations One organization survived, the other did not. A proactive board is the ultimate control.

11.2 AVOIDING OPERATIONAL LIABILITIES THROUGH RECORD RETENTION POLICIES

People in nonprofits frequently express concerns about record retention, with nonprofit listservs replete with questions about appropriate policies. Unfortunately, there is no magic bullet to solve this problem, but a few observations are warranted. You should recognize that records can be kept for too long, but they

41. S. Schultze, *Talker McGee Suspended for On-Air Obscenity*, MILWAUKEE J.-SENTINEL, Dec. 3, 2004; and WISCONSIN LEGISLATIVE AUDIT BUREAU, *supra* note 29, at 28.

42. C. Spivak and D. Bice, *George Kin Aboard OIC Gravy Train*, MILWAUKEE J.-SENTINEL, Nov. 13, 2004.

43. VIRCHOW KRAUSE & COMPANY, CERTIFIED PUBLIC ACCOUNTANTS, MANAGEMENT LETTER (Dec. 15, 2005), made available by the state of Wisconsin.

can also be destroyed too soon. Adopting a rule that all records will be kept for 30 years is not the right answer, nor is adopting a rule that all records will be destroyed immediately following their first review. The objective of any record retention policy is to focus on specific categories of records, taking a "Three-Bears" (just-right) approach with respect to each category of records.

(a) BASICS. All organizations have a record retention policy. It is either a formal policy reviewed by a team of lawyers or an informal one under which people destroy records when they are tired of looking at boxes piled to the ceiling. Although the latter approach may be the easiest and least costly in terms of immediate administration costs, it is filled with perils, including exposure to criminal liability for obstructing justice[44] and potential civil sanctions for *spoliation* (destruction or alteration).[45] Consequently, every nonprofit board should require management to implement a written record retention policy and mandate continuous compliance with its terms.

Most record retention discussions are triggered by two legal concerns. As already noted, people want to know when they can safely destroy documents without running afoul of legal rules designed to protect potential evidence necessary in regulatory audits, lawsuits, and government investigations. The other basis for concern is the myriad of government statutes and regulations mandating that records be kept for specified periods of time. Both of these concerns are appropriate motivating factors, but an organization should adopt a policy first and foremost so that information needed to conduct its activities is available and can be readily located. For example, insurance companies may require a social services agency providing mental health counseling to keep patient records for a set period of time as a condition for reimbursement. Some state statutes could also require these same social service agencies to retain client medical records for a specific but different period of time. Notwithstanding insurance company and state statutory requirements, the agency needs those records to be able to serve its clients. Those designing a record retention policy should not lose sight of operational needs when they focus on contractual and legal requirements.

(b) THE POLICY. There is no standard record retention policy. Whatever its form and content, every policy should be in writing and made available to all employees. The process of creating a policy should start with an inventory of all documents that flow through the organization. Each document should then be evaluated to

---

44. 18 U.S.C. 1519.
45. Prudential Insurance of America Sales Practices Litig., 169 F.R.D. 598 (N.J D.C. 1997), where the judge said:

> While there is no proof that Prudential, through its employees, engaged in conduct intended to thwart discovery through the purposeful destruction of documents, its haphazard and uncoordinated approach to document retention indisputably denies its party opponents potential evidence to establish facts in dispute. Because the destroyed records in Cambridge are permanently lost, the Court will draw the inference that the destroyed materials are relevant and if available would lead to breach of a claim.

determine how long the organization is legally required to keep it and how long users in the organization require access to it for operational reasons. Appropriate schedules should be developed summarizing this information. Retention and destruction of documents should then proceed in accordance with these schedules. As you will see, the policy must contain procedures to place a hold on the destruction of relevant documents when litigation or investigations are foreseeable, imminent, or in process. Finally, the procedure should have features that document the destruction of documents. If at all possible, the organization should audit its document retention procedures to ensure that employees are following them.

Document retention schedules can take the form of spreadsheets, with hundreds, if not thousands, of items and related retention periods, or they can be simple categories in which to group functionally related documents. One expert, Donald Skupsky, has developed a complete methodology built around functional categories that he believes can greatly simplify the retention process,[46] allowing a typical organization to monitor between 70 and 100 categories of documents.

Someone in the organization should be charged with overseeing the policy. This will often be the organization's general counsel. Employees with questions should be given timely access to the individual who can answer retention questions. Procedures should also be in place to keep the person who administers the program aware of pending investigations and litigation so that he can ensure that holds are placed on documents when the circumstances warrant.

(c) THE JUDICIAL PERSPECTIVE ON DOCUMENT DESTRUCTION POLICIES. The courts generally do not object to a document destruction policy if the organization adopts it in good faith, it is "reasonable considering the facts and circumstances,"[47] and it is consistently followed.[48] The policy should never be adopted when the organization is facing major litigation or an investigation or when either is foreseeable.[49] To be reasonable, the policy should serve legitimate business purposes[50] and the retention periods should approximate industry standards

46. DONALD S. SKUPSKY, RECORDS RETENTION PROCEDURES: YOUR GUIDE TO DETERMINE HOW LONG TO KEEP YOUR RECORDS AND HOW TO SAFELY DESTROY THEM! (Information Requirements Clearing House 1994), available from ARMA.

47. Lewy v. Remington Arms Co., 836 F.2d 1104 (8th Cir. 1988).

48. For the general proposition that the courts do not object to "valid" document retention policies, see Arthur Andersen v. U.S., 544 U.S.__ (2005).

49. Rambus v. Infineon Technologies *AG*, 220 F.R.D. 264 (E.D. Va 2004), with the court noting:

> Although Rambus has presented evidence that, in concept, it structured its document retention program like a lawful program and that it had valid reasons for adopting the policy, these arguments tend to ignore the vital question at issue: whether Rambus intentionally destroyed documents notwithstanding that it anticipated litigation. In other words, even if it was merely instituting a valid purging program, even valid purging programs need to be put on hold when litigation is "reasonably foreseeable."...
>
> Moreover, Rambus' privilege log illustrates that Rambus was developing both a patent litigation strategy and its document retention program at the same time.... Thus Rambus clearly anticipated some type of litigation at the point it destroyed documents.

50. *Id.*

unless the organization has very good reasons for adopting a different period.[51] Of utmost importance, the policy should be followed consistently.[52] This means that documents are regularly destroyed in accordance with developed schedules. The natural inclination may be to notify users that a batch of documents is about to be destroyed, giving them one last chance to indicate that they still need the documents, but this is inadvisable because many users will have second thoughts about the destruction when notified, resulting in inconsistent and selective destruction.

Organizations also need to focus closely on how they handle compliance reminders. If a reminder is sent just before a lawsuit or investigation is commenced and documents are destroyed, the organization may be accused of encouraging employees to destroy evidence in anticipation of the litigation or investigation. This is what people generally believe resulted in Arthur Andersen's downfall. On the one hand, Andersen's officials claimed that the reminder was just a routine call for compliance. The government, on the other hand, argued that this was a signal to start the shredding that ensued. At a minimum, any policy that calls for periodic destruction should provide for scheduled reminders (e.g., quarterly or annually), with the same language used in each reminder. In the event of litigation or an investigation, the organization may want to suspend the reminder notice or modify it to make clear that those in possession of documents related to the litigation or the investigation are not to destroy relevant documents.

(d) DESTRUCTION IN THE FACE OF EXISTING, IMMINENT, OR FORESEEABLE LITIGATION OR INVESTIGATIONS. In some instances, records are destroyed before the commencement of a lawsuit or a government investigation without any evil intent—in other words, with no knowledge or suspicion that the document is a "smoking gun." That destruction, albeit innocent, will be viewed by the nonprofit's legal adversary or government investigator in the worst possible light. If the nonprofit can point to a clear organizational policy and regular compliance with that policy, it will be in a much better position to counter allegations of wrongdoing. This assumes that the organization viewed the document no differently than all of the other documents that were destroyed pursuant to the scheduled destruction. As noted, the hallmark of a good document destruction policy is scheduled destruction in the ordinary course of business—in other words, consistent and routine adherence to the policy.

---

51. S. Schoenfeld and R. Rasalingham, *Document Retention Polices Have Long-Term Benefits: Goal Is to Ensure Important Information Is Kept as Long as Necessary and No Longer*, N.Y. LAW J., Nov. 18, 2002.

52. C. Chase, *To Shred or Not to Shred: Document Retention Policies and Federal Obstruction of Justice Statutes*, 8 FORD. J. CORP. & FIN. L. 721 (2003).

At times an organization will learn of a lawsuit or government investigation shortly before a scheduled destruction of relevant documents. Despite the retention policy and the regular schedule of complying with it, the organization must preserve those documents. Clearly, if a United States Senator says his committee plans to subpoena documents or a lawyer calls as a matter of courtesy to inform the organization that a lawsuit will be filed, the organization is on notice and must preserve the documents. Suppose, however, that the organization discovers that an employee has taken an action that could generate a civil lawsuit but that the organization knows of no specific lawsuit when it becomes aware of the action. At that point a lawyer should be consulted before destroying any relevant documents.[53]

In many instances the person who will benefit most from destroying documents that pose potential liability is the person in control of the documents. This is obviously a problem because the person may also be the first in the organization to know that an outside investigation or lawsuit is on the horizon. Any well-designed document retention program needs to address this possibility. This may mean routinely changing custody of documents, creating a system for notifying an independent person when documents are retrieved from storage, and making routine backups.[54] The organization's general counsel should play an integral role in the process.

(e) DIGITAL DOCUMENTS. When the discussion turns to document retention policies, people naturally think of paper, but many, if not most, documents are now

---

53. *Compare* Willard v. Caterpillar, 40 Cal. App.4th 892 (1995), where the court said,

> Therefore, if Caterpillar destroyed documents which were routinely requested in ongoing or clearly foreseeable products liability lawsuits involving the ... tractor and claims similar to [plaintiff's], its conduct might be characterized as unfair to foreseeable future plaintiffs. However, the document destruction at issue began more than 10 years before [plaintiff] was injured and evidence disclosed only one other accident involving on track starting ... [S]uch remote prelitigation document destruction would not be commonly understood by society as unfair or immoral.

with Carlucci v. Piper Aircraft, 102 F.R.D. 472 (S.D. Fla. 1984), where the court imposed sanctions on the aircraft manufacturer in a case involving the crash of an airplane in 1976. Until 1974, the defendant did not have a document retention policy. Prior to that, certain flight test reports were ordered to be purged from the records by a supervisor—long before the accident giving rise to the litigation. The judge in *Carlucci* wrote:

> Therefore, I conclude that the defendant engaged in a practice of destroying engineering documents with the intention of preventing them from being produced in law suits.... I am not holding that the good faith disposal of documents pursuant to a bona fide, consistent and reasonable document retention policy can not be a valid justification for a failure to produce documents in discovery. The issue never crystallized in this case because Pipe, utterly failed to provide credible evidence that such a policy or practice existed.... By deliberately destroying documents, the defendant has eliminated the plaintiffs' right to have their cases decided on the merits. Accordingly, the entry of a default is the only means of effectively sanctioning the defendant and remedying the wrong.

54. See Prudential Ins. Co. of America Sales Practices Litig., 169 F.R.D. 498 (N.J. D. 1997), in which the judge wrote:

> [I]t became an obligation of senior management to initiate a comprehensive document preservation plan and distribute it to all employees.

computer-generated and stored in digital form.[55] Any document retention policy must address digital documents, particularly e-mail records. The courts have largely said that digital records are no different than paper-based records for purposes of discovery.[56] Consequently, any organization utilizing computers and digital communication (which, as a practical matter, is virtually every organization) must design its systems to permit cost-effective recovery of digital information. This requires consultation with the organization's lawyers, equipment vendors, and IT consultants. There can be legal issues over which party should bear the cost of recovering documents,[57] what storage media will be subject to review,[58] whether the requested form of data is reliable,[59] and what form the search methodology will take.[60] No organization should operate under the mistaken assumption that none of its electronic records will be subject to discovery.

To manage this process, those outside the IT department must have a basic understanding of the existing backup and storage processes. Are documents backed up on local hard drives or through a network centralized storage system? No one should confuse *backup copies* with *record retention.* Backing up does not categorize or analyze the information in a useable format when the

---

55. In Collaborative Navigation of the Stormy e-Discovery Seas, 10 RICH J. LAW. & TECH 53 (2004), Robert Brownstone cites a number of expert opinions regarding the prevalence of electronic documents. One leading group of experts on the subject suggested that 70 percent of corporate records may be stored in electronic form and 30 percent of electronic information is never printed to paper. Another expert suggested that in many companies, 90 to 95 percent of all information is stored only in electronic form. Whatever the actual percentage, there is little doubt that a significant portion of corporate documents never find their way to paper. For additional information on the first group of experts, see SEDONA CONFERENCE, THE SEDONA PRINCIPLES: BEST PRACTICES, RECOMMENDATIONS & PRINCIPLES FOR ADDRESSING DOCUMENT PRODUCTION (Jan. 2004). For additional information regarding the second claim, see W. Leibowitz, *Digital Discovery Starts to Work*, NAT. LAW J., Nov. 4, 2002.

56. For a general discussion of electronic discovery, see L. Arent, R. Brownstone and W. Fenwick, *E-Discovery: Preserving, Requesting & Producing Electronic Information*, 19 SANTA CLARA COMPUTER AND HIGH TECH LAW J. 131 (2002), as updated on the Web in June 2003. In Linnen v. A.H. Robins Company, 10 Mass L. Rep. 189 (Mass. Super. Ct. 1999), Judge Brassard wrote:

> A discovery request aimed at the production of records retained in electronic form is no different, in principle, from a request for documents contained in an office file cabinet. While the reality of the situation may require a different approach and more sophisticated equipment than a photocopier, there is nothing about the technological aspects involved which renders documents stored in media "undiscoverable."

57. For an eight-factor test designed to determine which party should bear the cost of particular discovery, see Rowe Entertainment v. William Morris Agency, 205 F.R.D. 421 (S.D.N.Y. 2002). *See also* Zubulake v. UBS Warburg, 216 F.R.D. 280 (S.D.N.Y. 2003); and *In re* Air Crash Disaster at Detroit Metropolitan Airport, 737 F. Supp. 396 (E.D. Mich. 1989), addressing whether the requesting party was required to pay the other party's cost of providing the records in a certain format. For an in-depth discussion of this issue, see 10 RICH J. LAW. & TECH 53, which is a symposium issue on electronic discovery.

58. Public Citizen v. Carlin, 184 F.3d 900 (D.C. Cir. 1999), upholding the National Archivist's decision to store archival records in paper rather than digital form despite the fact that searching the records would be much easier if they were archived digitally. See also *In re* Bristol-Meyers Squibb Litig., 205 F.R.D. 437 (D.N.J. 2002).

59. Heveafil Sdn. Bhd. v. United States, 2003 WL 1466193 (Fed. Cir. 2003).

60. *In re* Honeywell Int'l Securities Litig., No. M8-85 WHP, 2003 WL 22,722,961 (S.D.N.Y. 2003), ordering PriceWaterhouseCoopers to produce documents in digital form despite having previously provided them in paper form, and then to provide proprietory software to permit the other party to search the digital records.

backups contain hundreds of thousands, if not millions, of documents cataloged merely by their position on the tape or creation date. Going back to the paper analogue, this backup process is no different than picking up all paper in an office and literally throwing it into a steamer trunk; the paper is no longer on the floor, nor is it in any usable order. If a computer system is centralized, are temporary backups performed and separate archival copies created? How often are temporary backup tapes overwritten? Is the backup of e-mail handled differently? Any policy will be problematic if it is developed without a clear understanding of existing practices.

If the organization has an existing policy with respect to paper-based documents, it must factor that policy into the process it applies to digital records. For example, if an organization has a policy that requires all documents relating to contracts to be retained for five years, it should apply that same standard to the same type of digital records. A court might well ask whether failure to apply the same retention rules to digital records makes the policy unreasonable or selective.

THE SEDONA GUIDELINES: GRAPPLING WITH TOUGH QUESTIONS

* * *

As should be readily apparent, the questions posed by electronic documents in the record retention process are complex. The legal system has dealt with these issues for at least three decades, but it is just beginning to resolve conflicting objectives. The system does not want people to destroy documents that could be important later. Yet preserving everything on backup tapes in raw form may be just as good as destroying the information, given the cost of culling through massive amounts of data to locate a particular document. Should a document retention system force users to cull and segregate records worth retaining from the chatter that pervades most e-mail? Should tools be developed that let computers make decisions by using a tagging system? Is it appropriate to utilize technology that automatically destroys (as opposed to just deletes) information unless the user acts within a relatively short time to remove it from the path of destruction?

A think-tank/study-group has been convened to address these and other questions. Known as The Sedona Conference Working Group on Electronic Document and Production, this group of lawyers, technologists, consultants, and members of industry have been studying those and other questions. In September 2005, the group issued THE SEDONA GUIDELINES: Best Practice Guidelines & Commentary for Managing Information & Records in the Electronic Age (available for free download for personal use at http://www.thesedonaconference.org). Anyone who is truly interested in developing an approach that comes to terms with document retention in the electronic age would be well-advised to review this document, as well as to begin following the activities of this innovative group. Excerpted next (with the permission of The Sedona Conference) is a discussion of the tough issue of systematic document destruction and routine destruction of e-mail (footnotes omitted).

3. An organization need not retain all electronic information ever generated or received.

Comment 3.a. Destruction is an acceptable stage in the information life cycle; an organization may destroy or delete electronic information when there is no continuing value or need to retain it.

Courts routinely acknowledge that organizations have the "right" to destroy (or not track or capture, whether or not it is consciously deleted) electronic information that does not meet the internal criteria of information or records requiring retention. See McGuire v. Acufex Microsurgical, Inc., 175 F.R.D. 149, 155-56 (D. Mass. 1997) (in the employment context, while there is no broad right to "broom clean" internal investigation files or edit personnel records "willy-nilly," employers may call for and edit drafts, and discard them where there are errors made by someone other than the accuser; "to hold otherwise would create a new set of affirmative obligations for employers, unheard of in the law—to preserve all drafts of internal memos, perhaps even to record everything no matter how central to the investigation, or gratuitous")...

Comment 3.b. Systematic deletion of electronic information is not synonymous with evidence spoliation.

Proper destruction of electronic records or other information consistent with a reasonable approach to managing information and records is not synonymous with spoliation of evidence or obstruction of justice. Absent extraordinary circumstances, if an organization has implemented a clearly defined records management program specifying what information and records should be kept for legal, financial, operational or knowledge value reasons and has set appropriate retention systems or periods, then information not meeting these retention guidelines can, and should, be destroyed. Destruction of this information is not spoliation of evidence. See Willard v. Caterpillar, Inc., 40 Cal. App. 4th 892, 921 (1995) ("good faith disposal pursuant to a bona fide consistent and reasonable document retention policy could justify a failure to produce documents in discovery"), overruled on other grounds by Cedars-Sinai Med. Ctr. v. Superior Court, 18 Cal. 4th 1, 74 Cal. Rpt. 2d 248, 954 P.2d 511 (1998); Lewy v. Remington Arms Co., 836 F.2d 1104, 1112 (8th Cir. 1988)....

Comment 3.c. Absent a legal requirement to the contrary, organizations may adopt programs that routinely delete certain recorded communications, such as electronic mail, instant messaging, text messaging and voice-mail.

Unless there is an applicable retention obligation imposed by statute or regulation, or there is a legal hold imposed by virtue of litigation, audit or investigation (see Guideline 5), organizations can legitimately prescribe retention (or deletion) periods for recorded communications, such as electronic mail, instant messaging, voice over IP, text messaging and voice-mails. There are several ways to approach the management of these communications. Some organizations impose space requirements (e.g., 1 MB limit for e-mail boxes where users are unable to send new messages once the limit is reached). Others impose time restrictions (e.g., all non-foddered e-mails more than thirty days old will be automatically deleted). Indeed, organizations can set up Instant Messaging so that archiving of the typed conversation is not allowed and the text disappears when the session is closed. Other organizations have used a hybrid approach, which provides that most communications are to be deleted within a prescribed number of days, but communications that have a true business critical nature can be retained for a longer period in public or shared folders. For example, if there is a construction project, e-mails relating to that construction project may be maintained for the life of the project in a public or shared folder, but should be deleted after the conclusion of the project.

As noted earlier, the selection of any particular solution involves complex and competing policy issues best resolved by careful discussions among an interdisciplinary team. For example, while the IT group may effectively advocate a policy against using a network for individual archiving, employees can often archive messages on their own local hard drives (e.g., with .pst files for e-mail within a Microsoft Outlook environment). This ad hoc "work around" will result in additional time and cost if the scattered information needs to be retrieved or reproduced. Organizations that rely heavily on e-mail may find it difficult to implement a strict disposal period without sufficient safeguards to protect against the loss of important information. This highlights how important it is for organizations to adopt policies, procedures and processes that best meet their business needs, while satisfying their legal obligations.

In addition, there may be some circumstances where an organization is legally obligated to retain all forms of communications. For example, the investment industry is under a requirement to maintain for a specified period all communications with certain investment customers. Alternatively, some organizations actually use e-mail to document specific transactions and, therefore, the e-mail itself might be a transactional record that should be retained under the tax laws and regulations. Before implementing a policy regarding the automatic destruction of electronic communications, the organization must have a good understanding of its legal obligations as well as its business practices.

Moreover, any organization that regularly deletes data based on a regular time period may need to be able to suspend such automatic deletion (i.e., as part of a legal hold) for some or all users, or otherwise provide a retention process or mechanism, as may be necessary to comply with preservation obligations. See generally John C. Montana, Legal Obstacles to E-Mail Message Destruction (ARMA Int'l Educ. Foundation 2003). Furthermore, organizations that adopt a time or space based approach should consider that the varying usage levels of different employees may result in the disparate application of policies and inadvertent loss of valuable information unless there is adequate education and effective procedures to cull records from non-relevant information. Indeed, a policy that routinely deletes "old" data (such as e-mail messages) without any other protections can be analogized to destroying boxes in a warehouse based on where they are on the shelf without any regard to the contents.

* * *

(f) COPIES. Although document retention policies may inadvertently eliminate what might have been smoking guns from an organization's records, that consequence should be a by-product rather than the primary reason for adopting a record retention policy. As noted, if a company adopts a policy just to rid itself of known smoking guns, the courts are unlikely to respect the policy and take the position that it was either adopted in bad faith or fails to serve legitimate business purposes. Eliminating the potential smoking gun is, however, one of the allures behind these policies; although no one would admit to that when advising a court that the policy furthers legitimate business needs. Moreover, people focused on eliminating a potential smoking gun by establishing otherwise legitimate policies should not be lulled into a false sense of security. Although official or archival copies of documents may be destroyed as scheduled, copies that were circulated and recopied or attached to e-mails might survive. Even if the organization's policy provides for destroying those copies, it is difficult to guarantee that all copies actually have been destroyed, particularly when employees frequently change employers or work in home offices. Those adopting record retention policies hoping to eliminate smoking guns are living in a fool's paradise.

Furthermore, no one should lose sight that evidence can take many forms, including depositions and court testimony. To illustrate, assume that a board ignores a situation that everyone knows is dangerous because the organization does not have the money to address the problem. The board may agree to keep a record of the discussion out of the minutes (or management may take comparable action) for fear of creating evidence that a subsequent injury was foreseeable. What should be obvious but for some reason often is not is that the lawyers are going to depose board members and the organization's employees. In all likelihood, the truth will come out even if it is not in writing.

(g) E-MAIL. There will always be those who can provide oral testimony regarding actionable behavior, but there is little doubt that e-mails pose problems even when there is otherwise no basis for finding wrongdoing. Studies have shown that people put less thought into e-mails than they do into writing business letters or communicating during meetings. People also tend to be more colloquial and off the cuff when communicating through e-mail. As a consequence, what is often an innocent note easily can be misconstrued in view of subsequent events. Even when it is permissible to destroy e-mails under a reasonable record retention policy, actually destroying them can be difficult given paper copies, backup tapes, and individual hard drives. With these realities in mind, organizations should adopt an e-mail policy, one that arguably reduces the use of e-mail. In fact, after 10 to 15 years of experience, some individuals and organizations are doing just that.[61]

But e-mail is clearly here to stay so any policy must involve controlling rather than eliminating e-mails. Probably the most important aspect of any policy is to limit what is addressed in e-mails. Clearly, scheduling meetings, notifying people that someone will be out of the office, and responding "yes" or "no" to factual questions is appropriate. However, organizations should discourage e-mail pertaining to (1) matters that are either headed for or currently the subject of litigation, (2) controversial or major issues, (3) employment-related matters such as evaluations, hiring, and termination decisions, and (4) matters that are not for general discussion.

---

61. G. Burns, *You've Got Mail Trouble: Liabilities Make Quick, Easy Communication Tool More Dispensable*, CHI. TRIB., Aug. 14, 2005. Just the fact that this article appeared on the front page (above the fold) of the Sunday edition of a major newspaper is evidence that concerns over e-mail have jumped from cautious corporate lawyers and consultants to managers and employees.

Employees should be instructed to use clear and meaningful subject lines. Because individuals in many organizations regularly receive 200-plus e-mails a day, people tend to ignore those that are not clearly labeled.

People should also be discouraged from replying to e-mails when the reply becomes part of a chain. These communications become very difficult to read. Moreover, to the extent that destroying e-mail is permissible, these replies keep individual e-mail messages alive by repeating them in multiple messages. Most important, employees should constantly be reminded that deleting an e-mail is quite different from destroying it.

Even when there is a policy to reduce the number of e-mails, deciding which should be retained is difficult. Some statutes now specifically require that e-mails pertaining to certain matters be retained, but that is not the general rule. Assuming there is no statute mandating retention, an organization can probably destroy many e-mails shortly after they are created because the content does not constitute a record under the organization's retention policy. For example, office chatter regarding meeting downstairs for lunch or car pooling need not be retained.

The question becomes more difficult if we consider internal e-mails regarding a contract negotiation. Must the 1,000 e-mails leading up to the decision or just the one that summarizes the terms of the final contract to the respondent be kept? Preliminary e-mails are arguably more akin to telephone conversations than to records. Assuming we can arrive at a standard defining which e-mails must be retained, is it advisable to have a policy requiring the originator to print out the e-mail and forward it to the organization's archive? If not, who will be charged with capturing that critical e-mail? Someone outside the negotiation process, such as someone in the IT department, lacks not only the time but also the context for identifying critical e-mails on a backup tape containing hundreds of thousands of emails.

Every organization should discuss this issue with its legal counsel to assess acceptable current practices. Any e-mail retention policy must focus on the cost of retrieving e-mails in the event of litigation and a discovery demand. That policy should be addressed when the organization purchases or licenses its e-mail system rather than when it receives a discovery request.

(h) OTHER ISSUES. A record retention policy must address protecting documents from destruction by external forces such as fire, flood, and theft. The specifics of any program will depend on the facts and circumstances. Nonprofits should consider off-site storage, microfilm or digital imaging, fireproof vaults, alarm and sprinkler systems, and routine creation of duplicate copies.

Retention policies must also address privacy and security issues. Organizations undertaking military research pursuant to federal grants must consider security clearances. Hospitals, treatment facilities, and employers must ensure that they keep patient medical records confidential, as prescribed by the Health

Insurance Portability and Accountability Act (HIPAA). Organizations should limit access to employee reviews, Social Security numbers, and background checks or risk facing lawsuits predicated on invasions of privacy and identify theft. This brings us to the act of destroying documents when they are scheduled for destruction. Virtually everyone has seen the highly effective television ad for a paper shredder in which the identity thief greets the returning homeowner by name while picking through trash cans awaiting curbside pickup. Documents should not be dumped in the garbage when they are destroyed. Industrial-strength paper shredders and outside contractors can be used to destroy not only the documents but also the information in them.

(i) CRIMINAL ACTS. As already noted, under certain circumstances, document destruction is a criminal offense. As part of the Sarbanes-Oxley Act of 2002,[62] Congress enacted a tough document destruction statute that provides as follows:

> Section 1519. Destruction, Alteration, or Falsification of Records in Federal Investigations and Bankruptcy.
>
> Whoever knowingly alters, destroys, mutilates, conceals, covers up, falsifies, or makes a false entry in any record, document, or tangible object with the intent to impede, obstruct, or influence the investigation or proper administration of any matter within the jurisdiction of any department or agency of the United States or any case filed under title 11, or in relation to or contemplation of any such matter or case, shall be fined under this title, imprisoned not more than 20 years, or both.[63]

This provision is extremely broad, making it difficult to predict exactly when a prosecutor will invoke it. Nonprofits (and their officers and directors) having dealings with the federal government should, however, appreciate this provision's potentially broad reach. Although the heading speaks of federal investigations, the actual language refers to the "proper administration of any matter within the jurisdiction," going well beyond criminal investigations. Consequently, organizations and individuals should keep that potential reach in mind when they apply for federal grants, respond to requests for information from federal officials, and otherwise communicate with the federal government.

Everyone should focus on the inchoate nature of the "investigation or proper administration" language. There is no qualifier, such as "pending," "imminent," or "known." There is potential for liability under the statute if someone destroys documents out of fear that the information may some day come to light during an investigation, even if officials currently have no information that would spark an investigation. To some extent, this concern is speculative because the statute is relatively new. Regrettably, the legal commentary in this area focuses on existing or foreseeable investigations, possibly creating the impression that it is permissible to destroy evidence before an event occurs that could give rise to a

62. Pub L. 107-204, 116 Stat. 745
63. 18 U.S.C. 1519.

lawsuit or investigation. Section 1519 clearly calls that contention into question. Moreover, the isolated and selective destruction of evidence could subject the participants to conspiracy charges, violate of legal duties, or result in other serious and negative consequences.

Section 1519 is just one example of the many statutory provisions at both the federal and state levels that address obstruction of justice and related crimes. The procedural rules governing both civil and criminal actions also contain sanctions for inappropriate behavior during the discovery process. The law permits certain adverse inferences to be drawn when documents are destroyed or altered (referred to as *spoliation* in civil matters) in anticipation or during the course of litigation. Legal treatises have been written on the subject and will be useful to lawyers responding to questions about document destruction rules, but the basic operating rule is really quite simple: The more you want to destroy a document because of its explosive nature, the more hesitant you should be to proceed, particularly if you are acting without the advice of experienced legal counsel. People actually go to jail for obstructing justice but rarely for making an honest but embarrassing mistake. As all too many people have learned, it is the cover-up, not the crime, that results in jail sentences.

(j) ASSESSING A DOCUMENT'S VALUE. Rather than taking a haphazard approach to document retention, the nonprofit should first categorize documents as to their value. The American Association of Records Managers (ARMA) has identified the following four basic categories or values for records: (1) legal, (2) audit/fiscal, (3) operational, and (4) historical/archival.[64] The retention policy with respect to a particular document depends largely on the document's classification within the ARMA scheme, with the understanding that a document can be included in more than one category at any given time and its classification can change over time.

Documents with legal value are those that either must be kept by law or may be required during the course of litigation or a government investigation.[65] Any document in this category should be kept as long as statute or regulation requires, until the litigation is complete (including appeals), or, in the absence of litigation or a government investigation, the potential for litigation or investigation is terminated, which is normally tied to the relevant statute of limitations.

Documents with operational value are those required to carry on a nonprofit's daily business.[66] These documents should be retained as long as they are needed, provided that they are not also included in another category. For example, consider an employee handbook, which should be kept for as long as the book

64. ARMA International, Developing and Operating a Records Retention Program (ARMS 1989). The names for these categories appear to change from time to time. For example, in ARMA International, Guidelines for Managing E-Mail (ARMS 2000), the category names are slightly different.

65. ARMA International, Developing and Operating a Records Retention Program, *supra* note 64, at § 3.2.

66. *Id.*, at § 3.1.

reflects the organization's current policies. These policies typically change over time as the organization issues supplements. The organization should periodically issue a revised handbook, collecting the outdated copies to avoid confusion. At that point, although the old version has no operational value, it may still have legal value: It states employment policies and practices for a particular period that could be pertinent should an employee bring an employment practices lawsuit. Moreover, statutory record retention periods could apply to the outdated handbook.

Documents with audit/fiscal value relate to the nonprofit's financial transactions[67] and include most documentation generated by an accounting system (e.g., invoices, credit files, checks, payment authorizations, and receipts). At a minimum, these documents should be retained until audit work involving them is completed or until they are no longer needed to support or substantiate tax returns. The retention policy should recognize that some of these documents may also have operational or legal value. For example, a receipt could include important warranty language, so although it may no longer be needed to verify that only authorized amounts were paid to the vendor, the receipt could be required to make warranty-related claims such as the repair of the item.

Documents with historical value are much more difficult to define because this determination depends on the type of organization. All organizations may want to retain the personnel files and biographical information for people who rise to the top. Organizations may want to retain materials generated by marketing and advertising campaigns, such as print or video ads, brochures, and product samples. An arts organization, for example, may want to retain posters announcing performances or exhibitions, ticket samples, performance programs, and catalogs. Research organizations may want to retain patent applications, project reports, and important studies, although they are outdated. The value assigned to historical documents is linked to the institutional memory that the organization wants to create and preserve, making their retention largely discretionary. Organizations should recognize the potential importance of many documents to future historians trying to tell the story of human progress over the ages. While the organization has discretion, it should act responsibly when it exercises this discretion.

To summarize, there is no easy way to determine how long to retain documents. People designing a retention program must identify each type of document the organization generates, assign each document type to one or more of the four categories, and then, having identified the document's value to the organization, assess how long the document will have value. These days, the easy availability of digital scanning and storage mitigates the fear of drowning in paper, which eliminates one reason many give for wanting to destroy documents.

---

67. *Id.*, at § 3.3.

(k) LEGALLY MANDATED MINIMUMS. Some people will still want specific timeframes for various categories of documents despite the preceding discussion. Obviously, if a government contract or a regulation requires a document to be retained for a fixed period of time, that time period should be used, but not all documents should be destroyed based on the minimum required period of time. For example, the IRS requires taxpayers to maintain permanent records to support the information reported on tax returns. Many lawyers, focusing on the worst-case six-year statute of limitations, advise clients to retain tax returns and supporting records for at least seven years. However, in some instances, tax returns and supporting records contain information that can be useful for preparing returns for many years to come or in defending tax return positions years after the statute of limitations seemingly make them irrelevant. In the nonprofit context, this can include information supporting public charity status, which can require up to five years of prior data (meaning that old returns may be relevant eight or nine years after the year that they are filed). If unrelated business income tax (UBIT) is an issue, the nonprofit may need to determine its cost basis for purposes of calculating depreciation. That could make keeping tax records for 10, 20, or more years highly advisable.

Do not confuse *statutory retention requirements* with *statutes of limitation,* which technically do not address document retention but focus on when a party with legal rights can no longer assert those rights. As a practical matter, statutes of limitation influence the retention period set for specific documents, which can cut both ways. An organization may want to keep documents at least through the expiration of a relevant statute of limitations so that it can defend itself if sued. At the same time, those documents could also support the other party's case. Although the organization might, as part of a good faith record retention policy, set a period shorter than the expiration of the statute of limitations, the courts may find a duty on the organization's part not to destroy certain documents even when no specific litigation is imminent or foreseeable.[68]

Ascertaining the statute of limitations for a particular type of legal claim can be difficult for several reasons. First, limitation periods are scattered throughout the law so actually finding the pertinent statute can be difficult. Second, there may be more than one potential legal theory for making a claim, each with a different statute of limitations. Third, although an actual statute may limit the claim to three years, under certain circumstances the courts are given discretion to toll the statute of limitations.[69] In other words, a three-year statute of limitations may actually run longer if a court ascertains that it should be tolled for some reason. Finally—and this makes record retention policies difficult to replicate in different jurisdictions—the statue of limitations for the same claim under the laws of different states can vary widely. For example, when it comes to claims

68. Reingold v. Wet N' Wild Nevada, 944 P.2d 800 (Nev. 800); and *Carlucci, supra* note 53.

69. For a discussion of tolling in the event of violations of fiduciary duties, see Letter from New York Attorney General Eliot Spitzer to Florence A. Davis, Presient of the Starr Foundation (Dec. 14, 2005).

under contracts, some states have a four-year statute of limitations while others have a ten-year statute of limitations.

NOT ALL ADVICE IS WORTH FOLLOWING: A SIMPLISTIC APPROACH TO RECORD RETENTION IS ILL ADVISED

* * *

One person on a listserv asked for advice about designing record retention policies for "small" nonprofits. Another person responded with the following solution: Each year the organization should place all of its documents in a box on a shelf in its store room. At the end of the first seven years, throw out the contents of the oldest box. The process should be repeated annually, sliding the boxes down the shelf.

While well intentioned, charitably speaking, this advice is ill advised. It is rooted in the incorrect notion that "small" organizations should be excused from burdensome and expensive administrative procedures because there is no value to that effort. The far more appropriate response is that an organization unable to take actions that are legally required or sound from a control standpoint should seek a merger partner or transfer its assets to another charity.

Back to document retention policies. Everyone is looking for that magic number—in the consultant's case, seven years. Here are several reasons why there is no magic number.

Obstruction of Justice. Although Arthur Andersen's widely publicized criminal conviction for its actions in the Enron matter was overturned by the Supreme Court in May 2005,[70] the statute that was the basis for the initial conviction is still on the books and is still good law. Moreover, Sarbanes-Oxley added a new document destruction statute that is in some respects broader than the statute involved in the *Andersen* case. While there may be debate as to exactly when an organization must cease destruction in the case of a criminal investigation, there is no question that if it receives a subpoena, document destruction activities must cease. The consultant's policy, at least as stated, does not adequately consider obstruction of justice issues. People go to jail for violating these statutes.

Sanctions in Civil Suits. There are also sanctions in civil proceedings for destruction of documents once there is some indication that the documents may be relevant to the litigation. For example, a judge may instruct a jury that it is allowed to draw unfavorable inferences from the destruction. Again, as stated, the consultant's policy does not consider civil litigation.

Documents Have Value. Setting aside court proceedings, documents have value to organizations. Does it really make sense to dispose of:

- Real property deeds?
- Satisfactions and releases of mortgages, which could be very important for establishing clear title when the underlying property is sold?
- Records that OSHA requires to be maintained for 30 years, documenting employee exposure to toxic chemicals? That requirement might not be relevant to many nonprofits, but it certainly could be relevant to a medical research organization.

---

70. Arthur Andersen *supra* note 48.

- Basic contracts that can include extended warranties or may be subject to a ten-year statute of limitations? What about construction contracts, for which the law might provide rights for latent design defects discovered many years after construction is complete?
- Asset purchase records for depreciable property used in an unrelated trade or business?
- The organization's IRS Form 1023, which the organization is required by law to furnish to members of the public on request?
- Information that supports the organization's entire accounting system?
- Insurance policies written on an occurrences basis?
- Client medical or treatment records?
- Board meeting minutes or articles of incorporation?

These rhetorical questions should make clear why a one-number approach to document retention simply does not work or make sense.

Shorter Destruction Cycles May Be Legal and Sensible. An organization can dispose of documents not required to be held beyond a certain period of time if the organization has a document retention policy that is applied on a regular and consistent basis (subject, of course, to a litigation suspension policy). Given the prevalence of employment practices litigation, why would an organization not want to avail itself of the opportunity to dispose of employment-related records that are not required to be held seven years?

Do Not Focus Just on Paper. The consultant's document-retention policy is much too papercentric. What about information on hard drives? What about all those e-mails stored on computer-storage tapes and servers?

Account for Multiple Copies. The consultant's document-retention policy assumes that only one copy of a document exists. What about the copies that Ted or Sally made? An organization that routinely disposes of documents pursuant to a bona fide record retention program must consider copies that others may have made.

This consultant may argue that the policy is a practical one because it is limited only to small social services agencies, such as organizations serving children. Although these agencies may not have UBIT problems, how will the agency in 14 years respond when a former seven-year-old brings an action in tort against the agency alleging that it did not take adequate precautions when it hired that counselor who raped or molested the child? Where are the background checks? Where are the checklists and timesheets that show counselor monitoring? Where are the counselor's reviews? Where is the proof that the seven-year-old was even enrolled in the agency's programs? All that stuff was in Box 2, the contents of which have since been discarded twice as part of the seven-year cycle.

The suggested policy treats records as a costly nuisance with no value to the organization. Those who share this viewpoint should review a number of publications published by ARMA, which provide an excellent framework for assessing the value of particular classes of documents to an organization.

* * *

(l) RETENTION PERIOD RESOURCES. Those charged with developing a record retention policy should examine publications available through ARMA for assistance in constructing retention periods, particularly the legally required retention periods. Donald Skupsky has written a book entitled *Recordkeeping Requirements: The First Practical Guide to Help Your Records ... What You Need to Keep and What You Can Safely Destroy!* The primary problem with this book is that it is now more than ten years old, making some additional legal research necessary. In addition to providing a solid foundation in record retention, the book contains sample retention periods for common business records. Those looking for something more current (but more expensive) should consider Mr. Skupsky's *Legal Requirements for Business Records*, an electronic book that identifies legal retention periods for a wide variety of records and includes the text of the actual statutes regarding retention. Undoubtedly, some law firms have also developed form retention policies that they will be willing to help an organization customize. Those starting down this path should also contact the appropriate trade associations.

People will still demand quick and dirty answers despite the perils of ignoring the preceding analytical framework. The following table should be a good starting point for many organizations (assuming that they review it with their legal counsel before implementing it and recognizing that these are only rules of thumb that need to be tailored to specific jurisdictions and to the organizations operating within them):

Record Source	Record Type	A Reasonable Retention Period
Business records in general	Uniform Preservation of Private Business Records Act	Several states have adopted the Uniform Preservation of Private Business Records Act. For example, Illinois imposes a three-year retention period[a] for business records[b] unless another law expressly provides for another retention period or the conditions on which records may be destroyed. Before designing a program, state law should be reviewed for comparable legislation.
Accounting records	General ledger	Permanently[c]
	Invoices, petty cash receipts, expense records, travel reimbursement and authorization	Depends on demands of internal and external auditors, but these documents may also be included in other categories of documents to be retained
	Records supporting receivables and payables	At a minimum, for a period based on the statute of limitations for the underlying transaction
Bank statements and checks	Routine transactions	At least seven years[d]
Business licenses and permits		See the rules governing specific license; at least through the date of expiration, plus any audit period
Construction documents	Blueprints, plans, designs	At least until the underlying property is disposed of plus any applicable statute of limitations[e]

Record Source	Record Type	A Reasonable Retention Period
Contracts and agreements	Minor contracts entered into in the ordinary course of the organization's activities	At a minimum, for the term of the contract plus the applicable statute of limitations. Remember that contract renewals may refer to earlier contracts and that statutes of limitation vary from state to state.[f]
	Major contracts like acquisition agreements, key licenses, and joint venture agreements	While owned, used, or engaged, plus any relevant statute of limitations. These documents support ownership claims to critical assets.
	Warranties and service contracts	At least one year following the expiration period, or if later, the statute of limitations applicable to the underlying contract
Corporate records	Articles of incorporation and bylaws	Permanently
	Meeting minutes (director and member)	Permanently
	Director consent resolutions	Permanently
	Notices and certificates for annual meetings	Permanently
General correspondence	Routine	At least three years, but always with a focus on whether a particular piece of correspondence is includable in another category that requires a longer retention period, or there is a legally mandated retention period
	Major contracts	Permanently, particularly if there is an ongoing relationship
Environmental records, studies, and filings		Consult with a qualified attorney
Financial statements	Year-end audited financial statements	Permanently
	Monthly or quarterly statements or board summaries	As long as possible, but no less than six years. Typically, this information is computer-generated so it can easily be saved in Adobe Acrobat file format. Organizations should keep these documents indefinitely so they retain the ability to prove a long-standing fraud.
Grants	Generally	For at least the length of the grant and any audit periods, but no less than required by the grant

Record Source	Record Type	A Reasonable Retention Period
	Federal grants subject to OMB Circular A-110	For at least three years from the submission of the final expenditure report, with different rules for awards that are renewed quarterly or annually[g]
Insurance policies	General Liability, errors & omissions, and other policies covering losses	As a general rule, permanently because subsequent policies may refer back to those policies, or occurrences may be covered by those policies
	Property	For at least five years after the disposition of the property
	Material supporting a claim	See policy terms and state law
Records relating to current or future federal investigation		At least until the investigation is complete—indefinitely[h]
Real estate	Deeds	While the property is held, plus the statute of limitations for the transaction involving the disposition of the property[i]
	Title policies	While the property is held plus the latter of (1) period specified immediately above and (2) the expiration of the period for making any claims
	Easements	While the property is held plus the statute of limitations for the transaction involving the disposition of the property[j]
	Leases	While the property is subject to the lease plus any statute of limitations on enforcement
	Checks or wire transfers for major transactions like acquisitions of real property or major equipment	At least for as long as the property is held but preferably permanently
Sales and use tax	Receipts invoices, exemption certificates, and information necessary to prove exemptions	At least until the expiration of the relevant statute of limitations

Record Source	Record Type	A Reasonable Retention Period
	Sales and use tax returns	At least until the expiration of the applicable statute of limitations
Tax documents	Notice of employer and taxpayer ID	Permanently
	IRS Form 1023/1024 and determination letter	Permanently
	Federal tax returns (IRS Form 990)	At least seven years, but keep in mind that prior returns can contain important basis and carry over information, so the longer the better.[k]
	State tax returns	Statute of limitations plus two years.
Trademarks, patents, and copyrights		At least through expiration date, plus any statute of limitations on infringement or related actions.
Employment-related records		
Age Discrimination in Employment Act	Job applications, resumes, promotion, demotion, and transfer documentation, applicant test papers, results of physical exams, and job advertisements	One year from the date of the personnel action to which the record relates.[l]
Davis Bacon Act	Required payroll records maintained by contractors subject to the Act	Three years following the completion of the contract.[m]
Drug and alcohol testing	Positive tests results or refusals to take test, and equipment calibration tests	For at least five years.[n]
	Drug Free Workplace Act	Unspecified.

Record Source	Record Type	A Reasonable Retention Period
EEOC records	Any personnel or employment record, including but not limited to requests for reasonable accommodation, employment application records and any other records having to do with hiring, promotion, demotion, transfer, lay-off or termination, rates of pay or other terms of compensation and selection for training or apprenticeship	For a period of one year from the date of making the records or the date of the personnel action involved, whichever occurs later. In the case of an involuntary termination, the record must be kept for a period of one year from the date of the termination.[o] There may be instances where two years is required[p]
ERISA	Employee benefit plan information, including annual reports and summary plan description	For a minimum of six years after the filing date of such documents.[q]
	Records needed to determine benefits payable under ERISA plans	Until the benefits are fully paid; in other words, indefinitely.[r]
Fair Labor Standards Act	Payroll records, employment contracts, collective bargaining records, and sales and purchase records	For at least three years.[s]
	Records on which wage computations are based (e.g., time cards and piece and work tickets), wage rate tables, and records of additions or deductions from wages paid	For at least two years.[t]

Record Source	Record Type	A Reasonable Retention Period
Family and Medical Leave Act	Information and records pertaining to FMLA leave, including documentation describing policy and dates FMLA leave taken	For at least three years.[u]
FICA and FUTA	Records relating to compliance with the Federal Insurance Contribution Act and the Federal Unemployment Tax Act	For at least four years after the due date of such tax for the return period to which the records relate, or the date such tax is paid, whichever is later.[v]
Immigration	I-9s	For a minimum of three years following the commencement of employment or one year following termination, whichever is later.[w]
OSHA	Records related to job-related illness and injury—OSHA Log 300, Form 301, and annual summary	For a minimum of five years following the year for which the record relates.[x]
	Employee medical records	For a minimum of thirty years following employment.[y]
	Employee exposure records (monitoring exposure to toxic substances)	For a minimum of thirty years.[z]
State Employment and Safety Law	State laws also have employment, anti-discrimination, work safety, and other employment-related record retention requirements	Must review applicable state law. Under no circumstances should anyone assume the state retention period is the same as the federal retention period.

Notes to Table:

a Section 2 of the Illinois Uniform Preservation of Private Business Records Act, which specifically excludes corporate minutes books from the requirements.

b A *record* or *business record* includes "books of account, vouchers, documents, cancelled checks, payrolls, correspondence, records of sales, personnel, equipment and production, reports relating to any and all of such records, and other business papers." Illinois Uniform Preservation of Private Business Records Act § 1

[c] This retention period is much longer than the suggested period in many retention schedules. Given the computerization of accounting records, there does not seem to be a good reason for destroying this information, particularly because portions of it may be helpful in prosecuting a fraud (e.g., employee theft) that has been ongoing for many years. While people are concerned about how records could be damaging if introduced as evidence in litigation, this type of accounting information is factual in nature and numeric. Moreover, at some point in the future if someone is buying assets, as part of due diligence, he may want access to this information.

[d] *Id.*

[e] Consider a nonprofit that has a new building constructed. After five years, it decides to sell the building because it needs a larger facility. As part of that sale, the nonprofit may have to make certain representations and warranties. If the building subsequently collapses (a bit extreme, but there could be a major defect), the buyer might sue the nonprofit for breach of one of the warranties. The nonprofit may have claims against the builder or architect for latent defects or errors in design.

[f] Some states have a four-year statute of limitations on contracts; others have a ten-year period. Neither of these numbers should be viewed as representing maximum or minimums; the law of the applicable state must be reviewed.

[g] Office of Management and Budget, Circular A-110, Uniform Administrative Requirements for Grants and Agreements with Institutions of Higher Education, Hospitals, and Other Non-Profit Organizations, 64 Fed. Reg. 54,926, at ¶ 53 (Sept. 30, 1999).

[h] 18 U.S.C. 1519.

[i] In all likelihood, the deed will be publicly recorded with a register of deeds so there will be a copy in the public records.

[j] *Id.*

[k] There seems to be little reason except space limitations to dispose of tax returns, which should not be too problematic given the typical size of a tax return. As noted in Chapter 6, the three latest returns must be made available to the public on request. One retention schedule specified a seven-year period; another specified a four-year period.

[l] 29 C.F.R. 1627.3(b)(1).

[m] 29 C.F.R. 5.1, 5.5, and 5.6(a)(2).

[n] 49 C.F.R. 382.401. Such testing is required by the United States Department of Transportation. There are other relevant federal regulations. Moreover, there may be state requirements.

[o] 29 C.F.R. 1602.14.

[p] 41 C.F.R. 60-250.80.

[q] Employee Retirement Income Security Act of 1974 (ERISA), Pub. L. No. 93-406, 88 Stat. 829, at §§ 107 and 209 (1974).

[r] 29 U.S.C. 1059.

[s] 29 C.F.R. 516.5.

[t] 29 C.F.R. 516.6.

[u] 29 C.F.R. 825.500; and 29 C.F.R. 516.5.

[v] 26 C.F.R. 31.6001-1(e)(2).

[w] 8 C.F.R. 274a.2.

[x] 29 C.F.R. 1904.33. The record-keeping rules are quite involved. There are partial exemptions from recordkeeping for employers with ten or fewer employees and for businesses in certain industries. See 29 C.F.R. Part 1904, for additional details.

[y] 29 C.F.R. 1910.1020(d)(i). There are a number of exceptions to this rule for more routine issues such as health insurance claims and minor first aid.

[z] 29 C.F.R. 1910.1020(d)(ii). Medical records arising from actual exposure to toxic substances may be subject to the retention rule; *see* 29 C.F.R. 1910.1020(d) (i).

(m) FACTA—METHOD OF DESTROYING "CONSUMER" (EMPLOYEE AND JOB CANDIDATE) INFORMATION. Any nonprofit organization that uses a consumer report for a business purpose is subject to the requirements of the portion of the Fair and Accurate Credit Transactions Act of 2003 (FACTA),[71] which calls for the proper

71. Pub L. 108-159, 117 Stat. 1952, codified at 15 U.S.C. 1681w(a)(1).

disposal of information in consumer reports[72] and records to protect against "unauthorized access to or use of the information." All nonprofits should seriously consider adopting the disposal procedures mandated by FACTA for all sensitive records that they destroy, but the law applies only to information obtained from a consumer reporting company[73] if that information is used—or is expected to be used—in establishing a consumer's eligibility for credit, employment, or insurance, among other purposes. Examples of consumer reports include credit reports, credit scores, and reports businesses or individuals receive that contain information relating to employment background, check-writing history, insurance claims, residential or tenant history, or medical history.

To illustrate, if a nonprofit asks a job applicant to supply a resume or fill out a form, when the nonprofit destroys that document, it need not follow FACTA-mandated procedures. However, if the nonprofit contracts with a third-party agency for a credit check, criminal background check,[74] or employment history, any information the nonprofit receives from that third-party must be destroyed in accordance with procedures mandated by FACTA.

The standard for the proper disposal of information derived from a consumer report is flexible; it permits a nonprofit to determine what measures are reasonable based on the sensitivity of the information, the costs and benefits of different disposal methods, and changes in technology. The following are among the reasonable measures for disposing of consumer report information: (1) burning, pulverizing, or shredding papers containing consumer report information so that the information cannot be read or reconstructed,[75] (2) destroying or erasing electronic files or media containing consumer report information so that the information cannot be read or reconstructed,[76] and (3) retaining a third-party document destruction contractor to dispose of the documents in accordance with FACTA,

---

72. 15 U.S.C. 1681a(d), defining a "consumer report" as follows:

> The term "consumer report" means any written, oral, or other communication of any information by a consumer reporting agency bearing on a consumer's credit worthiness, credit standing, credit capacity, character, general reputation, personal characteristics, or mode of living which is used or expected to be used or collected in whole or in part for the purpose of serving as a factor in establishing the consumer's eligibility for (A) credit or insurance to be used primarily for personal, family, or household purposes; (B) employment purposes; or (C) any other purpose authorized under § 1681b.

73. 15 U.S.C. 1681a(f), defining a "consumer reporting agency" as follows:

> The term "consumer reporting agency" means any person which, for monetary fees, dues, or on a cooperative nonprofit basis, regularly engages in whole or in part in the practice of assembling or evaluating consumer credit information or other information on consumers for the purpose of furnishing consumer reports to third parties, and which uses any means or facility of interstate commerce for the purpose of preparing or furnishing consumer reports.

74. Interestingly, the Federal Trade Commission press release announcing the issuance of regulations under FACTA makes no reference to criminal background checks, but the statutory language defining the terms *consumer report* and *consumer reporting agency* certainly can be construed to encompass such background checks. Therefore, it is wise for any nonprofit to treat these documents as if they are subject to FACTA. *See* Press Release, Federal Trade Commission, FACTA Disposal Rule Goes into Effect June 1 (June 1, 2005).
75. 16 C.F.R. 682.3(b)(1).
76. 16 C.F.R. 882.3(b)(2).

but only if the nonprofit conducts due diligence on the contractor and its procedures.[77] Due diligence includes (1) reviewing an independent audit of a disposal company's operations and/or its compliance with FACTA procedures, (2) obtaining information about the disposal company from several references, (3) requiring that the disposal company be certified by a recognized trade association, or (4) reviewing and evaluating the disposal company's information security policies or procedures.

FACTA addresses the act of destroying the document, focusing on the how it is done. It has nothing to say about the "when." Before destroying any document covered by FACTA, a nonprofit must determine the document's value to the organization and whether any law requires that it be retained.

(n) CONCLUSIONS. The digital world has made document destruction extremely difficult for every organization. The same information may reside on multiple hard drives, located both in and outside the organization, and in file cabinets and home offices. There is no question that every organization must develop and implement a document retention policy, but given the ease of copying, no organization can expect to totally control its documents. Those who view the policy as a way to legally destroy information that could potentially prove to be harmful during the course of litigation or a government investigation must be particularly cognizant of this reality. The criminal laws regarding document destruction are clearly shrinking, if they have not eliminated, the ability of organizations to rid themselves of a smoking gun, particularly once the document has been identified as such. Even assuming that the organization can legally destroy it, the more troublesome the document, the more likely it is that there is a copy outside the organization's control. This brings us back to the central thesis of this *Guide*: Good governance and controls are critical for any nonprofit because there will likely be a clear record when there is wrongdoing. Given the critical need for control and information, a nonprofit's board should ensure that its document retention policy not only preserves documents having value to the organization, but also ensure that the information in those documents is reviewed by the people in the organization who are part of the overall control process.

Mechanics of the ACLU's Document Retention Policy Show the Difficulties in Implementing Any Policy

* * *

The initial reaction to the headline "Concerns at A.C.L.U. over Document Shredding," might well be that there is a scandal or a cover-up.[78] In a week that brought the Supreme

77. 16 C.F.R. 882.3(b)(3).

78. S. Strom, *Concerns at A.C.L.U. over Document Shredding*, N.Y. Times, June 5, 2005.

Court's decision in the Arthur Andersen case and the revelation that Deep Throat was former FBI Deputy Director, Mark Felt, Stephanie Strom of the *New York Times* artfully offered evidence showing why record retention policies are difficult for organizations to design and implement.

Strom's June 5, 2005 article revealed an internal dispute at the ACLU over record retention. The ACLU has a long-standing record retention policy, according Strom's article. As a watch-dog organization, a strong and well-thought-out policy is particularly important: Should not the ACLU be held to the same standards that it demands of everybody else, particularly government officials?[79] Consequently, any diminution in the ACLU's policy is of concern both to the public and those running the ACLU.

For present purposes, the controversy serves to illustrate the problems facing all nonprofits when it comes to record retention policies. The ACLU's policy enumerated documents that could be destroyed without creating a record and those that had to be forwarded to the archivist.[80]

The controversy was sparked when the ACLU began placing shredders throughout its offices several years ago. After policy proved to be controversial, there was a partial reversal of that policy. However, several key officials retained their shredders. An attempt was made to document what was being shredded with these machines, but the *Times* article suggests that the logging procedure did not adequately track everything that was shredded.[81]

Some of the shredding appears to have been motivated by concern over Social Security numbers, salary information, and other personnel information falling into the wrong hands, permitting identify theft. This demonstrates that a variety of factors are at play in any record retention policy. Any organization must retain vital records that are required to be kept by law, but all organizations also have an interest in preventing identity theft. Moreover, all organizations should and must be concerned about cover-ups of clear wrongdoing, be it employment discrimination or national security. Out of those concerns comes what could mistakenly be viewed as a trivial dispute over whether there should be one centralized shredder or a shredder in every office. This seemingly mundane office management issue demonstrates how the simple placement of equipment carries clear signals to the staff. Does the organization place decision authority in every employee's hands, or does it want to send a message that the organization is so serious about its document retention policies that it wants to centralize decision-making authority?

To a certain extent, that entire debate is a red herring. An evildoer does not need a document shredder to destroy documents. Moreover, a mechanical shredder does not address e-mail or computer files, which one recent study said accounted for more than 80 percent of the documents in corporate America. Nevertheless, centralization does send a message and creates an ethic in the workplace: "We take record retention very seriously, so if you get caught destroying evidence as part of a cover-up, do not expect us to stand behind you."

* * *

11.3 AVOIDING OPERATIONAL LIABILITIES FROM EMPLOYMENT PRACTICES

Both anecdotal evidence and a number of surveys identify employment practice litigation as the largest source of liability for nonprofit organizations. This

79. *Id.*
80. *Id.*
81. *Id.*

should not come as a surprise. One federal employment law desk reference refers to 19 major federal labor laws.[82] Anyone who begins to examine these laws will quickly find many other federal laws affecting employment relationships. Federal law clearly has not preempted state employment law, and, in many instances, you will find that state statutes address the same issues. No employer can limit its analysis of minimum wage requirements, whistle-blower protections, or antidiscrimination laws to federal law.

When there are laws, there is litigation. According to one survey, about 60 percent of all United States companies face employee lawsuits annually. For its 2004 fiscal year, the United States Equal Employment Opportunity Commission (EEOC) resolved more than 85,000 employment-related claims, with more than $250 million in payments being awarded to disgruntled employees.[83] These numbers do not include a vast amount of private litigation or actions brought by state regulators. According to a 2004 press release from Jury Verdict Research, an independent firm that compiles and analyzes jury verdict statistics, the national compensatory jury award median for employment practice liability cases was $250,000.[84]

Volunteer directors are sometimes named as defendants in these suits although a volunteer has protection under the federal Volunteer Protection Act, its state analogues, and state nonprofit corporation acts. (See Chapters 4 and 12.) These lawsuits can be brought under federal or state employment laws. The focus here is federal law, including the Fair Labor Standards Act,[85] the Americans with Disabilities Act, the Age Discrimination in Employment Act, and the Family and Medical Leave Act.[86]

(a) EMPLOYMENT AT WILL. Before focusing specifically on a wide number of statutes designed to protect employees, let's first consider an employee's right to a job. Clearly, the terms of an employment or union contract govern whether and under what circumstances an employer can terminate an employee. In the absence of such a contract, most jurisdictions view an employee's employment to be at the will of the employer. In other words, the employer can terminate the employee at the employer's discretion both for cause and without it. This doctrine was originally rooted in the notion that an employment arrangement is a voluntary one and

82. Amy DelPo and Lisa Guerin, Federal Employment Laws: A Desk Reference (Nolo 2002).
83. United States Equal Employment Opportunity Commission, All Statutes FY 1992-FY 2004, *available at* http://www.eeoc.gov/statsall.html.
84. Press Release, Jury Verdict Research, Jury Verdict Research Releases Employment-Practice Liability Study: Employment-Practice Jury Awards Rise 18%, Discrimination Awards Fall Slightly (May 17, 2004).
85. 29 U.S.C. 201 et. seq.
86. 29 U.S.C. 2601 et. seq.

that the employee holds the right to terminate it when the employee sees fit. The courts concluded that employers should have the same right.[87]

One employment-law attorney has noted[88] that too many employers place far too much reliance on this century-old doctrine, ignoring the significant erosion that has taken place over the two decades.[89] According to this attorney, many employers mistakenly believe that they can dismiss at will if they have included language in employment applications and employee handbooks stating that the employment arrangement is at will. These employers fail to recognize the significant body of federal legislation (and state counterparts thereto) that we will consider in this section. For example, state law may permit a nonprofit to dismiss an at-will employee without cause, but federal (and, in all likelihood, state law) prohibits dismissal based on race or marital status. There are also federal and state laws that bar dismissal for whistle-blowing and organizing a union, among other actions. Some jurisdictions also grant certain employees rights when an organization decides to cease existence[90] or leave the jurisdiction.[91] These rights might not prevent dismissal, but they can impose notice and other requirements on the employer.

Quite apart from federal overlays on the doctrine, many jurisdictions have recognized specific exceptions to the at-will rule itself. For example, in many jurisdictions, an at-will employee can bring a wrongful termination lawsuit if the dismissal is against an established public policy.[92] For example, state law may grant an employee the right to bring a wrongful discharge action if the employee is discharged following a refusal to break the law or the filing of a workers' compensation claim.[93]

Probably more troublesome to the average employer is the "implied contract" exception to the employment at-will doctrine. In many jurisdictions, an employer can be sued for wrongful termination of an employee who claims that the employer inadvertently entered into a contract with an employee through oral[94] or written statements.[95] Nonprofits should be careful when using employee

---

87. In Payne v. Western & Atlantic R.R., 81 Tenn. 507 (1884), the court defined the doctrine as follows:

> [Employers] must be left, without interference to buy and sell where they please, and to discharge or retain employees at will for good cause or bad cause, or even for bad cause without thereby being guilty of an unlawful act per se. It is a right which an employee may exercise in the same way, to the same extent, for the same cause or want of cause as the employer.

88. J. Burns, *The Top Ten Ways to Guarantee Employee Lawsuits*, 27 EMPLOYEE RELATIONS L. J., at 84 (Winter 2001).
89. D. Ballam, *Employment-At-Will: The Impending Death of a Doctrine*, 37 AM. BUS. L. J. 653 (2000).
90. For example, the Worker Adjustment and Retraining and Notification Act, codified at 29 U.S.C. 2101-2109, requires certain employers to give notification regarding certain layoffs.
91. *See, e.g.*, Conn. Gen. State, Title 31, Chapter 555, §§s 31-51n and o.
92. See C. Muhl, *The Employment-At-Will Doctrine: Three Major Exceptions*, MONTHLY LABOR REV. (Jan. 2001), for a list of these jurisdictions as of October 1, 2000.
93. Palmateer v. International Harvester Company, 85 Ill.2d 124, 421 N.E.2d 876 (1981); and Petermann v. International Brotherhood of Teamsters, 174 Cal.App.2d 184 (1959).
94. Toussaint v. Blue Cross & Blue Shield of Michigan, 408 Mich. 579, 292 N.W.2d 880 (1980). The oral statements in this case pertained to job security.
95. Pine River State Bank v. Mettilee, 333 N.W.2d 622 (1983). The written statements also pertained to job security and appeared in an employee handbook.

handbooks, particularly ones based on standard forms, because of the variations in their legal status in different jurisdictions. For example, some jurisdictions may respect disclaimers but others may not. In one instance, a handbook contained a disclaimer (declaring an at-will relationship) but it also contained a three-step disciplinary procedure.[96] The court held that the employees were at-will employees but were entitled to the benefits provided by the procedure. Similarly, some courts have held that a list of specific grounds for dismissal can preclude an employer from dismissing an employee for other reasons.[97] Along these same lines, organizations that use probationary periods should ask the following two questions: (1) If our employees are truly at-will employees, why is there a need for a probationary period? and (2) Does the existence of a probationary period have implications for the classification of employees who are no longer on probation?

The third exception to the at-will doctrine is based on an implied covenant of good faith and fair dealing—with about one-fifth of the states recognizing this exception.[98] In essence, this exception imposes a duty of good faith and fair dealing when an employee has performed his duties admirably and given the employer no basis for the dismissal.[99] Not surprisingly, of the three exceptions, this is the one that has gained favor in the fewest jurisdictions. This exception is generally invoked when the employer terminates the employee to deprive the employee of benefits that are close to "vesting,"[100] but this is not the only basis.[101]

Although a nonprofit's employees may be at-will employees, the exceptions to the at-will doctrine, as well as a patchwork of federal and state employment regulations, provide practical limits on the ability of the nonprofit to terminate an employee without being subjected to litigation. This means that a nonprofit employer must handle all employment decisions, particularly termination decisions, with care and foresight. Let's now consider several important components in that patchwork of statutory laws that grant even at-will employees certain rights and limit employer rights.

(b) FEDERAL ANTIDISCRIMINATION STATUTES. An employee who believes that he has been the subject of discrimination can look to what is referred to as *Section 1981*[102] or to Title VII of the Civil Rights Act of 1964.[103]

96. Butler v. Walker Power, 137 N.H. 432, 629 A.2d 91 (1993).
97. For a general discussion, see Mark Rothstein, Charles Craver, Elinor Schroeder, and Elaine Shoben, Employment Law, at 749-51 (Thomson West 2004).
98. *Id.*, at 765.
99. K-mart Corporation v. Ponsock, 103 Nev. 39, 732 P.2d 1364 (1987).
100. Mark Rothstein, Charles Craver, Elinor Schroeder, and Elaine Shoben, *supra* note 97, at 765-67.
101. *See, e.g.*, Merrill v. Crothall-American, 606 A.2d 96 (Del. 1992), involving an employee who was placed in a vacant position with the understanding that he would hold the position indefinitely. However, he was fired when the employer found the permanent replacement that the employer had begun looking for beginning two days after the fired employee had originally filled the vacant position.
102. 42 U.S.C. 1981.
103. 42 U.S.C. 2000; and 29 C.F.R. 1600 et seq.

(i) Section 1981. Section 1981 is the more open ended of the two federal laws prohibiting discrimination because it is not administered by a federal agency. An employee who has a complaint simply files a lawsuit in federal court. Given its enactment immediately following the end of the Civil War, Section 1981 focuses, not surprisingly, on racial discrimination. It has been interpreted to include ethnic discrimination.[104] Section 1981 applies to all employers regardless of size and covers all workers. It focuses on contracts in general, not just employment relationships. Consequently, Section 1981 covers work-based relationships that may not be defined as employment (e.g., a partner in a law or accounting firm or an independent contractor). There is a question as to whether at-will employees (those without a contract) are covered by Section 1981, although the majority of courts apply Section 1981 to such arrangements.[105] Section 1981 has been interpreted to (1) prohibit race-based discrimination in hiring, promotion, or discharge practices, (2) compensation, and (3) conditions and privileges of employment. It has also been extended by Congress to cover racial harassment in the workplace.[106] Finally, for the statute to be applicable, the discrimination must be intended; that is, a showing of discriminatory impact without intent or purpose to discriminate is insufficient under Section 1981.[107]

(ii) Title VII of the Civil Rights Act of 1964. A number of other federal laws prohibit discrimination in the workplace, but the first one to specifically address employment was Title VII of the Civil Rights Act of 1964.[108] It applies to all private employers with 15 or more employees.[109]

BASIS FOR FINDING DISCRIMINATION

For the most basic action for discrimination under the Civil Rights Act of 1964, a person must establish each of the following three facts: (1) the person is a member of a protected class, (2) the person was subject to an adverse employment action, and (3) the adverse action occurred because the person was a member of a protected class.[110] Title VII prohibits discrimination based on "race, color, religion, sex, or national origin." Discrimination based on age and disability is addressed in other federal statutes. Title VII currently does not prohibit discrimination on the basis of sexual orientation, but some state laws do.

Employers clearly cannot discriminate when they make a hiring decision, but the term *adverse employment action* encompasses many more types of decisions,

---

104. St. Francis College v. Al-Khazraji, 481 U.S. 604 (1987).
105. THOMAS HAGGARD, UNDERSTANDING EMPLOYMENT DISCRIMINATION, at 144 (LexisNexis 2000).
106. See 42 U.S.C. 1981(b) added by Congress to overrule Patterson v. McClean Credit Union, 491 U.S. 164 (1989).
107. General Building Contractors Association v. Pennsylvania, 458 U.S. 375 (1982).
108. 42 U.S.C. 2000e, et. seq.
109. 42 U.S.C.2000e-(b). As a technical matter, the employer "must be engaged in industry affecting commerce." Nonprofits should not be misled by the reference to "commerce." As the courts have interpreted this phrase, virtually every entity will be deemed to "affect commerce."
110. 42 U.S.C. 2000e-2(a)(1).

including decisions affecting (1) termination, (2) compensation, assignment, or employee classification, (3) transfer, promotion, layoff, or recall, (4) testing, (5) use of company facilities, (6) training, (7) fringe benefits, (8) pay, retirement plans, and disability leave, and (9) other terms and conditions of employment.[111] The fact that someone is terminated or does not receive the same pay as someone else, however, is not sufficient to bring legal action. The employer's reason for taking the adverse employment action must be because the employee or applicant was a member of a protected class. An employer defends against a charge of discrimination by showing that the employee failed to establish one or more of the three factual conditions necessary for a cause of action. This typically means demonstrating that the adverse employment action was based on legitimate nondiscriminatory motivations, but the reasons cannot be pretextual—in other words, empty arguments that mask the employer's true motivations.

Employee lawsuits claiming discrimination take two basic forms. Under the first, an individual alleges an act of discrimination. To prove his case, the employee can use direct evidence (e.g., a letter from an employer stating that the employer does not hire women) or indirect evidence. Cases involving indirect evidence have an elaborate set of burden-shifting rules.[112] This is where the issue of pretext arises. Under the second form,[113] a group of individuals claims that the employer has discriminated against them as a class. Here the parties focus on statistical evidence as well as conduct that is "fair in form, but discriminatory in operation."[114] It should not be surprising that the law in this area is vast and complex with multifaceted tests and analysis. Those interested in delving deeper are advised to examine an employment law treatise for the details.[115]

Federal law also forbids sexual harassment[116] and discrimination based on disability,[117] age (age 40 or more),[118] and pregnancy.[119] The law also makes it illegal to retaliate against an individual for filing a charge of discrimination, taking part in an investigation of possible employment discrimination, or opposing discriminatory practices.[120]

All organizations should recognize that even at the federal level, the laws against discrimination are a patchwork and that the rules applying to different forms of discrimination have discrepancies. In one sense, the easiest way to avoid trouble is not to discriminate. Unfortunately, even employers with the

---

111. 42 U.S.C. 2000e-2(a).
112. McDonnell Douglas Corp. v. Green, 411 U.S. 792 (1973).
113. These suits are based on a violation of 29 U.S.C. 2000e-2(a)(2).
114. Griggs v. Duke Power, 401 U.S. 424 (1971).
115. *See, e.g.*, Mark Rothstein, Charles Craver, Elinor Schroeder, and Elaine Shoben, *supra* note 97. For a more detailed version of this book, see the version published by Thomson West as part of its Practitioner Treatise Series.
116. Meritor Savings Bank, FSB v. Vinson, 477 U.S. 57 (1986). See 29 C.F.R. 1604.11 for additional details.
117. Americans with Disabilities Act of 1990, which is codified at 42 U.S.C. 12101 et. seq.
118. The Age Discrimination in Employment Act, which is codified at 29 U.S.C. 621 et. seq.
119. Pregnancy Discrimination Act, which is codified at 42 U.S.C. 2000e(k).
120. 29 U.S.C. 2000e-3.

best of intentions can become the subject of a lawsuit because of a supervisor's actions, inadvertent language in an employee handbook, or a policy with unintended disparate impact. Consequently, these discrepancies can become important. For example, the prohibition against raced-based discrimination applies to employers with 15 or more employees, but the law against aged-based discrimination applies to employers with 20 or more employees.[121] In short, our brief discussion of the issues surrounding discrimination is just that—brief. The nonprofit needs an expert on its team if it is to successfully avoid lawsuits in this area. That expert may be someone in its human resources department or outside counsel.

Exemption for Religious Discrimination

Religious organizations have legitimate reasons for discriminating on the basis of religious affiliation. Congress recognized this fact, adding the following exemption to Title VII:

> This subchapter shall not apply ... to a religious corporation, association, educational institution or society with respect to the employment of individuals of a particular religion to perform work connected with the carrying on by such corporation, association, educational institution, or society of its activities.[122]

The Supreme Court has interpreted this exemption as being available even when the position in question is not religious in nature.[123] For example, a religious organization could require a janitor to be an adherent to its religious doctrine without having engaged in otherwise prohibited discrimination under Title VII. The Court first acknowledged that Congress had refused to distinguish between secular and nonsecular positions, and then upheld that refusal as reasonable in order to avoid entangling the courts in line drawing. Of course, any organization taking advantage of this exemption must review applicable state law. This provision does not permit religious organizations to engage in other forms of discrimination, such as that based on race or gender. This discussion addresses only permitted religious discrimination in employment, which was considered also in Chapter 8.

The Claims Process

To the extent that the claim is brought under federal law, the claimant must first file with the EEOC (except for charges brought under the Equal Pay Act).[124] For Fiscal Year 2004, the EEOC reported that 79,432 charges had been filed with it.[125] Roughly 35 percent of these charges were race-based and 30 percent were

---

121. 29 U.S.C. 630(b).
122. 42 U.S.C. 2000e-1(a).
123. Corporation of Presiding Bishop v. Amos, 483 U.S. 327 (1987).
124. Statement posted on the United States Equal Employment Opportunity Commission Web site, *available at* http://www.eeoc.gov/charge/overview_charge_filing.html (viewed Aug. 30, 2005).
125. Statistics posted on the United States Equal Employment Opportunity Commission Web site, *available at* http://www.eeoc.gov (viewed Mar. 22, 2005).

sex-based.[126] On an annual basis, the EEOC takes to court between 350 and 450 claims on behalf of complainants.[127] It notifies the employer within ten days after a complaint is filed.

The EEOC performs a "triage" on the complaints it receives, first investigating instances in which discrimination is likely to have occurred. It has a mediation program and may ask the parties to voluntary agree to participate in it to resolve the dispute. If the case proceeds without mediation, the EEOC continues to investigate and either concludes that discrimination occurred or closes the case. If the EEOC finds discrimination, it will seek a remedy for the employee through conciliation. If that is not successful, the EEOC has the right to file a lawsuit against the employer. If the EEOC closes the case because it does not find any discrimination, it issues a "Right to Sue Letter," starting the 90-day period during which the employee can file a suit.[128]

The employee can also seek redress under applicable state employment laws. These laws may also provide for an administrative process. This greatly complicates the matter, but the EEOC and the states have worked out accords to minimize duplicate investigations and costs to all involved.

Court Proceedings

The EEOC's administrative process resolves the dispute without the need to file a lawsuit in the majority of the cases. When a matter proceeds to federal court, the employer often makes a motion for summary judgment. The judge then examines the complaint by assuming all the factual allegations are true. If the judge determines that the employee has failed to state a viable claim based on that assumption, the case will be dismissed. If the judge determines that the claim is viable, a trial is scheduled.

Remedies

An employee may seek hiring, reinstatement, reasonable accommodation, promotion, back pay, front pay, or other relief that will make him "whole" if discrimination is demonstrated. Remedies also may include reimbursement for legal and expert witness fees and court costs. Under most laws enforced by the EEOC, the employee can seek damages for intentional discrimination for actual monetary losses, future monetary losses, and mental suffering and inconvenience. Punitive damages are available if the employer acted with malice or reckless indifference.[129]

(c) FAIR LABOR STANDARDS ACT. The Fair Labor Standards Act (FLSA) imposes a variety of rules on employers, including nonprofits. In addition to setting minimum

---

126. *Id.*
127. *Id.*
128. 29 C.F.R. 1601.28
129. Statement posted on the United States Equal Employment Opportunity Commission Web site, *available at* http://www.eeoc.gov/charge/overview_charge_processing.html (viewed Aug. 30, 2005).

wage and overtime rates, the act also regulates the employment of children and various other matters.

(i) Covered Employers. The FLSA does not contain a blanket exemption for Section 501(c)(3) organizations or other types of nonprofits. Moreover, even if a nonprofit is not covered by the FLSA, it should make sure that no state counterparts are applicable to the organization.

The rules defining coverage are complex and are anything but straightforward; their focus is interstate commerce, revenue levels, and employee activities.[130] Unless a nonprofit affirmatively determines that it is not subject to the FLSA, it should assume that it is, recognizing that this assumption is likely to be correct. Those who are inclined to "play close to the line" on this issue should be extremely cautious, as this excerpt from a 2001 memorandum prepared by the United States Administration for Children and Families suggests:

> Although it has been generally understood that grantees which are public agencies are subject to the FLSA, there has been some lack of clarity about the applicability of the FLSA to grantees that are private non-profit or for-profit agencies. After consultation with the United States Department of Labor (United states DOL), we have now established that private non-profit and for-profit agencies operating Head Start or Early Head Start programs are subject to the requirements of the FLSA by virtue of being engaged in the operation of a "pre-school." In addition, we have learned that over the past year, several private, non-profit Head Start grantees have been found out of compliance with FLSA standards and have been required to take corrective action, *including payment of back wages to employees.*[131]

---

130. To illustrate, Section 206 of Title 29 of the United States Code requires that employers pay a minimum wage to an "employee who in any work week is engaged in commerce or in the production of goods for commerce, or is employed in an enterprise engaged in commerce or in the production of goods for commerce." Section 203(s)(1) defines "Enterprise engaged in commerce or in the production of goods for commerce" as an enterprise that:

> (A)(i) has employees engaged in commerce or in the production of goods for commerce, or that has employees handling, selling, or otherwise working on goods or materials that have been moved in or produced for commerce by any person; and (ii) is an enterprise whose annual gross volume of sales made or business done is not less than $500,000 (exclusive of excise taxes at the retail level that are separately stated);
>
> (B) is engaged in the operation of a hospital, an institution primarily engaged in the care of the sick, the aged, or the mentally ill or defective who reside on the premises of such institution, a school for mentally or physically handicapped or gifted children, a preschool, elementary or secondary school, or an institution of higher education (regardless of whether or not such hospital, institution, or school is public or private or operated for profit or not for profit); or
>
> (C) is an activity of a public agency.

Nonprofits should not focus too heavily on the notion of "commerce" because it is much broader than its possible plain meaning might suggest. Those who regularly use the phone or mails can be deemed to be engaged in commerce.

131. Administration for Children and Families of the United States Department of Health and Human Services, Applicability of the Fair Labor Standards Act (FLSA) to Head Start and Early Head Start Grantees (May 3, 2001).

(ii) Hours and Overtime Rates. As noted, the FLSA sets minimum wage and overtime standards applicable to hourly and certain salaried employees.[132] The FLSA distinguishes between "exempt" and "nonexempt" workers.[133] Employers are required to pay nonexempt workers a minimum hourly wage plus overtime when the work week exceeds 40 hours. Currently, the federally mandated minimum wage is $5.15 per hour,[134] but each state has an analogue to the FLSA, and some states set a higher minimum wage.[135]

(iii) Exempt and Nonexempt Employees. The critical issue for any employer is correctly classifying workers as exempt or nonexempt employees. There are a number of categories of exempt employee including several that are of particular interest to certain nonprofits. For example, employees of certain camps and religious or nonprofit educational conference centers are exempt from the minimum wage and maximum hour requirements.[136] Certain resident house parents are also exempt but only from the maximum hour requirement (not to the minimum wage requirements).[137]

Probably the most important exemption is for certain executive, administrative, and professional personnel,[138] including certain computer professionals[139] and outside salespeople.[140] Under Department of Labor classification tests, an employee is considered to be an exempt employee if the employee's employment satisfies each of the following tests: (1) the employee is paid a predetermined and fixed salary, not an hourly wage that is subject to reductions because of variations in the quality or quantity of work performed (the "Salary Basis" test),[141] (2) the amount of salary paid meets minimum specified amounts (the "Salary Level" test),[142] and (3) the employee's job duties primarily involve managerial, administrative, or professional skills as defined by Department of Labor regulations (the "Duties" test).[143] Anyone who relies on this simple statement of the exemption is making a serious mistake because of the breadth of the regulations. The regulations contain specific rules pertaining to executives, administrative employees, learned professionals, creative professionals, teachers, those with

132. 29 U.S.C. 201, et. seq.
133. 29 U.S.C. 213(a).
134. 29 U.S.C. 206.
135. The Department of Labor Web site includes a list of the minimum wages for each state. *See* UNITED STATES EQUAL EMPLOYMENT OPPORTUNITY COMMISSION, *supra* note 125. As an example, according the Department of Labor, the District of Columbia has set the minimum wage at $7.00 (as of Feb. 1, 2006), but check for changes.
136. 29 U.S.C. 213(a)(3).
137. 29 U.S.C. 213(b)(24).
138. 29 U.S.C. 213(a)(1). The regulations outlining the details of this exemption can be found in Part 541 of Title 29 of the Code of Federal Regulations.
139. 29 C.F.R. 541.400.
140. 29 C.F.R. 541.500.
141. 29 C.F.R. 541.602.
142. 29 C.F.R. 541.600.
143. 29 C.F.R. 541.100 through. 504.

concurrent duties, and many other individuals who under some circumstances could be considered to fall within the "executive, administrative, and professional" rubric. Just to provide a sense of the type of analysis that might be required, consider the exemption for creative professionals. The head of an advertising agency's "art concepts" department may qualify for exemption as a creative professional, but the $20 per hour graphic artist who designs layouts based on sketches and specifications provided probably does not qualify for the exemption.[144] Classifying employees can be particularly difficult in the case of part-time employees and administrative assistants.

(iv) The Work Week—Regular Rate. Employers have also discovered that correctly calculating an employee's regular (hourly) rate for overtime can be difficult. The hourly rate is not necessarily the stated dollars paid per hour; certain nondiscretionary payments, which can include annual and retention bonuses, must also be considered, depending on how such payments are structured.[145] The regulations include extensive discussions regarding the classification of bonuses.[146]

For purposes of measuring whether more than 40 hours are worked during a work week, *work week* is defined as a fixed and regularly recurring period of 168 hours (seven consecutive 24-hour periods). Thus, the period need not coincide with a calendar week.[147] Averaging of work weeks is not permitted, so working 20 hours one week and 60 hours the next week does not eliminate the employee's right to overtime for the 60-hour week.[148] The FLSA does not require that overtime be paid just because the work occurs on a Saturday, Sunday, or holiday.[149] Nor does it preclude the payment of compensation in the form of a salary, but it does require that regular rate (calculated from the salary) be at least equal to the minimum wage rate.[150]

(v) Illustration. To illustrate a classic problem under the FLSA, consider Greenburg Social Services, a Section 501(c)(3) organization. It has 25 employees, including Jerry Wiseman, the administrative assistant to Wendy Jones, Greenburg's executive director. Wiseman is a salaried employee earning $45,000 per year. He runs Greenburg on a day-to-day basis while Jones is out fundraising and making speeches. Jones schedules a 90-minute meeting with Wiseman each day, during which he informs her about operational matters and she instructs him

---

144. 29 C.F.R. 541.302.
145. 29 U.S.C. 207(e) defines the regular rate as being based on all enumeration paid to the employee, but excluding eight specific items. Qualified wage payments are defined in Part 531 of Title 29 to the Code of Federal Regulations.
146. 29 C.F.R. 778.208 et. seq.
147. 29 C.F.R. 778.105.
148. 29 C.F.R. 778.104.
149. 29 C.F.R. 778.113.
150. 29 C.F.R. 778.109.

about what he should focus on. Wiseman is very busy and often works through lunch while he reviews reports and writes letters for Jones's signature.

Jones takes a position with a much larger social services agency at double her current pay. Wiseman had always hoped to assume Jones's position, but the Greenburg board brings in Tanya Treadwell as the new executive director. Shortly after Treadwell assumes her new role, Wiseman leaves Greenburg under controversial circumstances. He brings legal action against Greenburg, alleging that it violated FLSA regulations. He claims that he was not an exempt employee because he did not actually exercise discretion and independent judgment with respect to matters of significance[151] but only did what Jones told him to do. He now wants time and a half for all the lunch hours, nights, and weekends he worked.

This type of suit, particularly if a number of employees are involved, can be a nightmare for an agency with a very tight budget, so its board must make sure that the human resources department or other appropriate individual is up to date on FLSA compliance. Any compliance program should mandate an annual (or more frequent) review of FLSA compliance and employee classifications and the person responsible for FLSA compliance should make an annual report to the board. As in all employment-related matters, the organization needs to be cognizant of applicable state requirements.

(vi) Job Training. Some nonprofits run job-training programs. Although they may not consider their unpaid trainees as employees, these individuals may be considered employees for purposes of the FLSA. Long ago, the Supreme Court set out a six-factor test to avoid having a trainee classified as an employee under the FLSA.[152] The following are the relevant factors:

- The training must be similar to that which would be given in a vocational school, although it includes actual operation of the facilities of the employer.
- The training must be for the benefit of the trainees.
- The trainees cannot displace regular employees but should work under their close observation.
- The employer that provides the training must derive no immediate advantage from the activities of the trainees. Although apparently not an absolute requirement, the case for nonemployee status is improved if the training on occasion actually impedes operations.
- The trainees must not necessarily be entitled to a job at the conclusion of the training period.

---

151. 29 C.F.R. 541.200(a)(3).

152. Walling v. Portland Terminal Company, 330 U.S. 148 (1947). The Department of Labor continues to rely on this test. *See, e.g.*, United States Department of Labor, Opinion Letter FLSA 2004-16: Pre-employment Training and Employment Relationship (Oct. 19, 2004).

- The employer and the trainees must understand that the trainees are not entitled to wages for the time spent in training.

The issues surrounding training programs can be complex in the case of so-called welfare-to-work laws programs because of the interactions between the FLSA, other federal statutes, and state and local laws.

(vii) Child Labor Laws. The FLSA also regulates employment of individuals who are under 18 (child labor), dividing the labor into farm and nonfarm.[153] For nonfarm work, a nonprofit subject to the FLSA employing children is subject to the following limitations on child labor.

- Sixteen- and seventeen-year-olds may perform any nonhazardous job for unlimited hours.[154]
- Fourteen- and fifteen-year-olds may work outside school hours in various nonmanufacturing, nonmining, nonhazardous jobs under the following conditions: no more than 3 hours on a school day, 18 hours in a school week, 8 hours on a nonschool day, or 40 hours in a nonschool week.[155] These youngsters may not begin work before 7 AM or end after 7 PM, except from June 1 through Labor Day, when evening hours are extended to 9 PM.

Under a special provision, 14- and 15-year-olds enrolled in an approved Work Experience and Career Exploration Program (WECEP) may be employed for up to 23 hours during school weeks and 3 hours on school days (including during school hours).[156] There are special exceptions to these age limitations for certain activities, including gathering evergreens and making evergreen wreaths. Every organization must also make sure that it is complying with applicable state laws that can be even more restrictive.

By regulation, employers must keep records of the dates of birth of employees under age 19, their daily starting and quitting times, their daily and weekly hours of work, and their occupations.[157] Employers may protect themselves from unintentional violation of the child labor provisions by keeping on file an employment or age certificate for each young worker to show that the youth is the minimum age for the job.[158] Certificates issued under most state laws are acceptable for this purpose.

(d) FAMILY AND MEDICAL LEAVE ACT. In 1993, Congress enacted the Family and Medical Leave Act (FMLA),[159] granting eligible employees up to a total of 12

153. 29 U.S.C. 203(l) and 212.
154. 29 C.F.R. 570.117 and 118.
155. 29 C.F.R. 570.35.
156. 29 C.F.R. 570.35a.
157. 29 C.F.R. 516.2(a).
158. UNITED STATES DEPARTMENT OF LABOR, EMPLOYMENT LAW GUIDE, at 19 (Publication OASP-01, Apr. 2003).
159. 29 U.S.C. 2601, et. seq.

work weeks of unpaid leave during any 12-month period for (1) childbirth or adoption, and care of a newborn, (2) care of an immediate family member (spouse, child, or parent) with a serious health condition, and (3) medical leave when the employee is unable to work because of a serious health condition.[160] In the case of childbirth and adoption, the child must be the employee's. Leave to care for a newborn child or for a newly placed child must conclude within 12 months after the birth or placement.[161] Leave under the FMLA is unpaid.

The FMLA applies to most employers who employ 50 or more employees for each working day during each of 20 or more calendar workweeks in the current or preceding calendar year.[162] Only employees who have been employed by the employer for at least 12 months, have been employed for at least 1,250 hours of service during the 12-month period immediately preceding the commencement of the leave, and are employed at a qualified work site are eligible for leave under the FMLA.[163] A qualified work site is a location or within 75 miles of a location where at least 50 employees are employed.[164] The 1,250 hours include only hours actually worked for the nonprofit.[165] Paid leave and unpaid leave, including FMLA leave, are not included.[166]

A *serious health condition* includes an illness, injury, impairment, or physical or mental condition that involves impatient care or continuing treatment as outlined in applicable regulations.[167] Ordinarily, unless complications arise,[168] the common cold, flu, earache, upset stomachs, and normal dental disease are not considered serious illnesses. Substance abuse can be a serious health condition, but absence because of an employee's use of the substance, rather than for treatment, does not qualify for FMLA leave.[169]

While the leave is unpaid, an employer is required to maintain group health insurance coverage, including family coverage, for an employee on FMLA leave on the same terms as if the employee had continued to work.[170] Thus, an employer who paid 60 percent of the health insurance premium for the employee under a plan must continue to pay 60 percent of the premium during the FMLA leave.[171]

---

160. 29 C.F.R. 2612(a)(1).
161. 29 C.F.R. 825.201.
162. 29 U.S.C. 2611(4).
163. 29 U.S.C. 2611(2)(A).
164. 29 U.S.C. 26111(2)(B).
165. 29 C.F.R. 825.110(c). The calculation of the hours is made using the principles established under the Fair Labor Standards Act.
166. Question and Answers at the Department of Labor Web Site at http://www.dol.gov/elaws/esa/fmla/faq.asp.
167. 29 C.F.R. 825.114.
168. Miller v. ATT Corp, 250 F.3d 820 (4th Cir. 2001).
169. 29 C.F.R. 825.114(d).
170. 29 C.F.R. 825.209.
171. 29 C.F.R. 825.210.

The FMLA may be good social policy, but it poses potential problems for any employer because, by and large, it does not consider the employer's needs in determining whether leave is available to an eligible employee. The employee's work must still be performed while he is on leave. This may mean temporary hires or paying regular staff overtime and can quickly become an expensive proposition for a nonprofit with an already constrained budget. Failure to comply, however, can result in litigation, so the board and executive director should make sure that the human resources department or appropriate administrative person is aware of FMLA requirements.

The FMLA permits employees to take leave on an intermittent or reduced basis.[172] Intermittent leave is leave taken in separate blocks of time due to a single qualifying reason. A reduced leave schedule is a leave schedule that reduces an employee's usual number of working hours per work week, or hours per workday. A reduced leave schedule is a change in the employee's schedule for a period of time, normally from full-time to part-time. Leave for periodic chemotherapy (several days a month) or physical therapy (a bi-weekly session) are two examples of intermittent leave.

As noted, FMLA leave is unpaid, but employees may choose or employers may require the employee to use accrued paid leave to cover some or all of the FMLA leave taken.[173] Accrued paid vacation or personal leave can substitute for any of the situations covered by the FMLA. The substitution is limited by the employer's policies governing the use of such leave. If an employee were entitled to 12 sick days per year and took three days off in January for the flu, the employee would still be entitled to his full 12 weeks of FMLA leave, assuming neither the employer nor the employee designated the three days as FMLA leave. FMLA leave and workers' compensation leave can run together, provided that the reason for the absence is due to a qualifying serious illness or injury and the employer properly notifies the employee in writing that the leave will be counted as FMLA leave.[174]

An employee must provide the nonprofit at least 30 days' advance notice before an FMLA leave is to begin if the need for the leave is foreseeable based on an expected birth, placement for adoption or foster care, or planned medical treatment for a serious health condition of the employee or of a family member.[175] If 30 days' notice is not practicable because of the lack of knowledge of when leave will be required to begin, a change in circumstances, or a medical emergency, notice must be given as soon as practicable.

172. 29 C.F.R. 825.203.
173. 29 C.F.R. 825.207.
174. 29 C.F.R. 825.207(d)(2).
175. 29 C.F.R. 825.302.

A nonprofit may require a medical certification issued by the employee's health care provider when a leave is predicated on "serious illness."[176] The FMLA provides the nonprofit the opportunity to contest the certification through additional determinations, but the certification process is structured to discourage the nonprofit from contesting the basis for leave unless there is serious concern with fraud.[177]

From the nonprofit's standpoint, the most important requirement may be the one requiring the employer to notify the employee in writing that the requested time off will be counted toward the annual FMLA allowance.[178] There had been much litigation as to whether the employee was entitled to additional time if the employer failed to give the notice. The Supreme Court finally ruled that no additional time had to be provided.[179] However, the Court's opinion indicated that in some instances a failure to give notice could so prejudice the employee's rights so as to warrant a different result.[180] The Court also noted that the FLMA does provide for equitable relief. Consequently, a well-counseled organization should always provide the notice.

An employer is permitted to choose any one of the following methods for determining the "12-month period" in which the 12 weeks of leave entitlement occurs: (1) the calendar year, (2) any fixed 12-month "leave year," such as a fiscal year, a year required by state law, or a year starting on an employee's "anniversary" date, (3) the 12-month period measured forward from the date an employee's first FMLA leave begins, or (4) a "rolling" 12-month period measured backward from the date an employee uses any FMLA leave.[181] From the employer's standpoint, the last two options are preferable. To see why, consider the nonprofit that takes the most obvious course by selecting the calendar year. This would permit an employee to begin a leave on October 12, 2005, end it on December 31, 2005, and then begin a new 12-week leave beginning January 1,

---

176. 29 C.F.R. 825.305.

177. 29 C.F.R. 825.307.

178. 29 C.F.R. 825.301(c).

179. Ragsdale v. Wolverine World Wide, Inc., 535 U.S. 81 (2002).

180. The Court did note the availability of equitable relief under § 2617 of the FLMA. It also stated:

> Section 825.700(a), Ragsdale contends, reflects the Secretary's understanding that an employer's failure to comply with the designation requirement might sometimes burden an employee's exercise of basic FMLA rights in violation of §2615. Consider, for instance, the right under §2612(b)(1) to take intermittent leave when medically necessary. An employee who undergoes cancer treatments every other week over the course of 12 weeks might want to work during the off weeks, earning a paycheck and saving six weeks for later. If she is not informed that her absence qualifies as FMLA leave–and if she does not know of her right under the statute to take intermittent leave–she might take all 12 of her FMLA-guaranteed weeks consecutively and have no leave remaining for some future emergency. In circumstances like these, Ragsdale argues, the employer's failure to give the notice required by the regulation could be said to "deny," "restrain," or "interfere with" the employee's exercise of her right to take intermittent leave.
>
> This position may be reasonable, but the more extreme one embodied in §825.700(a) is not.

See Duty v. Norton-Alcoa Proppants, 293 F.3d 481 (8th Cir. 2002), for a possibly illustrative case.

181. 29 C.F.R. 825.200(b).

2006. A rolling period would prevent this back-to-back planning. If the employer fails to choose one of the permitted measuring periods, the employee is permitted to use the period that provides the employee the most favorable outcome.[182]

Upon return from FMLA leave, an employee must be restored to his original job or an "equivalent" job, which means virtually identical to the original job in terms of pay, benefits, and other employment terms and conditions.[183] This can be difficult for employers when, during the course of the leave, they learn for one reason or another that the employee on leave was incompetent. Consider a bookkeeper who takes 12 weeks of FMLA for a heart transplant. If the temporary replacement discovers that the bookkeeper was stealing money or had made no accounting entries for the last eight months, the employer can terminate the bookkeeper during the leave period without violating the FMLA. On the other hand, the employer cannot terminate the bookkeeper just because it prefers the temporary bookkeeper and would like to hire that person as a permanent replacement. Every employer should consult an employment attorney before terminating any employee on FMLA leave, even one who is discovered to have been stealing or grossly incompetent.

Under an important exception, an employer may deny job restoration to salaried eligible employees, referred to as *key employees,* if such denial is necessary to prevent substantial and grievous economic injury to the nonprofit's operations.[184] A key employee is a salaried FMLA-eligible employee who is among the highest paid 10 percent of all the employees employed by the nonprofit within 75 miles of the employee's work site. Those interested in denying restoration to a key employee should look closely at the definition of *substantial and grievous economic injury* in the regulations and relevant case law.

There will be cases when the employee uses up the FMLA 12-week allotment but needs more time before returning to work. As a practical matter, the employer probably does not want to quibble over three additional days if the request is legitimate. However, suppose that the serious medical illness will persist for 12 more weeks or indefinitely. In this case, the employee has no rights under the FMLA to restoration to the former or another position.[185] However, the employer's obligations may be governed by the Americans with Disabilities Act, discussed next.

(e) AMERICANS WITH DISABILITIES ACT. The Americans with Disabilities Act (ADA)[186] prohibits employers from discriminating against qualified individuals with disabilities in job application procedures, hiring, firing, advancement,

---

182. 29 C.F.R. 825.200(e).
183. 29 C.F.R. 825.214.
184. 29 C.F.R. 825.216(c).
185. 29 C.F.R. 825.214(b). See Sarno v. Douglass Elliman, 183 F.3d 155 (2nd Cir. 1998), which also illustrates how disputes over FMLA restoration can become disputes under the Americans with Disabilities Act.
186. 42 U.S.C. 12101. et. seq.

compensation, job training, and other terms, conditions, and privileges of employment.[187] The ADA covers employers with 15 or more employees.[188]

(i) Disability Defined. An individual with a disability is a person who (1) has a physical or mental impairment that substantially limits one or more major life activities, (2) has a record of such an impairment, or (3) is regarded as having such an impairment.[189] A qualified employee or applicant with a disability is an individual who, with or without reasonable accommodation, can perform the essential functions of the job in question. To fully understand this definition, it is necessary to distinguish between an impairment and a disability. An *impairment* is the manifestation of a physical or mental problem or deficiency; it becomes a disability only if it substantially limits one or more major life activities. To illustrate, Bob Watson has a permanent knee impairment that results in pain when he walks more than ten miles. He is impaired, but he is not disabled because his impairment does not restrict a major life activity; the average member of the population does not walk more than ten miles at a time.

In assessing whether someone is disabled, the employer is permitted to consider mitigating factors. For example, someone who has high blood pressure corrected with medication or someone who wears a corrective lens is not considered disabled.[190] This raises the question whether someone who chooses not to mitigate a disability that can easily be mitigated is considered disabled.

For purposes of the ADA, the following conditions are *not* disabilities: transvestism, transexualism, pedophilia, compulsive gambling, and pyromania.[191] Conditions that do *no*t qualify as impairments (and consequently are not disabilities) include homosexuality and bisexuality,[192] but employers should be careful about discriminating on those two conditions (or other types of sexual orientation) because state laws and the terms of grants may prohibit such discrimination. The EEOC has indicated that economic or cultural disadvantages, prison records, and common personality traits do not constitute disabilities for purposes of the ADA.[193] A person who is HIV positive is considered disabled.[194] Temporary conditions do not constitute disabilities.[195] For example, an employee who sprains a wrist that will heal within several weeks is not considered to be impaired.[196] Personality traits that are typically viewed negatively (e.g., impatience, poor impulse

187. 42 U.S.C. 12112(a).
188. 42 U.S.C. 12111(5)(A).
189. 42 U.S.C. 12111(8).
190. Murphy v. United Parcel Service, 527 U.S. 516 (1999); and Sutton v. United Airlines, 527 U.S. 471 (1999).
191. 42 U.S.C. 12211(b); and 29 C.F.R. 1630.3(d).
192. 42 U.S.C. 12211(a).
193. United States Equal Employment Opportunity Commission, EEOC Compliance Manual, at § 902.2(c) (March 1995).
194. Bragdon v. Abbott, 524 U.S. 624 (1998).
195. United States Equal Employment Opportunity Commission, *supra* note 193, at § 902.4(d).
196. *Id.*, at § 902.4(d), Example 2.

control) are not considered impairments unless they are manifestations of an underlying impairment (e.g., bipolar disorder).

(ii) Reasonable Accommodations and Undue Hardship. The ADA requires employers to make reasonable accommodations to applicants and employees with disabilities so that the applicants and employees can perform the essential functions of the job in question. Reasonable accommodations may include, but are not limited to, (1) making existing facilities used by employees readily accessible to and usable by persons with disabilities,[197] (2) job restructuring, modifying work schedules, and reassignment to a vacant position, and (3) acquiring or modifying equipment or devices, adjusting or modifying examinations, training materials, or policies, and providing qualified readers or interpreters.[198]

An employer is not required to make a reasonable accommodation[199] if the accommodation would impose an "undue hardship" on the operation of the employer's business. *Undue hardship* is defined as an action requiring significant difficulty or expense when considered in light of factors such as an employer's size, financial resources, and the nature and structure of its operation.[200] An employer is not required to (1) eliminate an essential function of the job, (2) lower quality or production standards to make an accommodation, or (3) provide personal use items such as glasses or hearing aids.[201] The interaction of reasonable accommodation and undue hardship standards may require an employer to take actions well beyond providing specialized equipment. Specific examples follow.

- *Modification of Workplace Policies.* An employer may be required to modify workplace policies to accommodate someone with a disability. To illustrate,[202] Yellow Housing Development Corporation, a Section 501(c)(3) organization, has a policy prohibiting its employees from eating or drinking at their workstations. Jane Mellon is an insulin-dependent diabetic. She requests that Yellow Housing waive its eating prohibition and permit her to eat a candy bar or drink orange juice at her desk should she accidentally take too much insulin (which without the food or drink could cause her to go into insulin shock).Yellow Housing must modify its policy to grant this request unless it involves an undue hardship, and it is difficult to see how it could.
- *Marginal vs. Essential Job Functions.* An employer need not eliminate the essential functions of a particular job to accommodate a disability, but the employer may be required to alter or adjust marginal functions if such

197. 42 U.S.C. 12111(9)(A).
198. 42 U.S.C. 12111(9)(B).
199. 42 U.S.C. 12112(b)(5)(A).
200. 42 U.S.C. 12111(10).
201. Equal Employment Opportunity Commission, Enforcement Guidance: Reasonable Accommodation and Undue Hardship under the Americans with Disabilities Act (Oct. 17, 2002).
202. *Id.*, at Question 24.

a change is a reasonable accommodation. To illustrate,[203] Brett Museum of Fine Art is located in a four-story modern structure. Larry Gallagher, a member of the museum's four-person janitorial staff, wears a prosthetic leg that enables him to walk very well, but climbing steps is painful and difficult. Although he can perform his essential functions without problems, he cannot perform the marginal function of sweeping the steps located throughout the museum. The marginal functions of a second crew member include cleaning the small kitchen in the employee's lounge, which is something Gallagher can do. The museum can switch the marginal functions performed by these two employees as a reasonable accommodation. It is difficult to see how this change could result in undue hardship to the museum.

- *Granting a Leave of Absence.* As previously noted, when certain conditions are satisfied, employees are entitled to a maximum of 12 weeks of leave under the FMLA. An employer may be required to grant a disabled employee a leave of absence as a reasonable accommodation under the ADA independent of the 12-week period under the FMLA.[204] In the case of ADA-related leave, the employer is entitled to take into account whether granting the leave imposes undue hardship (not a permissible inquiry under the FMLA). Moreover, the employer must allow the individual to return to the same position (assuming that there was no undue hardship in holding it open) if the employee is still qualified (i.e., the employee can perform the essential functions of the position with or without reasonable accommodation). If holding open an employee's position during a leave is an undue hardship under the ADA or the employee is no longer qualified to return to the original position, the employer must reassign the employee (absent undue hardship) to a vacant position for which he is qualified.

  To illustrate,[205] Kim Watkins is an employee of Duncan College. She has epilepsy and now requires brain surgery as part of her treatment. Because of the nature of the surgery, Watkins will require 13 weeks of leave for the surgery and rehabilitation. She is eligible under the FMLA for 12 weeks of leave (the maximum available), so this period of leave constitutes both FMLA leave and a reasonable accommodation. Under the FMLA, Duncan College could deny Watkins the thirteenth week of leave, but because she is also covered under the ADA, Duncan College cannot deny the request for the thirteenth week of leave unless it can show undue hardship. The college may consider the impact on its operations caused by the initial 12-week absence and other undue hardship factors.

203. *Id.*, at Question 16.
204. *Id.*, at Question 21.
205. *Id.*, at Question 21, Example A.

The courts have had some difficulty addressing the question of indefinite leave. They agree that a short-term leave of absence is a reasonable accommodation, but apparent disagreement exists as to whether an indefinite leave or a fixed-length, but protracted one is reasonable.[206] Until the Supreme Court addresses this issue, employers will have to live with some uncertainty.

- *Reassignment to Vacant Position.* The ADA includes reassignments to vacant position as a reasonable accommodation. The position must be equivalent to the old position in terms of pay, status, and other relevant factors. Assuming no undue hardship and the absence of other reasonable accommodations, an employer must reassign a disabled employee to a vacant position if the employee is qualified for it. The employer need not provide the employee training necessary to qualify for the position (except for training that it would provide to all employees before starting the position in question). The EEOC treats reassignment as the accommodation of last resort; it requires employers to first consider reasonable accommodations that would permit the employee to remain in his current position.[207]

  To illustrate, Krista McCoy is a kindergarten teacher at Tombstone Elementary School (K-8), a private school. The school's job description requires kindergarten teachers to be able to lift a 20-pound child. During summer vacation, McCoy is hit in a pedestrian crosswalk by a man driving an SUV while talking on a cell phone. She is paralyzed from the waist down and must use a wheelchair. McCoy is qualified to teach kindergarten through fifth grade. The school does not require those teaching second grade to be able to lift a certain amount of weight because children above a certain age do not require lifting. Assuming there are no other reasonable accommodations that would permit McCoy to continue as kindergarten teacher, the school must offer her the position (currently vacant) as a second-grade teacher (assume the pay and status are similar to that of a kindergarten teacher). The analysis can become complicated as the facts change, however. Suppose, for example, that there is not currently a vacant position but there might be one in the not-too-distant future.

---

206. For an excellent discussion of this issue, see R. Howie and L. Shapero, *How Long Is Enough—Leaves of Absence as a Reasonable Accommodation under the ADA*, 29 EMPLOYEE RELATIONS L. J. 33 (Fall 2003). The article cites a number of cases reflecting different philosophies, but these cases should be checked to determine whether there have been further developments in the applicable jurisdiction. Cited cases include Wood v. Green, 323 F.3d 1309 (11th Cir. 2003); EEOC v. Yellow Freight System, 253 F.3d 943 (7th Cir. 2001); Kimbro v. Atlantic Richfield Co., 889 F.2d 869 (9th Cir. 1989); and Myers v. Hose, 50 F.3d 278 (4th Cir. 1995). A leading treatise seems to view the law as more predictable than Howie and Shapero, stating:

> Similarly, courts have not required employers to provide open-ended, unpaid leaves of absence for disabled employees.

See LEX K. LARSON, 9 EMPLOYMENT DISCRIMINATION, at 154-32 (Matthew Bender 2005).

207. EQUAL EMPLOYMENT OPPORTUNITY COMMISSION, *supra* note 201, in the section labeled "Reassignment."

Although these accommodation categories are major ones, they certainly are not the only ones. There are literally hundreds, if not thousands, of court decisions addressing the question of reasonable accommodation. The decisions often are highly factual, sometimes reflecting conflicting views among the various federal circuit courts. Consequently, any nonprofit navigating these waters should do so by relying on the advice of a qualified attorney.

(iii) An Interactive Process. An employer is obligated to make a reasonable accommodation only if the employer is aware of the disability.[208] As a practical matter, this means that an employee with a "hidden" or latent disability needs to inform the employer of that disability (e.g., a mental impairment that is not readily apparent). On the other hand, one commentator cautions employers against waiting for the employee to request an accommodation when the employer is aware of a need for one.[209] According to the EEOC:

> The employer and the individual with a disability should engage in an informal process to clarify what the individual needs and identify the appropriate reasonable accommodation. The employer may ask the individual relevant questions that will enable it to make an informed decision about the request. This includes asking what type of reasonable accommodation is needed.
>
> The exact nature of the dialogue will vary. In many instances, both the disability and the type of accommodation required will be obvious, and thus there may be little or no need to engage in any discussion. In other situations, the employer may need to ask questions concerning the nature of the disability and the individual's functional limitations in order to identify an effective accommodation. While the individual with a disability does not have to be able to specify the precise accommodation, s/he does need to describe the problems posed by the workplace barrier. Additionally, suggestions from the individual with a disability may assist the employer in determining the type of reasonable accommodation to provide. Where the individual or the employer are not familiar with possible accommodations, there are extensive public and private resources to help the employer identify

---

208. United States Equal Employment Opportunity Commission, The ADA: Your Responsibilities as an Employer. The Appendix to 29 C.F.R. 1630 provides as follows:

> Employers are obligated to make reasonable accommodation only to the physical or mental limitations resulting from the disability of a qualified individual with a disability that is known to the employer. Thus, an employer would not be expected to accommodate disabilities of which it is unaware. If an employee with a known disability is having difficulty performing his or her job, an employer may inquire whether the employee is in need of a reasonable accommodation. In general, however, it is the responsibility of the individual with a disability to inform the employer that an accommodation is needed. When the need for an accommodation is not obvious, an employer, before providing a reasonable accommodation, may require that the individual with a disability provide documentation of the need for accommodation.

The courts have generally placed the burden on the employee to make the employer aware of the disability and the need for a reasonable accommodation. *See* Gaston v. Bellingrath Gardens, 167 F.3d 1351 (11th Cir. 1999); and Taylor v. Principal Fin. Group, 93 F.3d 155 (5th Cir. 1996). *See also* Lex K. Larson, *supra* note 232, at 154-21; and J. Sheffield, *Navigating Current Trends under the ADA*, 31 Employee Relations L. J. 3 (Summer 2005).

209. See J. Sheffield, *supra* note 234, at 8.

reasonable accommodations once the specific limitations and workplace barriers have been ascertained.[210]

The EEOC has acknowledged that "the employer providing the accommodation has the ultimate discretion to choose between effective accommodations, and may choose the less expensive accommodation or the accommodation that is easier for it to provide."[211] Unfortunately, just before the EEOC makes this statement, it also states that the "preference of the individual with a disability should be given primary consideration" if "more than one of these accommodations will enable the individual to perform the essential functions."[212] If an employee rejects a reasonable accommodation that would enable him to perform the essential functions of the position, he will not be considered a qualified individual with a disability,[213] although employers should be careful because they will almost inevitably find themselves arguing over whether the accommodation was "reasonable" or posed an "undue hardship."

(iv) Job Applicants. Job applicants may be asked about their ability to perform specific job functions but not about the nature or severity of a disability. Consequently, an employer may ask about education, training, skills, and whether the applicant can satisfy the job's requirements or essential functions and skills. An employer may not ask an applicant about the use of medications or prior workers' compensation history.[214] There is one important exception to the rule against asking questions about disability as part of the application process. According to the EEOC,

> [w]here it seems likely that an applicant has a disability that will require a reasonable accommodation, you may ask whether s/he will need one. This is an exception to the usual rule that questions regarding disability and reasonable accommodation should come after making a conditional job offer. Example: During a job interview, you may ask a blind applicant interviewing for a position that requires working with a computer whether s/he will need a reasonable accommodation, such as special software that will read information on the screen.[215]

The EEOC explains this exception in great detail in an appendix to its regulations.[216] Anyone desiring to pursue this line of questioning should review the appendix and consider consulting with a lawyer. Although the EEOC says it is permissible, the intention behind such questioning, particularly if the questions are not phrased properly, could easily be misconstrued.

---

210. UNITED STATES EQUAL EMPLOYMENT OPPORTUNITY COMMISSION, *supra* note 208.
211. 29 C.F.R. 1630, Appendix.
212. *Id.*
213. 29 U.S.C. 1630.9(d). *See* Keever v. Middletown, 145 F.3d 809 (6th Cir. 1998); and Hankins v. The Gap, 84 F.3d 797 (6th Cir. 1996).
214. 29 C.F.R. 1630, Appendix.
215. UNITED STATES EQUAL EMPLOYMENT OPPORTUNITY COMMISSION, THE AMERICANS WITH DISABILITIES ACT: A PRIMER FOR SMALL BUSINESS.
216. 29 C.F.R. 1630, Appendix.

As should be apparent, written job descriptions and requirements can be important because such descriptions provide a clear standard against which the employer can assess the applicant. Assuming that there was no intent to discriminate, an employer is in a much better position when it turns down a disabled job applicant if the employer can point to a job description that requires applicants to have taken certain courses directly related to the job performance and the disabled applicant has not taken them but other applicants have. However, the description is helpful only if the employer adheres to it in hiring and employment considerations.[217] The description may be counterproductive if the employer employees other people in the same position (or hires someone) that do not satisfy the criteria.

Applicants cannot be asked to take a medical exam before an offer of employment is made.[218] An offer may be conditioned on the results of a medical examination, but only if the examination is required for all entering employees in similar jobs (and is conducted after the offer is made).[219] Medical examinations of employees must be job related and consistent with the employer's business needs.[220] The deferral of medical exams is intended to make it easier to identify pretexts for denying employment. If an exam were part of the process that led to the basic employment decisions, applicants would have a more difficult time determining whether the employment decision was made on the merits or constituted discrimination.[221] The results of medical exams must be kept confidential and in separate medical files.[222]

The reasonable accommodation requirement extends to the hiring process. Consequently, an employer should be prepared to provide applicants written materials in accessible formats (e.g., large print, Braille, or audiotape) or provide readers or sign language interpreters.

Employees and applicants currently engaging in the illegal use of drugs are not covered by the ADA when an employer acts on the basis of such use.[223] Tests for illegal drugs are not subject to the ADA's restrictions on medical examinations,[224] but other laws, particularly state laws, may come into play. Employers may hold illegal drug users and alcoholics to the same performance standards as other employees.[225] Before testing for drugs, an organization should review state law and any applicable collective bargaining agreements or other contracts.

---

217. J. Burns, *supra* note 88, discussing why consistent applications of policies is important.
218. 29 U.S.C. 1630.13(a).
219. 29 U.S.C.1630.14(b).
220. 42 U.S.C. 12112(d)(4); and 29 C.F.R. 1630.14(c).
221. J. Sheffield, *supra* note 208, at 15.
222. 42 U.S.C. 1630.14(c)(1); and 29 C.F.R. 1630.14(c)(1).
223. 42 U.S.C. 12114(a).
224. 42 U.S.C. 12114(d).
225. 42 U.S.C. 12114(c)(4).

(v) Concluding Comments. As should be apparent, the ADA poses significant legal challenges for any employer, even one with the best intentions. We have only scratched the surface. Treatises have been written on the many issues posed by the ADA, making legal counsel highly advisable.

(f) AVOIDING PROBLEMS—CASES. Notwithstanding the very real complexities described, the entire issue of discrimination/harassment is somewhat of a no-brainer. Setting aside the risk of employment practices litigation, no organization should want harassment or discrimination in the workplace because a hostile work environment fosters employee turnover, lower productivity, and poor attitudes. Despite even the best of intentions, no organization can avoid these issues completely. After all, every organization deals with human beings, and people have their individual "issues." In any employment law handbook, guide, or newsletter, you will see references to court cases proving that discrimination and harassment have not been eradicated. The following cases involve nonprofits and the lessons that can be learned from them.

(i) Case 1: Rely on Specific Performance Deficiencies in Dismissals. Any time an organization dismisses an employee, it should be able to support the decision with specific facts, as the case involving a hospital foundation charged with violations under the Family and Medical Leave Act aptly demonstrates. An employee brought a claim against the Memorial Foundation of Allen Hospital under the FMLA. The foundation had dismissed him upon return from two weeks of family leave. Not surprisingly, that triggered a lawsuit claiming that the dismissal occurred in retaliation for taking family leave. The foundation claimed that the employee had not been doing her job, which in part consisted of acknowledging contributions to the foundation from donors. The issue had been raised before she started her leave. While she was on leave, another employee found evidence that more than 400 donations had not been acknowledged, with one of those donations being for $136,000. Memorial Foundation was able to document the facts that formed the basis for the dismissal, and, consequently, escaped liability even when the firing took place in close proximity to the exercise of the employee's rights under the law.[226]

(ii) Case 2: Use Job Postings. Regularly advertised job openings may be useful in defending against an employment discrimination suit. In one case, the employee, who was 50 years old, alleged that she was passed over for two positions. One of the women who received a position allegedly had less education, less experience, and had been employed by the school for less time than the employee who filed the complaint.[227] The school had not posted the position. Consequently, the school argued that because the applicant had never applied

226. Smith v. Allen Health Systems, 302 F.3d 827 (8th Cir. 2002).
227. Keen v. D.P.T. Business School, 2002 U.S. Dist. LEXIS 232 (E.D. Pa. 2002).

for the position, the school could not have discriminated in denying her the position. The court relaxed the standards that would otherwise apply because the employer's promotion procedures were informal, secretive, and subjective. In this particular case, the employee did not ultimately prevail, but the school could have reduced its litigation risk had it had a more transparent promotion policy—in other words, one that included posting open positions.

(iii) Case 3: Review Employee Guides. In the *Memorial Foundation of Allen Hospital* case, the foundation had an employee handbook that described a progressive employee disciplinary system. The foundation dismissed the employee without adhering to that system. The employee argued that the handbook constituted a contract, and the foundation was in violation of the contract. This claim shows why employers need to take employee handbooks seriously. The employer may not view the handbook as creating a contract, but a disgruntled employee can look to it for anything that supports the complaint. In this case, the foundation had specifically reserved the right to deviate from its disciplinary system, so the court did not hold the foundation to the handbook's terms.

(iv) Case 4: Handle Workforce Reductions with Care. In an effort to cut costs, the University of Wisconsin Press, a nonprofit organization affiliated with the University of Wisconsin System, dismissed four employees ranging in age from 46 to 54. The decisions were made without relying on employment evaluations, consultation with managers, or discussion with the dismissed workers. The duties of the employees in question either were assumed by younger workers or by new hires, who also were younger persons. The press wrote a justification for the terminations after the decisions had been made. This document refers to "pre-electronic" era skills that would have to be brought "up to speed." There were also remarks about the press needing a new "vision" that would require "agility." The jury apparently concluded that the press had equated agility with youth. The Seventh Circuit upheld the jury verdict against the UW Press for willful violations of the Age Discrimination in Employment Act.[228]

This case offers an important lesson: Any organization that works backward, first making the decision and then justifying it, is asking for trouble. The decision to fire the four workers appears to have been a "seat-of-the-pants" decision, without a review process to reach an impartial decision. With e-mails, backup systems, and other digital resources, any organization will have trouble passing off an after-the-decision report as having been written before the actual decision was made. There is simply too much digital evidence.

228. EEOC v. Board of Regents of the University of Wisconsin System, 288 F.3d 296 (7th Cir. 2002).

(g) UNIFORMED SERVICES EMPLOYMENT AND REEMPLOYMENT RIGHTS ACT OF 1994. Federal law grants broad employment-related protection to individuals who serve in the military-uniform services.[229] Under Uniformed Services Employment and Reemployment Rights Act (USERRA) of 1994, employers cannot discriminate in employment decisions based on someone's military status.[230] The law covers virtually all United States employers[231] regardless of size. Similarly, it protects almost all employees,[232] including part-time and probationary employees.

Anyone who believes that his rights under USERRA have been violated has the option to sue. However, an administrative process can be commenced instead by filing a complaint with the Veterans' Employment and Training Service (VETS) of the Department of Labor. If VETS is unable resolve the matter, it can be submitted to the Department of Justice for possible legal action on behalf of the aggrieved person. Those in the Department of Justice who handle these matters are vigilant. Employers want to avoid invoking their ire; compliance is the best way to avoid trouble.

The law defines "service in the uniform services" broadly. It protects those serving in the Army, Navy, Marine Corps, Air Force, Coast Guard, and Public Health Service commissioned corps, as well as the reserve components of each of these services.[233]The law also applies to federal training or service in the Army National Guard and Air National Guard. Under the Public Health Security and Bioterrorism Response Act of 2002, certain disaster response work (and authorized training for such work) is considered "service in the uniformed services" as well.[234]

Under the law, a preservice employer must reemploy covered employees returning from a period of service in the uniformed services if each of the following conditions is satisfied[235]: (1) the person held a civilian job,[236] (2) the person gave advance notice to the employer that he was leaving for service[237] (unless the circumstances made notice impossible or unreasonable),[238] (3) the cumulative period absence due to military service did not exceed five years;[239] (4) the person was not released from military service under dishonorable or other

229. For an overview, see S. Richey, *Employers' Responsibilities and Duties to Today's Citizen Soldiers*, 29 Employee Relations L. J. 46 (Spring 2004).

230. 38 U.S.C. 4311.

231. 38 U.S.C. 4303(4).

232. 38 U.S.C. 4303(3).

233. 38 U.S.C. 4303(13) and (16). For what appears to be a comprehensive list of covered persons and service, see United States Department of Labor Veterans Employment and Training Service, A Non-Technical Resource Guide to the Uniformed Services Employment and Reemployment Rights Act (Mar. 2003) *availalble at* http://www.dol.gov/vets/whatsnew/uguide.pdf.

234. 42 U.S.C. 300hh-11(e).

235. 38 U.S.C. 4312(a).

236. 38 U.S.C. 4313.

237. 38 U.S.C. 4312(a)(1).

238. 38 U.S.C. 4312(b).

239. 38 U.S.C. 4312(a)(2).

punitive conditions,[240] and (5) the person reported back to the civilian job in a timely manner or submitted a timely application for reemployment.[241]

The law establishes a five-year cumulative total on military service with a single employer, with certain exceptions allowed for initial periods of obligated service, required training for reservists and National Guard members, and other specified circumstances.[242]

Under USERRA, restoration rights are based on the duration of military service rather than the type of military duty performed (e.g., active duty for training or inactive duty), except for fitness-for-service examinations. The person seeking reemployment must act in accordance with the following schedule:

- *Covered Service of Less than 31 Days Service.* The employee must apply for reemployment by the beginning of the first regularly scheduled work period after the end of the last calendar day of duty, plus time required to return home safely and an eight-hour rest period, or, if this is impossible or unreasonable, as soon as possible.[243]
- *Covered Service of 31 to 180 Days.* The employee must apply for reemployment no later than 14 days after completing military service, or, if this is impossible or unreasonable, as soon as possible.[244]
- *Covered Service of 181 Days or More.* The employee must apply for reemployment no later than 90 days after completion of military service.[245]
- *Covered Service-Connected Injury or Illness.* Reporting or application deadlines are extended for up to two years for persons who are hospitalized or convalescing.[246]

The law outlines what position must be made available to the returning member of the military; it is not necessarily the same one that the person occupied before leaving. The law applies an escalator principle, requiring that the returning person actually step back onto the seniority escalator at the point that he would have occupied had he remained continuously employed. Finally, the law defines the positions that a person is entitled to based on a length-of-service schedule. This principle requires the employer to make reasonable efforts to qualify the person for the position.[247]

240. 38 U.S.C. 4304.
241. 38 U.S.C. 4312(a)(3).
242. 38 U.S.C. 4312(c).
243. 38 U.S.C. 4312(e)(1)(A).
244. 38 U.S.C. 4312(e)(1)(C).
245. 38 U.S.C. 4312(e)(1)(D).
246. 38 U.S.C. 4312(e)(2).
247. *See* United States Department of Labor Veterans Employment and Training Service, *supra* note 233, at 6-8, for complete details.

Employers are not required to reemploy a person if the circumstances have changed, making it unreasonable or impossible to do so.[248] Examples include cessation of the business and workforce reductions that would have included the person in question. Reemployment is also excused if it would cause the employer undue hardship.[249] The Department of Labor has stated that undue hardship can include the expense or difficulty of employing someone due to service-connected disabilities but then goes on to set forth a three-part reemployment scheme that requires reasonable efforts to accommodate disabilities and reemployment in other positions, among other requirements.[250] Any employer with questions regarding reemploying someone who incurs or aggravates a disability in military service should consult an attorney because of the sensitive issues posed by disabled veterans and questions regarding the application of USERRA, as well as the ADA. Finally, an employer does not need to reemploy someone who held a position for a brief, nonrecurrent period and had no reasonable expectation that the employment would continue indefinitely or for a significant period.[251]

A reemployed person is entitled to the seniority and other rights and benefits based on those that would have accrued had the person continued in the employ of the employer during his military service.[252] The law also contains detailed provisions regarding employee benefit plans and rights thereunder. For example, a reemployed person must be treated as not having incurred a break in service under a pension plan.[253] Another notable provision in USERRA grants individuals leaving for military service COBRA-type rights even when their employers are not covered by COBRA.[254] According to the Department of Labor,

> If a person's health plan coverage would terminate because of an absence due to military service, the person may elect to continue the health plan coverage for up to 18 months after the absence begins or for the period of service (plus the time allowed to apply for reemployment), whichever period is shorter. The person cannot be required to pay more than 102 percent of the full premium for the coverage. If the military service was for 30 or fewer days, the person cannot be required to pay more than the normal employee share of any premium.[255]

A person who is reemployed under USERRA may not be discharged without cause for one year after the date of reemployment if the person's period of military service was more than 180 days.[256] If the person's military service was for

248. 38 U.S.C. 4312(d)(1)(A).
249. 38 U.S.C. 4312(d)(1)(B).
250. United States Department of Labor Veterans Employment and Training Service, *supra* note 233, at 9. *See* 38 U.S.C. 4313(a)(3).
251. 38 U.S.C. 4312(d)(1)(C).
252. 38 U.S.C. 4316(a).
253. 38 U.S.C. 4318(a)(2)(A).
254. 38 U.S.C. 4317.
255. United States Department of Labor Veterans Employment and Training Service, *supra* note 233, at 11.
256. 38 U.S.C. 4316(c)(1).

31 to 181 days, he may not be discharged without cause for six months after reemployment.[257]

(h) OTHER LAWS TO CONSIDER. Nonprofits should also consider several other employment-related laws.

(i) Fair Credit Reporting Act and Background Checks. As noted elsewhere in this *Guide,* nonprofits should use background checks when the situation warrants. However, to the extent that those checks rely on a "consumer report," the nonprofit must comply with the terms of the Fair Credit Reporting Act (FCRA).[258] Unlike many other federal laws that govern the employment relationship, the FCRA applies to all employers regardless of number of employers because its basic focus is on consumers.

A *consumer report* is a report, written or oral, by a consumer reporting agency[259] that bears on a consumer's creditworthiness, standing, or character, as well as on the consumer's character, general reputation, personal characteristics, or mode of living if it is, among other things, used for employment purposes. The FCRA also specifies a special category of consumer report, termed an *investigative consumer report,* which is defined as a consumer report, obtained and based on interviews with neighbors, friends, or associates, addressing general reputation, personal characteristics, and mode of living.[260] To be a consumer report, the person providing it must be acting in a third-party capacity; in other words, as someone who did not have the relationship with the consumer being reported on. Consequently, when a nonprofit calls an applicant's former employer for a reference check, it is not obtaining a consumer report. When a nonprofit asks an employment or consumer reporting agency to obtain credit histories, criminal background checks, interviews with acquaintances, driving records, and other personal information, however, it has most likely requested a consumer report.

Before a nonprofit requests a consumer report from a consumer reporting agency, it must notify the applicant in writing what the report may be used for—the document used to convey this information must contain no other information[261]—and the nonprofit must obtain the applicant's written consent.[262] If the consumer report is an investigative consumer report, the nonprofit must make additional disclosures.[263]

257. 38 U.S.C. 4316(c)(1).
258. 15 U.S.C. 1681 et. seq.
259. 15 U.S.C. 1681a(f).
260. 15 U.S.C. 1681a(e).
261. 15 U.S.C. 1681b(b)(2)(A)(i).
262. 15 U.S.C. 1681b(b)(2)(A)(ii).
263. 15 U.S.C. 1681(d).

If the nonprofit plans to take an action adverse[264] to the applicant, it must provide the applicant a copy of the report and a summary of the applicant's rights under the FCRA, as prescribed by the Federal Trade Commission (FTC), before taking the action.[265] After the nonprofit has taken the action, it must provide the applicant an adverse action notice if the information in the report affected the decision.[266] This notice must include the following:

- The name, address, and phone number of the consumer reporting agency that supplied the report.
- A statement that the consumer reporting agency that supplied the report did not make the decision to take the adverse action and cannot give specific reasons for it.
- A notice of the individual's right to dispute the accuracy or completeness of any information the agency furnished and to an additional free consumer report from the agency upon request within 60 days.[267]

Up to this point, we have focused on FCRA requirements and the hiring process. However, FCRA's requirements relating to employment go beyond hiring; they apply to employment, promotion, reassignment, and retention decisions.[268] Consequently, nonprofits must adhere to the FCRA when they factor such reports into employment decisions. As you have likely come to anticipate, state FCRA analogues must also be considered.[269]

(ii) The Immigration Reform and Control Act. Nonprofit employers are required to comply with the Immigration Reform and Control Act.[270] It is illegal to hire or recruit unauthorized aliens.[271] To verify employment eligibility, the

---

264. 15 U.S.C. 1681a(k).
265. 15 U.S.C. 1681b(b)(3).
266. 15 U.S.C. 1681m.
267. Federal Trade Commission, Using Consumer Reports: What Employers Need to Know.
268. 15 U.S.C. 1681a(h).
269. Seyfarth Shaw LLP, Employment Practices Loss Prevention Guidelines: A Practical Guide from Chubb, at 43 (rev. Jan. 2005), as made available by the Chubb Group of Insurance Companies.
270. 8 U.S.C. 1324a et. seq.
271. *Id.* Section 1324a provides, in pertinent part, as follows:

(a) Making employment of unauthorized aliens unlawful

(1) In General. It is unlawful for a person or other entity

(A) to hire, or to recruit or refer for a fee, for employment in the United States an alien knowing the alien is an unauthorized alien (as defined in subsection (h)(3) of this section) with respect to such employment, or

(B)

(i) to hire for employment in the United States an individual without complying with the requirements of subsection (b) of this section or

(ii) if the person or entity is an agricultural association, agricultural employer, or farm labor contractor (as defined in section 1802 of title 29), to hire, or to recruit or refer for a fee, for employment in the United States an individual without complying with the requirements of subsection (b) of this section.

nonprofit must have all workers complete Form I-9 (with exceptions of workers hired before November 6, 1986, and continuously employed by the same employer, independent contractors, and certain individuals performing casual employment).[272]

An employer's obligation to complete the Form I-9 process does not arise until the applicant has been hired. Because of laws prohibiting discrimination based on national origin, employers should not begin the Form I-9 process during the pre-employment period, as the United States Department of Homeland Security has specifically stated: "The I-9 process may not be used to prescreen employees for hiring."[273] The process permits employees to satisfy the information requirements with a number of different documents. The employee is the one who has the option to select which document will be presented to the employer when the requirements provide that one of several documents will suffice.[274] When there are different options, an employer cannot require the employee to provide multiple forms of verification.[275]

The nonprofit must retain the Form I-9 for each worker for either three years after the date of first hire or one year after employment has ended, whichever is later.[276] On Form I-9, the worker must indicate that he is eligible to work in the United States because he is either a citizen or national of the United States, a lawful permanent resident with a green card, or an alien authorized to work in the United States. The worker is required to provide documents verifying both his identity and eligibility for employment; Form I-9 lists the various documents that are acceptable.

Workers must complete Form I-9 within one business day of the day of hire,[277] but the United States Citizenship and Immigration Services indicates that an employer can terminate an employee who does not produce the required documents or a receipt for replacement documents within three business days of the date employment begins.[278] To be valid, a receipt for a replacement document must be for a document that was lost, stolen, or damaged (as opposed to a receipt showing initial application for the document). The replacement document must be presented within 90 days of the hire.[279]

A nonprofit must accept verification documents if they appear on their face to be genuine and relate to the person presenting them, but it may not rely on copies

---

272. United States Citizenship and Immigration and Naturalization Service, Form I-9, Instructions.

273. UNITED STATES CITIZENSHIP AND IMMIGRATION SERVICES (OFFICE OF BUSINESS LIAISON), EMPLOYER INFORMATION BULLETIN 102: THE I-9 PROCESS IN A NUTSHELL (Mar. 16, 2005).

274. *Id.*

275. *Id.*

276. ABOUT FORM I-9, EMPLOYMENT ELIGIBILITY VERIFICATION—WHAT SHOULD BE DONE WITH FORMS I-9 AFTER THEY ARE COMPLETED?, *available at* http://uscis.gov/graphics/howdoi/faqeev.htm.

277. ABOUT FORM I-9, EMPLOYMENT ELIGIBILITY VERIFICATION—EMPLOYEE'S RESPONSIBILITY REGARDING FORM I-9, *available at* http://uscis.gov/graphics/howdoi/faqeev.htm.

278. UNITED STATES CITIZENSHIP AND IMMIGRATION SERVICES, QUESTIONS AND ANSWERS, *available* at http://uscis.gov.

279. *Id.*

of these documents. For most nonprofits, compliance with the Form I-9 process is a mere formality, but they should have a system for compliance and record retention.

(iii) Workers' Compensation. Obviously, nonprofits will want to comply with applicable state workers' compensation laws by obtaining the necessary workers' compensation coverage (or satisfying their obligation with other risk-financing tools, such as captive or self-insurance, if permissible). Nonprofits need to be particularly careful in making sure that they have appropriate insurance coverage (be it workers' compensation or other appropriate coverage) for volunteers. Depending on state law, the nonprofit may be required to provide workers' compensation coverage for certain volunteer workers, but the majority of the states exclude run-of-the-mill volunteers from mandatory coverage.[280] Workers' compensation coverage can be an issue when individuals participating in drug, alcohol, or other rehabilitation programs are required to work as part of the rehabilitation.[281] In some cases, nonprofits have been held responsible for these individuals under workers' compensation laws.[282]

Employers who encourage or sponsor employees to participate in after-hours community service programs should ensure that they have adequate insurance coverage should a court determine that the employer is responsible for any injuries sustained by the employee while volunteering his time. In one case, the lower court held that the voluntary service occurred outside the scope of employment, meaning that the volunteer-employee would not be limited to recovery under the employer's workers' compensation coverage.[283] That court was subsequently reversed, with the Indianas Supreme Court concluding that the volunteer-employee's claim was covered by workers' compensation, thereby significantly limiting the potential recovery.[284] The disagreement between the two courts in

---

280. For example, a number of states require workers' compensation coverage for volunteer firefighters and ambulance drivers. Many states exclude run-of-the-mill volunteers from mandatory coverage, but the definition of a "volunteer" has created issues.

281. For example, see Dixon v. Salvation Army, 2005 Ark. LEXIS 48 (Jan. 20, 2005), where, as a condition to being admitted to an alcohol treatment program, the participant agreed to attend services on Sunday and Wednesday and live at the rehabilitation center for 16 weeks. He engaged in 40 hours of work each week, receiving a beginning stipend of $7 per week. The participant was housed and fed at the facility at no cost as part of the program. The court stated that "[w]here a person engages in conduct that might be considered work, but does it to further his own benefit rather than to further the benefit of another, the person is not an employee." Based on the facts, the court concluded the participant was not an employee for workers' compensation purposes.

282. *See* Anderson v. Homeless and Housing COA, 135 S.W.3d 405 (Ky. 2004), in which the court ruled that the "claimant" was covered while working for the Homeless and Housing Coalition of Kentucky when helping to build houses for Habitat for Humanity; and Hoppman v. Workers' Compensation Appeals Board, 277 Cal. Rptr. 116 (Cal .Ct. App. 1991), finding that a "worker" received too much compensation to qualify as a non-worker under California's "aid or sustenance" exemption from mandatory coverage.

283. Knoy v. Cary, 794 N.E.2d 572, 578 (Ind. Ct. App. 2003). The defendant was not the employer but a fellow employee; the plaintiff alleged that his fellow employee caused the injury.

284. Knoy v. Cary, 812 N.E.2d 791 (Ind. 2004).

this case demonstrates why relying only on workers' compensation coverage may be unwise.

If state law[285] does permit a nonprofit to elect to include volunteers in the group covered by its workers' compensation policy, the nonprofit should seriously consider electing inclusion.[286] Such coverage requires payment of an insurance premium, but it arguably caps the nonprofit's exposure should a volunteer be injured—although plaintiffs' lawyers have tried to work around those caps. In the absence of workers' compensation coverage, the volunteer can seek damages under general legal principles, giving the organization far greater exposure to liability.

There are two ways to approach workers' compensation problem as it pertains to volunteers. The easier is to talk with an insurance broker who handles workers' compensation insurance. The other is to read the applicable statutes. For our purposes, the critical issue is to recognize that volunteer service raises liability and insurance coverage issues. Finally, when an independent contractor performs work for a nonprofit, the organization should require the necessary certifications from the contractor indicating that the business and its employees are covered by workers' compensation insurance.

(i) PREVENTIVE MEASURES. Many of the laws discussed here have laudable objectives. The cumulative effect of these laws can cause nonprofit organizations to cower at the prospect of endless lawsuits, making it difficult for them to operate. Although many of the laws considered here confer specific rights and benefits, the particular law chosen as the basis for a specific lawsuit often represents the most logical basis, in view of the facts and circumstances, to package larger grievances concerning the work environment. Not surprising, the same measures that can be taken to reduce the likelihood of successful litigation under one employment law will prove to be helpful in reducing litigation under all employment laws because these measures have a beneficial effect on the workplace as a whole.

(i) Avoiding Diversity-Related Complaints. Organizations face the following two questions: (1) What type of work environment do they want to offer their employees? and (2) How can employers minimize employment-related litigation? Fortunately, the answers to both questions dovetail. Four decades ago, many people might have disputed the assertion that diversity makes for a more congenial and productive workplace. Today, most employers and employees

285. It appears that Section 3363.6 of the California Labor Code permits such an election, but this should be confirmed by someone who has practical experience with California's workers' compensation regime.

286. Several commentators have suggested that it may be better to cover volunteers under general liability insurance policies rather than workers' compensation policies because injuries to volunteers that are covered by workers' compensation could adversely affect experience ratings, resulting in an increase in workers' compensation insurance premiums. That may be true, but that is also true with respect to injuries to employees. Moreover, these commentators do not explain why claims made under general liability policies will not have an equivalent effect on the future premiums paid for that coverage.

would agree that diversity in the workplace is a worthy goal from both cultural and productivity standpoints. Inevitability, employers can reduce the costs associated with employment practice controversies as they implement programs that foster diversity as part of their efforts to improve productivity and foster a better working environment. Here are a few basic steps that should be considered to minimize employment-related lawsuits:

- Implement an ongoing diversity training program/process for the organization's entire workforce.
- Develop procedures permitting employees to make harassment/discrimination complaints and concerns known to appropriate people within management. The process should be structured to minimize employee concerns about retaliatory action.
- Develop procedures for handling employee harassment/discrimination complaints in a transparent and consistent manner.
- Implement procedures for systematic follow-up when an employee registers a complaint.
- Describe in writing actions that will be taken against employees who engage in harassing or discriminatory actions.
- Consider an employee handbook, but recognize that it must be kept current.
- Post all job openings and advertise within the organization.
- Require all job applicants to complete an application form that has been reviewed by legal counsel versed in employment law so that the application does not ask for inappropriate information.
- Document all hiring and employment-related decisions, describing the factual basis for each decision.
- Implement and consistently apply a performance review process based on clearly enunciated standards.
- If the organization must undergo a workforce reduction, retain a consultant experienced with downsizing to properly handle the process. Do not eliminate the positions of the highest-paid employees because in many instances, pay is correlated with age, opening the organization to age-discrimination suits.
- At least once a year, all employment practices should be audited to ensure that what the organization is actually doing what it believes it is doing.

In short, just having a written policy declaring that the nonprofit is an equal-opportunity employer is not sufficient.[287]

287. J. Burns, *supra* note 88, at 64-65.

(ii) Conducting Job Interviews and Developing Application Forms. Certain questions cannot or should not be asked during a job interview or on a job application because they do not elicit information relevant to the hiring decision, and, consequentially, may be evidence of discrimination in hiring. As a general rule, any organization interviewing job applicants should avoid asking the following questions during job interviews and on written application forms.

Category	Questions to Avoid
Age related	How old are you? What is your birth date? When did you graduate from high school or college?
National origin	Where are your parents, grandparents, or other relatives from? Is your name of a particular origin?
Marital status	Are you married, single, widowed, or divorced? Do you have a significant other or a "love interest"? What is your sexual orientation? Is that your maiden or married name?
Gender status	Are you pregnant? When will you go into production? Do you plan on having children? How many children do you have? How old are your children?
Racial status	What race are you? What color is your skin, eyes, or hair?
Religious affiliation	What religion are you? What days off will you need for religious observance?
Health	Do you have AIDS or cancer? How healthy are you? How often are you sick? Are you in good health? How many days were you absent from work last year because of illness? Have you ever filed for or received workers' compensation benefits? Are you currently taking any medications?
Disability	Are you disabled? (Keep in mind that the rules change after an employer makes what is termed a "conditional job offer")[a] Do you drink alcohol?

Category	Questions to Avoid
Criminal activity/ record	Have you ever been arrested or convicted of a crime? (See subsequent comments.) Have you ever been convicted of a misdemeanor?
Military record	What type of discharge did you receive from the service?
Photographs	Can we have a photo of you?

[a] UNITED STATES EQUAL EMPLOYMENT OPPORTUNITY COMMISSION, *supra* note 215; and UNITED STATES EQUAL EMPLOYMENT OPPORTUNITY COMMISSION, JOB APPLICANTS AND THE AMERICANS WITH DISABILITIES ACT (Dec. 31, 2003), which provides as follows:

> The ADA prohibits employers from asking questions that are likely to reveal the existence of a disability before making a job offer (i.e., the pre-offer period). This prohibition covers written questionnaires and inquiries made during interviews, as well as medical examinations. However, such questions and medical examinations are permitted after extending a job offer but before the individual begins work (i.e., the post-offer period).
>
> 9. What are examples of questions that an employer cannot ask on an application or during an interview?
>
> Examples of prohibited questions during the pre-offer period include:
>
> - Do you have a heart condition? Do you have asthma or any other difficulties breathing?
> - Do you have a disability which would interfere with your ability to perform the job?
> - How many days were you sick last year?
> - Have you ever filed for workers' compensation? Have you ever been injured on the job?
> - Have you ever been treated for mental health problems?
> - What prescription drugs are you currently taking?
>
> 10. May the employer ask me these questions after making a job offer?
>
> Yes. An employer can ask all of the questions listed in Question 9, and others that are likely to reveal the existence of a disability, after it extends you a job offer as long as it asks the same questions of other applicants offered the same type of job. In other words, an employer cannot ask such questions only of those who have obvious disabilities. Similarly, an employer may require a medical examination after making a job offer as long as it requires the same medical examination of other applicants offered the same type of job.

What should be apparent is that even in a post-offer setting, questions regarding disabilities should be asked with great care and should be dictated by business necessity rather than idle curiosity.

In some instances, the organization has a legitimate reason for asking a question that is generally viewed as prohibited. For example, if state law requires a bartender to be at least 25 years old, the organization should be able to ask the individual whether he will be able to provide proof of age. However, such questions should first be cleared with an employment lawyer.

The EEOC has also issued a number of notices pertaining to the use of arrest and conviction records. As a general rule, an organization cannot use prior arrests or convictions as an absolute bar on hiring because such a policy has a disparate impact on some protected groups, but conduct that indicates unsuitability for a particular position may be a basis for denying employment.[288] In a 2001

288. UNITED STATES EQUAL EMPLOYMENT OPPORTUNITY COMMISSION, NOTICE N-915-061, ENFORCEMENT GUIDANCE: PREEMPLOYMENT DISABILITY-RELATED QUESTIONS AND MEDICAL EXAMINATIONS (Sept. 7, 1990).

publication, the United States Department of Labor notes the prohibition against an absolute bar but then refers the reader to applicable state laws that might preclude an employer from considering someone with an arrest or conviction involving a particular category of offense (e.g., a sex crime involving a minor).[289] As always, every organization engaged in hiring should contact an employment law attorney before asking questions related to disabilities or prior arrests or convictions in a job interview or on an application form. A quick review of the EEOC's Web site will lead to numerous documents and guides that reflect the complexities now inherent in making sure the hiring process complies with the law.

(iii) Conducting Performance Reviews. Every organization should establish a performance review process that it clearly communicates to employees. This process should have these basic objectives: (1) to provide a documented record for all promotion and termination decisions and (2) to ensure consistency in all promotion and dismissal decisions. Ad hoc decisions inevitably lead to lawsuits, particularly when the employee is a member of a protected class. Any actions leading to discipline should be documented so that if the employee is dismissed, a clear record supports the action.

Performance reviews should be conducted at least annually. At least two employer representatives should be present. If warnings are issued, the consequences flowing from those warnings should be clearly articulated to the employee. Depending on the format, it may be advisable to have the employee sign the review.

(iv) Protecting Whistle-Blowers. Any employer who retaliates against an employee who brings a discrimination or harassment complaint is subject to liability under a number of federal antidiscrimination laws including Title VII of the Civil Rights Act of 1964,[290] the Age Discrimination in Employment Act,[291] and the Family and Medical Leave Act.[292] The employer also should be concerned about violating statutes (both federal and state)[293] that protect whistle-blowers who disclose more general violations of the law.[294] One of the more notable statutes is Section 1513(e) of Title 18 of the United States Code, which provides as follows:

> Whoever knowingly, with the intent to retaliate, takes any action harmful to any person, including interference with the lawful employment or livelihood of any person, for providing to a law enforcement officer any truthful information

289. United States Department of Labor, From Hard Time to Full Time: Strategies to Help Move Ex-Offenders from Welfare to Work (June 2001).

290. 42 U.S.C. 2000(e).

291. 29 U.S.C. 623.

292. 29 U.S.C. 2615.

293. Literally hundreds of state statues provide protection to whistle-blowers. Those who want state-by-state details should review (and update) E. Callahan and T. Dworkin, *The State of State Whistleblower Protection*, 38 Am. Bus. L. J. 99 (2000).

294. For an example, see 31 U.S.C. 3703(h), the Federal False Claims Act.

relating to the commission or possible commission of any federal offense, shall be fined under this title or imprisoned not more than 10 years, or both.

This statute was added to federal law by the Sarbanes-Oxley Act,[295] and it clearly applies to all nonprofits, their directors, officers, employees, and volunteers. Section 1513(e) is broad in scope. *Interference, any action,* and *whoever* are hardly limiting terms and phrases. What is particularly frightening about this statute is the ten-year prison term that a violation can bring.

Officers and directors must be careful in dealing with an employee who blows the whistle to federal agencies, such as the IRS or agencies that disburse federal grants and awards. The reported violation may not initially appear to be a criminal offense, but documents are often filed under penalties of perjury or there may be criminal violations under wire or postal fraud laws. Only time will reveal the scope of this new protection for whistle-blowers, but the term *law enforcement officer* could be construed to include those working for a wide variety of federal agencies, including the Internal Revenue Service, Federal Election Commission, and the Justice Department. As usual, organizations must also consider applicable state laws.[296]

People are always concerned about the potential liability that whistle-blowing poses for any nonprofit if the whistle-blower is harassed, but no one should overlook the importance of whistle-blowing to the governance process. An organization's board should welcome any assistance in identifying fraud, theft, and other inappropriate behavior by senior executives and managers. As discussed in Chapter 5, the 2004 survey by the Association of Fraud Examiners reported that organizations with employee tip or hot-line programs often experience significantly reduced losses from financial frauds.

As an example, consider a dispute involving the Chicago Manufacturing Center (CMC), a Section 501(c)((3) organization that helps small- and medium-size manufacturers improve business performance by providing information technology services. CMC received a significant amount of its funding from the National Institute of Standards and Technology (NIST), an agency of the Department of Commerce. The dispute involved William Fanslow, a CMC employee, who filed a claim against CMC under the whistle-blower provisions in the Federal False Claims Act,[297] claiming that CMC had retaliated against him for reporting alleged misappropriations of federal funds to a federal official. The district court ruled in favor of CMC on a motion for summary judgment, resulting in the Seventh Circuit's review of the case.[298] The Seventh Circuit examined the evidence by assuming for purposes of the review that all of the allegations were true.

---

295. See note 62, *supra*.

296. For an example, see the Illinois Whistleblower Reward and Protection Act.

297. Federal False Claims Act, *supra* note 294.

298. Fanslow v. Chicago Manufacturing Center, 384 F.3d 469 (7th Cir. 2004).

Fanslow had learned during the course of his employment that two management-level employees were working on a new venture, referred to as MFR.Net. Fanslow believed that the two employees planned to "spin-off [MFR.Net] and get rich off of it." According to the court's opinion:

> Fanslow observed CMC's resources being diverted to MFR.Net in the form of travel and labor expenses, legal fees, computer hardware, and equipment. Fanslow identified several individuals who billed their time to CMC while they worked exclusively on MFR.Net.... He believed that these were unallowable costs under CMC's nonprofit funding structure.
>
> Fanslow voiced his concerns to a federal official named Ned Ellington at a conference sponsored by NIST in November 1999. While at a session on e-business strategy, Fanslow heard Ellington announce that NIST did not want its centers engaged in any type of spin-off dot com enterprises.

The court's opinion then continues to detail Fanslow's version of events. He eventually was fired, leading to the lawsuit.

Unfortunately, the Seventh Circuit never discussed whether the MFR.Net venture was an appropriate CMC venture or whether nonprofit resources were being diverted to a for-profit venture that would benefit the two CMC employees personally. Instead, the Seventh Circuit simply concluded that additional fact finding was necessary, remanding the case to the district court for further action.

Nowhere in the court's opinion is there any mention that Fanslow tried to contact CMC's board of directors. That is the critical fact for our purposes. Fanslow was making allegations that, if true, potentially threatened a significant funding source for the nonprofit. He was also raising issues that could jeopardize the organization's tax-exempt status or trigger IRS sanctions. Every board should want to know about such allegations, but the challenge facing any board is to devise a system that generates timely information that can be investigated. This can mean designating a person in the organization (the human resources or general counsel's office if there is one) to receive tips. The process should allow for a telephone number, box or mailing address to be provided for anonymous tips or retain an outside agency to receive and process them. Whatever the system, the board must be clear that any harassment of whistle-blowers will not be tolerated. Encouraging employees to communicate while offering protection to them not only minimizes organizational liability under whistle-blower statutes but also helps ensure that the board will be able to react before it has a public crisis on its hands.[299]

299. Keep in mind that the Seventh Circuit's focus in *Fanslow* was on whether there was a showing of harassment. The case's procedural posture required the court to view the factual allegations in their best light from Mr. Fanslow's viewpoint. The court never reached a conclusion as to whether there was fraud or inappropriate activities. This should not be surprising because the Federal False Claims Act's harassment provision does not require that the whistle-blower's allegations be true. In short, the focus is on the four corners of the case and the lessons it holds rather than the validity of Mr. Fanslow's underlying concerns.

(v) Conducting Background Checks and Screening. We will consider background checks and screening later in this chapter. Some general comments[300] are nevertheless in order. Background checks and screening are generally legal. Nevertheless, before conducting a background check, a nonprofit should obtain prior written consent from the applicant. At least one court has held that an applicant's refusal to undergo screening can be a ground for not hiring, but no one should rely on this case until more precedent develops. Before implementing any program, the organization must review applicable state laws directly governing background checks as well as state privacy laws.

At least two companies provide computer-based screening systems that permit nonprofit employers to verify Social Security number, address, and criminal, credit, workers' compensation, motor vehicle, and employment histories in a matter of seconds. The cost is relatively inexpensive, ranging from $10 to $30 per check, but problems can arise if the prospective employer uses the information in an inappropriate manner.

Organizations should be careful when they rely on credit check histories. These may be permissible and appropriate for employees such as cashiers or bookkeepers who will be handling money, but credit checks may pose invasion of privacy issues when they are used as a general screening device.

As already noted, organizations must consider the EEOC's policy regarding the use of criminal arrest and conviction records. If the nonprofit is hiring a truck driver, the driver's motor vehicle record is relevant, particularly if it includes serious traffic offenses. If, on the other hand, someone is arrested and convicted for shoplifting in high school but has had an unblemished record for the last 20 years, using the shoplifting conviction to automatically eliminate the person can be problematic.

If a criminal background check is warranted, the nonprofit should not rely exclusively on the FBI's National Crime Information Center database, which is notorious for gaps. Service providers can quickly check state and local criminal databases. If a background check does produce evidence of a problem, the organization should attempt to verify the information for accuracy (but such verification should take privacy and defamation considerations into account).

By and large, polygraph testing is illegal.[301] Under no circumstances should polygraph tests be administered in the screening process unless the nonprofit has a written legal opinion that such tests are permissible. There may be times when national security or other reasons permit the use of a polygraph test, but such testing is prohibited for the nonprofit employee who works for a social services agency, museum, or day care center.

In implementing background check procedures, the organization should strive for consistent application of the procedure. If they are required of all employees, the executive director's best friend should be subjected to a background check

---

300. For additional details, see Lester R. Rosen, The Safe Hiring Manual (Facts on Demand Press 2004).
301. 29 U.S.C. 2001 et. seq.

when he applies for a position with the organization. It is also important to protect a person's privacy rights. Applicants and employees may have the right to sue if information is widely disseminated.

Although background checks pose some litigation risk, some people argue that every employee should undergo a basic check. These advocates point out that employers are increasingly being sued for wrongful hiring decisions involving the hiring of applicants with documented problems (e.g., violent criminal records) who then harm someone while performing their job functions. Employers must balance the risks of doing and not doing background checks.

(j) EPL AND DIRECTOR LIABILITY. In the vast majority of cases, nonprofit directors should be able to rely on the federal Volunteer Protection Act (VPA), state analogues thereto, or limitations on liability provided in nonprofit corporation statutes to protect them from liability arising from the organization's employment practices (see Chapter 4). A plaintiff's lawyer may choose to sue the entire board as a matter of course, but volunteer directors who regularly attend board meetings and who are not involved in the organization's day-to-day activities should be at little risk. This is particularly true if the suit involves an isolated dispute arising from the relationship between a manager and a subordinate. Nevertheless, directors should exercise sound judgment and care when discharging their duties. As noted in the discussion of the VPA, its protection is not ironclad. A director who acts willfully or in bad faith can lose the VPA's protection. Alternatively, the plaintiff may argue that the director was acting personally rather than in his capacity as a director—this argument being an attempt to remove the protection provided by liability shields under some corporate statutes.

11.4 AVOIDING OPERATIONAL LIABILITIES FROM VOLUNTEER SERVICE

Volunteers are a very important resource for many nonprofit organizations. Without them, some nonprofits would not be able to survive, yet many nonprofits ignore the legal issues associated with volunteers. This may be due, at least in part, to the perceived "halo effect" that attaches to those who volunteer.

Throughout this *Guide*, we have considered a number of issues that pertain to volunteers as part of more general discussions. The following are some specific do's and don'ts[302] that nonprofits relying on volunteers need to consider:

- In selecting volunteers, utilize written job descriptions, a written application, and appropriate interview procedures.
- Many laws regulating employment practices prohibit various forms of discrimination. Often the terms of these laws apply only to employees. Even

302. The list that follows is based in significant part on points made by Eleanor A. Evans, an attorney with CAPLAW, during a presentation entitled *Working with Volunteers: Legal Issues and Best Practices* at the June 15-16, 2005 CAPLAW National Training Conference held in Chicago, Illinois.

when these laws permit what would be inappropriate practices if a nonprofit's volunteers were paid, such discrimination may not be permissible under less well-known laws. For example, nonprofits taking advantage of federal grant money cannot discriminate based on inappropriate factors when administering the grant.

- Consider preparing a handbook for volunteers that defines relevant duties and procedures. Specifically, it should address political activity while volunteering, confidentiality issues, and grievance procedures.
- Avoid offering employees the opportunity to volunteer, such as participating in keeping a particular roadside free of litter. Such volunteer programs are best avoided because they pose potential problems under the Fair Labor Standards Act if participation is not completely voluntary.[303] If a nonprofit insists on sponsoring such a program, it should first consult with counsel, consider having the employee sign a statement that participation is voluntary, and schedule participation so that it does not coincide with regular working hours. Participation should never be coerced, nor should it be discussed during or factor into performance reviews. Of utmost importance, an employee who volunteers should not perform the same tasks that he performs as part of his regular duties. For example, a secretary who works 9 to 5 should not be asked to provide volunteer secretarial services to support the work of outside volunteers who are working on a fundraising campaign.
- Evaluate volunteer efforts on a regular basis. Procedures should be in place for dismissing volunteers who do not work out. The evaluation standards and procedures should be outlined in the volunteer handbook.
- A nonprofit that is subject to a union contract should make sure that its use of volunteers does not violate the terms of that contract.
- Comply with child labor laws when utilizing young people as volunteers. This may mean limiting the hours worked, obtaining employment certificates, and prohibiting participation in certain activities. This area can be confusing; if your organization cannot obtain a clear answer, the best course is to comply with maximum hour limitations and limitations on the type of work that minors can perform.
- Obtain a written parental consent for minors who volunteer. That consent should clearly outline the work to be performed and basic procedures and expectations, such as who is responsible for making sure that the child arrives home safely following volunteer service.
- Before reimbursing volunteer expenses (particularly meals and travel) or giving gift cards or other honorariums, assess whether such gifts or payments could cause the volunteer to be treated as an employee under tax or

303. 29 C.F.R. 785.44.

labor laws or under the VPA. Nonprofits that provide room and board to "volunteers" who are participating in job training or drug and alcohol treatment programs should carefully examine potentially applicable federal and state laws to properly assess the status of these individuals under such laws.

This list does not repeat points discussed elsewhere in this *Guide*. You also will want to take a close look at Chapter 12 regarding insurance.

11.5 AVOIDING OPERATIONAL LIABILITIES FROM SERVICE TO CHILDREN

On September 20, 2004, the Catholic Diocese of Tucson filed a voluntary plan of reorganization under Chapter 11 of the United States Bankruptcy Code.[304] The filing was motivated by 22 pending lawsuits against the Diocese alleging sexual abuse.[305] There has been much speculation whether other Catholic Dioceses in the United States will make similar filings. This is a rather extreme step for a nonprofit to take to save itself.

The Catholic Church is not the only nonprofit that has had to deal with legal problems arising from dealings with children. The Middlesex County district attorney obtained a grand jury criminal indictment against the Trustees of Groton School for failing to report a sexual assault against one student by other students.[306] The district attorney was most likely trying to send a message because the penalty for the violation is only $1,000. The board of trustees subsequently pled guilty and paid a $1,250 fine.[307] Although the fine was relatively small, the conviction could be problematic for any institution should other incidents occur if the institution does not take appropriate action to address the underlying issues.

The Child Abuse Prevention and Treatment Act[308] requires certain federal grants to states to be contingent on the state's having a law requiring specific persons and entities to report child abuse on learning of an incident. According to the National Association of Counsel for Children, every state has enacted mandatory reporting laws.[309] These laws are cataloged on the Administration of Children & Families (United States Department of Health & Human Services) Web site.[310] The board of any organization that has regular contact with children

304. Press Release, Bishop of Tucson, Most Reverend Gerald F. Kicanas, D.D (Sept. 20, 2004).

305. *See* Disclosure Statement Regarding Plan of Reorganization, Roman Catholic Church of Tucson, as the Debtor, filed in U.S. Bankruptcy Court for the District of Arizona (Sept. 20, 2004).

306. Press Release, Middlesex District Attorney, Groton School Indicted for Failure to File 51A Report to DSS (June 7, 2004).

307. *Massachusetts: Groton Board Pleads Guilty*, N.Y. TIMES, Apr. 26, 2005.

308. 42 U.S.C. 5101.

309. National Association of Counsel for Children Web site at http://www.naccchildlaw.org.

310. The catalog is mandated by law and is *available at* http://nccanch.acf.hhs.gov/index.cfm.

should ensure that the organization complies with applicable state law. This requires adopting procedures that encourage whistle-blowers to report incidents.

Many people are aware that a number of schools and day care centers have been embroiled in lawsuits alleging child abuse, but they may be surprised by the large number of newspaper articles reporting sexual abuse allegations involving children. The message is clear: Any nonprofit that has contact with minors as part of its routine activities must take child and sexual abuse issues seriously. Such organizations include day care, foster care, and health care (including mental health) providers, schools, homeless shelters, youth sports and recreational leagues, teams, and organizations, and providers of other services to children and young people. Many organizations confronted with allegations involving child sexual, physical, or emotional abuse never recover from the allegations. Obtaining insurance coverage in this area is becoming increasingly difficult and expensive.

The focus here is on children and teenagers, but organizations providing services to the elderly or other dependent or vulnerable populations should have similar concerns and adopt procedures similar to the ones discussed.

(a) BASIC STEPS. Although every situation is unique, a board of directors should consider taking these steps:

- Requiring detailed background checks. This is one of the first recommendations made to prevent child abuse.
- Requiring at least two adults to be present at all times when children are involved, particularly when the nonprofit is providing services to a child whose special needs make him particularly vulnerable.
- Establishing a written procedure for addressing allegations of inappropriate behavior. No organization wants to improvise in dealing with specific allegations.
- Considering surveillance. Organizations should proceed with caution and only with the advice of counsel before engaging in any surveillance. Federal and state privacy laws and a collective bargaining agreement must be addressed before setting up any surveillance system.[311]
- Adopting procedures to keep track of children. This is designed to avoid situations in which children are left overnight on school buses or behind on school trips. Head counts, checklists, nametags, identifying clothing, and inspections are all simple to implement.

---

311. *See* § 8(a)(5) of the National Labor Relations Act. In Colgate-Palmolive Co, 323 N.L.R.B. 515 (1997), the National Labor Relations Board found that the use of hidden surveillance cameras to investigate workplace and employee theft was a mandatory subject of collective bargaining because the "installation of surveillance cameras is both germane to the working environment and outside the scope of managerial decisions lying at the core of entrepreneurial control." *See also* Brewers and Maltsters, Local Union No. 6 v. NLRB, 414 F.3d 36 (D.D.Cir. 2005).

- Developing guidelines and procedures for required notification to authorities when there is a reportable incident.
- Having the board regularly discuss safety, sexual and child abuse, and related issues.

(b) EMPLOYEE AND VOLUNTEER SCREENING. Screening employees and volunteers[312] inevitably comes up when an organization considers steps to take to prevent child abuse. Screening requires the nonprofit to walk a difficult line. On one hand, the nonprofit faces liability if an incident occurs that could have been prevented through employee and volunteer screening, but no screening was conducted. On the other, actual or prospective employees and volunteers can sue the nonprofit if the screening process is improperly administered or if the information obtained from it is improperly communicated. Any nonprofit embarking on a screening program should seek counsel from an attorney who has experience dealing with these issues.

(i) Screening Defined. Screening can encompass a wide variety of techniques, including law enforcement background checks, review of sex offender lists, and references from prior employers. As a general rule, requiring employees to take a polygraph is illegal.

The organization may want to use several screening techniques in tandem because not all are equally reliable. In particular, employers should be cautious when relying on employment references. Past employers are just as concerned about lawsuits for defamation as are prospective employers, so past employers are often reluctant to speak forthrightly. However, there are techniques to improve the quality of the information received through references. One expert suggests avoiding questions that are too general, that are leading, or that lend themselves to yes/no answers.[313] This same expert suggests an initial contact by telephone, with the caller identifying himself and his position and describing the job. The organization should not place too much emphasis on sexual offender registries. Anecdotal evidence indicates that many people who are required to register never do. Obviously, more screening is better than less, but at least one court has held that an organization is not required to undertake every screening technique in the panoply of available options.

To be meaningful, the particular screening tools must be tailored to the employee's or the volunteer's duties. Consequently, an organization should first have a clear job description before interviewing employees or volunteers.[314] If

312. The legal duty to screen is not tied to the payment of consideration for services. Nonprofits can also have an obligation to screen volunteers who work with children if the risks and circumstances otherwise warrant screening. *See* Broderick v. King's WayAssembly of God, 808 P.2d 1211 (Alaska 1991); Infant C. v. Boy Scouts *of* America, 391 S.E.2d 322 (Va. 1990); and Big Brother/Big Sister of Metro Atlanta v. Terrell, 395 S.E. 241 (Ga. App. 1987).

313. John Patterson, Staff Screening Tool Kit, at 76 (Nonprofit Risk Management Center 2004).

314. *Id.*

the job requires that the employee come in contact with children but have no involvement with financial matters, the organization should consider screening through criminal background checks and sexual offender registries. It also might want to use a detailed personal interview and call employment references, particularly when the applicant's prior employment also required contact with children. However, a credit check might not be an appropriate screening technique.[315]

(ii) Failure to Screen. There is no question that a nonprofit organization can be held liable if it fails to screen employees or volunteers and that failure results in an incident.[316] If state law requires mandatory background checks or requires employees or volunteers to be licensed, a nonprofit that fails to comply clearly faces the liability imposed by the statutory regulation. This could be a monetary fine or loss of an organizational license to conduct the regulated activity. Such liability is most likely to occur when a state or locality requires day care providers or school bus drivers to be licensed. At a minimum, nonprofits should screen to ensure that employees and volunteers have complied with applicable licensing requirements. Obviously, screening should be performed when initially retaining the employee or volunteer, but organizations should adopt procedures to periodically confirm that licenses are still valid.

Organizations can also be held accountable in an action brought by the injured party. In this type of lawsuit, the plaintiff most likely will be required to establish that (1) the organization owed a duty to the child, (2) the potential risk of harm to the child was foreseeable, (3) the organization failed to take reasonable precautions to protect the child from the foreseeable harm, and (4) the organization's failure to take reasonable actions was the proximate cause of the injury. In addition to disputing the plaintiff's assertions, organizations often argue that the employee or volunteer[317] was not acting in such capacity, and therefore, the organization did not have control over the actions.

To illustrate, consider Troubled Teens, a nonprofit organization that provides counseling to teenagers who have been involved in crime. Troubled Teens hires four child psychologists with expertise in treating troubled teenagers. It checks educational records to confirm that each applicant has the degrees shown on the person's resume, but Troubled Teens undertakes no further screening because it assumes that its educational requirements will effectively screen out any bad actors. Six months after it hires Dr. Brody, Johnny Hoodman, a 16-year-old reports to another staff member that Dr. Brody invited him and two other boys to Brody's home, where Dr. Brody plied the boys with liquor and then molested

315. Guillermo v. Brennan, 691 F. Supp. 1151 (N.D. Ill. 1988); and Welsh Manufacturing v. Pinkerton's, 474 A.2d 436 (R.I. 1984).

316. As to the question of liability from a negligent hiring decision, see Ponticas v. KMS Investments, 331 N.W. 2d 907 (1983), one of the often cited cases in this area. As for specific cases involving nonprofits, see John Patterson, *supra* note 313, at 29–30, for a list of cases involving nonprofits.

317. Restatement (Second) Torts § 308 (1965).

them. During the course of the ensuing investigation, Troubled Teens discovers that Dr. Brody is a registered sex offender with a history of molesting his patients. Hoodman's parents bring a suit against Troubled Teens, arguing that the organization had a duty to screen applicants and that failure to review sex offender lists maintained by the state was a violation of that duty.

Setting aside the law for a moment, no organization should be surprised that parents would sue it under the circumstances described in the hypothetical case. Such suits are reflexive responses. Nor can any organization predict whether the parents will prevail in any given suit. Each case depends on the particular facts. Troubled Teens is likely to respond that the molestation did not occur in its facilities so Dr. Brody was not acting in his capacity as its employee.[318] The rejoinder from the parents will be that Troubled Teens put Dr. Brody in contact with their son. It simply is not clear which side will prevail. To complicate matters, suppose Dr. Brody had never registered as a sex offender, so checking the state registry would not have uncovered prior incidents.[319] Taking the facts one step further, suppose that Troubled Teens called Dr. Brody's previous employers and none of them mentioned any prior incidents. Questions involving causation, duty, and foreseeability are fact dependent, making their outcome unpredictable.

Hopefully this hypothetical demonstrated the difficulty of predicting whether screening is legally mandated under common law doctrines. Clearly, not all courts apply the same rule. There are several theories for assessing negligence. One court may conclude that any organization dealing with children must screen because the possibility of molestation is foreseeable. Another court may be unwilling to impose liability for off-premises sexual activities of employees because such activities are deemed to be outside the control of the employer. Still another court may find an employer liable for negligent hiring if it fails to take reasonable efforts, including screening, to detect an unfit employee.[320] Finally, another court may conclude that screening is a sufficient defense if it is undertaken, rejecting any requirement that other tools be utilized.[321]

A nonprofit obviously must screen or perform background checks when a state statute mandates them. In the absence of a statutory requirement, each nonprofit having employees or volunteers who regularly come in contact with children as part of their duties should discuss the legal merits of screening with its

---

318. *See* Doe v. Boys Clubs of Greater Dallas, Inc., 907 S.W.2d 472 (Tex. 1995). In this case an organization escaped liability because, in part, molestation did not occur at its facilities, but this may not have been the only reason. Even when the molestation takes place on the organization's premises, it is not clear that all jurisdictions will hold the organization accountable under the doctrine of respondent superior. *See, e.g.*, Jeffrey Scott E. v. Central Baptist Church, 197 Cal. App.3d 718 (1988).

319. Juarez v. Boy Scouts of America, 80 Cal. App.4th 876 (2000) in which the court rejected a claim based on the assertion of a negligent hiring process. The court stated, "The conclusive determination that there was no information accessible to the Scouts that would cause them to suspect that Paz had a propensity to molest children is fatal to Juarez's causes of action based on these theories, even if such a common law duty existed." The court did hold that there were triable issues of fact as to whether the Boy Scouts failed to take reasonable measures to protect Juarez from sexual molestation.

320. Evan F. v. Hughson United Methodist Church, 8 Cal. App.4th 828 (1992)

321. *Big Brother/Big Sister of Metro Atlanta, supra* note 312.

legal counsel. As a general matter, screening employees and volunteers who regularly come in contact with children, teenagers, disabled people, and the elderly is warranted. The fact that a nonprofit took this action should provide at least some protection in the face of highly charged allegations, but there are no guarantees in this area.

(iii) Designing the Procedures. When a nonprofit decides to use screening procedures, it must be mindful of job applicant, employee, and volunteer rights as they relate to the screening process. They have rights to privacy under the United States Constitution, common law, and statutory law. Organizations should be particularly sensitive about using or disclosing any information in a way that could result in a defamation claim by the applicant. Applicants also have rights under federal and state employment discrimination laws that can be violated if the screening process is not correctly administered. It is critical that the nonprofit work with an attorney who has knowledge of local law. The following are just a few steps that an organization should consider:

- The organization should use an appropriate job application, and applicants should be required to certify that all statements in it are true and accurate.
- All screening procedures should be documented in writing, including procedures to protect the confidentiality of the screening results.
- The organization should clearly define the categories of people who will be required to undergo screening.
- The organization should define in advance what findings will result in disqualification.
- The behavior being screened should have a direct relationship to the job function.
- Polygraph tests should not be used in screening unless the organization has received a written legal opinion stating that the testing does not violate the Employee Polygraph Protection Act[322] and state analogues. As a initial reference point, employee polygraph testing should be viewed as illegal.[323]
- The screening procedure should be applied in a uniform and consistent manner.
- One person who has undergone appropriate training should be in charge of the screening process.

322. Employee Polygraph Protection Act of 1988, Pub. L. 101-649, 102 Stat. 646, *codified at* 29 U.S.C. 2001. Many states have adopted additional laws prohibiting polygraph tests.

323. 29 U.S.C. 2006 sets out a number of exceptions to the rule. They are tied to national defense, national security, and FBI contractors. There is also a limited exemption for ongoing investigations involving economic loss or injury, but the conditions that must be satisfied before that exception can be relied on are detailed.

- The screening process should be administered in a way that protects the applicant's privacy. For example, a screening interview or psychological exam should be conducted behind closed doors.
- Screening results should be disclosed only on a need-to-know basis. If the organization uses a hiring committee, it may not be advisable for everyone on the committee to know every detail, particularly if the committee is a large one.
- Screening results should be communicated to authorized personnel in a secure fashion. Interoffice routing envelopes and e-mail communications should be avoided.
- The nonprofit should obtain the written consent of the applicant before using invasive screening tools such as background checks, psychological interviews, or reference checks.[324]

Given the myriad of employment laws and job candidates' general awareness of their rights, all screening procedures have their perils. An organization should not hesitate to pay the legal fees to obtain adequate legal counsel in designing and implementing its screening program. Several thousand dollars may seem like a lot to pay a lawyer for advice, but that amount will pale in comparison to the legal fees necessary to defend just one lawsuit. Those who want to develop their plan in-house and then have it reviewed by an employment lawyer should review John Patterson's Staff Screening Tool Kit, published by the Nonprofit Risk Management Center. The kit is detailed, provides checklists, forms, questions, and much insightful information of critical importance to many nonprofits. It is affordably priced.

11.6 AVOIDING OPERATIONAL LIABILITIES IN THE WORK ENVIRONMENT

Nonprofits may be doing good, but they are still workplaces. As such, they are subject to the Occupational Safety and Health Act of 1970, administered by the United States Department of Labor through the Occupational Safety and Health Administration (OSHA). Regulations require each employer to provide a workplace that is free from serious hazards, examine workplace conditions to ensure that they conform to OSHA standards, ensure that employees have and use safe tools and equipment, establish operating procedures and communicate them so employees follow them, and make appropriate reports to OSHA. OSHA recommends that employers adopt the following four-point program as part of their efforts to comply:

- Management should first set policy, assign responsibility, and involve employees.

324. See John Patterson, *supra* note 313, at 27, 50, 54, 56, 78, and 80, and Chapter 9, which is not paginated.

- Both management and employees should continually analyze the workplace to identify current and potential hazards.
- Organizations should adopt methods to prevent and control existing or potential hazards.
- Managers, supervisors, and employees should be trained to understand and deal with work site hazards.

Workplace safety is a laudable goal notwithstanding regulatory requirements. It is also a topic that is beyond the scope of this *Guide*, but you should recognize that your organization is not exempt from OSHA just because the organization is a nonprofit. Furthermore, OSHA is not the only set of rules that should be of concern. Other federal agencies, as well as state and local governments, impose workplace safety requirements.

11.7 AVOIDING OPERATIONAL LIABILITIES FROM RESTRAINTS ON TRADE—ANTITRUST

When people hear about the antitrust laws and restraints on trade, they first think of large oil companies and manufacturers. At first, the possibility that any of these laws could apply to nonprofits is counterintuitive, but a review of case law under federal antitrust law leaves little doubt that nonprofits need to incorporate antitrust considerations into their basic decision-making process. Several of the leading Supreme Court cases interpreting federal antitrust law have involved nonprofit entities. Judge Posner explained why the antitrust laws should apply to nonprofits, stating:

> Non-profit status affects the method of financing the enterprise ... and the form in which profits ... are distributed and it may make management somewhat less beady-eyed in trying to control costs.... But no one has shown that it makes that enterprise unwilling to cooperate in reducing competition.[325]

Antitrust law is very difficult to discuss because of the integration of legal rules and economic analysis. Although the economic analysis is just another form of fact finding, it is clearly much more complex than the typical fact finding that permeates legal decision making. Further complicating matters are the periodic shifts in federal enforcement philosophies that occur when the political winds change in Washington, D.C. The statutory language may remain constant, but its interpretation can dramatically change the administration of the antitrust laws.

For purposes of this *Guide,* these difficulties limit our analysis to simply identifying situations in which a nonprofit should suspend its efforts until it has an opportunity to speak with legal counsel.

---

325. Hospital Corp of America v. FTC, 807 F.2d 1381 (7th Cir. 1986), as quoted in JAMES FISHMAN AND STEPHEN SCHWARZ, NONPROFIT ORGANIZATIONS: CASES AND MATERIALS, at 1007 (Foundation Press 2000).

(a) OVERVIEW. Before focusing on a specific rules, several points should be made. First, the focus here is federal prohibitions against restraints of trade, but every organization must adhere to applicable state laws.

Second, violations of many laws that we have considered throughout this *Guide* carry civil penalties and fines. In many cases, those charged with administration will simply give the violating entity a "slap on the wrist" if the behavior is corrected. Violations of antitrust law, however, entail potentially severe criminal penalties. White-collar prisons are full of corporate executives who have violated these laws. Additionally, penalties can include severe monetary fines, including treble damages in private antitrust suits.

Finally, we do not focus on the jurisdictional issues inherent in the federal laws. Jurisdiction under the Sherman Act[326] is tied to the Commerce Clause. Consequently, it apples if the restraint (or possibly just the business) affects interstate activity.[327] Anyone reading the case law will see that what often looks like isolated activity turns out to affect interstate commerce. The magnitude of that affect is largely irrelevant. Given the seriousness of the consequences flowing from violations of federal antitrust laws, nonprofits should not rely on jurisdictional touchstones as shields against liability.

(b) UNREASONABLE RESTRAINTS OF TRADE: THE SHERMAN ACT. The Sherman Act prohibits all contracts, combinations, and conspiracies that unreasonably restrain trade. Whether an act unreasonably restrains trade is a question of fact. The courts have divided violations into two categories for analytical purposes. The first category focuses on *per se* restraint, violations that so clearly restrain trade that they have been deemed unreasonable restraints as a matter of law. If a restraint falls into a per se category, the defendant is not permitted to argue its particular restraint is reasonable. Probably the best example is price fixing. The list of per se violations includes allocation of customers or territories among competitors, minimum resale price maintenance, certain tying arrangements, and group boycotts.

The second category requires an analysis of the conduct to ascertain whether the conduct restricts competition in some significant way but has no overriding business justification. This is referred to as a *rule of reason* analysis. Under this analysis, the person complaining that he has been injured by a restraint of trade must demonstrate that the alleged restraint produced adverse, anticompetitive effects within the marketplace. This typically means showing price increases, declines in supply, or declines in quality. This can be difficult to prove, so the courts have permitted those complaining of injury to demonstrate that the entity accused of restraining trade has market power (i.e., the ability to raise prices

326. 15 U.S.C. 1.

327. Summit Health v. Pinhaus, 500 U.S. 322 (1991); McLain v. Real Estate Board, 444 U.S. 232 (1980); and Cordova & Simnpietri v. Chase Manhantan Bank, 649 F.2d 6 (1st Cir. 1981). For a general discussion of the issue, see HERBERT HOVENKAMP, FEDERAL ANITTRUST POLICY: THE LAW OF COMPETITION AND ITS PRACTICE, at 761-65 (West Publishing 2005).

above the level that would prevail in a truly competitive market). If this can be established, the burden then shifts to the person accused of restraining trade to demonstrate that the challenged conduct promotes competition. In addition to the per se and rule of reason analyses, the courts also apply a "quick-look" analysis, which is really a middle ground analysis.[328]

(i) Price Fixing. Probably the most universally understood restraint of trade is price fixing. It is viewed as a per se violation of the Sherman Act. Nonprofits do not generally sell light bulbs or oil, but many sell services. Any of the following actions is illegal under the Sherman Act:

- Two hospitals agree to charge $1,000 for a certain medical test.
- Five universities agree to increase their tuition 10 percent this year.
- Six social services agencies in Omaha, Nebraska, agree to limit pay for social service workers with a master's degree in social services to $40,000 per year.
- Three nonprofit hospitals agree that they will not charge more than 105 percent of their direct costs for open heart surgery.

These examples involve "naked" attempts to fix price. Competitors can also engage in price fixing by indirect means, but there still must be evidence of collusion. For our purposes, the critical issue is how to stay out of trouble. To illustrate, assume that Joe Fox, the executive director of Brown Art Museum, is considering an increase in the museum's basic admission fee from $10 to $15, but he is concerned that Blue Art Museum, which is just five blocks west of Brown, will leave its fee at $12. This could attract some of Brown's patrons who refuse to pay the $15 fee. Fox decides to call Clara Harper, executive director of Blue Art Museum, to suggest that both museums will come out ahead if Harper also increases the fee for admission. Harper should immediately end the conversation and probably contact Blue Art Museum's general counsel.

Less obvious cases pose greater risks because the participants may not realize that they are engaging in illegal activity. To continue with our museum example, assume that the Association of Bricksville Museums has a monthly lunch meeting to discuss common problems. At the meeting, the following conversation takes place at a table occupied by officials from six different museums:

Joe Fox: Business has been good. Paid attendance is up 20 percent this year.

Clara Harper: Joe, you're right. We're up 25 percent. Tourism has really come back.

Linda Lorenz: Us too. In fact, we were thinking of upping our basic admission fee by $3.

---

328. United States v. Brown University, 5 3d 658 (3rd Cir. 1993).

Clara Harper: I hadn't thought about that, but it isn't a bad idea. Why leave prices low when the demand is there?

Joe Fox: You two are right. I'm going to go back and talk to our board of directors.

Notice that nobody has expressly agreed to fix a price, but inferences of collusive pricing activity certainly could be drawn if admission prices at all three museums suddenly jump. This discussion should not have taken place. The two other museum officials seated at the table would have been well advised to get up and walk out of the meeting when Linda Lorenz first began to talk about admission fees.

So to be clear, competitors—be they hospitals, museums, or social service agencies—should not talk about prices, methods for setting prices, costs, discounts, warranty terms, credit terms, or other matters that affect price. There may be exceptions to this rule, but they should be relied on only after consultation with qualified legal counsel.

People who want proof that nonprofits can run into trouble for fixing prices should consider the major enforcement action the FTC brought against nine elite universities because of their agreement concerning the determination of financial aid for incoming students. Such aid was properly viewed as a price discount when the veil of helping those in need was removed. The Tenth Circuit wrote:

> Since the Overlap Agreement is a price fixing mechanism impeding the ordinary functioning of the free market, MIT is obliged to provide justification for the arrangement.[329]

The court then remanded the case for a full-scale rule of reason analysis. Before that occurred, MIT entered into a settlement with the FTC[330] (the other schools had settled earlier), which permitted the schools to coordinate financial aid activities subject to a set of new guidelines.

(ii) Allocation of the Market. It is also a per se violation for competitors to divide a market, agreeing that one competitor will service this group of customers and the other will service another group.[331] To illustrate, consider North Hospital and South Hospital, both nonprofit hospitals. Each uses an expensive diagnostic machine to test for a particular form of cancer. If the two act competitively, each

---

329. *Id.*

330. Press Release, Massachusetts Institute of Technology, Settlement Allows Cooperation on Awarding Financial Aid (Jan. 5, 1994).

331. Palmer v. Brg of Georgia, 498 U.S. 46 (1990); United States v. Topco Associates, 405 U.S. 596 (1972); and Blackburn v. Sweeney, 53 F.3d 825 (7th Cir. 1995). Although the specifics of the *Topco* decision have been criticized, the Court did provide a concise statement regarding its treatment of territorial divisions, summarizing the law as follows:

> This Court has reiterated time and time again that "[h]orizontal territorial limitations ... are naked restraints of trade with no purpose except stifling of competition." Such limitations are per se violations of the Sherman Act.

will be able to charge $500 per test, which is $100 below the cost of administering the test. Recognizing the problem, North Hospital and South Hospital agree to forgo expensive advertising as a way to reduce cost and to draw a geographic line along the river that divides the city. South Hospital will provide tests only to people who reside south of the river, and North Hospital will provide tests only to people residing north of the river. This division will permit each hospital to charge $700 per test. This is a per se violation of the Sherman Act.

As is often true with anticompetitive behavior, the collusive aspect is not always so blatant. Let's assume the two hospitals have not bought the expensive diagnostic machines yet, but each is considering the purchase. After a thorough analysis, each hospital independently concludes that the market can support only one machine profitably. Therefore, the two hospitals decide to form a joint venture that will acquire one machine. In attempting to maintain the status quo, they further agree that the testing facility will refer patients testing positive to the respective hospitals based on geographic location. This makes perfect sense because patients who live on the north side of town would have naturally gravitated toward North Hospital for their test and treatment and patients who live on the south side of town would have naturally gravitated toward South Hospital for the same.

This example raises two basic issues under the antitrust law. Anytime competitors consider entering into a joint venture, they must consider whether that venture could be construed as a violation of the antitrust laws. The FTC has issued a series of guidelines regarding joint ventures between health care providers. Setting aside the agreement on referrals, the joint venture between North and South Hospitals is probably permissible under those guidelines, given the FTC's statement that:

> Most hospital joint ventures to purchase or otherwise share the ownership cost of, operate, and market high-technology or other expensive health care equipment and related services do not create antitrust problems. In most cases, these collaborative activities create pro-competitive efficiencies that benefit consumers. These efficiencies include the provision of services at a lower cost or the provision of services that would not have been provided absent the joint venture. Sound antitrust enforcement policy distinguishes those joint ventures that on balance benefit the public from those that may increase prices without providing a countervailing benefit, and seeks to prevent only those that are harmful to consumers. The Agencies have never challenged a joint venture among hospitals to purchase or otherwise share the ownership cost of, operate and market high-technology or other expensive health care equipment and related services.[332]

This statement creates a safe harbor that sets requirements that, if satisfied, will not result in the FTC or Department of Justice challenging the venture on

332. Federal Trade Commission, Statement of Department of Justice and Federal Trade Commission Enforcement Policy on Hospital Joint Ventures Involving High-Technology or Other Expensive Health Care Equipment.

antitrust grounds. The statement then provides an analytical framework for assessing whether a joint venture poses a potential problem when it does not satisfy the safe harbor. Before North Hospital and South Hospital enter into the joint venture, they should assess its status under the FTC's Statement.

This joint venture contains an agreement to divide the market as part of its terms. Although the basic joint venture may not pose a problem under the FTC statement, the parties have gone beyond operating a testing service to a division of the market for treatment. This is not permissible.

Anyone making an even cursory review of antitrust law will quickly see that antitrust issues lurk everywhere in the health care field. This same type of problem also could arise in a university setting, with, for example, several universities agreeing to develop computer-based training courses through a joint venture. That venture might be permissible under antitrust law, but it would run into trouble if the universities then agreed to allocate students using those programs.

(iii) Group Boycotts or Concerted Refusals to Deal. A group boycott involves an agreement to refuse to deal with someone. Clearly, an individual nonprofit's decision not to purchase goods or services from a particular vendor is not a restraint of trade. However, if the nonprofit asks others to join it, hoping to drive prices down, this most likely is a per se violation of the Sherman Act, particularly if the boycott participants possess market power. To illustrate a boycott that could be viewed as a restraint of trade, consider the four legal aid societies that operate in Verde County. Together, these four nonprofit organizations perform 90 percent of the defense work for low-income individuals accused of crime in Verde County. As a result of recent natural disasters that have attracted record levels of contributions to disaster relief organization, the four legal aid societies have seen a 45 percent decline in their contributions, making it impossible for them to maintain their current level of services. To address the problem, they collectively advise Verde County that they will cease performing any legal aid services unless the county increases by 20 percent the fees it pays these organizations for their efforts. This is in all likelihood an illegal boycott under the per se rule.[333]

While the legal aid boycott was designed to affect pricing decisions, some economic boycotts by nonprofits have clear political aims. The courts have been unwilling to extend the antitrust laws to these boycotts on grounds that to do so would violate First Amendment rights[334] or that the boycott is a noncommercial activity.[335] For example, the Eighth Circuit refused to apply the Sherman Act to a boycott organized by the National Organization for Women against states that had not ratified the Equal Rights Amendment. Any organization arguing that its boycott is entitled to protection under the First Amendment should be careful: The eye of the beholder often lacks objectivity. In a case similar to the earlier

333. FTC v. Superior Court Trial Lawyers, 493 U.S. 411 (1990).

334. NAACP v. Calibourne Hardware, 458 U.S. 886 (1982).

335. Missouri v. National Organization for Women, 620 F.2d 1301 (8th Cir. 1992). For a more complete discussion of this issue, see HERBERT HOVENKAMP, *supra* note 327, at 240–41, on which this discussion is based.

example involving the legal aid societies, the participants unsuccessfully argued that their boycott had a political element.[336]

(c) OTHER RESTRAINTS—DO NOT BE MISLED BY LISTS. We have focused on common restraints on trade. The prohibition under the Sherman Act is on restraints on trade, not specifically enumerated acts. One recent case[337] involving a nonprofit illustrates the potentially broad reach of the Sherman Act. Virginia Vermiculite, a mining company, brought suit against Historic Green Springs, a Section 501(c)(3) land preservation organization, arguing that Historic Green Springs had conspired with W.R. Grace Company, another mining company, to restrain trade when Historic Green Springs accepted a donation of valuable mineral lands from Grace.

Historic Green Springs prevailed in its efforts to obtain a dismissal of the lawsuit,[338] but Virginia Vermiculite's arguments do have at least some superficial appeal. Grace and Virginia Vermiculite were competitors in the vermiculite mining market. Not surprising, Grace did not initially want to sell the land to its competitor, despite the fact that Virginia Vermiculite was a logical buyer.[339] To ensure that the mineral rights would not somehow fall into Virginia Vermiculite's grasp, Grace imposed certain restrictions on the gift of the land, to which Historic Springs agreed.[340]

While the Fourth Circuit Court of Appeals held that accepting a gift does not constitute concerted action on the part of a donor and the donee, the case demonstrates how a competitor might respond if it believes that the actions of a nonprofit have placed it at a competitive disadvantage. What is most notable about the case is the absence of the usual price fixing, market allocation, or boycott allegations—the typically enumerated actions that create liability under the Sherman Act.[341] As a practical matter, few nonprofits need to worry about such creative assertions under the Sherman Act. At the same time, all nonprofits should keep the Sherman Act's general prohibition against restraint of trade in mind as they enter into increasingly common ventures with for-profit entities that do have competitors.

(d) PRICE DISCRIMINATION—THE ROBINSON-PATMAN ACT. The Robinson-Patman Act prohibits various forms of price discrimination.[342] Setting aside a number of exceptions and definitional issues, at its core, this act requires sellers to sell a

---

336. FTC, *supra* note 333.

337. Virginia Vermiculite, Ltd. v. Historic Green Springs, 307 F.3d 277 (4th Cir. 2002).

338. *Id.*

339. Virginia Vermiculite, Ltd. v. Historic Green Springs, 144 F. Supp. 558 (W.D. Va. 2001); and O. Chloe, *A Missed Opportunity, Nonprofit Antitrust Liability in Virginia Vermiculite, Ltd.v. Historic Green Springs*, 113 YALE L. REV. 553 (2003). See findings of fact numbers 1, 2, 27, 86, 89,169, and 184 in the district court's opinion.

340. *Virginia Vermiculite, Ltd., supra* note 339, findings of fact numbers 218–20.

341. Just to be clear, there was no basis for such traditional allegations.

342. 15 U.S.C. 13(a).

particular product to everyone at the same price when differential pricing would injure the competitive marketplace. For our purposes, the act's most relevant provision carves out a special exception for nonprofits, permitting schools, colleges, universities, public libraries, churches, hospitals, and charitable institutions not operated for profit to purchase their supplies without regard to the price discrimination rules otherwise applicable under the Robinson-Patman Act.[343] This provision has permitted nonprofit hospitals to purchase pharmaceutical goods at discounts not available to others.

The critical requirement is that the supplies be for the use of the nonprofit. This requirement has predictably generated the bulk of the litigation under this provision. Other buyers have challenged whether a nonprofit's use of the good is for its own use. For example, in one case, the United States Supreme Court held that drug purchases by a nonprofit hospital are for its "own use" if the drugs are dispensed for inpatient treatment, outpatient treatment when the patient has left the hospital (provided the use is for a limited and reasonable time and continues hospital treatment), and to physician staff members for their own use (if dispensation furthers the hospital's functions).[344] However, the hospital was not considered to be using the drug for its "own use" when a former patient wanted to renew a prescription.

(e) ANTICOMPETITIVE MERGERS—THE CLAYTON ACT. Section 7 of the Clayton Act prohibits mergers and acquisitions if the effect of the transaction "may be to substantially lessen competition, or to tend to create a monopoly."[345] Quite clearly, this is a determination that goes beyond the scope of this *Guide*, yet, nonprofits should recognize that the limitation on mergers and acquisitions that may reduce competition does apply to nonprofits.[346]

As a practical matter, this limitation will not be an issue for two small social service agencies in New York, Los Angeles, or Chicago that want to merge to achieve economies of scale. Large organizations or those in small markets have to be more careful. The FTC has challenged mergers involving nonprofit hospitals as being anticompetitive. Such a challenge is not out of the question if two local educational institutions were to consider a merger.

Nonprofits serving small markets such as rural communities may actually need to be more careful than those serving large urban markets because the assessment of competitive impact is not made in the abstract but with a focus on the particular markets being served by the entities in question. Consequently, when a nonprofit participates in a merger or acquisition, those charged with handling the legal aspects of the transaction should consult an antitrust lawyer. Given the fact that the nonprofit will in all likelihood need to notify the state's

343. 15 U.S.C. 13c.

344. Abbott Laboratories v. Portland Retail Druggists, 425 U.S. 1 (1976).

345. 15 U.S.C. 18.

346. *See, e.g.*, University Health, Inc., 115 F.T.C. 880 (1992); and The Reading Hospital, 113 F.T.C. 285 (1990).

attorney general and need court approval, these transactions will already involve hefty legal fees.

Large nonprofits must comply with the premerger notification requirements in Section 7A of the Clayton Act (referred to as the *Hart-Scott-Rodino notification requirements*). These requirements are intended to provide the FTC the opportunity to review the competitive impact of large transactions. While detailed scope provisions need to be reviewed, as a rule of thumb, the prenotification requirements are triggered only if one of the entities involved has $100 million or more in annual sales or total assets and the other entity has $10 million or more.[347] Notification is required in any event if the value of the transaction exceeds $200 million.

(f) TRADE ASSOCIATIONS AND RESTRAINTS ON TRADE. Trade associations clearly serve legitimate purposes, including education, standard setting (e.g., safety), and trade promotion. They also provide a coordinated vehicle for industry lobbying.[348] However, as Adam Smith pointed out long ago:

> People of the same trade seldom meet together, even for merriment or diversion, but the conversation ends in a conspiracy against the public, or in some contrivance to raise prices.[349]

From an antitrust perspective, trade associations pose two sets of issues. The first set involves the members. As previously noted, members cannot use the association to cleanse what would otherwise be illegal activity. Consequently, association meetings cannot be an occasion for the discussion of industry pricing practices. The following statement from DaimlerChrysler Corporation's Corporate Guide for Antitrust Compliance nicely summarizes how people should respond to inappropriate comments:

> Discussions at trade association meetings about prices, terms or conditions of sale, and restrictions on dealing with customers or suppliers are among the topics that are prohibited. DaimlerChrysler personal must not participate in any such discussions. If these topics arise, object immediately. If the discussion continues, leave the meeting and request that your departure be noted in the minutes. Any incidents like this should be reported to [DaimlerChrysler's Office of General Counsel].

The second set of issues pertains to the trade association itself. A trade association can be charged with antitrust violations if it engages in certain activity. Individuals and firms who have been denied membership in trade associations have been able to demonstrate that such denial violated the antitrust laws. While

---

347. 15 U.S.C. 18a(a)(2). For additional details, see 16 C.F.R. 801.
348. United Mine Workers v. Pennington, 381 U.S. 657 (1965); and Eastern Railroad Presidents Conference v. Noerr Motor Freight, 365 U.S. 127 (1961).
349. ADAM SMITH, AN INQUIRY INTO THE NATURE AND CAUSES OF THE WEALTH OF NATIONS (Random House 1937), as quoted in ABA SECTION OF ANTITRUST LAW, AN ANTITRUST GUIDE FOR TRADE ASSOCIATION PROFESSIONALS AND MEMBERS (2004).

membership requirements serve to limit participation to people with common interests, they also serve to exclude people. If not properly drawn, such requirements can be anticompetitive by denying to otherwise qualified individuals the accreditation necessary to compete in the marketplace. Consequently, the association must ensure that those setting membership requirements do not have hidden, anticompetitive agendas. Membership issues can also arise concerning how nonmembers are treated and how member expulsion is handled. For example, a trade association could run into trouble if it sponsors a major trade show but excludes nonmembers from participating if participation is potentially important to competing in the market.[350] Similar issues arise when an association undertakes standards setting. The standards cannot be designed to achieve anticompetitive objectives.[351]

Those managing the trade association must be concerned about association liability for the acts of its members that are part of its officially sanctioned activities.[352] The United States Supreme Court provided an excellent rationale for imposition of association liability:

> Furthermore, a standard-setting organization like ASME can be rife with opportunities for anticompetitive activity. Many of ASME's officials are associated with members of the industries regulated by ASME's codes. Although, undoubtedly, most serve ASME without concern for the interests of their corporate employers, some may well view their positions with ASME, at least in part, as an opportunity to benefit their employers. When the great influence of ASME's reputation is placed at their disposal, the less altruistic of ASME's agents have an opportunity to harm their employers' competitors through manipulation of ASME's codes.
>
> Only ASME can take systematic steps to make improper conduct on the part of all its agents unlikely, and the possibility of civil liability will inevitably be a powerful incentive for ASME to take those steps. Thus, a rule that imposes liability on the standard-setting organization—which is best situated to prevent antitrust violations through the abuse of its reputation—is most faithful to the congressional intent that the private right of action deter antitrust violations.[353]
>
> [Footnotes omitted]

Those running trade associations should keep this ruling in mind when they structure the association's activities. They should use written agendas for meetings, set procedures, review actions by committees, provide equal access to members of the industry, adopt procedures to respond to complaints, and take other meaningful actions.

---

350. Associated Press v. United States, 326 U.S. 1 (1945).
351. For a general discussion of standard setting, see HERBERT HOVENKAMP, *supra* note 327, at 233-39.
352. American Society of Mechanical Engineers v. Hydrolevel Corp., 456 U.S. 556 (1982).
353. *Id.*

(g) PERMITTED RESTRAINTS—COVENANTS NOT TO COMPETE. A nonprofit organization can generally use one important restraint on trade to its benefit, but subject to certain limitations. This is a covenant not to compete in an employment contract. Such a clause is commonly used in the business community to limit the ability of employees to compete with their former employers. There is no reason that a nonprofit should not consider such an agreement under appropriate circumstances. Specifically, such an agreement could be used to prevent a development director from jumping from one nonprofit to another with a similar mission and then contacting the donors he developed for his former employer.

The natural reaction of those who have never considered a covenant not to compete is similar to that of a kid in candy store. "Let's make it for 20 years." That is where the potential problems with such covenants lie. Although the laws in many states sanction them, these same laws are unwilling to enforce unreasonable covenants (or portions thereof), recognizing the need for an individual to earn a living and perform his profession. Various states apply different rules for purposes of enforcing covenants not to compete. The different approaches fall into two basic categories. In some states, if a covenant not to compete is unreasonable, the courts will simply rule that no part of it is enforceable. In other states, the courts will apply a "blue pencil" test and enforce the agreement to the extent that it is reasonable. For example, if a covenant provides for no competition for ten years and the court determines that only a two-year period is reasonable, the court will "redraw" the covenant, holding it valid for a two-year period of time. Some states regulate covenants not to compete by statute rather than relying on a court's assessment of appropriate public policy.

It is impossible to provide a safe harbor for reasonableness. However, most lawyers familiar with the subject would advise that a period much beyond a year or two is unreasonable except in extraordinary circumstances. Nobody should be surprised if the lawyer recommends an even shorter term.

The jurisdictions that refuse to enforce any portion of an unreasonable covenant are sending a clear message to employers: The employer overreaches at its peril, and the courts hope that this results in some degree of self-restraint on the part of employers. Nonprofits would be advised to limit their use of covenants not to compete to key employees and consultants. Courts are unlikely to enforce such covenants against the average janitor or secretary.

We have focused on covenants not to compete from the standpoint of time. They can also include territorial restrictions. The employer should be reasonable in defining the territory. Assuming that there is a valid reason for a restriction in the first place, a covenant restricting the executive director of a small New York social services agency from working for a similar agency in California would be hard to justify as reasonable. Along these same lines, a covenant limiting a development director from contacting current or potential donors with whom he has had contact in the last year might be reasonable. A covenant that prevented him from soliciting people who are not existing donors of his now-former employer and with whom he has never had contact does not seem to be reasonable.

The board of directors would be remiss if it did not consider a covenant not to compete when the interests of the nonprofit need to be protected. But in doing so, it should be sure to discuss the reasonableness and propriety of any covenant with a lawyer. Quite apart from the legality, the board should also consider the potential impact on the organization's ability to hire qualified personnel.

11.8 AVOIDING OPERATIONAL LIABILITIES ARISING FROM EVENTS

Many nonprofits sponsor street fairs, festivals, conventions, and other events to raise money and increase their visibility. We will examine a typical street festival to illustrate the issues and perils arising from such fundraising events.[354]

Imagine the typical street fair. It is a hot, sweltering weekend in July. The Downtown Chamber of Commerce, a Section 501(c)(6) organization, is sponsoring its annual July Fourth Festival. The festival drew 5,000 people when it was first staged in 1967. Today, it brings 600,000 people to the downtown area. The attractions are ethnic food, beer, street clowns and entertainers, fireworks, a marketplace, continuous entertainment on five stages, and a 10K midnight run. Each night, two nationally known bands headline the main stage. The chamber funds all of the entertainment with the proceeds from ticket sales for beer and food. Total revenue this year is expected to exceed $3 million.

As this example should make clear, small fundraising events can gradually turn into big business, requiring months of planning. This is true although the event takes place only once a year for a few days. The organization's board needs to adopt the proper mindset: It is running a business. The organization's business must comply with all applicable laws. Rather than relying on kind-hearted regulators to bring "inadvertent" violations to its attention, the organization's board, through the staff, should aggressively identify legal requirements and make sure that the organization complies with them. This may require the organization to retain outside legal counsel sooner than the board might expect.

(a) SECURITY. One of the first business concerns should be to ensure that there is adequate security for the event. Uncontrolled crowds can be dangerous. Returning to the hypothetical case, the Downtown Chamber of Commerce needs to have a security force in place. If the event is an integral part of the community, the organization may be able to request police assistance. In many cases, the organization must supplement police assistance with its own security force. This can mean hiring off-duty police officers (assuming that this is permissible under city ordinances and union rules governing the police force) or retaining security through a third-party provider. As a general rule, organizations should make every effort to obtain security assistance from an established third-party provider with an excellent reputation.

---

354. This is an area where the author has particular experience, having advised two nonprofits on major events for a number of years.

Assume, however, that a local company offers to provide festival security for $135,000, but Leroy Franks, a CPA who is a member of the chamber's board, convinces the board to hire 50 off-duty police officers at $20 per hour to provide security at a total cost of $50,000. He proposes to have the chamber cut a check payable to each officer at the end of the festival. To avoid income tax withholding hassles, Franks has each officer sign a short-form agreement stating that the officer is an independent contractor. By approving this plan, the board has made a number of potentially serious mistakes.

(i) Issue 1: Employment Taxes from the Organization's Perspective. Just saying that each member of the security force is an independent contractor does not make it so. Franks is correct in concluding that if the members of the security force are treated as independent contractors, the chamber is not responsible for wage withholding or employment taxes (FICA and FUTA). However, the distinction between "employee" and "independent contractor" status for tax purposes is a question of fact and has created a great deal of controversy. Do not assume that part-time or temporary arrangements lead to independent contractor status. The IRS and state taxing authorities rely on a multifactor test to determine whether an individual is acting as an independent contractor. Probably the most important factor is whether the individual or the "employer" controls how the individual performs his duties. If, for example, the chamber tells each member of the security force when to report for duty, what area he should cover, and what he should do if there is a problem, members of the security force may be deemed to be employees of the organization rather than independent contractors. Another important factor is whether the individual provides his own tools. If the chamber provides uniforms (e.g., a T-shirt labeled "Security") and communications equipment (e.g., walkie-talkies) to the off-duty officers, it is even more likely that they will be classified as employees.

One solution is to contract with a third-party provider. In the example, the chamber rejected an established company in favor of a more informal arrangement with off-duty police officers. Assume instead that the chamber had addressed the withholding issue by looking to a point person to supervise the security staff. This person might be an off-duty police officer who acts as a coordinator for the security force ("I know 20 guys I can assemble to help you out. You give me the cash and I will take care of everything else.") Unfortunately, this arrangement is ambiguous if the coordinator refuses to sign agreements or receipts. The chamber may still be considered to be the employer.

If the chamber wants to rely on Franks's proposal, it could file IRS Form SS-8 with the IRS, seeking a determination of the status of the security force members. The form should be reviewed by legal counsel before it is filed. This is a straightforward solution to the withholding problem, and, with one big caveat, every organization should consider taking advantage of this procedure. Before filing the form, the organization should make sure that its house is in order. If the organization has been treating a number of others as independent contractors who could be reclassified as employees, filing this form could result in the IRS's asserting tax deficiencies. In other words, filing the form may be equivalent to "sticking its head in the noose." There have been instances in which the IRS has sought to recover back taxes spanning more than ten years and amounting to hundreds of thousands of dollars.

Employee or Independent Contractor: The IRS's Take

* * *

According to the IRS[355]

> An employer must generally withhold income taxes, withhold and pay social security and Medicare taxes, and pay unemployment tax on wages paid to an employee. An employer does not generally have to withhold or pay any taxes on payments to independent contractors. To determine whether an individual is an employee or an independent contractor under the common law, the relationship of the worker and the business must be examined. All evidence of control and independence must be considered. In any employee-independent contractor determination, all information that provides evidence of the degree of control and the degree of independence must be considered. Facts that provide evidence of the degree of control and independence fall into three categories: behavioral control, financial control, and the type of relationship of the parties.
>
> Behavioral Control Category. Facts that show whether the business has a right to direct and control how the worker does the task for which the worker is hired include the type and degree of:
>
> - Instructions the Business Gives the Worker. An employee is generally subject to the business' instructions about when, where, and how to work. All of the following are examples of types of instructions about how to do work.
>   - When and where to do the work.
>   - What tools or equipment to use.
>   - What workers to hire or to assist with the work.
>   - Where to purchase supplies and services.
>   - What work must be performed by a specified individual.
>   - What order or sequence to follow.

The amount of instruction needed varies among different jobs. Even if no instructions are given, sufficient behavioral control may exist if the employer has the right to control how the work results are achieved. A business may lack the knowledge to instruct some highly specialized professionals; in other cases, the task may require little or no instruction. The key consideration is whether the business has retained the right to control the details of worker's performance or instead has given up that right.

---

355. Internal Revenue Service, Publication 15-A, Employer's Supplemental Tax Guide (rev. Jan. 2005). The language is quoted almost directly from this publication, but has been modified slightly for brevity.

- Training the Business Gives the Worker. An employee may be trained to perform services in a particular manner. Independent contractors ordinarily use their own methods.

Financial Control Category. Facts that show whether the business has a right to control the business aspects of the worker's job include:

- The Extent to Which the Worker has Unreimbursed Business Expenses. Independent contractors are more likely to have unreimbursed expenses than are employees. Fixed ongoing costs that are incurred regardless of whether work is currently being performed are especially important. However, employees may also incur unreimbursed expenses in connection with the services they perform for their business.
- The Extent of the Worker's Investment. An independent contractor often has a significant investment in the facilities he or she uses in performing services for someone else. However, a significant investment is not necessary for independent contractor status.
- The Extent to Which the Worker Makes Services Available to the Relevant Market. An independent contractor is generally free to seek out business opportunities. Independent contractors often advertise, maintain a visible business location, and are available to work in the relevant market.
- How the Business Pays the Worker. An employee is generally guaranteed a regular wage amount for an hourly, weekly, or other period of time. This usually indicates that a worker is an employee, even when the wage or salary is supplemented by a commission. An independent contractor is usually paid by a flat fee for the job. However, it is common in some professions, such as law, to pay independent contractors hourly.
- The Extent to Which the Worker can Realize a Profit or Loss. An independent contractor can make a profit or loss.

Relationship Category. Facts that show the parties' type of relationship include:

- Written contracts describing the relationship the parties intended to create.
- Whether the business provides the worker with employee-type benefits, such as insurance, a pension plan, vacation pay, or sick pay.
- The permanency of the relationship. If the "employer" engages a worker with the expectation that the relationship will continue indefinitely, rather than for a specific project or period, this is generally considered evidence that the "employer" intent was to create an employer-employee relationship.
- The extent to which services performed by the worker are a key aspect of the regular business of the company. If a worker provides services that are a key aspect of the "employer's" regular business activity, it is more likely that the "employer" will have the right to direct and control his or her activities. For example, if a law firm hires an associate, it is likely that it will present the attorney's work as its own and would have the right to control or direct that work. This would indicate an employer-employee relationship.

The independent contractor/employee issue is actually even more involved than this passage suggests due to a number of special provisions in the Internal Revenue Code, as well as due to specific industry practices. Anyone desiring more detail will find it on the IRS Web site or should consult an attorney.

* * *

We will not return to the independent contractor/employer issue again, so let's digress for a moment. This issue is not limited to special events. Recently, an arts council in Indiana lost an appeal of an unemployment tax case brought by the Indiana Department of Workforce Development over the proper classification of art school teachers who had significant independence. The department successfully questioned the classification of 75 instructors as independent contractors, arguing that they were employees.[356] Not surprising, the department's analysis was very similar to one used by the IRS. This issue comes up frequently with part-time teachers, student interns, medical interns and residents, and other common types of workers being misclassified. Every board should make sure that its organization is correctly characterizing members of its workforce; otherwise, the organization can incur an unexpected tax liability after grant money has already been spent. Unfortunately, the opinion in the *Arts Council* case did not provide the monetary details. If each of those instructors were paid $2,500 per year, the tax liability would have been somewhere in the neighborhood of $5,000 in back taxes, assuming the case did not result in the IRS attempting to collect FICA, FUTA, and Medicare taxes. An organization should not pay taxes that it does not owe, but if it plans to take an aggressive position, its board should first fully consider all of the implications in doing so and then reserve some money in the event a government body successfully challenges its position.

In case there are lingering doubts about employment taxes issues for part-time or temporary employees, the following quote from IRS Publication 15 (January 2005) should lay them to rest:

> For federal income tax withholding and social security, Medicare, and federal unemployment (FUTA) tax purposes, there are no differences among full-time employees, part-time employees, and employees hired for short periods. It does not matter whether the worker has another job or has the maximum amount of social security tax withheld by another employer. Income tax withholding may be figured the same way as for full-time workers. Or it may be figured by the part-year employment method explained in section 9 of Publication 15-A.[357]

(ii) Issue 2: Employment Taxes from the Directors' and Officers' Perspectives. Issue 1 focused on the risks posed to the organization when it fails to withhold on wages paid to employees. These problems can extend to so-called responsible persons employed by or acting on behalf of an organization.[358] Returning to the earlier example, Franks personally could face liability if the chamber ran into financial difficulties. He could well be considered a responsible person because he appears to have had some control over employment taxes and financial matters. Under the Internal Revenue Code, responsible persons can be held personally liable for income, Social Security, and Medicare

356. Bloomington Area Arts Council v. Department of Workforce Development, 821 N.E.2d 843 (In. App. 2005).
357. Internal Revenue Service, Publication 15 (Circular E), Employer's Tax Guide (rev. Jan. 2005).
358. I.R.C. §§ 6672 and 7501.

taxes that should have been withheld ("trust fund taxes").[359] Most states have comparable provisions for state employment taxes and state income taxes withheld from salaries.

Many directors and officers are surprised to learn that the withholding requirements (and responsible person liability) apply to nonprofit organizations, including Section 501(c)(3) organizations. In one case, a prominent tax attorney, who represented the members of a board that failed to collect and remit trust fund taxes, reported that the directors collectively settled with the IRS for an amount approximating $50,000. This attorney did a good job because the IRS apparently was seeking more than $100,000 from the group. The board members were all volunteers.

(iii) Issue 3: Workers' Compensation Insurance. Many states require employers to maintain workers' compensation insurance. If the organization fails to maintain such insurance, some states hold certain officers and directors personally liable for damages resulting from injury to workers. Now focus on Franks's security force. Suppose someone stabs, shoots, or takes a swing at a member of the force? The chamber should obtain the necessary coverage even if it takes the position that the workers are independent contractors for tax purposes, particularly because the coverage is not expensive or difficult to obtain. Even if the festival runs for only a few days and the organization has no other employees (meaning no experience rating), it should be able to obtain coverage (often through a state-organized fund).

The United States Department of Labor has prepared a very useful summary of the workers' compensation laws of all 50 states.[360] Its Web site indicates that the survey is current through January 1, 2003. Each nonprofit should consult legal counsel or an insurance professional rather than relying on the DOL summary, but the summary is a good starting point.

(b) FOOD SALES. It goes without saying that any organization is looking at significant liability if it serves potato salad or sushi that has been sitting unrefrigerated in the sun for hours. Organizations and their boards should take great precaution when they serve food or beverages, particularly when they are sold. This is true even when the organization contracts with third-party vendors to provide food service. As is often the case, common sense will go a long way toward preventing a disaster, but someone must take the initiative. The board should ask the questions, and the officers and employees should implement health and safety precautions.

---

359. I.R.C. § 6672(a), which provides as follows:

> Any person required to collect, truthfully account for, and pay over any tax imposed by this title who willfully fails to collect such tax, or truthfully account for and pay over such tax, or willfully attempts in any manner to evade or defeat any such tax or the payment thereof, shall, in addition to other penalties provided by law, be liable to a penalty equal to the total amount of the tax evaded, or not collected, or not accounted for and paid over.

360. The summary is *available at* http://www.dol.gov/esa/regs/statutes/owcp/stwclaw/stwclaw.htm.

PRECAUTIONARY STEPS: FOOD SALES

* * *

Any organization selling food as part of a fundraising event should take the following steps:

- Obtain any necessary license and request the health department to inspect the facilities during both the setup and the event. The tendency is to avoid contact with regulators, who are often viewed as troublemakers. Asking regulators for assistance demonstrates that the organization took reasonable precautions to prevent food poisoning and other illness.
- Avoid amateur chefs, home cooks, and pot luck preparation. Instead, the nonprofit should contract with licensed and experienced restaurants and vendors for food service and obtain certificates of insurance from them (naming the organization and its directors and officers as additional insured). This step poses problems for the PTA bake sale, but that can easily be addressed by asking people to purchase the goods or by soliciting donations from local bakeries in exchange for sponsorship recognition.
- Lease adequate refrigeration systems, or make sure that vendors have such equipment.
- Request that food servers and preparers leave jewelry, studs, and piercings at home, shower before reporting for work, avoid artificial finger nails, and wear hair nets when appropriate. Also, set a dress code that includes clean clothes, shoes, socks, and shirts. The organization should consult with legal counsel to ascertain whether any of these actions could pose employment practice issues.
- Provide adequate containers and serving plates to avoid cross-contamination (e.g., storing raw chicken with cooked chicken). If food will be transported, make sure that there are adequate heating and cooling capabilities.
- Provide adequate facilities for cleaning cooking utensils, pots and pans, and other food preparation gear.
- Provide adequate potable water for cleaning people, dishes, and work surfaces, including hot water for sanitation.
- Schedule times for cleaning the cooking facilities, including all surface areas.
- When cooking or grilling food, make sure ventilation is adequate. There should also be fire protection equipment near the grills and stoves. Make sure that tent flaps, decorations, and tablecloths are a safe distance from any open flame.
- Require that meat thermometers be used for testing the temperature of grilled foods.
- Provide adequate sanitation facilities for food servers, including portable sinks, liquid soap, and sanitary gloves. Post signs reminding food workers about sanitation.
- Use disposable dishes, utensils, napkins, and cups. If at all possible, make sure that straws, ketchup, mustard, and relishes, as well as utensils are prewrapped so that someone grabbing for a straw does not contaminate the others.
- Restrict access to food preparation facilities to authorized personnel. Keep babies and small children off counters where food will be served or stored.
- In the case of events spanning multiple days, make sure leftovers are destroyed instead of served the following day (consider contracting with a local food bank for daily donations of excess food, assuming laws are in place that protect the organization from liability).

- When dishes contain multiple ingredients that are not readily apparent, post the ingredients so individuals with allergies can adequately assess whether they can consume the food. In recent years, there has been much public discussion about peanut allergies, particularly in the context of airline passengers. Those same considerations obviously are an issue for any event where food is served.
- Avoid toothpicks and other decorations that could be swallowed.
- Do not use pesticides or bug sprays around the food service area.
- Make sure there are adequate bathroom facilities. Local ordinances may impose specific requirements.

* * *

While our focus has been on festival-style events, all of these recommendations are relevant for an employee cafeteria, a museum or hospital restaurant, or a catered lunch at a directors' meeting. The board should require written contracts and procedures when the organization opts for third-party vendors.

(c) LIQUOR AND DRAM SHOP LAWS. Most lawyers would ban alcoholic beverages from events if they had their druthers. That is easy advice to give, but there are the realities of outdoor events such as the July 4 weekend sponsored by the Downtown Chamber of Commerce. There will be beer because July is hot, people like beer, and beer represents big dollars for many nonprofits. Given that reality, there should be absolutely no question in anyone's mind that the organization, all third-party vendors, and all personnel will adhere to all legal requirements regarding alcoholic beverage sales. This means obtaining the necessary licensing, retaining qualified and licensed servers, requiring valid age identification, and adopting rules and guidelines for identifying and dealing with those who have had too much to drink.

In recent years, many event organizers have moved to centralized age verification, issuing a nontransferable bracelet at one tightly controlled location to those who are 21 and over. Centralizing this process should eliminate the maverick volunteer server who "remembers when he was 19." Will teenagers and sympathetic adults circumvent this system? Absolutely—but the organization will have taken a step that will help minimize underage drinking. One further step is limiting the number of beers that can be sold to one person at any given time. This will not totally prevent 22-year-olds from buying beer for their underage friends, but it should greatly curtail the practice.

As for obtaining licenses, start early. There can be a lengthy review and approval process. It is also important to draw distinctions between types of liquor permits. Specifically, there may be one permit required for beer sales by volunteers at a festival sponsored by a Section 501(c)(3) organization, but a different one required if the organization is using a paid vendor to sell the alcohol. Someone should make sure months in advance that the paid vendor has the necessary permits. In the case of a street festival, the organizers should assume the police or other enforcement agents will inspect the licenses.

At events like the Downtown Chamber of Commerce's July Fourth Festival, local owners may want to sell alcohol by placing stands in front of their bars. This can be tempting for everyone involved because the bar has a preexisting liquor license and the organizers may view a partnership with the bars as a means to avoid more formal compliance. The organizers should be cautious before relying on such a plan. In such situations, the nonprofit may want its volunteers or employees to staff the alcohol concession, but a bar owner's liquor license may require that only its employees can sell alcohol. Furthermore, liquor licensing regulations often restrict outdoor sales or permit sales only within so many feet of a licensed establishment. These requirements can pose a problem when the establishment is on a side street or around the corner from the nonprofit's event.

Finally, the nonprofit should check "open-container" laws to make sure that drinking in public is permissible. This should not be much of a problem for the Downtown Chamber of Commerce. After all, the licensing process will *probably* consider any prohibitions against drinking in public. However, circumstances could limit drinking to a specific facility or park area. In this case, the nonprofit should provide adequate notice to its patrons.

(d) FUN RUNS, MARATHONS, CARNIVALS, AND OTHER EVENTS. Life would be no fun if everyone avoided all risk. Nonprofit organizations and their boards often sponsor fun runs, contract with carnivals, and hold baseball or soccer games to raise money. Nothing anybody says will stop organizations from sponsoring these events, nor should it. Some basic common sense can go far toward preventing a human tragedy for a participant followed by a financial one for the organization.

Planning a Fun Run

* * *

The Downtown Chamber of Commerce sponsors a 10K midnight fun run in conjunction with its July Fourth Festival. It and other organizations should take the following steps:

- Cancel the event if the temperature is 110 degrees in the shade. The organization should schedule and publicize alternative dates should conditions warrant postponing the scheduled event.
- Ensure that adequate emergency personnel are present. A doctor or paramedic should be on site, but if this is not feasible because the event is a small one, the organization should notify the nearest hospital emergency room. If the event is a large one (e.g., 40,000 marathon runners), the organization should have ambulances on site with prearranged procedures for treating and transporting distressed runners. The organizers of large athletic events should also consider on-site medical facilities, such as a first aid station staffed with a trained medical staff.
- Ensure that the course is well designed, lighted, signed with directional arrows, and policed. If the course includes city streets, arrangements should be made with the

police and department of transportation to temporarily close them to traffic as appropriate. In the case of an evening run or bike ride, the participants should be required to wear protective reflective gear.

- Line race courses with water stations. As for appropriate spacing of these stations, the Road Runners Club of America (RRCA) offers the following advice on its Web site:

> Particularly during warm weather. Aid stations should be located every 2-3 miles in races over 5 miles in length. Water should be provided with an electrolyte replacement drink as an option. Wet sponges are recommended.[361]

- Hot weather is an obvious concern. However, information posted on the RRCA Web site indicates that health issues can also be associated with cold weather races. The RRCA publishes a 162-page bound and illustrated handbook entitled "Handbook to Club and Race Administration," which should be of interest to nonprofits regularly staging athletic (particularly running) events.
- Ban participants' use of headphones and cell phones (except in the case of an emergency) because they are distractions and could lead to collisions.
- Encourage proper training as part of the publicity for the event. Limit participation to those who have preregistered.
- Require each participant to sign a statement that clearly describes the risks being assumed and that releases the organization and all its directors, officers, employees, and agents from liability. Do not assume, however, that the release will eliminate liability.[362]

* * *

In the case of a fun run, the preventive measures described in the feature will help counter claims that the organization and its directors were negligent if a death or serious injury occurs. All of this assumes that the organization has liability insurance coverage in place. If it does not, it should obtain appropriate coverage before the event, and all officers, directors, and volunteers should be named as additional insured.

These safety suggestions can clearly serve as a starting point for organizations sponsoring walks, bike rides, or water-related events such as triathlons. There are often national trade groups servicing organizations that regularly sponsor particular types of activities. These organizations often provide their members with extensive advice to reduce liability from events. For example, Little League Baseball, Incorporated, the trade association for little league groups, has an excellent Web site that includes a safety newsletter available to anyone who wants to read it.[363] Near the newsletter is a link to a Child Protection Program.

361. http://www.rrca.org/publicat/howstart.html.

362. *See, e.g.*, O'Connor v. United States Fencing Association, 260 F. Supp. 2d 545 (E.D.N.Y. 2003), where the court held that a particular liability waiver was unenforceable

363. http://www.littleleague.org/newsletter/index.asp. The June 2005 newsletter contains articles discussing league safety plans, preventing and dealing with heat illness, preventing injuries from mowers, responses to health and safety questions from a doctor who specializes in sports medicine, responses to general questions, trips for safely traveling to tournaments, and tips from readers. In short, the information is available if organizations without special expertise or experience simply take the time to look for it. With the Web, the amount of time required is often miniscule, particularly when considered in terms of the return on the effort.

If the organization is sponsoring a carnival, make sure the appropriate city agency inspects the rides. Contract with reputable organizations; obtain references in writing and certificates of insurance. This is particularly important when animals are involved (e.g., a small circus or a petting zoo). If animals are involved, consider whether animal rights activists will pose security, publicity, or other issues.

(e) CELEBRITIES AND MUSICIANS. Celebrities and musicians can pose significant operational and legal risks to any organization that utilizes their services. To illustrate, consider the following facts: This year, the Downtown Chamber of Commerce has booked Magic Jones and the Street Interns as the headlining act for the festival's main stage. Magic is a nationally known R&B performer that commands $30,000 per performance. He and the Interns are expected to draw 15,000 beer-drinking festivalgoers, more than justifying the performance fee. Although there is no admission charge to see Magic and the Interns, the chamber expects to sell beer at $4 per cup. The chamber signed a standard form contract provided by Magic's agent that requires the chamber to pay Magic $15,000 in advance, and the remaining $15,000 immediately before the show.

In booking Magic and the Interns, the chamber has put itself in a weak negotiating position. What happens when Magic announces to the chamber's lawyer backstage that he is not feeling good, but an additional $5,000 will cure his ills? Remember that 15,000 fans have been sitting in 90-degree heat drinking beer for the last five hours. In all likelihood, the chamber is going to pay. To a certain extent, if it wants Magic and the Interns, there is nothing it can do about this. However, the chamber should recognize the position it is in before it signs the contract. At a minimum, it should know whom it is dealing with. While local musicians may not have the marquee power of a nationally known act, local musicians reside in the jurisdiction (making a lawsuit much easier), and they need to be concerned about their reputation in the community. If the chamber is using a talent agency to book the acts, it should use a reputable one with a large roster of acts. This agency will be much more sensitive to protecting its reputation than Magic's brother in-law, who handles only Magic. The agency will also be more interested in repeat business.

Here are several other tips for dealing with entertainers, including a very important one regarding income tax withholding requirements.

- The nonprofit should not overlook income tax withholding issues. Many states require that the event sponsor withhold income and other taxes from the payments to entertainers who do not reside in the state. This is just practical tax administration.
- Musician contracts are notorious for what often seem to be ridiculous requirements regarding dressing room conditions and amenities such as food and drink. The organization should be aware of this and abide by the contracts terms.

- Entertainers often sell T-shirts, CDs, and other paraphernalia at the performance site. The organization should check with its legal counsel to ensure that the arrangement governing these onsite sales does not expose the organization to sales tax liability.
- Check local sound abatement ordinances. The practical way to address these issues is work with the local alderperson or municipal-event coordinator.
- Make sure the entertainer has the necessary musicians' union clearances.

These precautions apply equally to celebrity speakers, athletes, and authors.

(f) ASCAP, BMI, AND SESAC LICENSING. In the United States, music composers are entitled to compensation for the public[364] performance of their compositions. Rather than enforcing their rights themselves, composers generally join one of three performance rights societies. The two better-known societies are ASCAP and BMI, both nonprofit organizations. The third is SESAC, a for-profit entity that specializes in certain categories of music. These organizations enforce copyrights and remit fees (minus expenses) to the composers.

Under this system, an organization that uses music in a public performance must enter into licenses with ASCAP, BMI, and/or SESAC. There is no blanket exemption under the copyright laws for nonprofit organizations. Licensing is required for both live performances and broadcasts of recorded music (even when the organization owns the record albums or CDs). Both ASCAP and BMI have successfully asserted composer rights against retail establishments playing background music and businesses playing music while a caller is on hold. Licensing is required even when the composer performs his own songs. The promoter or event producer, not the performer, is the one required to obtain the license.

A nonprofit engaging in public performances of music should enter into the appropriate licenses with ASCAP, BMI, or other relevant performance rights society. Unfortunately, entering into a license with one society does not eliminate the possibility that a license from another is also required. Licensing depends on music selection. If the works of only BMI composers will be performed, then only a BMI license is required. In a festival setting or when different artists are involved, however, it could be necessary to obtain licenses from both BMI and ASCAP.

In the absence of a public performance, an organization has no obligation to compensate the composer, raising the question of what constitutes a "public" performance. Under the law, a performance is public if occurs at a place open to the public in which a substantial number of persons outside a normal circle of family and its social acquaintances is gathered or the composition is transmitted or communicated by means of any device or process so that members of the public can

364. 17 U.S.C. 106(4) grants a copyright owner (in this case, the composer), the exclusive right to perform the copyrighted work publicly.

hear it.[365] Clearly, a public performance encompasses a performance of music in a concert hall for a large group of people (but without regard to whether an admission fee is charged). It also includes radio broadcasts and recorded music played over a speaker system in a restaurant. It would not include an employee listening to music on his MP3 player through headphones on his employer's premises.[366]

The copyright laws provide several very narrow exceptions useful to some nonprofit organizations. First, a nonprofit educational institution does not need to worry about licensing to the extent that a musical work is performed by instructors or pupils in the course of face-to-face teaching activities.[367] The issues surrounding licensing become much more difficult once an organization moves beyond music instruction in the classroom, particularly in the distance learning arena. Schools must focus on all requirements that must be met before this exemption applies. For example, performances by a school band at a college football game open to the public would not qualify for this exemption. However, a performance would likely qualify if a nonprofit school brought in a famous pianist to conduct a master class with students, provided the instruction is limited to "classroom situations" and there is no audience.[368]

Second, a religious organization does not need to worry about licensing to the extent that a nondramatic musical work is performed in the course of services at a place of worship or other religious assembly.[369] A performance is not exempt just because it takes place in a house of worship. It must be part of a religious service. Consequently, a church would need to license rights if it staged a secular fundraising concert featuring its famous pipe organ.

The performance must be part of a religious service, but the music need not necessarily be religious in nature. That means a church could include a Beatles song as part of its services without obtaining licensing. If the music is termed "dramatico-musical," it must be religious in nature to qualify for the exemption. This brings religious oratorios, cantatas, and musical settings of the mass into the exemption, but secular music from dramatic works such as musicals, plays, motion pictures, and operas are not covered by the exemption, even if they have a religious theme.[370] Although the exemption's focus is on the performance at a religious gathering, the exemption is available while the religious services are conducted in an auditorium, outdoor theatre, or the like

---

365. See 17 U.S.C. 101 for the complete definition.
366. This is probably not a "public performance," but if it were so considered, it would qualify for the exemption in 17 U.S.C. 110(5), which probably also applies to people who have radios or CD players at their desks but do not use headphones. However, the use of radios and CD players has generated litigation when the use goes beyond personal use.
367. 17 U.S.C. 110(1).
368. H.R. REP. 94-1476, 94th CONG., 2d SESS. (1976). See also MELVILLE B. NIMMER AND DAVID NIMMER, NIMMER ON COPYRIGHT § 8.15 [B] [4] (2005).
369. 17 U.S.C. 110(3).
370. H.R. REP. 94-1476, *supra* note 368. See also MELVILLE B. NIMMER AND DAVID NIMMER, *Supra* notes 368, at § 8.15 [D] [1]

(as opposed to in a consecrated house of worship).[371] Because the exemption contemplates people in attendance in the house of worship, a church considering broadcasting the series over a radio network should consult legal counsel regarding licensing.

Third, and of more general interest, certain nonprofits are exempt from licensing requirements to the extent that a particular performance is (1) without any purpose of direct or indirect commercial advantage and (2) without any payment of any fee or other compensation for the performance to any of its promoters, performers, or organizers, but only if (a) there is no direct or indirect admission charge or (b) the proceeds, after deducting reasonable production and performance costs, are used exclusively for educational, religious, or charitable purposes and not for private financial gain.[372] The copyright owner can preclude reliance on the (b) prong of this exception if it provides written notice at least seven days before the performance.

This exception should be helpful to charities but not necessarily to other types of nonprofits. For example, it is arguably not available to a trade association because the association serves commercial purposes. Even if a trade association prevailed on that argument, if it charged an admission fee, it is unlikely that it could argue that the net proceeds went to educational, religious, or charitable purposes. As a practical matter, it is unlikely that the performers would perform without charging a fee.

Moreover, charitable and educational organizations cannot rely on this exemption if they contract with a third-party promoter to sponsor a concert series to which tickets are sold. In that case, although the charity's share of the net proceeds may further charitable or educational purposes, the promoter is still receiving a fee, and this exemption never applies when the performers receive a fee. In the case of a benefit concert, organizations that want to take advantage of this exemption must be careful how the arrangement is structured. Under no circumstances should the performer charge a fee and then donate it back to the organization. Is reimbursement of actual travel expenses compensation?

To understand the full scope of this exemption, we must address an apparent redundancy in the provision. There is an overarching requirement in the exemption that there not be direct or indirect commercial advantage. At first, this initially appears to make the prong of the exemption that permits paid admissions somewhat superfluous. The legislative history clarifies this otherwise apparent redundancy, indicating that the reference to proceeds in the (b) prong of the test is to admissions, while the overarching commercial advantage language refers to a profit motive that goes beyond admissions. In fact, this legislative history refers to long-standing case law that has its roots in a Supreme Court decision holding that the copyright holder was entitled to payment for performance of his compositions in a restaurant setting where there was no admission charge.[373]

371. *Id.*

372. 17 U.S.C. 110(4).

373. Herbert v. Shanley Co., 242 U.S. 591 (1917).

Consequently, a museum would be required to pay for performance rights if musicians performed music while patrons ate in a restaurant despite the fact that the net proceeds from food sales are used for charitable purposes. This museum would also have to pay for the use of recorded music unless it either licensed it through an agency that had packaged the clearances with the license or qualified for a special exemption applicable to small spaces.[374] The issue becomes far more difficult in the case of student concerts during which the school has a concession stand where it sells cookies and soft drinks during intermissions. Is this during the performance? Does it create an indirect commercial advantage? Certainly, a good case can be made that it does, particularly if the concession area is open only in conjunction with a performance (compare that to a vending machine that is in a hallway and is used throughout the day regardless of whether there is a performance).

Any organization seeking to take advantage of any of these exemptions under the copyright laws should consult an attorney specializing in intellectual property rights. This discussion has focused on performance of musical works. There is an entirely separate set of licensing considerations when the work is a dramatic work such as a play or an opera. Another set of issues must be addressed when a nonprofit puts together a benefit CD or other physical media for sale.

When the question of music licensing comes up, someone on the nonprofit board inevitably will say, "They are not going to come after us. We are a nonprofit doing good things. Why throw away money on licensing?" Plug your ears (or at least tie yourself to the mast) and do not listen to this siren call to disaster. The performance rights societies are very aggressive in monitoring performances and suing those who do not comply with licensing requirements. They will threaten to sue or will sue your organization, ask for what seems to be astronomical damages, and then may negotiate a settlement providing for future compliance and a hefty payment.

(g) SUMMARY. Events come in all forms, shapes, and sizes, making a one-size-fits-all discussion dubious at best. Each organization and its board must assess the specific risks associated with its fundraising activities and events. Fireworks displays, hot air balloon festivals, travel tours, and various other fundraising efforts pose their own unique risks and problems. The best way to approach these events is work with legal counsel and talk with other organizations that have sponsored similar events. Nonprofits will also find a discussion with their insurance broker helpful.

---

374. 17 U.S.C. 110(5). People wanting to avail themselves of this exemption should read it very carefully because some issues regarding whether the entity is a "food service or drinking establishment" must be addressed.

11.9 AVOIDING OPERATIONAL LIABILITIES FROM CONFERENCE HOTELS AND RENTED FACILITIES

Many nonprofits sponsor annual conferences. Typically, the nonprofit enters into a contract with a hotel for conference services that includes food service, conference and meeting rooms, and discounted room rates for conference attendees. The agreement with the hotel may contain risk-shifting clauses. For example, the nonprofit may assume responsibility for damage caused by its or attendees' use of the facilities, including hotel rooms. In some contracts, the nonprofit may be asked to waive any rights of subrogation against the hotel in the event that the hotel is responsible for any event that results in damage or injury to the nonprofit or an attendee. This means that the nonprofit and its insurer cannot seek reimbursement from the hotel or its insurer for out-of-pocket costs and expenses that the nonprofit or its insurer are required to cover.

To address this risk shifting, the nonprofit should have its lawyer review any agreements to identify such clauses. It should then request that offending clauses be eliminated from the contract, using the number of hotel rooms that the conference is likely to fill as its principle bargaining chip. The large national business hotel chains may have ironclad policies against modifying standard contract terms. In such event, the nonprofit should assess whether it has adequate coverage under its general commercial liability insurance policy or other policies. A nonprofit should follow this same advice any time it is rents facilities, whether they are for an office or for events.

11.10 A LESSON FROM THE FEDERAL SENTENCING GUIDELINES

This chapter has focused on operational liabilities to minimize exposure to loss. Throughout this discussion, the nonprofit's senior management has been identified as primarily responsible for minimizing exposure to liability. Although senior management will delegate various tasks to others in the organization, it is ultimately accountable.

As you undoubtedly know by now, the board also has a role in preventing loss. It should constantly monitor exposure by asking management to report pertinent information. If the board believes that management has not adopted the right policies or that polices need to be modified, it should state this clearly to management. As anyone who operates a business knows all too well, managers get caught up in day-to-day minutia. The board has the opportunity to be more reflective, and it is critical that the board take advantage of that opportunity.

One need only take a cursory look at the recent amendments to the Federal Sentencing Guidelines to realize the importance of board involvement in the governance process. Chapter 8 of the guidelines establishes those guidelines applicable to organizations that are convicted of a crime under federal law. Just to be clear, *organization* includes a nonprofit entity, but for present purposes, the criminal aspect of the federal guidelines should not be the primary focus. What should be of interest are the mitigating factors that courts are instructed to consider. The guidelines look for an "effective compliance and ethics program," which, in part, requires the "organization's governing authority to be knowledgeable about the content and operation of the compliance and ethics program and exercise reasonable oversight with respect to the implementation and effectiveness of the compliance and ethics program."[375]

Obviously, if a nonprofit does commit a crime, having a compliance and ethics program in place will be an important factor in the court's sentencing decision. Of far more significance, however, is the general call for greater participation by boards in organizational governance, with a focus on controls designed to curb potential liability. That is exactly the role laid out for the board in this chapter.

375. United States Sentencing Guidelines Manual, at § 8B2.1(b)(1)(A) (2005).

CHAPTER 12

RISK SHIFTING, INDEMNIFICATION, AND INSURANCE

We saw the risk we took in doing good, But dared not spare to do the best we could Though harm should come of it.

ROBERT FROST[1]

1. *Exposed Net* in MOUNTAIN INTERVAL (1920).

The last chapter focused on common operational risks, and Chapter 4 examined director and officer duties and the potential consequences when those duties are breached. In this chapter, we will focus on shifting the costs of those risks to others. Because this *Guide* focuses on board governance, the chapter begins by examining how board members and officers can shift their exposure to liability either to the nonprofit itself or to an insurance company. The discussion then shifts to how the nonprofit can use insurance to shift operational risks.

12.1 RELATIONSHIP BETWEEN INDEMNIFICATION AND D & O INSURANCE

Small nonprofits often believe they cannot afford directors' and officers' (D & O) insurance. Consequently, the directors often are asked to rely on state statutes or the federal Volunteer Protection Act of 1997[2] for protection from liability. This may be a legitimate strategy in terms of liability from third-party suits, but it fails to protect directors from liabilities asserted by state regulators, the IRS, and the nonprofit itself. Furthermore, an active plaintiff's bar has made filing a lawsuit second nature. Even when directors ultimately prevail, they still must incur the costs of defending themselves, making D & O insurance coverage particularly important. Just defending a suit can cost well in excess of $100,000.

Large museums, hospitals, educational institutions, and social service agencies have plenty of assets, and therefore, they can afford D & O insurance premiums. Nevertheless, even large organizations may ask their current directors and officers to rely on indemnification provisions in corporate bylaws rather than D & O insurance. Although these organizations may have plenty of assets, those assets may not be available to the directors and officers who must respond to a

2. PUB. L.105-19, 111 STAT. 219. This act is discussed in more detail in Chapter 4.

lawsuit for breach of their duties. Under many indemnification clauses, a director or officer can seek only recovery following the resolution of a lawsuit. By then, the director may no longer be a highly regarded board member as the result of unfavorable court testimony and media portrayals. Unless a statute or agreement mandates indemnification, the director is at the mercy of the organization's discretion.

Because many corporate bylaws provide for indemnification, we first examine indemnification in detail. We will then consider D & O insurance.

12.2 INDEMNIFICATION

As noted, the superficially appealing solution to concerns over liability is to rely on indemnification rights provided under corporate bylaws or state statutes. The right to indemnification simply means that if the director or officer experiences a covered loss, the nonprofit will reimburse the director or officer for that loss.

Certainly, no one should reject such protection. Neither should anyone be fooled by what can be very illusory rights. Indemnification is only as good as the assets that secure the obligation. An organization can intend to indemnify a director against every conceivable claim, but that intent is worthless if the organization has only $100. When it comes time for the director or officer to seek indemnification, the assets of the nonprofit may already have been depleted by creditor claims, tort claimants, or just poor management.

(a) INDEMNIFICATION—LEGAL ISSUES. Any rights that directors and officers have to indemnification arise under specific statutory regimes that either require indemnification or permit the nonprofit to provide indemnification.[3] As of January 1, 2003, 31 states permitted some form of indemnification to a nonprofit director for losses he incurred when he acted in his capacity as a director.[4] Some states have adopted provisions capping director liability to the corporation but only if the corporation elects to apply the cap.[5] Given the many approaches to indemnification, directors and officers should read the specific language before

---

3. Directors should not look to common law rights for indemnification protection. See M. Fremont-Smith, GOVERNING NONPROFIT ORGANIZATIONS: FEDERAL AND STATE LAW REGULATION, at 227–28 (Belknap Press 2004), stating:

> [I]n the majority of states the extent to which indemnification is under common law is uncertain and depends on the 'somewhat bizarre application of the principles of charitable trusts, agency or contracts.

See Texas Society v. Fort Bend Chapter, 590 S.W.2d 156 (Tex. Civ. App. 1979), holding that there is no common law right to indemnification.

4. FREMONT-SMITH, *supra* note 3.
5. Revised Model Nonprofit Corporation Act (1987), alternative provision § 2.02(b)(5). See Va. Code, Title 13.1, Chapter 13.1, § 13.1-870.1A, providing:

> A. Except as otherwise provided in this section, in any proceeding brought by or in the right of a corporation or brought by or on behalf of members of the corporation, the damages assessed

relying on it. Executive directors often say to directors, "Do not worry; the corporation's bylaws provide for indemnification."As is often the case, however, the devil is in the details.

The California statute authorizing nonprofit director and officer indemnification is an excellent example of how the details can eviscerate meaningful protection. Even nonlawyers should read the accompanying statutory language; the critical phrases have been italicized.

Section 5238 of the California Nonprofit Public Benefit Corporation Law

(b) A corporation shall have power to indemnify any person who was or is a party or is threatened to be made a party to any proceeding *(other than an action by or in the right of the corporation to procure a judgment in its favor, an action brought under Section 5233, or an action brought by the Attorney General or a person granted realtor status by the Attorney General for any breach of duty relating to assets held in charitable trust)* by reason of the fact that such person is or was an agent of the corporation, against expenses, judgments, fines, settlements and other amounts actually and reasonably incurred in connection with such proceeding if such person acted in *good faith* and in a manner such person *reasonably believed* to be in the best interests of the corporation and, in the case of a criminal proceeding, had *no reasonable cause to believe* the conduct of such person was unlawful. The termination of any proceeding by judgment, order, settlement, conviction or upon a plea of nolo contendere or its equivalent shall not, of itself, create a presumption that the person did not act in good faith and in a manner which the person reasonably believed to be in the best interests of the corporation or that the person had reasonable cause to believe that the person's conduct was unlawful.

(c) A corporation shall have power to indemnify any person who was or is a party or is threatened to be made a party to any threatened, pending or completed *action by or in the right of the corporation, or brought under Section 5233, or brought by the Attorney General or a person granted relator status by the Attorney General for breach of duty relating to assets held in charitable trust*, to procure a judgment in its favor by reason of the fact that such person is or was an agent of the corporation, against expenses actually and reasonably

---

against an officer or director arising out of a single transaction, occurrence, or course of conduct shall not exceed the lesser of:

1. The monetary amount including the elimination of liability, specified in the articles of incorporation or, if approved by the members, in the bylaws as a limitation on or elimination of the liability of the officer or director; or
2. The greater of (i) $100,000, or (ii) the amount of the cash compensation received by the officer or director from the corporation during the twelve months immediately preceding the act or omission for which liability was imposed.

incurred by such person in connection with the defense or settlement of such action if such person acted in *good faith*, in a manner such person believed to be in the best interests of the corporation and with such care, including *reasonable inquiry*, as an *ordinarily prudent* person in a like position would use under similar circumstances. No indemnification shall be made under this subdivision: (1) In respect of any claim, issue or matter as to which such person shall have been adjudged to be liable to the corporation in the performance of such person's duty to the corporation, unless and *only to the extent that the court in which such proceeding is or was pending shall determine* upon application that, in view of all the circumstances of the case, such person is *fairly and reasonably* entitled to indemnity for the expenses which such court shall determine; (2) Of amounts paid in settling or otherwise disposing of a threatened or pending action, with or without court approval; or (3) Of expenses incurred in defending a threatened or pending action which is settled or otherwise disposed of without court approval unless it is settled with the approval of the Attorney General.

(d) To the extent that an agent of a corporation has been successful on the merits in defense of any proceeding referred to in subdivision (b) or (c) or in defense of any claim, issue or matter therein, the agent shall be indemnified against expenses actually and reasonably incurred by the agent in connection therewith.

(e) Except as provided in subdivision (d), any indemnification under this section shall be made by the corporation only if authorized in the specific case, upon a determination that indemnification of the agent is proper in the circumstances because the agent has met the applicable standard of conduct set forth in subdivision (b) or (c), by: (1) A *majority vote of a quorum consisting of directors who are not parties to such proceeding*; (2) Approval of the members (Section 5034), with the persons to be indemnified not being entitled to vote thereon; or (3) The court in which such proceeding is or was pending upon application made by the corporation or the agent or the attorney or other person rendering services in connection with the defense, whether or not such application by the agent, attorney or other person is opposed by the corporation.

Notice the hurdles that await anyone seeking indemnification. If the suit is brought by a third party other than the attorney general (or someone granted relator[6] status), the director who is unsuccessful in his defense is entitled to

6. As we have already seen, members of the general public are generally denied standing to challenge the directors and officers of charitable institutions over their stewardship of charitable assets. If a member of the public believes there has been wrongdoing, his remedy is to bring it to the attention of the state's attorney general. The attorney general, however, can then turnaround and authorize this or another appropriate person to commence legal action on behalf of the attorney general. This deputy is said to have *relator* status. For additional information, *see* FREMONT-SMITH, *supra* note 3, at 324–36.

indemnification for expenses, judgments, fines, settlements, and other related amounts, but only if he acted in good faith and reasonably believed that his action was in the best interests of the nonprofit. Even then, the indemnification must be authorized by either a majority of disinterested directors, the members, or a court after application by the appropriate parties. If the suit is by the nonprofit itself or by the attorney general (or someone granted relator status) to protect charitable assets, the unsuccessful director is entitled only to indemnification for reasonable expenses incurred in the defense. However, this holds only if the good faith and prudence standards are met, and then only if, depending on whether there has been adjudication or settlement, one of certain designated parties approves.

The very fact that nonlawyers are overwhelmed by this statutory scheme demonstrates the potential perils facing anyone hoping to rely on it. The California statute does not provide reliable protection given the required determinations regarding conduct and required approvals. This same observation holds true for many other state statutes, as well as for the specific provisions adopted by many nonprofits as part of their organizational documents.

(b) INDEMNIFICATION—QUESTIONS TO ASK. As already noted, when most in need of the protection provided by an indemnification clause, a director may find himself asking for help from a board or court that no longer views him as worthy. To be blunt, this director may find himself taking a long walk off a short plank. Every director and officer should ask the following questions before relying on an indemnification clause:

- What assets will be available for funding indemnification?
- Is indemnification automatic, or must it first be approved by the board, the members, or a court?
- If indemnification is automatic but only under certain circumstances, do clear rules define those circumstances?
- Does indemnification include legal defense costs?
- Does indemnification provide for advancement of legal defense and related costs?
- Is indemnification limited to legal defense and related costs, or does it also include adverse judgments, fines, and penalties?
- How are settlement costs and payments treated?

(c) THE PROBLEM POSED BY LOSSES. There is no guarantee, even when a director or officer has thought through all issues posed by indemnification rights, that the corporation will honor its obligations. As noted, when losses occur and a director or officer is sued, that person may be "out of favor" with those who control the corporate purse strings or those in control might put a different gloss on the facts.

Consider a case involving the American Society for Testing & Materials, a standard-setting organization.[7] The organization sought a declaratory judgment when an individual who served as a volunteer on an ASTM standard-setting committee requested indemnification for settlement and defense costs arising from an antitrust lawsuit brought against him, his employer, and ASTM. The ASTM board refused to pay the indemnification, taking the position that the antitrust action was not based on the volunteer's participation on an ASTM committee but were actions taken on behalf of his employer.[8] The court ruled in favor of the volunteer and his employer, but he had to go to great lengths to obtain what he was entitled to.

This case and the questions posed in it demonstrate why D & O insurance is often preferable to indemnification. Even then, the volunteer may become involved in a similar dispute with the insurance company over whether the particular loss is covered by the policy's terms.

12.3 D & O INSURANCE

The best protection against liability as a director or officer is insurance. Do not operate, under a common misconception: Homeowners and personal umbrella insurance policies generally do not provide liability coverage for service as a volunteer director or officer—although there are exceptions. Moreover, lawyers and accountants should not assume that their professional malpractice coverage protects against liability arising from volunteer activities. Professional liability insurance policies often exclude liability from service as a director or officer. In short, volunteer directors and officers seeking insurance coverage for their duties as directors and officers should rely on a D & O insurance policy rather than other types of policies.

(a) COST AND AVAILABILITY. In the mid-1980s, an insurance crisis made obtaining D & O insurance difficult, particularly for directors of publicly held companies. Even though that crisis has long passed, a myth developed that obtaining D & O insurance for nonprofit directors and officers is difficult. That myth is unwarranted, at least as far as conditions exist in 2006.

A number of insurance companies and brokers staffed exhibit booths at a 2004 nonprofit risk management conference. Many of these representatives were clear that neither their underwriting standards nor the premiums would significantly impede the average nonprofit in its efforts to obtain affordable D & O insurance coverage. When asked what a $1 million D & O policy would cost, one representative said cost for a nonprofit with $1 million of revenue would be

7. American Society for Testing & Materials v. Corrpro Companies, U.S. Dist. LEXIS 16,678 (E.D. Penn.).
8. The court's opinion is unclear on this point. It refers to the complaint filed by the plaintiff in the underlying antitrust lawsuit but does not provide clear details regarding the specific allegations in the complaint.

just under $800 per year. Another representative from a top-of-the-line company indicated that the cost under similar circumstances would be about $1,000, and the nonprofit has the opportunity to obtain reimbursement in the form of premium rebates for qualifying expenses (those aimed at reducing risk, e.g., director training). As these two examples suggest, the premiums for D & O insurance are typically based on revenue (in the case of foundations, asset value). None of the carriers had particularly rigorous or detailed underwriting requirements when D & O insurance was the exclusive focus. Although no one was explicit, many companies appear to be much more interested in selling other types of insurance to nonprofits, viewing D & O insurance as an entrée. Regardless of how insurance companies market it, D & O insurance should be viewed as an essential from the board's standpoint.

(b) BASIC CONSIDERATIONS WHEN EVALUATING A D & O POLICY. There are two basic components to a D & O policy: the duty to indemnify and the duty to defend. The duty to indemnify is the insurance company's agreement to cover losses arising from claims covered by the policy. This is the aspect of D & O insurance that is foremost in the minds of the directors and officers. The second aspect is equally, if not more, important. This duty to defend has two distinct elements. The first is to pay the cost of defending the claim; the second is to actually mount the defense. It is critical that both aspects of the duty to defend be considered.

(i) The Insured. The *insured* is the party covered by the policy. Each director and officer should review the provisions that define the insured to ensure that he is covered. At least one major company automatically includes the insured's spouse if the sole reason the spouse is named in the suit is because of the spouse's status as such. This is a good idea, as is including estates and successors. Some policies include a large number of additional insured, including people acting in their capacity as employees and volunteers. This is generally viewed as favorable, but those serving as directors want to look carefully at the adequacy of the policy limits. The fewer the number of covered individuals, the more coverage that is available to each insured.

Under some policies, the coverage extends to past, present, and future individuals serving in the covered positions. This expansive time frame is particularly important because it gives a director the freedom to resign at any time should he disagree with the organization's direction. For example, if the board is acting recklessly, even though a particular director may have defenses based on his individual actions, he may want to resign as soon as possible to minimize the likelihood that he will be named in a lawsuit. This director still wants the protection offered by the D & O insurance coverage. Although coverage for past directors is helpful, it could prove to be illusory under certain circumstances. For example, a director might decide to resign because he disagrees with the policies that he believes will lead to financial troubles. If he is correct, the nonprofit may not be able to afford continued coverage at a time when events are most likely to lead to lawsuits. Or the nonprofit might take an action following the director's resignation that leads to a claim that exhausts the policy's limits. That is not a problem if there are no other claims, but suppose the first lawsuit is followed by a second one that does involve an action that the director took part in? One solution is for the director to buy an individual D & O policy, but as a practical matter, few directors are likely to do so. Those who do purchase them typically serve as compensated directors on multiple boards. No one should operate under the faulty belief that an individual policy will be available once trouble is on the horizon.

(ii) Policy Limits. When buying an insurance policy, a nonprofit must distinguish between the overall policy limits and the limits on recovery for any one claim, wrongful act, or interrelated act. For example, a policy might provide a maximum recoverable amount of $2 million. That sounds like a lot, but the policy could also provide that the recovery for a claim arising out of any one incident is limited to $250,000. As a general rule, the preference should be for higher rather than lower limits on any one incident. Low limits could be particularly troublesome when the claim is made against multiple insured. A $250,000 limit may be sufficient if only one director is named, but if ten are named, that amount seems much smaller. As you will see, when deciding on coverage amounts, the insured should consider whether the defense costs reduce the policy limits or are in addition to them.

(iii) Indemnity Coverage. In evaluating a D & O insurance policy, the organization and those covered by it should identify the specific exposures it covers. Such coverage is referred to as the *indemnity* and is likely to be in the definition of "wrongful act" or other equivalent term. For example, one policy insures against wrongful acts, defined as follows:

> Any error, misstatement, misleading statement, act, omission, neglect, or breach of duty committed, attempted, or allegedly committed or attempted by an Organization or Insured Person, individually or otherwise, in their Insured Capacity, or any matter claimed against such Insured Person solely by reason of serving in such Insured Capacity.[9]

Anyone who stops reading after this definition has made a foolish decision. All policies also provide *exclusions* from coverage. They limit the coverage that would otherwise be provided under the broad language in the preceding quoted language. The *interaction of the coverage* and *the exclusions* define the actual

9. Chubb Group of Insurance Companies, Form Type 14-02-2009 (ed. 5/96). This specimen policy language is provided for illustrative purposes only. The precise coverage afforded by any policy is subject to the terms and conditions of the policy as issued.

coverage. To illustrate, some policies exclude fines or penalties. Few people would argue with this exclusion as a general proposition, but what about penalties or required reimbursements under the intermediate sanctions, a potential liability we considered in Chapter 6? One insurance policy restores the coverage for those liabilities under its definition of "loss," providing as follows:

> [T]he amount that any Insured becomes legally obligated to pay on account of any covered Claim, including but not limited to:...
>
> (v) Excess Benefit Transaction Excise Taxes in an amount not to exceed the sublimit set forth in Item 2(B) of the Declarations for this Coverage Section, but only if and to the extent that indemnification by the Organization for Excess Benefit Transaction Excise Taxes is not expressly prohibited in the bylaws, certificate of incorporation or other organizational documents of the Organization.[10]

Most, if not all, policies exclude coverage for deliberate or willful fraudulent acts and violations of law. Nobody should be surprised by this fact, but some exclusions may have a more practical import. Specifically, one policy issued by a large insurer excludes claims based on the insured's gaining a profit to which he was not legally entitled. This provision could be a problem for directors who have engaged in conflict-of-interest transactions, particularly if the board has not adhered to state law requirements regarding transactions tainted with conflict. Moreover, just because an organization has complied with state law does not necessarily mean that the D & O policy will cover a claim that subsequently arises out of a transaction that seemed to have been appropriate when the board validated it. The policy just referred to probably would cover such a loss because of the phrase "legally entitled to," but other policies might formulate the exclusion differently.

Given the significant number of employment-related lawsuits, many insurers now offer coverage that integrates D & O and employment practices liability (EPL) coverages. There is little question that an organization and its directors and officers want EPL coverage. The question is whether integrating it with the D & O policy makes sense. The directors and officers should also consider more specialized coverage when it is appropriate. This could include coverage for exposure under securities law if the organization issues securities (e.g., tax-exempt bonds or interests in low-income housing partnerships) and exposure to board members in their capacity as directors and officers that could arise from the sale of liquor or dealings with children or other dependent classes of individuals.

(iv) Deductibles and Co-Insurance. Everyone is undoubtedly familiar with the concept of an insurance deductible. Automobile and homeowner's policies generally include deductibles or copays. Usually, the first dollars of loss up to

---

10. Chubb Group of Insurance Companies, Form Type C33778 (ed. 10/2004). This specimen policy language is provided for illustrative purposes only. The precise coverage afforded by any policy is subject to the terms and conditions of the policy as issued.

the specific deductible amount are the responsibility of the insured. D & O policies also have deductibles. As with personal insurance, the trade-off is between premiums and dollar risk retained by the insured; the more risk that the insured retains, the lower the premium. Each director and officer should know what the deductible is and how it will be applied. The potential impact can depend on whether the deductible is applied on a per incident or per insured basis.

Some D & O policies provide a coinsurance provision in lieu of or in addition to a deductible. Under such provision, the insured agrees to assume a certain percentage of the loss. To illustrate, assume that Victoriaville Women's Health Clinic (WHC) purchases a D & O insurance policy with a 20 percent coinsurance clause. If it experiences a $1 million loss, the insurer is responsible for only $800,000 of that loss. Coinsurance can be viewed as a deductible, but it provides WHC a greater incentive to actively assist with the resolution of the claim. To see why, assume the insurer and WHC settle the $1 million claim for $500,000. With a $200,000 deductible, WHC bears $200,000 of the $500,000 settlement, but with a 20 percent coinsurance clause, it bears only $100,000 of it. Of course, based on these facts, the WHC would have been better off with a $50,000 deductible rather than a 20 percent coinsurance clause, assuming that the premiums are equal. Insurers will naturally price the policy based on the size of deductibles and the presence of coinsurance. While WHC may resist a coinsurance clause because it does not want to be a "full partner" with the insurance company in the loss, the insurer will increase the premium to the extent that it agrees to eliminate the coinsurance clause. All other things being equal, the insured's cost for shifting risk should be reduced if the insurance company believes the insured has incentives to cooperate in the resolution of any claim.

(v) Claims Notification. To recover under a policy, the insured must file (report) a timely notice with the insurance company. Someone else is likely to be responsible for filing the notice, but directors should be familiar with this procedure so they can ensure that one has been timely filed. Depending on the policy, the notice requirement could be triggered by a written demand for monetary damages, the threat of legal action, the commencement of a civil proceeding, regulatory notice, or numerous other events. An untimely notice can result in the loss of otherwise available coverage.

Many nonprofits are reluctant to file a notice or make a claim for fear of increased premiums, adverse publicity, and any number of other reasons. This can be a mistake, as one school district[11] discovered when it failed to file a required notice after first learning that an employee had embezzled money.[12] The policy in question was a fidelity policy, but the lessons apply equally to any

---

11. Although the school district is a governmental entity, for our purposes, it could have just as easily been a college or social services agency.
12. A.L. Cowan, *Failure to File Timely Insurance Claim May Cost Plundered School System Millions*, N.Y. Times, Dec. 6, 2005.

insurance policy. In this case, the school district wanted to avoid adverse publicity. Moreover, with a known theft of only $250,000, the board hoped to recover the loss from the employee. A subsequent audit estimated that the theft involved at least $11.2 million.[13] As a result of the failure to provide notice, three of the school district's four insurers refused to pay claims. The fourth reserved its rights to deny the claim. The insurance companies were arguably justified because prompt notice would have permitted them to commence a timely investigation, making it more likely that the stolen funds would be recovered. The action on the part of the former school board members generated lots of criticism resulting in a lawsuit by the school district against the former school board members.[14] The lesson should be clear: err on the side of premature notice.[15]

The policy should be reviewed to determine when the nonprofit is deemed to have notice of a potential claim. Few would argue that an organization is unaware of a potential claim when the general counsel or vice president of risk management first learns about an issue that could give rise to an insurance claim. However, the nonprofit wants to make sure that a reporting requirement is not triggered when a mailroom clerk becomes aware of facts, but understandably does not appreciate their insurance implications. Granted that is an extreme example, but what about the case where the person responsible for the problem attempts to cover it up? The insured should make sure that the notification provisions do not work to its disadvantage under those circumstances.

It is particularly important that an organization not attempt to resolve or defend against a demand or suit on its own. Insurance policies generally require that the insurer have significant input, if not control, over the defense of a lawsuit. By attempting to resolve the matter without notifying the insurer and permitting it to exercise its rights, the organization (and the covered individuals) may well lose the benefit of coverage. This is true even if the nonprofit has retained the right to defend the lawsuit or select legal counsel.

(vi) The Duty to Defend. Every nonprofit should make sure that its insurance covers legal defense costs, which can be significant. Nonprofits naturally will focus on attorneys' fees, but they should make sure that policies cover the

---

13. *Id.*
14. Id. Once again, this particular case resulted in a lawsuit against public officials, but the school board members could have just as easily been members of a nonprofit's board.
15. Certainly a board is acting with prudence if it *factors* future premium costs into a decision whether to file a notice or a claim, but the board should not reflexively rule out filing a notice or claim. If the full loss is known, the board certainly can undertake a cost-benefit analysis, particularly if the size of the deductible means that there will be no recovery. Boards should recognize, however, that there can be a difference between filing a notice and filing a claim. Filing a notice may impact rates, but probably not to the same degree as filing a claim. Moreover, the insurance company brings more to the table than just a deep pocket. If the board decides to forego notice to the insurance company, the board must handle the matter, which can mean out-of-pocket legal fees, investigative expenses, and director time. If the matter is turned over to the insurance company, many of these costs are immediately shifted to the insurance company.

cost of expert witnesses, investigative studies, and other expenditures typically incurred in a lawsuit.

When setting total claims coverage, the covered persons should determine whether the maximum dollar coverage is reduced by covered defense costs. If coverage is reduced (the defense costs are said to be inside the policy limits), the policy's maximum limits should be increased accordingly. It is important that each director and officer also determine whether the insurance company will advance these costs so that these individuals do not have to finance the defense themselves.

As noted earlier, who mounts the defense is also an issue. As a practical matter, both the insured and the insurer participate in the defense, but some issues should be addressed. First, who selects defense counsel? Some policies allow the insurer to select counsel; others permit the insured to do it. In many cases, the other party will have approval rights. Large nonprofits may insist that they have the right to select counsel because they have a history with a particular law firm that understands their operations. Small nonprofits may have less leverage in negotiating, but they are likely to have less experience with litigation. In fact, the small nonprofit may actually be better off relying on the expertise of its insurer in identifying qualified counsel.

Polices also address the rights of the insured and the insurer to enter into a settlement. Because a large portion of a recovery typically comes out of the insurer's pocket, it is unlikely to provide the insured the unconditional right to approve a settlement (unless the settlement is within the limits of the deductible). This does not mean that the insured does not have an interest in approving a settlement. After all, if the settlement exceeds the policy limits or includes payments for claims not otherwise covered by the policy, those costs are the insured's responsibility. Even if the settled amount is within the policy limits, it reduces the policy's future coverage. The insured should also be particularly concerned about settlement if there is a coinsurance clause.

Given the possibility of disagreements between the insured and insurer over whether to settle, the insurance industry has developed a concept referred to as the *hammer clause*. While many skeptics believe that anything referred to with this term in an insurance policy cannot be favorable to the insured, in point of fact, it can be. A hammer clause clearly recognizes that both the insured and the insurer have legitimate interests in deciding whether to settle a lawsuit. Insurance companies are likely to be more objective about litigation risks than the insured. After all, they participate in far more litigation than any individual insured. For the insurance company, litigation is just another day at the office. For the insured, litigation is a highly personal and threatening event.

Under the typical hammer clause, the insured retains the right to determine whether to settle a claim, but the insurance company receives protection from irrational insureds who want to litigate to the bitter end. The insurance company acknowledges the insured's right to control whether to settle the litigation. Under a typical hammer clause, if the insured turns down a settlement offer that the insurance company wants to accept, the insured must assume subsequent costs. The insured is entitled only to obtain a payment from the insurance company for the liability arising from the dispute equal to the amount of the settlement the insured rejected (assuming it was within the policy limits).

The following is a portion of language from a nonprofit D & O policy that illustrates how one insurance company couches its hammer clause:

> If the Defense Outside the Limits of Liability Option is not purchased as set forth in Item 5 of the Declarations of this Coverage Section, in the event an Insured in any Claim withholds consent to a Proposed Settlement, the Company's liability with respect to such Claim shall not exceed: (i) the amount of the Proposed Settlement plus Defense Costs incurred up to the date of the Insured's refusal to consent to the Proposed Settlement; plus (ii) seventy percent (70%) of any Loss, including Defense Costs, in excess of the amount referenced in paragraph (i) above, incurred in connection with such Claim; subject in all events to the applicable Retention and Limits of Liability for such Claim. The remaining thirty percent (30%) of Loss, including Defense Costs, in excess of the amount referenced in paragraph (i) above shall be borne by the Insured's uninsured and at their own risk, notwithstanding anything to the contrary contained in Subsection 11(a) Allocation.[16]

(c) A-SIDE, B-SIDE, AND C-SIDE POLICIES. When reviewing a D & O policy, a nonprofit and its directors should focus on whether the policy covers the directors and officers (A-side coverage), the entity's obligation to indemnify its directors and officers (B-side coverage), or the entity for its own liability (C-side coverage). Each coverage can be packaged as part of one policy or as separate policies. A-side coverage generally considers indemnification rights so that it often applies to losses that the nonprofit is prohibited by law from indemnifying, chooses not to indemnify, or is simply unable to indemnify against because of lack of financial resources. Typical A-side coverage requires a director who is entitled to indemnification to look first to the nonprofit rather than the insured for protection against loss. The following is sample language from a nonprofit D & O policy that packages A-side, B-side, and C-side coverage as part of one policy (but refers to them as Insuring Clauses 1, 2, and 3:

> **Insuring Clauses**
>
> 1. **Individual Non-Indemnified Liability Coverage Insuring Clause 1.** The Company shall pay, on behalf of each of the Insured Persons, Loss for which the Insured Person is not indemnified by the Organization and which the Insured Person becomes legally obligated to pay on account of any Claim first made against the Insured Person, individually or otherwise, during the Policy Period or, if exercised, during the Extended

16. Chubb Group of Insurance Companies, Form Type C33778 (ed. 10/2004). This specimen policy language is provided for illustrative purposes only. The precise coverage afforded by any policy is subject to the terms and conditions of the policy as issued.

Reporting Period, for a Wrongful Act committed, attempted, or allegedly committed or attempted by such Insured Person before or during the Policy Period, but only if such Claim is reported to the Company in writing in the manner and within the time provided in Subsection 6 of the General Terms and Conditions.

2. **Individual Indemnified Liability Coverage Insuring Clause 2.** The Company shall pay, on behalf of the Organization, Loss for which the Organization grants indemnification to an Insured Person, as permitted or required by law, and which the Insured Person becomes legally obligated to pay on account of any Claim first made against the Insured Person, individually or otherwise, during the Policy Period or, if exercised, during the Extended Reporting Period, for a Wrongful Act committed, attempted, or allegedly committed or attempted by such Insured Person before or during the Policy Period, but only if such Claim is reported to the Company in writing in the manner and within the time provided in Subsection 6 of the General Terms and Conditions.
3. **Entity Liability Coverage Insuring Clause 3.** The Company shall pay, on behalf of the Organization, Loss which the Organization becomes legally obligated to pay on account of any Claim first made against the Organization during the Policy Period or, if exercised, during the Extended Reporting Period, for a Wrongful Act committed, attempted, or allegedly committed or attempted by the Organization or the Insured Persons before or during the Policy Period, but only if such Claim is reported to the Company in writing in the manner and within the time provided in Subsection 6 of the General Terms and Conditions.[17]

Directors should look carefully at how A-side (Clause 1) coverage interacts with B-side (Clause 2) and C-side (Clause 3) coverage, as well as indemnification rights, because such interactions can leave the director unprotected in certain instances. To illustrate, assume that Victoriaville Women's Health Clinic purchases a $2 million D & O policy providing A-side, B-side, and C-side coverage. If a $3 million claim is asserted against both the directors and WHC, depending on how the coverage is allocated over the three sides, the directors could be left uncovered. To use an admittedly unusual contract provision, assume that coverage is first made available for the C-side claim, the company's direct exposure to liability (as opposed to its obligation to indemnify the directors and officers). If the payments for those claims exceed $2 million, the directors would be without full protection.

Given that problem, directors should have a distinct preference for a separate policy providing coverage that is not shared with the entity. Such a policy could take the form of an "excess A-side policy," which provides additional coverage in the form of a separate limit that only comes into play if the underlying D & O policy's limits are exhausted. It may also provide coverage for slightly expanded categories of covered claims. The excess A-side policy becomes the primary policy to the extent that a loss falls into a broader coverage category that is not covered

17. *Id.*

by the underlying D & O policy. This is aspect of an excess A-side policy is referred to as "differences in conditions" (DIC) coverage.

If excess A-side coverage is not readily available or the parties simply do not want to incur the added expenses, the directors should seek "an order of payments clause." This clause provides that the A-side coverage has payment priority over the B-side and C-side coverage if the D & O policy is three sided. To illustrate, one nonprofit D & O policy provides as follows:

> In the event payment of Loss is due under this Coverage Section but the amount of such Loss in the aggregate exceeds the remaining available Limit of Liability for this Coverage Section, the Company shall:
>
> a. first pay such Loss for which coverage is provided under Insuring Clause 1 of this Coverage Section; then
> b. to the extent of any remaining amount of the Limit of Liability available after payment under (a) above, pay such Loss for which coverage is provided under any other Insuring Clause of this Coverage Section.
>
> Except as otherwise provided in this Subsection 13, the Company may pay covered Loss as it becomes due under this Coverage Section without regard to the potential for other future payment obligations under this Coverage Section.[18]

There are even policies that contain a third clause that provides priority to the B-side coverage over the C-side coverage.

The potential issues lurking in A-side coverage can be exacerbated by the bankruptcy of a nonprofit, which can cause the policy to be treated as an asset of the bankruptcy estate and freeze the directors' rights. These interactions are clearly an issue in D & O policies providing coverage to directors of publicly traded corporation. They also can be an issue for nonprofit directors when wrongful termination suits name directors and the entity. They can also apply to suits claiming violations of securities laws such as those alleging fraud in the marketing of tax-exempt bonds or partnership interests in a low-income housing tax credit syndication. Depending on how it is written, excess A-side coverage could be a solution to this problem.

While A-side and B-side coverage may each seem separate, in practice, they operate in tandem. The insurer often requires the nonprofit to agree to a "presumptive indemnification" clause, which requires the nonprofit to provide the maximum legal level of indemnification. This can require the nonprofit to amend its bylaws or articles of incorporation to include discretionary rights to indemnify directors and officers under the particular state's nonprofit corporation act. If a claim occurs, the directors and officers typically look to the nonprofit for indemnity. In turn, the nonprofit looks to the insurer for reimbursement of payments under the indemnification provision. Consequently, to the extent that there

18. *Id.*

is a coverage shortfall because the claims exceed the policy's limits, the shortfall is often reflected in a conflict between the A-side and B-side coverage, on one hand, and the C-side coverage on the other.

If a nonprofit acquires C-side coverage, it should be careful not to rely too heavily on it. Specifically, entity-level coverage under a D & O policy can provide the entity protection against governance-related claims and securities law–related claims. However, this coverage is not a substitute for the traditional coverage included by professional errors and omissions, comprehensive general liability, workers' compensation, automobile, or other common and necessary coverages. At the same time, entity-level coverage under a nonprofit D & O policy is likely broader than entity-level coverage under a D & O policy for a major *Fortune* 500 company; the latter's coverage could be limited to violations of the securities laws.

(d) TIME FRAME—TWO BASIC APPROACHES. Just as important as the types of coverage is the coverage period. Most policies have a one-year term—that is the easy part. Does the policy cover only claims made during that one-year period for events that occurred then, or does it apply to any claims arising from events that occurred during that year no matter how far in the future those claims are asserted? The insurance industry addresses this issue by categorizing its policies as "claims-made" or "occurrences policies." This distinction is critical.

(i) Claims-Made Policies. Under a pure *claims-made* insurance policy, the insured has coverage for claims that it reports to the insurance company during the policy period.[19] Be careful: The terminology used by various insurance companies is not consistent, due in large part to the treatment of claims attributable to events occurring before the policy's inception. The task is to focus on the specific policy's provisions.

To illustrate the basic concept underlying a claims-made policy, assume that Better Social Services Agency obtains D & O insurance on a claims-made basis with the policy-period running from January 1, 20X5, to December 31, 20X5. Also assume that the directors are sued on March 1, 20X5, for an action they took on December 10, 19X8. A pure claims-made policy would cover this claim. The question to ask is whether the claim was made (against the insured) during the policy period and reported (by the insured to the insurance company) within the specified reporting period. Theoretically, the focus is *not* when the event giving rise to liability occurred.

Notwithstanding the theoretical aspects of a claims-made policy, the insured must review a first-time claims-made policy before assuming that it covers claims made during the policy period that are attributable to events occurring

19. Emmett Vaughan and Therese Vaughan, Fundamentals of Risk and Insurance, Glossary Definition (John Wiley 2003); and Melanie Herman, Coverage, Claims & Consequences: An Insurance Handbook for Nonprofits, Glossary Definition (Nonprofit Risk Management Center 2002).

before the policy's inception. Insurance companies often set a "retroactive date"[20] and cover only claims based on events occurring *after* that date. If the organization is a new one, the retroactive date is often its date of incorporation. If the organization is an existing one that had been covered under an occurrences policy, the retroactive date is likely to be the date on which the claims-made coverage began. If the organization had claims-made coverage with another insurer, the retroactive date should go back at least as far as the retroactive date in the prior claims-made policy; otherwise, the nonprofit will have gaps in coverage for earlier events.

In all likelihood, the policy will exclude claims based on events known to the insured when it applied for coverage. For example, if the board knows that the state's attorney general plans to bring an action against it for a breach of its duties, the board generally cannot obtain coverage against the claim by buying a claims-made policy just before the attorney general files the suit. The insured must identify any known events as part of the application process, and they are excluded.

When a claims-made policy is renewed, the new policy should provide "prior acts" coverage. This means that the retroactive date is set so that events that lead to a claim during the current period but that occurred during a prior policy period are covered. This generally involves keeping the original retroactive date in place. In a sense, the annual premium payment can be viewed as the purchase of a policy extension rather than a new and distinct policy. Viewed this way, the claim and the event causing the claim both occur during the term of what could be described as an "extended" policy. This is a gross oversimplification because the terms of policies can change from year to year, particularly when the insurer changes. Consequently, the insured should review the policy terms on an annual basis.

What happens when the insured drops the basic coverage? This typically occurs when the insured is no longer involved in the activities that led to the need for the particular coverage. Not so surprising, the insurance industry has addressed this issue. Many claims-made insurance policies provide the insured the opportunity to purchase a "tail" or extended reporting coverage when the insured discontinues primary coverage. The tail provides coverage only for claims that arise from events that would have otherwise been covered by the basic policy but that are asserted during the tail period.

It is critical that the insured not engage in the particular activity during the tail period because it does not cover claims arising from that activity. To illustrate, let's assume that Victoriaville Women's Health Clinic purchases D & O coverage for its directors for 20X5. At the end of 20X5, it decides to discontinue the basic coverage for periods after 20X5, but it elects the available tail option. If the board is sued in 20X7 for an action it took in 20X5, the tail provides protection.

---

20. Emmett Vaughan and Therese Vaughan, *supra* note 19, at 590–91.

On the other hand, if the board is sued in 20X7 for an action it took in 20X6, the tail does not provide coverage.

The obvious question: How many future months or years should the tail cover? There is no hard-and-fast rule, but a significant factor in determining the length is the statute of limitations that governs the liabilities that the basic policy covers. As an example, if the policy covers liabilities that can be asserted up to three years following occurrence of the event giving rise to the liability, the tail coverage should be for at least a three-year period following the end of basic coverage. Determining when the statute of limitations expires can be tricky, so organizations should err on the side of tail coverage that exceeds the statute of limitations. One of the reasons the determination can be tricky is because courts will sometimes "toll" (suspend) the running of the statute of limitations. In other cases, courts will conclude that the statue of limitations starts running from a later date than expected.

Keep in mind three important points when you analyze tail coverage. First, the tail is negotiated as part of the underwriting process. The insured should know that it has the tail coverage before it purchases the policy so that it can (1) evaluate the tail's cost and (2) be sure that if claims are made during the regular policy period, the insured cannot be denied the tail protection. Second, the premium for tail coverage becomes more expensive as the tail's term increases. Third, tail coverage is priced as a percentage of the annual premium (e.g., 400 percent of the annual premium for 5 years of tail coverage). Consequently, the cost of comparable tail coverage increases each year as basic premium rates increase.

(ii) Occurrences Policies. Under an occurrences policy, the insured is covered for losses attributable to events occurring during the policy period regardless of when the insured becomes aware of the liability,[21] assuming the insured provides timely notice to the insurance company.

Unless the insured acquired special coverage (sometimes referred to as "prior acts" coverage) that relates to events occurring prior to the first year of coverage, claims made during the policy period from events occurring before the policy's inception are not covered under an occurrences insurance policy. The focus is on when the event giving rise to the claim occurred; if it occurred during the policy period, the insured is entitled to coverage with respect to the resulting claim.

To illustrate, assume that Better Social Services Agency is formed on January 1, 20X3. It obtains D & O insurance on an occurrences basis; coverage is applicable to events occurring during the 20X3 calendar year. Due to unexpected revenue shortfalls, the board decides to discontinue coverage at the end of 20X5. If the attorney general brings an action against the board on March 1, 20X6, for an action it took on April 15, 20X3, the board is covered under the policy. However, if the attorney general brings an action against the board on March 1, 20X5, for an action it took on February 1, 20X2, it does not have coverage.

---

21. See note 19, *supra*.

(iii) Which Is More Desirable? Some technical differences clearly exist between claims-made policies and occurrence policies. The relevant question involves whether there is a material difference between the two types of policies. The answer depends on whether the nonprofit or the insurance company is asking. Assuming that the premiums are equal, an insurance company would much prefer to write claims-made insurance coverage. With occurrences coverage, the insurance company agrees to insure against losses attributable to events occurring during a given year no matter when the claim is made; it is open ended. With a claims-made policy, the insured bears the risk that claims based on events occurring during the policy period will be made long after the policy has expired. Of course, competition will force the "claims-made" insurance company to offer optional tail coverage provisions. But the pricing of tail coverage is adjusted each year to reflect experience and inflation, thereby shifting the cost of the uncertainty to the insured.

The insurance company's perspective can provide insight into which coverage type nonprofits would prefer. Again assuming the premiums are equal, a nonprofit purchasing D & O insurance should prefer an occurrences policy to a claims-made policy because it knows that coverage for events occurring during a particular period are covered no matter when the associated claims are asserted.

Because of optional tail coverage, prior acts coverage, and other contract terms, it is possible to obtain equivalent coverage under either form of policy. The critical task for the nonprofit is to review the policy so that it knows what it is purchasing and that no gaps in coverage exist. As a general matter, D & O insurance coverage for nonprofits and their directors and officers is written on a claims-made basis.

(e) NOTEWORTHY CLAUSES. Few people like to read an insurance policy, and many people simply rely on the judgment of the organization's insurance advisors in selecting a policy. This should be avoided. Although individual directors probably are not in a position to negotiate the terms of a corporate policy, each director should know the policy terms and understand specific clauses. After all, by serving, each director is exposing his personal assets, although as Chapter 4 demonstrated, that exposure in most cases will not be significant (with the exception of defense costs). Ideally, each director's attorney should also review the policy, particularly the noteworthy clauses, but few directors are willing to pay for that review. The issues that these clauses pose may not be familiar to the average director, but they are important and should be addressed by the person in charge of procuring insurance.

(i) The Allocation Clause. The fact is that not everyone involved in a lawsuit is fully covered by insurance. Consequently, the insurers, the insureds, and uninsureds defendants must address how to allocate common legal and other expenses. This can be particularly important to the insured when the defense costs are inside the contract because any defense costs allocated to the policy reduce the potential indemnity under it. An insurance company clearly has an interest in the allocation of these defense costs when it has agreed to cover those outside of the policy limits.

Insurance contracts specify the allocation of common defense costs between the insureds and uninsureds. To illustrate, assume that the cost of defending a lawsuit is $100,000, and both the insured and uninsured defendants share this common cost. Although the insurance company may have agreed to pay defense costs incurred by the insured, it would be unfair to require it to cover the full $100,000 when some of it redounded to the benefit of an uninsured defendant. The allocation clause addresses this by providing either a standard for determining the amount of common expenses that the policy will cover (including arbitration in the event the parties cannot agree on an allocation). One insurer avoids the issue of allocation entirely by paying all defense costs (as distinguished from the actual loss indemnity). Presumably, this insurance company offers this peace of mind at a slightly higher premium.

The question of allocation is not limited to defense costs. In some cases, only a portion of the loss is covered by insurance. For example, the entire board of a nonprofit may be sued for breach of its duties, but one director may be without coverage because he engaged in reckless conduct while the other directors were only negligent. In another case, there may be two claims, one of which is covered and one of which is not. In many cases, the settlement will not specifically allocate dollar amounts to a particular claim or defendant. Consequently, there must be a mechanism in the policy for determining what portion of the settlement the insurance covers. One policy contains an allocation clause that provides as follows:

> If both Loss covered under this Coverage Section and loss not covered under this Coverage Section are incurred by the Insureds on account of any Claim because such Claim against the Insureds includes both covered and non-covered matters, then coverage under this Coverage Section with respect to such Claim shall apply as follows:
>
> i. Defense Costs: One hundred percent (100 percent) of reasonable and necessary Defense Costs incurred by the Insured on account of such Claim will be considered covered Loss; and
>
> ii. Loss other than Defense Costs: All remaining loss incurred by the Insured on account of such Claim shall be allocated by the Company between covered Loss and non-covered loss based on the relative legal and financial exposures of the Insureds to covered and non-covered matters and, in the event of a settlement in such Claim, also based on the relative benefits to the Insureds from such settlement.
>
> If the Insureds and the Company cannot agree on an allocation of loss:
>
> i. no presumption as to allocation shall exist in any arbitration, suit or other proceeding; and
>
> ii. the Company, if requested by the Insureds, shall submit the dispute to binding arbitration. The rules of the American Arbitration Association

> shall apply except with respect to the selection of the arbitration panel, which shall consist of one arbitrator selected by the Insureds, one arbitrator selected by the Company, and a third independent arbitrator selected by the first two arbitrators.[22]

(ii) The Severability Clause. When a nonprofit applies for D & O insurance, it must submit a detailed application that permits the insurance company to assess the risks that it is insuring. This information forms the basis of coverage. Incorrect or false information can invalidate a policy.

Although the nonprofit is ostensibly supplying the information, a person actually completes the application. Depending on the nonprofit's size, that person is usually the CEO or treasurer (small nonprofits) or the vice president for risk management (large organizations). In the vast majority of the cases, the named insureds (you and the other directors, for example) are not in control of the application process, and this poses a potential problem for them: Each stands to suffer a loss if the policy is invalidated due to false statements in the application or the actions of one, but not all, of the insureds.[23]

To address this risk, many insurance policies contain "severability" clauses.[24] These clauses treat the insureds who had no knowledge of the misstatements as continuing to be covered by the policy despite the misstatements. Each covered person should make sure there is a clause in the policy that protects him from misstatements made by others.

A similar issue involves policy exclusions. For example, consider a board that is named in a lawsuit as a result of the criminal activity of one employee or director. Under the terms of the policy, even though the other directors had no knowledge of the criminal conduct, they could be without coverage depending on how broadly the policy exclusion for criminal acts is written. Because of that possibility, the nonprofit should make sure that exclusions do not eliminate insurance coverage for the innocent directors.

(iii) The Reaffirmation of Prior Applications Clause. It is one thing for a policy to require current directors and officers to live with the representations made in the current application for D & O coverage. It is quite another for these same directors and officers to be held accountable for representations made on

---

22. Chubb Group of Insurance Companies, Form Type C33778 (ed. 10/2004). This specimen policy language is provided for illustrative purposes only. The precise coverage afforded by any policy is subject to the terms and conditions of the policy as issued.

23. For an excellent article on the issues posed by severability clauses, see J. Tanner, *So Long, D & O Coverage: Policy Rescission—What the Insured Can Do*, 14 BUS. L. TODAY (Mar./Apr. 2005).

24. For examples of cases involving litigation over these clauses, see *In re* HealthSouth Corp Ins. Litig., 308 F. Supp. 2d 1253 (N.D. Ala. 2004); Cutter & Buck v. Genesis Ins., 306 F. Supp. 2d 988 (W.D. Wash. 2004); Wedtech Corp. v. Federal Ins. Co, 740 F. Supp. 214 (S.D.N.Y. 1990); Atlantic Permanent Federal Savings and Loan Assoc. v. American Cas. Co., 839 F.2d 212 (4th Cir. 1988); and Shapiro v. American Home Assurance, 616 F. Supp. 214 (D. Mass. 1984). For a case involving relief in the absence of a clause, see McGory v. Allstate Ins. Co., 527 So.2d 632 (Miss 1988). *See* D. Erlandson in RISK: LEGAL ISSUES IN INSURANCE COVERAGE (Fall 2003).

prior applications by former directors and officers. Nevertheless, some D & O polices require that the insureds reaffirm statements made in prior applications. Current directors and officers should demand that such reaffirmations be eliminated from the application.

(iv) The Insured versus Insured Clause[25] Insurance companies are not interested in paying claims based on intraorganizational disputes or collusion. Consequently, D & O insurance policies often exclude liabilities arising from disputes between directors or between directors and the nonprofit. Both organizations and covered persons should ascertain whether the D & O policy has an insured versus insured clause. Boards should be particularly concerned about such a clause if the executive director or other officers are covered under the same policy. This clause could eliminate coverage for the directors in the event of a wrongful termination suit by the exectuive director against the board.

It goes without saying that this exclusion has significant ramifications for derivative lawsuits and those brought by the corporation against directors and officers. For this reason, a careful reading of the D & O policy is critical.[26] An insured versus insured clause in certain situations can actually have a beneficial effect from the organization's standpoint (e.g., minimizing disputes among board factions by forcing them to weigh a negotiated resolution against the cost of resorting to the courts). However, directors and officers should attempt to eliminate the provision from policies because they stand to lose the most if the organization ever brings suit against them.

Some insurance companies recognize the potential problems that a broad insured versus insured exclusion can pose for the insureds, often eviscerating coverage. One company begins with a broad exclusion and then reinstates coverage for specific types of disputes between insured. This provision provides as follows,

> The Company shall not be liable for Loss on account of any Claim:...(c) brought or maintained by or on behalf of any Insured in any capacity; provided that this Exclusion 5(c) shall not apply to:
>
> i. a Claim brought or maintained derivatively on behalf of the Organization by one or more securityholders of the Organization or persons who are not Insured Persons, provided such Claim is brought and maintained without any active assistance or participation of, or solicitation by, any Executive;
>
> ii. a Claim brought or maintained by an Insured Person for contribution or indemnity, if such Claim directly results from another Claim covered under this Coverage Section....[27]

---

25. The insured versus insured clause may bring back memories of *Spy vs. Spy* from MAD MAGAZINE.

26. Stratton v. Hanson, 2004 U.S. Dist. Lexis 17613 (D. Mass.).

27. Chubb Group of Insurance Companies, Form Type C33778 (ed. 10/2004). This specimen policy language is provided for illustrative purposes only. The precise coverage afforded by any policy is subject to the terms and conditions of the policy as issued.

Although most people think of derivative suits in the context of high-profile shareholder litigation, many state statutes provide for them in the nonprofit arena. For example, the attorney general may be given power to bring an action against the directors on behalf of a nonprofit corporation. An insured versus insured clause could prove problematic for the nonprofit's directors if the attorney general is considered to be an insured. Under clause (i) of the language just quoted, the directors appear to be covered. Suppose, however, that one of the directors contacted the attorney general because that director objected to the behavior of his fellow directors? This is not a theoretical issue: In one very high-profile breach of duty case involving a nonprofit, some of the directors were hesitant about contacting the attorney general because they feared losing coverage for themselves because of an insured versus insured clause in the D & O policy.

(v) Employment Practices Endorsement. One recent book reports that the "vast majority of legal actions brought against nonprofits, nonprofit boards, and nonprofit managers and executives" are employment-related claims.[28] The cost of settling a wrongful termination suit can easily exceed $100,000 plus more than $100,000 in defense costs. Employment practices litigation refers to suits alleging protected-class (age, sex, and race) discrimination, wrongful termination, or sexual harassment, among other employment-related claims. EPL coverage is highly desirable given the propensity of these suits. The Chubb Insurance Company provides some sense the potential liability resulting from employment practices, reporting that:

> Not-for-profit organizations have become increasingly vulnerable to employee lawsuits. According to Tillinghast-Towers Perrin's 2004 Directors and Officers Liability Survey, 96 percent of the D&O claims against nonprofit organizations were brought by employees, while only 23 percent of claims against public companies were brought by employees. Of those employee claims against nonprofits, 36 percent were for discrimination and 21 percent were for wrongful termination, according to the Tillinghast survey.[29]

As a general rule, employment practices coverage is not included as part of the D & O policy but can be sold as a package with it. This package approach makes sense for a variety of reasons. First, if the board dismisses a key officer such as an executive director, each board member who voted for the dismissal could be named in a suit. Second, if the suit includes allegations of sexual harassment, the board may be named for permitting a hostile work environment to go unchecked. Third, aggressive plaintiff's attorneys in employment practices litigation may name the board as a matter of course. Although none of these

---

28. Melanie Herman and Leslie White, D & O: What You Need to Know (Nonprofit Risk Management Center 1998).

29. Press Release, Chubb Group of Insurance Companies, New Chubb Tools Help Not-for-Profit Organizations Manage Employee Lawsuit Exposure (Mar. 30, 2005); *available at* http:// www.chubb/corporate/chubb3622.html.

claims may actually be rooted in a breach of the duty of care, in fact the members of the board are named because they are directors. An integrated approach to D & O and EPL coverage eliminates possible adverse consequences from gaps in coverage when each policy assumes an unrelated policy covers the matter.

(f) INSURERS. Do not bother calling the insurance agency that handles your home or auto insurance to obtain D & O insurance coverage. This coverage is not considered a specialty line, but agents and brokers who specialize in home and auto insurance are unlikely to have much experience with D & O insurance. In fact, directors probably should not make the phone calls; that is best handled by the nonprofit. In case a director or officer wants to undertake some preliminary research, a number of companies specialize in this line of insurance. They include AIG, ANI-RRG (a Section 501(c)(3) insurance company), AON, Chubb Group of Insurance Companies, CNA, Great American, Hartford, Markel Insurance Company, Philadelphia Insurance Companies, Travelers, and Zurich North America.

(g) TAX CONSIDERATIONS ARISING FROM INDEMNIFICATION AND D & O INSURANCE. A number of important federal income tax considerations must be addressed before acquiring D & O insurance or indemnifying directors or officers. If the organization is a private foundation, all concerned must focus on the general prohibition against self-dealing.[30] In the case of public charities, the focus should be on the intermediate sanctions.[31]

(i) Private Foundations. In many if not most cases, the indemnification by a private foundation or payment of insurance premiums to cover the liabilities of a person in his capacity as a director or officer of a private foundation will not pose problems under the prohibition against self-dealing, but there can be exceptions.[32] In addressing these payments, the rules distinguish between noncompensatory and compensatory payments. The noncompensatory category includes indemnification and insurance payments that cover expenses reasonably incurred in proceedings that do not result from a willful act or omission by the director or officer that was undertaken without reasonable cause.[33] These payments are viewed as expenses for the foundation's administration and operation, not compensation for the directors' or officers' services.

The compensatory category includes indemnification or insurance payments that cover private foundation excise taxes, related penalties and correction expenses, and expenses that were not reasonably incurred or were for proceedings that resulted from a willful act or an omission by the manager undertaken

---

30. I.R.C. § 4941; and Tres. Reg. § 53.4941(d)-2(f)(3).
31. I.R.C. § 4958.
32. Treas. Dec. 8639 (Dec. 19, 1995).
33. Treas. Reg. § 53.4941(d)-2(f)(3).

without reasonable cause. Such payments are viewed as being exclusively for the benefit of the manager, not the foundation.[34]

The rules provide that noncompensatory indemnification payments and insurance premiums do not violate the prohibition against self-dealing, but that compensatory indemnification payments and insurance premiums are acts of self-dealing unless the the director's or officer's total compensation is reasonable when the payments and premiums are included in the total.[35] The rules further provide that treatment as compensation for the limited purpose of determining whether compensation is reasonable under the private foundation excise tax provisions is separate and distinct from determining whether such payments and premiums are includable in the director's or officer's taxable income.[36]

A private foundation should seek the advice of qualified legal counsel before providing D & O insurance coverage to its directors or officers. While the rules seem simple enough, they contemplate some rather difficult allocations when the protection is both noncompensatory and compensatory.[37] Moreover, any indemnification provision should be drafted to provide that payment is not required if the payment constitutes an act of self-dealing under the excise tax provisions.

(ii) Public Charities. Public charities do not need to worry about the excise taxes imposed on self-dealing transactions that are applicable to private foundations, but they should focus on the intermediate sanctions.[38] Under that regime, the basic question is whether the compensation paid to a director or officer is reasonable. In approaching the question of D & O insurance and indemnification payments, the regulations under the intermediate sanctions take an approach similar to the one taken by the private foundation rules pertaining to self-dealing, but the language is not identical, which could result in interpretative anomalies.

Although these rules do not expressly distinguish between compensatory and noncompensatory indemnification payments and insurance premiums, the regulatory approach relies on equivalent categorization. If the organization pays or reimburses a director or officer for (1) penalties, taxes, or expenses of correction under Section 4958, (2) any expense not reasonably incurred by a person involving a civil judicial or administrative proceeding arising from the person's performance of services on behalf of the organization, or (3) any expenses resulting from an act or failure to act with respect to which the person has acted willfully and without reasonable, cause, the organization must include the value of the payments in the determination of whether the director's or officer's total compensation is reasonable, unless the payments are excludible from gross income

34. Tres. Reg. § 53.4941(d)-2(f)(4).
35. *Id.*
36. Tres. Reg. § 53.4941(d)-2(f)(7).
37. Tres. Reg. § 53.4941(d)-2(f)(5).
38. I.R.C. § 4958.

as de minimis fringe benefits.[39] Inclusion of the benefit in compensation for purposes of testing whether it is reasonable does not determine whether the benefit is includable in the director's or officer's taxable income.[40]

When an insurance premium or indemnification is not described in the preceding paragraph, it most likely qualifies as a working condition fringe benefit under Section 132. As a result, the cost of such insurance or indemnification is simply excluded from the determination of whether the beneficiary's overall compensation is reasonable for purposes of the intermediate sanctions.[41] For example, a nonprofit does not have to include reimbursements for attorney fees in compensation for purposes of testing whether a director's compensation is reasonable under the intermediate sanctions if his actions were reasonable and did not exhibit willful misconduct.

(iii) Recipient's Income Tax Treatment. The value of the indemnification payments or insurance protection provided to an individual (including one who is not compensated) who performs services for a tax-exempt organization is not taxable to the individual (i.e., the payments are excludable from gross income) because such payments are considered "working condition fringe" benefits.[42] Consequently, private foundations and other tax-exempt organizations do not need to allocate portions of director and officer insurance premiums to individual directors and officers or include such allocable amounts in IRS Forms 1099 or W-2.[43] Indemnification payments permitted by law, whether made by an insurer or directly by the employer, are treated in the same manner as insurance premiums.[44] One caveat is required. The law does not permit a taxpayer to deduct penalties or payments made against public policy. Consequently, to the extent that an indemnification payment represents a reimbursement for a penalty or willful misconduct, the IRS could well assert that it is not a working condition fringe benefit, requiring that it be includable in gross income (unless it is viewed as a de minimis fringe benefit). A similar argument could be made with respect to the portion of an insurance premium that covers taxes or willful misconduct.

(h) EFFECT ON AVAILABILITY OF VOLUNTEER PROTECTION ACT COVERAGE. The Volunteer Protection Act limits the liability of volunteers, including directors.[45] To be considered a volunteer under the VPA, the person cannot receive (1) compensation (other than reasonable reimbursement or allowance for expenses actually

---

39. Tres. Reg. § 53.4958-4(b)(1)(ii)(B)(2).
40. Tres. Reg. § 53.4958-4(b)(1)(ii)(C).
41. Tres. Reg. §§ 53.4958-4(a)(4)(i) and 1.132-5(r)(3)(ii) and (4).
42. Tres. Reg. § 1.132-5(r)(3)(ii).
43. Tres. Reg. § 1.132-5(r)(4), Example.
44. V. Richardson and B. Brockner, *Private Foundation in the Mid-1990s with an Emphasis on IRC 4941 and 4945,* IRS Continuing Educ. Pub. (1995). The text accompanying this and notes 42 and 43 is based on their commentary.
45. See note 2, *supra*.

incurred), and (2) any other things of value in lieu of compensation, together in excess of $500 per year. (See Chapter 4 for an extended discussion.) Although the statute was enacted to address a liability insurance crisis, it does not specifically address whether D & O insurance is considered compensation or something of value. If the issue did arise, the volunteer could legitimately argue that the insurance should be viewed as paid for the benefit of the organization itself, or, at most, that the value of the insurance should be viewed as a reimbursement of a reasonable expense. Even if the volunteer did not prevail with those arguments, in many cases, the value of the insurance will be below $500. However, like the tax law, a plaintiff could raise questions of reasonableness if the value of the insurance exceeded $500. For example, garden-variety D & O insurance might be reasonable, but special coverage for the intermediate sanctions or self-dealing might not be. Although the possibility that D & O insurance could jeopardize protection under the VPA may initially be alarming to some directors and officers, if the coverage is broad, it is the insurance company that should be alarmed.

(i) CONCLUSIONS. Ordinarily, a director or officer of a nonprofit should ask for and obtain D & O insurance coverage. In many cases, you will find that indemnification provisions and state and federal statutes limiting volunteer or director liability will be available to provide you sufficient protection. You should understand, however, that even these protections often contain ambiguities, as do after-the-fact reviews that could be applied to deny the purported protection. In the final analysis, D & O coverage provides the most reliable protection. Even then, do not be Pollyannaish; insurance companies have been known to contest policyholder claims. Read the policy and insist on a reputable carrier.

12.4 IDENTIFYING AND SHIFTING ORGANIZATIONAL RISKS

So far, this chapter has focused on how nonprofit directors and officers can protect themselves from risk. Let's change the focus now and examine how a nonprofit can address its own risks. This means considering a risk management program and transfer of risk through entity-level insurance.

Some large organizations (e.g., hospitals and universities) have a risk management officer who focuses on nothing but managing risk, including the procurement of insurance. Other organizations assign these functions to the chief financial officer or treasurer who is a paid employer but who is also responsible for unrelated functions. Finally, there are the smaller nonprofits. The person responsible for finances in these organizations is in all likelihood the one who works with an insurance agent or broker, focusing almost exclusively on procuring insurance when it comes to risk management. While these small organizations naturally focus on "getting" the insurance in place, they should also focus on identifying an insurance agent or broker who is both a professional and familiar with the risks that nonprofits in general and the organization in particular face. The natural inclination for many start-ups is to ask one of the organizers to call his personal insurance agent. Hopefully this agent will refer this nonprofit to an insurance agent or broker who specializes in procuring insurance for commercial or preferably nonprofit entities.

All organizations should keep in mind the major distinction between brokers and agents: *Brokers* represent the insured; *agents* represent the insurance carriers. Consequently, brokers will have a slightly broader perspective than agents because they are not tied to particular carriers but theoretically work with the entire market of insurance carriers. Of course, brokers naturally develop preferences for and relationships with particular companies, so the notion that a broker will survey the universe of carriers for each client may be more illusory than real.

In addition to brokers and agents, nonprofits may want to consider retaining a risk management consultant. Hiring consultants may initially appear to be something that only large organizations can do because of their deep pockets. Small organizations should resist viewing consultants as a luxury. These organizations may not be able to afford or need a full-time risk manager on staff, but they can benefit greatly from a consultant who provides them perhaps 30 hours of time each year.

(a) RISK MANAGEMENT. Procuring insurance coverage is clearly a large part of risk management, but it is not the only aspect. To illustrate, consider Bolder Art Museum, a small museum in Chicago. It owns two paintings by Vermeer, four by Rembrandt, and one by Leonardo da Vinci. People travel to Chicago from all over the world to see these seven paintings. Each is priceless. Bolder has been able to obtain $100 million in insurance coverage for its collection, but experts value the collection at $400 million.

Although Bolder may be able to shift $100 million of risk to the insurance companies in the event of a theft or a fire, it has not eliminated the risk of a theft or a fire. There lies the distinction between risk management and insurance. In a sense, insurance eliminates risk to the insured by transferring it to someone else. If Bolder were a car dealer, shifting risk to an insurance company would be as good as eliminating the risk altogether. If two Honda Accords on the dealer's lot are stolen, the dealer will file a claim with its insurance company, receive a payment, and replace the two cars with two similar cars. However, Bolder cannot view insurance in quite the same light. If the two Vermeer paintings are stolen, it may collect $100 million under its insurance policy, but no amount of money will permit it to replace the Vermeers. Insurance can buy some solace for Bolder in the event of a theft, but if it wants to truly protect itself, it must focus on reducing rather than shifting the risk.

Although reducing and shifting risk are sometimes the same thing from the nonprofit's viewpoint any nonprofit that reduces risk should be able to pay a lower price to shift the remaining risk. Returning to the car dealer, the premium paid to shift the risk of loss from theft is likely to be lower if it houses its new car inventory in a building rather than on an open lot.

Reducing overall exposure to risk in a cost-effective manner requires an organization first to identify its risk(s). Then it must design its operations after undertaking a cost/benefit analysis to minimize risk. Only after it has reduced its risk to cost-effective levels should the organization consider transferring risk to someone else. Even after it has transferred risk, the organization must continue to focus on identifying risks and seeking ways to minimize its exposure to them.

Let's return to Bolder Art Museum. Having acknowledged that the seven oil paintings are irreplaceable, the museum should focus on minimizing theft or damage to them. This means thinking about all aspects of its operation, including the design of its building and types of materials used in it, the makeup of the security force, how the paintings are displayed, whether to install a video surveillance system, its hours of operation, whether paintings will be loaned to other institutions, and any number of other considerations. This analysis, if properly undertaken, will quickly become technical. For example, consideration should be given to the building's sprinkler system. Water might be appropriate for an automobile dealer's facility, but an alternative system might be necessary to avoid damage to Bolder's paintings. Consideration should also be given to gallery lighting, temperature, and humidity.

Among other considerations, Bolder's risk management program should focus on protecting the people who enter its building. This will involve signage, lighting, sanitation, and other considerations. When it considers its employees, the museum needs to design a safe workplace and ensure that its employment practices do not violate the law.

(b) INSURANCE POLICIES IN GENERAL. Insurance policies are contracts between an insured and an insurance company that permit the insured to shift risk to the insurance company for a premium payment. Virtually any risk can be shifted to an insurance company through an insurance policy. The issue is the cost. We have already considered D & O insurance. Keep that discussion in mind as you follow the discussion of other types of coverage. Many of the concepts developed as part of that discussion also apply here.

(i) Basic Form. While insurance policies take a wide variety of forms, they have the following five component parts: (1) declarations; (2) the insuring agreement; (3) conditions; (4) exclusions; and (5) definitions. Do not expect to see these five conditions necessarily laid out in this sequence. Each policy should be viewed as a unique contract, but often there are similarities between policies.

The declarations specify the insured, the insurance company, the premium, the policy period, and the policy limits. In other words, these are the basic facts. For example, the declarations for a general liability insurance policy issued to Vermilion Food Bank might appear as follows:

> **Insured**: Vermilion Food Bank
>
> **Insurance Company**: Big Insurance Co, a New York insurance company

Policy Period: January 1, 2005 (12.00 AM), until December 31, 2005 (11:59 PM)

Coverage Limits: $5 million in the aggregate during the policy period, $250,000 per occurrence

Premium: $10,000

The insuring agreement describes in broad terms the coverage provided by the policy. A typical commercial general liability (CGL) insurance policy states the indemnity in one sentence, providing that it will cover damages attributable to "bodily injury" or "property damage" resulting from an "occurrence" that takes place during the period in a "covered territory." The words in quotes are defined terms. The policy conditions define the rights of the insured and the insurance company, as well as the rules under which the parties to the contract agree to abide. For example, the conditions outline the procedures by which the insured will notify the insurance company of a claim under the policy. The conditions also define what actions the insured must take at the request of the insurance company. These include arbitration procedures, the relationship between the policy coverage and coverage provided by other insurance (whether the policy provides primary or excess coverage), procedures for premium audits, and a number of other matters.

The section of the policy defining terms tends to be lengthy and detailed. It does exactly what it says: It defines terms used throughout the policy.

Typically, the provision in an insurance policy defining covered losses is concise, making its coverage potentially very broad. The insurance policy then provides a long list of loss exclusions that effectively shrink the coverage. In one sense, the list of exclusions can be viewed as a negative from the insured's standpoint. However, these exclusions often include risks that the typical insured does not face. As a consequence, the exclusions serve to keep premiums reasonable. Viewed this way, the insured should use the list of exclusions as a checklist for specialized risks. If the insured has exposure to any of these excluded risks, it should then inquire about a special endorsement or consider a separate policy.

The review of a policy must focus on the interactions between these five basic components. For example, the definitions can effectively work as exclusions. To illustrate, "covered territory" is a defined term. If this territory is defined as including "the United States of America (including its territories and possessions) and Canada," this effectively excludes coverage for activity in Europe or Asia. If the nonprofit has overseas operations, it needs to obtain either an endorsement or a separate policy to cover general liability from its European or Asian operations. Similarly, the conditions and the declarations must be read together. For example, the policy may declare that it provides $250,000 of coverage per occurrence, but if it is an *excess* policy, the insurance company may not be liable for any amount if the primary insurance provides $250,000 per occurrence.

Although not one of the five component parts, the application for insurance may be the most critical "part" of any insurance policy. It is here that the insured answers questions designed to permit the insurance company to assess the risks that it is agreeing to insure. The application asks about the nonprofit's operations and activities, financial conditions, plans, and known claims and potential claims. The typical insurance policy requires the insured to state that all the information it has provided is truthful. The policy then contains language providing that the policy is voidable at the insurance company's election if there are misstatements in the application. Often there is a gap between the time that the application for insurance is made and the policy is issued. If intervening events cause the application to become misleading or false, the insured should advise the company (or the insured's agent or broker); otherwise, the contract language will make the issued policy voidable at the insurance company's election.

(ii) Defense and Its Costs. When reviewing an insurance policy, the nonprofit should pay particular attention to the terms for payment and defense under the policy. Some policies require the insurance company to pay defense and other covered costs as they are incurred. In this case, the insured never incurs out-of-pocket costs, assuming these expenses do not exceed the policy's limits and ignoring any deductibles or coinsurance. Other policies provide that the insurance company will indemnify the insured once the matter is resolved, forcing the insured to finance defense and other covered costs during what could be protracted legal proceedings.

Along these same lines, some policies impose a duty on the insurer to defend the insured. This means that the insurance company is responsible for shepherding the dispute through the litigation process. There is logic to shifting defense responsibility to the insurance company. After all, the insurance company has assumed exposure for the liability. Furthermore, insurance companies generally are more familiar with litigation than nonprofits. On the other hand, some nonprofits, particularly large and well-known institutions, may have gained special expertise in their industry over the years. In fact, they may have staff lawyers who have particular expertise with the liability at issue. Moreover, these institutions may want more control over the litigation out of concern for their reputations. Most importantly—and this applies equally to large and small nonprofits—the existence of insurance does not mean that the nonprofit is necessarily without exposure. If the litigation is handled poorly or the coverage limits are too low, the nonprofit may be forced to pay a portion of any settlement or judgment out of its own funds. Consequently, any insured has at least some reasons for wanting to control the litigation. Whatever the nonprofit's preference, it should focus on the provisions in the insurance policy that define who is responsible for litigation, including the approval of any settlements.

Finally, there is the issue of how defense costs and the policy limits interact. As noted in the discussion of D & O insurance, defending a lawsuit can be costly. As a consequence, covering these costs should not be a minor considerations in evaluating an insurance policy and its coverage. Some policies cover these costs but reduce the amount of coverage. Policies written on this basis are referred to as being "inside the policy limits." Other policies cover these costs without otherwise reducing the available coverage. Not surprising, policies written on this basis are referred to as being written "outside the policy limits." The premiums for these policies are more expensive, all other things being equal. The insured can make the necessarily adjustments in coverage if it is buying an "inside" policy, but to do so, it must first understand this aspect of the policy.

(iii) Primary, Excess, and Umbrella Policies. A nonprofit may need to procure more than one policy to obtain adequate insurance coverage for a particular exposure. This is because of policy standardization and an individual company's capacity to assume risk. Consider Vermilion Food Bank. It might determine that it needs $8 million of commercial general liability insurance (discussed in detail shortly). However, it might be unable to obtain that level of coverage for a number of reasons. The insurance company that writes the basic policy might decide that it wants to write only a standard policy providing $5 million of coverage because that is what the average insured wants. Or, the insurer might decide that a loss above $5 million is catastrophic in nature, and it does not want to insure catastrophic losses. Or, state insurance regulations might prevent the insurance company from writing coverage that exceeds $5 million—perhaps because of minimum capital requirements.

To meet its needs, Vermilion can purchase "excess insurance" that generally takes one of two forms. It can be written either as a separate policy with all coverage defined within the policy, or as a "following form excess insurance," in which case the policy will simply define its coverage by referring to the coverage in the primary policy. The insurance company providing this excess coverage may be able to do so because it has more capital or specializes in insuring catastrophic liabilities.

Excess insurance coverage has elements in common with the more familiar umbrella policy, but the two are different in two respects. First, an umbrella policy usually provides "excess" or additional coverage for more than one policy. It is not unusual for an umbrella policy to "sit on top of" a CGL policy and a commercial property policy. Second, umbrella policies often cover losses that the basic policies do not cover.

(iv) Marketing: Monoline, Packages, and Programs. Insurance coverage is marketed in a wide variety of forms. It is possible to acquire insurance to cover one particular exposure—a monoline policy. Two common forms of monoline insurance are commercial general liability insurance (liability to third parties) and commercial property insurance (covering the insured's property).

Alternatively, the insured can buy a "package" of policies. For example, many companies offer a package that includes commercial general liability and property insurance.[46] A package offers the insured two basic advantages. First, combined coverage usually has a reduced cost. Second, there is generally better integration among the component policies. There will, however, always be those who want to find the best of each component part.

Finally, an organization can obtain an even broader coverage package through a program."[47] Programs often focus on a particular industry, offering CGL and commercial property insurance with a number of other coverages appropriate to the industry in question. This sort of program is sometimes referred to as business owners' policies (BOP). The BOP is marketed to small and medium size businesses; several companies offer a specialized form for nonprofits.[48] Some companies offer programs to specialized types of nonprofits. For example, companies specialize in insuring religious congregations, affordable housing providers, and various sports and recreational groups (e.g., hiking and biking organizations, youth sports leagues).

(c) AVAILABLE COVERAGE. Let's now consider the basic types of coverage and policies available to nonprofits. Our discussion will focus on the basic monoline policies that nonprofits are likely to encounter and need. Keep in mind that any described coverage can be aggregated into packages or programs such as BOP; but no organization should ever assume that a specific program or package covers specific risks without first closely reading its terms. Your organization's insurance advisor will help the organization determine whether individual policies, or packages or programs make the most sense for it.

(i) Commercial General Liability Insurance. Every nonprofit should give serious consideration to obtaining commercial general liability (CGL) insurance coverage. This is general liability insurance that protects against bodily injury and property damage.[49] To illustrate, if the nonprofit is operating a legal services clinic, its CGL policy will protect the clinic against damages incurred by a client who is injured when the chair he is sitting in breaks, but it will not cover a malpractice claim by a client for faulty legal services. The contract language is very broad, but exclusions in the policy limit the coverage.

Each policy contains different exclusions; CGL policies generally do not cover liability from the operation of automobiles and other forms of transportation; damages to the insured's own property from fire, theft, or other casualties; liability arising from injuries incurred by employees in the course of their employment (workers' compensation or employer liability); or liability from employment practices. They also exclude coverage for punitive damages. These are just the basic exclusions. Some policies have more specialized exclusions

46. S. Mingo, *Is It a Program or a Package? Here Is How to Tell the Difference*, INSUR. J., Sept. 18, 2000.

47. *Id.*

48. MELANIE HERMAN *supra* note 19, at 170.

49. COUCH ON INSURANCE 3D § 129:2 (1997).

such as liability caused by pollution and serving alcohol. Schools and social service agencies need pay particular attention to the exclusions because they often include exclusions for liability arising from child abuse and sexual molestation. The insured can address exclusions by obtaining a specialized insurance policy.

The CGL policy has a long history. Until the 1940s, each insurance company issued its own version of the CGL policy, which made comparison between policies difficult.[50] In the early 1940s, the Insurance Services Office (ISO) introduced the first standardized CGL policy. There are competing standard-form policies, but the ISO standard is the predominant one. Insurance companies license the right to use the form.

The ISO CGL policy is written on both a claims-made and occurrences basis. The predominant policy form remains occurrences,[51] but when the potential losses being covered have their genesis in events that span decades, the insurance company may be willing to write the policy only on a claims-made basis. Recall the asbestos litigation of the last two decades to understand why insurance companies might be reluctant to write an occurrences policy.

An ISO CGL policy provides the following three specific types of coverage: (1) Coverage A—Bodily Injury and Property Damage Liability, (2) Coverage B—Personal Injury and Advertising Injury Liability, and (3) Coverage C—Medical Payments. Each coverage includes its own separate exclusions that are enumerated in the policy. Part A focuses on physical injuries to others and their property. It also creates a right and imposes a duty to defend any lawsuit seeking damages.

Part B focuses on personal and advertising injury. The phrase *personal injury* conjures images of people in slings and casts. However, physical injury is covered by Part A. The personal injury referred to in Part B includes slander, libel, malicious prosecution, and invasion of privacy. Advertising injury protects against losses arising from the promotion of a product or service. Part C provides coverage for medical payments incurred by the insured to provide medical assistance to individuals injured on the insured's premises regardless of fault. This coverage may exclude injuries to certain categories of people such as employees and other insureds. This is loss mitigation coverage, designed to remove any financial impediments for providing aid to someone who needs immediate medical attention.

A CGL policy provides an overall coverage limit as well as several per occurrence limitations and possible limitations for particular types of losses. There may be separate limitations, for example, for payments to any one person under Part C medical coverage, or limits for products liability. To illustrate, the policy can limit recoveries under it to $5 million during the policy's term and limit the amount that the insured can recover to $250,000 for any one occurrence. Assume that someone is injured on the insured's premises when a wall collapses and that this person receives a $6 million judgment against the insured. In this case, the

50. Melanie Herman, *supra* note 19, at 72.

51. Emmett Vaughan and Therese Vaughan, *supra* note 19, at 585–86.

insurance company is responsible for $250,000 of the $6 million judgment and the insured is responsible for the remaining amount. Obviously, limits vary from policy to the policy. Insureds should resist the natural tendency to focus exclusively on the overall limitation but should pay close attention to the specific dollar limitations on individual claims or occurrences, which may have far more practical impact when a loss occurs.

As is true of all insurance policies, the insured must pay close attention to the process of filing claims set out in the CGL policy. The insured must promptly notify the insurance company of an occurrence or event that could give rise to a claim as well as an actual suit. The insured must also provide the insurance company any relevant paperwork (such as notices or demands); authorize it to obtain records and other information; cooperate with it in the investigation, negotiation, settlement, or defense of the claim; and assist it in enforcing any claims or rights. The insured should not make voluntary payments, assume obligations, or incur any expense without the written consent of the insurance company, with an exception for the provision of first aid.

We considered the insured-versus-insured clause when we focused on D & O insurance. These provisions are often included in CGI policies, posing a potential problem. If a CGI policy includes volunteers as named insureds, a general insured-versus-insured clause could undermine the basic coverage protection provided.[52] Consider, for example, the individual who volunteers his services as a carpenter to a nonprofit to build houses for low-income individuals. Assume that the volunteer is not covered under the nonprofit's workers' compensation policy. If the volunteer sues the nonprofit because of an injury sustained while building a house, an insured-versus-insured clause could negate the nonprofit's insurance coverage. When negotiating with an insurance company over the terms of any CGI policy, the insured should try to eliminate any insured-versus-insured clause (or address the coverage of volunteers through an endorsement or special policy).

(ii) Workers' Compensation Insurance. Workers' compensation is a no-fault insurance system for handling work-related injuries. Each state has a statutorily mandated program that requires employers to cover an injured worker's medical expenses, lost wages, and disability. Under these systems, employers exchange the unpredictable and potentially high costs associated with tort-related litigation for predictable insurance premiums. Similarly, employees give up the uncertainties of litigation for clearly defined benefits.

Many state systems have been in place since the early part of the 20th century,[53] when the concept first gained popularity in the United States.[54] Not surprising, there is a fair amount of similarity between state systems, but as is always the case, each employer must consider the specifics of applicable state

52. D. Szerlip, *Commercial General Liability Insurance* in MELANIE HERMAN, *supra* note 19.
53. The first workers' compensation system was instituted by Germany in 1856.
54. The first workers' compensation legislation was enacted by the state of Wisconsin in 1911.

laws. As a general rule,[55] these laws do not distinguish between for-profit and nonprofit employers, so nonprofits should assume that they are subject to workers' compensation requirements. Some state systems may provide small organization more time to bring themselves into compliance, but nonprofits with only one or two employees should assume that they are required to obtain coverage unless a specific exemption is identified.

Financing the Benefits

Under the typical statutory system, the employer is required to buy workers' compensation coverage. Some states permit employers meeting certain requirements to self-insure. Often the coverage is purchased through private insurance carriers as part of an insurance package or program. If an employer is unable to obtain insurance from the private market, it can usually look to a state workers' compensation insurance pool. This pool often is composed of all companies authorized to write workers' compensation coverage in the particular state. A state agency typically assigns an insurance company from the pool to write the coverage for employers that cannot obtain coverage in the private market. These employers may not be entitled to certain premium discounts or dividends.

Not all states rely on private insurance. Some require employers to participate in a state-administered fund. The state often notifies new employers of its requirements when they first file tax registration forms or apply for basic business licenses. Some states require employers to provide proof of coverage before they issue various permits and licenses. New employers should affirmatively ask their insurance carrier or business advisers about workers' compensation requirements rather than relying on state notification.

Many state systems provide incentives to reduce workplace injuries. When there is a mandatory state pool, new employers typically pay predefined premiums based on the type of work their employees perform. These premiums reflect the pool's experience with claims by those engaged in similar activities. As the employer creates its own history, the premium will be adjusted to reflect the employer's experience.

Determining the Benefits

When an injury occurs on the job, no questions are asked. The state pool or private insurance company has an administrative process for awarding benefits to the injured employee. Those benefits are determined according to a predetermined schedule. Of course, disputes over which schedule applies or the nature or

55. According to Mark Rothstein, Charles Craver, Elinor Schroeder, and Elaine Shoben, Employment Law, at 600 (West 2004), "Idaho excludes nonprofit enterprises, and Arkansas, Missouri, and North Dakota exclude both charitable and religious employers." The laws of each of these jurisdictions should be reviewed before relying on this statement. Those interested in specific statutory authority should review § 72-212(6) of the Idaho statutes and § 11-9-102(11)(A)(vi) of Chapter 9, of Title 11 of the Arkansas Code. A brief review of online statutes did not uncover comparable provisions under Missouri or North Dakota law, but that review should not be considered conclusive.

extent of a permanent disability can result, but the system does not seek to determine fault for the injury in awarding statutorily defined benefits. Some systems do, however, deny benefits if the injury occurred because of "horsing around" or the employee was using illegal drugs.

Volunteers and Independent Contractors

Each nonprofit should pay particular attention to the definitions for *employee* and *employment* under the applicable statutes. Some states require the employer to cover certain independent contractors and employees of contractors. This can be true despite the fact that an injured person is employed by someone providing the services to the nonprofit under contract, although the nonprofit may have subrogation rights against the employer. One way that a nonprofit can protect itself is to require contractors to provide the appropriate certification that their employees are covered under their workers' compensation policy.[56]

Chapter 11 considered event liability, particularly pertaining to temporary security forces and food workers. A nonprofit may be responsible for providing workers' compensation for these workers even when they are independent contractors. Even if the nonprofit is not required to do so, it might want to treat these service providers as employees for workers' compensation purposes (assuming that is permissible). Doing so could foreclose the nonprofit's ability to argue that these workers are independent contractors for tax purposes, but in the long run, limiting its liability for injuries may be worth the inconvenience and additional tax costs. It may be possible for the nonprofit to elect into workers' compensation coverage for particular individuals when classification is unclear or ambiguous. In any event, the nonprofit should make sure that workers' compensation applies to these workers or that it has appropriate liability coverage in place.

A nonprofit relying on an exclusion for volunteers should make sure that honorariums or expense reimbursements do not preclude reliance on the exemption. There could also be an issue in the case of a person who makes a monetary pledge but satisfies it by providing "volunteer" services.[57] Social services agencies should be particularly careful when work-training or other program participants provide "free" labor but receive meals, shelter, or a subsistence stipend in return.[58] Nonprofits should not place too much reliance on waivers of coverage and self-serving contractual language.[59] Finally, individuals who originally were volunteers often become paid employees. Nonprofits should make sure that changes in status are reported for insurance purposes.

---

56. For a more detailed discussion of this issue, see Mark Rothstein, Charles Craver, Elinor Schroeder, and Elaine Shoben, *supra* note 55, at 602-03.

57. *Id.*, at 606.

58. Anderson v. Homeless and Housing COA, 135 S.W.3d 405 (Ky. 2004), holding that the claimant was entitled to workers' compensation benefits because he received more than just aid or sustenance for his services; and Hall v. Salvation Army, 261 N.Y. 110, 184 N.E. 691 (1933).

59. *See* Dixon v. Salvation Army, 160 S.W.3d 723 (Ark. Ct. App. 2004), *rev'd* 2005 Ark. LEXIS 48.

ADDITIONAL EMPLOYER INSURANCE COVERAGE

As part of private workers' compensation insurance packages, the insured may be able to procure additional employers' coverage that is sometimes referred to as *Part B coverage*. It is designed to protect employers from plaintiffs' lawyers who attempt to circumvent workers' compensation statutory caps on recovery.[60] For example, lawsuits have been brought by an injured worker's spouse. In other instances, an employee could sue a third party that caused the injury for tort damages rather than for damages under workers' compensation. This sets up the possibility that the third party can then seek recovery from the nonprofit employer.[61] Finally, some plaintiffs' lawyers have argued that the employee was functioning in a dual capacity. Part B coverage is designed to protect the employer against attempts to expand the recovery by circumventing the liability limitations under workers' compensation statutes.

(iii) Automobile Coverage. Both nonprofits and volunteers must be concerned about automobile liability insurance. The standard ISO CGL policy[62] does not cover liability resulting from the operation of an automobile (or other mode of transportation such as an airplane or boat).

Obviously, the nonprofit should make sure that it has comprehensive automobile liability coverage. This insurance should cover liability arising out of the ownership, maintenance, and operation of the nonprofit's vehicles by its employees. The organization should also consider coverage for "hired vehicles" (leased, rented, or borrowed) and "nonowned vehicles" (owned by an employee or volunteer). Such coverage protects against liability that results from the use of a vehicle not owned by the nonprofit. Typical examples include use by employees or volunteers of their own vehicles while serving the nonprofit (nonowned vehicles) or rental of a vehicle by an employee acting on behalf of the nonprofit (hired-vehicle coverage).

The nonprofit should determine whether its automobile policies cover volunteers. To illustrate why, consider the volunteer who uses his SUV to make deliveries for a nonprofit. Although the volunteer is driving his own vehicle, he is acting as the nonprofit's agent. In 2005, a Milwaukee, Wisconsin, jury awarded $17 million to an 82-year-old man who was left a quadriplegic when a volunteer for the Legion of Mary ran a red light and crashed into the man's car.[63] The four-decade-long volunteer was delivering a statue of the Virgin Mary when the accident occurred. The relationships between the Legion of Mary (apparently a volunteer group), the local parish, and the Milwaukee Catholic Archdiocese are not entirely clear, but newspaper accounts indicate that the award was against the Archdiocese.[64] The Volunteer Protection Act clearly provided no protection

60. See EMMETT VAUGHAN AND THERESE VAUGHAN, *supra* note 19, at 582.
61. Dole v. Dow Chemical Company, 331 N.Y. Supp. 2d 382, 282 N.E.2d 288 (1972).
62. See EMMETT VAUGHAN AND THERESE VAUGHAN, *supra* note 19, at 587.
63. D. Nunnally, *Church Told to Pay $17 Million: Archdiocese Found Liable for Volunteer Who Caused Crash*, MILWAUKEE J.-SENTINEL, Feb. 18, 2005.

to the Legion of Mary, the parish, or the Archdiocese. This case demonstrates why boards should be concerned that their organizations have adequately addressed vicarious liability through risk management policies and insurance coverage. Finally, the nonprofit should make sure that its policy includes uninsured motorist coverage. This permits the nonprofit to recover damages when its employee or agent is not at fault, but the other party is either uninsured or underinsured.

(iv) Commercial Property Insurance. CGL insurance covers damage to someone else's property by the nonprofit's employees and other agents but not to the nonprofit's property. Depending on how the exclusions are written, a CGL policy may not provide coverage for liability to property the nonprofit leases.[65] To cover its own property, the nonprofit must obtain property insurance, which may be written as a basic, broad, or special form policy. The *basic form* commonly covers fire, explosions, storms, smoke, riots, vandalism, and sprinkler leaks. A *broad form* commonly expands basic coverage to include damage from broken glass, water, and falling objects. Neither the basic nor the broad form commonly include theft. These policies are referred to as *specified perils policies* because they list the perils they cover. To cover theft, the nonprofit must look to a *special form* policy, which may be written on an open-peril basis; that is, it covers all losses except those that are specifically excluded.[66] This coverage is more expensive because it is more inclusive.

COMPUTING THE RECOVERABLE AMOUNT

Probably the most important issue to be addressed under commercial property insurance is valuing the loss. There are two basic approaches to the process: valuation based on replacement value and valuation based on actual cash value. To illustrate, assume that Vermilion Food Bank has a warehouse with a $2 million value (it is 20 years old and has a 20-year remaining useful life). If the warehouse was completely destroyed, Vermilion would have to spend $5 million to replace it. If Vermilion's insurance policy provided for the value of the loss to be measured by the warehouse's replacement cost, the insurance company would have to pay Vermilion $5 million, assuming that it actually replaced the warehouse and that the policy coverage limits exceed $5 million.

As an alternative to replacement value coverage, Vermilion might consider insurance that values the loss using the warehouse's actual cash value, determined by identifying the building's replacement value—in this case $5 million—and

---

64. S. Schultze, *$17 Million Verdict Against Archdiocese over Crash Upheld*, MILWAUKEE J.-SENTINEL, Apr. 19, 2005.

65. One of the typical exclusions in a CGL policy is for assumptions of liability through contract. This can prove to be a difficult provision to understand when it is read in conjunction with leases that attempt to assign liability for property damages. The important point is to recognize that leases pose an issue and to be sure the treatment of damage to leased property under a CGL policy is clear.

66. EMMETT VAUGHAN AND THERESE VAUGHAN, *supra* note 19, at 554.

then subtracting an allowance for depreciation. In this case, the warehouse was destroyed with half of its useful life remaining, so the $5 million replacement cost would be reduced by $2.5 million to reflect accumulated depreciation (assuming depreciation occurs ratably). That means the Vermilion would be entitled to a $2.5 million recovery, assuming that this amount is within the policy limits.[67] Obviously, there are variations on these determinations, but the basic concept should be clear. Not surprising, replacement coverage is more expensive than actual cash value coverage.

Coinsurance Clauses

The insurance industry uses coinsurance clauses to encourage organizations to fully cover the value of the property in question. In exchange for purchasing the threshold level of insurance, the insured's premium is calculated at a reduced rate. These clauses can be difficult to understand but can significantly impact coverage by making the insured a coinsurer if the actual coverage drops below the agreed-upon level. To illustrate how such a clause operates, let's return to the example involving Vermilion Food Bank. Assume that its property insurance policy has a coinsurance clause, making the reduced premium rate contingent on procuring coverage at least equal to 80 percent of the property's actual cash value, or $2 million (80 percent of $2.5 million).[68] If Vermilion carries only $1 million of coverage when the building is destroyed, it is entitled to recover only $500,000 for the loss. This amount is determined by multiplying the covered loss ($1 million) by a fraction having as its numerator the amount of coverage in place ($1 million) and as its the denominator the amount of required insurance ($2 million).

What is puzzling about the coinsurance clause is why an insured would agree to an 80 percent requirement if it were knowingly going to underinsure the property. The answer is that it would not knowingly do so. That is the point of the clause—to keep the insured vigilant and honest. The determinations under the clause are made at the time of the loss. The insured may have valued the property at the time of the valuation at an incorrect amount, or inflation may have increased it's value. Another possibility is that the insured may have improved the property but failed to increase its insurance coverage. One way to deal with the coinsurance clause is to ask the insurance company to agree to a clause that specifies the value of the property so that the coinsurance clause can be suspended. The organization must make certain that if an agreed-upon value clause is used, it not be allowed to expire.

Expanding Coverage Through Endorsements

We considered basic, broad, and special form coverage at the outset of this discussion of commercial property insurance. When a building burns down, the

---

67. *Id.*, at 162-63.
68. This focuses on actual cash value ($2.5 million) under the insurance contract rather than fair market value ($2 million). As is always the case, the nonprofit should examine the terms of the contract to determine how the property is valued for purposes of applying the coinsurance clause.

entity likely incurs other losses. The fire can destroy valuable papers as well as employee or volunteer property, cause the nonprofit to relocate its operations on a temporary basis, and—most important—interrupt the nonprofit's operations, thereby reducing revenue. Think of all the nonprofits operating in New Orleans immediately before Hurricane Katrina hit in August 2005. They could obtain coverage for these and other exposures by adding a policy form to a commercial property package or program or obtaining a separate policy. This is where proper risk assessment can be very important.

When considering business interruption insurance,[69] a nonprofit should determine what additional expense it could incur as the result of the disaster. Possible expenses include costs to relocate to a temporary location, to reconstruct business records, and to pay shipping premiums incurred if inventories must be restocked on a rush basis, salaries to key employees whom the nonprofit does not want to lose, and overtime and lease and/or mortgage payments. The organization also will likely lose profits from forgone activity. Given that one of the primary purposes behind business interruption insurance is to provide the funds necessary to begin operations as soon as possible following a disaster, the insurance should provide for payments within a day or two following the disaster.

As is true with all insurance, the insured must establish the value of the losses it claims under business interruption insurance. To do this, the organization needs numerous financial records. For obvious reasons, it should store duplicate copies (paper or digital) offsite. According to one expert, this insurance can be quite expensive, often necessitating coinsurance. Typically, the insurance company will cover 80 percent of the loss. The premium will generally be based on a percentage of the profit and extra expenses covered by the policy.

Other Specialized Policies

By tradition, special coverage has been necessary for steam, boiler, and other mechanical systems. A number of insurance companies specialize in this coverage. These policies cover losses due to explosions or other catastrophic events that result in injury as well as business interruption losses. A significant portion of the premium covers inspection services in order to minimize catastrophic events.

Some companies offering such policies have added coverage for damage to electrical, computer, and telecommunication equipment resulting from short circuits, electrical arcing, power surges, breakdowns, and operator errors. These policies also include a variety of services designed to help the insured prevent losses.

(v) Errors and Omissions Insurance. Errors and omissions insurance policies cover losses that can occur when a professional gives faulty advice that

69. This term is used loosely here. The organization may have to obtain several endorsements or separate policies to cover all contemplated expenses.

results in harm. Most people recognize that doctors and lawyers carry malpractice insurance, which is a special form of errors and omissions insurance. Obviously, a nonprofit that provides medical or legal services (e.g., family planning or legal aid clinics) should have this coverage even if each professional providing the services has an individual policy. Ultimately, the employer is responsible for all of its employees' acts. When dual coverage exists, the organization should discuss this fact with its insurance advisor to coordinate the coverages. Without coordination, the employer and professional could pay higher premiums than necessary. Moreover, dual coverage could result in a costly dispute between the carriers as to which carrier must respond to a claim.

Defining a Professional

In recent decades, the legal system has expanded the concept of *professional* well beyond lawyers, accountants, architects, doctors, and engineers. The courts have looked to the following definition in a 1968 decision by the Nebraska Supreme Court[70] to assist them in defining who is a professional:

> [The] act or service must be such as exacts the use or application of special learning or attainment of some kind. The term "professional"... means something more than mere proficiency in the performance of a task and implies intellectual skill as contrasted with that used in an occupation for production or sale of commodities. A "professional" act or service is one arising out of a vocation, calling, occupation, or employment involving specialized knowledge, labor or skill, and the labor or skill involved is predominantly mental or intellectual, rather than physical or manual.... In determining whether a particular act is of a professional nature or a "professional service," we must look not to the title or character of the party performing the act, but to the act itself.

Obviously, this definition encompasses far more than just traditional professions. It could be construed to encompass psychologists and counselors (e.g., drug rehabilitation and suicide prevention), job and career counselors, social workers, construction supervisors and consultants, community planners, and environmental consultants.

Many nonprofits providing services are not always as careful as they should be with respect to limiting the provision of those services to the professionals on staff. For example, a legal services clinic might give more responsibilities to law student interns than a law firm would. A clinic in that position should make sure that the interns' activities are covered by its errors and omissions policy.

An insured's CGL coverage typically excludes professional services. An insured that obtains errors and omissions coverage to fill the coverage gap should make sure that the two policies define "professional" in the same manner. One insurance writer[71] pointed to a case in which a substance abuse counselor was

---

70. Marx v. Hartford Accident & Indemnity, 183 Neb. 12, 157 NW. 2d 870 (1968). This case was cited in David Szerlip, *Commercial General Liability Insurance* in Melanie Herman, *supra* note 19, at 83-84

71. David Szerlip, *Commercial General Liability Insurance* in Melanie Herman, *supra* note 19, at 83-84.

providing treatment to a client who went into a rage. The client tripped, hit his head, and died. The patient's family sued both the nonprofit and the counselor for wrongful death. The nonprofit filed a claim with its errors and omissions carrier, which denied it because the carrier viewed the loss as arising from a "slip and fall" incident covered by the CGL coverage. As you might have guessed, the CGL insurer claimed that under the definition of professional activities in its policy, the loss was attributable to professional activities and, therefore, not covered by the CGL policy. The nonprofit eventually prevailed and recovered under the CGL policy. A number of reported cases involve similar disputes.[72] The lesson is that nonprofits should consider obtaining CGL and errors and omission coverage from the same insurer so that policy language is coordinated (although even then, the language should be reviewed). Indeed, in recent years, many insurance companies have refused to write CGL coverage for a number of nonprofits unless they also write the professional liability (errors and omissions) policy because they do not want to be entangled in coverage disputes with other carriers.[73]

PUBLICATIONS, MEDIA, AND THE INTERNET

Employees of nonprofits frequently prepare pamphlets, books, and standards for use by their members who may be rendering professional services or for clients seeking advice. These nonprofits must consider obtaining publishers' or authors' liability coverage, another form of errors and omissions insurance. Such policies should include coverage for errors and omissions, defamation, and copyright and other infringement. It should also cover Web-related activities. It could be that the CGL policy's Part B coverage provides adequate protection, but this should be verified. Note that there is a difference between (1) defamation and copyright infringement and (2) an error or omission. Both should be covered. This can require adding endorsements to the CGL policy or obtaining more specialized media insurance coverage.

(vi) Sexual Abuse and Molestation. Insurance covering a nonprofit's liability arising from sexual abuse and molestation is not as easy to obtain as other types of insurance because of the explosive nature of sexual abuse allegations. Given recent scandals, including the ones involving the Catholic Church, people tend to think of children when the phrase "sexual abuse" is used. Certainly, children are subject to sexual abuse and molestation. This can create exposure for schools, youth sports programs, child care centers, and other nonprofits that regularly come into contact with children. But nonprofits that have regular contact with the mentally ill, aged, or other people who depend on others to meet their basic needs have exposure to liability from sexual and physical abuse.

---

72. *See, e.g.*, McMillian Co. v. Aetna Casualty & Surety, 601 A.2d 169 (N.H. 1991); and Atlantic Mutual Insurance v. Continental National American Insurance, 302 A.2d 177 (N.Y. 1973).

73. David Szerlip pointed this out to the author in a January 20, 2005 e-mail. See note 71, *supra*.

Naturally, a nonprofit must be concerned about liability arising from the actions of its employees, volunteers, and clients (e.g., a resident of homeless shelter who rapes or molests a child) whose actions could make it accountable. Unless a nonprofit has an unusual CGL policy, it should not expect basic liability policy to cover such events. A general CGL policy commonly excludes an entire class, such as day care centers, from coverage. Furthermore, these policies often exclude liability arising from the sexual misconduct of employees, volunteers, and others. To protect against liability arising from abuse and molestation, the nonprofit likely must obtain specialized coverage. Many nonprofits have found this coverage difficult to obtain even for a high price. Some insurers simply will not cover these organizations.

At a 2004 nonprofit insurance conference, one insurance company representative discussed the way her company approaches sexual abuse and molestation coverage. Before pricing insurance, the underwriters spend considerable time reviewing the nonprofit's hiring, monitoring, and training procedures. She indicated that the underwriters want to make sure that if an incident occurs, the nonprofit is able to successfully defend itself because of the seemingly "bulletproof" precautions in place to prevent and, if need be, detect an incident. She indicated that although the policy limits are higher than likely defense costs, the philosophy underlying the coverage is to finance the successful defense of a lawsuit and to use the excess to cover a catastrophic but unlikely recovery. Do not take this as the universal approach to underwriting or pricing: it is only one person's view. Nevertheless, it has a great deal of logic.

If your organization is unable to obtain a liability policy that covers sexual abuse and molestation, the board should immediately assess and improve its safeguards. This could mean performing better background checks, providing more training, or extending the procedures to monitor and protect individuals. If liability insurance is not available, the board also should consider whether to continue current operations. That suggestion may seem extreme, and many people who work with children will be appalled at the suggestion. However, as fiduciaries, this is a question that the board must consider.

(vii) Fidelity Insurance and Bonds. There is no question that far too many nonprofits experience losses from employee theft and embezzlement. As noted, many of these losses could have been prevented through better financial and internal controls. However, unscrupulous employees can steal significant amounts of money from a nonprofit even with the best internal controls in place, particularly if two or more employees collude. Nonprofits can purchase fidelity insurance to protect against such losses. As a general rule, these policies protect only against theft by the organization's employees. If the organization is concerned about theft by independent contractors or other third parties, it should obtain special coverage through a policy endorsement or a separate policy.

Fidelity policies take one of two basic forms. They can either apply to certain persons or positions or be written as a broad-form policy, which covers all employees. The latter is preferable. Although covering the bookkeeper and individuals who handle money is only logical, the universe of employees who steal and embezzle extends beyond the obvious categories.

Claims for Theft Only

Generally speaking, claims can be made only for thefts by employees who take the action for their or a third-party's financial gain. Fidelity policies do not cover losses from an employee's negligence. For example, if an employee accidentally leaves cash unsecured and it is stolen, the organization cannot file a claim under its fidelity insurance policy.

Fidelity policies do not cover claims for general inventory shrinkage, accounting errors, or disputes over salaries. For example, in one case,[74] the bookkeeping department accidentally miscoded information in a payroll program, resulting in the overpayment of one employee for an extended period of time. The organization finally discovered the error and confronted the employee who immediately disappeared. Coverage was denied based on the absence of a "manifest intent" on the part of the employee.

Exclusion for Prior Criminal Record

Policies often exclude coverage of an employee who has a prior criminal record involving theft or other acts of dishonesty, but anecdotal evidence suggests that these exclusions vary from policy to policy. Some policies deny coverage if the organization knows of the past deeds but hires the person anyway. Other policies do not preclude coverage if the employer does a background check or undertakes other due diligence that fails to discover disqualifying past deeds. As is always the case, the organization must read the policy exclusions and due diligence requirements carefully. It should also keep in mind that those writing insurance policies may not consider the organization's obligations under laws prohibiting discrimination against those with a criminal record. For this reason, organizations cannot blindly incorporate coverage requirements into their employment practices.

Timing of Notifications and Claims

Organizations must pay particular attention to the notice and claims filing procedures under fidelity policies because of the nature of financial crimes. Many of them go undetected for months or years. Even when an organization suspects a problem, it may take several weeks or months to uncover the misdeeds and identify them as crimes rather than accounting errors. Further complicating the matter is the care that must be taken before accusing an employee of a crime. It is not unusual for a dispute to arise between an employer and its insurer over whether amounts stolen after certain facts were known are covered or whether the insured failed to provide notice to the insurance company on a timely basis.

---

74. ABC Imaging of Washington v. Travelers Indemnity Company of America, 820 A.2d 628 (Md. App. 2003).

Such problems can be exacerbated when the discovery occurs shortly before or after a policy expires or commences, coverage changes, or one insurer is replaced with another.

To illustrate the potential problem, assume that the board of directors of Vermilion Food Bank is reviewing the monthly financial statement at its December 19, 20X5, meeting. Jasmine Deluca notices that Vermilion's cash and marketable securities balance has declined from $1 million to $900,000 since October. She asks the treasurer to investigate. By coincidence, Vermilion has applied for fidelity insurance coverage from Big Insurance Company. Under the policy, coverage commences January 1, 20X6. On January 10, 20X6, after much effort, the treasurer discovers that Tom Odell has stolen $200,000 from Vermilion through a phony billing scheme and that $125,000 of the theft occurred before January 1, 20X6. When Vermilion files its claim for the $200,000 loss, Big Insurance could refuse to pay the claim. It could argue that Vermilion knew about the loss in 20X5, when Jasmine Deluca asked about the cash balance, but it failed to disclose that information on its application for insurance. The problem with Big Insurance's reasoning is that the decline in the cash balance could have occurred for any number of legitimate reasons. For example, Vermilion's chief procurement officer could have bought a large amount of canned goods at a significant discount by placing the order before a certain date.

Big Insurance also might argue that $125,000 of the loss is not covered by the policy because the events giving rise to that portion occurred before the policy period. Faced with this argument, Vermilion should look closely at how the phrase "occurrence of loss" is defined in the policy and interpreted by the courts. Is the occurrence of loss the criminal act or the discovery of it? Big Insurance also might argue that no portion of the loss is covered because the crime was ongoing at the policy's inception. Again, Vermilion needs to look closely at the policy's language.[75]

Another issue involves whether the annual renewals of policies create a continuous policy with one recovery limit or separate policies, each with its own recovery limit. To illustrate, assume that an insured has a fidelity policy providing $250,000 of protection each year for any loss. The policy, which is subject to annual renewal, contains a clause that any occurrence during the policy period is recoverable if discovered within one year following the occurrence. In the third policy year, the insured discovers that in each of the three policy years, an employee stole $250,000 through an elaborate scheme. Is the insured entitled to a $250,000, $500,000, or $750,000 recovery? One court concluded that the language in insurance contracts was ambiguous as to whether the arrangement created three separate policies or one continuous one. It denied coverage for the

75. These are no theoretical arguments. For recent cases interpreting contract language in light of events occurring close to the inception or termination of coverage, see Resolution Trust v. Fidelity & Deposit, 205 F.3d 615 (3rd Cir. 2000); Gulf USA v. Federal Insurance (D. Idaho, 1999); and Ellenberg v. Underwriters at Lloyds, 187 B.R. 785 (Bankr. N.D. Ga. 1995).

first policy period because of the one-year discovery limitation (recall that the discovery occurred in the third policy), but it treated the policies for the second and third years as separate policies, permitting recoveries up to the limits under each policy.[76]

Fidelity policies do provide for satisfaction of a claim even when the opportunity for the theft arises because of weak or nonexistent internal controls, but the insurer is likely to take the system of internal controls into account in pricing the premiums.

(viii) Employment Practices Insurance. As already noted, employment practices (EPL) coverage can be purchased as part of a D & O policy or as a stand-alone policy. According to a book published by the Nonprofit Risk Management Center, purchasing the package as part of a D & O policy may actually result in broader coverage for the nonprofit against employment practice claims.[77] However, when the coverage is combined, the nonprofit should consider adjusting the policy's limits upward because two distinct (albeit overlapping) risks are being covered by the policy.[78] Under no circumstances should a nonprofit rely on its CGL policy for employment practices coverage unless the policy specifically addresses EPL coverage. In many cases, CGL policies specifically exclude liability for employment practices. If the policy does not contain a specific exclusion, the nonprofit is most likely buying a lawsuit with the insurer if it expects coverage.

Employment practices insurance is of relatively recent vintage, first becoming significant in the early 1990s.[79] Insurance companies found a receptive market at that time because of recent amendments to the Civil Rights Act of 1964 and the enactment of the Americans with Disabilities Act. Survey after survey points to employment practices litigation as a costly expense of doing business. Nonprofits are clearly not immune from such litigation.

Wrongful Act Defined

Wrongful acts covered under an EPL policy can be defined by one of two approaches. Under the first, the policy enumerates specific acts, such as violations of state and federal employment discrimination and sexual harassment laws, as wrongful acts. The second is to provide for coverage for all losses connected with employment practices other than specifically excluded items. The latter approach favors the employer because plaintiffs' lawyers have a myriad of theories to choose from when pursuing an employment practice lawsuit. For example, there may have been a violation of the Civil Rights Act of 1964. However, the plaintiff's lawyer may also argue that the employer negligently hired the

---

76. Karen Kane, Inc. v. Reliance Insurance, 202 F. 3d 1180 (9th Cir. 2000).

77. Melanie Herman, *supra* note 19, at 112.

78. R. Mak, *What Do You Know about Your EPLI Coverage?*, N.Y. Law. J., Oct. 12, 2004.

79. Melanie Herman, *supra* note 19, at 111.

supervisor who violated the act. In other words, the plaintiff's lawyer is seeking a recovery predicated not only on the specific rights created under the Civil Rights Act but also on common law duties owed by an employer to its employees.

However the policy is written, the nonprofit employer should make sure that it covers specific violations based not only on the basic federal and state employment practices laws but also other bases. Employees have recovered damages under a variety of tort theories, including negligent hiring, hostile work environment, wrongful termination, invasion of privacy, infliction of emotional distress, slander and defamation, and interference with contractual relationships. There have also been recoveries under some less known statutes, including one that covers the treatment of employees on leave for participation in the military and reserves. Employees have also focused on contract law related to violations of employment contracts, employee handbooks, and benefit plans. Moreover, employers should take a forward-looking approach when they review policy language to ensure that coverage is broad enough to include emerging theories for claims. Examples include discrimination against people who are gay or lesbian, have criminal records, or abuse substances.

As a general rule, insurance policies exclude losses from intentional acts on the part of the insured. These exclusions can be particularly troublesome when they are included as part of an EPL insurance policy because, unlike a fire or a flood, the actions generating the claim are sometimes intentional.[80] Any nonprofit shopping for EPL coverage should try to limit if not eliminate the exclusion's scope. For example, the organization should ask that actions of individual employees be distinguished from intentional actions of the organization so that the exclusion does not operate if the loss arises from an isolated event involving one employee harassing another. If there must be an exclusion, it should apply only to intentional infliction of damages as opposed to intentional acts—although drawing that line may be difficult.

Punitive Damages

Juries sometimes award punitive damages in employment practice cases. When awarded, these damages can exceed actual damages several times. The insured should determine whether punitive damages are covered. Some insurance companies have traditionally shied away from offering this coverage because of the punitive nature of the losses.

Between 17 and 20 states prohibit insurance companies from covering punitive damage awards. Consequently, a nonprofit located in any of these states should not pay for coverage that cannot be provided. That is not to say that nonprofits in these states cannot buy protection against punitive damage awards. A number of insurance companies have used offshore insurers to circumvent state limitations or have written policy provisions on a "best-available coverage"

---

80. Chubb Group of Insurance Companies, Employment Practices Liability Insurance Brochure (December 2002) *available at* http://www.chubb.com.

basis.[81] Before committing to one of these options, the nonprofit should consider how it could enforce the provision if the insurance company refuses to pay a claim.

Claims Made

EPL insurance is written on a claims-made basis,[82] which results in fewer disputes between insurance companies and their clients over claims from facts that span many years. As noted, this means that to be covered, the claim must be made during the policy period. The fact that the event that gives rise to the claim occurred during the policy period is irrelevant if the claim is made after the policy period. As noted in the discussion of D & O coverage, this means the nonprofit should consider tail coverage options and focus on retroactive dates that could preclude coverage if the events in question occurred before the retroactive date.

Special attention should also be paid to the notification requirements in the policy.[83] The nonprofit may have notice of a potential claim long before an employee makes a formal complaint or files a lawsuit. This can be particularly problematic if the complaint is made to the supervisor accused of the misdeed, who then tries to cover up the problem. If at all possible, the nonprofit should attempt to negotiate language that requires insurance company notification only after the human resources department (or other appropriate person) becomes aware of the problem. Furthermore, the nonprofit should ask for some specificity as to what constitutes a complaint that requires insurance company notice. For example, it might ask that it be required to give notice only if the employee complaint is in writing or is made during a formal meeting requested by the employee.

Along these same lines, the nonprofit should pay close attention to the disclosure requirements in the insurance application.[84] A claims-made policy will, depending on the language, exclude coverage for losses pertaining to events that were known at the time the application was submitted but had not yet ripened into a formal complaint or lawsuit. Sometimes the events leading up to an employment practices lawsuit transpire over a ten-year period of time or longer. The employer may even have knowledge of some of the facts but believes that any problem had been resolved. These possibilities mean that a nonprofit should carefully focus on the disclosures it makes when it submits an application for insurance.[85]

Finally, the organization should focus on how policy limits are applied. For example, a $300,000 limit per loss on a policy providing $10 million of overall

---

81. R. Mak, *supra* note 78.
82. *Id.*
83. M. Lester and L. Bennett, *The Slippery Slope of Employment Practices Liability Insurance: Is It Worth the Money?*, EMPLOYMENT LAW ALERT (Feb. 1999).
84. *Id.*
85. The nonprofit also should discuss with its legal counsel how disclosures are made in the application for EPL coverage. Any disclosures could potentially come back to haunt the nonprofit if an employee seeks to discover the application and it contains less than artful language.

coverage may be acceptable when applied to a sexual harassment suit by one particular employee, but if multiple employees file suit based on one set of circumstances (e.g., the treatment of one class of employees or the interpretation of an employee handbook), the organization should ensure that the $300,000 limit applies on an employee-by-employee basis. Employment practices suits can take the form of class actions, which makes this a particularly important consideration when an organization has a large workforce.

Factor Prevention into Coverage

Unfortunately, all organizations face employment practices litigation. This means that employers are not transferring catastrophic risk when they pay premiums as much as they are simply financing the cost predictable losses. Thus, any nonprofit that has adopted procedures and programs specifically aimed at reducing EPL claims should ask that those procedures and programs be taken into account when the premium is set. Many insurance carriers also offer prepackaged training and other programs to reduce claims. Nonprofits that have not adopted their own programs and procedures should take advantage of insurance company offerings in an effort to reduce premium payments.

Nonprofits with excellent employment practices records should consider requesting a higher deductible (retaining more risk). They should also consider a coinsurance arrangement under which the insurance company would, for example, pay 70 percent of a claim and the nonprofit could cover the other 30 percent—but keep in mind that coinsurance may be a mandatory feature of any given policy.

(d) SPECIAL COVERAGES. As should be apparent, exclusions are an important aspect of any insurance policy. While organizations must carefully focus on a policy's exclusions to ensure that they have the coverages they believe, exclusions are not necessarily negative from the organization's standpoint. For example, most CGL polices exclude coverage for the sale of alcoholic beverages. This exclusion makes sense for many organizations because they do not sell alcoholic beverages. Why should an organization pay for superfluous coverage?

An exclusion does not mean that a risk is uninsurable. Returning to the previous example, organizations that do sell alcoholic beverages can obtain appropriate insurance coverage, but they need to obtain a special policy or an endorsement to a CGL policy. This permits the insurance company to better underwrite the risk by focusing on the unique aspects of the sale of such beverages. It also permits the more equitable pooling of these risks because only those subject to the risks pay to be covered against them. Finally, specialized coverage permits more focused contract language, which reduces the potential for coverage disputes.

Different types of specialized coverage are available to nonprofits. The trick is to know when it is needed. That often requires reviewing more general liability and property policies to determine what is excluded and talking with the organization's insurance advisors. This brings us back to basic risk management principles.

CHAPTER 13

EVALUATING YOUR ORGANIZATION

It is not enough to have a good mind. The main thing is to use it well
RENE DESCARTES[1]

If you have gotten this far (assuming you have worked from front to back), you have gathered lots of useful information. You now have the opportunity to apply that information to your organization. That organization may be one that is currently asking you to join its board or one that you have served for some time.

We will first consider a diagnostic survey that should help you evaluate your organization's policies and practices. After you complete it, we will examine a number of other approaches for evaluating your organization. These can be used by your organization's directors or officers as assessment tools. Each approach should provide some additional insights.

1. LE DISCOURS DE LA METHODE (1637).

13.1 THE SELF-ASSESSMENT SURVEY

The self-assessment survey is divided into ten topics intended to track the major chapters in this *Guide*. No feedback is offered here. Fortunately, the right answer is generally obvious, as the prescriptive action when your organization falls short should be. "No, our organization does not have internal controls. Well, maybe putting some in place would be a good idea." The questions assume you are serving as a member of the board of directors. When action is required, it should be undertaken primarily by the staff.

(a) SURVEY—ORGANIZATIONAL STRUCTURE

		Yes	No	N/A
1	Is the organization either incorporated under a state nonprofit statute or duly organized as another recognized form of legal entity?			
2	Have the steps to complete the incorporation process been completed and reviewed by qualified legal counsel?			
3	Does the organization have articles of incorporation and bylaws of comparable organizational and governing documents?			
4	Does each director have a current copy of the articles or incorporation and bylaws (or other governing documents) with all amendments?			
5	Are the president, vice president, treasurer, and secretary (or equivalent) positions currently filled?			
6	Is there significant overlap between directors and officers?			
7	If the organization has members, are their rights clearly defined?			
8	Does the organization regularly communicate with its members?			
9	Is there an annual members' meeting, and are procedures in place for providing timely notice of the meeting?			
10	If members vote at the annual meeting or other meeting, is appropriate information provided in advance?			
11	Is the organization able to obtain a quorum for member meetings?			
12	Is there an annual written report to the members?			
13	Is membership size driven by the self-interest of the staff?			
14	Is the organization in compliance with annual filing requirements under relevant state nonprofit corporation or other statutes?			

(b) SURVEY—DIRECTORS

		Yes	No	N/A
1	Is the board's focus on fundraising rather than oversight?			
2	Do more than one-third of the directors hold positions because of their fundraising ability or because of past or expected monetary contributions to the organization?			
3	Is the board chair independent of the executive director and management?			
4	Do board members bring a diverse range of skills to the board?			
5	Do board members bring a diverse set of viewpoints to the board?			
6	Are all director positions currently filled?			
7	Are board vacancies filled expediously?			
8	Does each director satisfy legal qualifications for directors and any organizational requirements in the articles of incorporation or bylaws?			
9	If there are designated positions on the board for certain constituencies (e.g., labor or government officials), are those positions held by qualifying individuals?			
10	Are there more than 15 director positions on the board?			
11	If there are more than 15 directors, is there an executive committee with clearly defined powers?			
12	Are director terms staggered so that *not* all directors stand for reelection at any one time?			
13	Are there limits on director terms (e.g., a maximum of three terms)?			
14	Is there a search committee for new directors, and is it independent of management?			
15	Does the organization have criteria for director eligibility?			
16	Is there a director's handbook?			
17	Is there new director orientation?			
18	Are there regular board meetings?			
19	Are there directors who consistently miss director meetings?			
20	If permissible, have telephone conference calls become a substitute for in-person board meetings?			
21	If state law permits director proxies, do the organization's practices and procedures comply with state law?			
22	Do members make decisions by e-mail, and if so, is this permissible under state law?			
23	Do board meetings and executive sessions comply with applicable open meeting requirements?			

		Yes	No	N/A
24	Does the organization's secretary prepare minutes for each meeting?			
25	Do the minutes describe each decision in sufficient detail, including the considerations behind the decision?			
26	Do the minutes adequately reflect director dissents from decisions?			
27	Does the organization's secretary maintain current and official copies of the organization's bylaws, and are draft versions properly marked and controlled?			
28	Is there a written agenda for each board meeting?			
29	If there is a written agenda, is it made available to the other directors more than a week in advance of the meeting?			
30	Is there an agreed-upon set of rules for conducting each board meeting?			
30	Do board committees (e.g., the audit committee) have charters?			
32	Do charters define each committee's powers and responsibilities?			
33	Do each committee's membership requirements comply with state law?			
34	Does the board receive regular reports from each committee?			
35	Does the organization have a written conflict-of-interest policy?			
36	If the answer to Question 35 is Yes, does the conflict-of-interest policy apply to directors, officers, employees, volunteers, third-party advisors, and independent contractors?			
37	Are all persons described in Question 36 annually required to review the conflict-of-interest policy and sign a written acknowledgment that they have reviewed the policy?			
38	When a director has a potential conflict of interest, does the board's process for handling it comply with validation procedures under state law?			
39	If the answer to Question 35 is Yes, does the organization have procedures in place to audit compliance with its conflict-of-interest policy?			
40	Does the organization routinely reward volunteer directors for their service by contracting for products and services from the directors and their businesses?			
41	If the answer to Question 40 is Yes, does the contracting process require the director to be the low-cost bidder in a competitive bidding process?			
42	Has the board considered a board retreat for long-range planning?			

(c) SURVEY—FINANCIAL OVERSIGHT

		Yes	No	N/A
1	Does the board receive interim and annual financial statements at regular board meetings (as opposed to summary financial information)?			
2	Do the financial statements that the board receives include a balance sheet, income statement, and cash flow statement?			
3	Do the financial statements provide a breakdown of the numbers using a restricted/unrestricted classification scheme?			
4	Do the financial statements include explanatory footnotes?			
5	Does the organization use a chart of accounts that properly reflects the organization's activities?			
6	Does the board receive budgets on a regular basis?			
7	Does the board regularly receive an analysis of budgetary variances?			
8	Does the chief financial officer regularly provide the board appropriate financial ratios for both the organization and similar organizations?			
9	Does the organization's chief financial officer present a financial report at each board meeting?			
10	Are the directors given a meaningful opportunity to ask questions about the financial report at each board meeting?			
11	Does the board have a finance committee?			
12	Does the board have an audit committee?			
13	Are members of the audit committee independent?			
14	Does anyone on the audit committee have financial accounting, audit, or internal control expertise?			
15	If the answer to Question 14 is No, has the committee sought the assistance of an independent outside advisor?			
16	Is the auditor's annual management letter discussed at a board meeting?			
17	Does the board follow up with management to make sure that management has adequately responded to suggestions in the auditor's management letter?			
18	Are the organization's financial records backed-up and stored off-site?			
19	If the organization has issued tax-exempt bonds, is it in compliance with all covenants, particularly with respect to those limiting private use of the facility?			

(d) SURVEY—FINANCIAL CONTROLS

		Yes	No	N/A
1	Is there a written code for ethical conduct that is distributed to all employees?			
2	Are there meaningful "whistle-blower" procedures in place to provide employees, contractors, service recipients, and donors the opportunity to report perceived wrongdoing to a person who is not in a position to suppress the report or retaliate against the person making it?			
3	As a general matter, are incompatible accounting, reporting, and custodial functions segregated?			
4	As a general matter, are the systems that are designed to produce accounting checks and balances audited on a regular basis?			
5	Is there a uniform chart of accounts?			
6	Are there multiple bank accounts and money market funds?			
7	If the answer to Question 6 is Yes, is there a meaningful reason for having each account?			
8	Are all accounts and financial assets either held or maintained as corporate accounts, with title vested in the nonprofit?			
9	Are multiple signatures/authorizations required for checks, wire transfers, and electronic transfers above a certain specified amount?			
10	Do the organization's financial institutions understand and adhere to the organization's signature policies?			
11	Do those who have check-writing authority perform other accounting functions?			
12	Are bank statements reconciled monthly by an employee who does not report to an authorized check writer or other authorized disbursement agent?			
13	Are all monetary disbursements except for minor cash disbursements from a petty cash fund made by check or other instrument?			
14	Are payments made based on submitted invoices that are appropriately marked as paid and filed following payment?			
15	Is there a list of approved vendors?			
16	Are cash and check deposits made on a daily basis?			
17	Are two people present when cash is collected and is a contemporaneous written record made of the amount collected?			
18	Has the organization considered video surveillance in the areas of its operations that regularly have material flows of cash?			
19	Does the organization use an independent third party to handle payroll transactions?			

		Yes	No	N/A
20	Does the organization exercise adequate control over the placement of and removal of employees into/from the payroll system?			
21	Are purchases of goods and services made using an authorization and purchase order system?			
22	If the entity engages in sales activity, is a cash register that generates receipts used as part of the sales process?			
23	If goods and services are provided (even if not for consideration), are invoices issued with duplicates sent to the accounting department?			
24	Are purchase orders, invoices, receipts, checks, and similar documentation prenumbered?			
25	Are inventory accounting records periodically confirmed through physical inventories?			
26	Are marketable securities either held in a safe deposit box or by a reputable financial institution that is a member of SIPC, or when appropriate, a separate corporate custodian?			
27	Are physical assets inventoried, and when appropriate, fitted with identity tags (laptop computers)?			
28	Is there a gift-acceptance policy?			
29	Are procedures in place for ensuring compliance with the terms of restricted gifts?			
30	Is there a process for authorizing write-offs of receivables (including pledges)?			
31	Are decisions to write off receivables based on standards and a decision process that is *not* controlled by the person(s) authorizing the extension of credit?			
32	Is the disposition of physical assets subject to authorization by someone who does not have custody of the assets?			
33	Is there an investment committee or other group that makes investment decisions and authorizes trades?			
34	If funds are managed by independent investment managers, is there a process for auditing their activities and auditing investment balances?			
35	If funds are managed by independent investment managers, are the assets held in segregated custodial accounts by a third party?			
36	When employees leave the organization, is there a procedure in place for revoking authorizations, collecting keys, changing combinations, and collecting assets held by the employee (credit cards, laptop computers, etc.)?			
37	Do employees have business credit cards?			
38	Are entertainment and travel expense authorization procedures in place?			

		Yes	No	N/A
39	If the executive officers have discretionary expense account authority, are standards in place to prohibit expenditures on entertainment and travel that would be viewed as inappropriate or excessive?			
40	Are discretionary entertainment and travel expenditures by executive officers regularly audited?			
41	Is there a budgeting process with periodic (monthly) review of variances?			
42	Were appropriate background checks performed on all employees when they were hired?			
43	Has the organization considered fidelity insurance or bonding employees?			

(e) SURVEY—INTERNAL CONTROLS (OTHER THAN FINANCIAL CONTROLS)

		Yes	No	N/A
1	Is there an employee handbook?			
2	Is the handbook kept current with a procedure in place for collecting and destroying outdated copies?			
3	Are employment practice policies in place?			
4	Is a formal procedure in place for employees to report violations of employment practice policies without fear of retaliation?			
5	When a violation of an employment practice policy is reported, is a procedure in place to correct the problem (including periodic follow-up with the complaining employee)?			
6	Are standards in place for disciplining an employee who repeatedly violates employment policies?			
7	If disciplinary standards are in place, are they applied consistently?			
8	Does the organization have a record retention policy?			
9	Does the organization's record retention policy deal adequately with electronic records?			
10	If the answer to Question 9 is Yes, has it been reviewed by a qualified attorney?			
11	When documents are authorized for destruction, does the physical or electronic destruction process ensure that an unauthorized third party cannot reconstruct them?			
12	Does the organization have procedures in place to protect documents that are relevant to current or possible litigation or government investigation?			
13	Does the organization have appropriate e-mail creation, retention, and destruction policies in place?			

		Yes	No	N/A
14	Does the organization regularly assess its risks?			
15	Does the board of directors have an independent compensation committee?			
16	Does the organization have a formal process by which to determine employee compensation?			
17	Does the organization use comparables or outside consultants to help determine compensation?			
18	If the organization uses outside consultants to assist in setting compensation levels, are the consultants chosen by the executive director or other interested employees?			
19	If the organization provides incentive compensation, does the board regularly assess whether the incentives properly align employee efforts with the organization's mission?			
20	Does the board regularly assess the business risks associated with achieving the organization's core mission by asking what could go wrong?			
21	If the organization is taking advantage of nonprofit standard mail rates, does it in comply with the various restrictions, including those on content and personalization?			

(f) SURVEY—TAX CONSIDERATIONS

		Yes	No	N/A
1	Has the organization obtained the appropriate Section 501(c) tax-exempt status and its state equivalent?			
2	Does the organization consider intermediate sanctions as part of its decision-making process?			
3	Do the organization's procedures for setting compensation permit it to rely on the rebuttable presumption under the intermediate sanctions?			
4	Do employee expense reimbursement policies qualify as accountable plans under the tax regulations?			
5	Do contracts with executives detail all fringe benefits, including club memberships, use of Blackberries, and access to personal chefs?			
6	Does the organization engage in activity that could be construed as prohibited political activity?			
7	Does the organization engage in lobbying activity or activities that could be construed as such?			
8	If the organization is a private foundation, does it have procedures in place to prevent self-dealing?			
9	If the organization is a private foundation, does it routinely review its activities in terms of excise taxes?			

		Yes	No	N/A
10	Does the organization routinely review its activities to determine whether any of them are subject to the tax on unrelated business income?			
11	Is the person who prepares the organization's IRS Form 990 (or IRS Form 990-PF) experienced in preparing these forms?			
12	Do the organization's directors and senior officers review the organization's annual IRS Form 990 (or IRS Form 990-PF)?			
13	Does the organization supplement its IRS Form 990 with information (e.g., a complete set of financial statements) that will help the reader understand the organization and the data included on the form?			
14	Does the organization have systems in place to provide required information to donors regarding charitable contributions?			
15	Does the organization have systems in place to preclude grants to organizations that support terrorism?			
16	Does the organization collect and remit trust fund taxes (e.g., income tax withholdings and the employee's share of FICA and Medicare) in a timely manner?			
17	Does the organization comply with all state sales and use tax laws?			
18	Does the organization obtain exemption certificates from all persons claiming that sales to them are exempt from sales or use tax?			
19	Does the organization regularly review claimed sales and use tax exemptions?			
20	Does the organization comply with all state property tax laws?			
21	Does the organization regularly review claimed property tax exemptions?			
22	Has the organization complied with all IRS and state bingo, raffle, and gambling reporting and withholding requirements?			
23	Has the organization paid excise taxes applicable to its gambling activities?			

(g) SURVEY—FUNDRAISING

		Yes	No	N/A
1	Does the organization have a fundraising and solicitation policy statement?			
2	Does the organization have a gift-acceptance policy?			
3	Is the gift-acceptance policy reviewed at least annually?			
4	Does the organization have a planned giving program?			
5	If the organization has a planned giving program, has it been reviewed by qualified legal counsel?			

		Yes	No	N/A
6	If the organization accepts interests in split-interest trusts, has it adopted a policy as to whether it will serve as a trustee?			
7	If the organization enters into charitable gift annuities, is it in compliance with applicable state insurance regulations?			
8	Are all internal and external fundraisers instructed to comply with the gift-acceptance policy (e.g., avoid making inappropriate promises on behalf of the organization)?			
9	Does the organization have a policy prohibiting both internal and external fundraisers from providing tax or legal advice?			
10	Do the directors discuss fundraising practices at least annually?			
11	Are the organization's fundraising activities and related promotional materials consistent with how the funds will actually be disbursed?			
12	Has the organization registered with the appropriate state and local authorities in each state in which the organization is soliciting contributions?			
13	Does the organization require that all pledges be in writing and made pursuant to a legally enforceable contract?			
14	In the case of major pledges, does the organization perform a background/credit check (due diligence) on the prospective donor before relying on the related pledge?			
15	If a major capital expenditure is to be financed by a pledge, is an appropriate portion of that pledge collected before the organization commits to all or a significant portion of the expenditure (e.g., enters into construction contracts or commences construction)?			
16	Does the organization properly account for pledges in its financial statements?			
17	Does the organization enforce its rights under pledges when not fulfilled promptly?			
18	If the organization honors donors by granting naming rights or other recognition, are the terms of the agreement clearly spelled out in appropriate detail?			
19	If the organization grants naming rights, does it protect itself with a "bad boy" clause permitting it to remove the name when appropriate?			
20	If the organization accepts restricted gifts, are the funds segregated, and the organization's accountants notified of the restrictions?			
21	Does the organization have in place a system to ensure compliance with gift restrictions?			
22	Has the organization adopted an appropriate spending policy with respect to its endowment?			
23	If the organization grants a security interest in its assets when it borrows money, does the grant of that security interest violate the terms of any restricted gifts?			

		Yes	No	N/A
24	Does the organization have procedures to protect donor privacy and safeguard donor information?			
25	If the organization uses paid fundraisers, are they registered with the appropriate state authorities?			
26	If the organization uses outside fundraisers, does it have a procedure for auditing their performance in terms of donor relations and perceptions?			
27	If the organization uses outside fundraisers, does it have an audit mechanism to ensure that all collected funds are remitted to the organization?			
28	Has the organization registered with the appropriate bingo/raffle regulators?			
29	If the organization is conducting Texas Hold'em or comparable poker tournaments, or Las Vegas-style gambling (e.g., blackjack, roulette, and craps), has it obtained a legal opinion that such hard-core gambling activities are legal?			
30	Do the organization's e-mail practices comply with CAN-SPAM?			
31	If the organization is the recipient of grants, does it provide each grantor all required reports and financial statements?			
32	If the organization has grants from the federal government, does it comply with applicable OMB circulars?			
33	If the organization is a faith-based organization, is it maintaining the required separation between its religious and social service activities?			
34	Does the organization post appropriate financial information (complete financial statements and IRS Form 990) on its Web site?			
35	When the organization make its financial information available (see Question 34), does it provide supplementary schedules that explain the information so that members of the public and press do not misconstrue the data or make inappropriate comparisons to other organizations?			

(h) SURVEY—REGISTRATION, REPORTING, AND DISCLOSURE

		Yes	No	N/A
1	Has the organization registered with the appropriate state charity regulators?			
2	If the organization is operating outside its state of incorporation, has it registered to do business with the appropriate regulators in each state?			
3	Has the organization determined that its governance structure complies with all requirements of each state in which it solicits contributions?			

		Yes	No	N/A
4	If an organization is soliciting charitable contributions through a Web site, has it considered whether registration in other states may be required?			
5	Does the organization post its IRS Form 990 (or IRS Form 990-PF) and financial statements on its Web site?			
6	Has the organization considered providing complete financial information to GuideStar so that the public has ready access to all relevant information?			
7	Does the organization provide its members and contributors an annual report describing its activities, plans, and financial status?			
8	Has the organization developed any measures that the board and contributors can use to assess whether the organization is achieving its mission?			
9	Do the measures referred to in Question 8 focus on financial data or outcomes?			
10	Does the organization comply with applicable lobbyist registration requirements?			

(i) SURVEY—EMPLOYMENT PRACTICES, VOLUNTEERS, AND ANTITRUST

		Yes	No	N/A
1	Does the organization have procedures in place to address an employee's concerns regarding employment practices?			
2	Has the organization trained employees who make hiring decisions (including those who conduct interviews) in how to conduct interviews and evaluate candidates?			
3	Does the organization have a nondiscrimination policy?			
4	If the answer to Question 3 is Yes, has that policy been incorporated into the organization's culture?			
5	Does the organization have a sexual harassment policy and appropriate training?			
6	If allegations of sexual harassment are made, does the organization have a process to investigate them?			
7	If the organization's employees are at-will, has the organization taken measures to ensure that status?			
8	Are the organization's employees properly classified for purposes of the Fair Labor Standards Act?			
9	Are hours and wage rates properly computed for Fair Labor Standards Act purposes?			
10	Has the organization provided its employees the necessary information regarding their rights under the Family and Medical Leave Act?			

		Yes	No	N/A
11	Does the organization properly notify employees when leave is considered to be Family and Medical Leave Act leave?			
12	Has the organization elected the method to be used to determine available leave under the Family and Medical Leave Act?			
13	Does the organization's hiring process comply with the Americans with Disabilities Act?			
14	Is the organization making appropriate accommodations for employees with disabilities?			
15	Has the organization addressed military leave?			
16	If the organization employs children (or uses them as volunteers), does it comply with child labor laws?			
17	Does the organization have in place a policy for recruiting, training, and evaluating volunteers?			
18	Are volunteers provided a handbook?			
19	Are there procedures in place for dismissing volunteers?			
20	Has the organization adequately addressed insurance (automobile insurance, workers' compensation, and other) issues pertaining to volunteers?			
21	Does the organization regularly review OSHA requirements?			
22	Has the organization reviewed applicable antitrust laws?			
23	If the organization is a standard-setting organization, do its procedures anticipate and comply with applicable antitrust laws?			
24	If the organization is a membership organization, do its membership requirements and expulsion procedures comply with applicable antitrust laws?			
25	Has the organization considered covenants not to compete for key employees and fundraisers?			

(j) SURVEY—RISK MANAGEMENT

		Yes	No	N/A
1	Does the organization have an ongoing risk assessment process?			
2	Does the organization have an insurance agent, broker, or consultant to assist it with insurance?			
3	Does the organization regularly review its insurance needs, including coverage, adequacy of policy limits, and deductibles?			
4	Does the organization have a system in place for timely notifying its insurers of potential claims?			
5	Does the organization have a commercial general liability insurance policy in place?			

		Yes	No	N/A
6	Does the organization address automobile insurance coverage for its employees, volunteers, and agents who drive vehicles on its behalf?			
7	Does the organization have workers' compensation insurance coverage in place?			
8	Does the organization have insurance in place that provides coverage for injuries experienced by volunteers?			
9	Does the organization have disaster recovery plans in place?			
10	Does the organization have business interruption insurance?			
11	Does the organization have a written policy regarding employment practices that clearly defines what behavior will not be tolerated?			
12	Does the organization provide all officers and employees regular employment practices training?			
13	If the organization's activities involve minors or other individuals who are unable to protect themselves (e.g., elderly, disabled, mentally impaired), has the organization carefully considered and implemented procedures to protect those individuals from harm, including sexual exploitation, other physical abuse, and kidnapping?			
14	Has the organization's legal counsel reviewed state law and the federal Volunteer Protection Act to determine to what extent these statutes provide liability protection to board members and other volunteers?			
15	Has the organization reviewed state law to determine the extent to which it can provide indemnification to directors and officers?			
16	Does the organization provide indemnification to directors and officers?			
17	If indemnification is discretionary, has the board adopted written guidelines defining when indemnification is available?			
18	Has the organization procured directors' and officers' (D & O) insurance for its directors and officers?			
19	Does the organization have adequate firewalls, e-mail filters, off-site data storage, and data backup routines?			

Hopefully this survey either has or will force you to take a hard look at your organization's governance, control, legal compliance, and risk management policies. Do not hesitate to share these results with other board members. The results should generate a good deal of discussion, which is the intent.

13.2 USING METRICS TO EVALUATE YOUR ORGANIZATION

For an entirely different approach to performance measurement, you might consider a shorthand mechanism to measure your organization's performance. This means returning to the financial ratio analysis considered in Chapter 5 but with a different focus.

(a) FOUR BASIC RATIOS. The following four indices are among those used by many people to evaluate charitable organizations: (1) charitable focus, (2) fundraising efficiency, (3) management efficiency, and (4) donor reliance. Although prospective donors often focus on these measurements, they also serve as useful management tools. However, all users should avoid slavish reliance on these measurements when comparing two or more organizations. Variations in accounting practices and organizational operations often account for differences.

(i) Charitable Focus. The *charitable focus* ratio is traditionally calculated as follows:

Program-Related Expenses ÷ Total Expenses

This ratio is easy to calculate and provides a quick snapshot of the percentage of expenses that directly affect mission. An interesting variation on this ratio uses the organization's total revenue as the denominator, and is calculated as follows:

Program-Related Expenses ÷ Total Revenue from All Sources

This ratio addresses revenues that are channeled to program-related activities by showing the percentage of each dollar of revenue raised that is directly used to fulfill the organization's charitable mission. If the organization uses the money to acquire permanent assets, or a significant portion of its income is subject to restrictions, the meaningfulness of the resulting number is open to question. To see why this is, consider an organization that receives a significant gift requiring that the income be accumulated for ten years. During the ten-year accumulation period, the income increases total revenues (the denominator), but the income cannot be spent. Accordingly, it does not make sense to assume that if the income is not reflected in program-related expenditures, it must have been used for administrative or fundraising expenses.

Expenditures for fixed assets also pose issues. Consider a museum that constructs a new building. It does not make sense to include the construction costs in program-related expenses because the funding for construction probably came from sources other than current year revenues. Part of the cost could have been financed from accumulated revenues, endowment, or loan proceeds. While a new building makes this point particularly clear, the same issue comes up with the acquisition of any capital asset. If any amount is reflected in program-related expenses, it should be depreciation expense. That results in a better matching of expenses with revenue.

Although restricted assets and capital expenditures initially appear to undermine the usefulness of this modified version of the charitable focus ratio, these issues are the ones that make this modified version more interesting than the traditional formula used to calculate charitable focus. To use the ratio, you must ask about restricted assets and capital expenditures. Both of those items raise important questions and policy considerations.

Both ratios are best used for organizations that collect money for immediate use and redistribution. Both ratios require accurate and thoughtful allocations of overhead expenses to program, fundraising, and administrative expense categories.

(ii) Fundraising Efficiency. The *fundraising efficiency* ratio is calculated as follows:

Fundraising Expenses ÷ Direct and Indirect Contributions

This ratio measures the cost of generating each dollar of charitable contributions. Comparisons should be made only between similarly situated organizations. The goal is to keep the percentage as low as possible while avoiding the misclassification of some portion of fundraising as program or administrative expenses.

Direct contributions include contributions from the public. Indirect contributions include contributions from other charities such as private foundations. If the organization has a planned giving program, the fundraising efficiency ratio should be modified by omitting those contributions and related costs from the numerator (or two ratios should be calculated). Of course, these numbers need to be isolated for both the charity in question and the universe of comparable charities, which may not be an easy task. In all likelihood, the cost components and relationships associated with planned giving programs differ from those associated with more public appeals.

Many organizations (e.g., arts organizations) have membership categories based on level of giving. A good case can be made that membership fees should be treated as contributions because members typically view them as such. If these fees are included, the charity should probably make the appropriate adjustments to eliminate the cost of the premiums and the quid pro quo payments from the calculation.

(iii) Management Efficiency. The *management efficiency* ratio is calculated as follows:

Management and Administrative Expenses
÷ Program-Related Expenses + Fundraising Expenses

This index measures the relationship of management and administrative expenses (organizational overhead) to all other expenses (the latter, in a sense, serve as a proxy for the organization's mission-related activities). Management and administrative expenses are excluded from the denominator because inclusion would be somewhat circular (measuring management of management). There are those who may prefer to include management expenses in or exclude fundraising expenses from the denominator. That is fine if the formula is applied consistently.

As with the charitable focus ratio, the management efficiency ratio probably is most meaningful for organizations that collect and immediately disburse money rather than use it to acquire operating or capital assets.

(iv) Donor Reliance. This *donor reliance* ratio is calculated as follows:

$$\text{Expenses} \div \text{Revenue} - \text{Contributions}$$

This ratio measures the organization's dependency on charitable contributions. If the ratio is higher than 1, the organization is either relying on debt financing or on contributions from donors to finance its activities. Even if it is using debt in the short term to finance its operations, in the long term it will need either to generate more cash flow from its operations or seek outside support in the form of the contributions. If the ratio produces a number lower than 1, the organization is able to use operating revenue to cover its expenses, thus making it less dependent on charitable contributions. One could make the case that fundraising expenses should be excluded from total expenses because if there were no charitable contributions, there would be no fundraising expenses. If the organization sells goods (e.g., a university's bookstore, a museum's gift shop, or a medical clinic's pharmacy), revenue and expense should probably be calculated net of the cost of goods sold.

Of all the ratios, this one is the most difficult to interpret, so let's consider several examples. Suppose the organization has no contributions from donors but receives $100,000 in operating revenue and incurs $100,000 in operating expenses. Its donor reliance ratio is 1, meaning that every dollar of revenue is being used to fund expenses. Although the organization does not depend on donor contributions per se, it is operating with little margin for error, particularly if its expenses are relatively fixed. Certainly, additional revenue from contributions would provide some comfort. If, on the other hand, the organization expends $100,000 on its activities and earns $300,000 in revenue, it is operating with a much higher level of independence from contributors. In other words, the closer this ratio is to 0, the better.

RESISTING THE LURE OF EFFICIENCY RATIOS

* * *

Anyone looking at the Web sites for many relief organizations following the December 2004 South Asia tsunamis was almost as likely to see a pie chart highlighting the percentage of contributed dollars that go directly to mission as they were to see pictures of devastated villages in Banda Aceh, Indonesia. This aspect of charitable solicitation not only deceives the public but also is ultimately harmful to the charitable sector.

Many of the corporate scandals making headlines over the last decade have been rooted in abuses of accounting rules. The investor community requires, with the help of the SEC and the accounting profession, clear and consistent disclosure of financial results so that companies can be meaningfully compared. The numbers that the charities disseminate describing their effectiveness in converting contributions into mission are not based on clear and consistent standards. Therein lies the deceptive nature of these percentages.

Charities have a fair amount of discretion in how they allocate overhead and classify expenses. Consider someone who works in the national office of a relief organization. It is possible to allocate 100 percent of his salary to overhead, or if the charity wants, ask him to keep track of his time and allocate it to specific programs—thereby converting what one charity might classify as general overhead into an expenditure on mission by another charity.

The relief organizations add an additional dimension to the fallacy of efficiency ratios. Although some of the relief organizations had people in South Asia, others collected money in the United States and allocated it to local NGOs in South Asia. Each type of organization serves an important role. However, any suggestion that these organizations can be compared through efficiency ratios is nonsense. Assuming comparison is even warranted, should the organization that channels money to other organizations not be required to include the overhead of its partner organizations into the efficiency calculations? The child wandering around in what was left of Banda Aceh did not receive any more food or shelter from the person who made the $1,000 contribution in San Francisco just because the administration of those funds takes place two entities removed from the donor.

Then consider the question of how to calculate these ratios. Should fundraising expenses be treated the same as management expenses? Should the expense number be compared against the organization's total revenue, its revenue devoted to program services, or some other denominator? Should investment income be included in the denominator? Should these numbers consider the distinction between restricted and unrestricted sources of revenue? Finally, to the extent that fundraising expenses are at issue, should there be an allowance for the impact of major capital campaigns, which will distort ratios for a single year (rather than some longer time period), and thus make comparisons meaningless? To simply ask these questions is to show the problem inherent with nonstandardized and poorly conceived measurements.

Of course, there will be those who say that a little deception is not such a bad thing if it raises more money for the victims of the South Asia tsunamis. Ironically, it is not the public but the charitable sector itself that is harmed by efficiency ratios. These meaningless measurements foster the notion that it does not cost anything to run a charity. Executive directors would like free secretarial, accounting, and information technology services, but that is not the reality of the marketplace in which charities must compete for talented people.

Furthermore, efficiency ratios foster the notion that anything not spent on water purification, shipping food, and protecting children against predators is a waste of money. Nobody in the public would want to learn that $20 of a $100 contribution had been stolen, but it takes money to implement and maintain internal controls that prevent theft.

Everybody hoped that a long time would pass before the next disaster. However, when the next one came—and *it* inevitably did in the form of Hurricane Katrina and a major earthquake in South Central Asia—everybody wanted the relief logistics in place. December 27, 2004, was not the time to identify qualified organizations and professionals in Indonesia, Sri Lanka, or Thailand. The necessary vetting process must be ongoing. Evaluating and building relationships takes money that probably looks more like management and administration than active disaster relief.

This obsession with efficiency ratios can lead to destructive behavior on the part of charitable organizations. One organization engaged in the South Asia relief efforts intended to devote 100 percent of the money raised to direct relief, with no allowance for organizational overhead. This organization stated explicitly that funds raised in response to the South Asia tsunamis were not be used to pay any portion of the salaries of long-standing employees who were directly involved in the relief efforts.

At first, this appears to be a very laudable policy, particularly in terms of honoring donor intent. However, the organization was simply "burning down the house to stay warm." As every for-profit business knows, you cannot price your product based on marginal costs and stay in business. That was exactly what this executive director was doing. Eventually, such behavior will affect mission. While the janitor who maintains the warehouse is the not glamour guy in this operation, every donor should want this organization to hire the best janitor. Contributions to buy food and medicine will go to waste if a poorly paid janitor fails to keep the warehouse at the right temperature or fails to combat rodent infestation. Unfortunately, at the root of such misguided policy are the meaningless efficiency ratios that too many in the charitable sector are selling to the public.

Charities need to do a better job of educating their contributors. Perhaps executive directors should bring their organization's janitor to the next fundraising function in addition to the highly visible doctor who went to South Asia and has heart-warming stories to tell. That janitor probably cares just as much as that doctor, and he may even have some interesting operational stories as well.

* * *

(b) APPLYING THE SYSTEM—CASE 1. To demonstrate the four ratios, let's consider the financial statements for the American Cancer Society and the American Heart Association, both of which were chosen because they are large, well-known charities. Each focuses on a major health issue that unfortunately confronts many Americans. One would expect the indices for the two organizations to be similar, but there were two surprises.

When applied to the American Cancer Society's 2001 financial statements, the four metrics yield the following results:

Charitable focus (total expenses as denominator)	73.23%
Modified charitable focus (total revenue as denominator)	68.58
Fundraising efficiency	19.42
Management efficiency	8.30
Donor reliance	15.00

The calculations did not distinguish between restricted and unrestricted assets or income. Furthermore, the calculation of fundraising efficiency excludes the value of contributed services because the valuations underlying that number is always open to question.

The American Cancer Society's five numbers are meaningless without a baseline for comparison. That baseline should either be the universe of charitable organizations with similar objectives and operations or the American Cancer Society's numbers as calculated for the prior five or ten years.

When applied to the American Heart Association's 2001 financial statements, the five metrics yield the following results:

Charitable focus (total expenses as denominator)	73.11%
Modified charitable focus (total revenue as denominator)	75.00
Fundraising efficiency	25.90
Management efficiency	7.31
Donor reliance	5.56

For our purposes, comparing these two organizations is sufficient, but a board member should ask the CFO to undertake a more comprehensive analysis, possibly computing the metrics for the March of Dimes, Epilepsy Foundation of America, the National Kidney Foundation, the National Multiple Sclerosis Society, and various other disease-centric charities. The CFO might go so far as to prepare an analysis showing the ratios for each organization and an industry average. In computing that industry average, the CFO should use a weighted-average methodology rather than simply taking the statistic for each organization, summing all of them, and then dividing the resulting number by the number of organizations in the surveyed universe. Even then, the CFO should attempt to make the necessary adjustments so that the raw accounting data are normalized. For example, if one organization shows the value of contributed services while another does not, some sort of adjustment is necessary for a meaningful analysis. Finally, the CFO should make sure that the each organization does, in fact, engage in the same types of activities. The bottom line is that the questions that must be asked to produce a sensible analysis are often more important than the numerical input.

Let's consider what conclusions we might draw from the various indices by examining two questions. First, can we conclude that the American Cancer Society is a better organization because its fundraising efficiency ratio (19.42 percent) is lower than the American Heart Association's fundraising efficiency ratio (25.90 percent)? The answer is that this would be an inappropriate conclusion to draw from this one number. It is true that roughly \$6.50 more out of every \$100 raised by the American Cancer Society *appears* to be channeled to its charitable mission and management efforts. Taken by itself, this might suggest that the American Cancer Society is more efficient than the American Heart Association. Then examine the management efficiency metric. Here the American Heart Association (\$7.31) has the edge; its cost of managing \$100 is roughly a dollar less than the amount for the American Cancer Society (\$8.30).

This is when the board members should ask questions about the underlying facts. The disparity between the two organizations might be attributable to overhead allocation formulas rather than actual efficiencies. The American Heart Association might be classifying more "management" overhead as fundraising expenses than the American Cancer Society, which could explain the disparities.

The board should find the answer to this question and other questions. Even though the board might conclude that the American Heart Association's fundraising is as cost effective as possible, it should still be concerned about what prospective donors might think. It might ask management to address these issues in solicitation materials.

Second, based on the management efficiency ratio, can we argue that the American Heart Association is actually a more efficient organization than the American Cancer Society? The answer, again is that it simply is not possible to draw that conclusion from one number. The one percentage point difference is too small and can be due to timing differences in recording expenses or income, different valuations or allocation formulas, or one-time stochastic events. On the other hand, if a donor is disturbed by the six percentage point difference between the two organizations when it comes to their fundraising efficiency metrics, the American Heart Association could use management efficiency ratios to counter the criticism. But every organization should be reluctant to make that argument because, as the old saying goes, "Two wrongs do not make a right."

Both organizations appear to depend heavily on charitable contributions according to the donor reliance index, but the American Cancer Society (15) appears to depend far more on donors than the American Heart Association (5.53). Recall that the donor reliance index measures total expenses against revenue from sources other than charitable contributions. As this number moves toward to zero (less than 1), the organization is able to cover its expenses from operating revenue and endowment income. Again, the analyst has to be careful. The difference between the two organizations could be due to a one-year aberration. However, after seeing these numbers, both boards might want to focus on reducing debt levels and increasing endowment income.

The point is that both organizations should use these ratios to probe all aspects of their operations rather than to brag about what may well be illusory differences. They must consider both interorganizational comparisons and intraorganizational comparisons over time.

(c) APPLYING THE SYSTEM—CASE 2. Now let's apply the system to the following art museums: the Museum of Modern Art (MoMA), Metropolitan Museum of Art (the Met), and Solomon R. Guggenheim Museum (the Guggenheim). Unfortunately, none of these institutions made its financial statements available on its Web site when the data were sought, so the financial data were taken from each organization's IRS Form 990. In one sense, this makes the calculations easier because the account names (lines on the tax return) were identical for all three organizations, but that apparent consistency, in all likelihood, is illusory. The pertinent question is whether each organization used the same expense allocations and individual revenue and expense classifications? Keep in mind that the financial data were taken from the latest statements available for each organization when the analysis was first undertaken, but the accounting periods were not identical. Here is the comparison:

	Guggenheim	Metropolitan Museum	MoMA
Charitable focus (total expense as denominator)	73.99%	85.58%	77.99%
Modified charitable focus (total revenue as denominator)	71.83	42.76	43.67
Fundraising efficiency[2]	10.77	5.40	5.80
Management efficiency	23.03	12.80	20.65
Donor reliance	2.84	.70	1.06

Once again, let's answer several questions to see what these numbers really reveal. First, can we conclude that the reason for the Met's low modified charitable focus is that it does not depend on donors to fund operations? The Met is the only museum of the three that had a donor reliance metric below 1, suggesting that it is covering its program expenses from income other than contributions and membership fees. Of the three museums, the Met has the lowest modified charitable focus ratio (42.76 percent). An unsophisticated user of these ratios might conclude that there is causation here. As the Met becomes less dependent on donors, it becomes less responsive to the public. There is some logic to that conclusion, but it is at least suspect and probably incorrect.

Significant issues underlie both the charitable focus and donor reliance ratios. First, the Met realized significant gains (some $203 million) from the sale of securities. It could certainly increase its charitable focus number by spending all of the gain from the sale of those securities now, but would that be prudent? The trustees apparently did not believe so, and anyone who wants to argue that point faces a tough counterargument.

Second, should a donor interested in artwork contribute to the Guggenheim because it has the highest modified charitable focus ratio? Drawing that conclusion from these numbers would be misguided. Of the three museums, many in the art world would argue that the Guggenheim lacks focus. In recent years, it has presented controversial exhibits (e.g., the Art of Motorcycle), which some consider to be commercial blockbuster shows that have little to do with serious art. This debate will be left to the public and art critics, but the fact that there is a debate aptly demonstrates that an organization's focus cannot simply be reduced to a number.

The problem with the charitable focus number is that it does not consider whether the institution is spending its money efficiently. It may be that an institution with a lower number is accomplishing the same tasks more efficiently. Furthermore, that institution could be building an endowment for future projects, whereas the institution with the higher number may not be setting aside enough money for a rainy day. Along these same lines, the institution with the lower

2. No adjustment has been made for the value of contributed services.

number could be prevented by the terms of restricted gifts from spending income currently. An unfavorable comparison should cause the directors to ask questions. They might discover that the differences are due to classification issues. That inquiry might also uncover significant operational deficiencies.

Third, can we conclude that the Metropolitan Museum should start spending more of its endowment? True, the Met appears to have the luxury of a strong endowment and operating income, permitting it to "ignore" annual contributions. However, this is probably far from the truth. As noted the Met's IRS Form 990 reveals more than $200 million of investment gains. The Met's investment advisor possibly thought the time had come to shift funds out of the stock market. If the advisor was correct, the Met will not necessarily have comparable investment gains in the coming years. If that is true, the Met is unlikely to perform as well on the donor reliance index next year. What this analysis really suggests is that the Met's donor reliance index should be examined over a number of years to better assess its meaning.

Regrettably, the IRS Form 990 does not distinguish between activity funded with restricted assets and revenue and activity funded with unrestricted assets and revenue. That information is included in the financial statements. The Met's financial statements might show that a significant portion of the investment gains were attributable to donor-restricted endowment funds that prohibit the Met from expending all realized gains. If that is the case, too much emphasis on the donor reliance index is unwarranted. The Met's investment gains also offer another lesson. The ratios should probably have been calculated marking unrealized investment gains to market for all three institutions.

As bears repeating, ratio analysis must be undertaken with a great deal of caution and skepticism. Raw numbers should not simply be accepted. As an aside, on the day this passage was revised, the MoMA opened its new facilities to the public. Had the preceding analysis been based on MoMA's financial data for the last several years, the results likely would have been quite different in view of MoMA's expansion. Further demonstrating the potential perils of such analysis, the original universe of museums included the Art Institute of Chicago, but it also operates a school, which makes any comparison particularly suspect.

Do the Financial Analysis for the Press and Donors or Live with the Consequences

* * *

On the eve of the 2005 Farm Aid concert, the *Chicago Tribune* ran a highly critical investigative report focusing on Farm Aid's finances.[3] Recall that Farm Aid is the charity founded

3. J. George, *Farm Aid Expenses Eat Away Donations: Only 28% of Revenue from Last Year Made It to Farm Families*, Chi. Trib., Sept. 17, 2005.

in 1985 by Willie Nelson, the highly regarded country singer. This charity provides aid to organizations assisting family farmers and works to increase public awareness of the problems farmers face. The article's headline proclaimed, *Farm Aid Expenses Eat Away Donations: Only 28% of Revenue from Last Year Made It to Farm Families* (September 17, 2005). This headline is misleading and unfair, but it is now out there. Moreover, the analysis undertaken in the article is superficial and based on faulty reasoning.

In arriving at the 28 percent number appearing in the headline, the reporter apparently compared Line 22 of the 2004 IRS Form 990 (Grants and Allocations) to Line 12 (Total Revenue). This is a dubious comparison because it assumes that Farm Aid's sole function is grant making. In fact, Farm Aid is in part an advocacy organization. It also provides direct assistance to farmers through a hot line. Although the reporter does note that analyzing numbers can be tricky, when all the cows came home, that difficulty did not temper the *Tribune*'s headline or much of the article's content.

Although just speculation, but the reporter was apparently attempting to assess Farm Aid's charitable focus (program-related expenses as compared to total revenue, or total expenses, if that is your preference). If that speculation is correct, the reporter should have compared program services (Line 13) to total revenue (Line 12). For the 2003 fiscal year, this shows 68.44 percent of revenue going to program services.

The *Tribune* article quotes a philanthropy expert as having said that at least 65 percent of revenue should be "given away" before a nonprofit is considered to be performing adequately.[4] In all likelihood the reporter misconstrued the answer to his question (or did not ask the right question). What the expert likely meant was that at least 65 percent of revenue (or total expenses) should be devoted to mission rather than fundraising and management. From that standpoint, Farm Aid passed the expert's benchmark. Although the article did not explicitly state, in all likelihood, its negative headline and tone stemmed from the incongruity between the 28 percent and 65 percent numbers. What is particularly notable is that when asked about her comments by a local newspaper, this expert indicated that she did not remember speaking to the *Tribune* and knew nothing about Farm Aid.[5]

Farm Aid's gross revenue for the fiscal year ending in 2004 was about $1.4 million. In this situation, it is difficult to understand why the leading newspaper in Chicago should focus on such a small charity's performance when the last available IRS Form 990 for Chicago's public television station WTTW showed a 67.23 percent charitable focus and the comparable return for Chicago's beloved Art Institute showed a 60.53 percent charitable focus. Both of these institutions are many times larger than Farm Aid and have a more direct impact on the Chicago community. Farm Aid outperformed both institutions based on the raw numbers, yet no one would seriously take the measure of WTTW or the Art Institute based on one ratio from one reporting period.

If the *Tribune* wanted to focus just on grants, the Art Institute gave just 8.13 percent of its Line 12 revenue away in the form of grants; again, it operates a school, so much of that could be in the form of scholarships, but that is only speculation. If charity is just about giving things away, then there ought to be a lot of people waiting in line to take home the Art Institute's signature collection of paintings.

The reporter seemed to be particularly troubled by the fact that in 2003, the Farm Aid concert took in $1,013,087 and had $853,833 in expenses, leaving just $159,254 for the organization's efforts.[6] The article quotes one expert who proclaimed, "That's not good. If I go to a concert, I would not like that at all." Again, there is no way to know the full context

---

4. *Id.*
5. M. Miner, *Neil Young Has a Cow: But He's Not Wrong about the Trib's Farm Aid Reporting*, CHI. READER, Sept. 30, 2005.
6. J. George, *supra* note 3.

behind that statement, but it is a surprising one. As all too many charities know, people often need incentives to encourage gifts. This often means holding elaborate fundraising events and parties that become loss leaders.

Once again, returning to the *Tribune*'s market: The 2003 IRS Form 990 for Chicago's famed Lyric Opera reports special events revenue on Line 9a as $1,432,827 and associated expenses as $1,641,722, producing a net loss of $208,895 from these special activities. It should be noted that the Lyric also reported $1,627,934 of associated revenue on Line 1a as charitable contributions. In one sense, these activities produced an economic profit if the charitable element is included as part of event revenue. On the other hand, the actual cost of the event appears to have exceeded the allocable portion of revenue representing the quid pro quo aspect of the admission. To be clear, there is nothing wrong or inappropriate with what the Lyric Opera has done. Again, what is puzzling is why the *Tribune* decided to focus on a small national organization instead of larger local ones operating in its hometown.

Undoubtedly, the article was inspired by the presence of the Farm Aid concert in the Chicago market the day after the article was published. If anything, the *Tribune* article proves that our highly touted celebrities are not as effective at changing society as they might wish or believe they are. If Willie Nelson and his friends deserve any criticism, it is for not being able to convert their star power into a bigger movement on behalf of farmers after 20 years of effort, but this can probably be said of many celebrities and their "pet" charitable organizations. Celebrity effectiveness is certainly a legitimate angle for a story, but that was not the article's focus. Clearly, the *Tribune*'s decision to investigate Farm Aid was legitimate, but the analysis must then be conducted with care. It must also provide context and disclose the limitations that were faced in reviewing the data.

Charities cannot prevent the press, "watchdog" groups, or donors from engaging in financial analysis, but charities can supplement their tax returns, donor marketing materials, and Web sites with statistics that anticipate the type of analysis undertaken by the *Tribune*. Charities can also provide their own comparative data, assumptions, and context. Of course, like journalists, the charity's analysis should be accurate and fair. If a charity that fails to anticipate the type of analysis undertaken by the *Tribune*, it is setting itself up for bad publicity, and in many cases, needlessly so. In the case of Farm Aid, the *Chronicle of Philanthropy* ran a very favorable article describing the organization's many accomplishments the same week the *Tribune* article appeared.[7] This article refers to a "lean budget," "expanded fundraising," and over two-thirds payout in grants over the organization's life. Had Farm Aid captured these statistics on its Web site, provided an activity-by-activity allocation of expenditures, and compared itself to benchmark numbers, it might have been able to avoid the unfavorable publicity splashed across the *Tribune*'s pages.

* * *

(d) CONCLUDING THOUGHTS ON RATIOS. There are good reasons for using financial ratios to measure the effectiveness and efficiency of any organization. The preceding discussion attempts to demonstrate why directors or potential donors should not place too much emphasis on any number without first fully understanding its component parts and what that number does not take into account.

---

7. M. Anft, *Cultivating a Broader Purpose: On Its 20th Anniversary Farm Aid Expands its Mission*, CHRON. OF PHILAN., Sept. 15, 2005.

A number of watchdog organizations are tossing such numbers out to donors in an effort to make them more thoughtful in selecting charities that receive their dollars. Regrettably, donors all too often focus on the raw numbers but ignore the caveats that accompany them. A board should obviously be concerned if the numbers do not accurately portray the organization's efforts and successes. This should and will affect an organization's marketing campaign, but that should never cause the organization to use false or fraudulent numbers.

13.3 INDEPENDENT REVIEW STANDARDS

There is a widespread belief that disclosure and transparency empower the public and grant-making organizations. If that is true, then the public and grant makers are in a position to change behavior by rewarding efficiency and effectiveness through contributions. Although this line of thought has some logic, its validity assumes that donors and grant makers pore over all of the data. That may be true for sophisticated grant makers and donors, but members of the public probably make their decisions based on glossy brochures and ads filled with images of starving children, abandoned pets, and sick people. In many cases, emotion—not numbers—drives the decision to give. If that conjecture is correct, then all of this disclosure could be nothing but a colossal waste of money.

Yet, a number of groups believe the public wants to make more informed decisions. These organizations act much like Wall Street security analysts, closely examining the data and then reporting their conclusions to the public. Among the organizations offering assessments are the BBB Wise Giving Alliance, the Maryland Association of Nonprofits, and Charity Navigator. These independent reviews are primarily for the benefit of donors, but charities should closely review them because the conclusions clearly affect public perceptions about individual charities.

Let's now consider three of the more prominent rating organizations.

(a) BBB WISE GIVING ALLIANCE. The Better Business Bureau Wise Giving Alliance is national charity monitoring organization that produces evaluative reports on national charities that specify if the charity meets or does not meet the *Standards for Charity Accountability*. There is no charge to the charity for the evaluation and the resulting reports are freely available on the give.org Web site. The Alliance selects charities based on the volume of inquiries received. National charities can also request to be evaluated. Inquiries about local charities are referred to the local Better Business Bureau serving that area. A charity is prohibited from making reference to the BBB Wise Giving Alliance name in its materials. However, charities that meet standards have the option of participating in a charity seal program if they execute a licensing agreement and pay an annual fee.

The BBB Wise Giving Alliance guidelines are worth any board's time even if the charity is not a national organization or is not interested in using the seal. There are currently 20 standards, broken down into five categories.[8]

Governance and oversight	The governing board has ultimate oversight authority for any charitable organization. This section of the standards seeks to ensure that the volunteer board is active, independent and free of self-dealing. To meet these standards, the organization shall have:
1	A board of directors that provides adequate oversight of the charity's operation and its staff
2	A board of directors with a minimum of five voting members.
3	A minimum of three evenly spaced meetings per year of the full governing body with a majority in attendance, with face to face participation.
4	Not more than one or 10% (whichever is greater) directly or indirectly compensated person(s) serving as voting member(s) of the board. Compensated members shall not serve as the board's chair or treasurer.
5	No transaction(s) in which any board or staff members have material conflicting interests with the charity resulting from any relationship or business affiliation.
Measuring effectiveness	An organization should regularly assess its effectiveness in achieving its mission. This section seeks to ensure that an organization has defined, measurable goals and objectives in place and a defined process in place to evaluate the success and impact of the program(s) in fulfilling the goals and objectives of the organization and that also identifies ways to address any deficiencies. To meet these standards, a charitable organization shall:
6	Have a board policy of assessing, no less than every two years, the organization's performance and effectiveness and of determining future actions required to achieve its mission.
7	Submit to the organization's governing body, for its approval, a written report that outlines the results of the aforementioned performance and effectiveness assessment and recommendations for future actions.
Finances	This section of the standards seeks to ensure that the charity spends its funds honestly, prudently and in accordance with statements made in fund raising appeals. To meet these standards, the charitable organization shall:
8	Spend at least 65% of its total expenses on program activities. [formula omitted]
9	Spend no more than 35% of related contributions on fund raising. Related contributions include donations, legacies, and other gifts received as a result of fund raising efforts. [formula omitted]

8. *Standards for Charity Accountability* reprinted with permission. Copyright 2003, BBB Wise Giving Alliance, 4200 Wilson Blvd, Arlington, VA, 22203. To access the full text of the Standards along with a detailed implementation Guide, visit http://www.give.org.

10	Avoid accumulating funds that could be used for current program activities. To meet this standard, the charity's unrestricted net assets available for use should not be more than three times the size of the past year's expenses or three times the size of the current year's budget, whichever is higher. [If an organization does not satisfy the numerical measures in 8, 9, or 10, it is given the opportunity to show that its use of funds is reasonable.]
11	Make available to all, on request, complete annual financial statements prepared in accordance with generally accepted accounting principles.
12	Include in the financial statements a breakdown of expenses (e.g., salaries, travel, postage, etc.) that shows what portion of these expenses was allocated to program, fund raising, and administrative activities.
13	Accurately report the charity's expenses, including any joint cost allocations, in its financial statements.
14	Have a board-approved annual budget for its current fiscal year, outlining projected expenses for major program activities, fund raising, and administration.
Fund raising and informational materials	A fund raising appeal is often the only contact a donor has with a charity and may be the sole impetus for giving. This section of the standards seeks to ensure that a charity's representations to the public are accurate, complete and respectful, both in whole and in part. To meet these standards, the charitable organization shall:
15	Have solicitations and informational materials, distributed by any means, that are accurate, truthful and not misleading, both in whole and in part.
16	Have an annual report available to all, on request, that includes (a) the organization's mission statement, (b) a summary of the past year's program service accomplishments, (c) a roster of the officers and members of the board of directors, and (d) financial information that includes: (i) total income in the past fiscal year, (ii) expenses in the same program, fund raising and administrative categories as in the financial statements, and (iii) ending net assets.
17	Include on any charity Web sites that solicit contributions, the same information that is recommended for annual reports, as well as the mailing address of the charity and electronic access to the most recent IRS Form 990.
18	Address privacy concerns of donors by (a) providing in written appeals, at least annually, a means (e.g., such as a check off box) for both new and continuing donors to inform the charity if they do not want their name and address shared outside the organization, and (b) providing a clear, prominent and easily accessible policy on any of its Web sites that tells visitors (i) what information, if any, is being collected about them by the charity and how this information will be used, (ii) how to contact the charity to review personal information collected and request corrections, (iii) how to inform the charity (e.g., a check off box) that the visitor does not wish his/her personal information to be shared outside the organization, and (iv) what security measures the charity has in place to protect personal information.

19	Clearly disclose how the charity benefits from the sale of products or services (i.e., cause-related marketing) that state or imply that a charity will benefit from a consumer sale or transaction. Such promotions should disclose, at the point of solicitation: (a) the actual or anticipated portion of the purchase price that will benefit the charity (e.g., 5 cents will be contributed to abc charity for every xyz company product sold); (b) the duration of the campaign (e.g., the month of October); and (c) any maximum or guaranteed minimum contribution amount (e.g., up to a maximum of $200,000).
20	Respond promptly to and act on complaints brought to its attention by the BBB Wise Giving Alliance and/or local Better Business Bureaus about fund raising practices, privacy policy violations and/or other issues.

The winter 2005 edition of the quarterly *BBB Wise Giving Guide* summarizes 519 national charity evaluations. Of those, 70 percent met the standards, with the remaining 30 percent falling short. There does not appear to have been one issue that consistently prevented a charity from meeting the standards.

(b) MARYLAND ASSOCIATION OF NONPROFIT ORGANIZATIONS' STANDARDS PROJECT. The Maryland Association of Nonprofit Organizations is a highly regarded state association (trade group) of Maryland nonprofit organizations. It has embarked on its "Standards for Excellence" project, which is a voluntary ethics and accountability code that has generated considerable interest. In fact, the Maryland Association has obtained grant money to replicate the project across the country.[9] Five other associations of nonprofit organizations (Louisiana, North Carolina, Ohio, Pennsylvania, and Georgia) were initially chosen as replication partners. They have adopted the program in one form or another,[10] with a number of other organizations expressing interest in it.

The program has now been expanded so that nonprofits from around the country can seek certification directly from the Maryland Association for a fee. A training component is also available. Those seeking certification should keep in mind that the standards were not designed as minimum benchmarks but reflect an attempt at excellence. As is typical with all tools for rating and evaluating the process, the value is in the process rather than the certification.

The program adopts a code of ethics and accountability that focuses on (1) mission and program, (2) governing board, (3) conflicts of interest, (4) human resources, (5) financial and legal accountability, (6) openness, (7) fundraising, and (8) public policy and public affairs. The Maryland Association offers a voluntary

9. In 2000, the Maryland Association received initial grants from the Surdna Fund and the Rockefeller Brothers Fund. It subsequently received $1.3 million in funding from the Carnegie Corporation of New York and Atlantic Philanthropies. See R. Mendel, *The Maryland Association of Nonprofit Organizations: Seeking "Standards of Excellence" for the Future*, CARNEGIE RESULTS (Fall 2005).

10. *Id.*

peer-review, certification program for nonprofit organizations demonstrating that they satisfy the standards. The project also has a technical assistance component.

The standards are available on the Maryland Association's Web site and can be purchased from the association for a nominal fee.[11] The standards highlight many of the points made throughout this *Guide*. They contemplate an active board of directors that is responsible for long-term and short-term planning, budgetary approval, establishing financial and personal policies, hiring the executive director, setting his compensation, and evaluating his performance. Under the standards, the board must be composed of at least five unrelated directors, with seven or more directors being preferable. Not surprising, the standards contain lengthy and thorough conflict-of-interest requirements.

The Maryland standards also focus on financial accountability by requiring an annual budget, an annual audit by an independent certified public accountant if revenues exceed $300,000, and accurate financial reporting. The organization must have written policies in place addressing investment of assets, internal controls, purchasing practices, and the use of unrestricted current net assets. On the legal side, the standards require compliance with a wide variety of laws, including lobbying and political advocacy, fundraising, and registration. The standards also call for periodic assessments of insurance coverage.

Like the *BBB Wise Giving Guide,* the Maryland standards place some emphasis on fundraising practices, setting out a novel yet defensible approach to assessing whether those expenses are too high. Specifically, the fundraising standards provide that, on average over a five-year period, a nonprofit should realize revenue from fundraising and other development activities that are at least three times the amount spent on conducting its activities. What is particularly commendable about this standard is its willingness to break away from focusing on annual numbers. After all, a particular fundraising campaign can straddle several years, resulting in mismatches between revenue and expenses. The standards also prohibit contingent fee arrangements (e.g., the fundraiser receives a certain percentage of each dollar raised). Probably the most refreshing standard is the one that requires organizations to curtail repeated mailings or telephone solicitations from in-house lists if requested.

(c) CHARITY NAVIGATOR. Like the BBB Wise Giving Alliance and the Maryland Association of Nonprofit Organizations, Charity Navigator[12] is a Section 501(c)(3) organization that evaluates charitable organizations. Unlike its two competitors, Charity Navigator takes a much more quantitative approach to evaluation. It focuses on two sets of ratios, one examining organizational efficiency and the other organizational capacity. Organizational efficiency considers how (1) program expenses compare to the operating budget, (2) administrative expenses compare to functional expenses, (3) fundraising expenses compare to overall

11. http://www.marylandnonprofits.org.
12. Charity Navigator maintains a Web site at http://www.charitynavigator.org.

expenses, and (4) fundraising expenses compare to charitable contributions. Organizational capacity focuses on revenue growth, program expense growth, and a working capital ratio (working capital divided by total expenses). To its credit, Charity Navigator has developed an elaborate rating system that focuses on peer groups. As of November 2005, it had evaluations for more than 4,900 of the largest charities in the United States.[13]

The information used by Charity Navigator is taken from IRS Form 990, so there are consistency and allocation issues when the data are used to compare two or more organizations. Charity Navigator acknowledges some of the limitations in using this data.[14] To mitigate single-year fluctuations, it examines data for up to five years. Clearly, Charity Navigator has attempted to respond to traditional criticisms of this type of analysis by developing a detailed analysis and measurement system. As a starting point, Charity Navigator's numbers are useful.

As discussed in various sections throughout this *Guide,* however, financial measurements can be misleading when qualitative factors and rigorous analysis are ignored—a point that those who run Charity Navigator probably do not disagree with. An organization could be spending 95 percent of its money on a variety of programs and receive a top rating but be "drilling dry holes" in oil-industry parlance. Who is to say that a few more dollars devoted to overhead might not vastly improve outcomes? To its credit, Charity Navigator indicates that it is working on methods for assessing how well an organization is fulfilling its mission.[15] The fact remains, however, that Charity Navigator's current approach punishes organizations that have overhead attributable to a solid control system.

Because Charity Navigator's assessments and rankings are widely available on the Web, charities and their boards should certainly examine its analyses, if only to be in a position to counter the rankings when warranted. Like all analysis based on ratios, Charity Navigator's analysis will have performed a useful function if it spurs an organization to dissect its numbers and undertake comparisons with other similarly situated organizations.

---

13. *Id.* See Web site.
14. For example, Charity Navigator states that:

> Givers should also recognize that there are a few limitations to our ratings. Most of these limitations result from the fact that the financial information on which we base our ratings is derived entirely from the IRS Forms 990 each charity files with the IRS. That information itself is limited in several ways.... Second, the IRS Form 990 requires accounting practices that differ in certain fundamental ways from those standards known as Generally Accepted Accounting Principles (GAAP). We rate charities based on financial information derived using standards that may be at variance with GAAP.

Elsewhere on its Web site, Charity Navigator addresses the challenges posed by restricted asset classifications.

15. Charity Navigator states on its Web site "The final limitation to our ratings is that we do not currently evaluate the quality of the programs or services a charity provides. As soon as we develop a methodology for doing so, we will." Elsewhere the site acknowledges that the problem with assessing quality is developing a uniform standard.

(d) CONCLUSION. As part of a self-assessment process, every organization should consider how it would rate under each of the three systems that have been considered. Each takes a different approach; that is, each provides different insights. Each organization should start with Charity Navigator, comparing itself to similar charities. Then each organization should use the two less quantitative systems, to ascertain whether the quantitative results make sense. Each system should be used principally for self-assessment. This process might make for a perfect session during a board retreat.

13.4 GRANTOR REVIEW STANDARDS

Several years ago, a local charity executive sent an e-mail to the author asking why his organization had been turned down for United Way funding.[16] What was surprising was the marquee nature of this charity. The e-mail highlighted the importance of review standards applied by grant makers. Although an organization can certainly ignore BBB Wise Giving Alliance, the Maryland Standards for Excellence, and Charity Navigator, it cannot ignore standards imposed by a grant maker. Grant makers are increasingly considering governance, financial controls, and more generalized internal controls as part of the grant-making process. Let's consider two sets of standards that apply to a wide variety of charities.

(a) THE COMBINED FEDERAL CAMPAIGN. Many charities choose to participate in the Combined Federal Campaign (CFC), the annual fundraising drive conducted by federal employees. In 2003, federal employees and military personnel raised $237 million. Essentially a public sector version of the United Way, the CFC has been in existence for over 40 years.

The CFC is the only program authorized to solicit in the federal workplace on behalf of charitable organizations (except for certain emergency/disaster relief campaigns responding to specific events). The campaign operates at both the national and local levels. The Director of the Office of Personal and Management (or a designee) oversees the overall campaign, and Local Federal Coordinating Committees (LFCC) conduct campaigns at the local level. Charitable organizations must apply to participate. They have the option to apply at the national or local level.

Charities or federations of charities are required to submit annual applications to participate in the campaign. Before a charity can participate at the national level, it must satisfy each of the following requirements, among others:

- Be a Section 501(c)(3) organization.
- Have provided or conducted real services, benefits, assistance, or program activities in 15 or more different states or a foreign country over the three-year period immediately preceding the start of the campaign year.

16. At that time, the author had no affiliation with United Way. The author has since served as a voluntary member of the United Way Metropolitan Chicago's Youth Impact Panel.

- Have no expenses connected with lobbying and attempts to influence voting or legislation at the local, state, or federal level or, alternatively, that those expenses would come within the limits of Section 501(h) of the Internal Revenue Code.
- Be a human health and welfare organization providing services, benefits, or assistance to or conducting activities affecting human health and welfare.
- Account for its funds in accordance with generally accepted accounting principles and undergo an annual audit of the organization's operations by an independent certified public accountant in accordance with generally accepted auditing standards. Such audit must show expenses by function.
- Provide a completed copy of the organization's IRS Form 990, including signature, with the application regardless of whether or not the IRS requires the organization to file this form.
- Provide a computation of the organization's percentage of total support and revenue spent on administrative and fundraising.
- If an organization's administrative and fundraising expenses exceed 25 percent of its total support and revenue, it must certify that its actual expenses for administration and fundraising are reasonable under all the circumstances.
- Be directed by an active and responsible governing body whose members have no material conflicts of interest and a majority of which serve without compensation.
- Prohibit the sale or lease of its CFC contributor lists.
- Make available to the public on request an annual report that includes a full description of the organization's activities and supporting services and identifies its directors and chief administrative personnel.

As an alternative to satisfying the national eligibility standards, an organization can seek eligibility to participate in a local LFCC campaign by submitting an application to the appropriate LFCC. The local eligibility requirements are similar to the national ones but are relaxed with respect to audits, size, and history of the organization. Specifically, applicants at the local level are not required to have provided services or benefits in 15 states or a foreign country over the prior three years. Those with annual revenue of less than $100,000 are not required to undergo an audit, and, hence, are not required to submit an audit report.

The eligibility requirements for participation in the campaign provide another set of standards that a board can use to evaluate its organization. These rules do not provide enough emphasis on governance or other legal matters, but they serve as a potential starting point, particularly for organizations seeking contributions from federal employees.

(b) UNITED WAY. The United Way has endorsed an entirely different approach to evaluating nonprofits. It focuses on program outcomes rather than controls or financial analysis.[17] This approach asks whether the organization is accomplishing its stated mission. Obviously, donors and grant makers want to know whether the organization is protecting its financial resources, but in the final analysis, they choose to fund the organization out of a desire to impact peoples' lives by enriching the human experience and solving social problems.

Under one formulation of the United Way model, volunteer evaluators are asked to apply what is termed in classic consultant jargon a *program logic model* to evaluate a particular program.[18] This requires the evaluator to identify program inputs, activities, outputs, and outcomes. Let's consider a job training program to illustrate how the program logic model operates. The program inputs are the resources used by the program. These can include money, the number of hours of instructor time, and computers. The program activities can be lectures, participant self-study, counseling, and role playing.

So far the model is relatively straightforward and intuitive. People have the most trouble differentiating the last two elements in the model, program outputs and program outcomes. As part of their fundraising efforts, many organizations highlight what the model refers to as *program outputs*. In the job training example, the outputs can be the number of students who complete the program or the number of lectures. In other contexts, it can be the number of young people receiving abstinence training or the number of meals served to homeless people during a month. Organizations often attempt to monetize their outputs. For example, it is not unusual to see a food bank proclaim that a $50 contribution will feed 50 people for one day, which translates into 150 meals. That information is useful, but it is only an intermediary step in assessing whether the program is successful.

Returning to the job training example, the fact that 100 people complete the program is interesting, but not necessarily meaningful. A basic question must be answered to assess the program's efficacy: How many of the 100 people were employed six months after receiving the training? The organization might go a step further, tracking the 100 participants so that it can determine how many were still employed three years later. In the case of the food bank, it might consider examining the nutritional and health benefits resulting from its efforts. If, at the end of six months, program participants have elevated levels of cholesterol or increased body fat percentages, the program may be feeding hundreds of people, but reducing their life expectancy. If that is the case, donors may want to reconsider their funding decision.

Focusing on program outcomes forces an organization to assess what it is trying to accomplish and whether its efforts are truly effective. In some sense, this is the most meaningful of all the evaluation tools or methods. The open-ended nature

---

17. According to representatives of United Way Metropolitan Chicago, staff members do undertake a traditional financial and governance review as part of the review process.
18. This discussion is based on materials distributed by the United Way of Metro Chicago to Agency Review Volunteers in December 2004, as updated in October 2005.

of the analysis turns off many people, however. Financial ratios create the illusion of certainty and ease of comparison. "We have to drop our administrative-expense-to-revenue ratio by two percentage points next year because our competition is only devoting 8 percent of its revenue to administrative expenses while we are devoting 10 percent." It is much more difficult to define what outcomes the organization is seeking when it designs programs to carry out its mission.

Boards, donors, and grant makers should be interested in assessing outcomes. All other things being equal, donors and grant makers would rather give to an organization that devotes 90 percent of its revenue to mission than to one that devotes only 50 percent to mission. This preference is the reason that many organizations stress their low administrative and fundraising expenses on their Web sites. But the more meaningful comparison is between an organization that devotes 80 percent of its revenue to mission and has 70 people per 100 trainees gainfully employed three years later and the organization that spends 90 percent of its revenue on training but has only 20 people per 100 trainees employed. In other words, the program logic model is an excellent tool for shifting the focus from administrative and fundraising expenses.

At the same time, although an outcomes analysis is a legitimate endeavor for any organization to undertake, it should not be used to the exclusion of other forms of evaluation. Every board should also analyze the organization's internal and financial controls, overall governance, and financial performance on an ongoing basis. After all, even good outcomes can be increased by more responsible and efficient use of resources.

CHAPTER 14

A FINAL THOUGHT

Patches, I'm depending on you, son, to pull the family through. My son, it's all up to you.

As sung by Clarence Carter, George Jones, and B.B. King[1]

There was an interesting exchange between the head charity regulator for one state and a member of the audience at a recent nonprofit law conference. The regulator had just finished explaining why each member of the board should be concerned with financial matters. The audience member disagreed, saying that financial matters were for accountants. According to this man, board members who are experts in the provision of social services should not be responsible for or concerned with financial matters. First acknowledging the practical limitations on taking action against inattentive directors, the regulator responded that his office was seeing ever-increasing levels of mismanagement by volunteer boards. He pointed to entire boards that had no idea that their organization was even generating a deficit. He calmly noted that inattentive directors are gambling with their organizations' assets and missions. The regulator concluded by assuring the audience member that some boards will lose the bet.

The last panel at this conference (and the only one devoted to financial matters) was charged with explaining why internal controls are a board issue. The audience member who had engaged in the earlier exchange got up and walked out just as the last panel began. Apparently, the regulator had not convinced him that financial matters are an issue for the entire board. Hopefully this *Guide* has caused those who share this man's viewpoint to think twice. Accounting and legal matters may not be interesting, but if "social service" people want to deliver social services effectively, they need to make an effort to understand this stuff.

Let's return to Chapter 1 and the Saratoga Performing Arts Center (SPAC). Recall that the incident that sparked the governmental investigation was a decision by the board to evict the New York City Ballet's participation. The investigation

---

1. Clarence Carter, *Patches*, *on* Patches (Atlantic 1970); and George Jones and B.B. King *on Rhythm Country & Blues* (MCA 1994). The song was authored by Ron Dunbar and General Johnson.

demonstrated that a numbers-driven analysis may well have reached the wrong conclusion[2]: Rather than being a financial drain, the ballet was arguably improving SPAC's bottom line. Here we have to engage in some speculation. If there were artsy types on the board who fought to keep the ballet, did they have the financial acumen to dispute the study prepared by those on the board who wanted to evict the ballet? Simply asking that question closes the gap between the regulator and the audience member. If board members who are mission experts want to effectively advocate their positions on mission, they must be willing to address financial, regulatory, and legal matters. Otherwise, those who are not mission experts will be in a position to advocate misguided positions, using opaque financial and legal arguments to impose their positions. Hidden agendas will prevail.

This *Guide* will have been a success if it has succeeded in demystifying the legal and financial issues affecting nonprofits for those who want to concentrate on "just the mission." If these people are willing to make the effort, they can use the information in this *Guide* not only to govern but also to more effectively fulfill the organization's mission. Hopefully, this *Guide* has also bridged a gap for those who bring some financial or legal experience to the organization but who are not versed in the unique aspects of the nonprofit world.

2. Recall from Chapter 1 that SPAC disputed the audit's final conclusion regarding the financial analysis but that the final audit continued to take issue with SPAC on this point.

ABOUT THE CD-ROM

INTRODUCTION

This appendix provides you with information on the contents of the CD that accompanies this book. For the latest and greatest information, please refer to the ReadMe file located at the root of the CD.

SYSTEM REQUIREMENTS

- A computer with a processor running at 120 Mhz or faster
- At least 32 MB of total RAM installed on your computer; for best performance, we recommend at least 64 MB
- A CD-ROM drive

NOTE: Many popular word processing programs are capable of reading Microsoft Word files. However, users should be aware that a slight amount of formatting might be lost when using a program other than Microsoft Word.

USING THE CD WITH WINDOWS

To install the items from the CD to your hard drive, follow these steps:

1. Insert the CD into your computer's CD-ROM drive.
2. The CD-ROM interface will appear. The interface provides a simple point-and-click way to explore the contents of the CD.

If the opening screen of the CD-ROM does not appear automatically, follow these steps to access the CD:

1. Click the Start button on the left end of the taskbar and then choose Run from the menu that pops up.
2. In the dialog box that appears, type ***d*:\start.exe**. (If your CD-ROM drive is not drive d, fill in the appropriate letter in place of *d*.) This brings up the CD Interface described in the preceding set of steps.

WHAT'S ON THE CD

The following sections provide a summary of the software and other materials you'll find on the CD.

CONTENT. The CD-ROM accompanying the *Guide* contains over 450 source documents. Many of the documents are referred to in the footnotes to the *Guide*.

You will find leading cases, IRS forms and publications, court pleadings and filings, statutory and regulatory material, congressional reports, governmental investigations and audits, and IRS Forms 990 for a variety of organizations. The documents have been organized by chapter. The individual documents are identified in the PDF document entitled:

Avoiding Trouble CD-ROM_Source Listing.pdf

APPLICATIONS. The following applications are on the CD:

- **Adobe Reader.** Adobe Reader is a freeware application for viewing files in the Adobe Portable Document format.
- **Word Viewer.** Microsoft Word Viewer is a freeware viewer that allows you to view, but not edit, most Microsoft Word files. Certain features of Microsoft Word documents may not display as expected from within Word Viewer.

Shareware programs are fully functional, trial versions of copyrighted programs. If you like particular programs, register with their authors for a nominal fee and receive licenses, enhanced versions, and technical support.

Freeware programs are copyrighted games, applications, and utilities that are free for personal use. Unlike shareware, these programs do not require a fee or provide technical support.

GNU software is governed by its own license, which is included inside the folder of the GNU product. See the GNU license for more details.

Trial, demo, or evaluation versions are usually limited either by time or functionality (such as being unable to save projects). Some trial versions are very sensitive to system date changes. If you alter your computer's date, the programs will "time out" and no longer be functional.

CUSTOMER CARE. If you have trouble with the CD-ROM, please call the Wiley Product Technical Support phone number at (800) 762-2974. Outside the United States, call 1(317) 572-3994. You can also contact Wiley Product Technical Support at **http://support.wiley.com**. John Wiley & Sons will provide technical support only for installation and other general quality control items. For technical support on the applications themselves, consult the program's vendor or author.

To place additional orders or to request information about other Wiley products, please call (877) 762-2974.

INDEX